ARTHUR M. WEIMER, Ph.D., University of Chicago, M.A.I., S.R.A., C.R.E., is Savings Association Professor of Real Estate and Land Economics, and Special Assistant to the President at Indiana University. He was for many years Dean of the School of Business at that institution. Dr. Weimer is President of Weimer Business Advisory Service, Inc., and is a director of several companies and organizations. He serves as consulting economist for the U. S. League of Savings Associations, and is a past president of the American Finance Association, Beta Gamma Sigma, and the American Association of Collegiate Schools of Business.

HOMER HOYT, J.D., Ph.D., University of Chicago, M.A.I., is President of Homer Hoyt Associates, consulting real estate economists. Dr. Hoyt previously taught economics at the Universities of North Carolina and Missouri, Columbia University, and Massachusetts Institute of Technology. A Member of the Supreme Court Bar, Dr. Hoyt has served as Principal Housing Economist of the Federal Housing Administration. His firm has conducted economic, market, and appraisal surveys for many nationally known real estate projects.

GEORGE F. BLOOM, D.B.A., Indiana University, M.A.I., S.R.P.A., is Professor of Real Estate and Real Estate Director at Indiana University. He has been active in the development of educational programs for the American Institute of Real Estate Appraisers and the Society of Real Estate Appraisers. He helped develop the Indiana State Approved Real Estate Salesmen's Course, and was founding president of the American Real Estate and Urban Economics Association. Dr. Bloom is Director of Real Estate Education of the Foundation for Economic and Business Studies, and Director of the Indiana Realtors Institute.

Seventh Edition

REAL ESTATE

ARTHUR M. WEIMER
INDIANA UNIVERSITY

HOMER HOYT
HOMER HOYT ASSOCIATES

GEORGE F. BLOOM
INDIANA UNIVERSITY

A WILEY/HAMILTON PUBLICATION

JOHN WILEY & SONS, New York · Santa Barbara · Chichester · Brisbane · Toronto

Library of Congress Cataloging in Publication Data:

Weimer, Arthur Martin, 1909-
   Real estate

   "A Wiley/Hamilton Publication."
   Includes bibliographies and index.
    1. Real property—United States. 2. Real estate
business—United States. I. Hoyt, Homer, 1896-
joint author. II.. Bloom, George F., joint author.
III. Title.
HD257.W45 1978   333.3'3   77-79170
ISBN 0-471-06878-0

PREFACE

The Seventh Edition is essentially a streamlined and updated version of the widely used Sixth Edition. Several of the introductory chapters have been combined and some of the discussions condensed. Much of the material has been updated and a number of new cases and study projects have been included.

We continue to provide a decision-oriented approach to the field of real estate. Basic concepts again are emphasized, especially in view of the problems encountered in the early and middle 1970's. Failure to recognize the importance of basic principles or to undertake careful location and market analyses accounted at least in part for many of these problems.

This volume, like its predecessors, gives special consideration to the physical, legal, and economic aspects of real estate. The analysis of economic, political, governmental, and environmental trends on national, regional, and local levels continues to be stressed. Real estate market analysis, location and risk analysis, and appraising methods are given careful attention.

Practical aspects of real estate decision making in the areas of building and land development, brokerage, property management, and finance are analyzed. The final chapters review some of the special problems in both the private and public sectors relative to housing, urban trends, commercial and industrial real estate, farms, forests, ranches, recreational land, and international real estate trends.

We emphasize the special characteristics of real estate decisions, especially the impact of income production at fixed sites. We indicate the relationships between the real estate business and other fields of business, as well as the importance of the social, political, economic, and environmental priorities of the American people for the real estate sector.

The book continues a forward-looking orientation. Discussions are presented in a manner designed to help students in the solution of future problems. Thus the "why" rather than the "how to" approach to the subject matter is again stressed. The cases and study projects, however, present much practical and current information. Review questions emphasize the major points in the text and cases for the student.

Suggestions for improving the book came from a number of those who used earlier editions. As a result we have tried to provide a somewhat more condensed and streamlined volume. We are especially grateful for this assistance.

ARTHUR M. WEIMER
HOMER HOYT
GEORGE F. BLOOM

ACKNOWLEDGMENTS

We wish we could recognize all of the persons who have contributed to the success of the various editions of this book, but this is not possible. Our indebtedness extends to former students, colleagues, and friends in business, government, and the academic community.

However, we must express thanks for the suggestions provided by Fred E. Case of the University of California, Los Angeles; E. Norman Bailey, University of Iowa; Robert O. Harvey, Southern Methodist University; Maury Seldin, American University; Arthur E. Warner, University of South Carolina; and Steven J. Martin and Thomas Earl Battle III, of Indiana University. The valuable assistance of Alex D. Oak of Paul I. Cripe, Inc., of Indianapolis, is gratefully acknowledged.

We are also indebted to the following faculty members of Indiana University: D. Lyle Dieterle, Edward E. Edwards, J. C. Halterman, Charles M. Hewitt, Edward J. Kuntz, John D. Long, E. W. Martin, Jr., John F. Mee, Robert R. Milroy, S. F. Otteson, D. Jeanne Patterson, W. George Pinnell, Richard L. Pfister, John H. Porter, Donald H. Sauer, Robert C. Turner, and L. L. Waters. Students in classes in Real Estate and Land Economics provided valuable feedback on text discussions for the Seventh Edition as well as the new study projects and cases. We appreciate the help of various practitioners in the field who criticized particular chapters. Their assistance is credited in specific notes or footnotes.

Assistance with the current edition or earlier editions was also provided by Lyle C. Bryant, Washington, D. C.; Norman Strunk, U. S. League of Savings Associations; Earl L. Butz, Robert C. Suter, and Ed Lott of Purdue University; Gail E. Mullin, Kent State University; Richard L. Haney, Jr., University of Georgia; and a number of others, including Ernest M. Fisher, Richard U. Ratcliff, David W. Thompson, George E. Price, David Price, Frank Flynn, L. Durward Badgley, Frederick M. Babcock, Paul I. Cripe, Albert E. Dickens, Carl F. Distelhorst, Richard May, and Herman O. Walther.

We are especially grateful to those who helped to ready the manuscript for publication, including Phebe Marshall, Kit Harahan, Charlotte Pitcher, Mary Holmes, and Doris Horn.

A. M. W.
H. H.
G. F. B.

CONTENTS

The Torrens System · **Acquiring Title to Real Estate:** Public· Grant · Devise or Descent · Adverse Possession · Private Grant Deeds · **Description of Property:** Rectangular System · Metes and Bounds · Subdivision · **Real Estate Contracts:** Contracts for Sale · Land Contracts and Related Arrangements · Listing Contracts · Leases · **Uniform Commercial Code**

Objectives of Decisions: Real Estate Administration · Highest and Best Use · **Special Characteristics of Real Estate Resources:** Income Production at Fixed Locations · Long Life of Real Properties · Real Properties as Large Economic Units · Interdependence of Private and Public Property · **Real Estate Value:** Utility and Scarcity · Value · Value and Price · Value and Cost · Value and Income · "Value Is a Word of Many Meanings" · **Supply Characteristics of Real Estate:** Supply of Properties · Supply of Property Services · **Demand Characteristics of Real Estate:** Impact of Incomes · Demand and Credit · Population and Real Estate Demand · Demand Dominant in Short Run

II. ANALYSIS FOR REAL ESTATE DECISIONS

Trend Analysis: Information Sources · Efforts To Provide Information · Evaluation of Information · **Economic Conditions and Real Estate Decisions:** Regions and Industries · Widespread Decisions · Localization of Income · Long-Term and Short-Term Outlook · Current Conditions · **Types of Fluctuations:** Secular Trends · Seasonal Fluctuations · Cycles · **Estimating Future Spending Patterns:** Consumer Spending · Business Spending · Government Spending · Foreign Spending and Receipts · Gross National Product Method · Flow of Income · Flow of Funds · Other Methods of Analysis · **Political and Governmental Areas for Analysis:** Special Interests · Viewpoint · Types of Regulations · Economic Stability · Inflation and Deflation · War and Peace · Conservation and Renewal · Environmental Priorities · Energy · Quality of Life · Consumer Interests · Equality vs. Excellence · Taxation · **Approaches to Urban and Housing Problems:** Housing Finance · Urban Renewal · Public Housing · Interest and Rent Supplements

Regional and Local Influences on Decisions: The Local Economies · Importance of Local Analysis · Type of Analysis Required · Definition of Region · **Approaches to Local and Regional Analysis:** Resources · Markets · Economic Relationships · **Location of Economic Activities:** Priorities · Combinations of Factors · Types of Cities · **Local Growth and Decline:** Specialization · Power To Grow · Limiting Factors · Changing Attitudes Toward Growth · **The Economic Base:** International Trade Theory · Basic and Service Activities · Outline of an Economic Base Analysis · **Input–Output Analysis:** Major Producing Sectors · **Other Techniques of Analysis:** Regional Accounts · Balance of Payments and Flow of Funds · Location Quotients · Improvement Efforts

7 Market Analysis   170

Market Factors in Decisions: Types of Markets · Demand, Supply, and Price · **Market Competition:** Informal Market · Nature of Exchange · Resources Allocation · Scope of the Market · **The Market in Theory:** Fundamental Concepts · Criteria of an Effective Market · Competitive Market Model · Real Estate Market Effectiveness · **Functions Performed by the Market:** Short-Run Market Changes · Longer-Run Changes · Land Use Determination · Planning and Zoning · **The Market in Operation:** Factors Conditioning Market Operation · Monopoly Elements · Market Variations · Demand Pressures · Inflexible Supply · Market Expansion · Market Contraction · National and Local Market Activity · Future Problems · **Major Features of a Market Analysis:** Purpose and Type of Market Analysis · Major Topics for Analysis · **Housing Market Analysis:** Housing Demand · Housing Supply · **Market Analysis for Business Real Estate:** Shopping Centers · Individual Stores · Office Space · Industrial Space

8 Location Analysis   204

Location Factors in Real Estate Decisions: Property Environment · Properties as Shares · Purpose and Extent of Analysis · Location and People · **Trends Affecting Structure of Land Uses:** General Trends · Competition Between Land Uses · Social and Political Competition · Redlining · Attitudes and Priorities · Anticipating Changes · **Urban Change:** Stages of Growth · Methods of Expansion · Influence of Topography · Land Use Patterns · Concentric Circles · Wider Dispersion · Sector Theory · Toward Ecumenopolis? · Individuality of Regions · Time Interval Maps · Land Use Changes · **Neighborhood Change:** Neighborhood Life Cycle · Types of Residential Neighborhoods · Density of Population · Main Points for Neighborhood Decisions and Analysis · Relative Marketability · **Commercial and Industrial Districts:** Central Business District · Outlying Centers · Isolated Outlets and Clusters · Industrial Areas · Analysis of Districts

9 Appraisals: The Income Approach   229

Appraisals and the Appraisal Process: Appraisal Process · Definition of Valuation Problems · Classes of Transactions · Physical Real Estate · Specific Property Rights · Date of Valuation · Location and Market Factors · The Three Approaches · Selection of Method · Method and Income · Business Profits · Direct Use · Method and Type of Property · Limitations of Appraising Methods · Investment Preferences, Cash Flow, and Depreciation · **Reconciliation of Results:** Factors Influencing the Judgment of Appraisers · The Use of Data · **The Income Approach:** Application of the Income Approach · Capital Investment Decisions · Estimating Income—The First Step · Estimating Expenses—The Second Step · Net Income · Capitalization · Methods and Techniques of Capitalization

10 Appraisals: Market Data and Cost Approaches   256

The Market Data Approach: Analysis of Subject Property · Selection and Analysis of Comparable Properties · Comparison of Subject and Selected

III.   REAL ESTATE DECISION AREAS

IV. SPECIAL PROPERTIES AND PROBLEMS

Office Space · Overbuilding Problems · Office Rentals · Office Building Occupancy · Types of Office Building Locations · Advantages of Various Office Building Locations · Demand for Office Space · Ownership and Management of Office Buildings · Insurance Company Experience · **Industrial Real Estate:** Central and Outlying Locations · Industrial Parks and Districts · Trends in Industrial Construction · Wholesale and Storage Warehouses · Demand for Industrial Space · **Selection of Industrial Locations:** Selection Factors · The Region · The Specific City Within the Region · The General Area Within the Metropolitan Region · The Specific Site

APPENDIXES

I

Introduction

We present a discussion of real estate decisions and decision makers in the first chapter. Comparisons are made between decisions in the real estate field and in other areas of business. A case study, "The Ambitious Student," at the end of the chapter helps to alert students to some of the kinds of decision problems that may be encountered. Also included is a study project which reviews the careers of several real estate entrepreneurs and illustrates some of the discussions in the chapter.

Because of the basic importance of the physical characteristics of real properties and their environment, these topics are considered in the second chapter. A study project at the end of the chapter presents a review of various architectural styles.

Real estate is not only a matter of land and buildings but of property rights in these physical objects; thus the legal aspects of real estate are reviewed briefly in the third chapter. Two cases illustrate several important problems: *Brown v. Southall Realty Company* and *Smith v. Old Warson Development Company.*

The final chapter of the introductory section considers the major economic characteristics of real estate. Both the physical and legal characteristics of real property have an important bearing on its economic worth, which depends primarily on income-producing capacity. Income may be derived from the direct use of a property, as in the case of a home owner, or a business firm occupying its own building, or income may take the form of monetary returns.

Income from real estate must be produced at a fixed site. Real estate comes in relatively large economic units and they have a long life. Local factors play a major role in real estate markets. These markets are characterized by relatively fixed supplies. Government on local, state, and federal levels has a major impact on the utilization of privately owned real properties. A study project is included to emphasize the major economic characteristics of real estate.

1

REAL ESTATE DECISIONS AND DECISION MAKERS

DECISION MAKERS

Nearly everyone participates to some extent in real estate decisions, since each of us uses real estate in some way every day. Some have only minor decisions to make such as deciding whether to rent a motel room for the night or buy a share of stock in a real estate enterprise. Others have major decisions to make, often involving many properties and large amounts of money. We may think of the primary decision makers in the real estate field as those who own real estate resources. In some cases owners are also users of properties; in other cases, ownership and use are separated. Users may exert major decision-making authority or occupy a minor role, depending on the situation.

Those who engage in various aspects of the real estate business are involved in a variety of decision-making activities. These decision makers include those who develop and subdivide, build, market, or finance real estate resources and operations.

Owners

Ownership has a wide range of meanings. In some cases the owner may have relatively little decision-making authority. Typically, however, ownership provides a major basis for controlling decisions. When ownership and use are combined, decisions are based on both the authority of the owner and his or her experience as a user of the property. When ownership and use are separated the ultimate decisions are made by the owner but he or she is likely to be influenced considerably by the recommendations of the user of the property. In some cases, the user may be able to specify very definitely the conditions under which he or she will make use of it and hence have a major influence on the owner's decisions. This is often the case when a long-term lease is being negotiated or when the user plans to improve the property in order to use it in some specific manner.

Real Estate Ownership

The ownership of real estate in this country is widely dispersed. Indeed, the opportunity to acquire ownership interests in real property was one of the main attractions for those who first settled in this country. Around two-thirds of our homes are owned by those who occupy them. Many people have a variety of investments in real estate. A high percentage of our farms are owned by those who operate them; a substantial number are owned by retired farmers. Many business firms own their places of business. Thus, there is relatively little concentration of real estate ownership in this country although there are some localities where old families, larger corporations, or major institutions control much real property. Inheritance taxes have brought about the breaking up of some holdings that might have resulted in large concentrations of ownership. Competition from other types of investments also has had an effect.

Owners of real estate exercise their rights to control property within certain broad limits imposed by government, notably those resulting from taxation, eminent domain, and the police power. (We will consider this topic at greater length in Chapter 3.) Governments at all levels also are important owners of real estate. Such ownership includes areas devoted to roads, streets, parks, national and state forests, conservation areas, military reservations, government office buildings, schools, and many others. The uses to which publicly owned real estate is put may have important influences on the ways in which private property is used.

The people in the real estate business may or may not be owners of real property. Some of them invest in properties on a long-term basis; others buy and sell properties in the hope of short-term gains.

Users of Real Estate

In terms of their decision-making importance we may distinguish between (1) owner users, and (2) nonowner users or those who typically lease properties for varying periods of time. The second group may be divided into (a) those who have widespread decision-making authority, such as those who use property under long-term leases or under leases which grant substantial powers to determine the ways in which property may be used and improved, and (b) those who use property under short-term leases or other limited arrangements—for example, a student who rents a room for a term, a newly married couple renting a small apartment for a month or two, or a business firm renting a storeroom on a temporary basis.

Those who lease property under arrangements which allow wide decision-making latitude stand in much the same relationship to real estate as owners.

Either directly or indirectly such users of property have a great influence on decisions. To some degree all users of real estate exercise some influence on owners through competition.

Buildings are constructed, modernized, equipped, repaired, and maintained in ways that will attract users. Sometimes users may spell out the specifications for development very precisely, as in the case of sale and leaseback arrangements. A large chain store corporation may buy a desirable location and sell it to a local investor provided he or she agrees to improve it in a specified manner and lease it back to the corporation under stated conditions.

Decisions related to real estate resources are similar in most respects to those made in relation to other resources or other areas of business. Some decisions are made on a logical and rational basis, others are the result of hunches, intuition, inspiration, or snap judgments. Decisions in the real estate field, however, are likely to be influenced by several sets of unique factors: (1) income from real estate resources must be produced at fixed locations; (2) long-term commitments usually are required; (3) real estate transactions typically involve relatively large amounts of money, and (4) private, public, and quasi-public interests are heavily interrelated; for example, streets and utilities are necessary to allow private real property to perform its functions, and taxes, laws, and regulations play an important role in the making of private decisions. In addition it should be noted that: (5) the real estate market differs from other markets because of the relative inflexibility of supply in the short run.

Decision Techniques

In recent years as business decisions have tended to become more rational in character, scientific methods have been used increasingly along with operations research and management science to aid decision makers. We will not undertake to discuss these topics except to suggest that they provide highly sophisticated ways of making use of information in arriving at rational decisions. When information is not available, imagination, inspiration, judgment, or so-called "heuristic" thinking often is used.

Even though the scientific method is used increasingly, it would be a mistake to draw too close an analogy between the scientific method and rational decision-making processes. Scientists seldom are concerned with taking action. Their objectives are to discover knowledge rather than to take action on the basis of it. The decision maker in business, whether in the real estate area or others, is trying to find programs which will lead to successful results. Decision makers may rely on models which are set up to help them. Various "decision rules" may be developed. The computer and other highly sophisticated equipment may be used along with mathematical techniques such as linear programming, game theory, and others. Decision makers often draw on information from the physical sciences and engineering, and from lawyers, statisticians, mathematicians, accountants, and specialists in many other fields.

Often, in the process of determining which decisions may be possible, a good deal of bargaining and negotiation is required. Compromises may be necessary.

In a final analysis, however, judgments must be made about an uncertain future. Decisions are forward-looking. They require that estimates be made about the future. Regardless of rational approaches or sophisticated techniques, we should recognize that the future can seldom be anticipated with great accuracy. Indeed it is this uncertainty that challenges all of us, especially those who have major decision-making responsibility.

Limitations on Decisions

In the real estate field as well as in others, the decisions of those who control finance, such as the executives of financial institutions, those who regulate activities, such as government officials, or those who control special resources, such as labor leaders, often have a major impact on decisions.

Along with all of us, major decision makers face many factors that are uncontrollable—the weather, fires, or other unpredictable occurrences. The term "state of nature" helps to define this area.

Those who make decisions can never be sure how competitors will act or react. Often "competitive strategies" are developed but they are limited by the strategies of competitors or the anticipated strategies of competitors.

Decisions will also be influenced by the values that are applied in given situations. For example, if the ultimate goal is to maximize return on investment, this may vary if one property or a number of properties are involved. Thus, it may be desirable to take a lesser return on one property in order to gain a better return on a block of properties. This is sometimes referred to as "suboptimizing."

Programs of Action

Business executives in general as well as those in the real estate field make decisions and also implement them. They are both "deciders" and "doers." It is almost impossible to separate these two roles.

In the modern corporation efforts are made to relieve the executive who carries major responsibilities of routine decisions. Thus, he or she is able to give primary attention to major decisions and to the more difficult programs required for carrying them out. The process of making decisions, putting them into action, and then re-evaluating them goes on continuously. It may be viewed as a "closed loop" with decisions, actions, feedback, review, and correction of the original decision or its continuation going on almost constantly.

One decision sets the stage for another or requires that still another be made. An action program often opens the way for new decisions and in turn for new programs. A review of the results of past decisions may indicate that new decisions are necessary and that new programs must be developed.

We tend to think of decisions as final. This is true in a literal sense, but we should recognize that we reappraise and review most decisions. We may modify them, change them entirely, or supplant them by new decisions.

In business, decisions are reviewed and reappraised almost continuously. For example, Mr. James may decide to lease space for his store. Even before he occupies the location, however, he may have found another one that offers greater advantages. He may then sublease the first location and occupy the new one. Decisions frequently are modified or changed, or canceled out. In some cases, of course, it may be impossible to change a previous decision. In the illustration above, for example, the manager may have found it impossible to take the new location if he were unable to sublease the first one. Even in this case, however, he may occupy the first location for a time and later be able to make a shift.

Management Process

In order to implement a decision it is necessary to develop *plans* for carrying the desired action into effect. Choices must be made between alternative plans. The plan selected in turn must be put into effect and this usually requires that various resources including land and buildings along with manpower, materials, money, and other things be *organized* so that the effort can be made with reasonable chances of success. In order to assure that an organized effort will be most likely to succeed, *controls* are established to evaluate the results and to modify the organized effort as required. These stages of planning, organizing, and controlling activities often are referred to as "the management process." It includes a continuing series of decision-making and decision-implementing activities, all of which get mixed up together.

THE REAL ESTATE BUSINESS

The real estate business includes a wide variety of enterprises. Many real estate brokerage firms are small operations. The office with one broker and a secretary is not unusual. Some brokerage firms attain fairly large size and offer complete real estate services. Some operate on a franchise basis. Building and development firms range from small- to very large-scale organizations. Investors may range from small to very large, including many types of financial institutions. Many people own and manage a few rental properties or lend money on the security of a home or two. Quite a number hold vacant land for future use. Banks, savings and loan associations, and insurance companies invest billions of dollars in real estate each year.

Of growing importance in the real estate field are the real estate departments of business firms. Some corporations engage in real estate operations in addition to those required for their own company purposes.

Functions of the Real Estate Business

Real estate enterprises exist because they perform useful functions for all of us, functions that people are willing to pay for. We may describe the principal functions of the real estate business as having three divisions: production (subdividing, developing, and building), marketing, and financing. We use the terms developing and building to describe the processes of preparing land for use, constructing buildings and other improvements, and making the completed properties available for use. Marketing includes the processes of putting real properties and property services into the hands of consumers. Brokerage and property management constitute the two main subdivisions of the marketing function. This function also includes promotion, advertising, and public relations activities. Financing provides for the channeling of a portion of the savings of the country into the production and use of real estate resources. Because of their long life, these resources require special types of financing arrangements.

In addition there are various specialized functions which facilitate the work of the real estate field. These include land planning, architecture and engineering, appraising and analysis, market research, real estate law, and others.

Production.   As producers of real estate resources, land developers and subdividers decide how a tract of land will be laid out and subdivided, the types of streets, sewers, and other facilities that will be provided and, by related decisions, tend to exercise a controlling influence on future decisions regarding the properties located there. Future owners and users may be able to make decisions only within a fairly limited range of possibilities. The builder plays an important role in real estate decisions in terms of both original construction and subsequent modernization and repair programs. A builder who does high quality work, for example, prevents the occurrence of many problems that may cause difficulties for both original and future owners and users.

Land development and building firms may be combined or conducted on a more specialized basis. Combined arrangements are of growing importance. Operations may range from a small builder who constructs a few houses a year to the developer of an entire new town.

Marketing.   Real estate brokers, by providing information for prospective buyers and sellers and by making available as wide a variety of choices as possible, also influence a broad range of decisions in the real estate field. They may also assist in making financial arrangements and thus exert additional influence on decisions.

Some brokerage offices specialize in the selling of particular kinds of property, such as residential, commercial, industrial, recreational, or farm properties. Others cover a broad range of activities and are known as full-service offices. Brokers are usually paid on a commission basis. They list properties for sale, promote sales, arrange for the closing of transactions, and carry on related activities.

Property managers may influence the decisions of both owners and users of properties by recommending programs of development, improvement, and effective use. A property manager is more than a lease broker although many start in this way. Usually a property manager acts for the owner in all matters pertaining to a property including the leasing of space, collecting of rents, selection of tenants, maintenance of the building and grounds, and related activities. He or she is usually paid on a commission basis based on a percentage of rentals collected. A property manager may specialize in the management of specific types of properties. Larger management firms, however, usually manage many types.

Those who engage in public relations, promotion, and advertising efforts often help to attract investments into the real estate field and to stimulate the sale and rental of properties.

Financing.   Those who engage in financing either as individuals or as executives of financial institutions play an important role in real estate decision making. Typically the equity or owner's investment represents a small percentage of total property value; the remainder usually is provided by borrowed funds. Sometimes the lender becomes a part owner—takes "a piece of the action." In other cases he or she remains a lender only. Of major importance in this area are commercial and savings banks, savings and loan associations, insurance companies, mortgage bankers, and individuals. Real estate investment trusts, pension funds, and other large pools of capital also play a role in this area.

Real estate financing usually is long-term in character and is accomplished by the use of mortgages or similar legal arrangements which provide for the pledging of greater or lesser degrees of interest in real property as security for loans. Sometimes leases are used as a means of financing as in the case of sale and leaseback arrangements. Construction loans are generally made for short-term periods during the building period but often are merged with long-term financing.

Special Functions

The many specialists who assist the various parts of the real estate business typically operate in an advisory capacity rather than as primary decision makers. This is generally true of real property lawyers, architects, engineers, land planners, appraisers, counselors, analysts of various types, and others. In general they advise the owners and users of property or those who develop and build, market, or finance real properties. These functions may be performed by individuals, professional firms, small businesses, or multinational corporations and major financial institutions. By providing expert information and counsel, specialists help to improve the efforts of real estate decision makers.

Appraising. Of the various specialists, the appraiser's position is unique in the real estate field. Because the market for real estate is not highly organized, it is often necessary to estimate the value of properties for various purposes. Appraisals or estimates of value serve as one of the major sources of information for business, personal, governmental, and institutional decisions pertaining to real property. Such estimates are often made by professional appraisers although others may at times undertake to do this. Because of the complexity of the appraisal process, the laws and regulations which require appraisals, and the policies of major financial institutions and corporations, more and more appraisals are being done by specialists. Such organizations as the American Institute of Real Estate Appraisers and the Society of Real Estate Appraisers have helped to develop training programs and professional standards of practice in this field.

Entrepreneurs. The entrepreneurial function in real estate is performed to a greater or lesser extent by all of the individuals and firms that participate in this field. Sometimes those who act as individual entrepreneurs are referred to as "operators." They may buy land and hold it until it is ripe for development, promote projects of various types, buy and sell property, change property from a lower to a higher use, or engage in other activities. Often brokers may operate on their own as well as for others; sometimes builders take an equity in their projects; even specialists may on occasion participate with the equity owner or take "a piece of the action" rather than the usual fee.

Organizations

As in other fields, activities may be carried on by individuals, partnerships, or corporations, or under other arrangements such as trusts and syndicates. In an individual proprietorship a single person serves as owner and operator. He or she may manage activities or hire others to do this or to perform other services. No legal formalities are needed except as may be required in the real estate field for brokerage or salespersons' licenses. In a partnership two or more persons are owners and may operate with varying degrees of formality. They are both individually and jointly responsible for all acts of the firm. Of special importance in real estate are limited partnerships; under this arrangement, the general partner or partners have overall responsibility, the limited partners are responsible only to the extent of their investments. The corporate form is widely used; financial institutions almost always are set up as corporations, although some may be organized as mutuals (also corporations).

Corporations. A corporation is a legal entity created by state or federal charter for the purpose of carrying on specifically authorized activities. There are corporations for profit and also those not for profit, the latter usually being established for educational, research, religious, or similar purposes. There may also be government corporations of various types.

In corporations organized for profit, the owners are the stockholders. Bonds may be issued to creditors. Bondholders have no ownership interest, although they may become owners in case of reorganization. Convertible bonds or debentures may lead to stock ownership. The owners of a corporation enjoy limited liability for the obligations of the firm—that is, liability is limited to their stock interests. Individual proprietors are personally liable for the obligations of their firms. Partners are liable for all of the obligations of the firm unless special limitations are established, and this type of arrangement depends on the statutes of the states where the partnerships are set up.

Since a corporation is a legal entity, it is taxed directly and its owners are also taxed on dividends received from the corporation (except in some small corporations whose owners may elect to be taxed as partners). This is not true of individual proprietorships and partnerships. Financial institutions are required to obtain federal or state charters in order to engage in business.

Usually no special licenses or other permissions are required to engage in land development or building activities. But, while the firm as such is not licensed, permissions usually must be secured to subdivide and improve land, especially when zoning laws are in operation; and building permits typically are required before construction can be undertaken.

Other Forms. We should note that a specific piece of real property may form the basis for an enterprise established in any of the above forms. For example, the ownership of a store building might be set up as a corporation, and this property could be purchased by buying a majority of the shares of the corporation.

Some real estate ventures are undertaken as syndicates. Usually this is done for a specific operation such as carrying out a major contract or developing a large tract of land. Syndicates may be made up of individuals or of several firms. The organization of a syndicate depends on the arrangements made to govern the interests of the syndicate members at the time it is established.

Trusts are often established for various purposes in the real estate field. An owner of property may establish a trust for his or her heirs. Title to the property is transferred to a trustee who administers the property in accordance with the trust agreement. The trust form may be used by owners of land to pool their interests with a trustee developing it; for example, a shopping center may be set up as a trust.

THE FRAMEWORK OF THE REAL ESTATE BUSINESS

The three functions of developing, financing, and marketing real estate must be performed regardless of how a society is organized. For example, in a dictatorship one huge government agency might perform all of them. Those in charge of such an agency would decide how much subdividing and building should take place, how the properties should be financed, who should be allowed to buy or rent them, and for how much. The government officials would be paid salaries rather than commissions, fees, rents, interest, or profits.

Private Sector

In an enterprise system these functions are organized through the market. Through competitive bidding, each person, within the limits of his or her economic resources, by buying or not buying, or by buying more or less, or by selling or not selling, or by selling more or less, helps to make the decisions which govern the development, financing, marketing, and use of real estate resources. Government, of course, has the responsibility for making market competition work and for supplementing it when necessary.

A large portion of the real estate business is carried on by private enterprises such as brokerage firms; management organizations; subdividing, development, and building companies; financial institutions; and individual entrepreneurs on a full- or part-time basis. In addition, however, federal, state, and local governments participate in varying degrees in real estate administration.

Public Sector

Government agencies, for example, establish the rules of the game within which the private firms and individuals operate. Government defines and protects property, organizes and enforces a system of private contracts (in effect a system of "private law"), provides protection for private owners in the occupancy and use of their property, and regulates the uses to which property may be put. Government also taxes property, provides various subsidies, conducts research, collects and disseminates information, provides counsel, facilitates the financing of property ownership and use, lends money, insures and guarantees mortgages, and also develops, leases, owns, and operates certain real properties. In addition, government may regulate the practices of those engaged in the real estate business by licensing laws and similar devices.

The relationships between business and government appear to be growing more and more complex. This is particularly true in the real estate field. No commodity except narcotics is more definitely regulated and controlled than real estate. In part this is because the concept of real property ownership is itself a creation of the law. Also, the close relationship between public and private property in the real estate field helps to account for this situation. Accessibility alone virtually requires the use of public property and private real estate in combination. In addition, the use of one property is likely to have significant effects on the use and hence the value of real estate located adjacent to it or nearby. The "neighboring effect" is of major importance.

Obviously the effectiveness with which government agencies are administered has a special bearing on the utilization of real properties. This is important on the federal and state levels, but in the case of real estate, especially important on the local level. Local government agencies may on occasion be hampered by limitations of funds or personnel, but they are tending to respond to the increasingly demanding requirements of the modern business community.

Quasi-Public Agencies

Another set of agencies of major importance in the real estate field includes trade associations, nonprofit organizations, mutual benefit societies, and a number of similar quasi-public institutions. These agencies carry on various activities such as providing information, advice, and assistance to member firms, lobbying, and other legislative activities. In addition, labor unions play a significant role, especially in the construction industry.

It is not easy to present a diagram showing the relationships among these heterogeneous groups of private enterprises, government agencies, and quasi-public organizations, but the accompanying chart may be helpful (see Fig. 1–1). This chart stresses the fact that when we think of the real estate business or of real estate administration, we must think of all of these agencies, rather than only of one or another type.

Government Agencies

Federal, state, and local agencies of government carry on a wide variety of activities that have a bearing on real estate administration. Some of the practices of the individuals and firms engaged in the real estate business are regulated—for example, by licensing laws. Some government agencies provide information and counsel. There are also some activities that are designed to stimulate or retard private activity.

The federal government does not regulate the real estate business specifically, other than to apply to it the regulations which are imposed on all business practices. Thus, antitrust laws and those regulating monopolistic practices apply in this area, as in others. Many of the informational activities of such federal agencies as the Department of Housing and Urban Development, Bureau of the Census, Department of Commerce, Bureau of

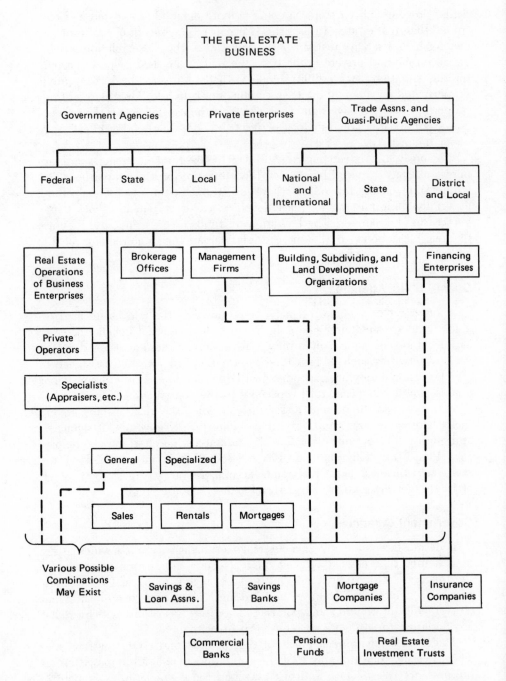

FIG. 1–1. General outline of the real estate business.

Labor Statistics, Department of Agriculture, and others are of importance to those engaged in real estate business.

Probably the influence of the federal government on the real estate business is felt principally through real estate finance. The work of the Federal Home Loan Bank System, including the Federal Home Loan Mortgage Corporation; the Veterans' Administration; the Federal Housing Administration; and the Federal and Government National Mortgage Associations has been of major importance.

Recently the impacts of the Occupational Safety and Health Administration, Environmental Protection Agency and ecology programs, and various consumer protection activities have increased in importance as have minimum wage laws, equal employment opportunity practices, energy conservation proposals, and others.

License Laws

State governments have special influences on real estate administration and practice through license laws. All of the 50 states have licensing laws in effect, as do the District of Columbia, the Territory of the Virgin Islands, and Guam. Five provinces in Canada also have effective licensing legislation.

A license law makes provision for regulating the practices of real estate brokers and real estate salespersons in the interests of the public. Typically, such laws require that each person desiring to carry on brokerage or other marketing activities in the real estate field secure a license, and that only persons with stated qualifications may obtain licenses. Usually the people licensed are divided into two classes, brokers and salespersons, with supervision being exercised directly over the brokers, who are responsible for the salespersons working for them. Provisions are made for machinery to administer and enforce the licensing laws, and for the revocation of licenses and imposition of penalties if the laws are broken.

License laws for their areas regulate the entrance of architects and engineers into their respective fields and thus have an effect on the real estate business. In addition, some state governments require that contractors and workers in the plumbing and electrical trades be licensed.

Local Regulations

Although there are many variations, local governments seldom regulate the real estate business directly but exercise profound influence on it by their tax policies, zoning and planning regulations, building codes, and related controls. Of special importance are building regulations, building permit requirements, regulations affecting the safety and health standards of buildings, changes in transportation systems and regulations, urban renewal programs, housing projects, and the like.

Trade and Professional Associations

Many trade and professional associations are of importance in the real estate field. The National Association of Realtors® and its affiliates, a nationwide organization, has branches in each state and in many cities. It includes such institutes, societies, and councils as the following: American Institute of Real Estate Appraisers, Institute of Farm Brokers, Realtors® National Marketing Institute, Institute of Real Estate Management, American Society of Real Estate Counselors, Secretaries Council, Society of Industrial Realtors®, International Real Estate Federation, States' Council, and Women's Council.

The National Association of Home Builders, The Society of Real Estate Appraisers, the National Association of Building Owners and Managers, the Manufactured Housing Institute, and the National Association of Building Manufacturers are important organizations in this field. In finance, a number of organizations carry on work of importance to real estate, including the American Bankers Association, U. S. League of Savings Associations, National Association of Mutual Savings Banks, Life Insurance Association of America, and Mortgage Bankers Association, plus others.

Most of these organizations strive to serve their members by representing them before the public, collecting and disseminating information, carrying on educational activities, undertaking such lobying and legislative activities as appear to be in the interests of their members, and conducting numerous related types of work. Of special importance are their attempts to raise the standards of business practice in their areas by educational programs, recognitions of various kinds, and restriction of membership to qualified personnel.

Organizations that play a leading role in educational activities include the Institute of Financial Education in the Savings Association field, the American Institute of Banking, the American Institute of Real Estate Appraisers, The Society of Real Estate Appraisers, the American Real Estate and Urban Economics Association, and others.

Realtor®

The efforts of the National Association of Realtors® to establish and maintain certain minimum standards of practice are deserving of special mention. In 1916 this organization adopted the term *Realtor*® as "a distinctive name" to be applied solely to persons who are members of a constituent board of, and as such having membership in, the National Association of Realtors®. This name may be used only by those who are affiliated with the Association. To the extent that members follow high standards of practice, this term acquires value in distinguishing them from other persons engaged in the real estate business.

IMPORTANCE OF REAL ESTATE DECISIONS

As we have indicated, each of us uses real estate every day. Real estate provides shelter, protection, comfort, convenience, privacy, and other things. Business firms need a place of business—a store, office, plant, or other parcel of real estate—in order to carry on operations. Farms and ranches, of course, rely heavily on real estate. Governmental, educational, religious, and cultural institutions all make use of real estate. We live in homes of many types. Our real estate resources—the homes, factories, office buildings, stores, shopping centers, farms, rights of way, roads, streets, parks, recreational areas, and other kinds—represent more than half of our national wealth.

Obviously, the decisions made with respect to resources of this magnitude have an important effect on the well-being of our people, the success or failure of business firms, and the general prosperity of the country. Effective utilization of real estate resources requires good decisions on the part of owners and users, whether they are home owners or the managers of business firms, those engaged in the real estate business, or the officials of government agencies and quasi-public institutions.

Improving Real Estate Decisions

Decisions made by business executives, government officials, or private citizens determine the amount and kind of real estate resources we have in the American economy and the effectiveness with which they are used. Thus, we may suggest that a major objective of studying this field is that of *improving decisions* relating to real estate resources.

Implementing Decisions

We are concerned, however, not only with the improvement of decisions relating to real estate but also with the *implementation* of such decisions. We are interested in the processes of putting decisions into effect. Hence, we might state the general objective of our study of this subject as the improvement of decision making and implementation of the real estate field, both with respect to the utilization of real estate resources and the operation of real estate enterprises.

Study Objectives

Your interest in this subject may arise from several sources. As a user, an owner or potential owner of real estate, or an investor in real property or securities based on real estate, you will need information about its uses and capacity to produce income. As an owner, manager, or employee of a business firm or a governmental or institutional agency, you will find a knowledge of this subject highly useful. If you are now connected with the real estate business or intend to engage in it, you have a particular interest in the study of this subject. As a voter, you are concerned with such problems as property taxation, land planning, zoning, environmental controls, slum clearance, housing programs, and the general efficiency with which we make use of our real estate resources.

METHODS OF STUDY

Real estate provides some unusual study opportunities in terms of the properties as well as the people engaged in this field of activity. Real estate markets are unique. And real estate involves many types of papers and documents.

Study of Properties

The study of the real estate field provides an unusual form of "laboratory work." The house or apartment building in which you live, a store, a farm, a vacant lot, or any other piece of real property with which you are familiar can serve as an excellent starting point for your study of this subject. You can use it as your own special laboratory for analyzing the various materials you will be studying, especially those that pertain to real properties and to the forces that affect the decisions of people regarding them. This should become your "study property."

Your home neighborhood and the town or city in which your study property is located may also be considered as a part of your laboratory. Decisions in regard to every parcel of real estate are affected by its surroundings, since it is a *share* in the community of which it forms a part. By carefully training your powers of observation, you can learn a great deal about the effects of economic, political, and social forces on the uses to which people put different types of real estate, on the trends of real estate values, and on business and personal decisions.

Study of People

Another interesting method of studying this subject is through discussions with people who are in one or another branch of the real estate business or who make real estate investments. Find out what their experiences indicate as the most important things to learn about real estate. Discuss career opportunities in real estate or related fields. Ask about current conditions in the real estate market and about potential market changes. Inquire about trends of land uses and new developments. Find out about real estate investment possibilities. Study major transportation changes and especially projected new developments. Consider changes in the central city, including urban renewal projects. Look into tax changes, zoning regulations, building codes, environmental controls, and related developments.

Study of Markets

Market forces, both national and local, have important effects on real estate. Such forces, of course, are the results of billions of decisions made by millions of people. Local market factors are especially important in their influence on residential real estate. Each local real estate market has its own unique characteristics. Even a small operator in the real estate field, whose interests may be centered in a single area, can often be of great help to you in gaining an understanding of local market conditions and trends.

Study of Documents

In addition, people who are actively engaged in business—especially those in real estate practice—will supply you with examples of the many forms and documents that are involved in real estate transactions. Sales agreements, listing agreements, deeds, leases, sales contracts, mortgages, deeds of trust, and many other documents are in constant use. It is often easier to learn about these from actual cases and situations than from merely reading descriptions of them in books.

Creative Thinking

One of the important abilities you should acquire through your study of this subject or others is that of producing ideas. Sometimes it is called creative thinking. Professor John F. Mee has summarized the steps in this process as follows: first, selection and definition of the problem; second, exploration and preparation; third, the development of partial solutions or hypotheses; fourth, the stage of incubating ideas, mulling over the problem, or engaging in "unconscious cerebration"; fifth, illumination or the appearance of the idea; and last, verification and application of the idea.[1] Mee also suggested the possibilities of "causative thinking," which involves developing an image of a desired future situation or event and then thinking back from it to identify the steps necessary to bring it about.

You will find it advantageous to improve your ability to think creatively and to stimulate your imagination and ingenuity. The creative thinking process is to a large extent an adaptation of the scientific method. Both inductive and deductive processes are involved, the former including the collection and analysis of pertinent information in order to arrive at a general summary or theory or principle. The latter includes the process of reasoning from a general principle or theory to a specific situation or problem.

Creative thinking is especially important in the real estate field. For

---

[1] John F. Mee, "The Creative Thinking Process," *Indiana Business Review*, vol. 31 (1956), pp. 4–9. See also Arthur Koestler, *The Act of Creation* (New York: The Macmillan Co., 1964), ch. 10.

example, it may provide the basis for developing a new subdivision, a way of financing a challenging project, or a method of selling a property that has been on the market for a long time.

Publications

Students of real estate must also know how to find and use the major types of published information that are available. You should learn how to use the library and should familiarize yourself with the more important services published, such as Standard & Poor's, Moody's, Prentice-Hall Real Estate Service, and others. Increasingly, reference materials are organized in such a manner as to permit the use of the computer in speeding up the processes of identifying and retrieving significant information.

Real estate transactions do not take place in a separate division of the business world but are a part of the total economic system. Consequently, you should cultivate the habit of reading current newspapers and magazines. *The Wall Street Journal, The New York Times* (especially the Sunday edition), and one or another of the weekly news magazines, such as *U. S. News and World Report, Newsweek,* or *Time* will be helpful. *Business Week* provides a good weekly summary of business developments, *Nation's Business* and *Fortune* are also good current publications to follow. *The Survey of Current Business* published by the Department of Commerce, the Federal Reserve *Bulletin,* the Federal Home Loan Bank Board *Journal,* and *Economic Indicators* published by the President's Council of Economic Advisers present summaries of business conditions. For regional and local information, the publications of Federal Reserve District Banks, Federal Home Loan Banks, and various university bureaus of business research are valuable.

Why vs. How

We emphasize the *why* rather than the *how* or *how to* aspect of the subject. This is not intended to minimize the importance of current practices in the business world or in the real estate field. Many current practices will be covered. It is well to recognize, however, that many business practices change in response to altered conditions, increased knowledge, legislative enactments, or for other reasons. In the short run, a how-to-do-things approach might be more valuable. In the longer run, however, a broader approach based on general concepts undoubtedly will be more practical, since it provides a basis for continuing growth and development.

SUMMARY

Decisions related to real estate resources are similar to other business decisions but are influenced by such unique factors as income production at fixed locations, long-term commitments, large commitments, close interrelationships of public and private interests and the special characteristics of real estate markets. Real estate decision makers are both "deciders" and "doers." They make decisions and implement them, hence are concerned with the management processes of planning, organizing, and controlling operations.

Principal decision makers are owners and users. The real estate business may be involved in primary or supportive decision-making activities. The major functions of the real estate business include production, marketing, financing, and specialized functions such as appraising, engineering, architecture, real estate law, and various analytical efforts. Some of those engaged in the real estate business may function as entrepreneurs or operators on their own; many others, from individuals to major corporations, may engage in a wide range of entrepreneurial activities.

The real estate business operates within a framework of private enterprises which function within a system of competition that is directed by laws and regulations on federal, state, and local levels. Many public and quasi-public agencies operate in this field. Of special importance are a variety of trade and professional organizations. Commissions which administer license laws play an important role. The term *Realtor*® designates someone who has met the qualifications established by the National Association of Realtors® which enforces a code of ethics to which members subscribe. (See Appendix B.)

Real estate decisions have an important bearing on our personal and business lives and on our society as a whole since each of us uses real estate every day. The general objective of our study of real estate is the improvement of decision making and implementing in the real estate field.

The study of this subject may be aided by the selection of a "study property" and by discussions with people actively engaged in the field. Efforts should be made to develop the ability to think creatively because of the importance of creative thinking in this area. Current publications and reports should be read regularly. The *why* rather than the *how to* approach is recommended in the study of this subject.

QUESTIONS FOR STUDY

1. What are the two classes of real estate decision makers? How do their goals differ?
2. Explain the statement that managers and administrators are both deciders and doers.
3. Explain why real estate decisions may differ from those in other fields.
4. What is meant by the management process?
5. Discuss the functions of the real estate business. Which organizations generally perform these functions?
6. How does the federal government influence real estate decisions?
7. How does competition act as a method of control in the real estate field?

8. How do the private and public sectors interact in the real estate area?
9. How are financing institutions likely to exercise influence on real estate decisions?
10. List the principal local governmental regulations that influence the activities of land developers and builders. Which regulations apply most directly to brokers?
11. Explain the functions of real estate license laws. Do you favor such laws? Why or why not?
12. How might license laws, building codes, and other regulations adversely affect the allocation of real estate resources?
13. Who can be designated as a Realtor®?
14. What is your major objective in studying this subject? What is the general purpose of such study?

SUGGESTED READINGS

FICEK, EDMUND F., HENDERSON, THOMAS P., and JOHNSON, ROSS H. *Real Estate Principles and Practices.* Columbus, Ohio: Charles E. Merriam Publishing Co., 1976. Ch. 1.

HINES, MARY ALICE. *Principles and Practices of Real Estate.* Homewood, Ill.: Richard D. Irwin, Inc., 1976. Ch. 1.

O'DONNELL, PAUL T., and MALEADY, EUGENE L. *Principles of Real Estate.* Philadelphia, Pa.: W. B. Saunders Co., 1976. Chs. 1 and 2.

SAMUELSON, PAUL A. *Economics: An Introductory Analysis* (10th ed.). New York: McGraw-Hill Book Co., 1976. Ch. 1.

SMITH, HALBERT C., TSCHAPPAT, CARL J., and RACSTER, RONALD W. *Real Estate and Urban Development* (rev. ed.). Homewood, Ill.: Richard D. Irwin, Inc., 1977. Chs. 1 and 2.

UNGER, MAURICE A. *Real Estate* (5th ed.). Cincinnati, Ohio: Southwestern Publishing Co., 1974. Ch. 1.

WEIMER, ARTHUR M., "Real Estate Decisions are Different," *Harvard Business Review* (November–December, 1966).

WEIMER, ARTHUR M., BOWEN, DAVID, and LONG, JOHN D. *Introduction to Business: A Management Approach* (5th ed.). Homewood, Ill.: Richard D. Irwin, Inc., 1974. Chs. 8 and 9.

WILEY, ROBERT J. *Real Estate Investment—Analysis and Strategy.* New York: The Ronald Press Co., 1977. Ch. 1.

CASE 1–1

The Ambitious Student

One of your student friends, John Robinson, a senior who was recently married, knows you are studying real estate and asks you to advise him in regard to his housing. You point out that you are in the very early stages of your study of this field. He takes the position that some knowledge is better than no knowledge and proceeds to present his problem.

John and his wife have been living in a small furnished efficiency apartment. The rent is $135 per month and they are renting on a month-to-month basis. They have about $4,500 available as a result of savings and wedding gifts. He says he knows that a lot of people make money in real estate so why shouldn't they buy a house, live in it for a year and then sell it for more than they paid for it or at least for as much as they paid and get free rent. Or he asks, why not buy a rooming house? His wife could look after it and he would have some time available to help her. Or why not buy a small apartment house—say a four-unit apartment?

You point out that you have already been convinced that there is no assurance of a specific property going up in value even though the general trends have been in that direction. You also suggest that much would depend on what may be available since this is a fairly small university town and the real estate market is not very extensive.

John reports that they recently met a young real estate broker who has several properties for sale. One is an old residence built in the later 1920's and fairly near the campus. It is owned by a retired faculty member who wants to move to a warmer climate. It has two bedrooms, living room, large kitchen, dining alcove, one bath, and a half basement. There is an old one-car detached garage at the back of the lot.

The lot has a frontage of 50 feet and a depth of 150 feet. It is on the west side of a paved street. The house measures 34 feet by 30 feet. Plastering is in fair condition; however, the bathroom should be replastered at an early date. The grounds are well maintained. There are several good sized shade trees. The legal description of the property is lot number 76 in Eroica's section 10, township 12 north, range 9 west, City of Eroica, Sunrise County, State of Illinois (known as 1776 North Upton Street).

Properties in this area are 50 years or more old. There is a small shopping center about four blocks away. The property is readily accessible to schools. It is priced at $19,750, but the owner would be willing to sell on a 12-year contract at 10 per cent interest with $3,500 down. The monthly payments would total $198.74 not including taxes and insurance. Repairs are estimated at $1,500 although part of this—perhaps one-third to one-half—could be accomplished on a do-it-yourself basis. Taxes are estimated at $378 and insurance at $92.

Upon inquiry you find that this house has been on the market for almost two years and you tell your friend that he may not be able to get his money out quickly if he takes a job elsewhere upon graduation. If he had to forfeit his contract, he would be paying a high rate of rent.

About this time you happen to notice an ad in the real estate section of the local paper describing a rooming house that is for sale and you call your friend's attention to this possibility as well.

The rooming house is located on South Seventh Street very near the campus. The offering price for the eleven-bedroom structure is $57,500. The original portion of the house is approximately 60 years old, with a five-year-old addition in the rear. The gross annual rentals, with 100 per cent occupancy, total $11,280. The entire house has been rented for the next summer and fall.

The building had originally been the home of the Kingery family, whose heirs had sold it in 1961 for $16,900. The new owner, a Mrs. Barringer, was housemother for a local sorority. She utilized her experience in turning the South Seventh Street property into a rooming house for university students. Five years ago, she added the new wing to the structure, nearly doubling the capacity. Desiring to move out of Illinois, Mrs. Barringer sold the property to the present owner, Robert Werneke, for $37,500 on a land contract. Mr. Werneke, because of ill health, wants to sell the property. Initially, he listed it for $59,500.

During the years Werneke owned the property, the following improvements were made: three new gas furnaces installed, exterior painted every other year, interior panelled and carpeted, much of the older furniture replaced, storm windows and screens replaced, structure checked for and protected against termites.

Werneke's problem in selling his property apparently stemmed from two factors. First, he wanted his cash at the time of sale; secondly, there was not a great deal of demand for older rooming houses such as the South Seventh Street property.

Werneke has indicated that he might sell on a land contract if he knew the buyer and if the down payment were sufficient. For a cash sale Werneke would probably accept an offer in the low $50,000 range because the property has been on the market for so long.

Figures supplied by Werneke, using some of his own estimates, are:

Rent schedule income		$11,280
Less 10% vacancy		1,128
Gross rent income		10,152
Expenses:		
Insurance	$ 315	
Taxes	900	
Utilities	1,382	
Management	500	
Maintenance reserve	500	3,597
Net income before depreciation		$ 6,555

Assuming he could buy the property for $50,000, with the owner taking a second mortgage for $10,000 at 10 per cent, you computed his financing requirements as follows:

Equity (down payment)	$ 5,000	
Mortgage 8%—20 yrs.	35,000	(70% of price, assuming property is appraised at price level)
2nd mortgage from owner at 10%—10 yrs.	10,000	
Total price	$50,000	

You pointed out to John that obtaining a $35,000 mortgage from a local financial institution would depend on whether the property would be appraised for $50,000 or more. You suggested that the capitalized value of the net income on the basis of 10 per cent in perpetuity would be $65,555. On a more modest 13 per cent basis, which might be more typical for this type of property, its capitalized value would be only $50,427.

Questions

1. Make John a list of the advantages and disadvantages of each of his alternatives.
2. If he buys the rooming house, what are some ways he can make up the difference between the $5,000 down payment and his $4,500?
3. What difference might a $65,000 or $50,000 appraisal of the rooming house have on the mortgage arrangements?
4. What is your recommendation to John?

STUDY PROJECT 1-1

Entrepreneurial Biographies *

A recent class of MBA students in real estate and land economics was given the opportunity to study the business biographies of seven men who had enjoyed outstanding success in this field. Success was defined rather broadly as outstanding achievement in any part of the real estate area and ranged over a wide variety of activities.

The men whose business biographies were studied in the order of their meetings with the class are as follows:

Max Karl, President, Mortgage Guaranty Insurance Corporation, Milwaukee, Wisconsin

John C. Hart, President, Gateway Corp., Indianapolis, Indiana

Guthrie May, President, Guthrie May and Company, Evansville, Indiana

Homer Hoyt, President, Homer Hoyt Associates, Washington, D. C.

James C. Downs, Chairman of the Board, Real Estate Research Corporation, Chicago, Illinois

A. D. Theobald, Chairman of the Board, First Federal Savings and Loan Association of Peoria, Illinois

Philip M. Klutznick, Chairman of the Board, Urban Investment and Development Corporation, Chicago, Illinois

It should be noted that these were not typical "organization men." Some of them had been involved in establishing their own enterprises. Some of them had worked for corporations or government agencies for varying periods. Several had spent some time in the military service. Some had served in professional capacities. For the most part, however, these were entrepreneurial types. They were selected in the hope that the class would be able to learn about entrepreneurship, especially in the real estate field, by direct association with entrepreneurs.

Not Defeated. Throughout these business biographies runs a constant theme of unwillingness to accept defeat. These people refused to acknowledge failure even when it seemed very close. They had a strong determination to succeed. To a man they were proof of Marshal Foch's famous statement: "No one is defeated who will not admit that he is defeated."

One of the outstanding illustrations of this was provided by Mr. Karl during the period when he was establishing the Mortgage Guaranty Insurance Corporation. In order to gain a national position quickly, he had decided to appoint a nationally recognized board of directors and this plan had been approved by those selected. Just a few days prior to the planned announcement of the new board, several members of the proposed board called Mr. Karl to indicate that they had decided not to go ahead with this plan.

Mr. Karl refused to accept this decision without making further effort. He inquired as to the basis for their position and upon learning that it resulted from the suggestion of one of their principal advisers, he asked who this man was and made a heroic effort to see him and to convince him of the validity of the new enterprise. In this he was successful. The new board was established according to plan and the Mortgage Guaranty Insurance Corporation as a result attained a national position in a relatively short time.

Mr. Downs started publishing his Real Estate Market Letter without any subscribers. He sent it to people he thought might have an interest in it. Even

* Arthur M. Weimer.

though recognition was a long time in coming, he persisted in this effort until the Letter came to be recognized as an important source of information. In turn it opened for him various other avenues to success.

Early in his career Mr. Klutznick was trying to assist a "clean up" administration in Omaha. The city desperately needed work projects. Every effort to secure federal grants proved to be frustrating since they required matching funds and Omaha had no funds available. Mr. Klutznick, who was serving as Assistant Corporation Counsel to the City of Omaha, found funds in the new public housing program which could be made available on a nonmatching basis. But this required the designation of certain areas as slum areas and the city government was reluctant to do this. After further efforts, however, the required procedures were adopted and a public housing program was developed in Omaha, the first west of the Mississippi River. This in turn brought Mr. Klutznick to the attention of those administering the public housing program and started him on a career in the housing field which included both extensive governmental and private activities.

Mr. Hoyt had a similar experience. He lost nearly all his holdings in the Chicago real estate depression of the late 1920's and early 1930's. This experience, however, caused him to try to find out why developments had occurred as they did and to determine whether Chicago real estate values might be revived. As a result he wrote his famous *100 Years of Land Values in Chicago* which was accepted as a doctoral dissertation at the University of Chicago. Thus he was able to finish a Ph.D. program he had started some years before. This in turn launched him into a highly successful career first with the Federal Housing Administration and then as a real estate consultant and investor.

After World War II when he returned from military service, Mr. Theobald found that a commitment to head an organization where he had been second in command would not be honored. He had no immediate alternative but to return. He persisted in his desire to be in a top leadership position and in a few months found an opportunity to take such a position.

Mr. May persisted with his new home building organization in the face of labor union problems. He often undertook ventures which his advisers and others believed could only lead to failure. Often when a venture looked bad in its early stages, he stayed with it, often committing further resources to it.

Mr. Hart refused to give in to disadvantages arising from the uneven enforcement of governmental regulations. He entered politics himself in order to correct some of the difficulties he encountered. He was as successful in politics and government as in business.

Innovative Approaches. The second major conclusion may be stated this way: Each business biography reflected a highly innovative type of person. These men were not limited by traditional approaches to problems nor to traditional solutions. When established methods and procedures failed, they invented new ones. When resources of the usual type were not available, they substituted others. They all had imagination and in varying degrees had creative ability.

The ability to innovate and indeed to invent new approaches to problems has already been illustrated in part in the preceding discussions. For example, Mr. Karl substituted a well-known national board for more traditional ways of developing a national market. He did not have the resources to launch a widespread promotional campaign but his national board in effect provided this for him. In turn the reputation of his new board served as a substitute for a lack of capital since the confidence which people in the mortgage business placed in these men was the equivalent of a substantial investment which could only be built over a period of time.

Mr. Hoyt adapted the techniques of the historian and statistician to the analysis of the real estate market. He designed ways of handling voluminous amounts of data prior to the days of the computer. He used maps in novel ways to summarize information. He patterned his investments after his sector theory of city growth, which was a new explanation of city growth and structure. Thus he combined business and academic innovations. He adapted the theory of international trade to economic base analysis for the appraisal of local economic conditions. This in turn contributed to many of his analytical studies as a real estate consultant.

Mr. Theobald used a community orientation as the basis for promoting the First Federal Savings and Loan Association of Peoria. He identified the growth of the association with the growth of the community. This gave him an unusual and attractive approach to the development of this savings and loan association.

Mr. Downs recognized early the possibilities in Florida real estate and the real estate in Hawaii. He saw the potential impact of the jet airplane on vacations at a very early stage. He was able to recognize early the potential in the prefabricated housing field and to capitalize on it. To get the required land he substituted a high price offer and longer-term financing for a lower price plus a large down payment and shorter-term financing.

Against the advice of many, Mr. Downs bought real estate bonds when they were selling for a few cents on the dollar, thus matching his judgment against that of others. He persisted in publishing his Real Estate Market Letter even though there seemed to be little demand for it. Ultimately it proved to be highly successful.

Mr. Downs undertook his first independent real estate management venture in a field where others were facing failure. His self-assurance undoubtedly was a major factor in his early success as a consultant.

Few of these entrepreneurs felt comfortable working for someone else. Many might be classified as "loners." All were highly independent in their beliefs and thoughts. They relied on other people but never in a final sense.

As a corollary to this, they all had great confidence in their own abilities. Not only were they unwilling to accept defeat as has been suggested, they believed in their capacity to succeed, even to the extent of being sure that success could not be denied them.

Learning from Experience. These men knew how to learn from their experiences. They made mistakes but seldom made the same mistakes twice.

Mr. Theobald recognized that he had been operating primarily as second in command prior to World War II when he was Vice President of the U. S. League of Savings Associations. During World War II he served on the staff of Tex Thornton who developed the famous "whiz kids" group which ultimately went to work for Ford. Theobald decided against going with this group on the ground that he would probably continue to be a second in command for a long time; he wanted to run his own operation soon. He sought another outlet for his energy and ability and soon found this in the First Federal Savings and Loan Association of Peoria.

Mr. Hoyt lost heavily because he bought at the peak of the boom; thereafter he was careful of his timing and adjusted his land commitments to his cash flow so as not to lose property because of a lack of cash. Also he avoided other types of investments than land, largely holding only cash or its equivalent and land.

Mr. Klutznick recognized that the kind of experience he had gained in public housing could be adapted to private developments and on this basis undertook the ventures that brought about the Park Forest Development and subsequently others.

Mr. May recognized that the command and leadership experience he had gained in World War II would enable him to operate his own business and thus he started a prefabricated housing business as a National Homes dealer rather than returning to his former job. Later he saw that experience in the housing field could be adapted to other fields.

Mr. Hart recognized that his work as an accountant for a building organization had provided him with the experience necessary to establish his own building organization. Later he saw that successful operations in the single-family home field could be adapted to apartment houses and commercial ventures. His accounting experience pointed the way to tax shelters in the real estate field.

Mr. Downs recognized that property management provided an open avenue to successful real estate investment. He learned that experience in real estate investments could be useful in developing other successful investments.

Forward Looking. To a man these entrepreneurs were forward-looking. They had the capacity to anticipate future developments and while they could not always clearly see the shape of things to come they operated on a forward-looking basis.

Mr. Hoyt's early recognition of the importance of the shopping center movement and its potential in terms of the emerging patterns of city growth is one of the best illustrations of this.

Mr. Theobald concluded that there would be no major depression and that the real estate market would expand substantially after World War II and this formed the basis for his successful operations.

Mr. May's ability to see the potential in prefabrication not only in his own town but in other cities was a major factor in his success. Ability to anticipate areas of growth along with problem areas served him in good stead.

Mr. Downs's recognition of the Florida and Hawaiian developments is a case in point as were Mr. Hart's abilities to see the potential in the northwest Indianapolis area.

All of these men had the capacity to plan. This ranged from planning day to day activities to long range planning. Many of these men liked to get to work early and plan their day before the office force assembled. Mr. Klutznick started this practice at an early stage and continues to follow it.

Mr. Hoyt writes constantly of the future, trying to probe potential developments at least to the year 2000.

Mr. Theobald is a continuous planner and he encourages planning on the part of his subordinates. He held special planning sessions of his staff typically away from the office so that they could jointly try to anticipate problems and potential developments. In this, incidentally, he hit on an interesting device for gaining recognition for his people by taking them to outstanding places such as well-known resorts. This not only appealed to the men, it also gave their wives special recognition among their friends at home.

This forward-looking attitude seems to be one of the characteristics of all these men. They try to anticipate potential developments. They look ahead rather than backward, although they use past experience as a guide to the future.

Summary. The real estate entrepreneurs covered by these discussions represented a wide diversity of experiences and types of people. Even so, there were many similarities in their careers and points of view. These men have been stubborn in their unwillingness to accept defeat. They have been innovative in their approaches to problems, seldom relying on standard or traditional methods. Typically they have enjoyed life largely through their work. These men have been highly independent in thought and action, almost to the point of being "loners" in some areas. With great confidence in themselves and their abilities they have often undertaken highly risky projects. They knew how to learn from experience and have used this knowledge in new projects. They have been forward-looking in outlook and attitude.

Questions

1. What common characteristics do these entrepreneurs possess?
2. Do these characteristics imply a "secret of success"?
3. What are the main differences among these entrepreneurs?
4. Which entrepreneur impressed you the most? Why?

2

REAL ESTATE RESOURCES AND THEIR PHYSICAL ENVIRONMENT

APPROACHES TO REAL ESTATE DECISIONS

One of the first things a real estate salesperson learns is the importance of selecting the proper route to a property when showing it to a prospective buyer. He or she knows that the same property approached from different routes often produces very different impressions. Similarly, the decisions that people make in regard to real properties are influenced greatly by the way they approach them and think about them.

Physical Approach

In Chapter 1 we suggested that you select a "study property." If we were to approach this property by one of the avenues leading to it, we would probably view it first as a physical entity, as land and buildings. This is the point of view of most people when they first think about real property. The land may be considered in terms of its size, type, topography, and such characteristics as the condition of the topsoil and subsoil, and accessibility to streets, roads, utilities, and various conveniences. The building may be viewed from the standpoint of size, type, design, condition, structural soundness, floor plan, mechanical conveniences available, relationship to the lot, orientation, and similar matters.

Legal Approach

If our approach to the property were by another "street" or point of view, however, we would look at it as a lawyer does and see it chiefly in terms of legal rights and obligations. To a lawyer the physical land and buildings have significance only to the extent that they represent *property rights*. These rights are evidenced by a great many types of legal documents and records. Many of these documents are recorded at the courthouse in the office of the local registrar of deeds or in the offices of similar officials. The property may be identified in a plat book. The owner or his or her attorney will have an *abstract of title*, which contains a detailed history of the transactions which have had a bearing on the title to the property. Thus, property rights, although intangible, have a certain appearance of reality to many people because they are represented by many types of written documents and official-looking pieces of paper. The legal characteristics of real estate are considered at greater length in the next chapter.

Economic Approach

If we approached your study property from still another "street" or point of view, we would look at it through the eyes of the business manager, investor, property user or owner, appraiser, or real estate broker. In this case, we would consider the physical land and buildings, of course, and we would also consider the property rights which the land and buildings represented. But we would view the property first and foremost as an economic resource, as a *vehicle of productivity* providing security, shelter, conveniences, privacy, and other services. In short, we would think of the property in terms of its *income-producing ability*, the dollars and cents which it may yield an owner over the period of its productive life, its contribution to the production and marketing activities of a business firm, or the direct satisfactions which an owner may derive from occupying it. This is the point of view with which we shall be chiefly concerned in our study of real estate decisions, resources, and operations. Our reason for stressing this point of view is the belief that factors relating to the income-producing ability of real properties are of primary importance in influencing the decisions of property owners and users. Income-producing ability is a reflection of a property's economic characteristics and environment as well as its relationship to the physical and legal environment.

Importance of Income

For our purposes, the land and buildings on the one hand and the property rights they represent on the other have significance chiefly through the direct satisfaction or the monetary income that may be derived from them. For example, good construction is important mainly because it is related to the ability of a property to produce money or real income. A sound relationship between the property and its environment will add to its income-producing ability. Similarly, property rights have significance chiefly as they facilitate or interfere with sound programs of property use.

Nevertheless, it will be necessary to study the physical characteristics of real property. Our main purposes in this connection will be to study the *income characteristics* of the physical land and buildings and their relationship to the physical environment, and to learn that portion of the language of the architect, engineer, developer, or builder which is essential to an understanding of the subject.

One of our primary purposes in considering the work of the architect and engineer as well as that of the lawyer is to learn to recognize those situations in which we should call on such specialists for advice on real estate decisions. To paraphrase an old axiom: "He who is his own lawyer, architect, or engineer has a fool for a client."

Characteristics and Classes of Land

In the early literature of economics, land was considered to be one of the three basic factors of production: land, labor, and capital. Land included everything furnished by nature, labor all human services, and capital all artificial or produced goods used in the production process.

There are serious questions about differentiating between land and capital as suggested by this classification. Natural agencies, for example, especially as used in production, are quite different from their original natural condition. Many costs have been incurred in order to make them useful. Indeed, such costs may on the average approximate the value of the natural agencies, thus suggesting that they are little different from most capital goods.

For our purposes we consider land in a physical sense as including the earth's surface; under some conditions we may also include the minerals below the surface and the air above the surface. Mineral and air rights are related to surface land through our system of land ownership but important qualifications often must be made in specific situations. A broad classification of land uses for continental United States is suggested in Table 2–1.

Building Classification

Buildings may be classified by type of use or in other ways. From the standpoint of type of use we may divide buildings as follows: farms and other rural buildings, residential, commercial and industrial, governmental, institutional, and other types. The vast majority of our buildings, of course, are located in urban areas but farm and other rural uses also account for many.

Farm buildings include farm residences as well as barns, silos, granaries, and other types. There are many nonfarm rural residences as well as a variety of country stores, small factories, recreational structures, and other kinds of buildings. In some cases large factories now locate in rural areas and some fairly large shopping centers may be found in rural areas near the intersections of major highways.

TABLE 2–1.   Major Uses of Land in the 48 States: Historic and Projected, 1949–2000

Land Use	Historic		Projected [1]	
	1949	1969	1980	2000
	Millions of Acres			
Cropland used for crops [2]	387	333	320	298
Cropland harvested	(352)	(286)	(292)	(272)
Forest and woodland [3]	601	603	591	578
Pasture, range, and other agricultural land [4]	768	767	771	782
Urban and related [5]	42	60	66	81
Other special uses and miscellaneous uses [6]	106	134	149	158
Total land area [7]	1,904	1,897	1,897	1,897

[1] Land use projections are derived from projections prepared for the Water Resources Council by the Economic Research Service, and the Bureau of Economic Analysis, Department of Commerce. Exclusion of data for Alaska and Hawaii significantly affects acreage of noncommercial forest, wasteland, and total land area, but has little effect on agricultural and commercial forest acreages.

[2] Cropland harvested, crop failure, and cultivated summer fallow.

[3] Excludes reserved forest land in parks, and other special uses of land. The total acreage of forest land in the 48 contiguous States was approximately 627 million acres in 1949 and 632 million acres in 1969.

[4] Permanent grassland pasture and range in farms and not in farms, land in crop rotation but used only for pasture or idle, and miscellaneous other land in farms.

[5] Area in urban places, highway and road rights-of-way, railroad rights-of-way, and non-military airports.

[6] Includes National and State parks and wildlife areas, national forest wilderness and primitive areas, national defense lands, State institutional sites, miscellaneous other special uses, and unclassified areas such as marshes, open swamps, bare rocks, sand dunes, and deserts.

[7] Change in total land area is attributable to changes in methods used in occasional re-measurements by the Bureau of the Census, and increases in the area of manmade reservoirs.

Source: Dept. of Agriculture, *Our Land and Water Resources,* Misc. Publication No. 1290 (Washington, D.C.: Government Printing Office, 1974).

Residential buildings may be divided by number of dwellings. Single-family, two- to four-family dwellings, and apartment houses with five or more units constitute the main classifications by number of dwellings. Apartments may be further subdivided as walk-up and elevator or as garden and high-rise types.

Industrial structures usually are classified as heavy manufacturing, light manufacturing, and warehouses. Sometimes they are classified by types of products being manufactured.

Commercial structures include all types of stores, office buildings, hotels and motels, recreational and service establishments. Sometimes commercial classifications are limited to structures used for wholesale and retail purposes with separate classifications for office buildings, service establishments, and the like.

Governmental structures include all types of buildings owned or operated by national, state, or local governments. Institutional buildings are owned or operated by educational, research, or religious organizations, foundations, or other groups. Some public utility buildings are classified separately, others are in combined units.

ENVIRONMENTAL DECISION FACTORS

Real estate decisions are influenced by land, buildings, and their physical environment. Land is a basic resource; how it is used has a major effect on the air, the water, and the general physical surroundings. Careful and systematic cultivation of the soil prevents erosion and keeps streams, rivers, and other bodies of water reasonably free of soil runoff. Appropriate methods for dealing with human, animal, and industrial waste prevent both water and air pollution. Congestion often leads to environmental problems. Heavy industry may contribute to the pollution of air and water unless appropriate standards can be observed that can also meet the economic requirements of production processes.

Government Regulations

Government regulations may influence the quality of our environment not only by the standards imposed as to disposal of wastes and related factors but also by zoning laws, building codes, traffic patterns and standards, density, and related requirements. General plans for the development of an area include the highway network, location of water and sewer mains, location and type of waste disposal systems, the placement of parks, schools, and other public facilities and many related factors. All of these have major effects on the physical environment. Plans and programs of development which avoid congestion and which make it easy for private citizens and enterprises to avoid contributing to environmental problems can mean much for long-term developments. In addition, the relative attractiveness of public buildings and other installations may determine the general quality of an entire area.

Land Development

Decisions related to plans for the development of land can affect not only the general attractiveness of an area but also the efficiency with which it can be used and the extent to which it maintains and improves the physical environment or adds to problems of pollution. Land planners and engineers thus have a heavy responsibility for our environment. Those who develop land and build structures also play a big role in determining the quality of the physical environment. Careful workmanship, effective use of materials, and appropriate combinations of land, buildings, and other improvements can do much to avoid environmental problems. Installation of good quality waste disposal systems, underground installation of electric wires and utilities, and general care in the development of an area are all important.

Physical Factors Affecting Income and Decisions

Those physical factors which affect property income are of primary importance in real estate decisions.

A listing of all physical factors that affect the income-producing ability of land and the buildings and other improvements on it would be an almost impossible task. We will direct our attention primarily to the following in this discussion: (1) land in terms of location, size and shape, topography, condition of topsoil and subsoil, and various physical factors in the property's environment; (2) buildings (including type of buildings in relation to the land), orientation, quality and durability, depreciation, types of construction, functional plan, style and attractiveness, and conformity to surroundings, and (3) other improvements.

LAND

Of the various physical factors related to land we will pay primary attention to those listed above. Because of the importance of land surveys we will consider this topic briefly as well.

Location

Although fertility is the principal factor in determining the income produced by agricultural land, the location or *situs* of urban land is of primary importance in determining its income-producing ability. Since no two points on the earth's surface are exactly alike, every piece of urban real estate is unique; it differs in some respect from others. In some cases the differences may be slight, in others of major importance. Each parcel of urban real estate is a part of a neighborhood or district; it is part of a city and region. To understand even a few of the important features of the relationships between location and income we will need to consider economic trends, industry potentials, city growth and structure, and the character of specific residential neighborhoods and commercial and industrial districts.

Location often means access or lack of access to various utilities and conveniences. Even the pioneer farmer had to have a road or a right of way over which he could carry his produce to market and bring back necessary provisions. The importance of accessibility tends to increase as our communities become more complex.

A farm may be diminished in value if it is split in two by an express highway to which it does not have access. Land at express highway intersections, however, has a high value for motels, shopping centers, and industries.

The value of a parcel of land is related directly to the ease or difficulty of access to roads and streets, transportation facilities, water and gas mains, sewers, and electrical and telephone lines. Similarly, such services as mail delivery, police and fire protection, and garbage, trash, and snow removal are significant.

Distances to schools, shopping centers, places of employment, churches, community centers, parks, and playgrounds are of special importance in considering the value characteristics of land used for residential purposes. Nearness to main arteries of pedestrian traffic and to parking areas is of major importance in the case of business sites. Nearness to transportation lines often is important to industrial sites. Increasingly, accessibility has meant ease of access by automobile or truck transportation. Both shopping centers and industrial parks illustrate this trend.

Size and Shape of the Land

Urban lot sizes are usually measured in square feet or the number of feet of frontage on the street and depth in feet. Farms and other rural real estate are measured in terms of acres (once acre equals 43,560 square feet) or sections (a square mile equals 640 acres). Size and shape affect the productivity of a parcel of ground. Obviously, a lot with only 30 feet of frontage cannot be used as the site for a tall office building or a large department store.

Size is an important factor in determining use, and use in turn has a very direct bearing on income-producing ability and hence on decisions. Size also determines effectiveness of use; the trend toward larger farms as agriculture has become more highly mechanized is an example. Value, of course, is not directly proportional to size. Up to a point, additions to the size of a parcel of land tend to increase its income-producing ability and hence its value; thereafter, such additions tend to be of diminishing importance. *Plottage* is the term used to describe the extent to which value is increased when two or more plots are combined.

The shape of the land parcel may determine the possible uses to which it may be put and hence affect its income-producing ability. While lots of irregular shape may often be used to advantage for residential purposes, regularity is usually desirable for business, industrial, or agricultural uses. Many developers of new residential areas plan lots of irregular shape, adapting them to curvilinear streets, cul-de-sacs, and park areas. This practice contrasts with the gridiron pattern formerly followed in subdivision planning. The gridiron pattern often resulted in oddly shaped lots when diagonal streets were involved.

The relationship between frontage and depth is important for many types of urban real estate. Few lots shorter than 50 or 60 feet in width are considered adequate for development of single-family detached residences. Lots used for business and industrial purposes vary greatly in width and depth, depending on the specific uses to which they are put,

Planned Unit Development

Efforts to improve the efficiency of land use have resulted in the concept of "planned unit development" (PUD). This involves the careful study of the interrelations among the various functions that are to be performed by a unit of land in order to get the maximum utilization of the land available. For example, instead of developing an area entirely with single-family homes on conventional lots, cluster-type housing may be used but arranged in such a way that adequate privacy is offered and provision is made for recreational, commercial, and other related land uses. More efficient land utilization will result. Recognizing the potential benefits of this concept of land development, many local zoning boards have added PUD zoning to permit greater flexibility of land use.

Topography

A study of topography includes a consideration of contour and slope, the direction and steepness of slope, and such things as gullies, streams, knolls, and ravines. These factors may have a determining influence on the uses which may be made of the land. Lots with steep slopes, for example, are not easily adapted to business, industrial, or agricultural uses. They may allow for attractive residential developments, although the cost of a house built on a sloping lot is usually greater than that of one constructed on a level lot. Note Figure 2–1 in this connection. Topography has an important bearing on drainage, soil types, erosion, the ease or difficulty of constructing streets or roads, and landscaping problems.

In addition to the topography of a specific land parcel, it is usually necessary to consider the topography of adjoining land, since drainage and related problems may be involved. Gently rolling land is usually considered desirable in residential neighborhoods and for farming operations, while level or nearly level land is more desirable in business and industrial areas.

It is well to give special attention to streams or bodies of water on or near a piece of land. The possibility of flooding is always an important consideration, and stagnant water may invite hordes of mosquitoes. Some streams are polluted or are in danger of it.

As a general guide to the study of the contour of a tract of land, consider on the one hand those factors which will be advantageous to its income-producing ability and on the other those things which will be detrimental. For example, drainage problems often require expensive tiling operations; steep lots may require the building of retaining walls.

Condition of the Topsoil and Subsoil

The condition of the topsoil and subsoil is of basic importance in determining the income-producing ability of farms. It also has a bearing on city lots. Surface and subsurface rock, clays which expand and contract

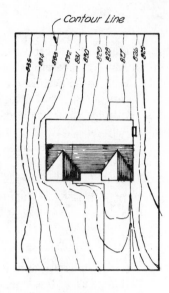
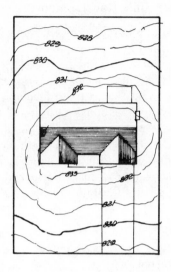

Plan View   *Plan View*

Construction on a side sloping lot   Construction on top of a slight knoll

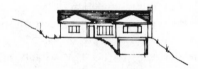

Front Elevation   *Front Elevation*

Construction on a side sloping lot   Construction on top of a slight knoll

FIG. 2–1. Topographical considerations related to house construction.

significantly, muck land, quicksand, and areas where fill material has been placed often create special problems in land use development. In some cities expensive piles must be driven to provide a bearing surface for any buildings of major size because of the unstable nature of the soil. If rock formations are encountered at a point only a few feet from the surface, it becomes expensive to excavate and to install water mains and sewer lines.

Further, certain types of soils have poor subsurface drainage characteristics and thereby introduce special problems in the construction of paved surfaces, underground utilities, basements, and individual sewage disposal systems. In areas where sanitary sewer service is not available, it is important to run percolation tests to determine the capability of the subsoil to absorb sewage where individual sewage disposal systems using absorption fields are contemplated.

The real estate decision maker should have a complete awareness of potential soil problems in a given area. The presence of such problems may have a significant impact on land use and development costs.

Physical Environmental Factors

The condition of the physical environment has an important bearing on the income-producing potential of real estate. For example, polluted streams, lakes, and ocean front as well as smog and other undesirable atmospheric conditions can affect large areas of land and hinder their development. Favorable or unfavorable weather conditions such as extreme cold or heat, hurricanes, heavy snowstorms, fog, and the like may have a bearing on various areas. Industrial wastes, trash dumps, open sewers, certain types of sewage disposal plants, and a variety of other environmental factors may have adverse effects. On the other hand, desirable environmental conditions can have a favorable effect on an area and on the properties located there.

Surveys

In connection with most land development activities, land transfers, and mortgage financing, surveys by licensed surveyors or engineers are often required. These surveys can be placed into three major categories: (1) boundary surveys, (2) topographic surveys, and (3) in-place surveys.

The exhibit for the boundary survey typically shows the distances and directions which describe the parcel of real property in question and is accompanied by a legal description of the boundaries. The location of section corner stones, power lines, property corner markers, fences, access ways, and other physical evidence of occupation relative to the boundaries is often shown on the survey as well as such items as easements of record. These surveys are typically required for land conveyance purposes.

Topographic surveys reveal through the use of contour lines (lines of equal elevation) the general contour and shape of the land. Locations of trees, structures, and roadways are often included on the topographic survey. Such surveys are utilized in the design of structures and other improvements related to a tract of land.

In-place surveys illustrate the location of existing structures and related improvements with respect to property lines, setback lines, and easements on a particular tract of land. These surveys are often done at the request of the mortgage lender to assure that the mortgaged property does not violate property lines, easements, setback lines, and the like. For single-family structures, the in-place survey is more often called a mortgage survey (see Fig. 2–2).

Additionally, surveys may be classified as staked surveys and unstaked surveys. Staked surveys require the actual staking of the property corners in the field; unstaked surveys utilize approximate boundary lines established

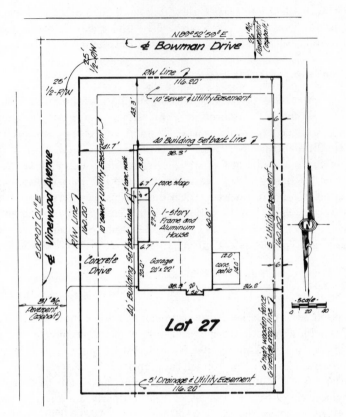

January 21, 19

Last Federal Savings and Loan Association
700 North Market Street
Indianapolis, Indiana 46204

Gentlemen:

I, the undersigned, hereby certify that the within plat is true and correct and represents a survey made by me on the 15th day of November, 19__, of real estate described as follows:

Lot #27 in Willow Creek Addition - Section Five, as per plat thereof recorded October 31, 1977, as Instrument #77-70273 in the Office of the Recorder of Marion County, Indiana.

Based thereon, I further certify that the building situated on the above described real estate is located within the boundaries of said premises. I have shown on said plat the distances from the sides and front of the building to points on the side lines and front line of the lot. I further certify that the buildings on the adjoining property do not encroach on the lot or real estate in question.

The property is improved with a one story frame dwelling, located at 5861 Vinewood Avenue, Indianapolis, Indiana.

FIG. 2-2.   Surveyor's plat of a city lot for mortgage purposes. (Courtesy Paul I. Cripe, Inc.)

by physical evidence such as fences, tree rows, and roads. The type of survey needed will depend on the purpose of the survey and the accuracy required. As an example, the mortgage survey is typically an unstaked survey and therefore cannot be used to establish property lines.

BUILDINGS

Except for parking lots and a few other uses, it is necessary to construct a building in order to earn income from urban land. Thus buildings should be thought of as the means by which the earning power of urban land is released. Considered in another way, the services of buildings and other improvements on urban land may be thought of as similar in some degree to the crops which are produced on farm land. Buildings are also important to farming operations but play a lesser role than they do in urban land uses.

In this section we will consider some of the physical characteristics which increase or diminish the income-producing ability of buildings and consequently have a bearing on real estate decisions. Land value arises from residual income, after expenses of operating the building, real estate taxes, and interest and depreciation on the cost of the building are deducted from gross income. If the wrong type of building is constructed, the value of the land may be reduced.

We should note that while a lot and a building together form a single income-producing unit, the building can be replaced while the land cannot. In the case of especially well-located lots, the land is one of the paramount supports of the value of the entire property. In other cases it is of lesser importance. In some cases land can be "made," as in Miami or Chicago, where water-covered areas have been filled in or steep hills have been graded down.

Type of Building in Relation to Land

It is desirable from both a private and public standpoint to have each piece of real estate developed to what is referred to in real estate circles as its "highest and best" use. This means that the maximum income-producing capacity of the land is realized by the type of improvement (usually a building) put on it. In some situations highest and best use may mean no building at all, as in the case of a parking lot or a cornfield.

One of the important considerations in developing a property to its highest and best use is a balanced relationship among land, buildings, and other improvements. The income-producing ability of a property may be greater or less than required to pay a return on the investment. This difference is often referred to by its appraisers as *improved value*.

For example, a building costing $500,000 to construct may be placed on a lot priced at $100,000. Faulty planning and improper improvement may result in a value based on anticipated returns of only $400,000. On the other hand, a proper combination of land and buildings based on careful planning by the architect, plus cleverness, imagination, and risk-taking by the promoter, may produce an income that will support a value of $800,000.

Some buildings represent an *overimprovement*—that is, a larger expenditure than can be supported by the site. Others represent an *underimprovement,* an investment that is not great enough to bring out the full income-producing potential of the site.

Orientation

The position of the structure on the land and the general relationship of the structure to the surroundings are usually referred to as its orientation. In solidly built business streets, of course, there is little latitude for special arrangements. Even in such cases, however, position on the street, easy access for customers, accessibility to delivery trucks, relationship to adjacent buildings, and the like are important factors in a property's income-producing ability. In the North, locations on the street facing the sun may command a premium; in the South the opposite is often true. An industrial building must be placed advantageously with respect to the movement of materials and workers into and out of the plant.

Orientation is a major problem in the case of residential buildings, particularly single-family homes. A house placed on the lot in such a way as to bring out the greatest potentialities of the entire property will be more valuable than an identical house located to lesser advantage. In addition, proper orientation to the sun, prevailing winds, and attractive and unattractive views are major considerations. Attention is often given to solar orientation in order to take greatest advantage of the sun's heat in the winter and protection from it in the summer. Also, houses should be located to advantage with respect to the local environment including lot lines, setback lines, and other houses in the area.

Quality and Durability

The quality of the workmanship and materials in a building has an important effect on its durability. If properly constructed a building will resist both the elements and usage over a long period of time and without incurring excessive maintenance costs. The durability of a building has a direct relationship to its life cycle—that is, to the period during which it can produce an income adequate to justify the investment involved. While the physical life of a building is usually longer than its economic life, there tends to be some relationship between physical life and the period during which satisfactory returns can be earned. These returns, of course, may be either in the form of monetary income or, in the case of an owner-occupied home, in direct usage.

It may be said in general that physical decay has not been a major factor in bringing the useful or economic lives of buildings to an end. Generally, buildings are demolished in order to make room for a higher land use. In-deed, the rate of obsolescence of buildings appears to be higher than it was several decades ago. Rapid changes in the structure of cities, especially under the impact of heavy automobile traffic, have brought swift changes in land values and in the economic usefulness of many buildings. Com-petition of outlying areas is affecting land uses in central business districts.

Depreciation

As we have indicated, the income-producing ability of a building tends to decline and its value to diminish with the passage of time, if other things remain equal. This process is called *depreciation*.

The American Institute of Real Estate Appraisers has pointed out that depreciation may be due to deterioration resulting from wear and tear and the action of the elements and to obsolescence which may be functional or economic. Functional obsolescence results from poor planning, design, or equipment and related factors "evidenced by conditions within the property"; economic obsolescence results from changes "external to the property," such as neighborhood changes, shifts in market preference, tech-nological advance, and the like.[1]

Of course, it should be kept in mind that economic forces causing appreciation in value may be at work along with those causing depreciation. For example, an older house, while suffering somewhat from physical de-terioration and obsolescence, may nevertheless increase in value over a period of time due to rapidly rising costs of material and labor used in constructing housing which provides similar services.

Types of Construction

The four main types of construction used in this country are wood frame, wall-bearing masonry, reinforced concrete frame, and steel frame. Another classification provides for two basic types of construction: skeleton frame and wall bearing. The former makes use of columns to transmit loads to the foundation; the latter uses the walls for this purpose.

Wooden frame construction, whether covered by weatherboarding or veneered with brick or stone, is the type most frequently used in building medium-priced houses (see Fig. 2–3). It is cheaper than other types, it can be built rapidly, and it is easy to insulate against heat or cold. Its chief disadvantage is susceptibility to fire. However, firestops, fireproof materials for insulation, aluminum coating, and flameproofed lumber help to reduce this hazard.

In masonry construction the exterior walls are of brick, stone, or concrete block. A brick wall may be of solid construction, or it may be built some-

---

[1] See *The Appraisal of Real Estate* (5th ed.; Chicago: The American Institute of Real Estate Appraisers, 1973), pp. 199–204. See also Richard U. Ratcliff, *Modern Real Estate Valuation* (Madison, Wis.: The Democrat Press, 1965), pp. 58–64.

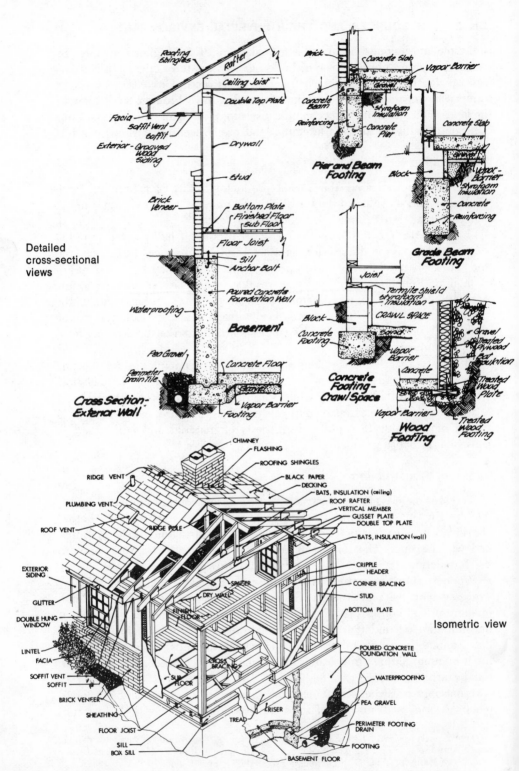

Detailed cross-sectional views

Roofing Shingles
Rafter
Ceiling Joist
Double Top Plate
Facia
Soffit Vent
Soffit
Exterior-Grooved Wood Siding
Drywall
Stud
Brick Veneer
Bottom Plate
Finished Floor
Sub Floor
Floor Joist
Sill
Anchor Bolt
Poured Concrete Foundation Wall
Waterproofing
Basement
Pea Gravel
Perimeter Drain Tile
Concrete Floor
Cross Section-Exterior Wall
Vapor Barrier
Footing

Brick
Concrete Slab
Vapor Barrier
Gravel
Concrete Beam
Styrofoam Insulation
Reinforcing
Concrete Pier
Pier and Beam Footing

Concrete Slab
Block
Vapor Barrier
Styrofoam Insulation
Concrete
Reinforcing
Grade Beam Footing

Joist
Termite shield
Styrofoam Insulation
CRAWL SPACE
Block
Concrete Footing
Board
Vapor Barrier
Concrete
Concrete Footing-Crawl Space
Vapor Barrier
Wood Footing
Gravel
Treated Plywood
Bat Insulation
Treated Wood Plate
Treated Wood Footing

CHIMNEY
FLASHING
ROOFING SHINGLES
RIDGE VENT
BLACK PAPER
DECKING
BATS, INSULATION (ceiling)
ROOF RAFTER
VERTICAL MEMBER
GUSSET PLATE
DOUBLE TOP PLATE
PLUMBING VENT
BATS, INSULATION (wall)
ROOF VENT
RIDGE POLE
EXTERIOR SIDING
SPACER
DRY WALL
FINISHED FLOOR
CRIPPLE
HEADER
CORNER BRACING
STUD
BOTTOM PLATE
GUTTER
DOUBLE HUNG WINDOW
LINTEL
FACIA
CROSS BRACING
SOFFIT VENT
SOFFIT
SUB FLOOR
BRICK VENEER
SHEATHING
FLOOR JOIST
SILL
BOX SILL
TREAD
RISER
BASEMENT FLOOR
POURED CONCRETE FOUNDATION WALL
WATERPROOFING
PEA GRAVEL
PERIMETER FOOTING DRAIN
FOOTING

Isometric view

FIG. 2–3. Wood frame construction. (Courtesy Paul I. Cripe, Inc.)

44

what thicker than a solid wall to allow for an air space between the outer and inner courses of brick. Often brick or stone is backed up with hollow terra-cotta tile or cement blocks. Masonry houses in the lower-price ranges usually have interior partitions and floor joists of wood. Steel joists may be used in more expensive types. Masonry structures tend to be more fire-resistant than frame types, and maintenance costs are typically lower. On the other hand, such structures are more expensive to build.

Reinforced concrete structures may have walls and floors of monolithic construction which are poured into place at the site, may be assembled from concrete block and precast joists and slabs, or may be constructed by a combination of these methods. Typically, steel reinforcing in the form of bars or wire mesh is submerged in the concrete while the concrete is wet to supply necessary tensile strength to the concrete. The chief advantages of concrete buildings are their permanency, fireproof construction, and low maintenance costs.

Steel-frame structures are similar in principle to wooden-frame buildings. Studs, joists, and rafters made of steel are used, eliminating shrinkage; when noncombustible insulating material and exterior covering are used, the structure will resist fire. Coverings may be of any of the usual building materials desired.

Functional Plan

Buildings are designed for many purposes, ranging from the functions of specialized industrial structures to those of small single-family residences. (See Fig. 2–4.) All of them provide protection against the elements, such as temperature extremes, rain, and snow. Nearly all provide some degree of comfort and convenience.

The development of an adequate functional plan for a building is largely the work of the architect and engineer. Careful design of spans, proper distribution of weight, adequate openings for doors and windows, correct width of corridors, suitable combinations of materials, and related factors are all involved. In recent years even low- and medium-priced single-family homes have been studied in terms of functions to be performed and the most effective arrangements of the exterior and interior of the structures for the performance of these functions. The functional plan of special-purpose buildings must reflect the specific use for which the structure is intended. General-purpose buildings aim at simple arrangements with a maximum of flexibility in the use of interior space.

Constant improvement in design is one of the important causes of obsolescence in existing buildings. The efficiency of one-story manufacturing plants with continuous assembly lines, for example, has rendered many multistory industrial plants obsolete.

Of special importance to the functional adequacy of modern buildings is the mechanical equipment that is used. The cost of such equipment is

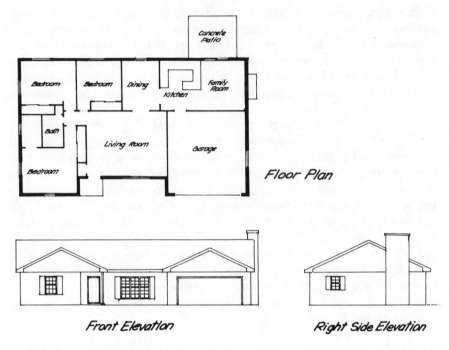

Floor Plan

Front Elevation   Right Side Elevation

FIG. 2–4. Several typical views included in a set of house plans.

now a major item, even in the construction of a small house. The adequacy, condition, durability, and operating economy of such equipment has an important bearing on operating costs and hence on the income-producing capacity of a building. For residences the most important types of equipment are plumbing and sewage disposal, heating and air conditioning, and electric light and power. Elevators are of major importance in many office, apartment, and store buildings. Indeed, the elevator was essential to the development of modern skyscrapers. Escalators are being used to an increasing extent. Industrial plants contain a wide variety of specialized equipment of many types.

Insulation against heat, cold, and moisture has become an increasingly important factor in the operating costs of a building. The rapidly rising cost of fuel has resulted in heightened emphasis on properly insulated walls, ceilings, floors, windows, entry ways, ducts, and plumbing.

Governmental regulation has also played an expanding role in assuring the functional adequacy of many buildings. Areas currently receiving attention include protection against fire, air pollution, and noise pollution.

Style and Attractiveness

The appeal of a building to prospective users and investors is an important element in its ability to produce future income. The factors that make up appeal are difficult to identify. We know that architects and engineers often are able to impart to a building an appeal that is over and above that arising from utilitarian and economic considerations alone. Often this appeal continues over many years. In such cases the building relates well to its environment. Style in a building is usually considered to be one of the factors that provide long-range appeal to users and investors. In this connection Condit says:

> . . . the word "style" is much abused. Yet its connotation is such that the critic and the historian of art can hardly avoid it. In architecture it represents or stands for those essential characteristics of construction, form, ornament, and detail which are common to all the important structures of any particular period in history. But it also stands for those technical and aesthetic qualities of the artistic product which grow directly, logically, and organically out of the conditions of human existence and out of the aspirations and powers of human beings. We rightly feel that the buildings of a certain style—if it is a genuine style—reflect in their form the realities of man's experience and the attempt to master and give emotional expression to those realities. These buildings are constituent facts of man's history, and their revelation is a part of truth itself.[2]

There may, of course, be wide variations in the tastes and cultural standards of prospective users and investors. These tastes will vary from time to time and from region to region. In general, however, experience indicates that buildings which are constructed according to the dictates of good taste are more stable in value over long periods of time than others. For example, houses constructed in accordance with sound architectural standards are not subject to the wide fluctuations in price which arise from the unsettling influences of fads and the temporary popularity of a particular style. The mark of good taste is simplicity. This is manifest in simple masses, simple roof lines, and restrained and well-chosen detail. Good taste and good architecture depend on simplicity. Beauty is not created by gingerbread and other incongruous and superfluous features and ornaments, but by good proportions and the proper use of materials.

Simplicity, balance, proper proportions, and quality of materials and workmanship, all considered in relation to the functions of the building, are the primary considerations in judging its attractiveness. It should be noted, however, that there are no absolute standards and that real estate value rests on what potential buyers, users, or investors *think* is attractive as well as on what may be considered attractive by experts.

Architectural Styles

Architectural styles vary widely. Most architects try to select the style which will express most adequately the use of the building. Recent trends

---

[2] Reprinted from *The Rise of the Skyscraper* by Carl W. Condit by permission of the University of Chicago Press, p. 1. Copyright 1952 by the University of Chicago.

have moved away from the limiting influences of some of the traditional
styles and toward greater emphasis on functional design. In the case of
houses, for example, it is possible to list a number of styles which may be
seen in our towns and cities every day, but in general many liberties have
been taken with the prototypes of these styles so that no hard-and-fast
classifications can be made.

We often refer to "English," "Spanish," "French," "colonial," or "modern"
houses, and to such special types as "Cape Cod," "ranch house," "Dutch
colonial," or "Southern colonial." All of these architectural styles are found
with many modifications and variations, but many houses of real distinction
cannot be classified by style. Indeed, the trend has been away from the
so-called traditional style and toward the modern or contemporary style.
This trend is even more pronounced for business and industrial buildings.

Consider the following statement:

. . . architecture is not just a way of packaging a rather large product to attract
potential impulse-buyers. Architecture is a system of organization, a way of putting things together.

And architecture—unlike "styling" or "packaging"—possesses another quality
that is of the greatest importance to any client or consumer: it only starts to live
after the job is done. A box of Kleenex tissue is through once it has been designed,
manufactured, sold and used up. The cycle is short, simple, direct. But a good
building is a living organism—it starts to do things of its own accord once it has
been born. "We shape our buildings," Winston Churchill has said, "and, after-
wards, our buildings shape us." [3]

Conformity

The degree to which buildings are compatible with their physical environment has a bearing on their value. We are talking here of general
conformity with respect to such items as the style of the building, remaining life of the structure, and in some cases the size of the structure. It
should be noted that factors of this type must be judged in terms of the
environment in which the building is found. Conformity may affect the
marketability of a property and hence its value.

OTHER IMPROVEMENTS

In addition to the main buildings, any other improvements which form
a part of a property have a relationship to its value. These other improvements may include (1) accessory buildings, such as garages; (2) walks,
driveways, and parking areas; (3) protective barriers; (4) terraces; (5)
service areas; (6) retaining walls; (7) landscaping, including lawns, trees,
shrubbery, and gardens; (8) fences; and (9) other types.

[3] Peter Blake, "Modern Architecture: Its Many Faces," *The Architectural Forum*
(March, 1958), pp. 77–78.

We shall not attempt to undertake a detailed discussion of these items. Their types, extent, and quality are points to consider when studying the relationship of "other improvements" to the earning power of a property and their impact on real estate decisions.

SUMMARY

We usually think of real properties as distinct physical units composed of land and buildings. As such, they possess many physical characteristics which may influence real estate decision makers. This is because physical characteristics affect income-producing ability, either directly or indirectly. The quality of the total physical environment has a bearing on income.

No two parts of the earth's surface are exactly alike, hence location is an important factor in determining the income-producing ability of real estate. For agricultural land, fertility varies from one location to another. In the case of urban real estate, some locations are more accessible than others, or have more favorable surroundings.

Although the value of a parcel of real estate is not directly proportional to its size, the size and shape of real properties are among the factors which help to determine value. Additions to the size of a piece of real property tend to increase its income-producing ability and hence its value up to a point. A large parcel of land may have, for some purposes, greater value than the sum of the values of the smaller land parcels of which it is composed. This is known as plottage value. The shape of the land parcels, as well as their size, often determines the possible uses for the properties, and thus influences their income-producing ability.

Other physical characteristics such as topography, topsoil and subsoil conditions, and accessibility to transportation and utilities may limit or determine land uses, and hence land values. The income-producing ability of a parcel of real estate also is influenced by the buildings upon it and their quality of construction, their style and attractiveness, size, orientation, and conformity with the surrounding area.

QUESTIONS FOR STUDY

1. What are the three approaches to the study of real property? How do they differ?
2. Develop a classification of existing land uses in the community in which your study property is located.
3. How do government regulations affect the physical environment of real estate?
4. Make a list of the physical factors affecting income-producing ability of real estate that would be most important if you were in charge of selecting a site for: (a) a television repair shop, (b) a new drive-in restaurant, (c) a golf course, (d) a new post office for your community.
5. What are the distinguishing characteristics of the principal types of construction?

6. If you were planning to build your own home, which factors would you consider most important in determining its orientation?
7. Give some specific examples of overimprovement and underimprovement of real properties.
8. Mr. Carey owns a vacant lot adjacent to his grocery store. This vacant lot has a frontage of 25 feet. Adjoining it is another vacant lot of equal size owned by Mr. Gibson, whose dry cleaning establishment is located on the next lot. Mr. Anderson offers Carey $5,000 for his lot, but says that if Carey can secure Gibson's vacant lot, he will pay $13,500 for the two lots. Can you explain why Anderson would offer more than twice as much for the two lots as he would give for one of them alone?
9. What is meant by "depreciation"? What is its effect on the income-producing ability of a building?
10. In planning your own home, would you prefer to buy and build on a level lot or a sloping lot? How might the value of the house be a factor in the choice of lots?
11. "We travel together, passengers on a little spaceship; dependent on its vulnerable reserve of air and soil; all committed for our safety to its security and peace; preserved from annihilation only by the care, the work and the love we give to our craft." (Adlai Stevenson) Do you think the Stevenson quotation has special significance? Why? How does this quotation apply to the use of real estate resources?

SUGGESTED READINGS

AMERICAN INSTITUTE OF REAL ESTATE APPRAISERS. *The Appraisal of Real Estate* (6th ed.). Chicago: The Institute, 1973. Chs. 9–12.

OLIN, HAROLD B., SCHMIDT, JOHN L., and LEWIS, WALTER H. *Construction: Principles, Materials & Methods* (3rd ed.). Chicago: The Institute of Financial Education, 1975. Secs. 101–1 to 101–10.

SMITH, HALBERT C., TSCHAPPAT, CARL J., and RACSTER, RONALD W. *Real Estate and Urban Development* (rev. ed.). Homewood, Ill.: Richard D. Irwin, Inc., 1977. Ch. 18.

STUDY PROJECT 2–1

Architectural Styles and Functional Utility *

Architectural Types. Most of the homes in this country are based on certain definite architectural types. (See following pages.) Thousands of good and bad hybrid combinations have evolved out of these recognized types. Perhaps the most universal classification is the colonial group—the New England Colonial, the Cape Cod, the Dutch Colonial, the Colonial of the Middle Atlantic colonies, and the Southern Colonial. Since the English were predominate in the first settlements along the Atlantic coast, it was natural that the Georgian architecture of eighteenth-century England should have directly influenced the colonial types in New England and the Middle Atlantic colonies which have become the basis of a purely American type.

* American Institute of Real Estate Appraisers, *The Appraisal of Real Estate* (4th ed.; Chicago: The Institute, 1964). Appendix B.

These are comfortable, homelike dwellings which are the result of a distinct type developed by New England carpenters attempting to imitate in wood some of the classic motifs of the Georgian houses of brick and stone which were so prevalent in their former homeland. They are generally of clapboard exterior, painted white, with shingle roof. They are characterized by excellent proportions in which openings are often treated with mouldings of refined detail.

This comes down to us from our earliest colonial days, and is a development of the one-story cottage. Generally, the main cornice line is at the second-story level, with a sloping roof, and sometimes with rooms on the second floor. Dormer windows are used. There is a detailed entrance feature with pilasters and cornices. These houses are most nearly correct when built of frame with clapboard or shingle walls, painted white. In some sections, however, stone is used for the first story, or even brick.

This style is recognizable at once by the double slope of its gambrel roof. Exterior walls may be either masonry or frame. Usually the entrance doorway is elaborately decorated and porches are at the side. It is well adapted for flat sites but is difficult to handle on a steep slope.

This type is descended from the more formal early colonial homes of wealthier families in the Middle Atlantic states. There are usually two full stories, sometimes with dormers to give light to a third floor space. Windows are divided into small panes. Simplicity and balance is the keynote. Woodwork is painted white or cream, with shutters usually in green.

Very similar to colonial and Georgian types, but usually distinguished by the use of two-story columns forming a porch which may be across the long facade or at the side.

The most formal of the colonial types. Balanced openings and chimneys predominate. Ceilings are usually higher than in the other colonial designs. Wings usually drop to follow the contour of the ground and are kept simple in detail. Porches, at front or side, are rather elaborate.

These stately, symmetrical, perfectly scaled Georgian houses are modern counterparts of the houses built in England during the reign of the four Georges. Extremely conventional in character, they require formal, park-like grounds for a setting.

A regional variation of the colonial, especially adapted for flat ground. It is informal in character, with the main section and its higher roof line dominating the design. The exterior stone walls are sometimes whitewashed and covered with plaster. Details are simple. Roof is either slate or wood shingle.

BINFIELD

9

These are rustic, informal, picturesque English houses with interesting exterior treatment and ornamentation of half-timber effects, carved wood, stone, and brick. In the original Elizabethan type, the exposed timbers on the exterior constituted the structural frame of the building. Between the half-timbering there is usually plaster. Roof slopes are quite steep and project at the ends with barges rather than cornices.

BINFIELD

10

Called "modern" to distinguish it from the other English types described, this has many of the marks of the earlier English styles, including the steep roof slopes with variegated and graduated slate or red tile, but with no cornices or eaves. Windows are mostly casements, wood or metal. It is especially suitable for sloping ground, the informal relation of rooms and spaces adding to the exterior effect.

This style as transposed to this country is especially suitable for larger homes where formality is desired. The design is characterized by verticality with exterior walls usually of stone or brick laid in formal pattern. Window and door trim are generally of dressed or cut stone. Windows are usually casements, and the roof is of slate spaced wide and thick to give the effect of a stone roof.

This is an adaptation of an English country or farm house characterized by informality relieved by sills, mullions, porches, and chimneys of stone dressed by a hammer. Details are generally fairly heavy. Windows are metal casements. The roof should be of variegated slate with irregular shapes, graduated from large sizes at the eaves to small at the ridge.

The Spanish in Florida and in their migrations through Mexico to the Southwest brought their sprawling type of home that gives protection from hot summer suns by its heavy tile roof and walls of adobe or stucco. With its enclosed patio it is designed for outdoor living.

Of the various French styles the most easily recognized is the small formal house, perfectly balanced, with high-pitched roof, capturing the spirit of the country estates of France.

If the site is large enough, this is a popular design, characterized by its round tower, generally used for the main stairway. Exterior walls are mostly of stone with both brick and dressed stone used at the openings, for the cornice, and for chimneys. Half-timbering is sometimes used as a relief.

An informal type using stone, painted brick, or stucco and varying considerably in adaptation and design. The example shown here has painted brick or plaster exterior walls with wood or stone around openings, and with half-timbering used as an accent. Roof slopes are steep and the roof is generally very informal in treatment.

Typical Italian details include completely framed windows and openings, circular heads over exterior openings, high windows and doors, and the red "S" shaped clay tile on the roof. Exterior surfaces may be masonry or plaster.

The two-story Monterey house is adapted from a style prevalent in the early Spanish era in California. It is characatrized usually by a balcony across the entire front of the building.

This style was derived from the early European modern trend. It is characterized by flat roofs and unadorned plain walls with geometric patterns of light and shade. Windows are large with corner window groups commonly used.

A new type of modern which can and does take many forms. It is designed to promote better living with close relationship to the outdoors and the site. It is designed to incorporate new construction methods, new materials, and new uses of old materials. Characteristics are overhangs over large windows, open planning, horizontal lines, and simple details. These houses may be one or two stories or split-levels to suit site conditions. Roofs may be flat, shed, gabled, or various combinations thereof.

These are modern ranch-type bungalows which sprawl out over their lot, providing the utmost in livability, light, and air.

Other architectural designs not pictured here but often encountered are the Mediterranean house, the Moorish house, and the Queen Anne. The first is closely related to the Italian type, having a tile roof, brightly colored canvas awnings shading decks and terraces, vast expanses of unadorned wall spaces, and massed forms created by circular stair towers. The Moorish house with its unusual minarets and pointed arches is unmistakable. The Queen Anne houses are identified by the baroque ornamentation which characterized the architecture developed during the reign of Queen Anne.

Questions

1. Which architectural types are most common in your area?
2. What are the major similarities and differences among the Cape Cod, Dutch Colonial, and Southern Colonial styles?
3. What are major differences among the four "English" styles?
4. What are the outstanding characteristics of the California Ranch, International Modern, and Contemporary styles? Can these be related to any of the more traditional styles?
5. Would an unusual architectural style have a bearing on a property's sales appeal? Why or why not?
6. Do most of the houses in your neighborhood comply with the traditional architectural types pictured? If not, what are the variations and do they affect the marketability of the houses?

Handwritten annotations:

21

1 New England Colonial
2 Cape Cod
3 Dutch Colonial
4 Modern Colonial
5 Southern Colonial
6 Georgian Colonial
7 Modern Georgian
8 Pennsylvania Farmhouse Colonial
9 English Half-Timbered (Elizabethan)
10 Modern-English
11 English Tudor
12 English Cotswold
13 Spanish
14 French Provincial
15 Norman French
16 French Farmhouse
17 Italian
18 Monterey
19 International Modern
20 Contemporary
21 California Ranch

3

LEGAL ASPECTS
OF REAL ESTATE

IMPORTANCE OF LEGAL FACTORS

The variety of regulations, laws, and governmental policies that have an impact on real estate is so great as almost to defy comprehensive classification and analysis. Try, for example, to prepare a list of all the regulations affecting your "study property."

Real estate is more closely regulated as to ownership and use than any other commodity, with the possible exception of narcotics. (See Study Project 4–1 on page 110.) This is due to the fact that private property rights in real estate are created, guaranteed, and enforced by government. Also, this situation may be explained by the so-called "neighboring effect"—the tremendous impact which the utilization of one piece of real property may have on another. In addition, real estate resources are an important part of our total environment.

Ownership

The ownership of real property is regulated by the laws governing titles and title transfers. Such regulation of ownership is in part the result of the gradual evolution of the common law and in part the product of legislative and administrative processes. Ownership is never "complete," since the exercise by government of the rights of taxation, eminent domain, or the police power may modify various private ownership interests substantially.

Income Production

The influence of legal and governmental factors on the income-producing ability of real property is profound. It ranges all the way from the definition and protection of ownership rights and the enforcement of contracts to the maintenance of full or nearly full employment conditions in our economy. Real estate is affected by all levels of government from the federal government to local townships, municipalities, and school districts. We should recognize that a major portion of the income from real estate each year is used for the payment of property and income taxes. Even so, we must also recognize that real property rights could not exist without government and that real properties would have much lower values without the opportunity to enjoy the protections and services of modern governmental organizations.

Not only governmental regulations and policies, but private agreements and regulations may also have important influences on real estate decisions and on the income-producing potential of real properties. We may think of all of the private agreements and contracts that involve real estate as constituting a system of private laws. In addition, such specific arrangements as deed restrictions or agreements of property owners' or condominium owners' associations may have important influences on real estate decisions.

Competition

Decisions relating to the uses of various real properties, the contracts and agreements of owners, users, investors, and others, the rate of development of properties, and the rationing of available space are all influenced by market competition. Indeed, competition is the principal method of regulating real estate resources in this country. Through competitively determined prices and rents, decisions are made regarding what will be produced, how much, and for whom. Competition, of course, is governed by numerous laws, regulations, and informal controls that make it possible for the market to function. Competition does not work automatically; indeed, there never was such a thing as completely unregulated competition, and there never could be, especially in our complex kind of economic system.

Real estate market competition is limited by special types of regulations, including laws affecting the transfer and financing of properties, zoning and land planning laws, building codes, subsidies, taxes, price and rent controls in some cases, government ownership, and other types of regulative methods.

Law and Real Estate Decisions

The value of a parcel of real estate may be divided among many interests, depending on the property rights represented by the land, buildings, and other improvements. A property may represent a wide variety of interests or *estates*. It may be owned by Mr. and Mrs. X, leased to Mr. Y, who in turn has subleased it to Mr. Z, who occupies it. Mr. A may hold a mortgage secured by the property, Mr. B may have the right to a path across it, and the public utility company may have the right to install utility lines on it. The degree, quantity, nature, and extent of interest which a person has in real property is that person's estate in the real property. Basically, the value of such rights depends on economic forces. In some cases the legal arrangements may limit decisions and programs regarding the utilization of the property and thus affect its value adversely. In other cases, legal arrangements may implement a sound program of property use.

The legal arrangements connected with property ownership, use, or transfer involve almost countless legal documents. The title, possession, or use of real property is usually evidenced by some written instrument. However, occupancy is notice to everyone of rights claimed in real property, and the rights of the occupant must always be ascertained.

Our interest in the legal aspects of real estate—in the papers and documents—arises from their effect on decisions of individuals and business and public officials. These decisions often turn on the economic implications of the legal arrangements which may be involved.

Use of Specialists

Those in the real estate business need to be familiar with the legal concepts and practices involved in real property ownership, use, investment, transfer, and financing. However, it is *not* their function to serve as substitutes for lawyers. Real estate entrepreneurs, brokers, and specialists have a place in the business community primarily because of their knowledge of *economic* forces and the application of such forces to specific business activities. They should know enough about real estate law to determine when situations require that competent lawyers be consulted. Such legal counsel is readily available.

There are relatively few people outside the real estate business who may be consulted in regard to the economic and business aspects of this field. It is in this area, therefore, that the real estate broker, manager, developer, appraiser, or mortgage lender tends to become a "professional" or expert in his or her own right. Hence, it is on the administrative and economic rather than on the legal and engineering phases of the subject of real estate that we concentrate our attention.

PROPERTY

Property may be defined in a nontechnical manner as the exclusive right to exercise control over economic goods. This right may be exercised by one or more persons, corporations, associations, or by the community at large.

Real vs. Personal Property

Property objects may be tangible or intangible. Even though they are intangible, they generally are described as *things*. Things may be divided into "things real" and "things personal." The land and all things permanently attached to it are considered to be realty, and all other things are personalty. The line of demarcation between the two is sometimes very hard to determine in practical situations, however.

Land is considered by the common law to have an indefinite extent upward as well as downward, so that the word *land* includes not only the face of the earth but everything under it or over it. A strict interpretation of the concept of property as including the surface of the land plus an indefinite extent upward would make air traffic impossible. Consequently the right to space above 1,000 feet in congested areas and 500 feet elsewhere is considered as similar to rights on a navigable stream. *Air rights* have been purchased above railroad tracks to provide space for buildings, as in the case of the Daily News Building, the Merchandise Mart, and the Prudential Office Building in Chicago and the Pan Am Building in New York.

Classes of Property

Between public property on the one hand and private property on the other, certain additional classes of property may be distinguished. One class is *common property*, which provides for the ownership of an undivided unit of land by a number of people who hold their interests by virtue of their ownership of adjoining private tracts. The New England common of an earlier period is an illustration of such an arrangement, as are the common areas in "planned unit developments" or in condominium developments.

Requirements for Private Property

The essential requirements for private property are (1) an owner, (2) a property object, which must be a thing of economic value, and (3) an organized government to protect and enforce property rights. Private property is essentially a matter of human relationships, a combination of rights and responsibilities which are recognized and sanctioned by the community.

RESERVATIONS ON PRIVATE PROPERTY

The exercise of the exclusive right of private property is subject to at least three reservations by the state. These reservations arise from eminent domain, taxation, and the police power. We should note also that private property for which there is no owner reverts to the state in accordance with the doctrine of *escheat*. Private property may also be limited by non-state type restrictions such as deed restrictions described later in this chapter.

Eminent Domain

Eminent domain is the right of the sovereign government to take private property for public use. In effect it is the right to compel a sale by the owner, since compensation is always paid. The private owner has no choice in deciding whether to sell or not to sell. He or she must sell if the property is *condemned* for public use. Eminent domain may be exercised by the federal government, by the various states, and by municipalities, or by semipublic corporations whose existence is regarded as essential to the welfare of the public.

Before this right is exercised, attempts are made, in practice, to purchase directly from the owners such properties as are required. This avoids the formal processes of condemnation, which often are costly. However, if the owner of any parcel refuses to sell, condemnation proceedings are instituted. The price is then fixed by the court, usually after hearing the testimony of expert appraisers. In the exercise of the power of eminent domain the government is not restricted to the property which is to be used directly for the public project involved. *Excess condemnation* is sometimes permitted by courts if this appears to be in the best interests of the public.

Public Ownership. Historically, we have been committed to the policy of encouraging private ownership of both urban and rural land. However, when public parks, schools, office buildings, army, navy, and air force installations, forest preserves, and the like are considered, our governments control a considerable amount of real property. In recent years special attention has centered on public ownership, often through the exercise of eminent domain, to cope with such problems as slum clearance, urban renewal, soil erosion, conservation, and environmental control.

When real estate is owned by government, several purposes may be served. For example, such properties may provide the basis for research and experimentation, or they may serve such purposes as income redistribution as in the case of providing improved housing for lower-income groups. Conservation of natural resources is often cited as a justification for public ownership. Control of the natural environment may require public ownership. Problems of water pollution may justify public ownership in some cases. Even so, we continue in general to encourage the private ownership of real property. A large majority of our families are home owners; most of our farms are owned by those who operate them; and a large percentage of our business firms own the land and buildings used for their installations.

Property Taxation

Taxation means the right to payments from citizens for the maintenance of the state. Property taxation means that the state may collect payments from a propery owner based on some relationship to the property, usually its value. If such payments are not made, the property may be sold by the state to satisfy the claim for taxes. Taxes may be thought of as interest payments on a mortgage that never matures and never can be paid off.

The extent of the tax burden varies between properties but in some cases represents as much as a third or more of annual gross rent. Because land ownership was a fair indication of ability to pay taxes during the early years of our country's history, property taxation came to be used widely by state and local governments. The federal government cannot impose direct taxes on real property. However, the federal income tax has an important bearing on many real estate transactions and in some cases may exercise a determining influence on decisions regarding the purchase, sale, leasing, or financing of real property. Although state and local governments now make use of other forms of taxation in addition to the property tax, a heavy share of the tax burden which such governments, notably local governments, impose is borne by real estate.

The relationships between governments and individual property owners arising from taxes have created numerous problems. Taxes are important to the politician as well as to the owner or user of the property or the investor in the property. As a result, our tax structure is complex, often illogical, and in many instances unfair to real property owners, users, or investors.

Types of Property Taxes. Taxes on real estate are of two principal types: (1) general property taxes imposed by states or municipalities and (2) those imposed by such special taxing authorities as sanitary districts or school districts. In addition, special assessments may be levied against a property owner to cover all or part of the cost incurred for paving streets, building sidewalks, or making other improvements directly affecting the property.

Tax Liens and Penalties. Taxes and assessments are liens on property, ranking above all others; in some cases they become personal claims against the owner as well. As we have indicated, the state is a persistent tax collector. If taxes are not paid when due, interest and penalties may be added. If payment is still not made, the taxing authority may either (1) sell the property and collect the tax out of the proceeds, returning the balance to the owner, or (2) sell the tax lien. Redemption periods are provided in many states. Thus, if a sale is made, the purchaser receives a "tax title," which ripens into full ownership if the property is not redeemed.

If tax liens are sold, the taxing authority is, in effect, selling its claim to another. In such cases, the purchaser pays the tax and looks to the owner of the property for reimbursement. In effect, the purchaser of a tax lien becomes the holder of a mortgage which is superior to all other claims against the property. If payment is not made within a stated period, varying greatly from place to place, the certificate matures and proceedings are carried out similar to those of foreclosure.

Tax Capitalization. One of the serious difficulties with our taxation policies affecting real estate is that they have tended to ignore the effects of taxes on different members of the community and on the uses to which properties are put. For example, when a tax of any sort is imposed on a piece of real estate, unless it receives benefits from government activity financed by the tax corresponding in value to the amount of such payments, the tax (or that portion of it which exceeds the accompanying benefits) will be *capitalized*, which means that the owner of a property at the time a tax is imposed pays it for all time, under the conditions outlined above. In other words, if taxes on a piece of real estate are increased without corresponding benefit, its sale value is decreased by an amount equal to the *capitalized value of all future tax payments.* This is true because the prospective buyer will consider the amount of the tax in determining how much he or she will pay—deducting a sufficient amount to allow for taxes. Thus, the present owner of the real estate pays the increased tax once and for all.

It is obvious that increases in real estate taxes which are not accompanied by corresponding benefits result in gross injustices to present property owners. It is equally obvious that removal of property taxes that have once been capitalized after a parcel of real estate has changed hands many times results in wholly undeserved windfalls to those who purchased properties after such taxes were imposed.

Police Power

The *police power* involves all regulations necessary to safeguard the public health, morals, and safety and to promote the general welfare.

The police power, in its broadest sense, includes all legislation and almost every function of civil government. . . . It is not subject to definite limitations, but is coextensive with the necessities of the case and the safeguards of public interest. . . . It embraces regulations designed to promote public convenience or the general prosperity or welfare, as well as those specifically intended to promote the public safety or the public health.[1]

In exercising the police power the state does not become the owner of property and it is not obliged to compensate private owners. From the standpoint of real property the most important use of the police power is found in zoning laws. These laws have far-reaching effects on the uses of real estate, as do building codes and related regulations.

Land Planning and Zoning.

Land planning and zoning, among the important examples of the exercise of the police power, are largely products of the present century, although some regulations of this type go back to ancient times. In this country several cities were planned at the time they were established, the most notable being Washington, D. C., under the L'Enfant Plan. In recent years the growth of both urban and environmental

[1] Sligh v. Kirkwood, 237 U.S. 52 (1914).

problems in many of our cities brought further development of land planning and zoning activities.

Land planning involves overall programs for development concerned chiefly with public or semipublic land uses such as roads, streets, parks, and related matters; it invades private property rights only in incidental ways. Zoning is a device for carrying out the plan with respect to land use and specifically limits the rights of private individuals, since it involves the regulation by districts under the police power of such matters as the height, the bulk, and the use of buildings as well as the use of land. Density of land use and hence of population may also be regulated. City, county, metropolitan area, state, and regional planning may all be involved.

Building Codes. Another illustration of the exercise of the police power is provided by building codes. Such codes are in force in most American cities. Regulations of this type are justified on the grounds of safety and health. Hence, the quality and strength of materials are usually regulated and controls leading toward fire prevention and sanitation are imposed. Regulations may determine the ratio between the height and thickness of walls, the spacing of girders, and allowable stresses. Sanitary and health regulations necessitate control over plumbing, vents, ventilation, room height, and similar matters.

Although building codes provide many protections for citizens, they have been subject to numerous criticisms. In some cases they are unduly complicated; sometimes they afford certain types of protection for local firms or unions; often they "make work" for certain trades; frequently they fail to recognize new materials or practices and thus retard progress in the building industry. Despite problems, however, progress is being made in these areas.

CLASSES OF ESTATES

Since it is possible to hold varying degrees of interest in land, lawyers have seen fit to divide these interests or estates into classes. The classification schemes commonly employed view these interests from one or a combination of the following: (1) quantity of interest, (2) *time* of enjoyment, and (3) *number* and *connection* of the interested parties.

Quantity of Interest

From the standpoint of quantity of interest, estates have been divided into those of *freehold* and those *not of freehold*. (See Fig. 3–1.) The concept of freehold has had a long historical development. It originally was synonymous with *possession*, but later came to be a more inclusive right than possession and was distinguished from it. Originally nonfreehold estates were considered as little more than contracts, although this

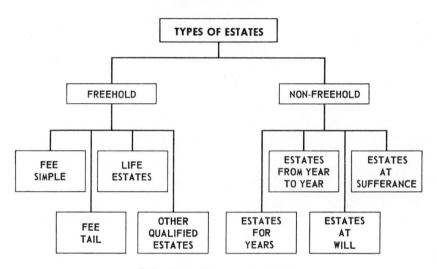

FIG. 3–1. Types of estates.

concept was broadened with the passage of time. Since feudal society required that someone always hold a freehold interest, the legal doctrine developed that "seisin [possession by virtue of feudal investiture] of land can never be in abeyance." Hence, with minor exceptions, there is always a freehold interest underlying an estate less than freehold. While this distinction between estates of freehold and those not of freehold is historical rather than logical, it helps to clarify the various types of interest which may exist. Freehold estates include the *fee simple, fee tail,* other qualified estates, and the *estate for life.* Nonfreehold estates include estates for years, from year to year, and at will and at sufferance, or those commonly called *leasehold* estates. In some cases a leasehold may be considered as personal property.

Freehold Estates

Fee Simple Estate. An estate in fee simple may be defined as the highest type of ownership in real estate known to law. The owner is entitled to the enjoyment of all the rights of the property. The terms *fee, fee simple,* and *fee simple absolute* may be considered equivalent.

A fee simple estate carries with it the right to use or not use the property in any way the owner wishes. He or she may sell it, give it away, will it to heirs or others, or trade it for other property. Furthermore, the property may be used in any way which will not interfere with the rights of other property owners within the limits established by the state, which were discussed above.

Fee Tail Estate. A fee tail or limited estate restricts the alienation of the property in that it must pass to descendants of the owner. Originally this device was used to insure the passing of land in a direct ancestral line. When liberalizing tendencies caused modifications of this condition, statutes were enacted which restored the limitation. Later changes provided that fee tail estates could be created which could be transformed into fee simple interests by appropriate court action. The fee tail estate has been abolished by legislative enactment in a number of our states.

Estates for Life. Estates for life or life estates are freehold estates in land and are limited in duration to the life of the owner, or to the life or lives of some other person or persons. Estates of this type cannot be transmitted by inheritance. Termination of a life estate depends on a future, uncertain event.

Thus, an estate so long as a specified person lives or during widowhood may be classified as a life estate. The life tenant may occupy the property or rent it to another and thus enjoy the income from it.

Estates for life are limited in time and involve a less complete form of ownership than the fee simple estate. Estates for life may be created either by act of the parties (conventional) or by operation of the law (legal). Of the former, there are estates granted by one party for his or her life, or estates granted for the duration of the life of another. In the first case the estate ends at the death of the grantee, and in the second, at the death of the party named.[2] Life estates created by operation of the law include *curtesy* and *dower*. Curtesy is the life estate of the husband in the real estate owned by his wife, while dower is the life estate of the wife in the real property owned by her husband. These estates are no longer recognized in some states. A number of states recognize the arrangement of *community property*. This provides that in the absence of a will the surviving husband or wife will receive half the estate and the heirs of the deceased the other half.

The right of homestead entitles the head of a family to an interest in the owned residence which is exempt from the claims of creditors. It is often referred to as homestead exemption. Statutes set limits to the amount of the exemption and usually require the filing of a written declaration of homestead. This type of interest has been created by statute, not through the common law.

Nonfreehold Estates—Leasehold Estates

The estates which are "less than freehold" include *estates from year to year, estates at will,* and *estates by sufferance.* These interests are commonly called *leasehold estates,* or rights of tenants as distinguished from those of a freeholder. An estate from year to year is a contract for a definite period of time—the period may be short or long. Estates at will are similar, but the duration of the lease depends on the will of both, as either party may terminate it. In the case of an estate by sufferance,

[2] This estate is technically called *estate d'autre vie.*

the term of a lease for a definite period has expired and the tenant continues to hold over without special permission. However, *periodic tenancy* is sometimes involved in similar situations; for example, leases which run from year to year and month to month are assumed to be renewed if the owner accepts payment after the expiration of the lease and if appropriate notice of its expiration has not been given. It is necessary to differentiate between these types of tenancy and a tenancy from one year or for one month.

Estates Classified as to Time of Enjoyment

Estates may also be classified as to time of enjoyment. As we have pointed out above, one may either be in immediate possession of an estate or expect to secure possession at some future date. The latter type of estates include *reversions* and *remainders.*

A reversion is the residue of an estate left with the grantor which entitles the grantor to possession after the end of another estate. For example, if X leases a property to Y for ten years, X has the reversion.

A remainder is the right of a person to interests which mature at the end of another estate. For example, if Jones grants a life estate to Brown and thereafter to Smythe in fee, Smythe holds a remainder. If such an estate passed to Smythe only if some obligation was paid or some other requirement fulfilled, Smythe would hold a *contingent remainder.* It should be noted, however, that a remainder must not be postponed for too great a period of time or it will be void because of the "rule against perpetuities." Usually this limits the postponement of estates to the lives of people who are living at the time the conditions are established.

Estates Classified as to Number and Connection of Owners

Classification of ownership by number and connection of interested parties results in two main groups of estates: *joint estates,* or what might be called co-owners, and *estates in severalty.* The latter are estates held by single owners, the former by more than one. In cases where more than one owner is involved, a number of possible arrangements may exist, the chief of which are *tenancies in common* and *joint tenancies.* If two or more persons own separate estates in the same property, each holding a distinct interest which may be sold or transmitted in any way, a tenancy in common exists. However, if two or more persons hold ownership in the same degree, acquired by purchase or grants, but not as separate shares, a joint tenancy exists. Joint tenancy is also distinguished by the doctrine of survivorship; that is, if one of the joint tenants dies, that interest passes to the survivor or survivors. While joint tenants cannot will their shares of such an estate, they may convey them while living. In such cases, however, a tenancy in common exists after such a grant. Any of the joint tenants may occupy the property without paying rent to the others, but if the property is leased to strangers, the rents are divided between the joint tenants. While the common law tended to favor joint tenancies, the present tendency is to favor the tenancy in common. In Oregon, for example, joint tenancies have been abolished by statute.

Another type of estate is tenancy by entirety. Since husband and wife are considered one person under the common law, each becomes the owner of the entire property when they take title to it together, and upon the death of either spouse the survivor is sole owner. Special statutes in the various states now fix interests of this type.

Business Ownership. In case real estate is transferred to a partnership, the individual persons composing the partnership become the owners of the property. Hence, when a business operates as a partnership, it is usually found expedient to acquire real estate under a business name or in the name of one or more of the individual partners. Under such an arrangement the partners are the equitable owners. Since a corporation is a separate legal entity, it may own real estate in much the same manner as an individual if given this power directly or by implication in its charter or certificate of incorporation.

The Condominium. A special type of real estate ownership is the condominium. It provides for a special, unique kind of property description. The condominium may be defined as the legal term for real property ownership which provides fee simple ownership of an individual apartment or other enclosed space in a building. It provides for the common ownership of such areas as halls, elevators, and recreational facilities that are part of the property by the owners of the individual units. Traditionally a fee simple title to land has meant the ownership of a certain area of the earth's surface that could be appropriately described. The condominium, in effect, makes possible the individual ownership, alienation, and mortgaging of a portion of the airspace occupied by an apartment or office several stories above the earth's surface.

CORPOREAL AND INCORPOREAL RIGHTS

In addition to the types of estates which may be held by the occupant of a property or *corporeal rights*, there may be certain nonpossessory interests in real estate, or rights held by those who are not entitled to actual occupation. The latter interests are called *incorporeal rights* and include (1) those rights which may ultimately develop into complete possessory or corporeal interests and (2) those which may not. Reversions and remainders, which have already been described, may be classified in the first group. In the second group of incorporeal rights in property, the most important are *easements* and *right of way*. Both include the right to make a limited use of land without taking anything from it or having possession, such as the right to pass over another's property. Sometimes these interests are classified as rights in another's property and include (in addition to easements and rents) profits and covenants running with the land, such rights as mortgages, statutory liens, and equitable charges or liens.

Liens

A lien is the legal right of a creditor to have a debt or charge paid or satisfied out of the property belonging to the debtor. Liens may be divided into specific and general classes, the former including mechanics' liens, taxes and special assessments, and mortgages, while the latter includes judgments, estate taxes, and the like.

Mechanics' Liens. Mechanics' liens protect those who furnish materials and labor for the improvement of a property by giving them a claim against it. Such liens are governed by statute and vary widely among the states. Typically such a lien affects only the property that is benefited by the materials and labor involved. Usually such liens are enforceable by foreclosure.

Tax and Special Assessment Liens. Taxes, of course, are liens on real property when levied against it, and the property may be sold to satisfy the claim. Special assessments, which generally arise when all or a part of the cost of public improvements is charged against the property which is benefited, may be collected in the same way. In addition, there are ways for federal or state governments to obtain a lien on a delinquent taxpayer's property even though the tax was not levied on the property. For example, the federal government may have unpaid income taxes made a lien.

Mortgages. While at common law a mortgage amounted to a conveyance of an estate to the mortgagee or lender, the conveyance to become void when the terms of the mortgage agreement were fulfilled, today the mortgage is considered more in the nature of a lien upon a property to insure the repayment of a loan or the performance of an act. In many states a mortgage is restricted, by statute, to a lien. If the loan is not repaid, the mortgagee may take the necessary legal steps involved in foreclosure in order to recover the claim.

Judgments. When judgments involve money awards, they become liens on the property of the debtor, and the property may be sold to satisfy the claim. Estate taxes or inheritance taxes are liens on the property of an estate, and such property may be sold to satisfy the taxes if they are not paid.

TITLE TO REAL ESTATE

While one may hold a wide variety of interests in real property, any owner must be able to prove ownership. Such proof or evidence of ownership is called *title*.

At one time the fact of possession was considered evidence of title, just as the possession of most personal property is considered evidence of ownership today. Because of the complexity of the interests which may exist in real property, written evidence of ownership became essential. False statements or errors of memory created so many problems that the Statute of Frauds was enacted in England in 1677. It provided that all agreements affecting the title to real estate must be in writing to be enforceable. The party refusing to perform the contract can be held if he or she signed the written memorandum, whether or not the other party signed. Similar requirements were established in each of our states.

Public Records

Not only was written evidence needed, but permanent public records were found to be essential to systematic recording of real property ownership and of the transactions involving such ownership. The "recording acts" have met this requirement. In each of our states there is provision for the recording of transactions affecting real property.

The registry laws do not make recording compulsory. They merely provide that recording of an instrument informs all who deal in real property of the transaction and that, unless an instrument is recorded, a prospective purchaser without actual notice of its existence is protected against it.

Such records have been set up for two purposes: (1) to preserve evidence of all instruments affecting title, and (2) to provide any person with notice of their existence and content. If the records are complete, it is possible to determine all claims against a property and all transactions affecting it. If any questions exist regarding outstanding claims, the title is termed "cloudy" or "defective" and is not "clear." In such cases the property is not readily marketable, since "a good and merchantable title" cannot be given.

Types of Records. Various records must be kept in order to preserve adequate information about the status of title. These include deed books, mortgage books, plat books, and other records which preserve information about judgments, tax liens, attachments, mechanics' liens, wills, estate administration, divorce, marriage, bankruptcy, special assessments, and similar matters. In addition, restrictions on the use of real estate established by zoning laws or deed restrictions also affect the status of titles to real property.

Place of Recording.   Recording must be made in the county in which the land is located. If a property lies in two or more counties, the instruments pertaining to it must be recorded in each. A land records office is usually located in each county or similar subdivision in the state, and the officer in whose charge such records are placed ordinarily is called the *recorder* or *registrar of deeds,* although in some states the clerk of the county or the county clerk keeps such records, and in others the auditor does this work.

Abstract of Title

The history of the title to a property may be traced by a study of those instruments in the public records which have affected it. Such a study is referred to as a *search of title.* It is usually made by abstracters or lawyers who prepare an *abstract of title* or an *abstract,* which contains a summary of the documents having a bearing on the history of the title to property. From this information it is possible for a competent lawyer to tell whether the title is *clear* or *defective.* The lawyer renders an *opinion of title.* This opinion may indicate that the title is clear or that certain matters must be cleared up before a purchaser can afford to take title to the property. The mere fact that an abstract is available is no assurance of good quality of title.

Title Insurance

Because of the many factors which may affect the title to a piece of real property and the countless risks which a purchaser may assume, title insurance companies have been established. In return for a premium such companies will assure that the title to property is clear, or that it is clear except for defects which are noted. Title insurance has been found to facilitate real estate transactions, since title insurance companies usually can act with greater speed in checking titles than individual lawyers and abstracters. Typically, such companies employ highly skilled personnel. Because of the care with which the work is done and the fact that risks are spread over many properties, it is possible to carry out transactions which might otherwise be blocked because of minor defects in title. Title insurance will pay for damages resulting from defects in title.

The Torrens System

A system of land title registration by which the state guarantees title has developed from the work by Sir Robert Torrens in Australia during the middle of the nineteenth century. This system is in use in a number of our states. In a sense it does publicly what title insurance companies do on a private basis.

This system of land title registration provides for the establishment of title in an owner once and for all when the owner makes application to a duly elected or appointed *registrar.* The registrar institutes court proceedings in order that any claims against the property may be made. If none is made or such as are made are settled, the title is decreed to rest with the applicant, a decree is entered in a book of registry, and a certificate of ownership is issued to the owner or owners.

The owner pays a fee which becomes part of a revolving fund and may be used to repay those who may have been cut off from their interests by the proceedings.

ACQUIRING TITLE TO REAL ESTATE

Property in real estate may be acquired in various ways, the most important of which are (1) by public grant, (2) by devise or descent, (3) by adverse possession, and (4) by private grant.

Public Grant

Title by public grant means that the federal government or a state issues a patent or grant to a private party. Much of the land originally held by the United States government was transferred to private ownership in this way.

Devise or Descent

Since one of the more important rights of property is the right to will it to survivors, a property owner may make a will. If the will is valid, the owner may dispose of the property as desired. Title secured in this way is called title by devise. After the death of the devisor the will is *probated*—that is, presented to a court for action. The property then passes automatically to those designated by the will if no one contests its validity. The right to convey property by will is subject to statutory limits which vary from state to state.

If a property owner dies intestate—that is, without making a valid will— the distribution of the property is governed by the statutes of the state in which the real property is located. Title acquired in this manner is said to be title by descent.

Adverse Possession

Title may also be acquired by adverse possession, that is, by occupying and using the property openly as if ownership actually existed for a specified number of years (varying from state to state.) Under modern conditions this is an unusual way to acquire real property.

Private Grant Deeds

The sale of property by one person to another is usually referred to as a *private grant,* and in such cases title is passed by the use of a *deed.*

CONSULT YOUR LAWYER BEFORE SIGNING THIS INSTRUMENT—
THIS INSTRUMENT SHOULD BE USED BY LAWYERS ONLY

THIS INDENTURE, made the   1st   day of   May   , nineteen hundred and
BETWEEN   WILLIAM J. JONES, residing at 115 Lenox Hill Avenue, in the City, County, and State of New York

party of the first part, and   JOHNATHAN WHITE, residing at 711 Front Street, in the City, County, and State of New York

party of the second part,

WITNESSETH, that the party of the first part, in consideration of ten dollars and other valuable consideration paid by the party of the second part, does hereby grant and release unto the party of the second part, the heirs or successors and assigns of the party of the second part forever,

ALL that certain plot, piece or parcel of land, with the buildings and improvements thereon erected, situate, lying and being in the Village of Lyons, in the County of Wayne, State of New York, and bounded and described as follows:

BEGINNING at a point on the southerly side of One hundred and seventh Avenue (Wayne Avenue) distant forty feet westerly from the corner formed by the intersection of said southerly side of One hundred and seventh Avenue with the westerly side of One hundred and thirty-fifth Street (Clinton Avenue) running thence southerly parallel with One hundred and thirty-fifth Street one hundred feet; thence westerly parallel with One hundred and seventh Avenue forty feet; thence northerly parallel with One hundred and thirty-fifth Street one hundred feet to said southerly side of One hundred and seventh Avenue and thence easterly along said southerly side of One hundred and seventh Avenue, forty feet to the point or place of beginning.

SUBJECT to covenants, restrictions and reservations contained in former instruments of record and to encumbrances of record.

TOGETHER with all right, title and interest, if any, of the party of the first part in and to any streets and roads abutting the above described premises to the center lines thereof; TOGETHER with the appurtenances and all the estate and rights of the party of the first part in and to said premises; TO HAVE AND TO HOLD the premises herein granted unto the party of the second part, the heirs or successors and assigns of the party of the second part forever.

AND the party of the first part, in compliance with Section 13 of the Lien Law, covenants that the party of the first part will receive the consideration for this conveyance and will hold the right to receive such consideration as a trust fund to be applied first for the purpose of paying the cost of the improvement and will apply the same first to the payment of the cost of the improvement before using any part of the total of the same for any other purpose.
AND the party of the first part covenants as follows: that said party of the first part is seized of the said premises in fee simple, and has good right to convey the same; that the party of the second part shall quietly enjoy the said premises; that the said premises are free from incumbrances, except as aforesaid; that the party of the first part will execute or procure any further necessary assurance of the title to said premises; and that said party of the first part will forever warrant the title to said premises.
The word "party" shall be construed as if it read "parties" whenever the sense of this indenture so requires.

IN WITNESS WHEREOF, the party of the first part has duly executed this deed the day and year first above written.

IN PRESENCE OF:

Wm. K. Murray   *William J. Jones*   (Seal)

FIG. 3–2a. Warranty deed. (Courtesy The Title Guarantee Company, New York.)

STATE OF NEW YORK, COUNTY OF New York ss:

On the 1st day of May 19 , before me personally came William J. Jones

to me known to be the individual described in and who executed the foregoing instrument, and acknowledged that executed the same.

(Seal) _Christopher Robin_
Christopher Robin
Notary Public, State of New York
No. 00-0000000
Qualified in New York County
Commission Expires March 30, 19

STATE OF NEW YORK, COUNTY OF New York ss:

On the 1st day of May 19 , before me personally came Deborah Behrmann the subscribing witness to the foregoing instrument, with whom I am personally acquainted, who, being by me duly sworn, did depose and say that he resides at No. 12 Mockingbird Lane, New York, New York; that she knows William J. Jones

to be the individual described in and who executed the foregoing instrument; that he, said subscribing witness, was present and saw him execute the same; and that he, said witness, at the same time subscribed her name as witness thereto.

(Seal) _Christopher Robin_
Christopher Robin
Notary Public, State of New York
No. 00-0000000
Qualified in New York County
Commission Expires March 30, 19

FIG. 3–2b. Warranty deed—reverse.

The principal requirements essential to the validity of a deed have been outlined by Kratovil as follows:

. . . the essential elements of a deed are a competent grantor, a grantee, recital of consideration, words of conveyance, adequate description of the land, signature of grantor and his spouse, and a delivery of the completed instrument to the grantee. In addition, a deed may (though it need not) contain warranties of title, recitals showing mortgages and other encumbrances, a date, witnesses, an acknowledgment, and documentary stamps. Delivery followed by filing or recording of the deed in the proper public office.[3]

The types of deeds which are used most frequently are the *warranty deed,* in which the seller warrants that the title to the property is "good and merchantable," and the *quitclaim deed,* which transfers only such title as the seller may possess. The grant deed is often used and may be classed between the warranty and quitclaim types. Also, there are various types of officers' deeds, such as the deeds given by sheriffs or other officials. In addition, there are trustees' deeds, executors' or administrators' deeds, conservators' or guardians' deeds, and related types. Since the most important is the warranty deed, you are urged to study Figure 3–2 with some care.

Deed Restrictions. In addition to such public controls of private property as may result from zoning regulations, building codes, and similar public programs, appropriate provisions may be inserted into the deeds by which properties are transferred, to further restrict property uses. Through deed restrictions private owners can limit the uses to which property may

[3] Robert Kratovil, *Real Estate Law* (6th ed.; Englewood Cliffs, N. J.: Prentice-Hall, Inc., 1974), p. 50.

be put, establish building restrictions, regulate land coverage, and control property in other ways. Such restrictions may be special, applying to only one property, or general, relating to an entire area.

Because of the attitudes of the courts arising from the long struggle to liberate land from feudal ties, there is a tendency to look with disfavor on restrictions that unduly limit the use and free transfer of real property. Thus, in cases of doubt the courts tend to favor the freer rather than the more limited use of property.

Deed restrictions may be enforced by the seller, or may provide that the restrictions run with the land and be jointly enforceable by seller and owner. In case of covenants running with the land, the usual remedy is a suit in equity to enjoin violations. Where restrictions are conditions upon which the deed is given, a reverter clause may provide that the property will revert to the seller if violations are claimed and can be proved.

DESCRIPTION OF PROPERTY

In order for real estate to be described in a sufficiently clear manner so that it can be located without question, several methods have been developed. Properties are legally described by one of two systems: The Rectangular System (Quadrangular Survey or Government System) and Metes and Bounds.

Rectangular System

After the Revolutionary War, the federal government had large tracts of undeveloped and uninhabited land. A new system of describing land was devised by a committee headed by Thomas Jefferson. The Continental Congress adopted this plan in 1785. It divided the land into a series of rectangles. This plan, designated the *Rectangular System* (or *Government System*) of survey, is in use today in 30 of the 50 United States (Fig. 3–3).

The township six miles square formed the basic unit of measurement in the Rectangular System. Townships are identified by surveying lines running east and west, called parallels, and north–south lines called meridians. North and south rows of townships are called ranges, and east and west rows are referred to as tiers. Within each township, sections are identified by numbers in accordance with the method illustrated in Figure 3–4. Farms are ordinarily identified with respect to their location in sections and townships.

Metes and Bounds

In those parts of the country which were not surveyed prior to being opened to sale to private individuals, the system of "metes and bounds" is used. The term *metes* refers to measures, and *bounds* to direction. For example, at a designated starting point, it is possible to indicate certain distances in various directions and return to the original starting point, thereby describing adequately a tract of land. (See Fig. 3–5.)

The key to the success of such description is the adequacy of the description of the original starting point. Some difficulty is encountered, for example, if bodies of water, trees, and other natural formations are chosen as starting points. In such cases the destruction of a tree or a *monument* will invalidate the property description. For the purposes of land description, such things as bodies of water or trees are refered to as *natural monuments*, and fences, houses, or walls as *artificial monuments*. In case of conflict, monuments control over metes and bounds.

Since there are possibilities for error, descriptions by metes and bounds usually contain the words "more or less," which give some protection in case a new survey does not coincide exactly with the original. These terms are usually interpreted by the courts within the limits of a reasonable standard.

Subdivision

Although a subdivision may be described by the rectangular system or by metes and bounds, plats typically are recorded.

When land is platted by a subdivider and a copy of the plat is made a matter of public record, the lots involved may be identified by block and number. Easements and restrictions may be included in the plat.

While the description of a property by the street and number of a house may be adequate for general purposes, a more detailed description is necessary when property actually changes hands. Indeed, it is usually considered advisable to have a careful survey made prior to undertaking purchase, mortgage lending, leasing, or improvement.

REAL ESTATE CONTRACTS

Almost all transactions involving the sale, purchase, or exchange of real estate result in the drawing of a contract. Such contracts in the real estate business may be of a number of types, including purchase and sale contracts, conditional sales contracts, land contracts, leases, and others.

The regulations governing contracts pertaining to real estate are similar to those governing contracts in general. The contract must be made by persons who are legally competent. There must be an offer and an acceptance. There must be a valid consideration. Each party must be obliged to do something. The object for which the contract is drawn must be legal.

In addition, however, contracts which involve real estate transactions must be in writing and must be signed by the parties who are to be bound

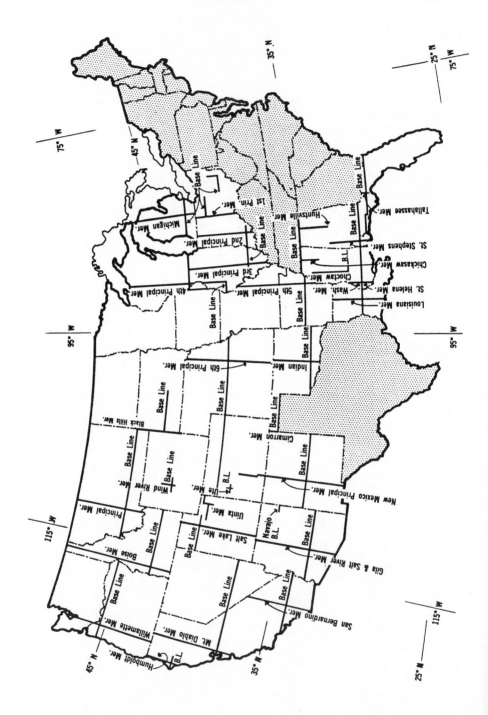

Meridians	Governing surveys (wholly or in part) in States of—	Longitude of principal meridians west from Greenwich ° ' "	Latitude of base lines north from Equator ° ' "
Black Hills	South Dakota	104 03 00	44 00 00
Boise	Idaho	116 24 15	43 22 31
Chicasaw	Mississippi	89 15 00	34 59 00
Choctaw	Mississippi	90 14 45	31 54 40
Cimarron	Oklahoma	103 00 00	36 30 00
Copper River	Alaska	145 18 42	61 49 11
Fairbanks	Alaska	147 38 33	64 51 49
Fifth Principal	Ark., Iowa, Minn., Mo., N. Dak., & S. Dak.	91 03 42	34 44 00
First Principal	Ohio & Indiana	84 48 50	41 00 00
Fourth Principal	Illinois[1]	90 28 45	40 00 30
Fourth Principal	Minn. & Wisc.	90 28 45	42 30 00
Gila and Salt River	Arizona	112 18 24	33 22 33
Humboldt	California	124 07 11	40 25 04
Huntsville	Ala. & Miss.	86 34 45	35 00 00
Indian	Oklahoma	97 14 30	34 30 00
Louisiana	Louisiana[2]	92 24 15	31 00 00
Michigan	Mich. & Ohio	84 22 24	42 26 30
Mount Diablo	Calif. & Nev.	121 54 48	37 51 30

Meridians	Governing surveys (wholly or in part) in States of—	Longitude of principal meridians west from Greenwich ° ' "	Latitude of base lines north from Equator ° ' "
Navajo	Ariz. & N. Mex.	108 32 45	35 45 00
New Mex. Principal	New Mexico	106 52 41	34 15 25
New Mex. Principal	Colorado	106 53 36	
Principal	Montana	111 38 50	45 46 48
Salt Lake	Utah	111 54 00	40 46 04
San Bernardino	California	116 56 15	34 07 10
Second Principal	Ill. & Ind.	86 28 00	38 28 20
Seward	Alaska	149 21 53	60 07 26
Sixth Principal	Colo., Kan., Nebr., S. Dak. & Wyo.	97 23 00	40 00 00
St. Helena	Louisiana	91 09 15	31 00 00
St. Stephens	Ala. & Miss.	88 02 00	31 00 00
Tallahassee	Florida	84 16 42	30 28 00
Third Principal	Illinois	89 10 15	38 28 20
Uinta	Utah	109 57 30	40 26 20
Ute	Colorado	108 33 20	39 06 40
Washington	Mississippi	91 09 15	31 00 00
Willamette	Ore. & Wash.	122 44 20	45 31 00
Wind River	Wyo.	108 48 40	43 01 20

1. Numbers are carried to fractional township 29 north in Ill., and are repeated in Wisc., beginning with south boundary of the State; range numbers are in regular order. 2. Latitude doubtful; is to be verified.

Note: East boundary of Ohio, known as "Ellicott's Line," longitude 80°32'20", was the first reference meridian, with township numbers counting from Ohio River, and range numbers in regular order. Township and range numbers within U.S. military land in Ohio are counted from south and east boundaries of tract.

FIG. 3–3. Meridians and base lines of the United States Rectangular System. The states shown unshaded, and Hawaii and Alaska, use the Rectangular System of survey. Each principal meridian and its base line is shown on the map, with location by longitude and latitude in the table. The shaded areas use metes and bounds surveys. (Courtesy Institute of Financial Education, U.S. League of Savings Associations.)

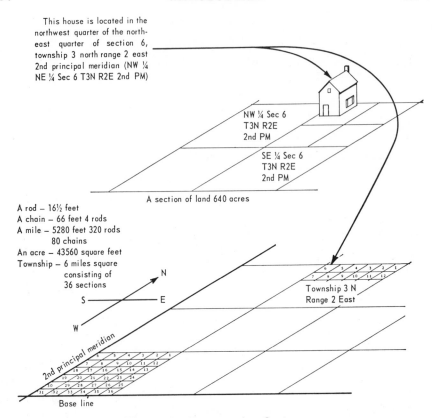

This house is located in the northwest quarter of the northeast quarter of section 6, township 3 north range 2 east 2nd principal meridian (NW ¼ NE ¼ Sec 6 T3N R2E 2nd PM)

NW ¼ Sec 6
T3N R2E
2nd PM

SE ¼ Sec 6
T3N R2E
2nd PM

A section of land 640 acres

A rod — 16½ feet
A chain — 66 feet 4 rods
A mile — 5280 feet 320 rods
          80 chains
An acre — 43560 square feet
Township — 6 miles square
          consisting of
          36 sections

Township 3 N
Range 2 East

2nd principal meridian

Base line

FIG. 3–4. Rectangular System.

by them. Real estate contracts differ in this regard from other types of contracts. This difference grows out of the provisions of the Statute of Frauds referred to above.

Contracts for Sale

Contracts for the sale of real estate are usually drawn in accordance with forms which are approved by a local real estate board or similar group. Typically, such contracts provide for a property description, a financial statement, a closing date and place, and signatures. In addition, such contracts should contain an exact statement of the kind of deed involved and an agreement regarding the evidence of title which the seller will furnish. It should be noted that real estate contracts are "specifically enforceable." The courts may force either party to a real estate contract to carry out an agreement exactly. However, this decision is discretionary with the court. If specific performance is not requested, the contract may be rescinded with adjustments in the monetary arrangements. Also, one party may sue the other for breach of contract and damages. The Real

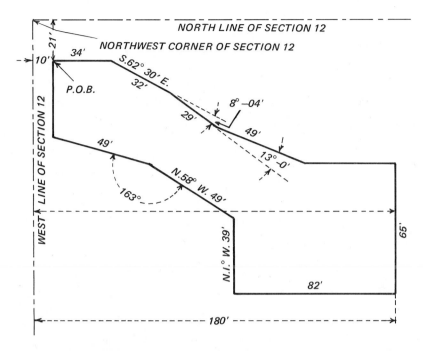

Commencing at the North West corner of Section 12, thence South along the section line 21 feet; thence East 10 feet for a place of beginning; thence continuing East 34 feet; thence South 62 degrees, 30 minutes, East 32 feet; thence Southeasterly along a line forming an angle of 8 degrees, 04 minutes, to the right with a prolongation of the last described course 29 feet; thence South 13 degrees, 0 minutes, to the left with a prolongation of the last described line a distance of 49 feet; thence East to a line parallel with the West line of said section and 180 feet distant therefrom; thence South on the last described line a distance of 65 feet; thence due West a distance of 82 feet to a point; thence North 1 degree West 39 feet; thence North 58 degrees West a distance of 49 feet; thence Northwesterly along a line forming an angle of 163 degrees as measured from right to left with the last described line a distance of 49 feet; thence North to the place of beginning.

FIG. 3–5.   A metes and bounds description traces the perimeter of a land parcel. Starting from a reference point, in this case tied to a rectangular survey, the direction and distances of segments of the boundary are described in order. (Courtesy Institute of Financial Education, U. S. League of Savings Associations.)

Estate Settlement Procedures Act specifies procedures to be followed in order to protect consumers.

Land Contracts and Related Arrangements

Land contract, or contract for deed, is the term used to identify a purchase and sale contract which provides for the payment of the purchase price in installments over a period of time. Sometimes similar arrangements are made under a *lease with option to purchase.* Such leases allow the tenants to purchase the property at a specified price within a stated period with the understanding that all or part of the rent paid will apply toward this purchase price.

Listing Contracts

There are four general types of listing arrangements: (1) *open listing,* in which the sellers may list the property for sale with a number of brokers; (2) the *exclusive agency,* in which the sellers give one broker an exclusive agency, but reserve the right to sell the property themselves; (3) the *exclusive right-to-sell contract,* which gives the broker the sole right to dispose of the property for a given period and if the owners sell the property themselves they still must pay the broker a commission, and (4) *multiple listing,* a system in which a number of brokers have an agreement by which any one of them may sell property for which another member of the group has an exclusive right-to-sell contract. Under such an arrangement, there is provision for dividing the commissions involved.

All of these contractual arrangements are best explained on the basis of when a commission is earned and by whom. In the open listing, the broker who completes the transaction earns the commission. Of course, the owners pay no commission if they sell the property themselves.

In the exclusive agency, either the owners or the one listing broker may sell the property. If the owners sell the property, no commission is paid. A commission is paid only if the broker negotiated the transaction. Under the exclusive right-to-sell contract, the listing broker qualifies for the commission regardless of who makes the sale.

Leases

Leases are agreements entered into by an owner or lessor with a tenant or lessee in which the possession of the property is granted to the tenant, usually for a specified period of time, in return for a stated rental.

Leases may be oral or written. In some states, leases for periods of more than one year must be in writing to be valid, while in some states oral leases are valid for as long as three years.

Property may be leased for a long period of time. There are leases that run for as long as 999 years. *Ground leases* are sometimes drawn up to run for long periods and allow the tenant to construct buildings or other improvements on the property.

Standard Forms. Because of the importance of the provisions of a lease, many real estate boards have drawn up standard lease forms, as have many business firms when the rental of property is an important part of their activities. In a transaction of considerable financial importance or involving any unusual rights of either lessor or lessee, it is advisable to have a competent real estate lawyer prepare the lease.

Types of Rents. Rents may be fixed for a flat rate, or related in some way such as *gross or net sales to the amount of business* handled by the tenant. Sometimes there is provision for a *graded* or *step-up lease.* In such cases, the rent is established at one level for a given period and then advances for another period. A reappraisal is sometimes required in such cases. As has been pointed out above, some leases contain an option to purchase. In some cases the lessee makes payments such as insurance and maintenance; this is called a net lease. If all types of payments are made by the lessee including taxes, it is termed a "net, net" lease.

Termination. Leases are terminated by expiration, by mutual agreement, by a breach of the provisions of the lease, or in other ways. Some leases are for an indefinite period and operate from month to month. Leases are important to the business of property management, and the details of lease agreements will be described in Chapter 14.

UNIFORM COMMERCIAL CODE

The Uniform Commercial Code has now been adopted in all of our states except Louisiana, which has adopted part of it. It has also been adopted by the District of Columbia and the Virgin Islands. Although it relates to the sale of goods and services and hence is not closely related to real estate law, there are a number of situations where it may be applicable. For example, such things would be included as a security interest in annual crops, fixtures, or goods before they become fixtures. There are many difficult problems involved as to the applicability of the code or traditional real estate law and they are too specialized for our consideration here. We should recognize the importance of the Uniform Commercial Code, however, and its potential significance for various real estate decisions.[4]

[4] See, for example, Paul T. O'Donnell and Eugene L. Maleady, *Principles of Real Estate* (Philadelphia: W. B. Saunders Co., 1975), Appendix D.

SUMMARY

Real estate is one of the most heavily regulated sectors of our economy, being subject to the direct or indirect regulations of federal, state, and local units of government. Private ownership of real estate resources is never complete, as this ownership may be modified by the governmental powers of taxation, eminent domain, or the police power. The exercise of these powers may therefore be a key factor in private decision making.

Real estate administration is conducted in an atmosphere of institutional arrangements and procedures which have developed within the legal system. Many legal details and legal documents are involved in the establishment of ownership or the transfer of ownership of real estate. Legal arrangements in some cases limit the utilization of property and thus reduce its income-producing ability; in other instances legal arrangements may promote sound property uses and enhance the value of real estate.

Property involves the right to exercise control over economic goods, including real estate resources. Various interests, or estates, in real property may exist and may be classified according to the quantity of interest, the time of enjoyment, or the number of interested parties. Also of importance are nonpossessory interests such as easements and rents.

The prudent individual or business manager will seek competent legal assistance in handling the detailed legal procedures involved in real estate transactions.

QUESTIONS FOR STUDY

1. Prepare a list of the various laws and regulations that have an effect on your study property and indicate their importance.
2. How could you establish proof of ownership of your study property?
3. Explain why organized government is necessary to the existence of private property. What is meant by eminent domain?
4. Why do we rely on real estate taxes so extensively? What are the principal types of real estate taxes? How significant are real estate taxes in the total tax receipts of state and local governments?
5. Explain the use of a tax lien.
6. Can a real estate tax be imposed upon all future owners of a specific property? Explain your answer.
7. What are the principal uses of the police power in regulating real estate?
8. Could an interest in real property exist that did not include either ownership or possession of the property? Discuss.
9. It is sometimes said that private property is a matter of human relationships. Explain.
10. Distinguish between "title" and "deed."
11. What is an abstract?
12. What is the purpose of title insurance?
13. What is the difference between a quitclaim deed and a warranty deed?

14. What are the principal methods of property description?
15. How are land contracts affected by the Statute of Frauds?
16. The owner of a building in which you intend to open a hardware store offers to negotiate with you either a flat-rate lease or a percentage lease. Indicate reasons why you might prefer one type of lease over the other.

SUGGESTED READINGS

KRATOVIL, ROBERT. *Real Estate Law* (6th ed.). Englewood Cliffs, N. J.: Prentice-Hall, Inc., 1974. Chs. 5–9.

LUSK, HAROLD F., and FRENCH, W. B. *Law of the Real Estate Business* (3rd ed.). Homewood, Ill.: Richard D. Irwin, Inc., 1975.

LUSK, HAROLD F., HEWITT, CHARLES M., DONNELL, JOHN D., and BARNES, JAMES A. *Business Law: Principles and Cases* (Third Uniform Commercial Code Edition). Homewood, Ill.: Richard D. Irwin, Inc., 1974. Ch. 30.

CASE 3–1

Brown v. Southall Realty Co.*

This was an action brought by Southall Realty (plaintiff) to evict Mrs. Brown (defendant) for nonpayment of rent. Mrs. Brown contended that no rent was due under the lease because it was an illegal contract. The trial court held for the landlord, Southall Realty. Judgment reversed on appeal, holding that no rent was owed by the tenant.

QUINN, JUDGE. The evidence developed, at the trial, revealed that prior to the signing of the lease agreement, Southall was on notice that certain Housing Code violations existed on the premises in question. An inspector for the District of Columbia Housing Division of the Department of Licenses and Inspections testified that the violations, an obstructed commode, a broken railing and insufficient ceiling height in the basement, existed at least some months prior to the lease agreement and had not been abated at the time of trial. He also stated that the basement violations prohibited the use of the entire basement as a dwelling place. Counsel for Southall Realty at the trial below elicited an admission from Brown that "he told the defendant after the lease had been signed that the back room of the basement was habitable despite the Housing Code Violations."

This evidence having been established and uncontroverted, Mrs. Brown contends that the lease should have been declared unenforceable because it was entered into in contravention to the District of Columbia Housing Regulations, and knowingly so.

Section 2304 of the District of Columbia Housing Regulations reads as follows:

No persons shall rent or offer to rent any habitation, or the furnishings thereof, unless such habitation and its furnishings are in a clean, safe and sanitary condition in repair, and free from rodents or vermin.

Section 2501 of these same Regulations, states:

Every premises accommodating one or more habitations shall be main-

---

* 237 A.2d 834 (Ct. App. D. C. 1968). Harold F. Lusk, Charles M. Hewitt, John D. Donnell, and James A. Barnes, *Business Law: Principles and Cases* (Third Uniform Commercial Code Edition; Homewood, Ill.: Richard D. Irwin, Inc., 1974), pp. 694–95.

tained and kept in repair so as to provide decent living accommodations for the occupants. This part of the Code contemplates more than mere basic repairs, and maintenance to keep out the elements; its purpose is to include repairs and maintenance designed to make a premises or neighborhood healthy and safe.

It appears that the violations known by appellee to be existing on the leasehold at the time of the signing of the lease agreement were of a nature to make the "habitation" unsafe and unsanitary. Neither had the premises been maintained or repaired to the degree contemplated by the regulations, i.e., "designed to make a premises . . . healthy and safe." The lease contract was, therefore, entered into in violation of the Housing Regulations requiring that they be safe and sanitary and that they be properly maintained.

In the case of *Hartman v. Lubar,* the court stated that:

> . . . the general rule is that an illegal contract, made in violation of the statutory prohibition designed for police or regulatory purposes, is void and confers no right upon the wrongdoer.
> . . . To this general rule, however, the courts have found exceptions. For the exception, resort must be had to the intent of the legislature, as well as the subject matter of the legislation.

A reading of Sections 2304 and 2501 infers that the Commissioners of the District of Columbia, in promulgating these Housing Regulations, were endeavoring to regulate the rental of housing in the District and to insure for the prospective tenants that these rental units would be "habitable" and maintained as such. . . . To uphold the validity of this lease agreement, in light of the defects known to be existing on the leasehold prior to the agreement (i.e., obstructed commode, broken railing, and insufficient ceiling height in the basement), would be to flout the evident purposes for which Sections 2304 and 2501 were enacted. The more reasonable view is, therefore, that where such conditions exist on a leasehold prior to an agreement to lease, the letting of such premises constitutes a violation of Section 2304 and 2501 of the Housing Regulations, and that these Sections do indeed "imply a prohibition" so as "to render the prohibited act void."

The result reached in this case is not typical of the attitude many courts would presently take. It is, however, becoming an increasingly common result in large cities where courts and legislative bodies are attempting to deal with "slum" housing.

Questions

1. Are Sections 2304 and 2501 of the District of Columbia Housing Regulations typical of current housing regulations?
2. Do you think regulations of this type will become more widespread?
3. Do you agree with the decision? Why or why not?

CASE 3–2

Smith v. Old Warson Development Co.*

This was an action brought by Frank and Catherine Smith (plaintiffs) against the Old Warson Development Company (defendant) to recover damages sus-

---

* 479 S.W.2d 795 (Sup. Ct. Mo. 1972). Harold F. Lusk, Charles M. Hewitt, John D. Donnell, and James A. Barnes, *Business Law: Principles and Cases* (Third Uniform Commercial Code Edition; Homewood, Ill.: Richard D. Irwin, Inc., 1974), pp. 673–74.

tained by the abnormal settling of a new house sold to the Smiths by defendant. The trial court granted defendant's motion for a directed verdict and the Smiths appealed. Reversed and remanded. The Court of Appeals filed an opinion reversing the trial court and then transferred the case up to the Supreme Court which affirmed the action the Court of Appeals had taken.

Old Warson Development Co. owned a tract of land in St. Louis which it subdivided for sale as residential lots. It had a home constructed on one of the lots which it sold to the Smiths in February of 1963. The sales contract contained the following provision:

> Property to be accepted in its present condition unless otherwise stated in contract. Seller warrants that he has not received any written notification from any governmental agency requiring any repairs, replacements, or alterations to said premises which have not been satisfactorily made. This is the entire contract and neither party shall be bound by representation as to value or otherwise unless set forth in contract.

Within a few months the Smiths noticed that the doors in a section of the house containing a bedroom and bathroom were sticking. Soon they noticed the caulked space between the bathtub and wall was enlarged. Eventually a space developed between the baseboard and the floor, and cracks developed in the wall. All problems were limited to the two rooms, which were constructed on a 4-inch concrete slab, completely surrounded by but not attached to, foundation walls. The remainder of the house rested on a foundation and experienced no difficulties. The slab had settled or sunk as much as 1¾ inches. Although the builder made some attempts to repair the visual problems, there was no attempt to correct the basic problem—the settling of the slab.

MORGAN, JUDGE. We accepted transfer of this cause after the filing of an opinion by the Court of Appeals, St. Louis District, because the result reached therein evidenced a departure, although limited, from a strict application of the doctrine of *caveat emptor*. The court's reasoning was expressed in an opinion by Smith, J., which was as follows:

> This appeal presents squarely the question of whether implied warranties of merchantable quality and fitness exist in the purchase of a new home by the first purchaser from a vendor-builder. We hold such warranties do exist.

* * *

. . . Although considered to be a "real estate" transaction because the ownership to land is transferred, the purchase of a residence is in most cases the purchase of a manufactured product—the house. The land involved is seldom the prime element in such a purchase, certainly not in the urban areas of the state. The structural quality of a house, by its very nature, is nearly impossible to determine by inspection after the house is built, since many of the most important elements of its construction are hidden from view. The ordinary "consumer" can determine little about the soundness of the construction but must rely upon the fact that the vendor-builder holds the structure out to the public as fit for use as a residence, and of being of reasonable quality. Certainly in the case here no determination of the existence of the defect could have been made without ripping out the slab which settled, and maybe not even then. The home here was new and was purchased from the company which built it for sale. The defect here was clearly latent and not capable of discovery by even a careful inspection. Defendant was the developer of the subdivision in which the house was located, and built this home to demonstrate to the public the type of quality residence which could be erected in the subdivision. It was held to the public as "luxurious" and was shown as a model to the public. Common sense tells us that a purchaser under these circumstances should have at least as much protection as the purchaser of a new car, or a gas stove, or a sump pump, or a ladder.

* * *

We turn to the "present condition" provision of the contract, and respondent's contention that that provision excluded any implied warranties. On its face it does not indicate that it has reference to implied warranties. Respondent contends that the language "Property to be accepted in its present condition unless otherwise stated in contract" is an exclusion of warranties. We cannot so interpret it. The reasonable interpretation of that provision is that vendor assumes no obligation to do any additional work on the house unless specified. Such a provision would preclude purchasers from insisting that the vendor promised to paint the house a different color, or add a room, or retile a bathroom or correct an obvious defect. We do not believe a reasonable person would interpret that provision as an agreement by the purchaser to accept the house with an unknown latent structural defect.

Questions

1. Do you agree or disagree with the discussion in this case? Explain.
2. Is the "implied warranty" concept being interpreted rather broadly in this case? Is this an example of broader consumer protections which have become popular in recent years?

STUDY PROJECT 3–1

The following questions and answers * were prepared by Earl A. Snyder who is a lawyer, appraiser, and real estate investment counselor. He has been on the faculties of American, Maryland, and Indiana Universities. Do you agree with his answers?

Q. What is the difference between a condominium and a cooperative? I maintain they're the same thing for all practical purposes.

A. I believe you're wrong. They're different. But they have some similar aspects.

Each is a form of ownership of real estate. The precise differences may vary because of statutory provisions in various states allowing the establishment of each.

Generally, a condominium is fee (absolute) ownership of space (a unit) in a multi-unit building, coupled with common ownership (along with other unit owners) of common elements of the building (e.g., stairways, halls, basement, land, etc.).

A condominium regime (it's called) is established under specific statutory authority (now increasingly called simply a Condominium Act but still called in some states, a Horizontal Property Regime Act). Each unit owner can buy, sell, mortgage and use his unit as he sees fit subject to restrictions contained in the document establishing the condominium (or horizontal property) regime and bylaws governing the regime (and, of course, general laws and regulations governing all units of that type).

Generally, a cooperative entails ownership of stock in a not-for-profit corporation which, in turn, owns the multi-unit building. Along with ownership of the stock, the cooperative owner gets a "proprietary lease"

* Used by permission of Earl A. Snyder.

granting him sole use and occupancy of space (a unit) in the building, coupled with use of common elements of the building (along with other cooperative stockholders).

The cooperative is established under specific statutory authority in only a few states. Usually it's established under general statutory authority providing for not-for-profit corporations to be organized. In a few states it's established simply as a mutual homes association. The cooperative stockholder can sell only his stock in the corporation or his interest in the mutual homes association (carrying with it his "proprietary lease"). His use and occupancy are limited by the basic cooperative document establishing the cooperative, and any bylaws. He has, generally, no mortgageable interest in his unit. There's only one mortgage on the entire building. It's the obligation of the corporation or mutual homes association.

Q. What is really meant by a freehold estate?

A. It's an estate of inheritance (fee estate, more properly called a fee simple or fee absolute estate) or a life estate (for the life of the grantee or grantor or some third person). A freehold contrasts with a leasehold estate, which is an estate for a specified period, e.g., a lease for a year or a certain number of years. Incongruously, a leasehold estate may be for 99 years which would normally be longer than a life estate, which is a freehold estate. A life estate could conceivably last only a few hours if the life on which it's based lasted only that long.

Q. I have an opportunity to buy some land near my home. The terms are that I'll pay nothing down and $250 per month, principal and interest at 8 per cent per annum for eight years. I will not get a deed until I've paid the full purchase price and all interest. Does this sound like a good arrangement?

A. I don't know about the value of the land, of course. I presume you're asking whether the fact that you're going to be making monthly payments without receiving a deed for the land is a "good investment" . . . assuming that the land is worth what you're paying.

There's no overweighing reason why buying the land on a "land contract" (sometimes called a "contract for deed") makes it a "bad investment." The seller is probably structuring the transaction this way because you're paying nothing down. If you default in your payments and he has to take back the land, it's simpler, quicker, and less expensive to take it back under a "land contract" than to be required to foreclose on a mortgage. (If you received a deed for the land now, you would doubtless have to execute a mortgage for the unpaid purchase price.)

The seller will probably insert a provision in the "land contract" asserting that if you default on the contract you agree to relinquish without the necessity for legal proceedings and all payments previously made will be retained by him as fair rental for the land, or as liquidated damages for breach of the contract, or both.

It would be a good idea to have the advice and counsel of an attorney versed in real estate before you sign the "land contract." He can advise you if there are any unfair provisions in the agreement, how to rephrase them to make them acceptable to you, and, generally, what your rights and obligations are under the agreement.

4

ECONOMIC CHARACTERISTICS OF REAL ESTATE

Real estate decisions, as we have seen, are influenced by a wide variety of forces. We considered some of the legal aspects of real estate decisions in Chapter 3 and the influence of land, buildings, and their physical environment on such decisions in Chapter 2. In this chapter we will review various economic characteristics of real estate decisions.

OBJECTIVES OF DECISIONS

Decisions typically are made to achieve one or another objective. In business such an objective usually has economic implications. What is considered "economic" depends on our concepts of economy, and economy in turn reflects relationships between input and output to obtain a desired objective. In a general sense, economy means getting as much as possible of what we want (in terms of objectives) by the use of the means (resources) available. Economics deals with the principles and concepts that explain the allocation of resources in the attainment of desired goals or objectives.

Both the economist and the manager or administrator are concerned with the effective utilization of resources in the attainment of desired objectives. Usually the economist serves in an advisory capacity while the manager is concerned with getting things done.

Real Estate Administration

As we have seen, administration or management may be described in terms of processes or major activities such as establishing objectives, setting up plans to achieve them, organizing resources, and controlling operations. Leadership, decision making, decision implementing, and related activities are all involved in these functions.

Real estate administration may be considered a special application of the processes of administration or management in general. In terms of objectives, our interest centers in those property owners and users (including individuals, families, business firms, or governmental and institutional agencies) as well as the objectives of those engaged in the real estate business, and the ends or goals of our society as a whole. We are also interested in the relationships between private and public objectives.

Objectives of Real Estate Enterprises. Business firms in the real estate field pursue objectives that are similar to those of business firms in other areas, such as survival, growth, and the attainment of recognition or a prestige position. In order to do these things, they must make a profit. Some firms attempt to maximize profits, others to gain a "reasonable" or other level of profit. Their specific objectives may vary widely, but it is virtually impossible to manage a business firm engaged in real estate or in any other field without a clear understanding of the objectives that are being pursued.

Objectives of Owners and Users. Similarly, the owners or users of real estate resources may pursue a wide variety of objectives. Many will try to maximize profits. Some will hope to achieve maximum monetary returns over the long run, others in the short run. Some will try to maximize satisfactions from the direct use of real properties. Objectives may be stated in terms of using real properties in connection with other resources to achieve a maximum total result, as in the case of a business firm using real estate and other resources in producing and marketing goods and services.

Highest and Best Use

To an important degree in the field of real estate, as in many other fields, the interests of the community as a whole are closely related to the activities of private real estate owners, users, brokers, managers, and investors. Despite differences in the reasons behind their decisions and actions, both the community as a whole and practical people in their private capacities demand the development of each parcel of real estate to its *highest and best use*. We should recognize, however, that this term involves some logical pitfalls and must be used with care. As we indicated in Chapter 2, it means the utilization of a property to its greatest economic advantage. The term has been defined in terms of *greatest net income*, *highest land value*, and *largest return in money or amenities over a period of time*.

In addition to economic factors, social and political considerations have a bearing on the meaning of "highest and best use." The term would have different meanings in a society organized under a dictatorship than in one organized on democratic principles. Even in our own society, the highest and best use of a property may change with shifting consumer preferences, improved techniques and equipment, a changing energy situation, or for other reasons. The market reflects changes in buyer preferences and production methods. Changing attitudes and techniques are also reflected in zoning laws, building codes, and other regulations governing the development and use of real property. For example, problems of air and water pollution reflect changing conditions and may have a bearing on highest and best use.

Social and Business Objectives. In our society, the owners of real property and those who own or manage various types of real estate firms are allowed to pursue their objectives within the general framework of our legal, governmental, and institutional arrangements. We allow this type of operation because we have found that in our competitive and democratic type of society the owners of real estate resources or real estate enterprises tend to serve the long-term interests of our society as a whole by pursuing their own best interests. This is not always the case, of course. For example, it is sometimes necessary to impose limits on the decisions of property owners through zoning laws to prevent the development of inharmonious land uses. Within certain limits, however, we rely on competition to regulate business activities for us and to assure buyers and users of goods value per dollar of cost. Similarly, democratic political processes assure a fairly direct response to the desires of both owners and users of properties.

A method of illustrating the relationships between the objectives of property owners, users, or managers on the one hand, and those of society on the other, is provided by an example from another field. We maintain a free press in this country and within very broad limits allow it freedom of expression. The objective of this arrangement is to disseminate the truth. This objective is achieved, not by requiring that all publications print nothing but the truth, but by allowing them (within the limits of the law of libel and other broad regulations) to print what they please. In this way we come very close to achieving our objective of disseminating the truth by means of freedom of expression and publication.

Private Objectives. Much the same thing may be said about the real estate field. By allowing owners of property to pursue their own objectives, to maximize income, or to develop properties to what they consider to be the highest and best use, general community as well as purely private objectives are served. In most cases such objectives are served better than if more direct and specific controls are set on the ownership, use, development, financing, or marketing of private real properties.

In general, the owners of real estate enterprises are allowed to pursue their own objectives under the discipline of competition which serves as a highly effective method of social control. It tends to bring about a blending of private and public objectives.

SPECIAL CHARACTERISTICS OF REAL ESTATE RESOURCES

Real estate resources include land and buildings plus property rights in these physical objects. These property rights represent income or income-producing potentials. These rights have value to the people who own, use, produce, finance, or market them.

Real estate resources include residential properties of many types: single-family houses, doubles, duplexes, three- and four-dwelling-unit structures, and apartments (walk-ups, elevator or high-rise buildings, garden apartments, and others). The general classification of business properties covers both commercial and industrial properties. Commercial properties include stores, office buildings, shops, places of amusement, and the like. Industrial properties include both light and heavy manufacturing installations and various types of warehouses and related properties. In addition, we may distinguish farms and other rural real estate, government and institutional real estate, and special-purpose properties.

As we have indicated, real estate resources have special economic characteristics:

1. Real estate is fixed in location; buildings cannot economically be moved from place to place.
2. Real properties typically have a long life, usually lasting for several decades or longer. As a result, the supply of real property is relatively fixed for any short-term period.
3. Real estate resources are available only in large economic units; even the smallest typically are valued at several thousand dollars and the most expensive may run into millions.
4. Access to real properties typically can only be provided by public facilities such as roads, utilities, and the like; thus there is great interdependence between private and public properties.

Income Production at Fixed Locations

All types of economic activity and decisions related to them are concerned with income—that is, the production of returns in excess of costs. Indeed, *income* has often been referred to as *the fundamental fact of economic life*. In real estate we are concerned with income but more particularly with the *localization* of income. In nearly all other types of business it is possible for the commodity or service involved to follow the market, to move to the point where the greatest income-producing potential exists. In the real estate field this is not true. The market must be induced to come to the property. Once a property has been developed, its future is dependent entirely upon its ability to command a market for its services at its specific location.

Thus, decisions relating to real estate turn largely on the analysis of income and estimates of income-producing potentials at fixed locations. Such incomes may be in the form of monetary returns or may result from the direct use of a property.

Unique Properties. Because of fixity of location, every parcel of real estate differs from every other one. It is unique within a changing economic framework. Not even a vacant lot is identical in every respect with an adjoining vacant lot.

As we have seen, physical structures differ with respect to condition, style of architecture, materials of construction, and in many other ways. Real properties also differ from each other with respect to distances from transportation lines, from places of employment, from civic and social centers, from other sections of the area, and from other parts of the country or the world. Decisions related to city properties are affected greatly by the "urban plant" which serves them—the system of streets, sewers, water mains, utilities, parks, playgrounds, schools, and the like. The extent of crime in a locality, adequacy of police and fire protection, and the general protection of the area all influence real estate decisions. Similarly, decisions related to rural properties are influenced by the availability and cost of public or quasi-public facilities and services. All are affected by the general physical environment and this varies greatly from locality to locality.

Neighboring Influences. Real estate resources can never escape the impact of economic, social, political, or physical characteristics which may affect them favorably or adversely. Thus neighboring influences are strong. If the street on which your home is located develops into a high-speed traffic artery, you cannot as a practical matter move even the house to a quieter or safer street. Nor can you move a house or any other piece of real estate away from unfavorable conditions in the physical environment such as smog or polluted waterways. Conversely, you cannot help but reap the benefits of any developments which reflect favorably on the city or the district or neighborhood in which your property is located.

Although fertility, topography, soil conditions, annual precipitation, length of the growing season, and temperature form the principal basis of the income-producing capacity of farm land, location or *situs*, as we have pointed out, takes priority in the case of urban land. As a specific area on the earth's surface, a land parcel is almost indestructible. Its usefulness and income-producing ability and hence its value can be reduced or eliminated. The desirability of location changes as conditions change. The fertility of farm land may decline with use. Thus, even if the land remains in a physical sense, it may lose all or nearly all of its economic value.

Limited Markets. Because of the fixity of location of real estate, its market tends to be more limited than are the markets for most other commodities. The market for owner-occupied homes typically is limited in geographic extent to a single city and often to a certain section of that city. The market for commercial and industrial real estate, however, is somewhat broader and may be thought of as at least regional in extent. Farm lands typically are bought and sold throughout a county or other relatively limited area. The market for a property varies somewhat with the point of view from which it is considered. Thus a New York investor might buy an apartment house in Chicago. The people who rented the apartments, however, would in almost all instances be Chicagoans.

Legal Implications. Fixity of location is the principal basis for the legal distinction between real and personal property, as we saw in our discussions in the preceding chapter. Also, fixity of location makes it possible to establish definite boundaries and to describe the property for legal and business purposes.

Long Life of Real Properties

Decisions relating to real properties are influenced greatly by the long life of these resources. Income expected ten years hence is worth less today than current income. This is because we discount the future due to the many uncertainties and risks that lie ahead and because of the waiting involved. As a site for buildings and other improvements, land is relatively permanent. Buildings and other improvements on the land have a longer life than that of most other commodities. Hence, investments in real estate tend to be fixed for long periods of time. It is not easy to change urban land from one use to another. If an apartment house is built on a lot, it usually remains there for many years, even if the market at times is depressed to the point where the owner cannot earn a satisfactory return on the investment.

Although agricultural land can be shifted from the production of one crop to another from year to year, crop rotation and other considerations may place limitations on land use.

Long-Term Implications of Decisions. Some decisions in regard to purchase, sale, or leasing of real estate are made for short-run purposes— for speculation, to provide space for temporary periods such as staying at a motel overnight, or to protect a position previously taken. Most such decisions, however, are made for longer-term periods. Even the leasing of a dwelling unit usually covers a period of a year, often longer; most commercial leases are for a term of years. Purchases are usually made with a long-term program of property use or development in mind. Some speculative purchases, of course, are long-term in character. Thus, the long-term nature of most real estate decisions is an important factor in understanding programs of property use and the operation of real estate markets.

Real Properties as Large Economic Units

The fact that real properties are relatively large economic units is one of the reasons for the existence of the real estate business. Brokers are needed to bring together buyers and sellers—investors in and users of various properties or property services. Property managers are essential to the operation of large buildings or blocks of properties. Since special financial arrangements usually are necessary in real estate transactions because of the large amounts of money involved, an elaborate system of financing has developed.

Interdependence of Private and Public Property

Rarely can a piece of real estate be used except in conjunction with some public land, and the interdependence of private and public land tends to increase as the community becomes more complex in structure and organization. In order to have access to private land, there usually must be either a public road or street or an easement providing a right-of-way over another private property. Since private arrangements of the latter type are usually difficult to make, we normally depend on public streets and roads for access to our properties. The proportion of the land area given over to public streets, alleys, parks, and similar uses increases as cities grow in size and complexity.

In addition to the problems of access to real properties, provision must be made for water, drainage, and disposal of sewage; for electricity, gas, telephones, and other utilities and conveniences; and for police and fire protection. Indeed, one of our problems in the future may center on channeling enough capital into public projects and properties to support private real estate resources. Problems of law and order, for example, may require substantially larger expenditures for police and fire protection.

REAL ESTATE VALUE

We all recognize that the value of real estate resources may change rapidly. This is also true of other resources. Unfortunately, there are no market quotations in the real estate field comparable to the daily reports of the major securities exchanges. Such reports, of course, are important to many business decision makers. Real estate decision makers, however, often find it necessary to ask that estimates of value or appraisals be made on various properties which are under consideration. Unlike stocks, which are homogeneous and represent interchangeable shares in the equities of companies, each property is unique. No two locations on the earth's surface are exactly alike. Relatively few properties are sold and bought in a given business day. In some communities relatively few properties are bought and sold in a period as long as a month. Since it is often necessary to call on real estate appraisers to make estimates of real estate values, they play an important role in this field.

Utility and Scarcity

Economists tell us that real estate, like other commodities, is valuable in proportion to its utility and scarcity. As an interesting case in point, consider the houses in one of the old western ghost towns. Many of these towns were established originally at points where new mineral deposits were discovered. People flocked there in the hope of amassing wealth. Real estate values, of course, rose rapidly. When the mineral deposits were exhausted, people moved on, leaving ghost towns to mark their earlier hopes. As a consequence, the real estate there became worthless because it no longer served a useful purpose and was available in greater quantities than the demands for it.

As a general rule people will demand what is important to them; what is important, however, tends to change from generation to generation. The modern supermarket might have faced early bankruptcy a few decades ago. The fertile prairies of Illinois were less valuable to the early settlers than to those who were able in more recent years to use improved machinery and technology. The value of a home cannot be measured entirely by what it will bring in the market; it may have a high subjective value to the family living in it even though its market value may be relatively low. By contrast the value of an office building will depend almost entirely on the rents it can command in the market.

Thus the value of real estate, like the value of other things, depends on its relative utility and scarcity. But the measure of utility and scarcity will vary with the times, the people, the community, and the technology involved. The term "value" needs to be considered in relation to community and individual standards, resources, and objectives.

Value

To the nation as a whole, value is a matter of the comparative importance to its citizens of the different things, including real estate, that are essential to its welfare according to its standards, but that do not exist in sufficient quantities to meet the demands for them. To an individual citizen, concerned primarily with a personal stake in the community, the value of a parcel of real estate depends fundamentally on how much of other things or the services of other things or persons can be obtained in exchange for a piece of real estate or the services which it renders.

Value and Price

In practice, the relative importance of real estate is reflected in prices, which are values translated into monetary terms, such as dollars, pounds, or whatever monetary unit is commonly used. Because the market for real estate is not highly organized, the prices paid for real properties may not coincide with their values at a specific time. Price and value will tend to be identical under conditions of perfect or near-perfect market competition. In such cases the full play of all forces having a bearing on the market results in prices which reflect with reasonable accuracy the values of the commodities that are traded.

Value and Cost

Costs must be borne in order to bring goods and services into the market. Costs are almost always necessary in order to produce income. Because of costs, goods and services tend to be scarce relative to the demands for them. In the case of real estate, the costs of new developments usually are large; costs must be borne in order to acquire a lot and hold it until it is ripe for development, and the costs of a building and other improvements usually are substantial. Owners or developers will not incur costs unless they think that incomes produced will be warranted by the required costs. Thus, when prices or rents are high relative to costs, people will tend to build; when low, no construction will take place. Thus, costs affect values and prices as they affect supply. Over the long run, costs and values tend to coincide, but at any given time costs may be well above or below values as reflected in selling prices or rents.

The fact that $40,000 was spent to buy a lot and build a house does not necessarily mean that the value of the property is $40,000. The expenditure would certainly be considered as one element by an appraiser in making a valuation. Such costs are important at the time they are incurred; once incurred, production costs are passive factors.

Value and Income

As we indicated above, income is the fundamental fact of economic life. Thus, it is important for us to think in terms of the income-producing ability of real properties in trying to determine their value. Real properties must produce income at fixed locations. This income may be received through the direct use of the property's services as in the case of an owner-occupied home or a store building owned by the merchant-occupant. In other cases incomes may be in the form of monetary returns—a landlord collecting rents or an investor receiving dividends on a property investment. Real properties produce income over relatively long periods of time, as we have pointed out. Future income is worth less than present income. We discount the future; a dollar a year hence is worth 94 cents now at an interest rate of 6 per cent. The risks involved over future time may be great and we also allow for these in evaluating future income. Thus, the present value of anticipated future income produced at a specific site may well be considered the most logical definition of real estate value.

Present value is indicated by the process of capitalization, that is, by reflecting future income in current worth. Thus, we may think of the property as its earning expectancy. As Frederick M. Babcock pointed out in his classical study of valuation, ". . . *the property is the earning expectancy,* and the capitalized figure—the total value—is a *derived* fact depending upon the future income stream in some manner." [1] This earning

---

[1] By permission from *The Valuation of Real Estate* by Frederick M. Babcock (New York: McGraw-Hill Book Co., 1932), p. 129. (Italics added.)

expectancy can be bought for a present amount. The size of this present amount will vary with the expected size and duration of the future income stream and the rate at which it is capitalized. Thus, if an investment is expected to earn an average of a thousand dollars per year in perpetuity and if investors were requiring a 10 per cent return, its value could be put at $10,000 (dividing $1,000 by .10).

If the future income stream could be predicted with accuracy and if a sufficiently broad market for real estate existed, there would be less difficulty in determining real estate values. In reality, valuations are affected by differences of opinion regarding future trends, the relative inefficiency of real estate markets, variations in the availability and cost of money, and related things. The future income stream will be influenced by governmental and political trends, general and local business conditions, market forces, and location factors. Consideration will be given to these topics in the next part of the book.

"Value Is a Word of Many Meanings"

The foregoing discussion emphasizes the validity of Justice Brandeis' remark, "Value is a word of many meanings." There is much confusion about value because the term has been interpreted in many ways, especially in the real estate field. For example, economists tend to identify value with market price, provided the price is set under genuinely competitive conditions. Appraisers tend to define value in terms of "warranted selling price," or the price that a willing buyer would offer and a willing seller would accept, neither acting under compulsion. The "most probable selling price" of a property has sometimes been stressed.

Appraisers help to resolve some of the difficulty by raising the question: "Value for what purpose?" The same property may at the same time have different values for different purposes. It may have one value in terms of a quick sale, another for longer exposure to the market, still others for mortgage lending purposes, tax purposes, and insurance purposes. Thus, a property does not have "one true value" as has sometimes been contended. Its value will vary with purposes and with the conditions that prevail at the time. It is imperative in discussing real estate values to clearly identify the kind of value under consideration.

SUPPLY CHARACTERISTICS OF REAL ESTATE

The supply of real estate is relatively inflexible. Additions to the supply are made in small increments, typically 2 or 3 per cent per year.

The supply of real estate available at any given time may be considered from two standpoints: (1) the *properties* themselves, and (2) the *property services* provided by these real estate resources.

Supply of Properties

Properties include all types of real estate: residential, commercial, industrial, agricultural, institutional, public, and special-purpose properties. They include the land, buildings, and other improvements as well as the legal rights represented by these physical resources.

Supply of Property Services

In a sense real properties may be thought of as "factories" producing services—shelter, protection, privacy, comforts, conveniences, and other services. For example, a hotel may be thought of as a producer of the various services it provides its guests. Once a property is improved, property services must be utilized or they will be wasted through depreciation and obsolescence. In this respect, property services may be compared to labor: the loss of a day of a worker's time is an irrevocable loss, as is the loss of a day of property utilization.

Supply of Real Estate Inflexible.

Because of the long life of real properties, the supply of real estate resources at any given time is relatively fixed.[2] These resources may be used more or less intensively, of course, and consequently the supply of *property services* is somewhat more flexible than the supply of *properties*. Even in terms of property services, supply is relatively fixed, however, since there are fairly narrow limits within which the property services from a given property can be expanded through more intensive use. Also, even though a property is not used, it tends to affect current market conditions by virtue of its being a part of the available supply.

Slow Additions to Supply.

The present supply of real properties has been accumulating over many years. The amount added in any one year represents a very small percentage of the total. If 2,000,000 nonfarm housing units are started in a year this represents only about 3 per cent of the total nonfarm housing supply.

The supply of commercial and industrial properties also is not expanded rapidly year by year. We have actually reduced the acreage under cultivation for agricultural purposes in recent years, although we have increased, of course, the intensity of use and expanded productivity through improved methods and machines.

When new construction declines to low points because of sluggish market conditions, the total supply of real estate is not reduced to any marked extent. The additions may be small but seldom are less than demolitions or losses from fire and other hazards.

---

[2] See Edward E. Edwards, "Real Estate Economics: A Return to Fundamentals," Study Project 4–1 at the end of this chapter.

Slow Deterioration of Properties.   Structures deteriorate with use and the passage of time. By 1980, for example, the remainder of the 20,264,000 dwellings built before 1920 will be at least 60 years old. Some of these will remain in good condition, but many will tend to deteriorate rapidly. Many of our present dwelling units have to be replaced every year.

DEMAND CHARACTERISTICS OF REAL ESTATE

The demand for real estate is based on a wide variety of considerations. It reflects the standards, attitudes, and objectives of individuals, families, business firms, government officials, and others. It indicates preference for real estate relative to other goods and services. In the case of commercial and industrial real estate, demand is a reflection of company policies based on estimates of the potential income-producing capacity of real property in relation to cost, including construction costs and operation expenses, and in relation to potential return from other resources. Industrial firms demand more real estate when the market for their products is brisk and market potentials are good. Commercial properties are in heavy demand when profit prospects are favorable. As a result of the adoption of long-range planning programs by many business firms, there is more of a tendency to buy real estate well in advance of current or short-term needs.

Impact of Incomes

The demand for residential real estate is largely a reflection of consumer incomes and income expectations. To a large degree the demand for residential real estate is similar to the demand for luxury goods. Minimum requirements for shelter could be met with very small expenditures. The demand for housing, however, is much more than a demand for shelter. It may include prestige factors; it may reflect the desire to attain the comforts and conveniences that are provided by modern living accommodations. The demand for residential real estate increases as consumer incomes or income expectations rise. This increase may be both for more space and for space of higher quality. Conversely, demand drops sharply when incomes or income expectations go down.

Demand and Credit

Residential real estate is in competition with other goods for the consumer's income. But the consumer's credit as well as income is involved. Credit is a major factor in the demand for commercial and industrial real estate. The demand for farm real estate is largely a reflection of both farm incomes and the credit position of farmers and investors in farm real estate.

Since real properties typically represent relatively large economic units, few buyers are able to pay for their properties as they are purchased.

Credit usually plays a major part in such transactions. The amount that a prospective buyer is prepared to bid for a piece of real estate depends to a marked degree on the amount the buyer can borrow. This is true of most home buyers and to a considerable degree of the buyers of commercial, industrial, and farm real estate as well. Except for loans arranged through friends, associates, or relatives, how much can be borrowed on a specific property depends on the attitudes and policies of the managers of lending institutions. Typically, financial institutions consider such factors as the following in deciding how much of a loan can be made to finance a specific transaction: (1) the borrower's income and income prospects, (2) the present and potential value of the property, (3) the purchasing power risk and the interest rate risk, (4) the relative attractiveness of other forms of investment, and (5) the legal restrictions surrounding financing arrangements.

Lending Policies. The policies of lending institutions are affected by market conditions. For example, their lending policies may tend to exaggerate the effect of incomes and income prospects on the demand for real estate. When incomes are high and income prospects are favorable, lending institutions tend to be optimistic about both the borrower's income and the value of the property. When incomes are declining and markets are sluggish, the policies of lending institutions tend to be very conservative.

The relative attractiveness of other forms of investments is an important factor in determining the availability of credit for real estate transactions. The availability of funds and the interest rate that must be paid are determined in part by conditions and events entirely outside the real estate market, such as the yield on government and corporate bonds and other investments. Relative attractiveness involves more than yield. There may be a preference for liquidity of investments, as is usually true during depression periods. At such times the funds available for real estate financing may dry up, even though high yields are offered, because investors place a heavy premium on liquidity.

Inflation tends to reduce the funds available for real estate investment since it leads to high interest rates. The real estate market does not compete effectively for funds under such conditions.

Government Influences. The lending policies of real estate financing institutions are closely regulated by state governments and the federal government. The importance of the federal government in this field has grown with the insurance of deposits and savings accounts, the insurance and guarantee of mortgages, and the increasing role of the Treasury and Federal Reserve in the money markets. The roles of the Federal Home Loan Bank System, including the Federal Home Loan Mortgage Corporation, the Federal National Mortgage Association, and the Government National Mortgage Association have expanded in recent years.

Thus at any given time the demand for real estate depends to a considerable extent on the willingness of financial institutions to finance property purchases. This is particularly true of residential real estate, but has considerable validity in the case of commercial, industrial, and farm property as well. The willingness of these institutions to make loans and the terms on which they may be made often are influenced substantially by the monetary and credit policies of the federal government.

Population and Real Estate Demand

If a rising population is accompanied by favorable income prospects, the demand for real properties and property services tends to be high. But an increase in population will not bring a rise in the demand for real estate if incomes are falling, unless there should be a sudden shift in the preference of buyers for real estate relative to other goods and services. Thus, the primary factors in real estate demand are considered to be incomes and the terms and availability of financing. However, population trends and movements may be clues to real estate demand when considered in relation to income trends.

The age distribution of the population is an important factor to consider as well as the trend of total population growth. If there are a large number of people of marriageable age, as will be the case for some years, demand for residential real estate will tend to be strong—assuming that income and financing conditions are favorable. As children reach school age, interest in single-family homes tends to rise. The trend toward fewer children per family in recent years undoubtedly shifted the demand from larger to smaller dwelling units. With a larger number of people in higher age groups and with the expansion of pension funds, both public and private, there is a growing market for small, efficiently designed town houses and apartments for retired persons and couples. There is also increased interest in locations in warmer climates.

Cities with growing populations usually have more active real estate markets than those with stable or declining populations. But there must be income-producing opportunities in a city to induce people to move there. Except for resort areas or "dormitory towns," people are attached to cities by good income prospects.

Demand Dominant in Short Run

Since the supply of properties and even of property services is relatively fixed, *demand* is the most important factor in determining market prices and rents during short-run periods of a year or two. When demand exceeds supply at current prices and rents, there is a tendency for prices and rents to move upward and to continue to advance for a prolonged period, since it takes a long time to add substantially to the supply available. When demand falls below supply at prevailing prices and rents, the market slows up and prices and rents fall and continue to decline for a long time.

Because of the relative inflexibility of supply and the informal nature of real estate markets, there probably never was a time when the markets were in balance. Tendencies toward balanced relationships among supply, demand, and price do exist, however, and it is the identification of these tendencies that is of greatest importance in analyzing real estate markets.

SUMMARY

Economic aspects of real estate decisions usually relate to the effective use of resources in the attainment of desired objectives. Properties should be developed to their "highest and best use."

Income is the fundamental fact of economic life. Real properties must produce income at fixed locations. Such properties have relatively long life, require long-term investments, and come in large economic units. There are significant interrelationships between public and private property. Real estate value reflects the relative utility and scarcity of real properties or their services. Value may be related to market price under conditions of effective competition, warranted selling price, most probable selling price, or the present value of future income. Value tends to vary with purpose, especially in the real estate field.

The supply of real properties available at any given time is relatively fixed. However, because of possible changes in intensity of use of real properties, the supply of property services tends to be more elastic than the supply of properties themselves.

With supply relatively inelastic, demand factors are the most important determinants of prices and rents in any short-run period. The expected profitability of investment in real estate as compared with investments in other resources is a key determinant of demand for commercial and industrial real estate. For residential real estate, consumer incomes are a major demand factor. Because of the high unit value of real properties, the terms and availability of credit also play a crucial part in determining the demand for real estate. Population trends and movements do not constitute a demand for real estate unless income and financing prospects are favorable, but population factors may provide clues to future real estate demand when considered in relation to incomes.

QUESTIONS FOR STUDY

1. What is meant by "highest and best use"? By economics? By administration?
2. How can private and social objectives be brought together?

3. Explain the importance of income production at fixed sites for real estate decisions.
4. In which respects can it be said that the supply of property services is more flexible than the supply of properties?
5. Indicate the ways in which fixity of location affects the income-producing capacity of real properties.
6. Give illustrations of changing social or political conditions that may affect the value of real properties.
7. What types of real estate (residential, commercial, industrial, agricultural, etc.) have the broadest market? Which types have the most localized market?
8. Why is credit an important factor in the demand for real estate? Which factors determine the availability of credit for potential purchasers of real properties?
9. In which ways does the value of private properties depend upon the existence of public properties?
10. What is the relationship between demand and value? Price and value? Cost and value? Income and value?
11. What is the value of a property that earns $1,000 per year at a capitalization rate of 10%? At a capitalization rate of 8%?
12. Smith has a choice between two properties. The asking price of each is $100,000. Property A earns a net cash flow of $10,000 per annum and property B earns a net cash flow of $12,000. However, because of increased risk, Smith must project a capitalization rate of 15% for property B, whereas a 10% rate seems appropriate for property A. What is the value of each to Smith?
13. Why are demand factors more important than supply factors in determining real estate prices and rents in any short-run period?
14. Describe the effect of a growing population on the demand for real estate. How may age distribution be an influence?
15. Which demographic variables other than population size and age distribution affect the real estate market? How?

SUGGESTED READINGS

AMERICAN INSTITUTE OF REAL ESTATE APPRAISERS. *The Appraisal of Real Estate* (6th ed.). Chicago, Ill.: The Institute, 1973. Chs. 2, 3.

HOYT, HOMER. *Dynamic Factors in Land Values,* Technical Bulletin No. 37. Washington, D. C.: Urban Land Institute, March, 1965. Reprinted in *According to Hoyt* (2nd ed.). Washington, D. C.: 1970. Pp. 513–27.

SAMUELSON, PAUL A. *Economics: An Introductory Analysis* (10th ed.). New York: McGraw-Hill Book Co., 1976. Chs. 4 & 8.

UNGER, MAURICE A. *Real Estate.* Cincinnati, Ohio: South-Western Publishing Co., 1974. Ch. 1.

STUDY PROJECT 4–1

A Return to Fundamentals *

[This study project is intended to stimulate some reflective thinking about the economic characteristics of real estate.]

Real estate prices behave quite differently in the market place than do prices of other economic goods. Why is this so? Can the differences be explained in terms of economic principles? Will an understanding of economic principles help to explain price behavior in the past? Will such an understanding help to predict future real estate prices?

A study of the behavior of prices for single-family homes leads to the conclusion that real estate prices can be explained and predicted in terms of five economic principles, which are as follows:

1. The supply of real estate is relatively fixed.
2. The demand for real estate is dependent in the first instance on income.
3. Effective demand is dependent largely on the availability and terms of financing.
4. The real estate market is a local, disorganized one.
5. The influence of government is very great.

These economic principles are well known and are not the discovery of the author. Perhaps, because they are so well known, they are frequently overlooked. This article, which deals with these five simple concepts only, may be considered a return to fundamentals in real estate economics.

Supply of Real Estate Relatively Fixed. This first principle hardly needs to be proved. Our present supply of real estate includes structures that have been built over a long period of years. The new structures added in any one year occasionally exceed in number the old structures that are torn down, but only in a building boom do they add as much as two or three per cent to the existing supply. When new construction ceases, the supply declines slowly, since neither government nor private enterprise can afford wholesale destruction of accumulated capital investment in real property.

Because the supply is relatively fixed, demand is the most important factor in determining price. When demand exceeds supply, as at the present time, real estate prices rise and continue to rise for quite some time, since there is little chance that the supply will catch up. Conversely, when demand falls below the existing supply, real estate prices fall and continue to fall or remain at low levels for a prolonged period.

The inflexibility on the supply side probably is such that there never is a time when supply and demand are equated. By the time an inadequate supply has caught up with a heavy demand, the demand has already shifted downward. On the low side, supply is never reduced to a depression-low demand, and the real estate market must wait until demand has again moved upward.

Demand for Real Estate Dependent in First Instance on Income. Real estate, as it is known in this country, is not a necessity of life, but a luxury. The amount of real estate actually needed for the bare necessity of shelter is very small. This is especially true when real estate is measured in terms of dollar value

---

* From Edward E. Edwards, "Real Estate Economics: A Return to Fundamentals," *The Appraisal Journal* (April, 1949). The opinions expressed herein are those of the author and do not necessarily carry the endorsement of the American Institute of Real Estate Appraisers.

rather than in dwelling units. The demand for dollars' worth of real estate, therefore, behaves very much like the dollar demand for any other luxury good.

What are the characteristics of the demand for luxury goods, particularly real estate? First, the demand for real estate increases sharply with increased personal incomes. In this connection, it must be remembered that the increase in demand is an increase in the dollars offered for real estate. This is not necessarily an increase in the number of houses demanded; in fact, it is more likely to be an increase in the dollars that the prospective buyer will put in a single house. An increase in total demand therefore may be accompanied by a decrease in demand for certain properties.

Second, the demand for real estate decreases sharply with falling off of personal incomes.

Third, the maintenance of demand, or the increasing of demand, except in periods of rising incomes, requires aggressive selling to meet competition of other luxury goods.

By putting the first two principles together, the conclusion may be reached that the most important factors in determining the price of real estate are the level of personal incomes and the competition of other luxury goods for those incomes. If the subject of real estate economics had to be reduced to a single theorem this would be it. The idea that real estate values over the long run must equal cost of construction is of little use in explaining the real estate market. Real estate prices practically never equal cost of construction; they are either higher or lower.

Effective Demand Dependent Largely on Availability and Terms of Financing. Most buyers of real estate enter the market with some money of their own and as much or more of some financial institution's money. The amount that they are prepared to bid for real estate is therefore largely dependent on the amount that they can borrow.

While it is true that most mortgage lenders apply some standards which relate the amount of the loan to the income of the borrower, these standards change from time to time. Unfortunately, the changing standards tend to accentuate differences in personal income levels rather than to equalize them. For example, lending institutions generally have been more liberal in periods of prosperity when the level of personal incomes is high than during depressions when the level of personal incomes is low.

The amount of funds which a financial institution will place in the hands of a prospective buyer of real estate is dependent not only on the borrower's income but also on the institution's judgment as to the appraised value of the property. Here again the judgment of the lending institution frequently rises and falls with the level of personal incomes. The result is that the action of the financial institutions tends to exaggerate the effect of changes in personal incomes on real estate prices.

There are, of course, many factors other than the level of personal incomes and appraised values which affect the amount of funds available for the financing of real estate. One very important factor is the relative attractiveness of other forms of investment. Mortgagors must compete in an open-money market for their funds. The availability of funds and the interest rate that must be paid are determined at least in part by conditions and events entirely outside the real estate market.

The relative attractiveness of an investment is not solely a matter of yield. All too frequently, in the past, this country has had periods when the investor would much prefer money in the bank or in a safety deposit box to any income-producing investment. This has resulted in a drying up of mortgage funds, hence a virtual elimination of the demand for real estate.

The influence of the financial institutions on demand for real estate is especially significant in view of the fact that the lending policies of so many financial institutions are regulated or influenced by federal government action. The insurance and guarantee of particular types of loans has a profound influence on the demand for real estate. The influence of the federal government on real estate prices is so important that it has been listed separately as one of the five factors necessary to explain real estate prices.

Real Estate Market a Local, Disorganized One. Real estate cannot be moved from one market to another, nor can demand be shifted from a market in tight supply to one having a surplus of properties. A vacant house in Indianapolis cannot be moved to Detroit, nor can a Detroit family solve its housing problem by moving to Indianapolis. Even within a single city separate markets exist for houses in different neighborhoods and for houses of different sizes and prices. For any given piece of property there are very few potential purchasers; for any prospective purchasers, there are very few properties that will satisfy their wants.

As a result, the so-called real estate market is in reality a large number of separate markets. One market may be enjoying a real estate boom while another is in a real estate depression. Comparable properties sell at widely differing prices, and there is no national market of investors and speculators to equalize prices as there is in securities and commodities.

Even within a single real estate market the equalization of prices is difficult if not impossible because of the cumbersome, slow, costly, and risky procedures involved in real estate transfer. Compared with a well organized securities or commodity market, a real estate market can only be described as highly disorganized.

Influence of Government Very Great. No other economic goods with the exception of narcotics is so greatly affected by government as is real estate. Perhaps this is inevitable in view of the fact that real estate after all is not a commodity but merely a bundle of rights created by government.

Until comparatively modern times only the state and local governments had much interest in real estate. In recent years, the federal government has moved rapidly into this field and its influence upon real estate prices is now of prime importance.

Real estate prices are affected by two more or less separate and distinct types of federal action. The federal government is now dedicated to the proposition that it must maintain a high level of personal incomes in this country. To the extent that the federal government's actions in this direction are successful, the demand for real estate is stimulated and a continuing strong demand is more or less assured.

But the federal government is not limiting its influence to the indirect effects of its full employment policies. It supervises the lending policies of many mortgage lending institutions. It guarantees and insures mortgage loans, it controls rents, it expedites the construction of new housing units, and at times it encourages public housing.

The actions of the federal government are not always consistent. The insurance of mortgage loans developed as a means of stimulating new construction during a depression, yet guaranty and insurance of mortgage loans continue during a period when there is full employment and runaway inflation is threatened. Rent control continues when there is a shortage of supply, and rationing is needed. Inconsistencies such as these are likely to continue. Perhaps politics is more important than economics, and no one should explain real estate prices except in political terms.

Summary. This discussion of real estate prices perhaps can be summarized in the form of a prediction of future real estate prices. Such a summary might read as follows:

The present real estate boom will not end because of new construction; it may end because of reduced demand. A reduced demand for real estate may come from a reduction in the national income, from a reduction in the proportion of personal incomes that people are willing to spend for housing in competition with other luxury goods. or from further tightening of real estate financing. No matter what happens, real estate prices will behave differently in each real estate market. Finally, the federal government, both directly in the field of real estate and indirectly in monetary and fiscal policy, will be a major influence.

On the assumption that the federal government will seek to maintain or increase the present level of personal incomes and to continue easy financing of home ownership, the prediction might be made that real estate prices will continue high on the national average, but that weak spots may develop in individual markets with changing local demands for real estate and widely varying increases in supply from new construction.

Questions

1. If demand for real estate advances, how will rents and prices be affected? Why?
2. If personal incomes of consumers were to double, would you expect expenditures on residential real estate to double? Explain.
3. How do financing terms influence the effective demand for real estate?
4. What are the chief characteristics of the real estate market? Why does the market for real estate differ from the market for automobiles?
5. Explain the impact of the federal government on real estate values.
6. Explain the statement ". . . real estate after all is not a commodity but merely a bundle of rights created by government."

II

Analysis for Real Estate Decisions

We discuss here the various types of analyses that may be used to aid the real estate decision maker. Chapter 5 covers economic and governmental trends, primarily on a national basis, and Chapter 6 discusses the analysis of regional and local trends. A study project at the end of Chapter 5 considers the outlook for the next 10 to 15 years. There is also an interesting case study of a hypothetical community named Bel Aire which helps to point up the discussion in Chapter 6.

Chapter 7 considers the general subject of real estate market analysis and outlines the major features of a market analysis with suggestions for applying them to different types of markets. A study project which reviews some of the history of real estate market activity helps to illustrate portions of the discussions in this chapter. There is also a case study of a State University's influence on the local housing market.

Chapter 8 considers location analysis and covers patterns of land use as well as the factors influencing neighborhoods and districts. Two case studies are presented: one involves a choice between neighborhoods; the second, a branch location for a department store. This part of the book ends with a discussion of appraising methods, Chapter 9 concentrating on the income approach and Chapter 10 on the market and cost approaches. At the end of Chapter 10 a complete appraisal report is presented for student analysis and discussion.

5

ECONOMIC AND GOVERNMENTAL TRENDS

TREND ANALYSIS

It is far from easy to analyze economic, political, and governmental trends and to determine their potential impact on real estate incomes, values, and decisions. Nevertheless, such analyses must be undertaken by real estate decision makers. Every economic and political development has a potential effect on real property. Those who make decisions regarding the purchase, sale, development, use, management, or financing of real estate find it necessary to try to anticipate economic and governmental trends, to estimate their potential impact on real property in general as well as on particular properties, and to arrive at decisions on the basis of such anticipations and estimates. The generation of income at fixed sites is influenced greatly by potential developments in the economic and governmental sectors of our society.

Information Sources

Although information about economic and governmental affairs is available in every newspaper and news magazine and on radio and television, it is hard to select the key information, weigh its implications, and determine its significance. Some assistance is available to the decision maker. For example, a number of trade associations operate in the real estate field and in related fields, as we noted in Chapter 1. Often they can provide pertinent information since they follow with considerable care all developments in New York, Washington, and other centers and state capitols. On the local level, real estate boards, chambers of commerce, and other business and citizens' organizations may be helpful. Sometimes economists can help in analyzing business conditions. Lawyers can often provide assistance in analyzing proposed legislative changes and in assessing their chances for enactment. It is often possible to secure help from members of Congress, senators, or legislative representatives in state or local government.

In some cases, various types of "public opinion polls" give indications of public attitudes and points of view although there are variations in their reliability. In addition, real estate decision makers usually follow closely the opinions of their own circles of acquaintances.

Efforts To Provide Information

Various federal, state, and local governmental agencies as well as educational and private foundations and other organizations carry on a broad range of research and information-producing activities in the real estate field. Of special importance is the Bureau of the Census and especially the Census of Housing. The National Bureau of Standards and the Forests Products Laboratory carry on continuing research. The Department of Housing and Urban Development, the Federal Reserve, and the Federal Home Loan Bank system are important sources of reports in the technical, market, and financial areas. Many states provide information about numerous subjects in the real estate area. Local government agencies often sponsor studies and publish many types of information. University divisions and bureaus of business and economic research often are sources of real estate, housing, and urban economics research reports and related information.

Evaluation of Information

Each of us can learn from the evaluation of research reports, headlines, news stories, and editorials, although this is far from easy.

Government officials or politicians sometimes issue statements that are designed to test public opinion. We should try to understand what is back of current reports and what the motives of government officials or politicians may be. We should think in terms of who exercises the real power in political and legislative campaigns. Elected representatives or public officials often have one eye on those who control important blocks of votes or who may provide financial support. Appearances may be deceiving in political matters.

ECONOMIC CONDITIONS AND REAL ESTATE DECISIONS

The general level of economic activity has an important bearing on the income-producing capacity and potential of real properties and hence on real estate decisions. The real estate sector of the economy is greatly influenced by the economy as a whole and, in turn, influences general economic conditions in varying degrees.

Regions and Industries

Not only are general conditions likely to influence real estate decisions, but conditions in specific industries, in regions, and in particular cities and local areas also have their impact. Conditions in specific industries or regions may be more favorable than conditions in the economy as a whole. Although local economic conditions tend to parallel general trends, special local situations may bring substantial deviations from such trends.

For a particular industry or line of business, it is necessary to anticipate changes in competitive conditions, market preferences, government regulations, taxes, and many other related factors. Regional economic trends often are hard to forecast due to possible changes in competitive conditions and in regional economic opportunities. It is even difficult to anticipate trends for a particular locality. A sudden shift in government policies or the decisions of a major corporation to withdraw its programs or investments may cause marked changes in the local economic outlook.

Widespread Decisions

Estimates of future trends for the economy as a whole or for an industry, a region, or a particular locality are far from easy to make. For the economy as a whole, estimates of future conditions involve predicting the decisions that will be made by some 70 million households, over 4 million farmers, and nearly 5 million business firms, as well as thousands of government officials on federal, state, or local levels. In some cases, it is necessary to anticipate the decisions of government officials in other countries, as well as the decisions of consumers, farmers, and businessmen abroad.

Localization of Income

Real estate decision makers will have as much concern with general economic and political trends, regional changes, and the prospects of various industries as those interested in other major fields of business activity. In addition, the real estate decision maker will emphasize the localization of income, as we have pointed out in various earlier discussions. The value of a particular piece of real estate may be influenced by anticipations as to general economic or political trends but it will be influenced especially by anticipated changes in the stream of income flowing into the local economy. Even within a local economy the effect of local trends on various parcels of real estate may differ markedly.

Long-Term and Short-Term Outlook

Real estate decision makers are concerned with potential changes both in the short run and in the longer term. Because of the long life of real properties, long-term trends may be somewhat more important in the real estate field than in others.

Thus, we pay special attention to projections of the longer-term future, including potential trends of development for the American economy as a whole and for some of its principal sectors to the year 2000.[1] Similarly, we are particularly interested in the long sweep of historical development. Often trends of development that have persisted for a long time may give keys to future potentialities. Of special importance for economic development are the education of the work force and the advancement of knowledge along with expansion of the work force, increased use of capital, more efficient operations, and economies of scale.

Current Conditions

An understanding of the current status of economic, political, and governmental activity and its relation to previous trends is essential for decision makers. They usually follow changes regularly through newspapers and more specialized publications such as *The Wall Street Journal* and *Business Week.*

One of the more important indicators of business activity is the level of industrial production. The Federal Reserve System makes monthly estimates of industrial production and publishes an index in the *Federal Reserve Bulletin.* This index is separated into various types of industrial activity which can be compared to each other or to the total.

Other general measures of business conditions which will prove helpful are the volume of employment and the level of personal income. Such information is published regularly in the *Survey of Current Business,* published by the Department of Commerce, the *Federal Reserve Bulletin,* and *Economic Indicators,* which we referred to in Chapter 1. Detailed data on population estimates are available in the Bureau of the Census' *Current Population Reports.* These same sources will provide information about corporate profits, proprietors' incomes, unincorporated business and professional income, and farm income. Information is also readily available in regard to business sales and inventories; manufacturers' sales, inventories, and orders; the number of firms in business; new firms started; and number of business failures—all of which are helpful figures when related to past levels. The *Survey of Current Business,* in addition, publishes data on retail trade, advertising, securities and security markets, and industrial activities and product lines.

[1] See, for example, Robert C. Turner, "Economic Growth—The Outlook for Ten and Twenty-five Years," Committee for Futures Studies, Indiana University, 1975. A summary of this study is presented as Study Project 5–1 at the end of this chapter.

TYPES OF FLUCTUATIONS

In considering the relationship of current activity to that of preceding periods, three major types of changes may be distinguished: secular trends, seasonal fluctuations, and cycles.

Secular Trends

A secular trend results from basic underlying forces, such as population growth or technological change, which exert a more or less steady influence on general economic activity or on an industry over the long run. For example, in the United States during the last six or seven decades, the total output of all goods and services (called *gross national product,* or GNP), measured in constant dollars, has increased *on the average* by about 3 per cent a year.

Note that we said "on the average." Substantial fluctuations may, and usually do, take place around the trend line. These are the cyclical and seasonal fluctuations. It is sometimes difficult to distinguish between a fluctuation which is cyclical in character and one which represents a basic trend change.

There are various methods of identifying the trend line of a statistical series. Regardless of the mathematical technique employed, however, they all require the exercise of judgment. Unless we make proper allowance for the secular trend factor, erroneous conclusions may be drawn regarding business conditions and prospects. For very short-term comparisons, however, trend can often be ignored.

Seasonal Fluctuations

With regard to seasonal fluctuations, little need be said. These are variations caused by factors associated with the calendar year: the weather, the varying lengths of months, holidays, conventional vacation periods, and so forth. Almost any measure of business activity exhibits some seasonal fluctuation. More houses are usually built in the spring and summer than in the fall and winter, and the reasons for this are obvious (at least in the northern part of the United States).

Again, there are recognized statistical techniques for identifying normal seasonal variation, and analysts should know what seasonal variation to expect in studying any phase of economic activity. Otherwise, they may be unduly discouraged or encouraged by what is, in fact, only a normal seasonal fluctuation. Analysts should be on the lookout, however, for any changes in seasonal patterns.

Cycles

Assuming that proper allowance has been made for trend and seasonal variation, the main concern of the analyst is with cyclical fluctuations.[2] We all know that the record of American business is one of ups and downs. At times, nearly all business firms have been prosperous and nearly all employable persons have been working. At other times, nearly everyone has found business poor, jobs scarce, and unemployment high. These swings in general business activity—through prosperity, recession, recovery, and prosperity again—are business cycles.

Before we go any further, we should dispose· of the notion that there is anything rhythmical about business cycles. They have varied in timing from about two to about twelve years. They vary even more in magnitude, all the way from the boom of 1929, followed by the deep depression of the early 1930's and the partial recovery of 1937, to the milder cyclical swings of 1948–49, 1953–54, 1957–58, 1960–61, 1969–71, and 1973–75. Unfortunately for the forecaster, each business cycle seems to be unique, and its length and amplitude are determined by a combination of forces never duplicated before and probably never to be duplicated in the future. In the past thirty years, largely because of the economic stabilizers, the amplitude of both business and real estate cycles has been less than previously.

ESTIMATING FUTURE SPENDING PATTERNS

It is not safe to project a trend into the future by purely mechanical means. It is necessary to analyze the fundamental forces at work and to draw some conclusions as to whether these forces will continue to operate in the future.

In an exchange economy, the level of business activity depends to a great extent on the volume of spending. The principal spending divisions are consumers, business firms, and governments. Besides information on past and current levels of spending, some guides to the future intentions of each of these three major spending divisions are available.

Consumer Spending

Since consumer spending currently makes up over 60 per cent of the total expenditures in our economy, this area requires special consideration when estimating future levels of business activity. The Federal Reserve has sponsored various studies of consumer buying intentions and the gen-

---

[2] Although a more detailed description may differentiate between major and minor cycles or between cycles and random fluctuations, we are using the term "cycle" in this general treatment of the subject to refer to the fluctuation remaining after removal of trend and seasonal factors.

eral financial condition of consumers. The Bureau of the Census, the Survey Research Center at the University of Michigan, and various industry groups also carry on studies of this type. These surveys are, of course, subject to the usual errors of sampling and to the risk that consumers may change their minds after the surveys have been completed.

Of special interest to us are reports on plans for home buying, current levels of home ownership, home mortgage debt, owner equities, and related information. Such information may be related to current levels of consumer income, volume of employment, and the terms and availability of financing for such items as consumers purchase.

In recent years, total consumer spending has reflected fairly consistent growth, although there have been some shifts among various types of expenditures. Even during periods of recession when unemployment rose and industrial production dropped, consumer spending held up reasonably well.

Business Spending

Another major area for consideration is the volume of spending by business. Business spending for wages and salaries is of major importance with respect to the level of consumer incomes. Investment by business firms in plant and equipment is especially vital to anyone seeking to forecast future business conditions. Plant and equipment expenditures usually rise when profit prospects are favorable and decline when they are not. Special programs such as tax inducements may also affect the volume of business spending.

The Department of Commerce and the Securities and Exchange Commission make a joint estimate of business plans for expenditures of this type, which is published in the financial newspapers and in the *Survey of Current Business*. McGraw-Hill, Inc. also makes surveys of business plans for plant and equipment expenditures and reports them in *Business Week*. As in the estimates of consumer spending, of course, these estimates may be affected by subsequent changes in plans.

The level of inventories and inventory plans are of special importance for the short-run analysis of business conditions. Low levels of inventory during periods of rapid expansion indicate the possibility of further advances in the volume of business activity. On the other hand, during a period of level or declining activity, a substantial rise in inventory levels may create instability because of pressure to reduce these levels. Information about inventories is reported regularly by the *Survey of Current Business* and also by the financial press.

It should be noted that improved methods of inventory control have enabled business managers to operate on relatively small inventories in recent years. Even so, inventories are an important factor in the short-run business outlook.

Government Spending

The third major area of spending is that of federal, state, and local governments. Information about the expenditure plans of state and local governments is not readily available, although past levels of expenditure are reported in the *Federal Reserve Bulletin* and the *Survey of Current Business.*

The earliest indication of future federal government expenditures is the President's Budget Message, submitted annually to each regular session of Congress. The analyst must subsequently follow the appropriation and tax actions of Congress to determine whether they coincide with the original request.

After Congress has acted, estimates of the timing and amount of receipts and expenditures of the federal government are reported in the financial news and in *Economic Indicators.* Funds are allocated by appropriations, but it is important to note expenditure plans, because the effect of federal government spending on business conditions depends largely on actual spending. A considerable period of time may elapse between appropriations and actual spending.

Foreign Spending and Receipts

In addition to spending by consumers, business, and governments, spending in foreign countries, balanced against receipts, may at times be significant. Although in the United States these items do not claim the attention that they do in such countries as Holland and England, they are a factor of growing importance in estimating business trends.

Gross National Product Method

In order to make more detailed and complete analyses of business conditions, the gross national product (GNP) method has been developed. In this procedure, the major income and expenditure (product) accounts in the nation are analyzed. The total is the sum of expenditures by the major groups outlined above. You will see summaries of the accounts regularly in the *Survey of Current Business* and in *Economic Indicators,* as well as in the Economic Report of the President and the *Annual Report* of the Council of Economic Advisers. They are useful for short- and longer-term projections and often help to estimate trends in various industries or sectors of the economy.

GNP Definition. Gross national product is the total value of all goods and services produced in the economy in any given period, usually a year. The method used by the Department of Commerce in calculating the official GNP figures avoids double counting by counting only the total value of final products and ignoring primary and semifinished products (except to the extent these add to business inventories). Calculated in this way, GNP indicates amounts actually paid in the market and therefore reflects price fluctuations as well as changes in physical output. (Allowances for changes in the value of the dollar are provided by the use of price deflators.) Prices not otherwise available are estimated for goods and services wherever possible and are included in the GNP calculation. This includes assigning price values to government services, the output of self-employed persons, food produced on the farm for home consumption, and the imputed rental value of owner-occupied dwellings. The major items are presented in Table 5–1.

TABLE 5–1. National Income or Expenditure, 1960, 1970, 1975
(Billions of Dollars)

	1975	1970	1960
Gross national product	1516.3	982.4	506.0
Personal consumption expenditures	973.2	618.8	324.9
Gross private domestic investment	183.7	140.8	76.4
Net export of goods and services	20.5	3.9	4.4
Government purchases of goods and services	339.0	218.9	100.3

Source: Economic Report of the President, and Annual Report of the Council of Economic Advisers, 1977.

Flow of Income

So far we have been concerned with a static concept, an accounting of the nation's total output in a given, finite time interval. The dynamic concept of the moving, changing flow of income through the economy is shown in Figure 5–1. The chart is intended to illustrate not what happens in any finite time period, but rather the process of change from one time interval to the next.

Flow of Funds

Another important method of analyzing the economy and projecting future business conditions is the flow-of-funds approach, showing the relationship between GNP purchases and the nation's debt structure. This approach was originally developed in the early 1950's and was subsequently adopted and refined by the Federal Reserve System. Quarterly data are reported each month in the *Federal Reserve Bulletin*, with a lag of about four months.

Other Methods of Analysis

Efforts are being made constantly to improve the methods available for analyzing and forecasting potential changes in economic activity or to develop new approaches to these problems. In addition to gross national

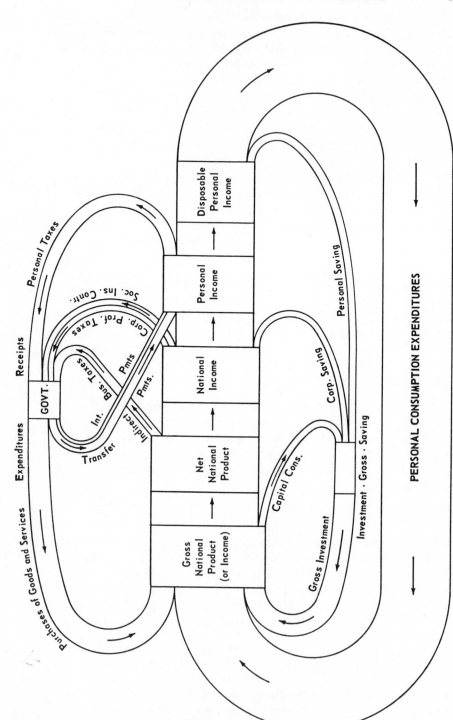

FIG. 5–1. The flow of money income and expenditures: the circular flow in a given time period. (Adapted from *America's Needs and Resources: A New Survey*, The Twentieth Century Fund.)

product and flow-of-funds, several other analytical methods are important, including "national wealth statistics," input–output tables, and balance-of-payments accounting.

Industry Analysis.   Many studies that undertake to make short- or long-run projections of a particular industry start with GNP projections and relate potential industry developments to them.   National markets, of course, are often related to consumer or business spending plans.   In some cases, a given industry bears a fairly fixed relationship to one or another national measure of economic activity.

In many cases we have accumulated a substantial store of statistical information about an industry.   The construction industry is a case in point. Good statistical data are available for new construction, both public and private, and for maintenance and repair activities.   Estimates can be made for, say, a year ahead, or for the longer-term future.

POLITICAL AND GOVERNMENTAL AREAS FOR ANALYSIS

It would be impossible to set forth all of the governmental and political areas that will be of concern to the real estate decision maker.   Consequently, we outline here some of the areas that are likely to hold substantial interest for those operating in this field.   We will review briefly various of the current issues and trends related to inflation and deflation, war and peace, economic stability, conservation and renewal, energy problems, environmental priorities, quality of life, and equality versus excellence.

Special Interests

We should note that while the bulk of regulations and controls are set up to serve the public interest, there are numerous cases where special-interest groups are trying to secure an advantage.   An example may be found in some of the building regulations which favor local builders and workers as against competition from other cities or localities.

As has been suggested above, things are not always what they seem to be in the governmental or political field.   Governmental machinery often offers opportunities for closely knit groups to exert their influence and secure competitive advantages over other groups that are not situated in as fortunate a position.   Such advantages usually last until the other groups become sufficiently organized to exert pressures for their own purposes. In most federal, state, and local governments these processes are going on more or less constantly. Their extent and nature are often difficult to determine without access to the kind of information that usually is *not* found in the official pronouncements.

Viewpoint

The analysis of governmental and political (or other) trends varies somewhat with the point of view of the analyst and decision maker. For example, the viewpoint of the private investor differs from that of the public official. The federal government official's outlook will differ from that of the local official. The point of view of a company executive differs from that of the home owner. As we have indicated, the viewpoints of buyers and sellers, borrowers and lenders, and owner users and nonowner users may differ widely. We need to remind ourselves from time to time of the variety of points of view from which real estate decision makers may consider their problems and their decisions.

Types of Regulations

It is often helpful to think in terms of the various types of regulations that may have a bearing on real estate. Although we tend to emphasize public regulations and controls, we should recognize also that various private regulations may be important. For example, deed restrictions are very important as are policies, programs, and regulations imposed by groups such as labor unions, property owners' associations, business associations, and others.

The various types of regulations and programs that affect real estate may also be divided according to whether they are of the *coercive* or *inducive* types. Coercive regulations typically are of the "thou shalt" or "thou shalt not" types, with penalties imposed for failure to comply. Inducive regulations accomplish their objectives by offering rewards for compliance or by providing information on the basis of which individuals will tend to make decisions that are in line with the public interest. Subsidies are generally of this type, as are the information-giving services of federal, state, and local governments, trade associations, universities, business firms, and private individuals.

Economic Stability

The general concept that it is the responsibility of the federal government to prevent extreme fluctuations in economic activity is rather generally accepted by the American people. Greater emphasis may be given in the future to stabilizing the value of the dollar. Maintenance of employment and incomes helps to strengthen the market for all types of properties.

Prior to World War II the declines in real estate prices, rents, and volume of activity were much greater than the average declines for other commodities. Thus, modification of the swings of the business cycle tended to benefit real estate. Even so, the use of monetary and credit policies to control the economy has from time to time created special problems for the real estate sector. It is not a good competitor for funds when interest rates are high and funds are scarce.

Inflation and Deflation

Historical trends in this country have been in the direction of gradual inflation. Downward adjustments in prices, of course, have occurred from time to time. But after each downward swing, prices typically have advanced to levels higher than previously.

This long-run tendency has been of great importance to real estate ownership and investments. Except for poorly located or improperly designed properties or those which were the victims of changes in the internal structure of land uses in our cities, the dollar investments in real estate over the years have tended to be maintained. The major problem has been the ability of owners and investors to hold on during depression periods.

An interesting case in point is the experience of the Home Owners Loan Corporation. Although over a million mortgages were financed during the depression of the early 1930's, by the time the Corporation was liquidated in 1952 it had been able to operate without loss and turned over nearly 14 million dollars to the Treasury.

War and Peace

International relations and defense programs are likely to have important effects on real estate decisions and on the income-producing ability of real properties in the foreseeable future. The unsettled condition of world affairs, the varying temperatures of cold to hot wars, and the many related uncertainties undoubtedly mean that the defense and related industries will continue to have an important place in the American economy. They may become a smaller percentage of the total GNP but undoubtedly will continue to be large in absolute terms. Much will depend on the degree of international stability or lack of stability that emerges in the years ahead. Factors of this type will complicate the making of decisions related to the long-term commitments involved in real estate ownership, management, and investment. Uncertainties often bring a movement of real estate investments from one part of the world to another.

Conservation and Renewal

As a nation, we have placed relatively less emphasis on private and public programs for conservation, reclamation, and renewal of real estate resources than have many older countries. We have generally been more interested in the development of new properties than in conserving or renewing old ones. Cutover timberland, eroded agricultural land, and the deteriorated condition of some of the "near-in" areas of our cities all reflect the pioneer tendency to abandon worn-out land or structures and to develop new resources. Presently greater interest appears to be developing, however, in programs to renew and conserve these resources.

We should recognize, of course, that there are some nonrenewable resources. For example, a natural recreational area may not be subject to renewal. The same thing is true of such resources as coal, petroleum, and natural gas. Renewable resources are subject to replacement either through natural processes or through human decisions and programs. Basic soil fertility may be destroyed but is also subject to renewal. Urban areas also may be renewed under certain conditions.

Environmental Priorities

In recent years, increasing attention has been given to the conservation of natural resources and to the preservation of the physical environment. Relatively more attention has been given to programs of flood control, soil conservation, reforestation, urban renewal, and related activities than previously. Programs in these areas are gaining more recognition by government agencies at all levels as well as by private investors and developers.

Concern about the physical environment has required that special consideration to be given to environmental factors in connection with industrial developments. Urban congestion has brought a variety of problems of air and water pollution as have various industrial processes. Residential developments are being planned with increasing attention being given to such factors as the preservation of natural advantages, overcrowding, provision of adequate waste disposal systems, and related factors. Increased environmental regulations on federal, state, and local levels have added to the costs of land development and building. Of special importance is the National Environmental Policy Act with the requirement that environmental impact statements be filed. Also of importance is the Clean Air Act. The National Environmental Protection Agency has played a role of growing significance.

Energy

Higher costs of energy and potential shortages have had significant effects on real estate. As a result there are greater advantages than previously for central locations. Greater attention is being given to conserving fuel, electricity, water and other resources. Buildings are insulated better than before. Some limitations have been set on local programs of expansion. The potential changes in the energy field—either favorable or unfavorable—are bound to have a major impact on real estate decisions.

Quality of Life

Although we continue to be interested in economic growth and expanding opportunities we have become increasingly concerned with the quality of life. Problems of the environment have come in for widespread attention. Social costs of economic growth are being assessed with increasing care.

Government programs for subsidizing research, disseminating information, and pursuing related activities have general widespread support. Programs undertaken in the interest of small business firms and farms are popular and help to guarantee a widespread distribution of economic opportunity. Continued support of our public school system, extending through universities, is one of the best guarantees that young people of ability will have a chance to rise on independent terms.

Security against illness, unemployment, and old age has come in for increased attention. Concern with the quality of life and security could impose limits on economic development if carried to extremes. Real estate decision makers, of course, must carefully assess the significance of trends of development in these areas.

Consumer Interests

Consumers have taken a more active interest in the real estate area. As a result, various laws have been passed such as truth in advertising, truth in lending, real estate settlement procedures, and others.[3] Many business firms have been giving increased attention to consumer relations and to warranties and guaranties. The National Association of Home Builders, for example, has developed a home buyers' warranty program and a somewhat similar program has been developed by the National Association of Realtors®. Real estate decision makers are giving increasing attention to consumer affairs.

Equality vs. Excellence

Our society has the difficult task of pursuing both equality and excellence, even though these are in some degree incompatible objectives. The pioneer community on the American frontier believed that "all men are created equal," but still insisted, "Let the best man win!"

Today we expect outstanding performance of scientists, managers, and government officials at the same time that we put restraints on them in the interest of equality. Standards of employment continue to move upward and there is greater intensity of competition both at home and abroad. We often take pride in some of our more exclusive residential developments but we are making efforts to include a wider distribution of income levels in our neighborhoods than formerly. We need the incentives that come from some exclusiveness, but cannot afford to allow this to emphasize inequality to a marked degree. This is particularly true if exclusiveness can lead to a stratified society.

At the present time tendencies toward increased equality may be noted

---

[3] See *Settlement Costs: A HUD Guide* (Rev. ed.; Washington, D. C.: Government Printing Office, 1976).

in the real estate field as efforts are being made to provide broader access to markets and to eliminate discrimination because of color, religion, or income with respect to housing. There is a growing emphasis on equality of results relative to equality of opportunity. Many people now believe they are entitled to equality of results.

Taxation

Of all the ways in which government programs and political trends affect real estate decisions none is more important than taxation. It has aptly been said that the power to tax is the power to destroy. The federal government does not tax real estate directly. This is in the province of state and local governments. Real property itself cannot be concealed. Hence, it seldom can escape from taxation.

Real estate investors have varying tax incentives to invest in real estate, including depreciation allowances and others. These vary with changes in the tax laws. Home owners may deduct mortgage interest when computing their taxes. Rents paid by business firms are, of course, considered an expense of doing business when computing taxes.

In addition, property taxes tend to be capitalized. As a result, any change in the tax burden of a real property has a direct effect on its value. An increase in the taxes on a residence of $100 would at a 10 per cent rate mean a loss of value of $1,000 unless benefits resulting from the tax expand in proportion to it.

Trends in Property Taxation. Historically, we have relied heavily on the property tax as a source of revenue for state and local governments. It continues as a prime support of local government programs and services; however, the property tax has been supplemented by other types, notably income and sales taxes. It may be that we are reaching the limits of taxes on real property for several reasons. First, the tax burdens themselves are already high; second, a substantial majority of homes are now owned by their occupants; and third, other sources of revenue are proving to be productive.

It is doubtful, however, that significant property tax reductions are likely to occur. In part this is due to the tax capitalization process which would mean that owners at the time of the reduction would reap a major windfall. In addition, it would be politically unpopular in some quarters to reduce such taxes. (As property ownership becomes more widespread, this situation may change.) About all owners and prospective owners of real property may hope for in the near term is the approximate holding of tax burdens at or near present levels.

APPROACHES TO URBAN AND HOUSING PROBLEMS

We have undertaken a wide variety of programs to try to cope with the growing complexity of our urban and housing problems. The Chicago

World's Fair of 1893 gave an early impetus to city planning and related programs. The reinstitution of the L'Enfant Plan for Washington in 1900 added widespread interest in this area. Concern about the slum problems of New York had brought a tenement house law as early as 1867 with a substantial revision in 1901. The first comprehensive zoning law, covering both land use and the height and bulk of buildings, was enacted in New York in 1916. In the same year traffic studies brought electrically operated traffic lights to Detroit. The federal government constructed some housing during World War I.

It took the depression of the early 1930's, however, to bring a major federal approach to many of our urban and housing problems. Efforts were made to encourage housing and to improve slum conditions which in turn were expected to expand employment opportunities. These efforts included a system of federal mortgage insurance through the Federal Housing Administration, the improvement of housing finance through the establishment of the Federal Home Loan Bank System, early programs in public housing and slum clearance, and related efforts. Following World War II came the establishment of broad programs of urban renewal. More recent years have seen both the expansion of these earlier programs and the addition of new ones, especially after the establishment of the Department of Housing and Urban Development in 1965. The recession of the mid-1970's combined with growing energy, environmental, and consumer problems brought a variety of governmental responses which were important for real estate and even more for housing.

Housing Finance

On the federal level, government probably has influenced real estate and housing decisions through programs of finance to a greater extent than in any other way. The general governmental functions related to the regulation of currency, credit, and financial institutions have an impact on the real estate sector through the work of the Department of the Treasury, Comptroller of the Currency, the Federal Reserve, the Federal Deposit Insurance Corporation, and related agencies. Because of the heavy impact of federal economic stabilization policies on housing, monetary and credit policies have had a special significance for the real estate field. The work of the Senate and House Banking, Housing and Urban Affairs Committees is of major importance.

A number of specialized agencies operate more directly in the area of real estate finance: the Federal Home Loan Bank System, the Federal Home Loan Mortgage Corporation, and the Federal Savings and Loan Insurance Corporation, the Department of Housing and Urban Development (HUD), which includes the Federal Housing Administration, Government National Mortgage Association, and other agencies. The mortgage guarantee programs of the Veterans' Administration have played an important role in real estate finance. Also of importance are the programs of the Federal National Mortgage Association, a semiprivate agency which helps to provide a secondary mortgage market. Market support programs through "tandem plans" of mortgage sales and purchases by the Government National Mortgage Association in cooperation with the Federal National Mortgage Association and the Federal Home Loan Mortgage Corporation have grown in importance. We will have more to say about these agencies in our more detailed discussions of real estate finance. We should note, however, that future governmental and political trends are likely to be influenced greatly by programs in the financial field.

The priorities enjoyed by these programs, of course, change from time to time. For example, federal mortgage insurance and guarantees appear to be somewhat less important than previously with the emergence of systems of private mortgage insurance. Concern about inflation has brought attention to the problems of providing some type of protection against interest rate and purchasing power risk. Today they are of greater concern than the more traditional areas of borrower, property, legal, and administrative risks usually associated with mortgage lending.

Special attention has been given recently to the possible restructuring of financial institutions. Changes of this type could have a major effect on real estate finance.

Urban Renewal

A variety of urban renewal programs have included efforts in the areas of land acquisition, replanning, demolition or rehabilitation, and resale. Bringing structures that are substandard or in a deteriorating condition up to acceptable standards and efforts at conservation and upgrading are parts of the renewal process. Modernization and repair efforts are sometimes included. In some cases complete rebuilding of areas has been undertaken either in cooperation with private developers or with provision of housing and other structures by direct federal or local government investment. For example, a number of firms have undertaken the redevelopment of land after it has been assembled and cleared by governmental or quasi-governmental authorities. Various universities, hospitals, and other institutions have taken increasing interest in urban renewal efforts. Urban homesteading has had some success.

Public Housing

Federal, state, and local efforts have been undertaken to provide housing directly by government investment and management. Many early projects were entirely the responsibility of the federal government. More recently federal and local government cooperation has been the rule in the public housing area. In some cases public housing projects have helped to rehabilitate deteriorating areas and have enjoyed considerable success; in others such projects have turned into "urban jungles" and appear to have generated worse problems than existed before efforts at improvement were made. Efforts to allow occupants of public housing projects to become owners of their dwelling units appear to hold some promise.

Interest and Rent Supplements

The 1960's saw the beginnings of below-market interest rate subsidies. These programs were expanded to include both interest and rent supplements. In general, provision was made for subsidies of rents which exceed 25 per cent of a tenant's income; in the home ownership programs subsidies typically were provided at about 20 per cent of a buyer's income.

SUMMARY

Real estate decision makers are influenced by economic, political, and governmental trends. Real estate is among the most highly regulated of all commodities; hence governmental and political trends are important factors in real estate decisions. The level of economic activity nationally, regionally, and locally is an important determinant of income from real property. Information must be evaluated carefully with due regard to both short- and long-run considerations.

Industry trends and regional patterns of economic change are also important. Because of the impact of economic conditions on real estate income, the analysis of such conditions provides a guide to decision making. Such analyses are usually based on data related to employment, income, production, and prices. Such data and related information are published in *Economic Indicators, Survey of Current Business, Federal Reserve Bulletin, The Economic Report* of the President and the *Annual Report* of the Council of Economic Advisers, in other government publications, and in the business and financial press.

Changes in economic activity may be the reflections of seasonal, cyclical, or secular trend influences. Each of these may be analyzed to advantage.

The level of spending is an important determinant of total business activity. Consumer spending makes up the largest single element of total spending, although this in turn is dependent largely on business expenditures for wages and salaries.

Areas for political and governmental analysis that typically have special interest for the real estate decision maker include economic stability, inflation and deflation, war and peace, energy, conservation and renewal, environmental priorities, quality of life, and the priorities given to equality on the one hand or excellence of performance on the other. Taxation is especially important in real estate decisions.

We have undertaken a variety of approaches to our urban and housing problems. Of special importance in these areas are programs of housing finance, urban renewal, public housing, and interest and rent supplements. Multiple approaches are followed increasingly and the rate of change requires that constant attention be given to new developments in these areas.

QUESTIONS FOR STUDY

1. Are real estate decision makers more concerned with local or national trends? Short- or long-term trends? Explain your answers.
2. How do general economic conditions affect the income-producing ability of real properties?
3. List the main indicators of current levels of general business activity.
4. What is meant by "gross national product"?
5. Distinguish among secular trend, seasonal fluctuations, and cycles in business activity. Explain why each of these might be important to the analysis of real estate markets.
6. Explain the importance of each of the following to the level of general business conditions: (a) spending by consumers, (b) government spending, (c) business spending for plant and equipment; business spending for inventories, (d) spending by foreign countries for U. S. goods.
7. Give examples of both coercive and inducive regulations.
8. Describe the probable impact on real estate of inflation and deflation in the future.
9. What effect will concern for the environment have on the use of real estate resources?
10. Explain how owners of real property would be affected by a reduction of taxes on real property.
11. Do you believe the federal government should make special effort in aiding home financing? Explain.
12. What programs have been undertaken by governmental and private groups to renew or improve the urban environment?

SUGGESTED READINGS

Economic Report of the President and *Annual Report,* Council of Economic Advisers (current issue). Washington, D. C.: Government Printing Office.

JACOB, DENNIS J., and THYGERSON, KENNETH J. "National Fiscal Policy and Housing," *Real Estate Issues* (Fall, 1976).

SAMUELSON, PAUL A. *Economics* (10th ed.). New York: McGraw-Hill Book Co., 1976. Ch. 14.

SMITH, HALBERT C., TSCHAPPAT, CARL J., and RACSTER, RONALD L. *Real Estate and Urban Development* (rev. ed.). Homewood, Ill.: Richard D. Irwin, Inc., 1977. Ch. 7.

TURNER, ROBERT C. *Economic Growth—The Outlook for Ten and Twenty-five Years.* Bloomington, Ind.: Committee for Futures Studies, Indiana University, 1975.

WEIMER, A. M., BOWEN, DAVID, and LONG, JOHN D. *Introduction to Business; A Management Approach* (5th ed.). Homewood, Ill.: Richard D. Irwin, Inc., 1974. Chs. 5, 6, 7, and 10.

STUDY PROJECT 5–1

Economic Growth—The Outlook *

We shall attempt here to estimate the probable economic growth prospects of the United States in the next ten years, and to give some more speculative estimates for the following fifteen years, that is, to the year 2000.

Two assumptions are implicit but very basic. The first is that the people in the United States, including notably business executives and political leaders, will find it possible to act in a responsible and rational manner and thus achieve in reasonable degree the economic objectives of which this nation is physically capable as, in the main, we have in the past. In other words, we are concerned with the potentialities for, physical limitations on, and technological problems that will need to be resolved for further real economic growth. We are not dealing with social and political theory, or on prospective developments in this area.

Second, it is assumed that the international scene will not change so radically as to render this analysis of United States capabilities irrelevant. This is a dangerous assumption. On one hand, it is evident to all that a new world of politics and economics is evolving. The atomic bomb, possessed by a number of nations in addition to the United States and the Soviet Union, poses an ever present threat to world peace. On the other hand, a partial *rapprochement* between the United States and both Russia and China seems to be underway. The decolonization movement and the rise of nationalism in some seventy new nations of the world has had dramatic political and economic effects, the recent oil embargo being only an example. The rising aspirations of the poorer countries of the world are having far-reaching consequences, particularly in their demands upon the United States for a redistribution of the world's output, notably of food. Conversely, raw material producing countries are increasingly using their leverage derived from these resources for both economic and political ends. No drastic curtailment of import availabilities has been assumed.

Population growth prospects vary greatly; in general, the richer countries are approaching stable populations, whereas in the poorer countries continued rapid population growth for several generations is a virtual certainty. These and many other changes that could be enumerated, plus others now unforseeable, may alter the pattern of international relationships so drastically as to undermine completely our calculations.

If the above-mentioned basic assumptions prove to be reasonably valid, however, some tentative conclusions regarding economic growth prospects in the United States can be drawn.

1. The population of the United States will continue to grow during most or all of the remaining years of the century. However, the rate of growth, currently 0.7 to 0.8 per cent a year, will diminish, especially after 1985. By the 1990's, the rate of population growth will be so close to zero population growth (ZPG) as to have economic consequences not materially different from those of absolute ZPG. Under some not unreasonable assumptions as to the fertility rate, absolute ZPG may be reached before the year 2000.

2. The labor force, however, will continue to grow at a rate not appreciably below that of the 1960's until the earlier 1980's, when a steady decline is in prospect. For the quarter-century as a whole, a growth in the man-hour input

* Adapted from the Preface and Summary of Conclusions, "Economic Growth—The Outlook for Ten and Twenty-five Years," by Robert C. Turner (Bloomington, Ind.: Committee for Futures Studies, Indiana University, 1975).

(Employed labor force × Average workyear) of about 1 per cent a year is in prospect.

3. Secular stagnation, predicted in the 1930's as the inevitable consequence of ZPG, is not a likely prospect, but neither is the possibility so small that it can be ignored.

4. Labor productivity will continue to rise, though at a lesser rate than in the past twenty-five years for reasons growing out of the points noted below.

5. The crucial limiting factor on further economic growth will be energy. Difficult energy problems are probable for the next decade, but assuming continued availability of petroleum imports, and with reasonable technological advance and effective conservation (especially of gasoline), they are not insurmountable and should not seriously impede further economic growth. The most difficult petroleum problem of the next decade is to devise means of protecting the nation from drastic damage in the event of another oil embargo. Higher prices of fuels in general, however, will contribute to inflationary pressures and will profoundly affect the economics of certain industries.

6. Beyond those data, energy problems will gradually but inexorably increase unless new forms of energy are found. So little is known about the potentialities of the fast breeder reactor, nuclear fusion, solar energy, and geothermal power that firm predictions are utterly impossible. However, there are reasons for hoping that solutions will be found. Especially if nuclear fusion could be harnessed, a host of other problems would be dramatically alleviated.

7. Water resources should not be a limiting factor on economic growth, except in the southwest corner of the United States. Costs of water are sure to rise, however, as pollution control and impoundment of water supplies become increasingly necessary.

8. With a few probable exceptions, minerals and metals will not seriously slow economic growth in the next twenty-five years. (Again, this conclusion assumes continued availability of imports of certain metals and minerals.) Beyond the next twenty-five years, however, problems will rise unless major technological breakthroughs occur, especially in developing substitutes for scarce metals and in energy. And in the meantime, the secular trend of metal prices is sure to be upward.

9. Forest products are not likely to inhibit further economic growth if (a) further progress is made in forest cultivation and management, and (b) major conservation gains are made. Price incentives should contribute greatly to conservation of forest products.

10. Agricultural land should not serve as a barrier to expanding source of food supplies, viewed as a strictly U. S. problem. However, world demands upon the United States are sure to mount. Substantial progress toward population control in the undeveloped countries is highly unlikely, and adequate technological advances in agricultural practices in these countries may not be made. Therefore, pressures on the United States to reduce its level of food consumption, especially of quality foods, in order to share its output with these countries, may be well-nigh irresistible.

The net effect is that the average rate of growth in the United States in the next twenty-five years will be below the 4 per cent average of the past twenty-five years, but a doubling of real GNP by the year 2000 is a reasonable prospect and, with luck, especially technological, somewhat more than a doubling is a possibility. A disproportionate share of the growth, however, will be in services of various kinds, including those supplied by governments, rather than in goods. Because further population growth is still in prospect, average family incomes will probably less than double, but it is not unreasonable to expect that average family incomes will permit a decent standard of living for all Americans, even allowing for the inevitable vagueness in the definition of "decent," by the year 2000.

Questions

1. What basic assumptions does Turner make in developing this study?
2. When will zero population growth (ZPG) be reached in the U. S.?
3. When will the labor force begin to decline?
4. Will labor productivity continue to advance?
5. What is considered to be the major limiting factor on future economic growth?
6. Is growth in the U. S. expected to be at a higher or lower or at about the same rate in the years ahead as in the past?

STUDY PROJECT 5–2

An Interview on Economic Forecasts *

Q. Must long-range economic forecasts be pessimistic?
A. Not necessarily—in fact, one may find less error on the optimistic side. The human race has the ability not only to adapt to changing conditions, but also to respond to them in a constructive way. I do not know how we will get along when there is no more oil in the world, if that ever happens, but I have no doubt that we will get along and I suspect that we might even do better.

As a matter of fact, I don't believe the world will run out of oil. The fear that we will run out will set in motion a number of forces that will prevent this from happening. Of major importance, steadily rising oil prices will make it profitable to find substitutes, not just for oil, but for the goods and services now dependent on oil. We are already seeing how this process works.

The greatest of our resources is the human mind and its capacity to produce new knowledge and know-how. Instead of being used up, knowledge expands day by day and year by year as inventions, innovations and other products of creative minds add to our storehouse of knowledge.

You might say that I am optimistic primarily because there are so many pessimists pointing out the many problems that will need to be solved. I would be much more pessimistic if we didn't know what at least some of the major unsolved problems are.

And I suppose, too, I am optimistic for the long run because in the long run we will have time to solve our problems. Time itself is a great resource. If we are able to combine time with knowledge and creativity, we have good grounds for optimism.

Q. Should we be less optimistic about the short-term future than the long-term?
A. Probably—too many of us have been taken in by the idea that stimulating aggregate demand through monetary and fiscal policies will bring full employment, and that full employment somehow will assure economic growth. We are beginning to see that this solution, like other pat answers to complex problems, has serious flaws. As we continue to learn that inflation rather than real economic growth is the more likely result of stimu-

---

* A. M. Weimer was the respondent in this interview, which appeared in *The MGIC Newsletter* (November 1975).

lating aggregate demand, I am confident that we will both define our economic problems more clearly and come up with better solutions. But that will take time and more knowledge. It will not happen in the short run.

Q. How can we assure continued economic growth?

A. The efficient production of most economic goods, including most services, requires work, equipment and intelligent direction. These are the three essential ingredients along with natural resources. We can substitute knowledge, technology and know-how for most natural resources over time. To produce more goods with less work—that is, to achieve economic growth—requires more effective work, more or better equipment, or more intelligent or more purposeful direction. (These same ingredients can also be applied to the development of a business firm or a private or public institution.) More abundant natural resources, of course, would also help us produce more goods with less work.

Policies for economic growth must therefore result, whether directly or indirectly, in *a more effective work force, a growing stock of more productive capital goods, and an increasingly effective management of these productive resources.* I am assuming we are not likely to discover great new reservoirs of natural resources, though this may be possible, either on "space ship earth" or in outer space. I am also assuming that we'll continue to add to our knowledge. So I'll stress our work force, capital equipment and management.

An effective work force would seem to be one that is willing and able to do the work that is required. It does not help us if people may be willing and able to do unskilled work, or even skilled work if such work is no longer required because of technological change. People must be willing and able to do the *new* kinds of work that a growing economy both offers and requires. Thus education and training, and *continued education and retraining,* are absolute essentials in a modern and growing economy. The more rapid the growth, especially if the result of technological change, the more essential the continued education and the retraining.

Questions

1. Are you inclined to be optimistic or pessimistic about the long-term future? Explain your position.
2. Would you tend to be more optimistic or less optimistic about the short-term than the longer-run future?
3. What are the basic ingredients of economic growth? Are they likely to be present as required in the years ahead? Explain.

STUDY PROJECT 5-3

Urban Decay *

Urban decay is one of the most serious economic and social problems facing the nation today.

Regardless of size, nearly every older city has been plagued to some degree by the flight of families and businesses, increasing crime and decreasing revenues,

* Adapted from "Better Housing Alone Won't Do Away With Urban Decay," *Savings and Loan News* (December, 1976), pp. 32–33.

health service and education difficulties, and a host of other problems. Unless something is done to reverse these forces, our central cities will become nothing more than large slums.

Although a complete estimate of the costs of decay is not possible, dollar figures alone wouldn't provide a full measurement anyway. The social costs of many of today's urban conditions must be added to the dollar losses resulting from deteriorating housing and declining real estate values.

Despite the difficulty of measuring the total cost of urban decay, we do know that it is potentially enormous. Consider, for example, the number of housing units that could be lost to urban neglect. In 1974, the latest year for which census data are available, slightly more than 22.5 million housing units were located inside central city areas. This represented 32 per cent of the nation's total occupied housing stock of 70.8 million units.

With these figures in mind, consider the problem of trying to replace 30 per cent of all the housing units in America if the nation is unsuccessful in developing policies to reverse the process of urban decay.

Most housing forecasts for 1976 suggest that 1.5 million housing units will have been produced by the end of this year. Thus, at this level of production, simply trying to replace the central city housing stock currently in place would take 15 years.

Because the resources for such a massive effort simply aren't available, our nation must find a way to reverse the process of urban deterioration and preserve the central cities.

Up to this point, the national approach to this problem has not been successful, partially as a result of the complexity of the problem itself. However, the greater shortcomings have resulted from the public policies adopted to deal with the problem.

During the 1960s and early '70s, it became fashionable to think in terms of solving our social problems through the federal government. Indicative of this approach were the efforts made to improve urban housing from 1968 to 1972.

During this period, the decay of the cities was blamed on the inability of low- and moderate-income households to buy new homes or rehabilitate older homes in urban neighborhoods. Consequently, public policy focused on a massive infusion of federal funds into the nation's central cities, providing large housing subsidies so that low- and moderate-income households could buy new homes.

At its outset, this federal subsidy boom accounted for nearly 11 per cent of the total housing units started in 1968. The boom peaked in 1970, when subsidized starts represented 30 per cent of all starts, and continued through 1972 before tailing off below the 14.1 per cent ratio of starts subsidized that year.

Although this boom succeeded in producing a great number of new homes for low- and moderate-income households in the central cities, it did not succeed in reversing or even stemming the process of urban decay. An unending list of scandals and abuses in the two major subsidy programs, sections 235 and 236, brought an end to the boom.

The lessons learned pointed up the fallacious nature of the "throw-money-at-a-problem" public policy approach to urban decay. Simply building low- and moderate-income housing in urban areas, it was learned, did not come to grips with the multifaceted problems of decay. In fact, many observers noted that the abandonments which resulted actually may have hastened the decay process in many central cities.

From 1973 to 1975, the subsidy failures brought an action void in the federal government's effort to solve the urban decay prbolem. Nevertheless, the past housing subsidy boom had created high expectations among community groups that the federal government was going to "do something" to reverse the forces of central city decay.

The "something" would have to be different, however, as even these groups came to acknowledge the failures of subsidies.

Realizing that federal money was not the solution for the urban decay problem after all, community groups began to look elsewhere for answers. Their efforts evolved into what could be called the "villains" approach, centering on the responsibility of the private sector to act to reverse the trends of urban decay.

The villains approach is a modern variation of the old "greed" theory used to describe the creation of slums and extensively reviewed by Richard Muth in his book on *Cities and Housing*. Like the greed theory, the villains approach develops the idea that the blame for slum housing and urban decay lies with the villains in the real estate and mortgage industries. A forceful exposition of this view is given in *The Ghetto Makers* by Jack Rothman.

The theory is that villains create slums through practices which keep funds from the central cities and make neighborhood maintenance impossible in these areas.

The first job is to identify the villains, which a number of community groups and politicians have pointed out to be the real estate and mortgage lending industries of our nation's major metropolitan areas. Once the villains are identified, so goes the theory, efforts can begin to force these interests to allocate large amounts of private capital for the central cities.

The first step in these efforts produced federal legislation late last year to require disclosures of mortgage lending activities in central cities. As these data became available for the first time on September 30, the villainizing efforts were initiated.

Not only do the news media play up lending data which reflect our nation's urban problem, few readers fail to infer that those providing the data are the villains responsible for the creation of slums. To blame urban decay on private market villains is like blaming bad news on reporters. The fact is that real estate brokers, appraisers and mortgage lenders are simply reporters documenting uban housing problems.

The villains approach is as bankrupt as the nation's previous subsidy program. It simply would substitute private lender dollars for federal dollars.

Both approaches view the urban housing problem in a vacuum. Both assume that dealing with decay simply involves building and rehabilitating housing in urban areas. Both represent a piecemeal approach to the decay problem.

As was shown in the case of the federal housing subsidy boom, the solution to urban decay is not new housing units. The solution lies in a comprehensive neighborhood approach to reverse the social and economic forces which create decay. The similarities between the villains and federal subsidy approaches doom the villains approach to failure.

The ultimate result of this new approach may well be a repeat of the losses suffered from the subsidized housing boom. Private lenders may either be destroyed or be forced to pass on their urban investment losses. The consumer-taxpayer will pay with federal tax dollars or with higher costs for obtaining mortgage money if this new villains approach is adopted.

Regardless of how the costs are passed on to the consumer-taxpayer, the approach's bankruptcy is assured. An effort aimed solely at putting more dollars into urban housing units cannot reverse the trend of urban decay. Recent experiences with federal subsidies clearly imply that simply providing dollars for central city housing is not the solution.

To address the issue of urban decay, we must identify all of the national problems which tend to have a major impact on our nation's central cities. Simultaneously, we must reduce unemployment, crime and energy usage while we improve education, transportation and housing revitalization in urban areas.

Just making a start requires that the nation adopt a public policy encompassing a comprehensive neighborhood approach to the urban decay problem. We must no longer think in terms of the urban "housing problem" or the urban "crime problem."

We must focus on the urban neighborhood. We must build desirable neighborhoods, not just housing units. The urban decay problem must be redefined as the inability of low- and moderate-income households to buy new homes or rehabilitate older homes in "desirable" urban neighborhoods.

The federal government has a crucial role to play as a catalyst in the effort to fight urban decay in general and the problem of urban housing in particular. Federal programs should be designed to stimulate many diverse neighborhood participants to unite in a coordinated effort to reverse urban decay. Several programs proposed or already in operation fit the catalytic mold, including:

• The proposed share-risk, or conventional loan co-insurance, program, which is designed to stimulate central city lending.
• The Neighborhood Housing Services program, which is uniting neighborhood residents, lenders and providers of city services in a common bond to reverse urban decline.[1]
• A proposed National Neighborhood Policy Act, which is designed to stimulate community organization activities.

In addition to these new catalytic program efforts, existing institutions such as the Federal Housing Administration must be revitalized. Similarly, we must maintain the existing institutions doing a good job for housing. In this regard, we must see that Regulation Q and the savings differential are maintained.

The current public policy approach to the urban decay problem holds little promise, whether federal or private funds or a combination of both are used. A comprehensive neighborhood approach is needed.

Catalytic federal programs designed to implement such a comprehensive approach are proving successful where they've already been initiated. Real progress in reversing the process of urban decay, however, requires the formal adoption of a comprehensive neighborhood approach to the problem.

Once such an approach is adopted, we could halt the efforts to place the blame for urban decay on selected villains. We could implement catalytic federal programs and begin a coordinated effort involving all neighborhood participants in the process of reversing urban deterioration.

Any hope of central city survival lies in such a comprehensive neighborhood effort.

---

[1] The Neighborhood Housing Services (NHS) Program is an effort to tie neighborhood residents, lenders, and providers of city services together. NHS programs function under the joint direction of the Federal Home Loan Bank Board and HUD under the aegis of the Urben Reinvestment Task Force. The NHS concept is in operation in approximately 30 cities and could, if expanded carefully, operate in 50 cities within the next year or so. It now involves the active participation of over 300 savings and loan associations, and has had some spectacular successes in terms of neighborhood revitalization and rehabilitation. It is illustrative of the blending of federal and local initiative that is absolutely necessary for a comprehensive approach to the preservation of much of the residential real estate in our central cities.

Questions

1. Why is a comprehensive approach to the problems of the older areas of our cities required?
2. Why have efforts to build low- and moderate-income housing failed to revitalize older areas?
3. What is the Neighborhood Housing Services Program?
4. Suggest recommendations for more effective approaches to the problems of older neighborhoods.

6

REGIONAL AND
LOCAL TRENDS

REGIONAL AND LOCAL INFLUENCES ON DECISIONS

As we have suggested, the real estate decision maker has a basic interest in the localization of income. Although economic activity in a region or locality may move parallel with general business conditions, there are often significant differences. For example, the Southwest and Southeast have grown substantially faster than the American economy as a whole in recent years. Similarly, regions and localities may have different political and governmental priorities.

The Local Economies

Of major importance for most real estate decision makers is the potential direction of economic, political, or governmental activity in a particular locality—a metropolitan area or city or rural community. Real estate decision makers are also interested in the outlook for smaller sections of a local economy—in the market for the type of property under consideration and in the neighborhood or district in which the property is located. Again, we recognize that there may be variations between the growth rates of local areas and various types of markets within them. There also may be differences in local political trends or problems.

Importance of Local Analysis

Interest in local economic and governmental activity results from a variety of decision problems. The multiplant firm has problems of locating and relocating branches. Chain store organizations are faced with decisions about alternative locations for their stores. Manufacturing companies do not always seek localities with strong growth potential; in some cases, a surplus labor supply or the availability of unused plant and equipment may be attractive. By contrast, retail organizations almost always seek locations with strong growth potential. All types of companies are interested in the quality and cost of local government.

Investors have choices between properties located in one part of the country or another, one locality or another, even one country and another. Life insurance companies and other large mortgage lenders, for example, often conduct local analyses.

From a local standpoint, builders and land developers may be concerned with the extent and timing of their projects. Owners of land have problems of holding, selling, or moving their investments to alternate locations.

Local mortgage lenders need bases for developing both short- and longer-term lending policies; government officials find it advisable to anticipate requirements for utilities, schools, and municipal services. Analyses and forecasts of local developments are helpful to these decision makers and to many others, ranging from home buyers to major investors.

Type of Analysis Required

The type of analysis undertaken will vary with the nature and complexity of the decision problem. In some cases relatively simple analyses of economic and governmental conditions may be adequate. In certain situations economic base analysis may serve the purposes of the decision maker. In others, more elaborate types of analysis may be called for. This does not necessarily mean that one type is "better" than another; one type may be more desirable in terms of its applicability to the specific decision problem.

Definition of Region

A region may mean almost anything that an analyst chooses it to mean. For example, a region may be defined as a traditional geographic region such as New England or the Pacific Northwest, an area such as the "Upper Midwest" or "Appalachia," a metropolitan area, or an area restricted by political boundaries. We may have a definition of a region in terms of ecology, natural resources, or climate. Some regions may be defined economically as in the case of a Federal Reserve District or in terms of their economic development interests or potential.

One analyst has suggested that "all regional classification schemes are simply variations on the homogeneity criterion and it is somewhat misleading to suggest otherwise. The only real question is what kind of homogeneity is sought." He suggests that a region may be homogeneous with respect to jurisdiction of a specific government or administrative agency, trade or function of the area, physical characteristics such as geography or natural resource endowment, economic or social characteristics, or boundaries for statistical purposes.[1]

Economic theory has developed a branch which is referred to as "regional analysis," or "regional economics." Those interested in this branch of study, however, have not always agreed on the way in which a region should be defined. Because the boundaries of a region are so difficult to specify without a reference point, each definition is meaningful primarily in terms of the specific purpose involved. For the purposes of real estate decision makers, regional analysis tends to be restricted primarily to local economies. Since the methods of analysis typically are similar, we do not try to distinguish here between different sizes of local economies. We consider "regional and local analyses" to refer mainly to local economies and the surrounding areas, depending on the type of decision problem under consideration.

APPROACHES TO LOCAL AND REGIONAL ANALYSIS

One may approach the problems of local and regional analysis from a variety of viewpoints; our main concern here is the real estate decision maker and consequently we tend to stress interests which are largely economic and governmental although not exclusively so.

Resources

We may analyze the local economy in terms of local resources. The future of a mining or lumbering town, of course, depends on the supply of its basic resources, their probable life, their competitive position, and related conditions.[2] We may consider the character of the labor resources in the local economy; the land resources, for example, the availability of desirable industrial sites; availability of capital and the ability to command it; and the presence of entrepreneurial, professional, technical, and related talent. Such community resources as schools, utilities, governmental services, and the like may also be considered. These resources provide the general conditions in which development may occur or fail to occur. Special problems may require analysis. Water pollution, smog, or other environmental problems may inhibit the future development of a facility. Unfavorable tax policies, poor governmental administration, or unfavorable local attitudes often require consideration.

In addition to studies of major local resources, industry studies may be undertaken, particularly of the more important industries in the local

---

[1] John R. Meyer, "Regional Economics: A Survey," *American Economic Review,* vol. 53, no. 1, pt. 1 (March, 1963).

[2] Homer Hoyt, *According to Hoyt* (2nd ed.; Washington, D. C.: Hoyt, 1970), pt. VIII; Charles M. Tiebout, *The Community Economic Base Study* (New York: Committee for Economic Development, 1962), pp. 18–19.

economy. Sometimes inventories of the industrial assets and liabilities of a local economy may be developed and analyzed.

Markets

We should note that it is possible to study the markets for the major resources of a local economy and thus to gain insights into its growth potential.[3] For example, the labor market, the land market, the capital market, or the market for special talents such as entrepreneurship, research ability, or leadership may be studied with varying degrees of intensity. Information about such markets may be related to the specific problems under consideration by decision makers. For example, the efforts of various local communities to induce business firms to locate in their areas may be more rational than often is supposed if it is recognized that local community leaders may be interested primarily in the entrepreneurial, leadership, managerial, and research talent that may be gained.

Economic Relationships

We might try to approach the regional or local economy as a subdivision of the national economy. For example, we might analyze local employment and income trends and make comparisons with national changes. Such indicators of economic activity as bank clearings, car loadings, electric power consumption, building permits and housing starts, and others may be analyzed and compared. If we tried to make use of GNP analysis, however, or other types of analyses useful on a national basis, we would soon encounter difficulties largely because local and regional economies are "open" and not "closed." That is, there are no reasonably well-defined economic boundaries.

Efforts are sometimes made to use regional accounts which resemble national income accounting; input–output analysis is attempted in some cases and flow-of-funds methods may prove to be useful. Most of these methods, however, are difficult to use because of inadequate data or because of the sweeping assumptions that typically are required.

Despite some theoretical and practical inadequacies, economic base studies have proved to be highly useful for the analysis of local economies. The economic base has been defined as follows:

The economic base of a community consists of those activities which provide the basic employment and income on which the rest of the local economy depends. An economic base study identifies the basic sources of employment and income and provides an understanding of the source and level of all employment and income in a community.[4]

[3] Wilbur R. Thompson, *A Preface to Urban Economics* (Baltimore: The Johns Hopkins Press, 1965).
[4] Tiebout, *op. cit.*, p. 9.

Later in the chapter we will consider the main elements in economic base studies and outline briefly the major features of input–output analysis. Before considering these topics it may be helpful to review some of the principal characteristics of local economies.

LOCATION OF ECONOMIC ACTIVITIES

The point at which a particular city will arise depends on factors which favor the establishment of activities which may give the city a competitive advantage over others. Usually topography has been the most important factor, although its effects have depended on whether military, political, social, or economic considerations were paramount.

Priorities

In modern periods a specific city is established at a certain point and expands in importance mainly because opportunities to secure employment and income are available. The sites of many older cities were determined largely by defense factors.

Toynbee says, for example:

Thucydides, in his introduction to his history of the Atheno-Peloponnesian War of 431–404 B.C., has observed that, in the archaic age of Hellenic history, the Greek city-states were pulled in opposite directions by the conflicting requirements of trade and defence. Trade called for a location of the city as close as possible to good food-producing land and to good water transport, which in the Aegean basin, means maritime transport, since in this region there are no navigable rivers. On the other hand, defence calls for a location out of the reach of pirates, brigands and invading armies, which in this region, means a location on a mountain island. Manifestly accessibility and security were difficult to combine, even for Greek cities that had become rich enough to be able to afford to provide themselves with artificial defences in the shape of man-made walls.[5]

In a few cases social and religious factors have played a dominant part in determining city location. Sometimes political situations have determined the location of cities. For example, the location of Washington was the result of military and political factors. Most of our cities, however, grew up at points which gave them *economic* advantages. Economic advantages of various locations may result from one of the following factors or combinations of them:

1. Trade routes and transportation breaking points
2. Access to raw materials
3. Access to rich markets

[5] Arnold Toynbee, *Cities on the Move* (New York and London: Oxford University Press, 1970), p. 29.

4. Power resources
5. Climate

Transportation. Some cities developed at transportation breaking points—for example, where land and water routes met. In such cases the availability of harbor facilities was the dominant factor. Cities often grew up at points where one type of water transportation met another—or where land trade routes intersected; air routes have tended to follow established locations but jet air travel has changed a number of old patterns. One writer has aptly stated:

It is when the transfer of goods is accompanied by a breaking of bulk or by a change of ownership, there being then added the complex mechanism of commercial exchange performed by importers, exporters, wholesalers, retailers, insurers, brokers, and bankers, that wealth is accumulated and localized, with consequent power to control business for local benefit.[6]

Raw Materials. Easy access to raw materials has often determined the location of a city because of the economies resulting from being near the sources of supplies. Generally, raw materials of great bulk which are costly to move have had more influence on the location of cities than other types of raw products. When such resources are exhausted, the towns which grow up near them decline, unless other economic opportunities develop.

Market Dominance. Frequently, points which give easy access to rich markets form natural places for economic development. For example, the development of New York City was in part due to the fact that there was an easy route from the West through the Appalachian Mountains to the East. Similarly, Chicago's growth was based on the richness of its market area, the upper Mississippi Valley.

Power Resources. Power resources have accounted for the rise of cities at certain specific points, the "fall line" in the East having resulted in the establishment of various cities because of the available water power. In more recent times, other types of power, particularly electricity, which can be transmitted for considerable distances, have eliminated the dependence of machinery on natural power. When methods of using atomic energy are further developed, the importance of the location of power resources may be eliminated entirely as a factor in determining city location and development. Until then, however, the availability and cost of energy will play an important role in local economic development.

Climate. Climatic conditions also have been of importance in determining city location. Sometimes climate favors certain types of industry,

[6] Richard M. Hurd, *Principles of City and Land Values* (New York: The Record & Guide, 1924), ch. 2.

the growth of cotton and woolen manufacture in areas with moist climates being a case in point. Space-age installations have largely gone to southern areas because of climatic factors. Climate usually has a more direct influence in determining the location of resort or amusement centers, such as Miami Beach or Honolulu.

Combinations of Factors

In general, no single factor accounts for the location of a city at a certain point. For example, the *exact* point where a town starts may be largely accidental, since any of a number of points in the vicinity might be equally desirable. New York's original location was due to a combination of advantages. And so was its phenomenal growth. As Raymond Vernon points out:

> The disposition among historians is to lay New York's rise to the Erie Canal; to the ice-free conditions of the East River, kept clear by its churning tides; and to a comparatively unobjectionable sand bar at the mouth of New York's harbor— a sand bar more manageable than at the mouth of the Delaware. There is also a disposition to give credit to something in the fluid social structure of New York's life, an indefinable quality which even then attracted off-beat businessmen in search of their fortunes. At any rate, whether or not New York's social structure was part of the lure, its early growth was almost certainly based on a lead in foreign trade.[7]

The original site of Chicago was a swamp; but the point at which Lake Michigan and the Great Lakes system came closest to joining the Mississippi River and its tributaries was a natural trade center, originally for the fur trade and later for other types of markets. The decisive factor undoubtedly was the Illinois–Michigan Canal; otherwise, development might have occurred farther south.

Types of Cities

Cities may be classified in various ways. For our purposes it is desirable to classify them on the basis of the major employment and income sources represented. Such a classification might take the following form:

1. Industrial cities, including those involved chiefly in the manufacturing and processing of commodities
2. Cities devoted principally to commerce, which include seaports, lake ports, river cities, and railroad and air terminals and junctions
3. Political cities, including all those for which the activities of a state government or the Federal government provide the basic income source

[7] Raymond Vernon, *Metropolis 1985* (Cambridge: Harvard University Press, 1960), p. 8.

4. Recreational and health resorts, as well as cities in which retired people reside
5. Educational, research, and cultural centers

Many cities, of course, include all or nearly all of these major activities, although one or two types may be predominant.

Extractive industries ordinarily do not produce the largest cities. Our largest cities typically are those with superior transportation facilities which place them in the main currents of trade. Manufacturing generally has developed in larger cities to a greater extent than in smaller places, and such expansion has in turn contributed to further growth. It should be noted, however, that some cities have grown very large without becoming great manufacturing centers. Kansas City, Denver, and Washington are cases in point. In recent years many manufacturing plants have been located in the countryside, away from major urban concentrations.

LOCAL GROWTH AND DECLINE

At an early stage in the development of economic thought Adam Smith pointed out:

The country supplies the town with the means of subsistence and the materials of manufacture. . . . We must not, however, upon this account, imagine that the gain of the town is the loss of the country. The gains of both are *mutual and reciprocal* and the division of labor is in this, as in all other cases, adjusted to all the different persons in the various occupations into which it is subdivided.[8]

Toynbee has made the following observation:

In the long run a city's imports and exports must balance each other in terms of value. The penalty for a chronic deficit would be the eventual cutting off of supplies and a consequent reduction of the city's population—ultimately to zero. In the past, cities that have paid their way have not imported more in value than they have exported, but they have brought in more in bulk than they have thrown out. . . . Consequently, in the course of time, their surface has risen in height.[9]

Specialization

Division of labor between town and country, region and region, industry and industry, and employment and employment continues to be a vital factor in explaining the character and direction of modern economic activity. Division of labor undoubtedly is the basis for the establishment

[8] Adam Smith, *The Wealth of Nations* (London: George Bell & Sons, 1908), III, p. 383. [Italics added.]
[9] Toynbee, *op. cit.*, p. 4.

of a local economy and the extent of its long-term growth. The economic base concept rests primarily on this principle, as we have pointed out.

Power To Grow

After a local economy attains a certain size, however, it may be able to maintain its growth, if not to augment it, because it has the economic or political power to command further support. A pool of labor, particularly if special skills are represented; a supply of capital or the ability to induce it to come to a locality; a group of community leaders and hard-hitting entrepreneurs and politicians; highly trained professional people, experts, and technicians—all may help to assure ongoing economic activity and even some growth. Substantial additional growth, however, may depend on specialization and advantages in interregional trade.

"Urban-Size Ratchet."   Thompson suggests that an "urban-size ratchet" is at work, that once a locality attains a certain size and economic importance it can continue to grow and expand because of diversification, a "blending of young, mature and decadent industries," the influence of power politics, the large amount of sunk, fixed capital invested, the importance of the local market itself, and the chance that growth processes are stimulated in a city of some size—"a large urban area is more likely to give birth to new industries at critical points in its life cycle than is a small urban area." [10]

Whether the growth process is self-regenerative or the result of special factors, inside or outside the locality, remains an open question and the answer probably varies with the character of the local economy. For example:

In a pattern which will appear many times during this account, growth fed on growth. For a time, New York's unique scheduled sailings, its "ship brokers," and its wholesalers could be matched nowhere else. . . . During the middle decades of the century, though New York's role as the national gateway continued to expand, its own heavy dependence on the sea was already beginning to shrink. The Erie Canal had opened up a new route through which New York could tap the wheatlands and forests of the Middle West. Bits and pieces of rail line were also beginning to be put in place, adding another means by which raw materials could be shipped east and manufactured products could move west to the new territories. [11]

Activities that had sprung originally from the port became independent; wholesaling took on the handling of domestic products as well as foreign trade; in finance, maritime insurance shifted to domestic property risks, foreign banking to domestic banking. In subsequent developments one

[10] Thompson, *op. cit.*, pp. 9–11.
[11] Vernon, *op. cit.*, p. 9.

type of growth gave way to another. New York's size probably aided in making these adjustments but explanations of these processes are not easy to nail down.

Variety of Economic Opportunities. The growth of Chicago from a hamlet of fifty people in the early 1830's to a metropolis of more than six million in a century and a half can be explained by a wide variety of economic opportunities. As one of the authors has pointed out:

> The advantage of the site of Chicago as a meeting place first of lake, river, canal, and wagon transportation, and then of lake and rail carriers in turn, made it the principal distributing and manufacturing center for a valley containing the richest combination of agricultural and mineral resources of the world that was being exploited for the first time. . . . The magnitude of the population was but the measure of the strength of the economic advantages of the site of Chicago, and of the economic resources of its hinterland—the Upper Mississippi Valley.[12]

And the growth of the Chicago region has continued, although at not as rapid a rate as for some other cities, notably in the South and West.

New Growth Sources. Growth comes not only from the expansion of present sources of income and employment but from new sources that may be developed. Thus, the capacity to attract new sources of employment and income deserves special attention. Such capacity typically will represent a combination of conditions ranging from availability of resources and markets to living conditions, quality of government, tax levels in relation to the services provided, quality of local leadership, environmental conditions, energy, competitive factors, and others. The competent real estate decision maker pays attention to the entire complex of factors that enables a locality to provide goods and services on terms that will compete with other cities and localities within a local climate or environment that is attractive and congenial.

Limiting Factors

While Chicago and New York were growing, some cities were declining in economic importance. Outstanding, of course, were certain mining and lumbering towns whose natural resources were exhausted. Some cities declined because others enjoyed an advantage in nearness to raw materials or to markets, availability of labor and capital, climate, political preference, or the drive and dedication of local leaders. Certain smaller cities lost their reasons for existence as improved transportation facilities enabled major cities to serve wider areas. Some cities were helped or hindered by governmental or administrative policies; e.g., differential freight rates and

---

[12] Reprinted from *One Hundred Years of Land Values in Chicago,* by Homer Hoyt, by permission of the University of Chicago Press, pp. 279–84. Copyright 1933 by the University of Chicago.

tax policies have had their effects on the growth of specific cities. In some cases the efforts of community leaders have stimulated city growth, while other cities failed of their potential because of inadequacy of local leadership.

As we suggested in the discussion above, an adequate supply of civic and social resources may help to stimulate economic growth. Thus, if a city possesses good local government, schools, hospitals and doctors, shopping facilities, and the like, new industries may be attracted to it. The lack of such facilities and services might repel business firms that are considering alternative locations for their new plants. The existence of difficult problems such as high crime rates, smog, water pollution, energy limitations, inadequate police and fire protection, and others often inhibit growth and development.

State and Local Tax Problems. State and local taxes relative to the government services provided often play a major role in the development of a region. Thus, analysts usually pay special attention to taxes and their impact on real estate decisions.

Where the state levies taxes on local real estate, it is to the self-interest of counties and cities to assess their properties at low valuations so that they will pay a lower share of state taxes. To overcome this, a state tax commission may make its own appraisal and may order the local assessments raised by a factor that is supposed to equalize assessments throughout the state. Uniformity of assessment among all types of property in cities is difficult to achieve because of political considerations. Single-family homes, since they contain the most voters, are usually undervalued in comparison with apartments and commercial or industrial properties.

Many different local taxing districts frequently overlap. There are school districts, sewer districts, local city governments, park districts, mosquito abatement districts, and others. Each district may impose taxes upon real and personal property to cover its costs. The tax on any specific property is a composite of local city taxes, county taxes, school district taxes, park district taxes, and others. All the taxes may be collected by one government authority and distributed to the others; or sometimes taxes must be paid separately to different authorities, such as the city and the board of education.

The need for reassessment of all the real estate in a given jurisdiction does not arise from the fact that real estate values change, but that they do not change uniformly. Some districts decline in desirability but they may still retain old levels of assessed values. Other new districts may have increased rapidly in value and are underassessed.

Relative Tax Burden. Differences in property tax burdens and in relative tax burdens often have a major impact on real estate decisions. There is a great difference in local tax burdens, not only between cities in different regions of the country, but even between local communities in the same metropolitan area. Such differences may be accentuated in the future since they are due to the following factors:

1. The number of surplus-producing properties such as stores, factories, vacant land, and high-priced homes compared with the number of low-valued single-family homes which typically do not pay enough in real estate taxes to cover their share of local government costs. One community in a metropolitan area may have the regional shopping center and most of the high-priced homes. Its taxes will be relatively low compared with surrounding communities.
2. The quality and quantity of local government services. In some suburban communities taxes are low because no sewer or water systems are provided and there is inadequate police and fire protection. Highways are provided by the state without local government cost. Taxes are high in some central cities not only because of the cost of sewers, water mains, and streets, but also because of heavy payments for social services.
3. The amount of tax-exempt property. A large amount of tax-exempt property throws heavier burdens on other property.
4. Homestead exemption. In Florida, homestead exemption gives extremely low taxes to low-value homes.
5. The amount of revenue-sharing subsidies, or grants-in-aid, or allocations of state revenues received from state income taxes, liquor license taxes, or gasoline taxes, or federal government aid for education, highways, or other purposes.
6. The amount of taxes collected locally from sources other than real estate, such as license fees, fines, local sales taxes, and so forth.

Zoning Regulations. On the local level of government, zoning and building regulations have a continuing influence on real estate decision makers and often require careful analysis. Increasingly zoning is carried out on a county-wide basis and may extend to entire metropolitan areas. Successful zoning laws and planning regulations typically conform to the general pattern of city growth and do not run contrary to such patterns. Some flexibility, of course, is usually needed since no one can be entirely sure of long-range land use needs.

We should recognize that zoning sets limits on competition and in effect establishes certain noncompeting areas as between types of land use. This is done because of the recognition that some land uses are incompatible and that orderly development cannot be relied upon to result from open market competition. Houston, however, has been able to operate without a zoning law. Typically residential districts are designated and divisions may be made as between single-family and multi-family dwelling house areas; commercial areas are marked out as are industrial areas. One type of land use is not permitted to invade another.

Virtual monopolies may be granted and substantial gains may be had by getting certain land rezoned. In some cases zoning is used to serve the purposes of a special group. For example, "snob zoning," which typically requires three to five acres per residence, may protect existing exclusive communities and prevent development of new areas by builders for the general market. Builders sometimes seek out communities with lenient zoning laws. Although the trend appears to favor more extensive zoning, there has been growing criticism of zoning practices. Experimentation is needed which will permit the more widespread use of competition as a regulator.[13]

Building Regulations. Building codes which usually regulate quality and strength of materials and allowable stresses, and make provision for various sanitary and health considerations, have been subjected to a considerable amount of study and criticism in recent years. Often they add unduly to construction costs. They usually fail to establish performance standards but rather impose a variety of detailed regulations and bureaucratic practices. They may be used to protect local workers and business firms and often they delay the introduction of new construction materials and methods. Changes may be slow in coming, however, since numerous special interests typically are involved.

Changing Attitudes Toward Growth

Many towns and cities, and even some states, are pursuing cautious policies with respect to future growth. Preferences range from no growth, growth to a specified level, and slow but limited growth, to as much growth as possible. Some communities discourage newcomers, using such slogans as "Don't come here to live" or "Come to visit but don't move here." In some places growth is limited by zoning, for example, through controlled rezoning of agricultural land. A few cities such as Boca Raton, Florida, have set ceilings on growth. Court controversies have erupted over slow growth or no growth policies; Petaluma, California, and Boca Raton are examples.

THE ECONOMIC BASE

The concept of the economic base was set forth by Werner Sombart in the 1920's and by Robert M. Haig as early as 1928.[14] Sombart pointed out the difference between "Städtegründer," which may be translated as *Town Founders* or *Builders*, and "Städtefüller," which may be translated as *Town*

---

[13] See, for example, Lyle C. Bryant and James McMullin, *Nonregulatory Strategies for Managing Urban Growth* (unpublished manuscript).

[14] W. Sombart, *Der Moderne Kapitalismus, Dritter Band: Das Wirtschaftsleben im Zeitalter des Hochkapitalismus* (2d rev. ed., 1927; 3d ptg.; Berlin: Duncker & Humbolt, 1955), 413; also R. M. Haig, *Major Economic Factors in Metropolitan Growth and Arrangement*, Vol. I, *Regional Survey of New York and Environs*, Regional Plan Committee, 1928.

Fillers. Homer Hoyt, co-author of this book, refined the concept of the economic base in a variety of reports and articles from 1936 onward and dealt with some of the essential ideas in the concept of the economic base or economic background in his *One Hundred Years of Land Values in Chicago,* published in 1933.

International Trade Theory

Essentially, the economic base concept rests on international trade theory and on the multiplier effect of "export" activity. The locality or region is viewed in relation to other regions and its potential growth is considered as dependent upon "basic" sources of employment or income, that is, *those that command income from beyond its borders.* For example, manufacturing activity, since its usually leads to "exportable" products, is considered "basic" and the service trades as "nonbasic" or supporting activity. The impact of the former, however, is multiplied through the latter since basic income will support some service activity (ratios vary widely—1 to 1 or 1½ to 1 are not uncommon).[15]

Basic and Service Activities

The terms town "founders" or "builders" and town "fillers" as used by Sombart are suggestive of the roles which various economic activities can play in local economic development. We should note, however, that "filler" or "service" or "nonbuilder" or "nonbasic" activities may at times help to attract town building activities and thus play a leading rather than a supporting role in local economic development. Availability of outstanding service activities or efficient local government can play a significant role in the economic development of an area. The extent to which local people are willing to invest their savings locally may have a bearing on the economic development of the area as well.

Outline of an Economic Base Analysis

For illustrative purposes we present here an outline of some of the major steps that may be taken in carrying out an economic base analysis of medium complexity. In summary these steps include: (1) determining the relative importance of major present and potential income sources; (2) analyzing each of the basic sources of income—manufacturing, trade, extractive industry, and other types; and (3) studying modifying influences—the size of the local market, quality of community facilities and services, governmental factors, and the general "climate" for local economic activities.

Relative Importance of Basic Income Sources. The sources of employment and income in a local economy are many and varied, but for

[15] Hoyt, *According to Hoyt, op. cit.,* pp. 548–86.

convenience of analysis they may be combined into the following primary groups: (1) manufacturing, (2) extractive industry, (3) wholesale and retail trade, and (4) special sources of income, such as political, educational, institutional, resort, or amusement activities. The stream of income brought into the city by people who receive pensions, rents, royalties, and interest from elsewhere should also be considered a part of the urban growth income. Few cities are supported by any one of these income sources alone; nearly all rely on a combination of various types.

Chicago, Detroit, Hartford, Cleveland, Milwaukee, and Baltimore are predominantly industrial cities; while New Orleans, Minneapolis, Kansas City, Omaha, and Portland are predominantly commercial centers. Miami and Atlantic City are chiefly tourist resorts. Washington is supported principally by the activities of the federal government. In St. Louis, Boston, and Philadelphia there is a fairly equal division of employment and income between trade and manufacturing. In Springfield, Illinois, and in Oklahoma City there is an extraordinary diversity of support from manufacturing, extractive industry, trade, and state institutions. Ann Arbor, Michigan, is primarily an educational and research center.

The first step in determining the economic potentialities of a city is to estimate the relative importance of each of the various sources of employment and income. Information concerning total employment, as well as the number employed in each of the main types of economic activity, can be secured from such sources as the Bureau of the Census, state employment services and their local branches, and chambers of commerce. Where more detailed information is desirable, assistance may be secured from the personnel departments of principal firms, and local labor unions. Information concerning payrolls is often available from census reports, local or state taxing authorities, and similar sources.

From one or a combination of these sources, total employment can be obtained and the per cent of the total engaged in each of the major types of economic activity outlined above can be computed. Efforts should also be made to determine whether any new sources of income are likely to develop in the near future, and their relative importance.

Analysis of Manufacturing.   In forecasting the trend of manufacturing activities in a locality as a source of future economic development, each type of industry should be studied in some detail. Attention should be given to such factors as the nature of the products manufactured by each firm, the location of raw materials, principal markets, trends of demand for the products, and the competitive position of each of the major establishments. Such factors as the competence of management, the character of the labor supply, and special local advantages or disadvantages should be considered. In addition, tax burdens, regulatory practices, the attitudes of local community leaders toward each firm, and the trends of local government policies generally merit consideration. Special attention should be given to competitive advantage of the location, diversification of industry, competitive position of the firm, and cyclical fluctuations. From the standpoint of future effects on real estate values, it is important to determine whether the industries located in a city will remain, advance in importance, decline, or move to another location.

Among the factors that tie an industry to a city are large plants, heavy fixed capital investments in new and modern machinery, the availability of a large body of skilled labor, favorable transportation rates, convenient access to raw materials, proximity to markets, favorable attitudes of local community leaders, and taxes that are favorable relative to government services provided.

Unfavorable conditions also require analysis. Environmental, energy, slum, or crime problems, for example, may cause an industry to move from an area or repel industries that might otherwise move there. Local policies that discourage growth may also be a factor.

There is always an element of risk if a city has great concentration of industrial activity along one specific line. If half of the workers in a city are employed in a single establishment, the whole structure of real estate values may collapse if that establishment moves away. If there are many establishments in the same industry, the risks are less; but the city may suffer because of a decrease in the demand for one of the locality's products or the rise of a competing product. In addition, single-industry towns are more likely to fall under the dominance of a relatively few businessmen or labor leaders, with the result that real estate values may suffer from shortsighted managerial policies or from prolonged strikes and industrial disturbances.

Analyzing Income from Trade. The prospects for future employment and income from trade in any city depend chiefly on the following:

1. The extent to which the city is expanding its trade area at the expense of competing cities or losing out in competition with such cities
2. The growth or decline of resources and purchasing power in the trading area
3. The potential growth or decline of population in the trading area

Diversification of types of trading activities and firms is not so important a consideration as in the case of industry, since we seldom find cities in which one or two stores serve all the needs of a trade area. Similarly, cyclical fluctuations in trading activities are not likely to be so marked as in the case of industry, although such fluctuations may occur.

Analyzing Other Income Sources. A forecast of employments and incomes which are dependent upon mines, oil wells, or timber resources requires an analysis of the probable future life of the natural resources involved and of the extent to which these resources can be utilized at prevailing or anticipated price and cost levels. Competition of the products of such extractive industries with other products of the same type should be considered, as should the possibility for the development of substitute products.

Financial institutions such as banks, insurance companies, and savings and loan associations may play a key role in the economic life of a community, either because income is brought into the area or because various types of economic activity are facilitated. The attitudes of financial lenders often have an important influence on local economic development.

Government and Education.   For several decades employment in governmental agencies has tended to expand. Incomes of government workers have advanced. Since the seats of governments, such as state capitals or county seats, are relatively fixed, the possibilities of changes of location of such governmental activities are remote. However, cities with a large number of federal agencies may lose or gain income as the activities of such agencies are expanded or diminished or as changes of location are made. The location and relocation of space and defense industries is an important factor in the future of a number of cities, especially in the South and West. The recent legalization of gambling in Atlantic City is a case in point.

Educational institutions are usually fixed in location and are not likely to move to other places unless exceptional conditions arise. Normally employment in such institutions is relatively stable. Recent expansion of educational activity may give way to more stable conditions because of lower rates of population growth. New institutions have been established in a number of places. Such developments may have a significant bearing on the future of an area both in terms of the employment and income that is generated and the increased attractiveness of the area for other activities.

Resorts and Retirement.   Employment and incomes derived from resort and retirement activities are subject to unusual fluctuations. Such areas are affected considerably by the trend of general business conditions, since their incomes tend to decline sharply in recession periods. To the extent that a resort enjoys a prestige reputation or is endowed with exceptional natural advantages, of course, it will tend to be affected less by business recessions than will other resort centers.

In a number of towns and cities, retired people represent an important source of income. The extent and stability of such income depend on the sources from which it is drawn. As more and more people qualify for pensions or build up retirement funds, incomes of this type will play an increasingly important part in the economic fortunes of many areas, notably those in favorable climates.

Local Conditions and Characteristics. Conclusions tentatively reached in regard to the future development of a city on the basis of a study of major income sources may be modified by favorable or unfavorable local governmental, environmental, energy, or crime conditions; tax burdens in relation to public services provided; quality of the school system; adequacy of community facilities, such as hospitals and cultural and entertainment programs; quality of business, labor, and political leadership; and relative position with respect to other cities in the region or nation.

Long-run analysis may require that consideration be given to the "multiplier" process. Some of the income earned by a manufacturing firm may be invested locally, some elsewhere; of that invested locally some may stimulate local activity, some may bring about further export activity. The propensity to invest locally can be estimated by developing assumptions on the basis of local data and experience.

Careful investigations may indicate which persons or organizations exercise the greatest influence and wield the major power in the local community. If it is possible to identify them, some estimate of their conception of the future of the city may be an important factor in predicting its potential growth. As we have suggested also, some growth may be locally generated. Productivity gains may be important in this connection.

INPUT–OUTPUT ANALYSIS

Input–output analysis has been adapted to the study of local economies; its future promise depends on the much-needed improvement in the accuracy and availability of data.[16]

Major Producing Sectors

This type of analysis revolves around the establishment of a model, in the form of a matrix, which highlights the sales of the output of each major producing sector to each major consuming sector of the economy, for example, the total dollar output of manufacturing which was consumed by the construction industry, by the power industry, and even by the manufacturing industry itself. This matrix can be constructed in any desired detail, for example, the manufacturing industry can be broken into heavy and light manufacturing, or an even finer classification such as the chemical industry, the petroleum industry, the steel industry, etc. The degree of refinement depends on (1) the industrial makeup of the area in question, (2) the availability of detailed data, and (3) the potential value of added research effort to the problem under analysis.

---

[16] Fundamentals of input–output theory were developed by Wassily W. Leontief as early as 1936. See his "Qualitative Input and Output Relations in the Economic System of the U. S.," *Review of Economics and Statistics* (August 1936).

Relative Importance of Sectors.   From an input–output matrix, it is possible to determine the relative importance of a particular line of economic activity to the community and its impact in sustaining other lines by its purchases. The earnings and expenditures of governments can be included as sectors of the economy as can the receipts and spending of households. As a matter of fact, these two sectors are usually estimated independently and are used as inputs to the model. To understand how an input–output matrix is developed, look at the oversimplified 5 ×5 matrix depicted in Table 6–1.

TABLE 6–1.   A Hypothetical Input–Output Matrix

Producing Sectors	Purchasing Sectors					Total Gross Output
	Agricul- ture	Manu- factur- ing	Power	Con- struc- tion	House- holds	
Agriculture	20	20	1	4	12	57
Manufacturing	5	30	2	3	45	85
Power	1	3	2	1	3	10
Construction	2	2	4	1	1	10
Households	32	50	6	11	4	103
Total inputs	60	105	15	20	6	265

Hypothetical Case.   Reading across, Table 6–1 yields the sales of each industry to every other industry. Thus, the entry in the second column of the second row reflects the sales of the manufacturing industry to itself. The entry in the fifth column of the second row reflects the amount the manufacturing industry sold to households. Total sales of the manufacturing industry are shown in the total gross output column.

The figures gleaned from reading down the column depict the purchases of each industry from every other industry. Thus, the entry in the first column of the second row reflects the purchases of the agricultural sector from the manufacturing sector. Since every sale is at the same time a purchase, it makes little difference on which basis the figures are gathered.

Projections.   In using this matrix for projective purposes, the household sector is usually considered as being exogenous to the model, that is, independent of the producing sectors, and is estimated first. The problem then resolves itself into estimating the production levels in each sector necessary to satisfy this household demand. This is accomplished by assuming that the production inputs will be combined in the same proportion in the future time period to produce a level of output as they were in the present period. Table 6–2 is a reconstruction of Table 6–1 in terms of the production coefficients which are then assumed constant.

Table 6–2 was derived by dividing each of the elements in a column by the first column total. Thus, by dividing the element in the second row of

TABLE 6–2.   Direct Inputs per Dollar of Output

Producing Sectors	Purchasing Sectors				
	Agricul- ture	Manu- factur- ing	Power	Con- struc- tion	House- holds
Agriculture	0.33	0.19	0.07	0.20	0.18
Manufacturing	0.08	0.28	0.13	0.15	0.69
Power	0.02	0.03	0.13	0.05	0.05
Construction	0.04	0.02	0.27	0.05	0.02
Households	0.53	0.48	0.40	0.55	0.06
Total	1.00	1.00	1.00	1.00	1.00

the first column (5) of Table 6–1 by the column total (60), we get 0.08. This means eight cents out of every dollar produced by the agricultural sector is consumed by the manufacturing industry. Similarly, 53 per cent of agriculture's output goes to satisfy household demands.

With an assumed household demand in some future time period, estimated by some other method and used as an input to the model (that is, spending by households is considered their "production" and hence an input), the problem reduces itself to finding the levels of production necessary to satisfy this demand—recognizing the interactions of the model. Thus, an increase in household demand for food of 20 per cent will occasion something different from a simple increase in agricultural output of $2.40 ($12.00 × 1.20 = $14.40) to $59.40. An increase in agricultural output must be accompanied by increases in manufacturing, power, and construction output. These increases in output of manufacturing, power, and construction must in turn be supported by higher production of their various inputs. These latter increases in production are called the indirect effects as contrasted to the $2.40 increase in agricultural output occasioned by the increased household demand for food which is a direct effect. The procedure resolves itself into one of successive interactions performed on a computer. The process is stopped when the indirect effects are of such magnitude that they have no appreciable effect on the level of the various outputs, that is, they are within acceptable limits.

Problems of Analysis.   Inadequate data often handicap the input–output analyst. There are also theoretical limitations, for example, the model must be considered one of stationary equilibrium so that time is of no consequence. This is because inputs, in reality, must be produced before they can be used for output and therefore current production in the model is connected not to current supply of inputs, but to previous periods of supply.

A problem also results from the fact that industries do not have identical production methods. Thus, output determines input only if the various firms expand and contract proportionally. Likewise, as firms within the industry produce multiple products, the theory must assume constant product mix for industry as output expands. Furthermore, the use of production functions designating given outputs for given inputs is more naturally applied to mining, manufacturing, and utilities than it is to other sectors such as trade, finance, and the household. Estimation for the latter sectors may involve considerable approximation.

The theory also assumes that if output is given, the level of input is uniquely determined. Such a model does not take into account the possibility of input substitution; and this effect may be significant. In addition, there is a problem of distinguishing between inputs used for current output and those used for investment in plant and equipment.

Many of the advantages of an input–output matrix are statistical. It enables the analyst to record in a rather concise fashion a large amount of information about a regional economy and the interrelations of its sectors. Further, it imposes a statistical discipline on data collection assuring consistency in the approach. The table itself helps to reveal where there are gaps in the data and it may be suggestive of ways to fill them.

OTHER TECHNIQUES OF ANALYSIS

As we suggested in the introductory sections of this chapter, various other methods may also be used to facilitate the analysis of local economies, including regional accounts, balance-of-payments, flow-of-funds, location quotients, or proportionality techniques, as well as others. Each of these methods may be highly useful for particular purposes.

Regional Accounts

The intricacy of relationships among regions complicates the development of regional accounts. As we suggested earlier, regions are "open" rather than "closed" economies. Many of our large corporations may have headquarters in one region, do a major part of their business in others or internationally, and yet make no separation on a regional basis. Domestic and international separations typically are made. Federal government receipts and payments are also hard to assign to regions.

Balance of Payments and Flow of Funds

The Federal Reserve carries on a number of regional analyses that develop data on a regional basis. The various Federal Reserve districts have used regional balance-of-payment and flow-of-funds methods. Studies of the flow of goods, services, and financial payments among regions have been developed from shipping and banking data and other sources. Although often lacking in some types of data, such flow studies often provide insights into the economic life of a region.

Location Quotients

Location quotients sometimes are helpful. In such analyses the percentage of an activity in a particular location (region, state, county) is compared with the percentage of the same activity in the nation as a whole. The Department of Commerce has made comparisons of this type using a proportionality technique to analyze various regional changes relative to the national economy.

Improvement Efforts

A number of students of local and regional economies are carrying forward a variety of efforts to improve both the theoretical and practical approaches to analytical and forecasting efforts. For example, efforts are made to study the multiplier effect in regional economic analysis. There are continuing efforts to re-evaluate and improve economic base analysis. Mathematical model building is being tried in a number of cases. The net effect of all these efforts should be to provide real estate decision makers with improved tools of analysis in the years ahead.

SUMMARY

Regional and local analysis provides valuable assistance to real estate decision makers. Managers of multiplant firms and chain store organizations can use such materials as well as investors in real properties, mortgage lenders, builders and land developers, and government officials. For these discussions, little effort is made to distinguish between regional and local economies since the purpose of the decision makers is largely the governing factor. Our primary concern is with the problems of the real estate decision maker, whose decisions are related to factors influencing the localization of income. Natural factors and division of labor help to explain the location of economic activity along with local advantages that attract people of special competence—leaders, entrepreneurs, scientists, and the like—capital, and special facilities. These factors also help to explain expansion in one place as against another. In addition, once a certain size is reached an "urban-size ratchet" may go into operation.

The economic base method provides a useful approach to analyzing local and regional economies. It involves the application of international trade theory to local economic analysis. The relative importance of various local income sources is determined, their future potential is analyzed, and local modifying factors are considered in estimating the future growth potential of a local or regional economy by means of the economic base method.

Of other methods in use, input–output analysis holds considerable promise if required data can be made more readily available. Regional accounts, balance of-payments, flow-of-funds, location quotients, or proportionality techniques are also used.

QUESTIONS FOR STUDY

1. How can local analysis help a real estate decision maker?
2. How does regional analysis differ from an analysis of general (national) business conditions?
3. Discuss the economic forces that cause cities to grow.
4. What is meant by an "urban-size ratchet" effect? Do you agree with this concept? Why or why not?
5. How important are local property tax problems for a real estate decision maker?
6. Explain how you would analyze income and employment from trade in your home town.
7. What is meant by "basic income sources" in the economic base model? What are the basic income sources for: (a) your home town? (b) the capital of your state? (c) the city in which your college or university is located?
8. What is meant by "urban service employment"? Can urban service employment contribute to city growth? Explain.
9. Why is diversification of manufacturing desirable?
10. Assume that you are to present a report on the topic "An Evaluation of Economic Base Analysis as an Aid to Decision Making." Prepare a brief outline of the main points you would want to make.
11. What are the advantages and disadvantages of the input–output method of analysis?

SUGGESTED READINGS

AMERICAN INSTITUTE OF REAL ESTATE APPRAISERS. *The Appraisal of Real Estate* (6th ed.). Chicago, Ill.: The Institute, 1973. Ch. 5.

HOYT, HOMER. *According to Hoyt* (2nd ed.). Washington, D. C.: Hoyt, 1970. Part VIII. Pp. 548–86.

ISARD, WALTER. *Methods of Regional Analysis: An Introduction to Regional Science.* Cambridge: The Massachusetts Institute of Technology Press, 1960. Chs. 5, 6, 8.

PFISTER, RICHARD L. *On Improving Export Base Studies.* Bloomington, Ind.: Indiana University Institute for Real Estate and Applied Urban Economics, 1975.

THOMPSON, WILBUR R. *A Preface to Urban Economics.* Baltimore: The Johns Hopkins Press, 1965. Chs. 1, 2, 4.

TOYNBEE, ARNOLD. *Cities on the Move.* New York and London: Oxford University Press, 1970.

CASE 6–1

Economic Base of Bel Aire

Bel Aire is located in an agricultural and mining area of a state having no large cities. Bel Aire is several hundred miles from a major industrial center. Employment opportunities have diminished and there has been a reluctance on the part of the residents to move on; hence, there is a surplus of labor in Bel Aire.

In the past half-century the rate of population growth in the town of Bel Aire has not kept pace with that of the rest of the nation. Except for the decade of the 1950's the population has decreased in every decade since 1940. By way of contrast, the nation as a whole has had significant population increases in the same period (see Table 1).

TABLE 1. Population Changes: Bel Aire and the United States

Year	Bel Aire	Per Cent Change	United States	Per Cent Increase
1970	12,000	−4	200,255,000	10.8
1960	12,500	−3.84	180,676,000	19.1
1950	13,000	+23.8	132,122,000	14.8
1940	10,500	−8.69	123,188,000	7.2

In Bel Aire at the last census the male population was slightly under the national average. There is a significant difference in age groups of the population of Bel Aire as compared with the rest of the nation. The percentage of preschool (under 5) and school age (5 to 19) population is under the national average, whereas the percentage of the older age groups (60 and over) is higher than the national average.

Approximately 95 per cent of the Bel Aire population are native-born caucasians. The median number of school years completed is slightly under the national average.

The major sources of employment by type of industry are agriculture, retail trade, mining, and manufacturing (see Table 2). The firms are small in size.

Bel Aire has an adequate urban plant.

TABLE 2. Employment in Bel Aire

	1975	Per Cent
Total employed	4,000	100
Agriculture	900	22.5
Mining	600	15
Construction	250	6.25
Manufacturing	450	11.25
Transportation	200	5
Utilities	100	2.5
Wholesale trade	50	1.25
Retail trade	850	21.25
Medical, educational, and professional services	300	7.5
Public administration	300	7.5

Questions

1. What type of industry do you think the Chamber of Commerce should try to bring to Bel Aire? Why? How might industry be induced to locate there?
2. Assume that two manufacturing firms will locate in Bel Aire next year. One plans to employ 300 persons and the other plans to employ 200 persons. After the plants are in operation, what number of basic employees would you expect? Nonbasic employees? What would be the effect of such a development on total population?
3. What do you consider to be the long-range prospects for the marketability of real estate in Bel Aire? What are the principal factors in determining long-run marketability?

7

MARKET ANALYSIS*

MARKET FACTORS IN DECISIONS

Real estate decision makers have a major interest in markets and locations since such factors have important influences on the income-producing potential of real properties and hence on their value. In this chapter we are concerned with market forces and with various suggestions for their analysis. In the succeeding chapter we consider local location factors.

Market changes and potential market changes play an important part in the decisions of real estate owners, users, investors, brokers, managers, builders, appraisers, mortgage lenders, mortgage insurers, buyers, and sellers. Government officials engaged in planning, zoning, slum clearance, the administration of taxes and public finance, and building codes, influence real estate market changes and trends.

Types of Markets

Because of the diverse nature of real estate markets and the wide variety of factors that affect them, somewhat different approaches to the analysis of residential, commercial, industrial, farm, and special-purpose real estate markets often are required. Even so, a number of general guides to market analysis are applicable to each of these types of real estate markets. We consider here some of the major characteristics of real estate markets, various analytical tools that may be used in analyzing them, kinds of data that are helpful, and the judgmental factors that often are highly important to the real estate decision maker.

Demand, Supply, and Price

In all types of markets, including real estate markets, the major factors involved are those related to demand, supply, and price. Note that price

---

* We are indebted to Michael Sumichrast, Chief Economist of the National Association of Home Builders, for reviewing this chapter.

is emphasized in our discussions along with supply and demand. Price is viewed broadly, however, to include rent, interest rates, special charges, and the like, depending on the market sector under consideration.

We discussed in Chapter 4 some of the major characteristics of the demand for real estate and the supply of real estate. You may wish to review that discussion.

MARKET COMPETITION

The basic force in markets is competition, and this is the key to understanding how markets work. Through competition, prices and rents (as well as interest rates) are set and the market performs its functions of allocating space, determining rates of development of properties, and determining land uses.

Informal Market

An owner wishing to sell a parcel of real estate offers it in the real estate market. A prospective buyer wishing to purchase or lease real property "enters the market" and attempts to secure the property or property services that will meet particular requirements. This market has no single geographical focus, but operates through scattered transactions of owners, brokers, and users of real estate resources or services. There is no organized exchange where real estate transactions take place, as in the case of the large security or commodity markets. "The market" is a highly informal series of negotiations ranging all the way from direct sales of properties by owners to complicated transactions in which numerous brokers and their principals participate.

Nature of Exchange

The market process arises from the *mutually beneficial nature of exchange*. If the owners of a house sell it for $34,500, they must want the money more than the house. On the other hand, the buyers must want the house more than the $34,500. Unless these conditions were present no sale or purchase would be made. Both buyers and sellers expect to benefit from the transaction at the time it is made. Later on, of course, changing conditions may prove that one of the parties to the transaction was benefited to a greater extent than the other. At the time of the agreement, however, both expected to benefit.

We should recognize that markets are made up of people, and more specifically, of people with economic capacity, that is, with available funds or the ability to command credit. The decisions of people are behind whatever happens in markets. Thus, when we refer to "market forces" we are really thinking of various actions that are being taken as a result of decisions made by people in connection with their personal, business, or governmental activities.

Resources Allocation

Competition for various kinds of space is a major factor in the setting of prices (and rents) and in establishing price relationships. This process largely determines how real estate resources are allocated among those who demand them, and it influences the rate of adding to and subtracting from the available supply.

Scope of the Market

Because of the fixed location of real properties we usually tend to think of the real estate market as being local in character, typically including only one city or community. While stores, factory buildings, homes, and farms cannot be moved from one locality to another, there are wide variations in the scope of the market for different kinds of properties or property services. Typically the market for owner-occupied homes is a local one. It is confined to the people living in the community or moving to that specific area. The market for resort property, however, may be widespread, since such dwellings are usually occupied for only a portion of the year and purchasers or tenants may come from any part of the country or the world. Income from property can be compared on a regional or national and often on an international basis. Thus, the market for investment properties of nearly all types tends to be regional and in some instances is national and international in scope. An investor in Chicago might buy a farm in Kansas. A New York investor might purchase an apartment house in Los Angeles.

The market for commercial and industrial property tends to be regional or national rather than local in scope. Large industries like General Electric, Ford, and U. S. Steel buy, sell, and lease real estate on a national and international basis. Chain store organizations analyze the population and purchasing power of numerous trade areas throughout the country, determine new store locations, the volume needed to support stores of various sizes, and the population and income required to achieve such volume.

THE MARKET IN THEORY

A market is a set of arrangements for bringing together buyers and sellers. The market process is commonly symbolized by specialized trading rooms where major dealers assemble daily for making transactions and where the transactions are all promptly reported to the public. However, it is only in connection with a few highly standardized and heavily traded items like wheat, cotton, copper, and the securities of large corporations that highly organized exchanges are found. Such highly organized exchanges are often used as illustrations of the general economic theory of markets. This is partly because they are dramatic, but mainly because the geographic concentration of transactions and the comparative freedom from other complications make it fairly easy, in connection with them, to visualize the basic principles that operate in all kinds of competitive markets. In other words, in the great exchanges, actual operations resemble very closely the competitive model of economic theory. It should be understood, however, that other markets, including the real estate market, follow the same model, though not so closely.

Fundamental Concepts

Of the general principles of market operation none is more fundamental than the tendency, in a given market as of a given time, toward uniformity of prices for like commodities. Other basic principles of general market operations are these:

1. When demand exceeds supply at the current price, price tends to advance. When supply exceeds demand at the current price, price tends to decline.
2. An advance in price tends to reduce demand and to increase supply.
3. Price tends to move to the level at which demand and supply are in balance.
4. An increase in demand, or a decrease in supply, will tend to raise price at least temporarily; a decrease in demand, or an increase in supply, will tend to lower price at least temporarily.

In markets where specialized trading rooms are characteristic, these tendencies are easier to observe, but their operation can be detected no less certainly in markets like that for real estate which are characterized by other means for getting buyers and sellers together. This is the case, for example, in the over-the-counter securities market, where major dealers, despite their separation, get together by telephone and wire services.

The departures from the model outlined above are considerably greater in the real estate market, where the complications include lack of standardization as well as separation of buyers and sellers. However, even in the real estate market the basic principles of market operation outlined above are in evidence.

In general, pieces of property approximately comparable in size, quality, and desirability tend to rent or sell for about the same prices at a given time in a given locality. Also, the rents and sales prices of properties of different sizes, qualities, or degrees of desirability tend to reflect more or less accurately these differences. While the processes by which adjustments take place do not operate as smoothly or as quickly as in the organized exchanges, they do regulate changes affecting real estate; and in a very fundamental sense they help to govern the uses of these resources.

Criteria of an Effective Market

In our preceding discussion we stressed the point that the real estate market corresponds in a general way to the theoretical model of market competition. It is equally important to understand how the real estate market departs from this model. In this connection we need to ask what are the criteria of a good or effective market. Competition can operate more easily if the goods involved are durable and capable of bearing long carriage, if they can be standardized, graded, and bought and sold from samples. Furthermore, a market requires good organization, preferably as a central exchange which is easily accessible to all and where offers to buy and sell can be cleared with a minimum of difficulty.

The more complete the knowledge which buyers and sellers possess of all forces bearing on the market, the more effective market competition becomes. Finally, buyers and sellers must be free from compulsion (as, for example, where some single group dominates the market) if competition is to be effective.

Competitive Market Model

In the model of a competitive market, sellers and buyers are numerous and they are seen as bidding against each other until a price is set at which the market is cleared. The action of any single buyer or seller in this model has only an infinitesimal effect on the market as a whole; but the interactions of all operators taken together create changes in supply, demand, and price. All that any individual buyer can do is to buy or not buy, or buy greater or smaller quantities, as prices change. All that an individual seller can do is to sell or not sell, or sell more or less. A producer can produce or not produce, or vary the amount of production. The quantities supplied will thus be changed and this will affect price.

Real Estate Market Effectiveness

The real estate market ranks comparatively low in effectiveness among various types of modern markets and contrasts in several ways with the model of a competitive market we outlined above. In the market for agricultural staples like wheat, for example, the conditions mentioned above as essential for a good market are approached rather closely; but they are found only to a limited extent in the real estate market. In general, real properties cannot be graded or bought and sold from samples. Also, dealings in the real estate market take place in terms of an assortment of legal rights which vary in details from case to case. In addition, every transfer of real property involves many papers, documents, and legal formalities.

In the case of some real estate markets, for example, the market for vacant and unimproved land, a single buyer may exercise a significant effect. This is due to the relative "thinness" of the market. A comparable situation is that of stocks traded in limited volume on the over-the-counter securities market.

FUNCTIONS PERFORMED BY THE MARKET

Real estate market operations contribute to the performance of at least three important functions which are essential to satisfactory business and community life. Consideration of these functions is helpful in gaining an understanding of market operations.

First, adjustments must be made to sudden changes in the requirements for space. Thus, rapid changes in the needs for space may result from such things as the establishment (or disestablishment) within a community of a private business or of a governmental agency. When changes in space requirements occur on short notice, as they usually do, it is obviously impossible to expand or contract the supply of buildings simultaneously. When such changes occur only on a temporary basis, expansion or contraction would not be desirable even if it were possible. Hence, the situation calls for apportioning existing quarters in as satisfactory a manner as is possible among all of those who need to use them.

Second, unless changes in land or building requirements are only temporary, the situation calls for expanding or contracting the space available in order to meet the changed conditions. Otherwise the people in the community would be subjected to prolonged inconvenience and economic loss.

A third function which has to be performed relates to land use determination and has as its objective the creation of a proper balance in the development of a community by arranging to have each parcel of land devoted to its most important use in relation to other parcels in the area. The efficiency of a city as an economic and social unit depends largely on the adequacy with which this function is performed in the light of the needs of the community as a whole.

In periods of national emergency, of course, the market allocation of real estate resources may be superseded by laws and regulations. For example, rent controls may be established and building materials may be rationed. As a result, the competitive market forces become largely inoperative and the allocation of real estate resources is undertaken by government authorities.

Short-Run Market Changes

Suppose City A, U.S.A., with a population of around 30,000 families, or about 100,000 people, is selected as the location for a new industry. As a result, suppose that approximately 1,000 families move to City A within a few months. Requirements for both business space and living quarters would expand suddenly. The situation would be complicated by the fact that the success of this industry may not be assured and investors may be unwilling to take the risk of adding new permanent housing facilities. Adjustments would be worked out, however, through market competition.

If a similar situation occurred in City B, located in a controlled society that did not rely on market competition, the processes of adjustment would be quite different. In both cases, it is apparent that the situation would call for a considerable amount of doubling up or crowding together of the prior residents to make room for the newcomers. In City B, this process would be attacked directly by administrative methods. The space would be catalogued and rationed out on some predetermined basis to those who had demands for it. In City A, similar results would be achieved through market competition. Rental levels would move upward to the point where the required adjustments would be made. Many families would be compelled to move to smaller quarters or to double up as rents advanced, thus making space available.

Illustration of Short-Run Changes. The various sets of conditions and the adjustments which would take place are illustrated diagrammatically in Figure 7–1. Curve D_1 represents the character of the requirements (or demand) for residential space as of some moment of time prior to the coming of the new industry. It simply shows the amount of space and other house services that would have been required by the citizenry at all possible levels of rent per unit [1] within the range of rents shown. The dotted curve D_2 shows the new character of requirements for residential space as of some moment of time after the coming of the new industry.[2] Both curves imply that any given group of people under specified conditions would use less space as a result of rent increases.

Curve S reflects the amount of space that would be made available for various purposes within a fairly short period of time (a month or so) at different levels of rent. It will be noted that the curve has practically no elasticity; in other words, under the condition shown, very little increase in the amount of space and property services available could be expected as a result of an increase in the level of rents.

If this diagram were drawn to reflect accurately the actual demand and supply conditions in City A at the time, it would indicate the direction toward which average rents would tend to move under each of the two sets of demand conditions stated. Under the conditions existing prior to

---

[1] In drawing a diagram of the sort presented here, which seeks to describe certain features of the market situation for an entire city, one is obliged to reduce all existing and potential building space to comparable units. Definition of such a unit in physical terms is almost impossible, but some such concept must be used in this connection. This diagram is based on *a priori* considerations and not on direct statistical data. For illustrative purposes, however, it should be helpful.

[2] It is important to note that curves D_1 and D_2 both represent sets of demand conditions *as of a moment of time*. As new families moved to the city and as incomes of families already there increased, a steady day-to-day movement to the right of the actual demand curve undoubtedly took place.

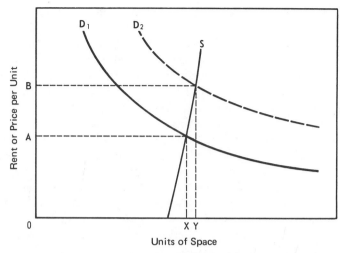

FIG. 7–1.   Short-run supply–demand relationships.

the advent of the new industry, the rent per unit would tend toward the *OA* figure; under the conditions reflected by the D_2 curve, rents would tend toward the *OB* level.[3] At any time, of course, average rents might actually be higher or lower than those points—but, should rents be higher, there would tend to be a higher percentage of vacancies; likewise, if rents were ever to fall lower, demands for space would increase and rents would be raised.[4]

Role of Demand in Short Run.   From the illustration it is apparent that when we are interested in knowing what will happen during some short period of time, such as a few months, as a result of a given change in the real estate market, demand forces are the determining factors, since supplies are relatively fixed.   Consequently, any short-run analysis of the real estate market requires that demand considerations be given greatest attention. Over longer-run periods this is not the case, as the following discussion will show.

Longer-Run Changes

The second function which the real estate market performs is that of adjusting the available supplies of space to changes in requirements which are expected to be permanent.   If a new industry moved into a city, there

---

[3] In the conventional language of economics, *OA* and *OB*, under the supply conditions represented by curve *S*, represent the equilibrium prices for the demand conditions represented by curves D_1 and D_2 respectively.   They are the prices which, under the conditions specified, will just clear the market.

[4] For a more complete discussion of demand, supply, and price relationships, see Paul A. Samuelson, *Economics* (10th ed.; New York: McGraw-Hill Book Co., 1976), chs. 20–24.

would be a tendency for rents to move upward, as we noted above. Now, if it became apparent after a year or two that this industry would succeed and remain prosperous for some time, this would provide grounds for expecting the level of rents to continue to a high plane and would give some assurance of higher than average profits to anyone who wished to construct new residential or office buildings in the city.

It is reasonable to expect that considerable building activity would result. The rapidity of the response would depend largely on how much the rent per unit in that city exceeded that in other cities. If the rent differential were large, adjustment would presumably be made in a shorter time than if the differential were smaller. (If diagrams are helpful, the supply curve in Fig. 7–1 would be drawn with a less sharply upward slope.)

Variations in the rate at which additional space is made available in a given real estate market depend not only upon variations in the rate of return on capital invested in real properties but also upon variations in the length of time allowed for adjustments to work themselves out. Differences in the rate at which supply may be increased in adjustment periods of different length reflect the fact that as soon as the rate of building in a given market exceeds the normal capacity of local builders and suppliers of materials, increases in that rate are possible only if greater remuneration is offered for those necessary services. Overtime must be compensated, allowances must be made for lower efficiency of operations, and laborers and tradespeople must be attracted from other cities.

Periods of active building often result in excessive supplies of space. Builders may continue to develop new properties even after demand has started to decline. The vacancy rate then increases and a considerable time may be required for readjustments to be made because of the long life of real properties.

Land Use Determination

In considering the ways in which market forces performed their first two functions, we must not overlook the fact that market competition is one form of social control. Frequently, some government action is necessary to harness the forces of competition, especially in the form of contract enforcement, the maintenance of order, and the limitation of forces tending toward monopoly. In the performance of its third main function, that of land use determination, the community must rely to a much greater extent on governmental action to direct and regulate the operation of competitive forces than in the case of the rental market.

If we take for granted a particular pattern covering the layout of streets, public transportation routes, boarding points, and the like, it can be said that rents and market prices obtainable for various tracts of land provide the most serviceable indexes of their relative importance to the community as a whole. Within this sphere, market competition, which tends to force land into the uses from which the greatest returns can be secured, affords the most workable device for deciding the alternative uses to which these land resources may be put. We should note that returns cannot necessarily be computed in dollars. In some cases esthetic considerations or sentimental attachments may be major factors in decisions related to land use. Such decisions, however, will also tend to be reflected in the market. While some other qualifications are necessary, such as those arising from a given type of income distribution, it may be said that the use which can pay the most for a given site is the use which will be most advantageous for the community as a whole.

This, of course, is not the whole story. We have assumed a *given pattern* for the street, transportation, and utility system. Had the basic plan been laid out on another basis or had the main transportation and utility lines been located elsewhere, altogether different parcels of land would have commanded the highest prices and rents.

Modifying Factors. Also, it may not pay to demolish an existing structure and build another until the present building is in a late period of its economic life. Tax depreciation factors may play a major part in a decision to demolish or not to demolish a structure. In addition, some land uses are very detrimental to adjoining properties. For example, a warehouse located in a residential area might bring great returns on the tract upon which it was built, but it might reduce the value of many neighboring properties. The net result might represent a loss in the total property values of the area.

The net loss in a property's value from the development of a particular parcel of land in a manner that is out of harmony with the character of the area in which it is located is likely to reflect a diminution in the economic welfare of the entire community. The effects are felt even beyond adjacent tracts of land, since the people who previously were the land users (and any potential users under the prior conditions) are now forced to seek new areas, which in all probability are less desirable than was the original district before the adverse development occurred. Furthermore, the very existence within an area of uncertainties as to whether such adverse developments may occur tends to exert a restraining influence on new investment and to make necessary a higher prospect of return before developments can be expected.

Planning and Zoning

These observations suggest the conclusion that the potentialities of individualistic competition in connection with land use determination can sometimes be realized to the fullest extent only if government or private groups act to minimize the dangers and risks arising from the manner in which particular owners may use their properties. This provides the economic justification for zoning, land planning, and private restrictions on land use.

Zoning is not always an answer to these types of problems, however. For example, zoning may result in an uneconomic arrangement of land uses if more land is zoned for designated uses than is required. If zoning authorities make use of market surveys, they may be able to adapt the regulations to the needs of the market. It would be desirable to do this without opening the door to' unlimited "spot" zoning.[5] Some markets—for example, Houston—have operated effectively without zoning.

THE MARKET IN OPERATION

A brief and general description of the forces operating in the real estate market, the principles explaining their relationships, and the functions which they perform may seem to imply that the competitive process brings about smooth adjustments among supply, demand, and prices. Such is not necessarily the case. Competition is the main regulative force, it is true; but the actual operation of the market is far from perfect or efficient.

Factors Conditioning Market Operation

The following are among the factors that condition the operation of real estate markets:

1. Each property is unique. Only one building can occupy a particular spot on the earth's surface. The degree of uniqueness varies. Row houses or town houses or standardized detached houses in a large homogeneous neighborhood are virtually interchangeable. In contrast, every 25 or 50 feet of land may change in value in a central business district. Also, we should note that a special-purpose building may be suitable for use by only one tenant.
2. Some properties are parts of estates or are involved in litigation, with restrictions on sale or lease so they cannot be sold or developed. Such properties, even though in desirable locations, are virtually out of the market.
3. Some owners have a sentimental attachment to their homes, farms, or other properties and refuse to sell for prices that reflect market conditions.
4. Some properties are leased for long periods and are not available for sublease or sale.
5. Buyers are often restricted to persons living in the city or neigh-

[5] Although it is not appropriate to discuss in detail here the relation of competitive forces to the problem of the social control of real estate, we should note that an important relationship exists between them. For example, in the case of the third market function which is discussed above, it should be noted that most programs for planning set the balanced and economical development of cities as their major goal. Of course, this goal can be achieved only by getting individual parcels of land assigned to their proper places in a comprehensive and generally satisfactory pattern. From what has been said, it should be apparent that the real estate market contains powerful forces which can be made to do a major part of this work if they are understood and skillfully harnessed.

borhood who are in a position to take advantage of bargains or the necessities of the seller.

6. Owners living outside of a city frequently are not familiar with local developments which may increase or diminish the value of their properties.
7. Prices are affected by the terms and availability of financing.
8. Oral agreements are not binding as in stock market or grain market transactions, so that a seller or buyer may not complete a transaction even though an obligation to pay a broker's commission may be incurred.
9. Whether the seller has a good title cannot be determined quickly as in the case of stocks or merchandise, so that a period of time must elapse before the title can be passed.
10. Real estate cannot escape local taxes as is often possible in the case of personal property.
11. The value of real properties is often affected greatly by changes in local zoning laws.
12. The value of any specific property is affected by the character of the neighborhood and the economic outlook.
13. Buildings are not standardized commodities like automobiles. They may have hidden defects or exceptionally favorable features.
14. There is no machinery for selling short in real estate markets.
15. While properties may turn over rapidly in periods of advancing prices, there may be long periods of low sales volume during periods of stagnation and decline.
16. Residential real estate has been subject to rent control in times of emergency, which checked the operation of normal market forces.
17. The value of real estate will be lowered by a high crime rate in the neighborhood. Property values depend on adequate police and fire protection.
18. Property values are affected by availability and quality of water, sewer systems, utilities, and highways.
19. Air and water pollution may have highly adverse effects on real estate values.

The nature of the real estate market is thus different from other types of markets. Yet its operation can no more be called exceptional than the operation of the stock market and the board of trade, which are themselves exceptional in the unusual homogeneity and standardized character of the articles in which they deal.

Monopoly Elements

In addition, the workings of the real estate market are sometimes modified considerably by the presence of certain elements of monopoly. For example, in some of our larger cities low-income groups have sometimes been limited to certain areas and this may give property owners a certain monopoly advantage.

It should be noted, however, that higher rents or prices in such cases are secured usually by crowding the available accommodations to a greater degree than is typical of similar accommodations in the broader market. As a consequence, even badly deteriorated rental properties may produce handsome returns on the investment represented. Special efforts are sometimes made by investors in such positions to protect themselves against further competition such as might arise from new housing developments designed for the occupancy of similar groups.

In some rural areas religious or social groups form closed communities in which land purchases are restricted to the members of a particular group or sect. Thus, such markets are limited.

Market Variations

As we indicated in earlier discussions, real estate markets can be classified according to types of properties, scope, and whether dealings are concerned with the purchase and sale of properties themselves or the rental of the services of properties for specified periods. While the rental and sale markets for properties are not mutually exclusive, both forming parts of a larger whole, the rental market is not characterized by the wide variations which occur in the buying and selling of properties themselves. In part this is due to the fact that the rental market partakes indirectly of the nature of a consumers' goods market and the sale market of a producers' goods market. Usually variations of market activities in consumers' goods are not as great as those in producers' goods.

However, the rental market influences selling prices and the rate of building. When a seller's market exists, prices may move high enough to bring about the production of new buildings. When new structures are made available, they remain on the market for long periods of time, since they usually last for many years. If more of these are produced than can be absorbed at prices characteristic of a seller's market, a long period of time is generally required for readjustments to take place.

Demand Pressures

An upward movement in the price of real estate services or rents and in the selling prices of real properties is normally the result of an increase in the demand for space. We have noted that, in short-run periods, demand conditions are of greater importance than those of supply. The basic elements in demand are income and the terms and availability of financing. When such an increase in demand and prices occurs, the stage is set for an expansion of activity. Expansion of economic opportunities usually is necessary to attract people or to increase their incomes. Similarly, a loss of such opportunities tends to depress the real estate market.

A rapid increase in the rate of population growth does not of itself cause an advance in real estate activity, for it must be accompanied by buying power on the part of the newcomers. Buying power includes consumer and business incomes, but depends also on the terms and availability of financing. Likewise, the lack of any sudden population growth does not necessarily prevent an expansion from occurring if incomes advance and financing terms are liberal.

Inflexible Supply

Wide variations in real estate activity can be explained largely in terms of the relative inflexibility of the supply of space. While people are willing to make a smaller amount of space go around in periods of recession by doubling up, they are unwilling to live under conditions such as this when their incomes increase. Also, business firms demand more and better space when their incomes advance. Under depressed conditions new construction will be at a standstill because it will not pay to build at the low existing rents. But, as the population and business firms expand in number and rent-paying capacity, the large supply of vacant units typical of depression periods is rapidly absorbed. When the percentage of vacant units reaches a low figure, rents begin to rise. Such an advance also forces up prices and values. The net rentals advance even more sharply than gross rentals because operating costs, interest charges, taxes, maintenance, and similar expenses are relatively fixed. Hence, the rate of profit is rapidly increased, and it becomes profitable to erect new buildings.

Market Expansion

In the early stages of expansion, construction of single-family houses predominates because many are constructed for those who have incomes sufficient to make down payments, even if the houses would not command rents sufficient to yield a normal monetary return on the cost. Similarly, business firms may expand plants or stores. As expansion progresses, however, it becomes profitable to construct apartment buildings, business blocks, industrial structures, shopping centers, and office buildings that are financed solely for pecuniary return.

As we have pointed out, net rents tend to rise more rapidly than gross rents. Costs usually do not move up as fast as rental levels. The period of construction usually begins with a period of easy credit. During such a period it may become quite easy to finance projects of various types.

As new buildings are erected, they absorb the vacant land. A land boom results, with subdividing activity proceeding first at a slow rate and then gathering momentum if the pressure of building on land continues to increase. Large areas may be added to the supply of land available to the city. It should be noted that as outward movement from the city center occurs, the area available increases in a manner comparable to the square of the radius of a circle.

Expenditures for public improvements tend to increase at the same time that the volume of building and subdividing gains in momentum. Sometimes public improvements may be made in advance of current or immediate future needs.

Market Contraction

At some time in the course of this period of expansion, demand begins to fall behind the rapid additions to supply which are being made available. It becomes difficult for the operators to lease or sell properties, and the sources of credit begin to tighten. The tightening of credit results in foreclosures; and unless the market continues to expand because of some increase in demand, an advance in the volume of foreclosures forecasts a period of decline. Many sectors of the real estate market may still maintain a peak level of activity. Construction of new apartments or stores may continue for some time at almost peak levels. There is as yet no marked decline in rents. Operating expenses are increasing, however, and foreclosures are likely to have an upward trend. The fact that real estate is financed more on a debt than an equity basis probably helps to intensify the variations that occur. Thus, those who finance real estate can make or break the market.

If foreclosures mount in volume as credits are tightening, the entire market is affected. It becomes impossible to sell properties without cutting prices. Land values begin to decline. Just as net rentals rose more rapidly than gross rentals in the early period of expansion, they now fall more rapidly because of the fixed charges involved. Hence, profits are wiped out and market activity falls to low levels.

The rate of recession in the real estate market will be intensified if there is a simultaneous recession in business generally. In that event incomes of tenants will drop and vacancies will increase as some families double up and others leave the city. Prospective marriages will be deferred in many cases. Business firms will reduce the space used. The result will be a rapid decline in rents. Foreclosures will increase rapidly, first on apartment and office buildings, because rents decline faster than operating expenses and owners soon find themselves unable to meet interest even on their first mortgages. Then, if a long recession ensues, the foreclosures will extend to single-family residences and owner-occupied business properties. Many owners of single-family homes will struggle to the limit of their ability to hold their homes. Others, especially those with thin equities, will give up at the first sign of recession. As a result of this process of attrition, the prices of real estate holdings are forced down.

A large volume of foreclosures is characteristic of depressed conditions in the real estate market. As a result of the foreclosure process, properties are refinanced and the financial wreckage is cleared away. Thus the stage is set for another period of expansion, which does not come automatically but which awaits some special impetus resulting in an increase in the demand for real estate resources.

National and Local Market Activity

Although activity in many real estate markets follows general national trends of business conditions, there are significant local variations. Regional differences account in part for some of these variations. The rapid expansion of the Southeast and Southwest has resulted in the acceleration of activity in the real estate markets of those regions.

Differences in the "mix" of economic activities in cities often result in local market experience that differs from general national or even regional trends. Usually cities that are largely dependent on the production of producers' goods will have wider swings in real estate market activity than those that rely largely on the production of consumers' goods. Also, cities with a diversified economic base typically enjoy greater stability of real estate market operations than those with less diversification, especially one-industry towns.

Major booms in real estate market activity are likely to come during periods of general business prosperity. Some cities, however, may experience only moderate expansion in such periods, while in others market activity may attain boom proportions. Local, regional, and industry factors largely account for the differences.

Future Problems

Numerous problems may cause future difficulties, despite generally favorable prospects. Some regions and some localities will fall far below national averages in terms of the growth that appears to lie ahead. Heavy taxation of real properties, energy shortages, the relatively slow introduction of improved construction methods and technology, labor problems, concern with the environment, the problems of slum and downtown areas, and the competition of many new goods and services for a portion of the income produced—all may cause difficulties. Beyond these, there is the general volatility of demand for real estate resources against relatively fixed supplies in short-run periods. These conditions continue to make possible wide variations in real estate market activity. The character of efforts to control variations in economic activity are bound to have their effect on real estate as well as other markets.

MAJOR FEATURES OF A MARKET ANALYSIS

In making an analysis of a real estate market, purpose often governs the type of analysis undertaken, the coverage of various topics, and the intensity with which the analysis is carried out. The priorities assigned to the topics and the emphasis given to them will vary with specific local situations. Our discussions here outline a number of the topics that are usually included in a market analysis. In specific situations, of course, not all of these may be covered or others may be included.

Purpose and Type of Market Analysis

As in the making of appraisals, the first step in the analysis of a real estate market is a careful definition of the problem. Why is the analysis being made? Is it to determine whether a builder should start a new project? Is an investor deciding on a major purchase or sale? Is a department store planning a new shopping center? Is a building manager trying to decide whether to raise rents? Is a mortgage lender planning to tighten financing terms? These questions and many others that might be raised suggest some of the variety of uses of market analyses.

The problems involved in making a market analysis generally will fall into two major groups: those pertaining to short-run objectives, and those pertaining to long-run objectives. For example a builder may be concerned with whether the houses to be built within the next six months can be sold. An investor or a lending institution, by contrast, may be interested in the income potential and stability of properties over the next decade or two or longer. Planning commissions may be concerned with problems requiring that estimates be made for different types of land uses for as many as twenty or thirty years ahead.

Definition of purpose assists in determining whether short- or longer-run considerations should be given primary attention, the sector of the market that needs to be stressed, and the intensity with which the market must be studied. For example, if several cities are located in close proximity, all of them may be included in a market analysis. On the other hand, a specialized problem may limit the analysis to a few areas or districts. Once purpose has been defined, we may proceed with a consideration of the principal factors bearing on market conditions.

Major Topics for Analysis

The main factors in the analysis of real estate markets may be listed as follows:

1. The general level of business activity affects real estate markets. For example, the recessions of 1948–49, 1953–54, 1957–58, 1960–61, 1969–70, and 1974–76 affected real estate markets of nearly all types in varying degrees.

2. The level of local business activity also requires consideration. Local business activity, of course, may deviate from general national trends because of special local factors. Usually there is some relationship between local business conditions and real estate market trends.

3. Of major importance for all types of real estate are changes in the employment and income sources of the community. Expansion of existing economic activities such as may result from new factories, new government agencies, new tourist attractions, and the like tend to increase market activity; the loss of employment and income has the opposite effect. Methods for analyzing changes of this type were outlined in the preceding chapter and are pertinent to nearly all types of real estate market analyses.

4. Financing terms and trends have a major influence on the demand for nearly all types of real estate. General and local mortgage market conditions form an integral part of almost every type of real estate market analysis.

5. While income and financing factors are of primary importance, population growth or decline tends to affect real estate markets. Not only are changes in the total population important, but also changes in the age distribution and composition of the population, as well as shifts of population within the market area. For example, a persistent movement to the suburbs may increase the demand for certain types of properties and bring a decline in the demand for other types, even though there are no changes in total population or in incomes.

6. Changes in the tastes and preferences of customers and potential customers may be highly important at current prices and rents.

7. The volume of building activity requires consideration, as well as construction cost levels and trends. Costs in relation to prices and rents have an important bearing on the rate at which additions will be made to the available supply. Also, the availability of improved lots and the cost of improving raw land usually should be considered.

8. Often the vacancy rate is the most important single indicator of real estate market trends. Rising vacancies usually indicate that the supply of existing space is greater than the demand for it. The rate at which vacancies are increasing or declining often provides the key to probable market changes. Closely related to vacancies in existing structures are the new structures that have not been sold or leased and remain on the market as an "overhang" for varying periods of time.

9. As we have suggested above, the interrelationships among prices, rents, and construction costs are important keys to market conditions and potential market changes. Wide differences between listing prices and final sales prices are especially significant.

10. The volume of market activity is reflected in the number of deeds recorded, the number of mortgages recorded, and the volume of foreclosures. Comparisons of present with past levels often provide good indexes of potential market changes.

11. Finally, all of the above factors must be studied in relation to each other and in relation to past developments. In this manner both short- and longer-range market trends may be identified and used as the basis for estimating future probable market changes.

General Business Conditions.   We have pointed out in several connections that local forces exercise important influence on the real estate market. This is especially true of the markets for residential real estate. We do not wish to imply, however, that general economic trends have only limited influence on local real estate markets.

In many cases local markets will follow national trends rather closely. This is usually true when the major sources of local income and employment represent a typical cross section of the American economy as a whole. In other cases local markets may deviate to some extent from national trends. This may be due to the types of employment and incomes represented or to special factors such as a rate of building that has been too rapid for local absorption, successful local efforts to bring in new industries, local financial policies that have unduly restricted building, unfavorable local government policies such as taxes, and many others.

Suggestions for analyzing general business conditions were outlined in Chapter 5. Estimates of general business trends usually precede the analysis of a specific real estate market. Then attempts are made to determine whether local conditions will follow closely or deviate significantly from general trends.

Local Business Conditions.   The real estate market of a locality will be influenced by the trend of local business conditions, which may be influenced in turn by general economic trends. Of the many factors to consider in studying local business conditions, the most important is the trend of employment and incomes. Such information is generally available from local chambers of commerce and from state employment services as well as from the personnel office of the major local employers. Frequently local chambers of commerce publish monthly data reflecting local business trends. Some universities publish monthly summaries of business conditions. In addition the various Federal Reserve Banks make available monthly reports covering business trends for the district served and for the more important cities in the district.

Besides showing employment and income, reports of these types frequently provide information on bank debits, department store sales, electricity production, newspaper advertising, car loadings, and similar information, as well as data on construction volume, real estate transfers, mortgages recorded, foreclosures, vacancies, and related materials more directly pertinent to the local real estate market.

Employment and Incomes.   Recent changes in employment or incomes have a vital influence on all phases of local real estate market activity. Of special significance, of course, are potential developments that are likely to strengthen or diminish the demand for specific types of properties. Such potential developments must be related directly to the specific market problem that is being studied. If local incomes are good and income prospects are favorable, the real estate market is likely to be active (unless there has been a great surge of building). Even though no new residents are attracted to the city, higher incomes will mean an increase in the demand for housing. Heavier spending will lead to greater demand for commercial property. Thus, demand for real estate can rise in a locality even though there has been no major increase in population. Similarly, demand will fall with a decline in incomes, even if there has been no loss of population.

Financing Conditions.   Next to incomes, the terms and availability of financing are the primary factors in determining the strength or weakness of demand for real estate. When financing is available on liberal terms and at low interest rates, the demand for property is strengthened. Rigorous financing terms tend to limit demand.

Financing conditions may vary between different sectors of the real estate market. Financing may vary between regions and cities.

As we have pointed out, the mortgage market does not operate independently of the other capital markets. Hence, the availability of financing for real estate projects is dependent in part on the alternative uses for funds in other types of projects.

Information in regard to the terms and availability of funds for real estate financing may be secured from such sources as the Federal Reserve *Bulletin, The Federal Home Loan Bank Board Journal,* the publications of the regional Federal Reserve Banks and Federal Home Loan Banks, from financial newspapers and magazines, and from institutions which engage in real estate finance, such as insurance companies, banks, and savings and loan associations. For example, *The Wall Street Journal* often carries quotations on GNMA, FHLMC, and FNMA offerings.

Population Changes.   Analyses of the local economy often provide a helpful approach to the prediction of future population trends. Past trends of population growth for census periods can be obtained from the U. S. Census of Population.

The best single method of estimating the current population of most urban areas outside of central cities is to ascertain the total number of new dwelling units that have been added to the given areas since the preceding census, as indicated by building permits. This total of new dwelling units may be multiplied by the average size of the family in the area in the last census to obtain the estimated additions to the population since that time. It may be preferable to secure data on the number of completed dwelling units added since the preceding census from the electrical inspector's or assessor's office, but these figures on completed dwelling units are not always available and they do not differ materially from building permit figures, since nearly all permits result in completed units. Allowance must always be made for vacancies, when the increase in population is estimated by new dwelling units. Conversions and doubling up may also be factors of importance.

The number of occupied housing units for each block in each city or urban area with a population of 50,000 or more is usually given in the United States Census of Housing. The population and number of occupied units, the median family income, and other data are usually available for each urban place of 2,500 population or more and for every county in all of the states.

Good alternative methods of estimating present population are based on the number of electric meters, since nearly every family has a meter, or on the number of water meters. The current population can be estimated by multiplying the present number of electric or water meters by the ratio of population to number of meters at time of last census.

Special Population Information. Information about births and deaths for each year can be secured from city or county offices. Differences can be computed for each year, thus indicating population changes due to natural causes. Relating this to total population changes indicates net migration to or from the area. Often, local chambers of commerce or similar organizations have information of this type available. Visitation programs for new arrivals to the city may provide useful information. Also, rough estimates can be made through listings in telephone directories or numbers of gas or electric meters connected or disconnected.

While the general trend of population is important, some information should be secured about the marriage rate, since this indicates the rapidity with which new families or households are being established. Adjustments should be made for divorces, although a divorce does not necessarily lead to a reduction in the demand for housing. In many cases divorces lead to an increase rather than a decrease in the demand for space. Information about the number of marriage licenses and divorces can be secured from county offices. Estimates may be made also of the rate at which other households are being established.

Changes in Preferences and Tastes. Consumers of real estate resources and services include the entire population and range from large corporations to single individuals. Within any real estate market, whether it is the market for industrial property in a certain city, the market for shopping center sites or subdivisions, or the market for rental housing, shifts may occur in the preferences and tastes of the customers involved. Such shifts may be very difficult to identify or to evaluate. Consumers of housing may be attracted by design or style changes; consumers of industrial real estate by efficient and convenient layouts of space; and consumers of retailing areas by ease of access and flexibility. At one time, one set of factors may be in favor; at another time, others will predominate.

Construction Volume and Costs. The rate at which new additions to supply have been made during recent years should be studied by securing figures from city offices on the volume of construction and the number of demolitions. Such data are made available for a number of cities by the Bureau of Labor Statistics and by several commercial services.

Conditions in the building industry should be analyzed carefully. The availability of labor resources and of building materials and their prices require special consideration. The availability of building sites and the prices of available land need to be determined. Also, special attention should be given to changes and potential changes in building technology since they may affect construction costs. The quality and competence of architects often is a factor of importance and should be related to quality and competence of builders and developers.

Data on construction costs can frequently be secured from the city building department. Local real estate boards often assemble data of this type. Several federal agencies publish information on construction costs for a number of cities, and various commercial organizations also supply such data.

Construction costs must be related to selling prices and rents in order to determine future rates of building. When prices and rents are sufficiently above costs to allow a substantial profit margin, building proceeds rapidly. As the spread is narrowed, the rate of building slows down. Less efficient builders are eliminated. When costs exceed sales prices or capitalized rental income, nearly all building ceases.

One of the important elements in building and developing costs is land and the cost of improving it. When the available supply of improved lots has been exhausted, builders may face very large outlays of funds in order to develop new areas. If the market does not exhibit signs of substantial strength, such large-scale projects may be postponed.

Vacancies. As we indicated above, the vacancy rate is one of the major indicators of real estate market conditions and trends. A surplus of vacant units will tend to retard price or rent increases even when demand is strong. Just what is meant by a surplus or deficit of vacant units cannot be defined exactly. The concept varies from one community to another and from one type of property to another. Normal vacancy for houses is usually considered as something less than 5 per cent, for apartments slightly over 5 per cent, and for business units it may run somewhat higher; but these are only rules of thumb which vary from one place to another.

Whenever the supply of vacant units exceeds a normal percentage, the market tends to be depressed. Competition of owners and sellers seeking tenants and buyers forces prices and rents downward and restrains new construction. A decline in the vacancy ratio, on the other hand, may be reflected in an upward movement of rents and prices.

Information about vacancies in various types of properties is frequently collected by local real estate boards. At times the Postal Service conducts vacancy surveys in various cities. Often local public utility companies or departments will assemble data concerning vacancies, and the publishers of local directories may gather information of this type at periodic intervals. Conferences with major property managers often provide useful data. It is desirable that vacancy ratios be computed separately for different classes of property, for it frequently happens that one part of a market will have a shortage of space while another has a surplus.

Price and Rent Trends. Any persistent changes in market prices or rents upward or downward reflect basic market conditions. Sometimes these movements are of short duration, but if they persist for a year or more it may usually be presumed that the trend will continue for a time.

On occasion real estate brokers test the market by advertising a popular type of property at a very reasonable price or rental. They are then able to gauge market conditions by the number of responses received to the advertisement.

Of special importance is the variation between listing and actual selling prices. Similarly, the difference between the rental rate asked and finally paid is a reflection of the strength of the market.

The length of time new properties remain on the market before being sold or rented indicates the strength or weakness of demand. When long periods are required to dispose of property, the market is weakening. This assumes, of course, that prices have been set on a reasonably competitive basis.

Market Activity and Trends. After the factors outlined above have been studied, it should be possible to make reasonably sound estimates of future market trends. This involves determining the present position of the market in relation to past conditions. Variations in market activity are reflected in the number of real estate transfers. Such information may be secured from the volume of deeds recorded in county recorders' offices. The number of mortgages recorded is available from the same sources, as is information about the volume of foreclosures.

Studies of these data covering fairly long periods of time are desirable. Data on deeds, mortgages, and foreclosures may be related to population trends; vacancy ratios; price, rent, and cost indexes; and the volume of construction. Such relationships provide a good indication of the present position of the market with regard to past periods.

Relative Prices and Relationships. Of major importance in studying market conditions and trends are *relative prices*. For example, construction costs may be rising, but rents and selling prices may be rising even more rapidly. Hence, further construction may be expected to take place despite the advancing costs. Furthermore, an upward or downward trend in prices and rents may cause buyers, investors, and property users to expect still further changes in the same direction and accentuate the trend that has been developing.

A reduction in financing charges may stimulate market activity, even though no other basic change has occurred. Favorable terms of sale, such as smaller down payments and longer periods in which to repay loans, may stimulate the market. Rising incomes may have only a limited effect if real estate rents and sales prices, as well as the prices of other goods and services, are moving up in proportion. In other words *real incomes* rather than monetary incomes deserve primary consideration.

HOUSING MARKET ANALYSIS

The analysis of a housing market involves application of the pertinent factors outlined above to the residential sector rather than to other sectors of the real estate market. After careful definition of the specific problem under consideration, the analysis proceeds to a consideration of the major demand, supply, and price factors involved.

Housing Demand

Expanding economic opportunities will bring people into a city from elsewhere and stimulate the demand for housing. Rising incomes even without expansion of employment may also lead to heavier housing demand. Thus, economic base and similar types of analyses are often helpful in housing market studies.

In relating income levels to housing demand, it is necessary to consider incomes in relation to house prices. As a rule, families cannot afford to pay more than about 2½ to 3 times their annual income for a house. Consequently, a good housing market analysis requires that an income distribution of the families in the area be secured. Data of these types are available from census materials by census tracts in metropolitan regions and for cities, towns, and counties. Such census reports also indicate the number of owner-occupied and rental units by price and rent brackets.

Closely related to income, cost, and price factors are financing considerations. If financing is available on easy terms, demand may be maintained even though incomes are not advancing. Conversely, if financing terms are not favorable, housing demand may be reduced rapidly, even though incomes are steady or advancing. Changes in the terms of financing may have an even greater impact on the market than changes in incomes because of the large proportion of borrowed funds that go into most house purchases. For example, extending the term of the mortgage reduces the monthly payments of the home buyer.

Housing Supply

The supply of new dwelling units can be estimated on the basis of new building permits and the number of water meters or electric meters added.

Data of this type can be broken down by districts and can be related to base periods such as those for which census materials are available.

A long period of strong building activity may indicate the possibility of a weakening market, especially if vacancies are rising and new houses are remaining on the market for long periods of time before being sold. Also, construction costs must be studied in relationship to current prices to determine whether it is likely to be profitable for builders to continue construction activity.

Efficiency of building and low sales prices will stimulate demand. Larger builders, both those with large-scale on-site operations and prefabricators, have been able to stimulate demand in this way. However, whenever market prices fall below the amount for which the most efficient builders can and will construct houses, few will be added to the supply.

As we have suggested above, changes in design or style may appeal to changing tastes and preferences of house buyers. Changes in technology may make design and style changes possible.

MARKET ANALYSIS FOR BUSINESS REAL ESTATE

Analysis of markets may be undertaken for a variety of business real estate. Here we will consider briefly shopping centers, individual stores, office space, and industrial space. Our discussions will be short and should not be considered as more than suggestive of the types of analyses that may be undertaken.

Shopping Centers

A market analysis to determine the soundness of a new shopping center requires consideration of special sets of factors in addition to those involved in the analysis of broader divisions of the real estate market. A general outline of a shopping center market analysis is presented below.

1. The size of the trade area is determined by the location of competing centers, by location of mass transportation routes, and by related factors. The time or distance from the center is not the vital factor. Families will drive long distances to reach a large shopping center if there is no similar facility near them. They will not drive even a short distance if they live within walking distance of a major shopping district. Most of the large regional shopping centers depend upon customers who arrive in automobiles. Families living near subways, elevated stations, or suburban railroad stations often prefer to shop in central shopping districts.

The size of the trade area varies with the type of center. It is broadest for a regional center with one or more large department stores, smaller for a center with a junior department store, still smaller for a center with a variety store as the principal unit, and only neighborhood-wide for a center with a supermarket and drugstore as the chief units. The size of the trade area can best be determined by taking a sample survey of housewives to determine where they shop.

2. After determining the extent of the trade area, the next step is to estimate the number of families in each census tract, community, or district of the trade area. This is accomplished by adding to the number of dwelling units shown by the most recent United States Census the number of new dwelling units added since that time as reflected by building permits, electric meters, or water meters.

3. The average family income in each census tract or community is estimated on the basis of U. S. Census reports. Adjustments for intervening years between the last census and the date of the market analysis can be made by applying the average increase in per-capita income for the state in which the center is located, using the midpoint of the income brackets as the average. Aggregate income of each community is determined by multiplying the number of families by the average income.

4. The next step is to estimate the volume of retail purchases for each type of store planned for the center as of the date of the survey. It is estimated that all families above the lowest income level spend about the same percentage of their incomes for clothing, shoes, furniture, and other fashion goods. The percentage of income which families spend in each metropolitan area in each type of store may be determined by relating total metropolitan area retail sales in each type of store to the total family income of the region or state as indicated by the U. S. Retail Census.

5. On the basis of questionnaires or sample surveys, an estimate may be made of the proportion of their income which families in the area will spend in each type of store planned for the shopping center in its first year of full operation.

6. The total sales of each type of store at the center being studied may be estimated by adding expected purchases from each segment of the trade area, taking into account the competition of other centers.

7. The store area required for the new center is estimated on the basis of expected average sales per square foot for each type of store. Parking area is calculated on a ratio of parking to store area.

8. The cost of constructing the center is estimated on the basis of current square foot cost for the number of square feet of store area required.

9. The rentals are estimated on the basis of percentages customarily paid by each type of store on the volume of sales.

10. The net return is estimated by deducting from the gross rents the annual charges for interest, maintenance of the buildings, real estate taxes, insurance, and allowances for vacancies and management fees.

11. The future sales at the center are based on estimates of the future growth of population and income of the trade area.

Individual Stores

Surveys may be made for single stores as well as for shopping centers. For example, a survey may be made for the purpose of determining whether a new drugstore or hardware store can thrive in a specific location. In this case, the competition of other stores must be noted, the extent of the trade area from which the local neighborhood draws customers estimated, and the number of families and income of the families in that trade area determined. From these data, the total purchases for the type of store under consideration in the trade area will be estimated. Knowing the experience of their own type or a similar type of store in other neighborhoods with similar populations and incomes, the store company will decide whether sufficient volume of sales could be developed to warrant paying the rents for which stores could be obtained in the given location.

It is always necessary to estimate the potential growth of the trade area. An important factor is the amount of vacant land suitable for new homes in that area. It is desirable to ascertain the future program of builders for new home construction and to consult with telephone company and electric power company engineers as to their predictions for the future growth of the specific neighborhood or trade area.

Office Space

The potential demand for new office space in a city may be estimated by determining the number of occupied square feet of office space per capita for the metropolitan region. This ratio must be determined for each city, since wide variations prevail. The amount of new office space potentially required may be estimated for each city on the basis of growth prospects and its prospects for development as a regional commercial and financial center.

Such general estimates, of course, should be related to current vacancy ratios, rents, construction costs, and the terms and availability of financing. Cycles in office building are of longer duration than those of general business. A period of overbuilding may produce a surplus of office space, which depresses rents and net income for a long time thereafter.

It has been estimated that 2 square feet of office space per capita is adequate for most "normal" requirements. Thus, any space above such a figure indicates the extent to which a city is a national or regional office center. For example, San Diego has 2.2 square feet of office space per capita; New York, 16 square feet; and Chicago, 7.5 square feet.

Industrial Space

In making surveys of available factory space, industrial buildings should be classified into one-story buildings and multistoried buildings. The buildings should also be classified as to age, condition, and location. There may be a surplus of space in old multistoried buildings but a scarcity of one-story factory buildings. There may be a surplus of downtown space and a scarcity of space in outlying areas. Special attention should be given to industrial districts. Rental rates or sale prices of buildings offered for rent or sale should be obtained. Usually surveys of this type are made by the utility companies with a view to attracting new industries to their region.

SUMMARY

This chapter presents general guides to the analysis of various real estate markets. It is essential to know the purpose for which any analysis is undertaken, and purpose indicates whether long-run or short-run considerations will be dominant.

Competition is the major force in markets. Demand, supply, and price (or rent) factors should be considered as well as their interrelationships. The market in theory helps us to understand the market in operation. Markets perform the functions of retaining space in the short run, adjusting supplies to demands over the long run, and determining land uses. In the analysis of any real estate market, the following factors are usually applicable:

1. General business conditions
2. Local business conditions
3. Employment and incomes
4. General population changes
5. Special population information
6. Changes in tastes and preferences
7. Financing conditions
8. The volume and costs of construction activity
9. Prices, rents, vacancy rates, and other indicators of market conditions as well as their interrelationships

These and related factors help in estimating potential future market changes. Factors related to income are of primary importance in estimating the demand for real estate; of almost equal importance are the terms and availability of financing.

Suggestions are presented here which relate to market analyses for housing, shopping centers, individual stores, and office and industrial space.

QUESTIONS FOR STUDY

1. Why is the market for owner-occupied homes more highly localized than the market for commercial or industrial property?
2. Is competition a type of social control? Explain.
3. List and explain the functions performed by real estate markets.

4. How does the real estate market differ from other types of markets?
5. How does the market serve as a rationer of space?
6. Compare and contrast the allocation of space under competitive market conditions and under administrative regulations.
7. How does the market determine which additions will be made to the supply of real properties or of property services? How does the market determine the amount of such additions?
8. What are the major factors that condition real estate market operations?
9. If demand in the real estate market rises, what will happen to prices and rents? Over the longer run what will happen to supply? Explain.
10. Is there usually a relationship between the volume of real estate activity and the level of local business conditions?
11. How do monopoly elements in the real estate market contribute to inner-city housing problems?
12. Describe the processes of expansion and the processes of contraction in real estate markets.
13. Why does the purpose of a real estate market analysis play such a large role?
14. List and explain the major factors to be considered in making a real estate market analysis. Which ones would you emphasize in making a market analysis of your home area?
15. Indicate the types of data in each of the following categories that you could profitably employ in making a market analysis: (a) population, (b) employment, (c) building costs, (d) financing, (e) incomes, and (f) vacancies.

SUGGESTED READINGS

BOYD, HARPER W., JR., and WESTFALL, RALPH. *Marketing Research.* Homewood, Ill.: Richard D. Irwin, Inc., 1972.
COUNCIL OF ECONOMIC ADVISERS. *Economic Indicators* (published monthly). Washington, D. C.: Government Printing Office.
MCMAHAN, JOHN. *Property Development.* New York: McGraw-Hill Book Co., 1976. Chs. 7–10.
SUMICHRAST, MICHAEL, and SELDIN, MAURY. *Housing Markets: The Complete Guide to Analysis and Strategy for Home Builders and Other Investors.* Homewood, Ill.: Richard D. Irwin, Inc. (Dow Jones), 1977.
Survey of Buying Power. Published annually in May by *Sales Management.*
WILEY, ROBERT J. *Real Estate Investment—Analysis and Strategy.* New York: The Ronald Press Co., 1977. Ch. 14.

STUDY PROJECT 7–1

An Interview on Real Estate in the 1970's

Q. Dr. Hoyt, the building industry sometimes remains depressed long after business activity in general has turned up. The popular explanation

---

* This interview was conducted with Dr. Homer Hoyt of Homer Hoyt Associates, Washington, D. C. It appeared originally in *The MGIC Newsletter.* Reprinted by permission of Mortgage Guaranty Insurance Corporation, April 1976.

seems to be that interest rates are too high. Is that your belief, too, or do you give more weight to other factors?

A. First, I assume we are discussing mainly the building of income properties—offices, apartments, shopping centers—rather than single-family homes, for it is in the income property area that the depression exists.

Now as to the reasons for the continued depression, I do not believe that interest rates and mortgage market conditions really have much to do with it. The real causes are about the same as they always have been when depression sets in, primarily overbuilding in the preceding period of prosperity.

As Shakespeare said, "There is a tide in the affairs of men which taken at the flood leads on to fortune." In the final stages of a boom, however, the momentum leads to overbuilding of condominiums, office buildings, and shopping centers in excess of the demand and requires a period of time for the excess supply of buildings to be absorbed. Foreclosures or periods of vacancies and operating losses must be faced.

Q. You must consider the building boom of the past several years unwarranted in terms of the economic factors involved. Is that correct?

A. Yes, that is correct. What we are seeing now is the ending of a long period of increasing speculative activity that began following World War II.

The boom began slowly, as at first there was a prediction of slow population growth, with a final limit on the population of the United States. However, the baby boom following World War II stimulated expectations of growth.

From 1948 to 1974, 19,000 planned shopping centers, of which 1,600 were large regional types, were built and successfully developed without any government subsidies. Industries sought locations near highways and railroad lines on vacant land on the fringe of cities where they could build efficient one story plants with land for surface parking. Apartment buildings, once confined to locations on subway and elevated lines in central cities, sprang up on highways or expressways outside the dense urban mass. Office buildings were erected in suburbs near shopping centers or in clusters near suburban centers.

New towns were planned. Office buildings in many cities were planned and built far in excess of demand. Real Estate Investment Trusts (REITS) flourished on borrowed money. Condominiums were constructed on a lavish scale, particularly in Florida and Ocean City, Maryland.

The day of reckoning came in 1974. There were 44,000 vacant and unsold condominiums in Florida, 28 million square feet of vacant office buildings in New York, and many vacancies in Atlanta, Chicago and other cities. By 1974, progress in the development of new towns stopped as there were 62,000 acres in these towns without any new construction.

The bottom in real estate may have been reached in March, 1976, but the question is how long will it take to absorb the oversupply of office space in New York, Chicago, Atlanta, and other cities? How long will it take to absorb the oversupply of condominiums in Florida?

Q. Before you answer these questions, Dr. Hoyt, let's clear up something about what you call the speculative boom. Did we really overbuild, or was the demand for real estate cut-off by the business recession, the break in the stock market, and the high rates of interest?

A. Of course the real estate depression is worse because of the decline in general business activity but don't forget that speculative activity in real estate had a great deal to do with the over-heating of the economy in 1972 and 1973, the unprecedented rise in interest rates and the eventual ending of prosperity. Also, the appraiser, the investor, the mortgage lender, and perhaps even the promoter or developer of a real estate project is supposed to know something about business conditions and movements of prices and interest rates. However, my judgment is that there has been overbuilding in the areas of the market we are discussing, and I arrive at this judgment from observation of actual projects and the decision processes that led to their untimely promotion.

But let me preface this part of my comments with an illustration from a sector of the market where overbuilding has not occurred, and this is the shopping center. Here we find a minimum of speculative frenzy and a maximum of application of sound principles of investment. Most carefully planned shopping centers were started, not on the hope of success, but only after actual lease arrangements had been worked out with credit worthy prospective tenants. As a result, few shopping centers are in serious trouble, and while the market may be near the saturation point, demand should continue to grow with the growth of the economy.

How different in the case of office buildings, for example. Almost in violation of the principles of economic base, new office buildings were promoted, financed and built in New York and other central cities with declining population, no new basic industries or services, and a deteriorating financial condition. Far from waiting until prospective tenants were committed, buildings were completed without any assurances of profitable occupancy. Little wonder that almost thirty million square feet of office buildings in New York have no tenants, and there are only a few tenants in some new office buildings in Chicago.

The situation may not be as bad as in Chicago during and following the Great Depression, when no new office building was built for almost 20 years. But the evidence of overbuilding is about as clear.

Q. Now let's return to the questions you said must be answered. How long will it take to absorb the over supply of office space in so many of our cities, and of condominiums in Florida?

A. I am afraid it will be a long, long time in some of our cities before there is enough demand for office space to justify the promotion of new office buildings. The current excessive supply is keeping rentals down, but construction costs continue to go up. Rentals will have to increase steadily to bring prospective income from a new building to a level justifying the required investment. By that time, construction costs will have moved up even more.

A few cities, of course, will be growing in terms of economic base, Houston being perhaps the best example, but many of our cities are seeing a leveling or even a decline in their basic economy. It is hard for me to imagine a reversal in the trend of corporations to leave New York City just because office space is abundantly available. But New York City is not unique among our cities in terms of limited growth potential. Too many office buildings have been built in most of our cities without thorough analysis of the city's economic base and future prospects.

As for the resort condominiums, long run trends toward ownership of second homes, plus continued population growth will eventually bring about the sale and occupancy of most units now unsold. Many structures, of course, are poorly located, and many may not be well planned or well constructed. After all, if careful thought had gone into the planning, many of them would not have been built at all. Still, I am reasonably optimistic about resort and retirement housing except in the short run.

Q. You haven't said anything about what many people think is the most depressed sector of the market, the building of rental apartments. Based on new housing starts, the multi-family sector has been struggling along at 70 to 80 per cent under the peak volume of three years or so ago, with little or no improvement in sight. What is the reason for the decline, and when do you expect a return to a more prosperous level?

A. The reason for the decline is the fact that at present rentals, construction costs and interest rates for new apartments do not yield a return on the investment. Rentals still are well below the levels required to justify additional construction. Vacancy figures suggest that demand may be catching up with supply, but long before many new projects will be started, the rental market must tighten to the point that rentals will rise somewhat proportionally to the increase in construction costs—including cost of construction financing—over the past three or four years. Eventually, of course, this will happen. New household formation will be increasing rapidly, not only because of the increase in population in the 21–35 age range, but also because of the increasing number of households of only one person. Time is the most important variable in rental housing, just as it is in office building, and there are sound reasons for optimism in apartment building in the long run.

Q. Dr. Hoyt, why doesn't inflation justify the building now of what may be a temporary over-supply of housing or office space in order to have available a lower cost supply a few years from now? Do you believe inflation is not going to continue?

A. Inflation will continue, in my opinion, but that is also the opinion of most other people, including those with money to lend or invest. The result of these inflationary expectations is that interest rates now include a premium for inflation, which in effect equalizes the cost of a structure built today and not utilized with the cost of one built after the market demands it. With equal cost, the risk involved in trying to estimate now just what will be most marketable some time into the future makes such a venture highly questionable.

Q. What about the new towns and the new town idea?

A. I may be overly pessimistic, but I am afraid it will be a long, long time before we will see much new investment in either the new towns already started or in brand new promotions. Even the more successful of the new towns such as Columbia and Reston near Washington, D. C., still have vacant tracts available for builders.

As our central cities, or most of them, continue to decline in population, I would expect the losses to be offset mainly by further growth of suburbs and especially of our smaller cities and even many small towns. The long time trend awaw from the small towns seems to be reversing, and although brand new towns might seem to be a better answer than growth of existing communities, the difficulties of developing new communities from scratch are almost insurmountable as compared with further development of places that already have a local government, an economic base, and an investment in community services such as schools, streets, sewer and water.

Q. Do you have any solution for the blighted areas, the abandonment of structurally sound buildings, and other problems of our central cities? Is movement to the suburbs and to smaller cities and towns the only answer?

A. How to reclaim the thousands of dwellings in the blighted areas of our cities is perhaps the most challenging problem facing the student of real estate today. I do not know the answer, but I am optimistic, again, in the long run, that our cities will survive, and that people in all walks of life may again find advantages in being city dwellers.

A more constructive approach toward the older city and its problems may be one of the good things coming out of the no-growth policies of some of our newer cities and the restrictions on growth in coastal areas, the refusal to grant zoning, the strict enforcement of environmental standards and other impediments to development in more open areas.

Q. Dr. Hoyt, you have had an interesting and successful life-time career in real estate. Based on your experience and observation, what advice do you have for today's real estate investor?

A. That's a difficult assignment, but for a short answer I believe I would say that there has been such a drastic change in the elements affecting real estate values that investment is now a new ball game. Some of the basic principles such as economic base, sector theory, and the discounting of future incomes to determine present value are still valid, as true as two and two make four. The big change is the investor's need to understand what is happening and likely to happen not just in a local situation, nor only nationally, but in a highly dynamic world which we no longer dominate. Knowing the formula will still be important, but what figures to drop in will be the interesting and rewarding side of investment.

Questions

1. Why is overbuilding such a big factor in determining the timing of a period of recovery in the building industry?
2. What are the major forces that lead to overbuilding?
3. What effect does anticipated inflation have on interest rates? What effect does this have on new construction?
4. Why does rent control or the threat of rent control tend to discourage new construction?

STUDY PROJECT 7–2

A Recommendation for Housing

December 10, 19__

MEMO TO: President J. A. Jordan, State University
FROM: John A. Parker, V.P. and Treasurer, State University

Recently we made some long-term projections of our enrollments. We concluded, somewhat reluctantly, that our long-term growth will be limited, and indeed, may decline somewhat by the last decade of the century. This conclusion is based on the assumption that our enrollment trends will tend to follow emerging general population patterns.

Accordingly, I recommend that we do not undertake to procure additional land for expansion. I also recommend that we do not build student dormitories or apartments for students or faculty members in the foreseeable future. I believe we can rely on the local housing market to meet any foreseeable student or faculty housing needs beyond those we are providing with our existing properties. We should, of course, continue to give special emphasis to the maintenance and repair, and, on occasion, modernization of our properties.

December 16, 19____

Memo To: John A. Parker, V.P. and Treasurer, State University
From: J. A. Jordan, President

Thanks for your memo of the 10th. I agree with your conclusions and recommendations and will put this subject on the agenda for our next Board meeting in January. Will you please be prepared to discuss your recommendations. Do you have any objections to sending copies of your memo of the 10th to members of the Board prior to the January meeting?

December 21, 19____

Memo To: President J. A. Jordan, State University
From: John A. Parker, V.P. and Treasurer

Thanks for your memorandum and your favorable comments. I would be pleased to have you circulate my memo of the 10th to the Board.

State University
The Bugle

January 21, 19____

State University, City

At its regular meeting today, the Board of Trustees of State University voted to discontinue the acquisition of land for expansion and to cease developing new dormitories or apartments, relying on the private market to take care of future needs.

In response to a question as to whether this meant the end of growth for State University, President Jordan said, "Our growth is more likely to be in the direction of quality than quantity in the future."

Sam Perkins, local real estate broker and builder, told this reporter that it was "high time" the university got out of the real estate business and left this to the private market.

R & R Realty Company
State University, City

Dear Student:

We have read with interest the new policy regarding dormitories and apartments which was announced in yesterday's *Bugle*. For several months we have been considering the development of a new apartment house near the campus. This announcement is encouraging.

The investors who are interested in this project have asked us to make a careful market analysis to determine whether to proceed and, if so, with what size of project.

Will you please outline for us how we should go about making a market analysis for this purpose, and indicate the type of data we would have to assemble.

I look forward to hearing from you.

                                  James D. Rorich, Jr.
                                  R & R Realty

Question

Prepare a reply to Mr. Rorich's letter.

8

LOCATION ANALYSIS

LOCATION FACTORS IN REAL ESTATE DECISIONS

We have pointed out repeatedly that a parcel of real estate may be thought of as a fixed but dynamic point within a constantly changing economic, social, and political framework. This framework is made up of the property's immediate environment, its local economy and community, and the broader national and international climate.

Property Environment

The real estate decision maker has a vital interest in a property's immediate surroundings and in its relationship to other parts of the local area and region. The property's environment and any special physical, economic, governmental, or social factors that may improve or impair this environment influence the decision maker. We usually refer to these various sets of relationships and particularly to those involving a property's immediate surroundings and its position relative to the local area and region as *location* factors. To a considerable degree, a property's income-producing potential is determined by location factors, conditioned, of course, by market changes and by trends in the local, regional, national, and international economies.

It is often said that the three main considerations in real estate decisions are: (1) location, (2) location, and (3) location. Thus, we will give special attention to location factors in this chapter.

Properties as Shares

An urban property may be thought of as a share in the local economy or city and also as a share in a specific area or sector of the city. A rural property may be considered as a share in its local community. The economic strength of a city or local economy provides basic support for the values of all of the properties located there. If the local economy expands, however, all properties will not be affected in the same manner or to the same degree; some will benefit greatly and some slightly, and some may be affected adversely.

Similarly, a piece of real estate may be thought of as a share in the immediate neighborhood or district of which it forms a part. A variety of factors are at work constantly to bring about favorable or unfavorable changes in the neighborhoods and districts and in major sectors of urban areas.

Purpose and Extent of Analysis

As is true of most types of real estate analysis, studies of location factors are governed to a considerable extent by the purpose to be served. A business executive may have one purpose to be served, a government official another, an individual home buyer still another. An analysis of a location may be undertaken in connection with a property appraisal. A business executive may be considering a location for a new branch office; a local official may be considering recommendations for changes in the zoning law; a newcomer to the city may be considering the purchase of a house that is for sale.

In some cases a quick inspection may be adequate. In others, detailed and extensive analyses may be required. A prospective home buyer may be interested in a relatively limited area, a mortgage lender may want to cover an extensive area. Purpose and type of interest, thus, will govern the analysis of a location.

Location and People

When we refer to locations we are likely to think in terms of land area, structures, and other physical factors. Although this is appropriate in a sense, we should remember that these physical factors have significance only as they serve the needs of people. When we refer to neighborhoods and districts, we mean primarily the people who live or work in such places. The people may be influenced by their physical surroundings, but in a final analysis the people control the types of buildings and other improvements that are found there. Thus, we are concerned with the factors that influence the decisions of people, either from a personal or a business standpoint, relative to real estate resources.

There is a tendency for us to think of impersonal forces as determining the future of specific localities. We refer to location factors, to market forces, political influences, and the like, often forgetting that when we do this we are really referring to the attitudes, points of view, interests, and objectives of specific persons. In combination, the opinions of large numbers of persons may appear to constitute an impersonal sort of force. Fundamentally, however, we are likely to reach false conclusions if we forget that real properties, neighborhoods, districts, the structure of cities or metropolitan areas all mean little or nothing unless we think in terms of the people who give importance to them. And it is the reactions, life styles, value judgments, hopes and fears of people that finally result in the assignment of values to real properties, and that give one neighborhood a better reputation than another or give one business district an advantage over others.

In the discussions that follow we often refer to the physical character-istics of neighborhoods and districts. This should not obscure the fact that we are considering factors which are likely to influence the judgments and decisions of people in respect to real estate resources.

TRENDS AFFECTING STRUCTURE OF LAND USES

We have tried to emphasize the importance of location factors in dy-namic rather than static terms. Thus it may be helpful to consider briefly some of the forces that are likely to hold particular significance for the real estate decision maker in the years ahead.

General Trends

Changes in per-capita incomes have implications for changes in ex-penditure patterns and future employment opportunities. Science and tech-nology are bringing major changes in communication patterns. New ma-chines, techniques, and processes are hastening the obsolescence of existing plant and equipment which in turn present new location decisions. Changes and potential changes in transportation patterns as well as in methods for bearing the costs of transportation are likely to have major effects.[1] Taxes and potential changes in tax burdens will continue to influence decision makers. Problems of air and water pollution are tending toward greater dispersion and distribution of activity. Energy problems, on the other hand, tend to favor concentration of activities. Changes in the values and life styles of people have a continuing bearing on real estate location de-cisions.

The character of urban growth may change. Further expansion of urban areas may slow down. There may be some tendency to slow down the outward trends as a result of transportation and energy costs. Also, cen-tral tendencies may be reinforced if it becomes possible to spread some of the costs now borne by the central city to suburban areas. Current trends, however, indicate continued suburban development.[2]

[1] See Paul F. Wendt, *Real Estate Appraisal: Review and Outlook* (Athens: University of Georgia Press, 1974), ch. 4, pp. 78–80; Sanders A. Kahn and Frederick E. Case, *Real Estate Appraisal and Investment* (New York: The Ronald Press, 1977), ch. 5.

[2] See, for example, Peter O. Muller, *The Outer City* (Washington, D. C.: Association of American Geographers, 1976), and Norton Long, "The City as a System of Perverse Incentives" in *Urbanization; Past and Present* (Milwaukee: University of Wisconsin, College of Letters and Sciences), Summer 1976, No. 2.

Competition Between Land Uses

Industrial and commercial locations have tended to spread more widely. Residential land uses have become somewhat more fluid; apartment houses are mixed up with single-family houses; town houses or row houses are found in a variety of areas. Shopping centers are being scattered throughout urban areas; often a shopping center is a key factor in the success of a new subdivision. Increasingly, industrial developments, many of which are not incompatible with residential uses, are found at scattered locations throughout the urban area. Concepts of "inharmonious" land uses appear to be changing.

Social and Political Competition

Although zoning laws and deed restrictions, as well as other types of regulations, tend to limit competition and channel it into specific directions, there continues to be intense competition between land uses and within classes of land uses. To some degree, zoning laws and related forms of regulation have become another form of competition among land developers, investors, and users. Developers tend to seek those jurisdictions in a metropolitan area that have a minimum of zoning restrictions as to lot size, type of use, utility requirements, and tax levels.

In other words, competition may take social and political forms. Labor and political organizations sometimes provide the basis for competition between land uses and between neighborhoods. Some efforts are being made to disperse rather than to concentrate low-income groups.[3] We should note also that many types of competition cannot be explained by economic considerations alone.

Governmental and political factors will continue to exert significant influences on the future pattern of land uses. Their general character may change; for example, there may be a resurgence of interest in local governmental and political activity. The effect of a heavier tax burden in one neighborhood than in a competing one will continue to merit the attention of the real estate decision maker as will such factors as fire and police protection, control of traffic, location of traffic arteries, zoning laws, and the cost of local governmental services relative to their quality.

Redlining

The so-called "redlining" controversy seems likely to continue for some time. This term refers to the alleged practice of excluding certain neighborhoods from consideration by lenders. In a broader sense it may include any failure or alleged failure to support a neighborhood with governmental, professional, or business services. Efforts to generate support for older neighborhoods appear to be increasing.

[3] The President's Task Force on Low Income Housing, "Toward Better Housing for Low Income Families" (Washington D. C.: Government Printing Office, 1970).

Attitudes and Priorities

Cultural factors and attitudes will play an important part in determining the future pattern of land uses, as we have already suggested. For example, we have had a strong trend toward home ownership; this may be modified, of course, but we are fairly certain that home ownership will continue to be highly acceptable in most areas and that neighborhoods of home owners may represent relatively stable areas. Efforts are being made to extend opportunities for home ownership to those in low-income groups. Attitudes toward private property, home ownership, "appropriate" locations for various lands uses, and many others are important in this connection. Prestige factors also change over time and their importance can easily be overlooked.

The tastes and preferences of people relative to real estate may tend to undergo changes. The two-house family is growing in importance. Weekend cottages combined with "near-in" apartments appear to be competing effectively with some types of suburban residences. There appears to be renewed interest in "near-in" locations in order to reduce commuting time. Many other changes may emerge as well. Increased leisure, broader social and cultural interests, longer life for many, and increased interest in political activities, notably on the local level, are likely to have effects on the location of various land uses. Also, broader opportunities on the part of all types of people to enjoy home ownership will be important.

Physical factors such as rivers, swamps, land contour, condition of soil and subsoil, and the like will continue to have a bearing on the location of land uses and the shifts that occur. Environmental and energy problems and controls probably will play a role of growing importance. Depreciation resulting from the physical deterioration of structures or from changes in use or fashion will have an influence, in part physical, in part social and economic. The existing transportation system has both physical and economic implications in regard to present and future land uses. Increased interest in conservation and in the preservation of older structures and neighborhoods is deserving of consideration.

Anticipating Changes

All this suggests that the future structure and pattern of land uses will be determined by a wide variety of factors, as has been the case in the past. To some extent, past trends will be helpful, but it will be important to anticipate, if possible, the major forces that will affect land uses and interrelationships between them in the future.

URBAN CHANGE

Our urban areas are highly complex arrangements of many types of land uses serving a wide variety of people. These urban areas are seldom static; they change constantly. For most American cities change has been stimulated primarily by growth. In some cases, however, change comes about as a result of decline. In some growing cities there are certain areas and sectors which do not share in the benefits of growth.

Efforts have been made to develop general principles and concepts that will help us to understand the processes of urban change. We will consider some of these efforts and their potential significance for the real estate decision maker.

Stages of Growth

As cities expand they tend to pass through certain stages of development. For example, a city in the initial stage of development is like a small country town.[4] Here there is little competition among various land uses. In general, the major business center is at the point of origin of the town, which may be a crossroads or a railroad intersection, the point at which a river meets the sea, or some similar focal point which caused original settlement there. A few light industries may grow up; if so, they are usually adjacent to the downtown business center. Hence the town will represent a very simple sort of organization.

However, when expansion continues beyond this stage, possible land uses increase in number and intensity. The area of the city will be expanded as a result of population growth, and the intensity of land use at various points will be increased. Various types of uses to which the land was originally put will give way to "higher" uses, or those which will yield a greater return per dollar of investment. For example, establishments which require relatively large areas in relation to business volume will tend to be crowded out of the central parts of a city because of the competition of other types of enterprises with greater rent-paying ability. Because the more powerful activities are able to force out other land uses, this competition for sites causes a constant movement within the city.

Such competition is most intense when the city is expanding. If a city is declining in economic importance, new demands for space are limited and only the most favored locations are able to earn substantial incomes. It is during periods of rapid growth that the most noticeable changes occur in the uses to which various parcels of real estate are put.

Methods of Expansion

A city may expand (1) by growing vertically through the replacement of lower structures with higher ones, (2) by filling in open spaces between settled areas, or (3) by extending the existing settled area.

[4] Professor N. S. B. Gras has pointed out that the form of the village may either be "nucleated," that is, of a very compact form, which is sometimes called a "heap village," or it may be "nonnucleated," that is, spread out, the houses usually being some distance apart and near the field surrounding the village. One example of this is the so-called "long-street village," which is fairly common in Europe, also in Quebec, Nova Scotia, and Maine. See Gras, *An Introduction to Economic History* (New York: Harper & Row, 1922), pp. 53–56.

When the settled area is expanded, growth may take several forms, the most important being (1) *concentric circle* or *ring growth* around the central nucleus; (2) *axial growth,* with prongs or fingerlike extensions moving out along main transportation routes; and (3) *suburban growth,* with the establishment of islands of settlements in advance of the main city area. These types of expansion are characteristic of most larger cities. Baltimore was for a long time a good example of ring growth, while New York, Chicago, and Detroit illustrate axial and suburban development.

When both ring growth and axial expansion occur, a star-shaped city structure results. As Hurd pointed out many years ago:

In their methods of growth cities conform always to biological laws, all growth being either *central* or *axial.* In some cities central growth occurs first and in other axial growth, but all cities illustrate both forms of growth, and in all cases central growth includes some axial growth and axial growth some central growth. Central growth consists of the clustering of utilities around any point of attraction and is based on proximity, while axial growth is the result of transportation facilities and is based on accessibility.[5]

Influence of Topography

A city located in the center of a level plain might be expected to grow outward in rings from the main point of origin. However, most of our cities were located at points where their growth was influenced by hills, rivers, and other topographical features. New York, located first at the southern tip of Manhattan Island, could expand only northward until ferries, bridges, and tunnels made growth in other directions possible. Chicago's growth to the east was stopped by Lake Michigan. In some cases the original topography of a site was changed by grading or filling when it became profitable to undertake such projects. For example, Boston was located on a rather narrow peninsula, but the filling-in of the Back Bay and similar areas provided space for expansion. The lake front in Chicago has been extended nearly a mile eastward from the Loop area. The original area of Miami Beach, Florida, was nearly tripled by pumping sand out of Biscayne Bay. In addition, topographical factors often govern the location of transportation lines, and these in turn influence the direction of city growth by accelerating axial and suburban developments.

Land Use Patterns

Although we can distinguish central and axial growth in our cities today, a much greater variety and diversity of land uses and changes in land uses have emerged than appeared probable even a few years ago. Few of the earlier theories or explanations of land use patterns are adequate for current

[5] Richard M. Hurd, *Principles of City Land Values* (New York: The Record & Guide, 1924), pp. 58–59.

and future purposes although they give us some keys to understanding the processes that have gone on. It has been pointed out, for example:

In the era of the Greek cities in the fifth century B.C. a city was considered an artistic creation which should maintain its static form without change. To take care of population growth, the Greeks sent out colonies, like swarms of bees, to found new cities on the ideal model. Plato said that the ideal city should not contain over 5,000 inhabitants, although he, himself was the product of an Athens with 250,000 population. In the Middle Ages most continental European cities were surrounded by walls and many, like Milan, Italy, preserved an unaltered form for hundred of years.[6]

Concentric Circles

The modern city tended to spread over wider areas as improved transportation made such dispersion possible. In the 1920's Burgess set forth his concentric circle theory in an effort to explain city form and structure. It is an interesting concept, though not too helpful today.

The typical process of the expansion of a city can best be illustrated, perhaps, by a series of concentric circles, which may be numbered to designate both the successive zones of urban expansion and the types of areas differentiated in the process of expansion.

He believed that each zone tended to invade the next one by a process called "succession." At the heart of his model was the "loop" with the financial and office district at the center and the central retail district surrounding and penetrating it. Beyond this, as he pointed out:

Encircling the downtown area there is normally an area in transition, which is being invaded by business and light manufacture. A third area is inhabited by workers in industries who have escaped from the area of deterioration but who desire to live within easy access of their work. Beyond this zone is the "residential area" of high-class apartment buildings or of exclusive "restricted" districts of single-family dwellings. Still farther out, beyond the city limits, is the commuter's zone—suburban areas, or satellite cities—within a thirty- to sixty-minute ride of the central business district.[7]

Wider Dispersion

Burgess' explanation was made obsolete primarily by the automobile; but other factors were at work as well, including rising incomes, advancing technology especially in transportation and communication, the require-

[6] Homer Hoyt, "Recent Distortions of the Classical Models of Urban Structure," *Land Economics* (May, 1964).

[7] Reprinted from *The City* by R. E. Park, E. W. Burgess, and R. D. McKenzie, by permission, University of Chicago Press, pp. 50–53. Copyright, 1925, by the University of Chicago.

ments for large amounts of space for single-story factory buildings, tax factors, and others. Noneconomic forces also played a part in this process.

The automobile made possible a wide dispersal of people over a metropolitan area, the wide separation of workers from places of employment, the rise of planned shopping centers with thousands being established, the outward movement of manufacturing, as such land uses found a variety of locations compatible with their needs, improved roads and freeways, and the general broadening of the urban land market.

Sector Theory

Another general theory of urban structure was developed by Homer Hoyt and set forth in 1939.

If an entire city is thought of as a circle, and if the different residential areas are thought of as wedge-shaped sectors pointing to the center, the high-rent or high-price areas of the city will tend over a period of years to move outward to the periphery in the path described by one or more of the sectors. Similarly, if a certain sector develops originally as a low-rent or low-price area, the balance of that sector is likely to be occupied by low-rent or low-price residences as expansion proceeds outward. The same tendency is typical of intermediate rent or price sectors.[8]

The sector theory is based on the following general tendencies:

1. The various groups in the social order tend to locate in rather definite areas according to their incomes and social positions. While efforts are being made to modify these tendencies, they continue to persist. The high-price and high-rent areas tend to attract the central business district to move in their direction.
2. The principal growth of American cities has taken place by new building at the periphery rather than by the rebuilding of older areas. Growth has tended toward higher ground, toward the homes of community leaders, and toward the open countryside.

Careful studies of past trends in the major sectors often provide keys to the understanding of future developments (see Figs. 8–1 and 8–2).

Also of interest in analyzing urban land use changes is the multiple nuclei concept developed by Harris and Ullman as a modification of the sector theory. They stressed the clustering of land uses, especially business uses, and the impact of transportation, topography, and related factors. Family preferences and social customs were considered as important factors in the location of residential land uses.[9]

---

[8] This theory was worked out by Homer Hoyt and first presented in a series of articles in the Federal Housing Administration's *Insured Mortgage Portfolio* (Washington, D. C.: Government Printing Office), Vol. I, Nos. 6–10. See also, his *The Structure and Growth of Residential Neighborhoods in American Cities* (Washington, D. C.: Federal Housing Administration, 1939).

[9] Chauncey D. Harris and Edward L. Ullman, "The Nature of Cities," *Annals* of the American Academy of Political and Social Sciences (November, 1945). See also Frederick E. Case, *Real Estate* (Boston: Allyn and Bacon, 1962), pp. 53–54; Homer Hoyt, *According to Hoyt* (2nd ed.; Washington, D. C.: Hoyt, 1970), pp. 616–21.

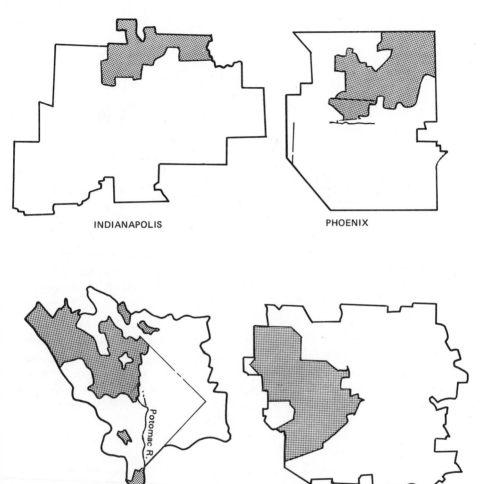

INDIANAPOLIS

PHOENIX

WASHINGTON, D.C.

HOUSTON

FIG. 8–1.   High-income sectors. (Adapted from ULI Technical Bulletin No. 55.)

Muller has emphasized the continuing outward urban expansion and the growing importance of suburban developments.[10] Figure 8–2 illustrates his concepts of urban expansion. He also stresses the influence of transportation changes (see Fig. 8–3). Muller says, "Urbanization trends

[10] Muller, *op. cit.;* see also L. H. Masotti, "The Suburban Seventies," *Annals* of the American Academy of Political and Social Sciences, vol. 422, no. 7, p. 151; J. S. Adams, "Residential Structure of Midwestern Cities," *Annals* of the Association of American Geographers, vol. 60, pp. 37–62; B. J. Berry, "Contemporary Urbanization Processes" in F. E. Horton (Ed.), *Geographical Perspectives and Urban Problems* (Washington, D. C.: National Academy of Sciences, 1973).

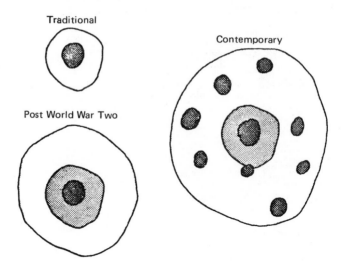

FIG. 8–2.   The changing spatial form of the twentieth-century American metropolis. [Reproduced from Peter O. Muller, *The Outer City* (Washington, D. C.: National Association of Geographers, 1976), p. 2.]

in the U. S. today indicate suburbia to be the essence of the contemporary American city. . . . suburbia in the late seventies is emerging as the *outer city*" (p. 1). He points out that there has been a significant shift from a single- to a multiple-core metropolis as shopping centers, suburban office buildings, industrial parks, and freeways have emerged to create new outlying urban centers. Examples include Newport Center in the Los Angeles area, Schaumburg northwest of Chicago, and Cherry Hill near Philadelphia.

Also of interest are recent efforts to revitalize the downtown areas of suburban cities. For example, many of the suburbs in the Chicago area are undertaking efforts to encourage the redevelopment of their central cities. Some try to develop pedestrian malls, others make provision for additional parking areas and try to encourage business for their downtown areas in other ways. The suburban cities as well as the major central cities have encountered problems in their downtown areas.

Toward Ecumenopolis?

Are we headed toward a single world city? This suggestion was put forth by Toynbee. He said, for example:

The megalopolises on all the continents are merging to form Ecumenopolis, a new type of city that can be represented by only one specimen, since Ecumenopolis is going, as its name proclaims, to encompass the land-surface of the globe with a single conurbation.

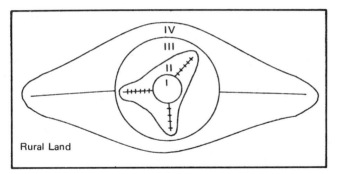

FIG. 8–3.   Intraurban transport eras and metropolitan growth patterns.
   I Walking–Horsecar Era (pre-1850–late 1880's)
   II Electric Streetcar Era (late 1880's–1920)
   III Recreational Automobile Era (1920–1945)
   IV Freeway Era (1945–   )
Source: Same as for Fig. 8–2, p. 5.

He goes on to suggest:

> Human affairs are already being swept toward Ecumenopolis by two currents, both of which are strong and which are both flowing in the same direction. Between them, they make the coming World-City a certainty. One of these two currents is the present rapid growth of the world's population, especially among the economically backward and therefore indigent majority. The second current that is making the Ecumenopolis is the simultaneous migration from the countryside into the cities which is taking place in the "developing" and "developed" countries alike.[11]

These concepts are intriguing. They may indicate the direction of future developments. On the other hand, new forces, not yet in evidence, may emerge which will modify the trends which Toynbee identifies.

In order to make estimates regarding future probable changes in the land uses of a city, it is necessary to study past developments with some care. Changes in the internal structure of a city occur slowly. Hence we cannot forecast future probable changes unless we can determine the major trends that have been in operation for a considerable period of time.

Individuality of Regions

The great diversity of American cities makes it difficult to set forth general explanations of land use patterns. The sector theory, however, may be helpful in anticipating land use changes, especially movement toward high-income locations. We should remember that all shifts in the patterns of land uses result from the decisions of people either as individuals or as

[11] Arnold Toynbee, *Cities on the Move* (New York and London: Oxford University Press, 1970), pp. 95–96.

officials of business firms or governmental or institutional agencies. What motivates them at a given time may be hard to anticipate. They may react in one manner in one region and in another way elsewhere. Hence, the pattern of every urban region tends to have its own unique characteristics and is deserving of special study. Even so, the sector theory often has been helpful to decision makers.

Time Interval Maps

One method for collecting information that may aid a decision maker is by the use of time interval maps. A photograph or a map of a city at a given moment of time fails to show the dynamic character of the city's growth. Several photographs taken at different time intervals or several maps for different periods reveal the processes of change. Thus, if the location of a certain type of area has changed from one period to another, it is possible to determine the direction and speed with which such movements have occurred by using devices of this kind.

Generally speaking, a period covering at least the time since the end of World War II should be studied. A detailed description should be worked out for a year around two decades ago. Earlier situations should then be compared with current conditions.

If it is possible to undertake careful and intensive research, specific information can be secured from such sources as the Sanborn insurance maps, which show locations of individual structures in many cities for periods as far back as the 1880's. Also, valuable assistance can be secured from the United States survey maps, which provide similar information. Older maps of cities can frequently be found that provide valuable data. City histories and old newspaper files often include accounts of the development of particular areas.

It is sometimes possible to compare recent aerial photographs of entire regions with those taken at a former period. Thus in recent surveys of the growth of the Washington metropolitan area, a comparison was made between aerial photographs taken currently with those taken in 1958 and 1937. The marked growth in the urban settled area which had taken place in that period and the direction of growth were clearly indicated.

In the absence of such specific material, or if pressure of time necessitates the use of less refined methods, sufficient information can often be secured by consulting older people who have a reputation for accuracy and good judgment and who are known to be well informed regarding the growth of the city. At least three different persons should be consulted. If there seems to be considerable disagreement among them, additional people should be questioned.

Land Use Changes

Regardless of the plan of attack adopted, a map (which may be referred to as a time interval map) for each period should be prepared which will indicate the areas occupied by (1) factories and heavy industries, (2) low-rent residential areas, (3) the chief central and outlying shopping or commercial areas, and (4) the more fashionable residential neighborhoods. From these maps a reasonably accurate picture can be secured of the major movements affecting each of these important types of land uses.

Such general maps should then be compared with maps showing the development of the internal transportation system of the city. Maps showing the transportation system at various periods of time can usually be secured from city offices or from the offices of those who are in charge of the transportation system. Similarly, comparisons should be made with existing zoning maps which indicate the restrictions applying to various areas of the city.

When the movements indicated by the maps have been studied and analyzed, the forces of city expansion may be noted and the probable future structure of the city may be estimated. It is generally possible to assume that existing uses will expand outward in the same sector and that the trend of past development will be continued into the future, unless important and powerful forces are in existence or are likely to develop which will tend to cause a change in such trends.

NEIGHBORHOOD CHANGE

The forces which cause people to reach decisions that bring about changes in neighborhoods are of three main types: (1) physical and functional depreciation, (2) the development of more intensive land uses, and (3) changes of residence. Physical wear and tear and the introduction of new materials, designs, and equipment tend constantly to make older structures less desirable places in which to live. As new houses are built, the older ones may lose out in competition with them.

Business uses sometimes invade residential areas. The relocation of an industrial district may affect a number of neighborhoods. There is some tendency for families to move as income increases. As people move into a neighborhood, they may or may not be absorbed without any significant change.

As a result of the operation of these forces, people are drawn to newer or more desirable areas (as measured by their standards). A number of population movements are taking place more or less constantly in our towns and cities.[12] Some families move into other apartments in the same building, others go next door, across the street, or around the corner. Still other families move long distances within the city or move to other parts of the country, while new individuals and families move into the city. It is estimated that each year about one family in five moves.

---

[12] See, for example, R. J. Johnson, *Urban Residential Patterns* (New York: Praeger Publications, Inc., 1971), especially ch. 8.

Neighborhood Life Cycle

Those interested in real estate value changes sometimes observe that houses do not wear out but neighborhoods do. Residential neighborhoods tend to pass through periods of early growth, maturity, and decline. A new neighborhood may be entirely built up by a developer, with all facilities complete and no intervening vacant lots. Where the area is subdivided and lots are sold to individual home builders, houses may be built on scattered lots. A development may be arrested with builders going to new areas where entire sections of new houses can be built. Sometimes the advantages of utilities and pavements in the older areas cause new houses to be built on the vacant lots at a later period.

There is no uniform rate of maturity or decline in neighborhoods. The Battery in Charleston, South Carolina, has maintained an attractive residential character for over 200 years. Suburbs often remain attractive for very long periods of time. Examples include various of the North Chicago suburbs, the Westchester County area near New York, and the Maryland and Virginia suburbs near Washington, D. C.

Neighborhoods may decline for many reasons; the buildings may become obsolete as to structure, architectural style, or lot area, people may move into and out of an area; or certain commercial or industrial establishments may expand and make the area less desirable for residential purposes. Changes in the character of schools may affect neighborhood decline.

The aging of the population may be a factor. As children grow up to marriageable age, they may find it difficult to buy homes in the old neighborhood or they may prefer to move to newer neighborhoods where their friends are living. As the old residents die new people will take their place.

In some cases families move from a central apartment to a suburban apartment, and then into a single-family home. When children reach school age, families tend to move from apartments to single-family homes.

It cannot be assumed that old residential neighborhoods decline in value after reaching maturity. Houses in old neighborhoods sometimes sell for higher prices than at the time they were built. Although the general tendency is to lose out in competition with newer ideas, there is growing interest in neighborhood preservation and property restoration.

Some residential neighborhoods are absorbed into new commercial developments. This is rather infrequent, as most central business districts have ceased to expand laterally. The requirement for parking areas near existing shopping districts, however, is creating a demand for old houses near established commercial areas at prices high enough to absorb the cost of the structures.

Thus there is no uniform rule as to the rate of change in a neighborhood, and each neighborhood should be considered in relation to the general pattern of residential land uses.

Types of Residential Neighborhoods

The largest proportion of the utilized land in our cities is devoted to residential purposes. However, these residential areas contain many different types of people, properties, and neighborhoods. Although the dividing lines between neighborhoods usually are not sharp, there are great differences between the deluxe residential suburbs at the one extreme and slums at the other.

Neighborhoods might be classified by the types of people who live in them; by type, location, age, and condition of structures; or in other ways. Nearly all of these factors are reflected, however, in the level of rents or prices typical of the various neighborhoods of a city. Hence, the following classification is based on two general levels of rents or prices: high, and lower and intermediate; in addition, types of structures and locations are reflected in the subclassifications. This is not a hard-and-fast classification, but will suggest the types of neighborhoods most generally found in our cities.

I. High Rent or Price Areas
   A. Apartment house or town house neighborhoods, located at desirable points
      1. On main mass transportation lines
      2. Near ocean, lake, or river fronts
      3. Near expressways
      4. In suburbs
   B. Single-family neighborhoods
      1. Axial developments
         a. Located along best transportation lines
         b. Located along desirable water fronts
      2. Self-contained areas
      3. Suburbs
      4. Country estates

II. Lower and Intermediate Rent or Price Areas
   A. Apartment house neighborhoods (urban and suburban)
      1. Garden types
      2. Walk-ups
      3. Elevator types
   B. Row house or town house areas (urban and suburban)
   C. Neighborhoods of two-family structures and small apartment houses (urban and suburban)
   D. Neighborhoods of single-family homes
      1. Suburban or peripheral developments
      2. "Near-in" areas
      3. Country towns

Density of Population

Ordinarily we think of overcrowded conditions as being undesirable for a neighborhood either from a social or an economic standpoint. In planning for the redevelopment of some of the slum areas of our cities, special efforts are often made to decrease population density. With careful planning, however, high densities can be accommodated as in the case of "platform cities."

The density of population in cities depends on (1) the size of the total population, (2) the speed of the city's internal transportation system, (3) types of structures, and (4) land coverage.

In ancient Rome, for example, a population of 1,000,000 was crowded into an area of five square miles. Most of the residential buildings were 5 or 6 stories high, and the streets were only 8 to 10 feet wide. While the population density in the central portion of our larger cities is still high, improved transportation and more careful land planning have helped to reduce the adverse effects of high densities.

Main Points for Neighborhood Decisions and Analysis

The following items are likely to influence decisions of owners, buyers, sellers, tenants, or investors and thus are the major points for neighborhood analysis.

1. Location of the neighborhood with respect to other land uses and the main lines of growth
2. Land use regulations such as zoning laws
3. The relative age of the neighborhood
4. The people in the area
5. The buildings and other improvements in the area
6. Transportation
7. Access to schools, churches, shopping centers, amusement places, and places of employment
8. Tax burdens and special assessments
9. Utilities, conveniences, and services including police and fire protection
10. Special hazards and nuisances

Relative Marketability

All of these factors have a bearing on the marketability of properties in the area. As a summary of these factors, it may be desirable to consider the degree to which typical properties in a neighborhood will be salable over a period of years and whether they will be more or less salable than similar properties in other areas. We should remember that the high-cost neighborhoods are not always the most stable areas.

As we have pointed out in the earlier part of this chapter, a careful analysis of the factors which have been discussed should provide a useful guide to real estate decisions. Such an analysis will be more reliable if proper allowances have been made for local applications of the general tendencies we have outlined.

COMMERCIAL AND INDUSTRIAL DISTRICTS

Although there are wide varieties of business (commercial and industrial) areas in our cities, they may be classified into five main groups. Commercial districts include: (1) central business districts, (2) outlying business and shopping centers, and (3) isolated outlets and clusters. Industrial districts are of two main types: (1) those used chiefly for heavy industrial establishments and (2) those used principally by light industry. Industrial districts may also be classified by location.

Business uses may radiate out from the center of the city along one or more main traffic arteries. Businesses which require larger amounts of horizontal space, special parking facilities, or large quantities of land are found along these streets. New and used automobile and accessory dealers, filling stations, food marts, supermarkets, and larger grocery stores, farmers' markets, tourist hotels and motels, and the like are located on such streets. "Near-in" parts of such streets may be thought of as a part of the central business district; those farther out may be classified with outlying business centers. Shopping centers may be found at a variety of locations in the metropolitan area.

Central Business District

The central business district is the functioning heart of the city. In it are concentrated the major retail, financial, hotel, service, and governmental activities of the city. The specialized land uses in the central business district typically include retail shopping areas, office buildings, hotels, theater and amusement sections, banks and other financial institutions, government buildings, and, on the fringe, the wholesale district and the light manufacturing area. Transportation routes usually lead to this center.

In the central business district the cost of doing business is high, competition is keen, good sites are at a premium, and there are chances for both great successes and great failures. Almost all kinds of business enterprise may be found there except those requiring large amounts of horizontal space or those dealing in commodities which are low in value in relation to bulk. The establishments with the greatest rent-paying ability obtain the choice sites, with the less desirable space going to other businesses. Generally speaking, the best parts of the central business districts are those with access to the greatest potential purchasing power, as measured by the quantity and quality of pedestrian traffic. Customers are drawn from all parts of the city and from its hinterland or market area, which may extend for many miles in all directions.

"100 Per Cent" Locations. The types of business which can afford to locate in "100 per cent" business locations and pay the highest rents are department stores, women's apparel stores, shoe stores, men's clothing stores, jewelry stores, drugstores, candy stores, and variety stores. Traffic counts are sometimes used to estimate the amount of business that may be generated at specific locations.

With the rapid development of shopping centers, the downtown areas have suffered in varying degrees from this competition. Certain functions, however, appear to be especially adapted to central business districts. These include department stores, highly specialized activities, financial institutions, major office headquarters, and theaters.

Outlying Centers

Outlying business and shopping centers include a variety of districts which may be miniatures of the central business district, regional and super-regional shopping centers, smaller community shopping centers, and neighborhood centers and clusters. Typically the outlying centers do not include transportation terminals. Parking space and the presence of good feeder roads and streets are of considerable importance to such a center.

Nearly all types of enterprises may be found in outlying centers. There has been a tremendous growth of shopping centers of many types. The choice sites go to the establishments with greatest rent-paying ability. Pedestrian traffic is much less significant than in the central area. Parking facilities are one of the major attractions.

Small neighborhood centers usually include only such establishments as appeal to the immediate needs of the people in the area, with little specialization of land use.

Isolated Outlets and Clusters

Isolated business outlets include single establishments doing business principally on a personal basis, as in the case of a delicatessen in the front of a residence or a beauty shop or dentist's office located in a part of a house or apartment. Increasingly, such stores as Sears Roebuck and various supermarkets occupy isolated locations. Isolated filling stations, restaurants, general stores, and repair garages are found on principal highways. Two or more such outlets may form a cluster of establishments which complement each other, such as a drugstore, supermarket, and shoe repair shop. Typically they develop on small parcels of land which are designated by zoning regulations for commercial uses and are quite limited in extent. However, the small town or village business cluster is more like the central business district in embryonic form. It usually serves the village and the surrounding countryside, but the establishments located there are not highly specialized.

Industrial Areas

Heavy industrial areas are being located to an increasing extent in peripheral areas and in the open countryside. Light industry may be found at almost any location. Some light industry may even be acceptable in or near residential neighborhoods. Often there is no noise or odor, grounds are attractively landscaped, and the number of employees is relatively small due to highly automated processes. Industrial districts and parks have developed extensively in recent years, typically in outlying locations.

Analysis of Districts

The analysis of commerical and industrial districts varies with the purpose being served. Purpose will govern the extent and intensity of the analysis, the factors given priority, and the types of data included. Usually analyses of this type are more detailed and specialized than those of residential neighborhoods, although there are wide variations in practice.

The more important forces to consider in analyzing various commercial districts include: (1) the economic potential of the region, (2) intensity of competition, (3) changes in the internal structure of the city, (4) physical factors, (5) transportation, and (6) government policies, including taxes, zoning and planning regulations, traffic controls, environmental and energy regulations, protections against crime, fire, and other hazards, and related policies and regulations.

Industrial districts will be affected by the same forces but their impact may vary somewhat. Both commercial and industrial areas will be affected by the economic development of the region as well as general directions of city growth and changes in the city's internal structure. We have considered these factors in our earlier discussions.

Transportation. Transportation facilities have always exercised great influence. There has been a significant development of industrial locations of various types along belt highways; for example, Route 128 in Boston, the Calumet Expressway in Chicago, and the Pennsylvania Turnpike north of Philadelphia. Heavy industries require adequate rail or water transportation, and their location and development depend to a large extent on the transportation facilities available and their cost.

Topography is of importance because it may control the development of new transportation lines. Energy problems and costs are of growing importance in business locations.

Land and Buildings. Industrial districts may be limited in their development by the amount and kind of vacant land available. Land costs often play a major role in decisions. Decision makers may be influenced also by the rate of functional depreciation of industrial buildings, since some structures of this type are superseded by more efficient ones in a relatively short time.

Regulations. Regulations pertaining to environmental factors are growing in importance. Relative standards and costs of waste disposal, for example, are entering more and more into location decisions. In most cities definite limits have been placed on the movement of commercial and industrial districts by city planning regulations and zoning laws. Restrictive tendencies have become more common.

Taxes.   Tax policies are of major importance in determining the future probable locations and developments of commercial and industrial districts. Tax burdens are one aspect of the whole problem of competition for sites and the relative costs of land.

Competition.   Commercial establishments usually can outbid industries in their competition for space. Industrial establishments often require large ground-floor areas, and only the light industries can operate economically in the upper stores of buildings. Hence, high land values are a handicap to heavy industrial development.

Outward Movement.   To escape high land values and high taxes, many industries have moved farther and farther from the centers of our cities. Industries now cover many parts of the countryside, much as farms did in an earlier period. Formerly it was necessary to consider nearness to the homes of workers, but improved transportation and especially the increased use of the automobile have largely eliminated this consideration in determining industrial and commercial locations. We may find some return of industry to central locations if land values decline sufficiently and if special inducements are provided.

SUMMARY

Location factors play an important part in real estate decisions. A real property may be thought of as a share in the local economy and also as a share in a particular area or sector of the local community. When a city expands, all properties do not participate in the benefits to the same degree; the reverse is also true. Factors likely to influence these interrelationships in future years include changes in per-capita incomes and resulting changes in expenditure patterns; the impact of science and technology on transportation, communication, energy, the environment, and the obsolescence of plant and equipment; governmental changes, notably in allocations of costs and benefits; changing competitive patterns between land uses; social changes and changes in the life styles, tastes, and preferences of people. General theories of city structure, notably the sector theory, may be helpful to the real estate decision maker.

As with any investigation, it is essential to know the purpose for which location analysis is undertaken. Such analysis may be needed for business, personal, institutional, or governmental decisions. Purpose also helps to determine the type and extent of the analysis.

A number of classifications of neighborhoods may be employed. This chapter has presented a classification based on levels of rents and prices. Neighborhood change is the result of the interaction of personal, business, and governmental decisions plus various historical or institutional factors. The primary forces behind these decisions are physical and functional depreciation, type and intensity of land use, and changes in residential patterns.

Many factors in the neighborhood environment will have important influences on decisions. They include location with respect to city growth, protections, types of people and buildings in the area, transportation, civic and social facilities, and governmental factors including regulations and police and fire protection, and taxes.

Neighborhoods tend to go through phases of growth, maturity, and decline. However, the time sequence of these phases is not fixed; some neighborhoods decline rapidly whereas other remain attractive for long periods of time.

Commercial and industrial districts are classified in this chapter into five main groups. In analysis of these districts the following factors are of importance: (1) changes in the economic potential and internal structure of the city, (2) transportation, (3) physical factors, (4) intensity of competition, and (5) governmental policies.

QUESTIONS FOR STUDY

1. Why is location such an important factor in real estate decisions? In the determination of property income?
2. Explain this statement: "An urban property may be thought of as a share in the local economy or city and also as a share in a specific area or sector of the city."
3. List the urban trends that seem most likely to affect the future structure of land uses. Which of these now has a major influence in your city?
4. Explain the changes in the character of the competition between land uses in recent years.
5. Which social and cultural trends may be expected to affect the pattern of land uses in the future? Which government and political factors? Which of these do you consider most important and why?
6. Explain the concentric circle theory of city structure set forth by Burgess.
7. Explain Hoyt's sector theory. How may it help to anticipate changes in land uses?
8. What are time interval maps? Explain their use.
9. Describe the principal forces causing changes in residential neighborhoods.
10. Make a list of the principal factors now affecting the neighborhood in which you live.
11. How do population movements affect the future of a neighborhood? In analyzing a neighborhood, which population factors would you consider most important?

12. How important is the availability of transportation for the future of a neighborhood? A shopping center? An industrial district?
13. What are the main forces that influence commercial and industrial locations?
14. As an investor, would you prefer to invest in industrial or commercial property? Explain.

SUGGESTED READINGS

American Institute of Real Estate Appraisers. *The Appraisal of Real Estate* (6th ed.). Chicago: The Institute, 1973.

Hoyt, Homer. *According to Hoyt* (2nd ed.). Washington, D. C.: Hoyt, 1970. Pp. 269–96, 587–621.

Johnson, R. J. *Urban Residential Patterns: An Introductory Review.* New York: Praeger Publications, Inc., 1971. Ch. 8.

Muller, Peter O. *The Outer City.* Washington, D. C.: Association of American Geographers, 1976.

Samuelson, Paul A. *Economics* (10th ed). New York: McGraw-Hill Book Co., 1976. Ch. 37.

Wendt, Paul F. *Real Estate Appraisal: Review and Outlook.* Athens: University of Georgia Press, 1974. Ch. 4.

CASE 8–1

A Neighborhood Decision

George Edwards has just moved to your city and has called several real estate brokers to help him find a house. He is in a hurry to make a purchase because he is scheduled for an overseas assignment which will take two or three months and he wants to get his family settled before leaving the country.

One real estate broker calls his attention to a 15-year-old house located in one of the older neighborhoods of the city. It has been on the market for several months. The neighborhood continues to be an attractive area despite its age. The properties are well maintained. Insofar as Mr. Edwards can determine, the people in the area are the kind with whom he and the members of his family would feel comfortable. Schools, churches, and shopping centers are readily accessible. There is a heavy traffic artery two blocks from the house which must be crossed to reach the school and the shopping center.

Taxes have been advanced in recent years and are now considered to be among the highest for any neighborhood in the city. A bus line is available at the high-speed traffic artery and the area is about a twenty-five-minute bus ride from downtown. The broker reports that fire and police protection are adequate. The area is zoned R-3 which means that multifamily buildings could be constructed. However, most of the land area is now used by single-family residences with a few doubles and it would be necessary to tear down older houses to make way for apartments.

The second property suggested by another broker, is less than a year old and located in a new neighborhood. It is approximately the same size, but has a three-car garage in contrast to a two-car garage for the older property. The development in which the newer property is located is fairly new and is only about a third built up at this time. The property has come on the market within the past week because the owner was transferred to another location. Mr. Edwards is assured that the limited extent to which the area is built up does not constitute a hazard. It is zoned R-1 which means single-family residential use only. The oldest house in the area is now about two years old so it is not possible to determine how stable the area will be. Most of those living there now are newcomers to the city.

A school is located about a mile away. There is no public transportation. Tax rates are relatively low since the area is located outside the city limits. No city police or fire protection are provided. The county sheriff and his staff are believed able to provide whatever protection may be needed. The city fire department will service the area but a special fee is charged. The property is accessible to city water, but not sanitary sewer.

The first property is priced at $47,500 and the broker believes an offer of $45,000 will buy it. The second is priced at $45,000 and there seems little likelihood of an adjustment since it has just come on the market.

Questions

1. Which property should Mr. Edwards buy? Justify your selection.
2. Which basic factors would you change in order to reach the opposite decision? Explain.

CASE 8–2

Lacey's Department Store

Lacey's department store had served the town of Edgewater for 75 years when Mr. Morgan, the company president, decided it was time to consider opening a second store in town. Edgewater had grown to a size of 125,000 and suburban shopping areas had begun to develop. Morgan was afraid that competition from these areas would draw business and profits away from downtown. He wanted to protect the profitability of the Lacey Company.

Last month, Morgan was approached by the agent of a real estate developer who was developing a large enclosed mall shopping center on the south side of town. It would be spectacular, he said, containing 40 stores, including Sears Roebuck and several other national tenants. It would be built at the intersection of two major highways, one of which was an interstate. Therefore, it would be of easy access to small towns in the Edgewater retail trading area. The agent said that he wanted Lacey's because it was a good department store and because of its fine local reputation.

Mr. Morgan also knew of an existing smaller shopping center on the north side of town that had expansion room that would be large enough for a department store. It was located well within the city at the intersection of two principal streets. There was also the possibility of locating a free standing store at a number of locations throughout the metropolitan area. One possibility would be on the west side where most of the higher-priced homes were located.

In the course of his investigation, Mr. Morgan accumulated the following information about the location possibilities. He realized that selecting the right location would be crucial to the success of his business.

South Side. The south side of town is largely industrial, but some housing has been developed outside the city limits. All the public housing in town is near the mall site. The location at the intersection of the highways is a definite advantage as far as rural shoppers are concerned, but it is not known how many residents from the north side will drive all the way through town to the mall. It is significant that Sears will be in the shopping area. The rent for Lacey's would be $120,000 per year plus 4 per cent of annual gross sales over $3,000,000.

North Side. The north side site is located at a major intersection and is convenient to a large number of townspeople. In a smaller shopping center, there will not be competition from as many other stores. Mr. Morgan thinks he can have a building built and rent it from the owner for a flat rate of 4 per cent of gross annual sales.

West Side. The site Mr. Morgan has in mind on the west side is also at the intersection of two principal streets. It is closer to the center of town than either of the other sides, but is nowhere near a highway. He figures the rent on a new free standing store there would run about $80,000 per year. One disadvantage is that there would be no other stores in the immediate area to help draw traffic.

Questions

1. What advantages and disadvantages of each location can be inferred from the information given?
2. At what level of annual gross sales would the rent on the south and west side stores equal 4 per cent of the gross?
3. At which site do you think Lacey's could do the greatest business? Why?
4. If you were in Mr. Morgan's place, what would your decision be?

9

APPRAISALS:
THE INCOME APPROACH*

APPRAISALS AND THE APPRAISAL PROCESS

In this chapter and the following one we will consider appraisals. Valuations or appraisals are important aids to real estate decisions. They provide one of the major bases for reaching real estate decisions and for developing programs of action for implementing such decisions. Thus, valuations are not usually ends in themselves. Appraisers do not make decisions. They provide information and forecasts which may aid business executives, government officials, or individuals in arriving at better conclusions and decisions than might otherwise be possible. For example, if a mortgage lender asks an appraiser to estimate the value of a property for mortgage lending purposes, it is not the function of the appraiser to decide on the merit of the specific mortgage arrangement that the lender has under consideration. The appraiser provides the lender with an estimate of the property's value. The lender decides whether to lend and if so, how much, for how long, and at what rates. An appraiser may help a seller to decide how much to ask for a piece of property or a buyer to decide how much to offer, but the appraiser does not make the final decisions.

Appraisal Process

The orderly procedure developed by professional real estate appraisers to help make reliable valuations is known as the "appraisal process."[1] The

---

* We are indebted to Jack K. Mann, MAI, of Jackson, Miss., for reviewing this chapter.

[1] *Real Estate Appraisal Terminology*, compiled and edited by Byrl N. Boyce, published by The American Institute of Real Estate Appraisers and the Society of Real Estate Appraisers (Cambridge, Mass.: Ballinger Publishing Co., 1975).

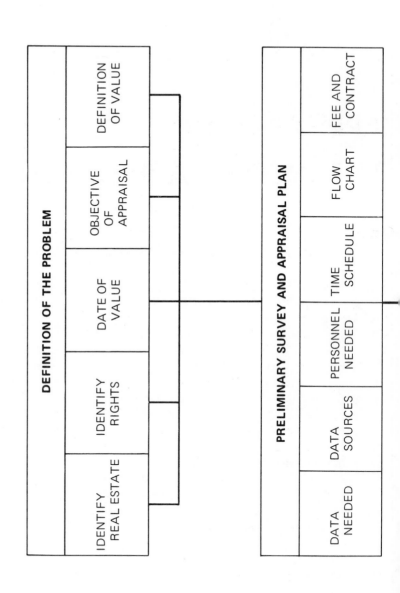

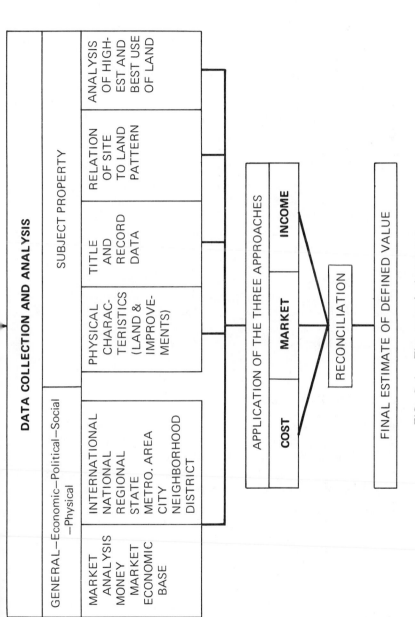

FIG. 9–1. The appraisal process.

appraisal process as presented by the American Institute of Real Estate Appraisers (AIREA) is outlined in Figure 9–1.

According to the Institute the appraisal process includes five major steps. The first is the definition of the problem with the physical characteristics of the land and buildings identified as well as the property rights pertaining to them, the date of the valuation, the manner in which the report is to be used, and the type of value to be appraised. The most common type of value is "market value" although many other kinds of value may be used depending on the appraisal problem to be solved.

The second step involves a preliminary survey and development of an appraisal plan.

The third step is the process of data collection and analysis. Information about the real estate is often divided into two main categories: (1) data which relate to location and market conditions; and (2) data related more specifically to the real estate being appraised.

Having collected and analyzed the available and pertinent data, the cost, market data, and/or income approaches are undertaken as the fourth step.

The final step in the process, according to the Institute, involves reconciliation (also referred to as correlation) of the results in arriving at a final estimate of the property's value as defined. After the completion of the appraisal process, the appraiser prepares a report, usually written, in either a narrative form or on a specified or standardized form that serves as the basis for the report.

Definition of Valuation Problems

The objective which an appraisal is intended to serve—the purpose for which it is made—is of basic importance, not only in defining value, but also in defining valuation problems. Other conditions that are of importance in defining valuation problems include *time*, the identification of the specific *property rights,* and the major physical and economic factors involved.

In general, however, the objective of the appraiser may be thought of as that of estimating the present market value of the income potential of a given property. Specific situations, however, may require that the appraiser estimate the price that may be obtained in a quick sale; the price that a prospective buyer should offer for the property or a partial interest in a property; and the value of the property for insurance purposes, for mortgage lending purposes, for damages suffered under condemnation proceedings, or for the solution of many other business or personal problems. Thus, definition of the specific valuation problem to be solved is an essential first step in the process of making an appraisal of the rights to a piece of real estate, recognizing that most appraisals are "market value" appraisals.

Classes of Transactions

Real estate transactions may be classified in many ways, but the following classification indicates the nature of the appraisal problem that is involved:

1. Transfer of ownership:
   a. Sale
   b. Purchase
   c. Trade
2. Extension of credit secured by real estate
3. Compensation for damage or loss:
   a. Through condemnation
   b. For damage compensable under property insurance contract
4. Taxation:
   a. Assessment for property tax
   b. Basis for depreciation allowance
   c. Basis for inheritance tax
5. Selection of a program of utilization [2]

Physical Real Estate

Another aspect to consider in defining the problem to be solved is the physical characteristics of the real estate. In the discussion of physical elements—land and improvements—in Chapter 2, it was emphasized that the physical elements are merely the "machine" for providing property services such as shelter, privacy, protection, and the like. Sometimes there is a tendency to overemphasize the importance of the physical property. It is tangible, as contrasted with the intangible legal and economic characteristics of the property. But it is essential to know and consider in the decision-making process the major physical characteristics of the property as outlined in Chapter 2.

Specific Property Rights

The definition of the problem includes an identification of the specific property rights involved. As we indicated in Chapter 3, a wide variety of interests may exist in the same piece of real estate. Usually the appraiser estimates the value of specified property rights rather than the value of the physical land and buildings. The physical property must, of course, be identified, but the "rights" to the use of the physical property are of much more concern. The appraiser may be called upon to estimate the reversionary right in a leased fee, the value to a tenant of a lease, the air

[2] Richard U. Ratcliff, "A Restatement of Appraisal Theory," *The Appraisal Journal* (January, 1964). See also in *The Appraisal Journal:* Richard U. Ratcliff and Bernhard Schwab, "Contemporary Decision Theory and Real Estate Investment" (April, 1970), and Richard U. Ratcliff, "Appraisal Is Market Analysis" (October, 1975).

rights over a piece of land, the value of an easement, and many other types of interests. The American Institute of Real Estate Appraisers points out:

Because the value of real property is not limited to the physical land and the improvements, the appraiser cannot define the problem precisely until he knows exactly what property rights are involved. Without this information his work may produce an estimate of value which is irrelevant to the problem.[3]

Date of Valuation

The date of the valuation is another important element in defining appraisal problems. In some cases the appraisal requires that a value estimate be made as of some specified date in the past, rather than in terms of the current date. Such situations often arise in the case of tax problems or valuation for the purpose of settling estates. It may be necessary to estimate value as of some future date as well.

Location and Market Factors

The major location and market characteristics of a property should be identified in defining the appraisal problem to help guide the analysis of data. Such factors as the following are important: relationships of the property to the surroundings; its relative position as a share in its neighborhood, district, and local economy; its potential economic life; the character of the income it will produce; the cost of producing this income; and related factors.

It may be helpful at this point to review several of the economic concepts which help to explain real estate value, in order to relate them to specific valuation problems:

1. Income is the fundamental fact of life.
2. Like other areas of business, real estate is concerned with income but more specifically with income produced at a fixed site.
3. Income production potentials can be translated into present values by the discounting process. Thus, the value of a real property may be defined basically as the present worth of the future income it may be expected to produce.
4. Future income may be derived from the direct use of a property or from monetary returns it may produce.
5. Estimates of the income that a property may produce require an analysis of:
   a. Governmental and economic trends.
   b. Regional and local economic trends.
   c. The property's real estate market.
   d. The property's location.
   e. The economic characteristics of the property itself.

[3] *The Appraisal of Real Estate* (6th ed.; Chicago: American Institute of Real Estate Appraisers, 1973), p. 53.

We have discussed each of these topics in the preceding chapters in this second part of the book. This chapter and the following one conclude that series of discussions. They draw on the background of these discussions of various types of analyses for real estate decisions.

The Three Approaches

Professional appraisers have developed three principal (or "classic") approaches to valuation problems:

1. Cost Approach
2. Market Data Approach
3. Income Approach

As we have suggested, the income approach fits best the logic of valuation theory, since all property value is derived from future income, whether such income is in the form of monetary returns or results from the direct use of the property. (The latter are sometimes called *amenity returns* in connection with residential property.) In many cases, however, there are practical difficulties in using the capitalized income method. For example, if you have occupied your own home for a number of years, it may be easier to make an appraisal by the *market data approach* than by capitalizing an estimated future income stream. Again, the appraisal of a public building requires almost inevitably the use of the *cost approach,* since neither income estimates nor comparable sales prices are likely to be available. In many cases (except for single-family owner-occupied homes) all three approaches are used in order that one result may be compared with another.

Regardless of the method used, however, the appraiser must always consider the objective of the appraisal, the property interest represented, the physical real estate and its economic or value characteristics, and the time at which the appraisal is to apply. In almost all cases the appraiser will find it essential to think in terms of the income-producing ability of a property even though the market data or cost approach is used. Obviously, the costs of developing a site and constructing a building would not ordinarily be undertaken unless anticipated monetary or direct returns were expected to exceed such costs. Similarly, prices, rents, and other pertinent market data reflect more or less accurately the market's estimate of the future income-producing capacity of properties.

Selection of Method

Three principal factors will guide an appraiser in the selection of the appraising methods to be used for a specific case. Much will depend on (1) the purpose of the valuation, (2) the type of income produced by the property or assumed to be produced under the use program that is projected, and (3) the kinds of data available for use.

In some cases the appraisal problem is stated in terms which specify the method to be followed. For example, an appraiser may be asked to estimate the present value of a lease, which clearly indicates the use of the income method, or to report the price which could be obtained for a property in a quick sale, which would require the use of the market method.

As we have indicated above, the availability of data sometimes dictates the choice of appraisal method. While decisions based on the availability of information may not always be logical, there are times when the appraiser has no alternative. Cases such as a public library, a government building, a hospital, a school, a grain elevator, an unused factory building, or a museum are likely to present data problems.

Method and Income

If the method is not defined, consideration is given to the type of income produced or assumed to be produced by the property. As has been suggested, two principal kinds of returns may be considered: (1) dollars, and (2) direct returns resulting from the use of the property by the owner. Babcock has pointed out how type of income may aid in selection of method.[4] If income is in dollars, it may be derived from several sources, the two main types being commercial rents and business profits.

Business Profits

If the property earns commercial rents, the income method is indicated; shopping centers are an example. If business profits are involved, they may be due entirely to the real estate or partly to the real estate and partly to the business enterprise. If profits are all due to real estate, the income method is preferred. To the extent that returns to the real estate and the business enterprise can be distinguished, the income method is considered preferable. However, if the returns on real estate cannot be distinguished from other returns, as in the case of a foundry or a railroad terminal, the cost method is generally used.

Direct Use

If returns are in the form of direct use of the property, the income method may be used if such returns can be translated rather accurately into dollars. If, on the other hand, returns from direct use cannot be translated into dollars, the selection of methods hinges on the extent to which market data are available. If there are sufficient market evidences

---

[4] Frederick M. Babcock, *The Valuation of Real Estate* (New York: McGraw-Hill Book Co., 1932), p. 184.

of value, as in the case of comparable properties, the market method would be selected. This is often the case in appraising a single-family owner-occupied residence. However, if there are few or no data available indicating market prices or rents for comparable properties, the cost method is followed of necessity. Typical illustrations of this situation are provided by the problems of appraising a library or a government building.

Method and Type of Property

As we have pointed out, the appraisal method should be adapted to the type of property. For example, in the case of a large department store on a principal corner of an eastern city, the lot and the building were both owned by the store, thus the property and the business were parts of a total unit. The building was suited for only one purpose, that of a department store. The valuation was derived by capitalizing the percentage of sales the department store could afford to pay as rent. On the other hand, in valuing the property on the opposite corner, an obsolete bank building, the valuation was developed by ascertaining the net rentals that could be obtained from stores on that corner and capitalizing these rentals. That is, an assumed use program was set up. The building in this case was regarded as of no value in appraising the best retail corner in the city, because it had to be wrecked to make way for the new stores from which the highest rent could be obtained. This is an illustration of developing a model of the highest and best use of the site for appraisal purposes.

Limitations of Appraising Methods

Acceptance of the concept that value is directly related to the present worth of future income does not mean, as some seem to infer, that all appraisals must be made by the income method. Because of specific objectives as defined in the appraisal assignment, the nature of the income, or the absence or inadequacy of data, it may be impossible in many practical situations to use the income method. This does not alter the basic nature of the appraiser's task. Regardless of the method used, the appraisal is an attempt to estimate the value of the earning expectancy. Most real estate decisions will be related to earnings but important modifying factors may be present.

It is often necessary to use sales prices of comparable properties as the basis of valuations and decisions since data may not be available on which estimates of the size or duration of a future income stream can be made. Sales prices of comparable properties, however, indicate what buyers and sellers in the current market believe the present value of that income stream to be.

Construction and development costs are important elements in the valuation of real properties and in decisions regarding them. They enter directly into the valuations of new properties and indirectly into value estimates of older properties. The owner of a vacant urban site can only secure a stream of income from the land, except in the case of parking lots or similar uses, by constructing a building and other improvements on it. If the building is constructed in an area where there is no demand for its services, or the demand is very limited, or operating costs are too high for the income produced, then the land may have a zero or even a negative income.

Properties located in declining areas present special problems because of the difficulty of estimating rate of decline, possibility of renewal efforts, and other uncertainties. Market prices of comparable properties often are helpful in the valuations of such properties since they reflect the opinions of buyers and sellers in regard to such uncertainties.

Investment Preferences, Cash Flow, and Depreciation

A typical appraisal may not in a specific situation reflect the special interests of an investor. For example, an investor may have little interest in the market value of a property but may be especially concerned with the cash flow that it may generate. Or it may be that an investor has a greater concern with the depreciation allowances that a property may generate. In some cases investors will instruct an appraiser as to their specific interests, in others they will look to cash flow and depreciation types of analyses as by-products of appraisals undertaken for other purposes.

RECONCILIATION OF RESULTS

After the appraisal problem has been clearly defined and the data collected and analyzed, the appraiser arrives at an estimate of value. In this process the appraiser will try to be as objective and as careful as possible in evaluating the information available.

Factors Influencing the Judgment of Appraisers

Although the making of value estimates should be an objective process, there is little doubt that appraisers frequently are influenced by the state of the real estate market at the time an appraisal is made and by popular opinions. During periods of prosperity, when the real estate market is very active and the income from real estate is high, appraisers may tend to project this favorable income situation far into the future. On the other hand, during periods of extreme depression, when the volume of sales is limited and the return on real estate is low, appraisers may forecast a continuation of this low-income condition for a long period of time.

Similarly, prevailing opinions regarding the character of certain neighborhoods or sections of the city or the popularity of one or another type of property may influence the judgment of appraisers. For example, appraisers may continue to predict an optimistic future for fashionable residential neighborhoods for some time after such areas have started to decline. Certain types of commercial property (for example, some downtown stores) which have had a long record of past success often are expected to continue to maintain such a record even though forces are in operation which will tend to limit their future earning power.

Competent appraisers try to avoid pitfalls of this type. They try to study objectively all of the factors which will affect the future income-producing power of the properties which they appraise. Other appraisers, however, do little more than rationalize the popular beliefs prevailing in the real estate market.

The Use of Data

The best protection for an appraiser against current market psychology is the use of factual information. As we have indicated above, many appraisers follow the practice of collecting voluminous files of data for use as an appraisal tool. However, appraisals are not the product of such data; they are the result of the appraiser's judgment. The data available are of importance because they help in formulating sound judgments. They supplement rather than supplant the judgment of the appraiser.

In order to use data, an appraiser or other analyst must understand the basic processes of collecting, classifying, and analyzing them. A considerable portion of appraisal data is statistical in nature, and its use is governed by sound statistical practice.

General Rules for Using Data. Such general rules as the following apply to the use of data:

1. *Isolated facts* are relatively useless. The facts used should have a direct bearing on the appraisal.
2. Observations must be sufficiently *numerous* to be representative.
3. The items of information collected must conform to *accuracy standards;* for example, *errors* should tend to cancel out rather than to be cumulative.
4. The sample collected must be *characteristic* of the area or problem or of the "universe," to use statistical terminology.
5. The data must be *classified* or *arranged* systematically, the basis of the classification varying with the purpose involved.
6. Analysis is carried on for the purpose of determining points of *similarity and difference* between items and classes or groups.

Too frequently, appraisers overemphasize one item of information and fail to put it into a proper relationship with other data. In many cases too few are collected; conclusions may then be based on information which is not typical. During a boom period nearly all information may be weighted in the same direction and reflect the immediate market situation and immediate future expectations only, rather than long-range trends.

Basically, the use of data means borrowing from the experience of others. The complexities of real estate value problems are so great that few people can carry enough information around in their heads to solve them. Programs of data collection, assembly, and analysis are growing in importance in the field of real estate valuation, aided by the expanding use of the computer and the calculator.

Although theoretical concepts have not changed a great deal, except for some refinements, more elaborate sets of relationships can now be developed in a practical manner through the use of the computer. It should be recognized also that major changes have occurred that complicate the application of various value theories and principles. For example, the old depth and corner influence concepts have little or no applicability for the modern regional shopping center. Recognition must be given to the increasing importance of governmental influences, ranging all the way from farm price supports, transportation developments, and zoning laws to general federal programs for the maintenance of long-term prosperity.

THE INCOME APPROACH

The capitalization of anticipated net incomes requires that estimates of revenues and expenses be made and that the estimated net income before depreciation be capitalized at an appropriate rate. While the procedures of appraisers vary somewhat, the three main steps usually involved in the process are these:

First, gross income is estimated by computing the total possible income at 100 per cent occupancy of the building and deducting for vacancies and collection losses.

In the second step, expenses are estimated, including allowances for replacement of certain items of equipment and parts of the building which must be replaced because of physical deterioration.

The third step in the use of the income method is capitalizing the net income (deducting estimated expenses from gross effective earnings) by applying the appropriate capitalization rate or rates. This phase of the process is not simple, even when net income is capitalized in perpetuity. The selection of an appropriate capitalization rate usually means the difference between a sound and an unsound decision. Even more complicated problems arise with the application of one of the residual techniques in which one rate is used for the income attributed to the land and another for the income assigned to the building. A more complete explanation of these techniques follows.

Application of the Income Approach

The practical difficulties in applying the principle of capitalizing income to actual real estate valuations and related decision problems in the business world are numerous. For example, it has been said by those who are critical of the income approach to valuation problems that the application of the present value concept involves dividing one unknown (the estimated future annual net income) by another unknown (the capitalization rate) to arrive at a third unknown (value).

Thus, if we assume that the annual net income of a particular piece of real property is $1,000 and that the rate necessary to attract investment into properties of this type is 10 per cent, by dividing $\dfrac{\$1,000.00}{.10}$ we find that the estimated value of this property on the basis of capitalizing its anticipated income at a 10 per cent rate is $10,000. (In this case income is capitalized in perpetuity; that is, $10,000 now is equal to $1,000 per year forever in terms of a 10 per cent capitalization rate.)

Although it is true that anticipated future incomes can never be known exactly, buyers, sellers, investors, developers, mortgage lenders, appraisers, and others concerned with valuation problems must make the best estimates possible of the future net income that a property can produce, for how long, and at what risk (probability that it will be earned). Similarly, while the capitalization rate that will exactly reflect future earnings in present value is unknown, an estimated rate can and must be applied. This process is little different from those which are followed in arriving at many other types of business decisions. For example, when a new product is available to a manufacturer, its income-producing ability and the risks involved are estimated, and the risks are discounted to the extent that is believed appropriate. On the basis of these estimates the manufacturer decides to produce and market the new product or to pass it by.

Capital Investment Decisions

Many business decisions involve similar types of postulates and analyses, notably capital investment decisions. As has been pointed out:

The situation in which a manager is working will tend to indicate the factors to which he or she gives greatest weight in arriving at capital investment decisions. For example, the manager may stress the period of pay-back. It may be important to recapture the investment at an early period. Or he or she may stress returns per dollar of outlay, without respect to the timing of the return. The manager may emphasize average annual proceeds per dollar of outlay (that is, giving consideration to the number of years and averaging the return per year). The manager may estimate average income on book value of the investment; that is, after depreciation has been charged against the investment. The method considered highly desirable by many managers is the discounted cash flow method, that is computing the present value of the earnings that will be secured over a period of time.[5]

Estimating Income—The First Step

Income estimates are based on the earnings record of the property as well as that of comparable properties, with proper allowances being made for probable future developments. That is, past earnings may be used as an indication of future earnings only if there is reason to believe that the future will be like the past with respect to the subject property. Past income is only a part of the data to be considered by the appraiser. That is why it is important to consider general economic trends, governmental and location factors, and local market trends, as well as the specific property being appraised. The difficulties of estimating the future income production of a property are emphasized by a review of urban real estate investment experience. Usually there have been rather wide variations in gross income and even wider variations in net income over a period of years. Estimates of income potential made during periods of prosperity tend to be unduly optimistic. Those made in periods of economic recession tend toward the conservative side.

In the process of projecting the rental schedule of the property being appraised, the appraiser looks at two kinds of rents—contract and economic. Contract rents are those which prevail because of a lease or other kind of contract and cannot, therefore, be adjusted. On the other hand, economic rents are those representative of the market based on the exposure of the property on the open rental market. The selection of competitive rents depends on the going rates of similar or comparable properties. For example, if two-bedroom apartments containing 700 square feet are renting in the market for $200 a month, the appraiser's conclusion should be that a similar apartment which is being appraised should rent for $200 a month, assuming everything else is comparable. Thus the economic rent is $200 a month. If the rents being collected by management are lower, then contract rent is less than economic rent.

Need for Careful Estimates. Since the anticipated future income is the most vital element in valuation, the appraiser should make a careful survey to determine probable future incomes. If an apartment property is being appraised, the appraiser should obtain prevailing rents in a number of comparable properties, ascertain the number of vacancies, and study location and market trends for the purpose of determining whether the

---

[5] Arthur M. Weimer, David Bowen, and John D. Long, *Introduction to Business: A Management Approach* (5th ed.; Homewood, Ill.: Richard D. Irwin, Inc., 1974), pp. 387–88. See also Richard U. Ratcliff, *Modern Real Estate Valuation* (Madison, Wis.: The Democrat Press, 1965), pp. 56–57, and Richard U. Ratcliff and Bernhard Schwab, Study Project 17–1, p. 500.

prevailing rents are likely to continue. The appraiser should determine also what would be a reasonable estimate of vacancy rate and collection loss.

In the appraisal of commercial properties, the appraiser should secure information about rentals on recent leases of comparable properties. Where properties are leased for long terms on net leases to responsible firms, the problems of estimating future income are much less difficult.

Estimating Expenses—The Second Step

In appraising, expenses are defined as all annual outlays involved in the ownership and operation of a property during the remaining economic life of the building except mortgage payment, allowances for depreciation, and federal income taxes.

Note that the personal income taxes of the owner are not chargeable to the building and that payments on the mortgage are not operating expenses. If either were included, it is obvious that a comparable property without a mortgage owned by a person in the 20 per cent tax bracket would have a higher value than one with a mortgage owned by a person in the 50 per cent tax bracket, yet both properties might bring the same amount in the open market.

Professional appraisers use three principal classes of expenses:

1. *Fixed Expenses.* The category of fixed expenses usually includes real estate taxes and property insurance. There may be other types of expenses which are not affected by the operation of the facility. Both taxes and insurance premiums generally are outside the control of even good management, whereas expenditures known as operating expenses may depend heavily on the efficiency of management and the type of tenants. Real estate taxes and other assessments are calculated on the basis of current rates and those which are likely to develop within the next year. Special assessments are frequently charged against properties for special services and must be included. Property insurance includes fire and extended coverage, liability, plate glass, elevator, rental loss, and other types which good management would include in the operation of a facility.

2. *Operating Expenses.* Operating expenses include all the cash expenditures in the actual operation of the facility such as utilities (electricity, gas, water, etc.), repairs and maintenance, supplies, wages and salaries, and a representative management fee for the management of the property. Note that no replacement or capital expenditure is included in this category. Maintenance includes the patching or repair of a roof in order to continue the operation of the facility. Painting and minor repairs are also included in maintenance.

3. *Replacements.* Replacements include those expenditures for major parts of the building which wear out or become obsolete and must be replaced in order to maintain the operation of the building. The replacement

of a roof is illustrative of this type of expenditure. Inasmuch as these expenditures are not usually annual, it is necessary to amortize or "to spread over a number of years" these particular items. For example, a furnace is considered to have a 20-year life and so the cost to replace a furnace is divided by the number of years of its expected life. Capital expenditures are defined as those which alter the structure, changing its use or remaining economic life.

Accuracy of Records. In estimating operating expenses, appraisers should be careful to determine the accuracy of the records placed at their disposal. It is usually advisable to compare figures for several similar properties or to consult the officials of real estate management firms who are usually intimately acquainted with operating expenses. In addition, care must be taken to include only annual charges; insurance, for example, is often paid for three-year periods and a division is necessary to reflect annual expenses. Such charges as special assessments may have only a definite number of years to run, and this must be reflected in future expense estimates.

As is the case with income records, the past experiences reported by records of operating expenses are supporting data only. They help to make possible estimates of future expenses, but past experience can be projected only when it appears that the future will resemble the past sufficiently to justify such a procedure. In estimating future operating expenses, allowances must be made for increased or decreased wages of building maintenance workers, higher real estate taxes, higher insurance costs, and higher or lower material costs for repairs whenever such increases or decreases appear probable. Also, the condition of the structure should be considered since this may affect operating costs.

Net Income

The ultimate objective of gross income and expense estimates is to produce a representative annual net income figure. Net income for appraising purposes may be quite different from that used by accountants, by the Internal Revenue Service, or by investors. It is referred to as Effective Net Income or Net Income Before Recapture and is the amount which is capitalized into a value figure.

Capitalization

As we have pointed out, the value of a property may be considered as equivalent to the present worth of anticipated future incomes. We have considered briefly some of the items which have a bearing on the income-producing capacity of real properties and on the expenses of producing such income.

In order to capitalize net income it is necessary to establish a rate which will reflect the risk involved in the particular investment being considered.

This rate should reflect the market for all types of investment. An analysis of the investment market should make possible the development of an appropriate rate for the property being appraised.

The Capitalization Rate. The "cap" rate is that rate used to convert a net income figure into a capital value figure. The accompanying illustration of the capitalization process is a very basic and simple one. Usually it is necessary to employ a more detailed technique than that of "capitalization in perpetuity."

Land earns returns in perpetuity; buildings and other improvements wear out sooner or later, and therefore, as with any investment which has a finite life, the investor wants a *return on* the investment as well as the *recapture of* the original capital over the period of the economic life of the depreciable asset. Thus, the capitalization rate for a building is composed of two components: the risk rate (representing the *return on* the investment) plus the recapture rate (representing the amortization each year of the original capital invested in the building).

The amortization of the investment in the building may be compared to an oil well or a gravel pit, which will be used up over a period of time. This is known as depletion. In real estate, we use the term "depreciation" since the asset can to some degree be renewed. In both cases investors recognize that they are investing in assets that are being used up at varying rates.

Capitalization Illustration. Assume that an investor owns vacant land which is leased at $12,000 per year net for 99 years. Such an investment may be relatively low in risk and the investor may be satisfied with a 6 per cent return. The conversion of $12,000 in perpetuity at 6 per cent produces a value figure of $200,000 ($12,000 ÷ .06 = $200,000). Since land is not a depreciating asset there is no need for the investor, as a form of self-protection, to "load" the "cap" rate with a percentage for recapture.

Now let us consider the value of an investment from the standpoint of entrepreneurs who leased the land described above in order to construct a building on it. Their primary investment is in the building since they do not own the land. Assume that the annual net income produced by the building after paying all expenses (including the lease on the ground) is $60,000. If an 8 per cent rate will be required to attract the investors into this type of investment and if the building will wear out (economically or physically or both) in 25 years, the investment in the building will have to be recaptured in that time, hence a 4 per cent rate per year will be used for this purpose (100% ÷ 25 yr. = 4%).

The appropriate capitalization rate for this building then is:

Risk rate	8%
Recapture rate	4
Capitalization rate	12%

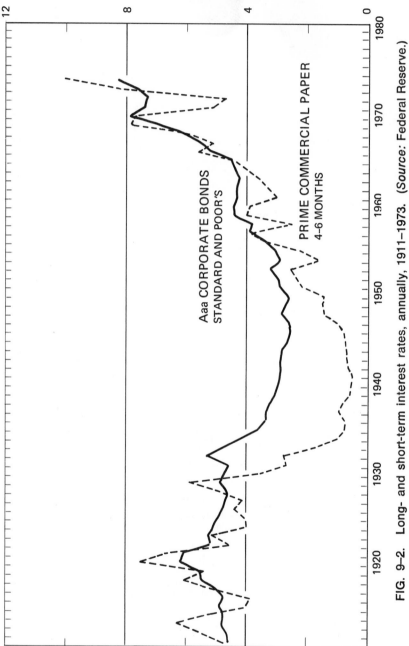

FIG. 9-2. Long- and short-term interest rates, annually, 1911–1973. (*Source:* Federal Reserve.)

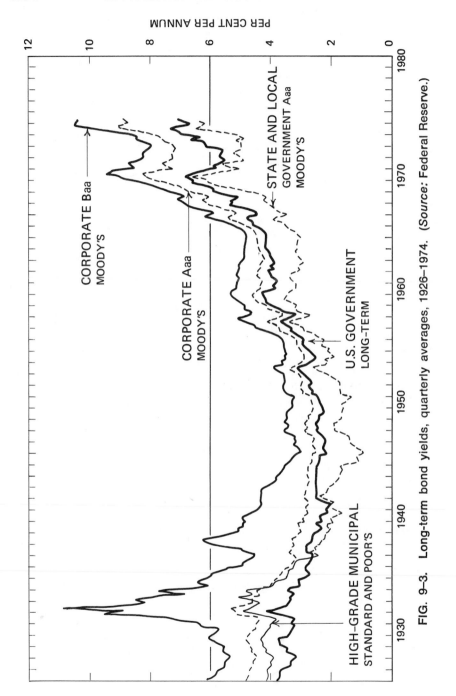

FIG. 9-3. Long-term bond yields, quarterly averages, 1926–1974. (*Source:* Federal Reserve.)

The capitalization process then involves dividing $60,000 by 12 per cent ($60,000 ÷ .12 = $500,000), indicating a value of $500,000.

Selection of Rate. The rate of interest is not the capitalization rate. Theoretically, the term *interest* is used to designate a *return* on capital, and may be composed of two parts: a riskless rate and the rate for risks assumed. Pure interest is riskless interest. The return on government bonds is the closest approximation to riskless interest which can be cited. Such rates vary from time to time. (See Figs. 9–2 and 9–3.) To this basic interest rate we must add an allowance for various risks in arriving at a total risk rate. Such additional risks will vary from property to property.

Incomes from properties with prospects for stable, continued returns merit low rates; those with great risks, higher rates. Such factors as marketability of the property, changes in business conditions, interest rate risk, purchasing power risk, investment preferences, and the like are important risk elements. Also, in some cases allowances are made in the development of the rate for the management of the investment.

It is obvious that a difference of 1 per cent in the capitalization rate will have a major effect on the value estimate. For example, if an investment is expected to earn a net return of $5,000 per year and is capitalized in perpetuity at 10 per cent, the resulting value estimate is $50,000. However, if it is capitalized at 9 per cent, the result leads to the higher estimate of $55,555. At 15 per cent the value estimate declines to $33,333.

Investor Opinions. How is an appraiser to know which capitalization rate to select? In most cases a rate is selected which reflects the opinions of investors at the time. This rate should indicate how much investors expect to receive as a return if capital is advanced on one or another type of property or how much more or less they expect if capital is invested in real estate as against alternative types of investment. In a sense the selection of a capitalization rate is based on an estimate of the opinions of real estate investors. Financial institutions as well as investors themselves provide data of this type for the use of the appraiser. The final selection of a rate will be an estimate, of course. However, it should be an estimate based on the most reliable information available to the appraiser.

Summation Method. Sometimes appraisers use a summation method in developing risk rates. For example, they may begin with as near a riskless rate as possible, such as the return on government bonds. To this may be added an allowance for risk, an allowance for lack of liquidity of real estate investments, and an allowance for the difficulty of managing the investment. Thus, to a return of 6 per cent on government bonds might be added 2 per cent for risk, 1½ per cent for non-liquidity, and 1 per cent for management—or a total rate of 10½ per cent.

Band of Investment Method. If comparable investments in real estate could be financed with a $40,000 first mortgage of 50 per cent of value at

8 per cent, a $20,000 second mortgage of 25 per cent of value at 10 per cent and if equity investors of the balance of 25 per cent would want 12 per cent, these may be related as follows:

	Amount	Per Cent of Total	Interest Rate	Weighted Average
First mortgage	$40,000	50%	8%	4 %
Second mortgage	20,000	25	10	2½
Equity	20,000	25	12	3
	$80,000	100%		9½%

The weighted average is calculated by multiplying, for the first mortgage, the 8 per cent interest times 50 per cent (.08 × .50 = .04 or 4 per cent), the percentage of the first mortgage to the total financing. This is repeated for the second mortgage and the equity, producing a risk rate for this type of property of 9½ per cent based on the market results and applicable to the property being appraised.

Methods and Techniques of Capitalization

Professional appraisers have developed many complex methods and techniques of applying the capitalization process. For our purpose, however, we will concentrate on two of those most widely used. The first, "direct capitalization," appears to be a very simple process but is, in reality, somewhat complex because of the importance of its component parts. The second, "straight-line capitalization using residual techniques," is more complex and demanding. Both are used by professional appraisers as are Mortgage Equity, Inwood, Investors, Perpetuity, and others.

Direct Method. The "direct method" of capitalization converts the net income projection from the property being appraised into a value by the use of an *over-all rate of capitalization* (known as OAR). The reliability of this method depends heavily on the proper development of OAR, which is taken from the market as reflected in like investment properties. The rate is developed from the relationship of the sales prices and net income of similar properties in the market. For example, if comparable property A recently sold for $200,000 and its net income was $20,000 at the time of the sale, the OAR would be $20,000 ÷ $200,000 = 10 per cent. If other comparable properties ("comps") produced OAR's of 9.8 per cent, 10.3 per cent, 9.9 per cent, 10.1 per cent, and 10 per cent, we might conclude that investors in the market were expecting an "over-all return rate" of approximately 10 per cent.

The direct method of capitalizing net income of the property being appraised is as follows.

Net income of property being appraised	$18,000
Overall rate from the market	10%
Market value ($18,000 ÷ .10)	$180,000

The indicated market value according to this approach is $180,000.

Straight-Line Method of Capitalization. The second method is the "straight-line method employing residual techniques." This method recognizes that the capitalization or "cap" rate for land may be different than for buildings. This method requires the development of a risk rate. Also, the appraiser must estimate the remaining economic life (REL) of the building as a basis for the recapture rate.

More difficult problems are encountered in appraising investments composed of combinations of land and buildings and perhaps other improvements. A property is a single income-producing unit, of course, but it is possible to make estimates of the proportion of the income which may be allocated to land on the one hand and to buildings and other improvements on the other.

Building Residual Technique. Assume that a small apartment house on a 100-foot lot earns a net return of $5,000 per year. If land in this area has been selling for $100 per front foot, one may estimate (by the market method) that the lot has a value of around $10,000 (100 feet × $100). If investors are expecting a return of 8 per cent on improved land ($10,000 × .08 = $800), then $800 of the earnings may be attributed to the land and the remainder to the building. The remaining $4,200 may be capitalized at a rate which will reflect recapture of the investment over the remaining economic life of the building plus the investors' expectations of earnings from such properties. If the remaining economic life of the building is predicted at 25 years, 4 per cent per year of the value of the building must be recaptured each year. If investors expect to get 8 per cent for the risk they assume on the investment, the capitalization rate for the building may be estimated as follows:

Risk rate	8%
Recapture rate	4
"Cap" rate	12%

The capitalization process then is: Net return for building $4,200 ÷ 12% "cap" rate = $35,000 for the market value of the building.

Land value	$10,000
Building value	35,000
Property value	$45,000

In the building residual approach the residual return is assigned to the building, to use appraisal terminology. The investors demand the same return on the building as on the land (8 per cent is the indicated risk). In addition the investors expect to recapture their investment over a 25-year period, the economic life of the building. The 25-year period calls for 4 per cent per year recapture rate. The capitalization rate is then developed by adding the 8 per cent risk rate to the 4 per cent recapture rate, producing a 12 per cent capitalization rate.

Land Residual. The example above applies more definitely to properties in mid-life or late life than to properties improved with new buildings. When the net income from a property has the characteristics of an annuity, the income must be processed in a different way. For example, an investor builds a commercial facility for a "Triple A" credit rating tenant who leases it on a 20-year term for $60,000 per year. Obviously, this is a comparatively low risk venture and the net income will be in equal annual installments over a 20-year period. The building is new and is the highest and best use of the land. The cost to construct the improvements was $500,000, a figure which has been substantiated as a fair and representative cost. The land, however, is an unusual piece of property with no sales of comparable sites available. In this situation it is reasonable to believe that "cost is value"—that the $500,000 cost figure is equivalent to value. In order to establish an estimate of the value for the land, the "land residual" technique and a "present value of level annuities" table may be used. A risk rate of 9 per cent is estimated for this investment.

Note that when the annuity tables are used only the risk (return on) rate is used; the use of a term of years (20 years in this example) incorporates the recapture (return of) provision.

Net income to the property		$60,000
Building cost (value)	$500,000	
9% for 20 years produces a factor of 9.128 (See Appendix C)		
Share required each year from net income to produce 9% return on investment of $500,000 and recapture that amount in 20 years ($500,000 ÷ 9.128 = $54,776)		
Income attributed to building		54,776
Net residual to land		$ 5,224

Net income of $5,224 to land capitalized in perpetuity at 9 per cent produces a capital value of $58,044. The value of the building, $500,000, plus the value of the land, rounded to $58,000, totals a value for the entire property of $558,000.

Other Methods and Techniques. A major and continuing problem facing the appraiser is the selection of a capitalization rate which will reflect the pattern of net income. Several mathematical models or assumptions may be set up, such as level annual returns to the end of the building's life or declining returns at different rates. Babcock, for example, has established four income premises and has set forth tables reflecting the different types of return under appropriate capitalization rates. Various other tables have been prepared based on different mathematical models or assumptions, including the Hoskold sinking fund and the Inwood tables. Almost any type may be used, if the appraiser understands the assumptions back of the tables and their meaning in the capitalization process.

In the Inwood method the principal is reduced each year by an amount equal to the periodic payment less the interest on the prior unpaid balance. The Hoskold method assumes that the portion of the investment returned each year is reinvested in a sinking fund at a lower rate of return; hence, the outstanding investment is not reduced.[6]

Ellwood Method.   Drawing on his experience as a mortgage loan officer, L. W. Ellwood developed a concept of valuation known as "mortgage equity."[7] This concept, popularly called the Ellwood Method, considers certain factors which may not be specifically recognized in other capitalization methods. Its primary contribution is the explicit recognition that most property is financed by a mortgage. The mortgage is usually repaid with level, periodic payments which include both a reduction of the mortgage principal and a payment of the interest on the remaining principal balance. As time goes by, the level payment includes a proportionately greater reduction of the principal because the unpaid balance declines, and consequently the interest payment thereon is lower. Therefore the value of the equity in the property, which is the difference between the value of the property and the unpaid mortgage balance, increases at an increasing rate over time.

The Ellwood Method recognizes the mortgage factor by taking into consideration both the amount of the mortgage as a percentage of the value of the property and the various terms of the mortgage. For example, if the loan is for a large proportion of the appraised value of the property and the amortization period is relatively long, the Ellwood Method reflects a higher value. In addition the Ellwood Method allows for the inclusion of an estimate of the change—either an appreciation or a depreciation—in the property's value over time. A projected decrease would, for example, result in a higher "cap" rate and thus a smaller present value estimate. Finally, the Ellwood Capitalization Tables include sections applicable to purchase–leaseback problems and to income tax shelters. In general, the mortgage equity concept incorporates in a more specific manner many elements which investors consider in making investment decisions.

SUMMARY

Appraisals or valuations are important guides to real estate decisions. The income approach most nearly fits the theoretical basis of real estate

---

[6] Babcock, *op. cit.*, pp. 534 and 561.
[7] L. W. Ellwood, *Ellwood Tables for Real Estate Appraising and Financing* (2nd ed.; Chicago: American Institute of Real Estate Appraisers, 1967), Chapter 1.

valuation. Its use, however, may be limited by lack of data or the difficulty of translating returns from direct use into monetary returns.

The steps in the capitalization method are: (1) gross income is estimated, (2) an estimate is made of expenses, (3) net income is established, and (4) net income is capitalized into value. The selection of the capitalization rate often presents difficult problems for an appraiser. Various methods may be used for developing the capitalization rate, including summation and band-of-investment methods.

Two widely used methods of capitalization are (1) the "direct method," which uses an overall rate of capitalization and (2) the "straight-line method of capitalization," which uses a residual technique.

Various other methods based on various models of anticipated income patterns may also be used. These include the Hoskold sinking fund and Inwood tables and the Elwood Method.

QUESTIONS FOR STUDY

1. Why is it important to know the purpose of a real estate transaction before making an appraisal? Outline the principal classes of transactions.
2. Define the appraisal process. Illustrate the steps of the appraisal process.
3. How might an appraisal made to estimate an asking price for a quick sale of a property differ from one made to aid in settling an estate? Explain.
4. Assume that your home is assessed for tax purposes at $8,500 and that you have been offered $25,000 for the property. You also know that the local savings and loan association will lend $17,500 on it. Which of these amounts indicates the property's value? Explain.
5. Which appraisal method would you use in appraising your study property? Justify your selection.
6. Which appraisal method would you use in the valuation of the house in which you live? Why is this method better than others?
7. If capitalization of future income is the appraisal method most consistent with the theory of value, why are other methods also used? For what purposes are these other methods applied?
8. Why is the capitalization of future income the approach most consistent with valuation theory? Why are other methods used?
9. How may types of income influence the selection of appraisal method?
10. What difference would it make in selecting a method if the return on the property were in the form of dollar payments or direct use?
11. If returns to a property are in the form of business profits, how may this affect selection of method? Illustrate.
12. List the steps typically followed in the income approach. Discuss and illustrate the principal difficulties in each step.
13. Outline the principal methods used to determine capitalization rates. Which one seems best from your standpoint? Why?
14. Gross income from a small apartment house is estimated at $30,000 and expenses at $18,000. Investors are expecting a 12 per cent return for investments of this type. What would be a value estimate for this property? Explain.

15. Suppose you knew that you could purchase the apartment house in Problem 14 with a 75 per cent mortgage at 8 per cent interest. You also expect the value of the apartment house to decrease by 20 per cent over the next 10 years. Would it be best to estimate the present value of this property using the Ellwood Method? Why or why not?

SUGGESTED READINGS

AMERICAN INSTITUTE OF REAL ESTATE APPRAISERS. *The Appraisal of Real Estate* (6th ed.). Chicago: The Institute, 1973. Chs. 1–4, 14, 15, and 21.

BABCOCK, FREDERICK M. *The Valuation of Real Estate.* New York: McGraw-Hill Book Co., 1932. Chs. 15–18.

ELLWOOD, L. W. *Ellwood Tables for Real Estate Appraising and Financing* (3rd ed.). Ridgewood, N. J.: Published by the author, 1970.

KAHN, SANDERS A., and CASE, FREDERICK E. *Real Estate Appraisal and Investment* (2nd ed.). New York: The Ronald Press Co., 1977. Chs. 2, 3, 6–14.

KINNARD, WILLIAM N., JR. *Industrial Real Estate.* Washington, D. C.: Society of Industrial Realtors, 1967. Ch. 12.

———. *Income Property Valuation.* Lexington, Mass.: Heath Publishing Co., 1971.

RATCLIFF, RICHARD U. *Modern Real Estate Valuation.* Madison, Wis.: The Democrat Press, 1965.

WENDT, PAUL F., and CERT, ALAN R. *Real Estate Investment, Analysis and Taxation.* New York: McGraw-Hill Book Co., 1969. Chs. 1, 2, 10.

WILEY, ROBERT J. *Real Estate Investment—Analysis and Strategy.* New York: The Ronald Press Co., 1977. Ch. 4.

CASE 9–1

An Appraisal and Investment Decision

Samuel Jones would like to buy an income property in his hometown of Centerville, Massachusetts. The two most likely possibilities are apartment projects. Both are being offered for sale by local Realtors® who provided income–expense data.

One, the Cambridge Arms, was built in 1928. Its 100 units are large and rent for $230 per month. When new, they were almost the only apartments of their type in town and were considered luxury apartments. Total operating expenses amount to $100,000 per year, netting about $176,000.

The other possibility, the Park Chateau Apartment Complex, was built in 1965. Geared toward young marrieds, these apartments are not nearly as large and ornate as those in Cambridge Arms. The 120 units rent for an average of $150 per month. Total operating expenses run about $80,000 per year.

Mr. Jones must decide which project offers a better investment opportunity. Park Chateau is very popular with the younger set and even has a waiting list so he feels it has a minimum of risk. Because mortgage rates on apartments are running around 9 per cent, he feels an overall capitalization rate of 12 per cent would be appropriate.

The Cambridge Arms represents a completely different situation. It is filled now, but that may be because there is a shortage of apartments in town. When newer ones are built, he feels that tenants will be drawn from the oldest existing units first. He is also wary of maintenance expenses on such an old building. Therefore he has settled on an overall capitalization rate for the Cambridge Arms of 15 per cent.

Questions

1. Using the income–expense figures provided, what are the indicated market values of the two projects?
2. Do you agree with Jones's capitalization rates? How would you change them?
3. Mr. Jones says his decision is made more difficult by the fact that the full-occupancy net for the Cambridge Arms is so much higher than that of Park Chateau. He computes it this way:

	Net Income	Market Value
Cambridge Arms	$176,000	$1,175,000
Park Chateau	136,000	1,135,000

Do you agree with these estimates? If he came to you for advice, what would you tell him?

4. In addition to operating expenses, new mortgage financing would be as follows:

	Loan	Interest	Term	Constant	Annual Payments
Cambridge Arms	$950,000	9½%	15 years	12.54%	$119,130
Park Chateau	900,000	9	20 years	10.80	97,200

How do these data affect your recommendation?

10

APPRAISALS:
MARKET DATA
AND COST APPROACHES*

THE MARKET DATA APPROACH

The Market Data Approach consists of two methods—direct market and the gross rent multiplier. The process of estimating value by the use of the direct market approach includes four principal steps: (1) analysis of the property under consideration; (2) selection and analysis of comparable properties; (3) comparison and contrast of subject property with attributes of the comparable properties or "comps," making appropriate adjustments in value based on the major elements of comparison, and (4) formulating an indicated market value of the property being appraised based on "comps" as adjusted.

Analysis of Subject Property

The property under consideration is analyzed in terms of its use and potential uses, characteristics of the land, characteristics of the structure or potential new structures, location factors, market trends, regulations and restrictions affecting the property, and related factors. The detail with which this analysis is carried out will vary with the type of property and purpose of the appraisal. In many cases, established forms are used; for example, savings and loan associations, insurance companies, banks and other mortgage lenders often indicate rather specifically the factors to be included in a property analysis. (See Fig. 10-1.)

* We are indebted to Jack K. Mann, MAI, of Jackson, Miss., for reviewing this chapter.

In making comparisons most appraisers are careful to consider the following four elements: the time of the sale, the conditions of the sale, the physical characteristics of the property, and its location, market, and related characteristics. Sometimes appraisers use a grid system to help make such comparisons and adjustments.

Selection and Analysis of Comparable Properties

Other properties having the same or nearly the same characteristics as the property being appraised, often referred to as "subject property," are selected. The appraiser has available or secures information about these properties to use for comparison with the subject property. Generally properties are selected for comparative purposes which have been bought and sold in the open market (without such compulsion as forced sales) and for which price information can be obtained. Other information which is used in the absence of price data includes listings or offers to sell, offers to purchase, and rentals. Only "arm's-length" transactions should be used. Recent sales data are much more reliable than those going back a year or more.

All information about the comparable properties is analyzed carefully. For example, sales data are considered with respect to the number of sales involved, the period of time covered, the terms of the sales (including down payments, financing arrangements, and the like), the motivating forces back of the sales, if discoverable, and the degree of market activity, including the rate of turnover of properties.

Comparison of Subject and Selected Properties

Comparisons between the subject property and comparable properties are made, either on an over-all ("chunk") basis or by the use of cubic- or square-foot units or other units of comparison, such as number of apartments or seats in a theater.

Appraisers follow various techniques in carrying out the process of making comparisons between properties. In some cases, detailed rating forms are used to assist in the process. Typically, comparisons are made at least with respect to the four elements of comparison listed above: (1) date of sale; (2) conditions of sale; (3) physical factors, including both land and buildings; and (4) location, market, and related characteristics.

1. *Time of sale* includes an analysis of the difference in market conditions including present and anticipated sales prices, rentals, ease or difficulty of financing, volume of transfers, preferences for various types of properties, construction costs, and anticipated changes in market trends (see Chapter 7). Degree of marketability, currently and in the future, is one of the major considerations in determining comparability of properties for appraisal purposes. Related economic factors include: (1) earnings, (2) operating expenses, (3) competitive position of the property, and (4) special features.

RESIDENTIAL APPRAISAL REPORT

To be completed by Lender

Borrower/Client		Census Tract	Map Reference
Property Address			File No.
City	County	State	Zip Code
Legal Description			

Sale Price $ _____ Date of Sale _____ Property Rights Appraised ☐ Fee ☐ Leasehold ☐ DeMinimis PUD(FNMA only ☐ Condo ☐ PUD)

Actual Real Estate Taxes $ _____ (yr) Loan charges to be paid by seller $ _____ Other sales concessions

Lender _____ Lender's Address

Occupant _____ Appraiser _____ Instructions to Appraiser

NEIGHBORHOOD

Location ☐ Urban ☐ Suburban ☐ Rural

Built Up ☐ Over 75% ☐ 25% to 75% ☐ Under 25%

Growth Rate ☐ Fully Dev. ☐ Rapid ☐ Steady ☐ Slow

Property Values ☐ Increasing ☐ Stable ☐ Declining

Demand/Supply ☐ Shortage ☐ In Balance ☐ Over Supply

Marketing Time ☐ Under 3 Mos. ☐ 4-6 Mos. ☐ Over 6 Mos.

Present Land Use _____% 1 Family _____% 2-4 Family _____% Apts. _____% Condo _____% Commercial

_____% Industrial _____% Vacant _____%

Change in Present Land Use ☐ Not Likely ☐ Likely (*) ☐ Taking Place (*)

(*) From _____ To _____

Predominant Occupancy ☐ Owner ☐ Tenant _____% Vacant

Single Family Price Range $ _____ to $ _____ Predominant Value $ _____

Single Family Age _____ yrs to _____ yrs Predominant Age _____ yrs

Note: FHLMC/FNMA do not consider the racial composition of the neighborhood to be a relevant factor and it must not be considered in the appraisal.

Comments including those factors, favorable or unfavorable, affecting marketability (e.g. public parks, schools, view, noise)

	Good	Avg.	Fair	Poor
Employment Stability	☐	☐	☐	☐
Convenience to Employment	☐	☐	☐	☐
Convenience to Shopping	☐	☐	☐	☐
Convenience to Schools	☐	☐	☐	☐
Adequacy of Public Transportation	☐	☐	☐	☐
Recreational Facilities	☐	☐	☐	☐
Adequacy of Utilities	☐	☐	☐	☐
Property Compatibility	☐	☐	☐	☐
Protection from Detrimental Conditions	☐	☐	☐	☐
Police and Fire Protection	☐	☐	☐	☐
General Appearance of Properties	☐	☐	☐	☐
Appeal to Market	☐	☐	☐	☐

SITE

Dimensions _____ = _____ Sq. Ft. or Acres ☐ Corner Lot

Zoning classification _____ Present improvements ☐ do ☐ do not conform to zoning regulations

Highest and best use: ☐ Present use ☐ Other (Describe) _____

Public _____ Other (specify) _____

	OFF SITE IMPROVEMENTS			Topo
Elec. ☐	Street Access: ☐ Public ☐ Private			Size
Gas ☐	Surface _____			Shape
Water ☐	Maintenance: ☐ Public ☐ Private			View
San.Sewer ☐	☐ Storm Sewer ☐ Curb/Gutter			Drainage
☐ Underground Elect. & Tel.	☐ Sidewalk ☐ Street Lights			

Is the property located in a HUD Identified Special Flood Hazard Area? ☐ No ☐ Yes

Comments (favorable or unfavorable including any apparent adverse easements, encroachments or other adverse conditions)

IMPROVEMENTS

Existing (approx. yr. blt.) 19 ___ No. Units ___ Type (det, duplex, semi/det, etc.) ___ Design (rambler, split level, etc.) ___
Proposed ___ Under Construction No. Stories ___

Exterior Walls ___

Roof Material ___ Gutters & Downspouts ___ None

Window (Type): ___ Screens ___ Combination ___ Storm Sash

Insulation: ___ None ___ Floor ___ Ceiling ___ Roof ___ Walls

BSMT.

Foundation Walls ___
Crawl Space ___ % Basement ___ Outside Entrance ___ Concrete Floor ___
Slab on Grade ___ Evidence of: ___ Dampness ___ Termites ___ Settlement

Floor Drain ___ Sump Pump ___ % Finished ___ Finished Ceiling ___ Finished Walls ___ Finished Floor

Comments ___

ROOM LIST

Room List	Foyer	Living	Dining	Kitchen	Den	Family Rm.	Rec. Rm.	Bedrooms	No. Baths	Laundry	Other
Basement											
1st Level											
2nd Level											

Finished area above grade contains a total of ___ rooms ___ bedrooms ___ baths.

INTERIOR FINISH & EQUIPMENT

Kitchen Equipment: ___ Refrigerator ___ Range/Oven ___ Disposal ___ Dishwasher ___ Fan/Hood ___ Compactor ___ Washer ___ Dryer

HEAT: Type ___ Fuel ___ Cond. ___ AIR COND: ___ Central ___ Other ___ Adequate ___ Inadequate

Floors	Hardwood	Carpet Over ___
Walls	Drywall	Plaster
Trim/Finish	Good	Average ___ Fair ___ Poor
Bath Floor	Ceramic	Cond. ___
Bath Wainscot	Ceramic	

Special Features (including fireplaces): ___

ATTIC: ___ Yes ___ No ___ Stairway ___ Drop-stair ___ Scuttle ___ Floored ___ Heated
Finished (Describe) ___

CAR STORAGE: ___ Garage ___ Built-in ___ Attached ___ Detached ___ Car Port
No. Cars ___ Adequate ___ Inadequate Condition ___

PORCHES, PATIOS, POOL, FENCES, etc. (describe) ___

PROPERTY RATING

	Good	Avg.	Fair	Poor
Quality of Construction (Materials & Finish)	☐	☐	☐	☐
Condition of Improvements	☐	☐	☐	☐
Rooms size and layout	☐	☐	☐	☐
Closets and Storage	☐	☐	☐	☐
Plumbing—adequacy and condition	☐	☐	☐	☐
Electrical—adequacy and condition	☐	☐	☐	☐
Kitchen Cabinets—adequacy and condition	☐	☐	☐	☐
Compatibility to Neighborhood	☐	☐	☐	☐
Overall Livability	☐	☐	☐	☐
Appeal and Marketability	☐	☐	☐	☐

Effective Age ___ Yrs. Est. Remaining Economic Life ___ Yrs.

COMMENTS (including functional or physical inadequacies, repairs needed, modernization, etc.) ___

FHLMC Form 70 Rev. 7/77   ATTACH DESCRIPTIVE PHOTOGRAPHS OF SUBJECT PROPERTY AND STREET SCENE   FNMA Form 1004 Rev. 7/77

FIG. 10–1. Residential appraisal report form.

VALUATION SECTION

Purpose of Appraisal is to estimate Market Value as defined in Certification & Statement of Limiting Conditions (FHLMC Form 439/FNMA Form 1004B). If submitted for FNMA, the appraiser must attach (1) sketch or map showing location of subject, street names, distance from nearest intersection, and any detrimental conditions and (2) exterior building sketch of improvements showing dimensions.

COST APPROACH

Measurements	No. Stories	Sq. Ft.
x	x	=
x	x	=
x	x	=
x	x	=
x	x	=

Total Gross Living Area (List in Market Data Analysis below)

Comment on functional and economic obsolescence: _____

ESTIMATED REPRODUCTION COST — NEW — OF IMPROVEMENTS:

Dwelling _____ Sq. Ft. @ $	= $
_____ Sq. Ft. @ $	=
Extras _____	=
	=
	=
	=
Porches, Patios, etc.	=
Garage/Car Port _____ Sq. Ft. @ $	=
Site Improvements (driveway, landscaping, etc.)	= $
Total Estimated Cost New	= $
Less — Physical | Functional | Economic	
Depreciation $ _____ | $ _____ = $ (	)
Depreciated value of improvements	= $
ESTIMATED LAND VALUE	= $
(If leasehold, show only leasehold value)	
INDICATED VALUE BY COST APPROACH	= $

The undersigned has recited three recent sales of properties most similar and proximate to subject and has considered these in the market analysis. The description includes a dollar adjustment, reflecting market reaction to those items of significant variation between the subject and comparable properties. If a significant item in the comparable property is superior to, or more favorable than, the subject property, a minus (-) adjustment is made, thus reducing the indicated value of subject; if a significant item in the comparable is inferior to, or less favorable than, the subject property, a plus (+) adjustment is made, thus increasing the indicated value of the subject.

ITEM	Subject Property	COMPARABLE NO. 1		COMPARABLE NO. 2		COMPARABLE NO. 3	
Address							
Proximity to Subj.							
Sales Price	$		$		$		$
Price/Living area	$		$		$		$
Data Source							
		DESCRIPTION	+(-)$ Adjustment	DESCRIPTION	+(-)$ Adjustment	DESCRIPTION	+(-)$ Adjustment
Date of Sale and Time Adjustment							
Location							
Site/View							
Design and Appeal							
Quality of Const.							
Age							
Condition							
Living Area Room	Total | B-rms | Baths	Total | B-rms | Baths		Total | B-rms | Baths		Total | B-rms | Baths	

MARKET DATA ANALYSIS

- Basement & Bsmt. Finished Rooms
- Functional Utility
- Air Conditioning
- Garage/Car Port
- Porches, Patio, Pools, etc.
- Other (e.g. fireplaces, kitchen equip., heating, remodeling)
- Sales or Financing Concessions

Net Adj. (Total) ☐ Plus; ☐ Minus | $ ☐ Plus; ☐ Minus | $ ☐ Plus; ☐ Minus | $

Indicated Value of Subject $ $ $

Comments on Market Data _____

INDICATED VALUE BY MARKET DATA APPROACH _____

INDICATED VALUE BY INCOME APPROACH (If applicable) Economic Market Rent $ _____ /Mo. x Gross Rent Multiplier _____ = $ _____

This appraisal is made ☐ "as is" ☐ subject to the repairs, alterations, or conditions listed below ☐ completion per plans and specifications.

Comments and Conditions of Appraisal: _____

Final Reconciliation: _____

This appraisal is based upon the above requirements, the certification, contingent and limiting conditions, and Market Value definition that are stated in

☐ FHLMC Form 439 (Rev. 9/75)/FNMA Form 1004B filed with client _____ 19 _____ ☐ attached.

If submitted for FNMA, the report has been prepared in compliance with FNMA form instructions.

I ESTIMATE THE MARKET VALUE, AS DEFINED, OF SUBJECT PROPERTY AS OF _____ 19 _____ to be $ _____

Appraiser(s) _____ Review Appraiser (If applicable) _____ ☐ Did ☐ Did Not Physically Inspect Property

FIG. 10–1. Continued.

2. *Conditions of the sale* relate to the circumstances under which the "comps" were sold. Based on the market value definition, the property being appraised is considered to be offered on the open market for a reasonable period of time and both the buyer and seller are making decisions based on reasonably full information and with no one operating under undue compulsion. Also, the buyers are expected to be fully qualified buyers with financial capacity to act. If the circumstances involved with actual sales of the "comps" are not "open market" then adjustments must be made or the "comp" not used.

3. *Physical factors* include: (a) site and accessibility; (b) size and shape of the lot; (c) size, style, and functional plan of the building; (d) condition of the building; (e) materials of construction; (f) number of apartments, rooms, offices, or other space units; (g) equipment in the building and its condition; and (h) life expectancy of the building and other improvements.

4. *Location, market, and related factors* include: (a) the general reputation of the neighborhood or district in which the property is located; (b) the desirability of the area as a place to live or do business; (c) the presence or absence of adverse conditions; and (d) the economic future of the city or area (see Chapters 5, 6, 7, and 8). Governmental and regulatory factors include: (a) tax rates and assessments, (b) zoning and building regulations, (c) deed restrictions, (d) traffic regulations, (e) police and fire protection, and (f) public improvements, such as streets, utilities, schools, and related facilities.

Gross Income Multipliers

In some cases, appraisers develop value estimates by comparing gross incomes of the property being appraised with like properties which have recently sold. This involves the use of a multiplier based on experience and "rules of thumb." One such rule of thumb is that value will be equal to 100 times gross monthly rent in the case of residential rental property. Such rules of thumb, of course, may be dangerous and misleading. The proper application of the gross income multiplier requires the development of an appropriate multiplier for the property being appraised. The reliability of the multiplier depends directly upon the quality of the data available. A large number of comparable sales should form the basis for a multiplier. Following is an example of the development of a multiplier:

Comparable Properties	Sales Price	Gross Income	Indicated Gross Income Multiplier
A	$100,000	$10,000	10.00
B	103,950	9,900	10.05
C	97,975	10,100	9.7

An indicated multiplier from these three examples would be in the range of 10. To complete the illustration, assume that the gross income of the property being appraised is $11,200. Then 10 times this figure produces an indicated market value of $112,000. More sales would be desirable, of course, to develop a more reliable mutiplier. The gross income figures used in this example are on an annual basis. For certain types of properties which are rented on a monthly basis, such as apartments, it is common practice to develop multipliers using gross monthly incomes.

Investors often base their decisions on some multiple of gross income, both in the real estate field and in other fields. In some cases appraisers use current gross incomes in this process and in others a stabilized or adjusted annual income is established. The multiplier varies with the type of property, economic life of the property, current investment preferences, and other factors.

Problems of Applying Multipliers.   The principal problem involved in the use of gross income multipliers arises from the fact that for many types of properties expenses do not change in the same proportion as gross incomes. That is, if gross rents advance, net incomes are likely to advance even more rapidly if many expense items, such as taxes and insurance, do not move up in the same degree or at the same rate as gross rents. The opposite is also true: When gross rents decline, net incomes may decline even more rapidly.

There is some justification for the use of gross incomes in the case of single-family residences, because expense ratios do not appear to vary in the same degree as in the case of larger residential or commercial properties.

When a value is estimated by using a rent multiplier, the selection of this multiplier must be made with care. Rent multipliers will vary between rental ranges; they will differ for properties in the same rental or value range, depending on the appeal and competitive position of such properties; and there will be variations depending on the remaining economic life of the property.

This process of valuation by the use of gross income multipliers may be considered a variation of the capitalized income method but more frequently is used in connection with the market method, since the multipliers employed may be developed by using data on the market prices of comparable properties and the relation of such prices to gross incomes.

Sources of Market Information

The most reliable sources of sales information are Multiple Listing Systems (MLS) which are in operation in most communities (see Chapter 13). Such a system usually requires its active members to assemble and share complete records, not only of listing prices but also of actual consummated sales.

Standard sources of information for other types of data are insurance atlases, showing the dimensions of the land and buildings; the assessor's record cards, which usually show dimensions of the land and buildings and the assessed valuation; city zoning maps; real estate atlases, showing the occupancy of each store in the principal shopping districts; the county recorder's records of leases and deeds; published accounts of transactions in newspapers and real estate magazines; files of real estate brokers and financial institutions; records of title companies; and interviews with brokers and clients.

Most appraisers follow the practice of building voluminous files of information. These are sometimes referred to as an appraiser's "data plant." The computer makes possible the storage and retrieval of a large volume of data. It may play a big role in future appraisal data plants.

THE COST APPROACH

The cost or "cost to produce new" method is used widely by appraisers. Many terms are used with reference to costs, including actual cost, historical cost, original cost, reproduction cost, cost to produce new, and replacement cost, to mention but a few.

Actual Cost

This term usually refers to the amount actually expended in the development or acquisition of a property. Hence, the same property may have different actual costs under different conditions; it may have cost $4,000 to acquire a lot and $20,000 to build a house—an actual cost of $24,000. However, the property may have been sold for $27,500 and this amount would then represent actual cost to the new owner.

Original Cost

This term often is intended to refer to the cost of construction rather than to subsequent sale price. Here again, however, problems arise. What is to be included in cost of construction? Will contractors' profits be included? Financing costs? Other charges? Also, there is the problem of accounting practice, which tends to identify original cost with the acquisition cost to the present owner.

Historical Cost

The concept of historical cost has also been used to designate original construction costs, but almost any cost which has been previously incurred is a matter of history and might properly be included in this term.

Cost Concept in Appraisals

Because of the many terms and meanings in common use, we need to define what we mean by cost in real estate appraisal practice. A number of terms have been used such as "estimated cost of replacement of building" and "required investment exclusive of land." The former refers to the costs involved in replacing a structure with a similar structure, whereas the latter includes all costs incurred in improving a site. In the later group are included (1) building costs, (2) carrying charges, (3) financial costs and interest, and (4) equipment and fixtures.

Difficult problems are involved also in deciding what to include in replacement or reproduction costs when buildings are in mid-life or late life. Most appraisers tend to use the terms cost of replacement and cost of reproduction synonymously, taking both terms to mean the present cost of a property of equivalent utility. The investor is concerned with an acceptable substitute and is not interested in a replica. For our purposes we will emphasize the "cost to produce new" concept and thereby avoid becoming involved in the types of conflicts that may arise out of different concepts of costs.

Bases of the Cost Approach

A "cost to construct new" estimate with land value added may be considered as establishing the upper limit of the value of a property. The *principle of substitution* serves as the basis for this position. There is an inherent danger, however, in accepting this conclusion without careful review.

When a new building is constructed, the owners would not ordinarily undertake the project unless they believed that the return which the new property is expected to earn would more than justify the costs incurred. Hence, it is quite appropriate in the case of a new structure (assuming highest and best use of the site) to compute a return on the investment required to improve the land and to impute the remainder of the anticipated income to the land, as we explained above in our discussion of the income method.

The appraisal of an older building raises the depreciation problem. *Current cost to produce less depreciation* is the principle applied to such properties in valuation by the cost approach. While investors are concerned with estimates of this type, there are many problems involved in the use of the cost approach in the case of older buildings. Market prices of comparable properties often provide more reliable guides in such cases.

When valuations are based on costs less depreciation, current construction costs should be used. As a general rule, when there are available sales data on a number of buildings of the same type as an older building being appraised, the market approach is preferable. It reflects obsolescence but does not exaggerate physical depreciation.

Despite these difficulties, there are cases in which the appraiser has no alternative but to use the cost method in the case of older properties. The purpose of the appraisal may necessitate the use of this method, or it may be found impracticable to proceed in any other manner because of the lack of pertinent data. If proper considerations are given to the problems and difficulties involved, reasonable value estimates may be made. This is likely to be true if it is possible to relate such data to market prices or to the income production of comparable buildings. Often, an older structure would not be replaced. In some cases, it might even have a negative value.

Backward vs. Forward View

The fundamental difficulty with the cost method, even in the case of new structures, is that the appraiser's view must of necessity be directed backward rather than forward. The income method stresses future probable returns; the cost method may emphasize past or current experience of the property rather than its future. The original decision to construct a building may have been made at a time when it was justified by expectations; however, subsequent events may justify the original expectations or prove them to be in error. The key to the solution of the problem is the treatment of depreciation in terms of the ability of the property to perform its functions in the future rather than only in terms of past events.

Steps in the Cost Approach

The steps in the cost approach are:

1. Market value of the land		$ x x x
2. Cost to produce the buildings new	$ x x x	
3. Less accrued depreciation	x x x	
4. Indicated market value of the building "as is"		x x x
5. Indicated market value of the property		$ x x x

In the appraisal of new properties, cost estimates may be based on a quantity survey of the actual expenditures involved, or unit cost methods may be used. Special factors may arise in specific cases which cause costs to be well above or below the average for properties of the type under consideration. Unit costs are based on averages which are reduced to square feet, cubic feet, or some similar unit.

In some cases blueprints are used as the basis for making cost estimates for buildings that are to be constructed. Appraisers usually do this by the application of a unit cost factor, with allowances for extras or deficiencies.

Building costs include all of the expenditures required to construct a building—costs of materials, wages, contractors' fees or profits, architects' and engineers' fees, and allowances for extras and contingencies. Sidewalks, driveways, landscaping, and the like are also included, as well as costs of accessory buildings. To these are added carrying charges, financial costs, and equipment costs.

Carrying charges include costs incurred during the period of construction and the time that elapses before the building is put into operation, such as taxes and insurance during construction, costs of working capital, and expenses involved in rental campaigns. Financing costs include interest on invested capital or borrowed funds during the construction period, as well as discounts, commissions, consulting fees, related legal expenses, and the like. Costs of such equipment which becomes a part of the real estate are included, although furniture and removable equipment may or may not be included, depending on the valuation problem involved.

Market value of the land is usually estimated by the comparative method, although the actual amount paid for the land may be a guide if it is comparable to current prices of similar sites.

As we have pointed out above, cost of construction new does not provide a usable result for the valuation of older structures unless allowances are made for depreciation, earlier defined as "loss in value from all causes."

Step 1: Land Value

The market value of the land is developed from actual sales, offers, listings, or leases of vacant land considered comparable to the land being appraised. The only source of land value is from the market inasmuch as land cannot be "produced" or "built" like buildings. Sales or other market information about similar sites provides a basis for estimating the market value of land for use in the cost approach and the capitalized income approach as well as the market approach.

Another method of determining land value is to set up a model of a hypothetical building that represents the best use of the site. The rents for this building are estimated on the basis of comparable rents in the vicinity, or sometimes by actual offers of responsible prospective tenants. Operating costs are estimated on the basis of comparable buildings. The land residual technique outlined in Chapter 9 in the discussion of the income method is then followed.

Plottage Value. If a city zoning ordinance requires that detached homes have a minimum frontage of 60 feet, a single 30-foot lot would have little or no value, but if two 30-foot lots were joined together they would have a greater value than the sum of the two lots as separate units. This increase of value obtained by combining lots into a larger tract is known as plottage value. Value increases in such cases until the assembled tract is large enough for the maximum utilization of the site.

Recent changes in land uses have increased the size of plots necessary for the highest and best use of land. Now it is considered desirable to acquire a number of blocks for one downtown project so that streets can be closed, and the buildings placed on the basis of 25 per cent land coverage, oriented so that they will have the best view, and provided with the maximum light and air.

Department stores have found that plottage value can be obtained by acquiring an entire block so that the values of the main street are carried over to the side street. Rockefeller Center in New York City obtained a plottage value by erecting a series of buildings on a tract of several blocks, which permitted open plazas and yielded higher rents for the office space than buildings with 100 per cent land coverage.

Step 2: Cost To Produce the Building New

There are three ways to develop current building costs. The first is national building cost services which provides monthly cost adjustments for prescribed types of buildings. The limitation of this source is that it applies only to major cities in the country and adaptations from it may not be reliable.

The second source is local contractors, architects, and engineers who typically maintain current data regarding costs for the communities in which they work. Obviously, this information would be current and applicable to the local community but the limitation is that there are no standard specifications for different kinds of buildings.

The third source is directly from the market in which a building of the type being appraised has recently been constructed. If the actual cost of such construction would be available, this would be an excellent and reliable source. The only danger of using this information is that the builder may be overly efficient or inefficient thereby producing lower costs or higher costs than other builders in the market.

It is important to remember that cost figures developed for the building being appraised must apply as of the date of the appraisal and be specifically applicable to the type and quality of the building being constructed. Also, the estimater must make a decision between reproduction costs and replacement costs at this point inasmuch as the consideration in the third step, the application of depreciation, depend upon the decision regarding the use of replacement or reproduction costs.

Step 3: Depreciation and Obsolescence

Buildings and the equipment in them wear out over time. This usually takes place gradually. This process is referred to as *depreciation* as we have seen and may be contrasted with *depletion* or the using up of a natural asset, commonly used in the case of oil wells.

Loss of value results not only from wear and tear but from the development of more and better buildings and equipment and from general economic changes. We typically use the term *obsolescence* to describe this process. Obsolescence, as we have seen, may be functional or economic, the former relating to conditions within a property, the latter to external changes. Physically a building may be in excellent condition but will lose value if another building (usually a newer one, but the time difference may not be great) performs the same function more efficiently or more attractively.

In recent years as rates of change have accelerated, value losses from obsolescence have grown increasingly important. Higher discount rates are required in connection with many real estate decisions in order to reflect higher risks of obsolescence.

Methods of Estimating Depreciation.   There are a number of methods in use for estimating depreciation, such as the straight line, weighted rate, reducing balances, and sinking funds; however, their application without modification is likely to result in wide margins of error because of the differences in the definition of depreciation and the variations in the care and maintenance of different properties.

The care and maintenance given to different properties are not reflected in many of the depreciation tables which are used. Two methods are often adopted to deal with this problem: (a) the quantity survey of observable depreciation with allowances for curable and noncurable defects, and (b) the effective age device.

QUANTITY SURVEY OR BREAKDOWN METHOD OF ESTIMATING DEPRECIATION. In this method, a survey is made of the building, and points of depreciation are divided into curable and noncurable classes; the net cost of making the repairs and alterations necessary to remedy the curable defects is then computed and added to the estimated loss in value due to noncurable defects. Physical deterioration and functional and economic obsolescence may be treated in this manner.

The professional appraiser applies the breakdown method in this manner: (a) physical deterioration, curable and incurable; (b) functional obsolescence, curable and incurable; (c) economic obsolescence, incurable. Physical deterioration refers to the physical condition of the building. This is a reflection of the wear and tear that have been endured and of how well the building has been maintained. Incurable physical deterioration describes those elements of the building which obviously have suffered so much from age that there is no way economically to cure the defect. The best example are footers and basement walls which show evidence of exposure to time. Examples of physical deterioration that are curable are floor coverings which wear out from use, painted areas that need resurfacing, and other similar items.

Functional obsolescence refers to loss in value because of loss of usefulness, sometimes referred to as "inutility." Curable functional obsolescence may include insufficient closet space in a house in which additional closets could be added at a reasonable cost. Incurable losses are those which cannot be economically cured, e.g., extremely low ceilings in a building which would affect the use of a room for display purposes, or as a meeting room, or for storage. There is no economic way to raise the ceilings, of course, thereby making this loss incurable.

Economic obsolescence is the appraiser's term used to indicate loss of value because of forces external to the property. These are typically location factors and there is no way to cure them. An example of this kind of depreciation is the $100,000 house built in a neighborhood of $30,000 houses.

OBSERVED OR EFFECTIVE AGE METHOD OF ESTIMATING DEPRECIATION. This method of estimating loss in value requires a knowledge of market conditions and an ability to relate them to a specific property or properties. The building being analyzed is compared with buildings of like condition and utility regardless of its chronological age. If adequate market data are collected and proper analyses can be made, this method may produce a very reliable estimate of total depreciation.

The effective age of a property may or may not coincide with the actual age (the number of years since construction). A building may be 15 years old and the average economic life for structures of the type under consideration may be 30 years, but the estimated remaining economic life of the building may be 25, years. Hence it more nearly resembles a five-year-old building than a 15-year-old building. An appropriate depreciation percentage then is 5/30 or 16⅔ per cent depreciated, rather than 50 per cent (15/30). This process of comparing the building being appraised with others of like utility may represent a reasonable reflection of the attitudes of consumers in the market. The method also has the advantage of forcing the appraiser to consider the future economic life of the building rather than its past.

Depreciation Tables

The application of depreciation tables often exaggerates the loss of value of well-maintained properties. There are examples of residential structures 50 years old that sell in the market for half of their present cost to build new, and yet, on the basis of the types of depreciation tables often used, would be almost valueless. Tests of all depreciation tables should be made by comparing market prices of old buildings with valuations based on current costs less depreciation. Rapidly rising construction costs, of course, offset many depreciation allowances, and structures over 20 years old have frequently sold for more than their original cost. When used, depreciation and obsolescence allowances should be deducted from the most recently available cost of construction estimates.

Valuation for Tax Assessment Purposes

The cost method is used widely in appraising real estate for tax assessment purposes. A land value map usually is prepared by estimating current front-foot values for every block in a city, with square-foot values being prepared for industrial properties and acreage values for certain vacant land. These values do not necessarily represent full market price, but they should reflect the relative desirability of the different residential neighborhoods in the city and the relative value of business and industrial properties. Usually the assessor consults with local real estate brokers to establish a proper relationship between land values.

The building values generally are estimated on a reproduction cost basis. All the buildings in the community are classified according to types, which are determined by materials of construction, quality, height, area, plumbing facilities, and related items. Then square-foot or cubic-foot costs are established for each type. This cost may be a percentage of the current cost, which is to be preferred, since that is the cost which may be most easily ascertained, or it may be the costs in what is considered a normal year.

After all the buildings in the city are classified by types, field staffs visit every property, classify it as to type, take its external measurements, note the material of construction, type and quality of equipment, and related items. The age of the building is determined for depreciation purposes, either from building permit records or from the architectural type and appearance of the building.

Assessments derived by the method of construction costs for buildings should be checked against recent sales. Properties that sell for less than their reproduction cost less depreciation plus land value are probably suffering from obsolescence for which allowances should be made.

The foregoing methods are generally used in wholesale assessments for taxation purposes. It is not possible to secure sufficient current sales data for all types of properties, particularly factories, office buildings, and large stores, to base assessments upon sales. In the case of commercial properties, rentals paid on current leases should be analyzed in making assessments. Valuations based largely on cost less depreciation can be related to values based on income by adjusting land values or the amounts allowed for obsolescence.

THE APPRAISAL REPORT

Appraisal reports may be relatively simple statements or involved and detailed reports, depending on the objective of the appraisal and the complexity of the problem. Many firms use standard forms for appraisal reports. In such cases the appraiser has a definite guide as to the requirements of the client. In some cases a brief statement in the form of a letter or memorandum serves as an appraisal report.

With the growing importance of appraisals and with the development of standards of practice by such groups as the American Institute of Real Estate Appraisers and the Society of Real Estate Appraisers, appraisal

FORMAT FOR THE APPRAISAL REPORT

Letter of Transmittal—

"As requested . . ."
Identify property appraised
Any other special comments needed

Part I—Introduction

  a. Title page
  b. Picture(s)
  c. Table of contents

Part II—Description, Analysis, and Conclusions

  d. Brief identification of property, legal description, rights being appraised, and objective of the appraisal
  e. Definition of defined value
  f. Date as of which the defined value estimate applies
  g. National (International) Market and Business Conditions Analysis—specifically as these factors affect the subject property
  h. Economic Base Analysis (city, region, area, and/or state)
  i. Analysis and application of real estate market conditions and trends—specifically as they apply to the subject property
  j. Neighborhood (District) Analysis—location factors, including zoning, utilities, trends, etc.
  k. Site description, analysis of functional utility, and statement of highest and best use (including zoning, utilities, taxes)
  l. Indicated defined value of the land
  m. Building description and analysis
  n. The cost approach—indication of defined value from this approach
  o. The market data approach (comparison)—indication of defined value from this approach
  p. The capitalized income approach—indication of defined value from this approach
  q. Reconciliation and final estimate of defined value
  r. Certification of value
  s. Limitations and qualifying statements, contingent and limiting conditions
  t. Qualifications of appraiser

Part III—Addenda

  u. Maps, plats, pictures
  v. Detailed statistical data
  w. Other detailed reports too long or complex to include in the body of the report
  x. Any other supporting data

FIG. 10–2. The appraisal report—general format.

reports have tended to become more standardized than was formerly the case. A suggested recommended format of a formal appraisal report is shown in Figure 10–2.

Main Parts of Appraisal Report

Usually a formal report contains three main parts: (1) an introduction, (2) the analysis and conclusions, and (3) the supplementary data in the form of appendixes or addenda. The introduction may include a brief description of the type of property being appraised; a photograph or photographs of the property; and in addition (if the report is of some length) a table of contents and title page as well as a statement of the appraiser's qualifications.

The second part, which is really the body of the report, usually includes the following: (1) purpose or objective of the appraisal, (2) legal description of the property, (3) property data (building and site), (4) location data, (5) market information, (6) a detailed outline of the value estimate, including reasons for selection of the approaches used and the main steps required in their application to the problem, (7) interpretation of the estimate, and (8) certification of the estimate.

The third part of the report includes maps, supplementary photographs, blueprints, floor plans, and other information. Materials of this type are ready for use if necessary but are supplementary to the first two parts of the report.

Current practices vary in the use of the letter of transmittal. In Figure 10–2 the letter is used only to "convey" the report to the reader. Many appraisers, however, use the letter of transmittal to summarize the report, pointing out major conclusions and matters of major importance in the appraiser's development of the conclusion.

The appraisal report, regardless of the type or format used, is the appraiser's sole vehicle to convince the reader of the logic of the procedure used in reaching a defensible conclusion. It should be clear, concise, and convincing.

SUMMARY

The Market Data approach to valuation problems enjoys widespread use. It is especially helpful when markets are active and information about sales is readily available. Careful comparisons are made between the subject property and similar properties for which market information may be available. Physical, location, market, and governmental factors are included in such comparisons.

In some cases gross income multipliers are used in connection with the market approach. Such multipliers are sometimes used also with the income approach. Appraisers often encounter special problems in the application of gross income multipliers.

Market data are of great assistance to appraisers. Often they build "data plants" to assist them in their work.

The cost approach includes an estimate of land value (usually by the market method), an estimate of the cost to produce the building or buildings and other improvements new, and if the building or other improvements are not new, this estimate is adjusted to reflect accrued depreciation. Various methods may be employed to make required adjustments for depreciation and obsolescence.

The cost approach has widespread use in valuations for tax assessment purposes. The cost approach often is used when lack of data prevents the application of another approach.

The results of a valuation are carefully reviewed and presented in the appraisal report. Appraisers are required to exercise careful judgment and to maintain an objective point of view. The appraisal report may be presented in greater or lesser detail, depending on the requirements of the appraisal. Typically such reports include an introduction, analysis, and conclusions, plus supplementary data.

QUESTIONS FOR STUDY

1. Outline the principal steps in the market approach. Illustrate each.
2. What are the principal problems likely to be encountered in using the market approach?
3. What does the gross income multiplier method have in common with the capitalized income method? How is it related to the market method?
4. Which of the three valuation methods would you recommend for use in the valuation of: (a) the administration building of your college or university? (b) your own home? (c) a newly constructed home that you might be interested in buying? (d) your local post office building? (e) your city's newest shopping center?
5. How may the age of a building influence the choice of valuation method?
6. Outline the main steps in using the cost approach. Illustrate.
7. Why is the cost method easier to apply to new than to older structures?
8. Discuss some of the difficulties involved in using this method for old structures.
9. Which methods do appraisers use in making estimates of depreciation?
10. Which one is best? Explain. Define straight-line, declining-balance, and sum-of-the-years'-digits techniques to reflect depreciation.
11. Why is the cost approach in valuations used for tax assessment purposes?
12. Explain how "the use of data means borrowing from the experience of others."
13. Outline the principal risks in using data. Illustrate each.
14. What is usually included in an appraisal report?

SUGGESTED READINGS

AMERICAN INSTITUTE OF REAL ESTATE APPRAISERS. *The Appraisal of Real Estate* (6th ed.). Chicago: The Institute, 1973. Chs. 14–17.

BROWN, ROBERT KEVIN. *Essentials of Real Estate.* Englewood Cliffs, N. J.: Prentice-Hall, Inc., 1970. Ch. 8.

DAVID, PHILIP. *Urban Land Development.* Homewood, Ill.: Richard D. Irwin, Inc., 1970. Pp. 87–111.

KAHN, SANDERS A., and CASE, FREDERICK E. *Real Estate Appraisal and Investment* (2nd ed.). New York: The Ronald Press Co., 1977.

KINNARD, WILLIAM N., JR. *Income Property Valuation.* Lexington, Mass.: Heath Publishing Co., 1971.

CASE 10–1

Appraisal of Westside Shopping Center

Mr. John Smith
1627 Lincoln Street
Metropolis, Indiana

Re: Westside Shopping Center
1350 West 15th Street
Metropolis, Michigan

Dear Sir:

At your request, I have examined the subject property for the purpose of estimating the market value as of March 30, 197_, for fee simple title free of encumbrance to the real estate which is more particularly described as Lots #25, 26, 33 and 34 of the West Manor Subdivision of a part of the northeast quarter of the northwest quarter of Section 17, Township 6 North, Range 3 West, in the City of Metropolis, Livingston County, Michigan, the plat of which is recorded in the Office of the Recorder of Livingston County.

I have inspected the subject property and the surrounding neighborhood and considered the factors affecting its market value. Based upon my knowledge of real estate values and my experience in this field and particularly upon the facts which relate to the subject property, the more pertinent of which are included in the attached appraisal report, it is my opinion that the market value of the subject property, as above described, is $275,000.

Respectfully submitted,
RICHARD I. BROWN, CPM, MAI

Identification of Property. Legal Description: The subject property is legalley described as:

Lots #25, 26, 33 and 34 of the West Manor Subdivision of a part of the northeast quarter of the northwest quarter of Section 17, Range 6 North, Township 3 West in the City of Metropolis, Livingston County, Michigan, a copy of which is recorded in the Office of the Recorder of Livingston County, Michigan.

Summary of Salient Facts and Conclusions

Land area	37,125+— square feet; 225 front feet
Building area	14,097+ square feet
Ratio of improved land to parking area	1 to 2.4
Market Value indication by replacement cost, less depreciation, plus land value approach	$272,000
Market Value indication by income capitalization approach	$277,000
Market Value indication by market approach	$274,000
Conclusion of Market Value	$275,000
Economic rent	Approximately $2.00 per sq. ft.
Estimated local taxes	$5,234
Estimated net operating income	$28,000+

Street Address: The subject property is known by the street address of: 1350 West 15th Street, Metropolis, Michigan.

Property Rights Appraised. The property rights appraised are those of fee simple title free of encumbrance. Liens, mortgages and other encumbrances, if any such exist, have not been considered as factors affecting value.

City Data. Metropolis, Michigan, is the county seat of Livingston County, Michigan. It is situated on State Roads #57, 66 and 83, U. S. Highways #40, 41 and 231 and Interstate 65. It is 50 miles northeast of Flint, Michigan.

The 1970 population, according to the U. S. Census, was 31,357, an increase of 11.3% over the 1960 figure. The population of Livingston County was 59,225 in 1970; 50,800 in 1960; and 36,534 in 1950.

Metropolis has several large factories of major corporations. These include General Motors, General Electric, RCA, and Bristol-Meyers. Total employment in industry is approximately 8,500 persons. Metropolis also has considerable employment in agriculture, meat packing, and mining. The Peabody and Ayrshire Coal Companies employ a total of approximately 900 persons.

Shopping areas in Metropolis are concentrated principally in three areas: Downtown, Eastgate Shopping Center on the east side at the intersection of U. S. 40 and Interstate 65, and Westside Shopping Center at 1250 West 15th Street. The pattern of shopping seems to be that major purchases are made downtown and that the outlying centers serve more for daily needs and convenience purchases.

Neighborhood Data. The subject property is bounded on the north by 15th Street, on the east by Madison Street, on the south by Con Rail and on the west by a service station. The area is characterized by high-density housing and numerous commercial establishments such as service stations, fast food franchises, and an automobile dealership.

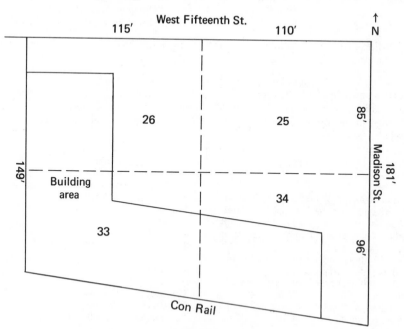

PLAT
Part of West Major Subdivision
City of Metropolis, Livingston County, Indiana

Exhibit A

Site Data. A plat of the site (Exhibit A) shows the property to be a trapezoid, having a frontage of 225 feet on the south side of West 15th Street, a west line running north and south 149 feet, a south line running diagonally northwest and southeast along the railroad right-of-way, and an east line measuring 181 feet. The total land area is computed to contain 37,125 square feet. The topography is level and at street grade. There are no descernible soil or subsoil conditions which would affect the highest and best use of the land or its marketability. City sewers, both storm and sanitary, city water, gas, electricity, and telephone are available at the site. Fifteenth Street has a platted width of 40 feet, is paved with concrete and has curbs, gutters and sidewalks on either side, as does Madison Street.

Zoning. The subject property is zoned B–3 which is a classification for "General Business Use."

Assessment and Taxes. Records in the Office of the Township Assessor indicate that the land is assessed at a total of $20,870, the improvements total $48,730, and the total assessment is $69,600 for the year 197_, payable in 197_. Taxes for this township are currently assessed at the rate of $7.52 for each $100 of assessed valuation. It is computed that the taxes for the year 197_, payable in 197_ for the subject property will amount to $5,233.92.

Description of Improvements. The improvements on the subject property consist of a one-story masonry structure with a flat roof and no basement, built along the south and west sides of the property. All of the walls except the south and west walls are faced with brick and those two walls are concrete blocks. The roof structure is designed so that there is a six-foot overhang projecting over the sidewalk, which runs in front of and on the ends of the building. All foundations are poured concrete slabs. Roofs are covered with tar and gravel, and the downspouts are aluminum. Part of the windows are double-hung and part are plate glass store windows all set in aluminum sash. The subject property is divided into thirteen storerooms.

Replacement Cost, less Depreciation, plus Land Value Approach. The nature of the subject property made it extremely difficult to find sales of comparable parcels of land in Metropolis. It was finally concluded that two transactions, adjusted, provide the best indication of the land value and they are described as follows:

#1. The Wampler Lot. This is designated as Lot No. 10 in West Manor Subdivision and has a frontage of 68 feet on the north side of Fifteenth Street, directly across from the subject property, and has a depth of 261.38 feet. It contains a total of 17,774 square feet and was recently purchased at a price of $57,500. The agreement with the former owner of the property is that he will remove the existing improvements at no expense to the purchaser.

$57,500/17,774 sq. ft. = $3.24 per square foot

At the date of purchase of this property, it was not zoned for commercial use and it is estimated that an adjustment of 110% in the sale price is appropriate to reflect this lack of zoning. The difference between the frontage and size of the Wampler Lot and the frontage and size of the subject property indicates that this lot lacks a certain plottage value which is possessed by the subject property and it is estimated that an adjustment of 115% is appropriate to reflect this difference. Total adjustment 126.5% × $3.24/ sq. ft. = $4.10/ sq. ft., the indicated value of the subject property.

#2. Property situated between 6th and 7th Streets and between Adams and Jefferson Streets, .containing a total of 78,870 square feet (which does not include all of the property in the block) was recently purchased as a site for a motel at a cost of $280,000.

$280,000/78,870 sq. ft. = $3.55 per square foot

At the date of purchase this property was not zoned for business use and it is estimated that an adjustment of 110% is appropriate to reflect this difference between this transaction and the subject property; $3.55/ sq. ft. × 110% = $3.90/ sq ft., the indicated value of the subject property by comparison with this transaction. Analyzing these two sales which appear to be the most nearly comparable of recent date, leads to the conclusion that the present market value of the subject property is $4.00/ sq. ft.

37,125 sq. ft. @ $4.00/ sq. ft. = $148,500

Site Improvements. The subject property contains a total of 37,125 sq. ft. of which 14,097 is improved with the building. This leaves a total of 23,028 sq. ft. of land area which is paved. It is estimated that the cost of this paving is 30¢ per square foot.

23.028 @ 30¢ = $6,908.40.

Improvements: By reference to *Boeckh's Manual of Appraisals* (6th ed.) page 331, it is found that the base cost of the building is $134,955.

Site Improvements	$ 6,908.40
Building	134,955.00
Total Replacement Cost New	$141,863.40

Say—$142,000

Depreciation. It is estimated that the total physical deterioration, both curable and incurable, amounts to approximately 10% of the replacement cost new or $14,186.

In analyzing the rent schedule, the tenancies and the operation of the subject property, it was concluded that the total functional obsolescence, both curable and incurable, amounts to $14,186.

Since the highest and best use of the land has been found to be in its present use as a shopping center and in view of the present and anticipated future population density in the immediate surrounding area, it is difficult to imagine a location which would be better for this type of an improvement and therefore it is concluded that the subject property does not suffer from economic obsolescence.

Physical Deterioration—10%	$14,186
Functional Obsolescence—10%	14,186
Economic Obsolescence	–0–
Total Depreciation	$28,372

Summary:

Land Value		$148,500
Replacement Cost of Improvements		
(rounded)	$142,000	
Less: Depreciation	28,372	
Depreciated Replacement Cost		113,628
Indicated Market Value		$262,128
Rounded to		$262,000

Market Data Approach. A careful analysis of the City of Metropolis failed to reveal any recent property sale reasonably comparable to the subject property in physical terms. One transaction was found on the south side of Third Street between Maple and Oak Streets. It is an automobile dealership. The actual selling price was $253,000, a figure which is in marked contrast with an offer of $278,000 which the seller refused to accept in January of 197_. It seems well established that this was a case of a distressed seller and that the transaction would be aptly described as a good buy. After careful consideration, it is estimated that this property could have been sold, granted a reasonable time, at a price of $280,000.

The gross monthly rental being developed by this property at the date of sale was $3,460. Dividing the adjusted sale price by the gross monthly rent gives a monthly gross rent multiplier of 81.

The actual monthly gross rents received from the subject property during the fiscal year ending 197_ amounted to $3,384.05. Multiplying this figure by the gross rent multiplier of 81 gives an indicated value of the subject property of $274,108.05.

Rounded to $274,000

Income Capitalization Approach

Annual Rent Schedule:

Room Number	Annual Rent
1	$6,500
2	1,800
3 & 5	4,020
4	4,200
6	1,920
7	1,400
8	1,836
9	2,564
10	1,800
11	2,100
12	2,700
13	9,800

Estimated Stabilized Operating Statement:

Income:		
Stabilized Rent (Adjusted from Annual Rent)		$40,608.66
Vacancy and Collection Loss (3%)		1,218.26
Effective Gross Rent		$39,390.40
Operating Expenses:		
Heat	$ 300.00	
Electricity	285.00	
Maintenance:		
Building Exterior	800.00	
Building Interior	650.00	
Building Lot	460.00	
Management	1,579.00	
Taxes:		
Gross Income	474.00	
Real Estate	5,234.00	
Insurance	930.00	
Miscellaneous	631.00	
		11,373.00
Operating Income		$28,017.40

An investigation indicates that mortgage money is generally available in Metropolis for an investment of this type at from 8 to 8¼ per cent. An adjustment for risk factors of the property being appraised raises this rate to 8½ per cent as an acceptable rate of return.

Operating Income	$28,017.40
Land Requirements ($148,500 @ 8½%)	12,622.50
Income Attributable to Improvements	$15,394.90
$15,394 capitalized at 12% (8½% + 3½% recapture)	$128,284.00
Plus land value	148,500.00
Total	$276,784.00
Rounded to	$277,000.00

Reconciliation and Conclusion. Each of the approaches to value contains certain inherent advantages and certain dangers. In the replacement cost, less depreciation, plus land value approach, the advantage is that it is particularly applicable to a property which reflects the highest and best use of the land and which is of relatively new construction. The danger in this approach lies in the difficulty in estimating accurately the degree of depreciation which a property has suffered and the greater the degree of depreciation suffered the less the reliability which can normally be placed upon this approach. The advantage of the market data approach is that this is the one commonly employed by buyers and sellers in the market place. The disadvantage is the difficulty of accurately comparing the known sales with the subject property and particularly in understanding the motivations of the buyers and sellers. The income capitalization approach is of particular value in analyzing properties of the type which are normally owned for the income stream which they produce. The disadvantage of this approach is the difficulty of estimating accurately the income and expense and supporting an opinion as to the proper rate of interest, since the operation of the capitalization process multiplies a small error in any of these items into an error of great magnitude in the final result.

The range of the three approaches is from $272,000 to $277,000 which is a variation of approximately 2% and both the high and low figures appear to have about the same degree of support. It is therefore concluded that the market value of the subject property, as of the appraisal date, March 30, 197_, is $275,000.

CERTIFICATE OF APPRAISAL

The undersigned certifies that:
1. He has personally inspected the subject property and considered the factors affecting its value.
2. He has no present or contemplated future interest in the property.
3. Neither his employment nor his compensation is contingent upon the values estimated herein.
4. This report has been made in conformity with the standards and rules of professional ethics of the American Institute of Real Estate Boards of which he is a member.
5. In his opinion, the market value of fee simple title free of encumbrance to the land, land improvements and buildings constituting the subject property as of March 30, 197_, is $275,000.

RICHARD I. BROWN, CPM, MAI

Date: April 20, 197_

Questions

1. What could be done to improve the quality of this appraisal?
2. How would the results of the income approach be changed if the net operating income were $35,000? If the capitalization rate were 7 per cent plus 2 per cent recapture rate?
3. What are the weaknesses of the market comparison approach in this case? What would be the result if the gross rent multiplier had been 94 and the monthly gross rent from the subject property $2,900?
4. What would be your conclusion in the replacement cost approach if the Wampler Lot had sold for $72,000 and the motel site for $310,000?
5. How does an appraiser arrive at a depreciation figure? Outline the advantages of each of the three methods that are in widespread use for estimating depreciation.
6. What is the present value of Westside Shopping Center's operating income over the next 30 years? (Assume it will remain constant.) Which capitalization rate should be used to determine this? (If the rate you choose is not in the table, round off to the next higher rate in the table.)
7. How does the present value arrived at in question 6 compare to the appraised value in the income approach?

III

Real Estate
Decision Areas

The chapters in this part consider various decisions in the production, marketing, and financing of real estate resources and services. The first two chapters cover production and include the subjects of subdividing, land development, and building. NASA's experimental "House of the Future" forms the basis of a study project.

Chapters 13 and 14 discuss real estate marketing, including brokerage and promotion and property management. Case studies help to illustrate some of the problems involved in real estate brokerage as well as the major principles and practices in property management.

The final three chapters of this Part deal with the general subject of real estate finance. Chapter 15 covers the major methods and instruments of finance. Chapter 16 considers the financial institutions and agencies operating in this field. The types of mortgage instruments which may be developed in the years ahead and the federal government's impact on the private mortgage market are the subjects of the study projects.

The final chapter considers the general subject of risk analysis. Supplementary materials offer a study of a borrower and an outline of contemporary decision theory.

11

PRODUCTION: SUBDIVIDING AND LAND DEVELOPMENT

DEVELOPMENT DECISIONS

The production of real estate resources is usually thought of in terms of the physical processes of land development, improvement, and building. These physical processes, while often intricate, have significance primarily because they provide people as families and as members of business, governmental, or social groups, or of institutional organizations with real estate resources and services. Thus, the developer of a large project is in effect the developer of a community. A few developers have produced entirely new towns. Even the developer of a small subdivision creates at least a part of a neighborhood.

The manner in which land is developed—the size of the lots, the types of streets installed, the services and utilities provided, the quality and price level of the houses built, the business and community facilities provided, and related factors—all have a bearing on the kind of community or neighborhood that ultimately will result. Thus, early decisions have long-range effects. They may have a major role in determining the general quality of life in the area.

Short-Range and Long-Range Interests

Typically, those who develop and sell land are interested primarily in providing properties that will be immediately attractive to potential buyers and hence readily salable. The concern of the real estate broker is similar to that of the original subdivider: the primary interest is in immediate sales. In both cases, however, the long-term success of these firms depends on the effectiveness with which the properties serve the needs of the buyers.

The interests of financial institutions and other investors are almost always of a longer-term nature. This is because the funds which are advanced are typically repaid over a great many years. Similarly, the interests of property managers tend to be of a long-term nature.

Long-term investors and mortgage lenders are thus concerned that the properties developed and the communities and neighborhoods of which they are to be a part will continue to be desirable places in which to live and work over a number of years. Properties that remain desirable over long periods of time represent less financial risk than other properties.

Production Alternatives

If you were going to buy an automobile, you would probably visit one or more dealers, select the type and model you wanted, pay in cash or arrange the necessary financing, and drive the car away. You would hardly think of manufacturing it yourself or having it built entirely to your order.

If you wanted a house, however, you might consider these alternatives: you could go to a builder or a real estate broker and buy a house, either a used one or a new one, in somewhat the same way you would buy a car. Or you might buy a lot, install a water and sewage-disposal system, build a road, buy the necessary materials, and construct a house, either by your own efforts or by engaging a contractor to do the work for you. You might arrange for a manufactured house dealer to put it up for you. You might buy a lot in a subdivision that had been carefully planned and in which all of the various utilities and streets had been installed. The developer of the subdivision might also be a builder and might agree to build a house for you, either one planned by your own architect or one constructed from plans the builder had available.

Much the same type of situation would face a business firm wishing to develop its own place of business. A piece of land might be bought and a contractor engaged to erect the desired type of structure. Or a developed lot in an industrial park or district or a shopping center might be leased or bought and arrangements made for constructing a building.

Production Processes

In the real estate business the production of real estate resources is usually thought of as including only the processes of land development and building. Of course, in an economic sense the production of real estate resources or services includes all of the processes of developing the site and constructing the improvements, as well as financing, marketing, and property management. It involves the creation of facilities for the production of income at fixed locations, whether these incomes are in the form of direct use of the property, as in the case of an owner-occupied home, or a place of business that is owned by the firm, or in the form of monetary returns to an investor.

Management of Building and Development Firms

Business firms engage in subdividing and land development activities in various ways. Frequently, such activities are combined with building operations. In some cases, an individual buys land and holds it for future development, sometimes subdividing it and installing the necessary facilities, sometimes selling it to others who do this. In some cases, several persons form a syndicate to engage in land development. Sometimes a real estate brokerage firm undertakes to develop land and sell the lots, or contracts with the builder to provide completed properties for sale.

Land development and building enterprises may be individual proprietorships, partnerships, or corporations. They may be operated as syndicates or trusts or in other ways. Some of the largest of our corporations have gone into land development and building operations with varying degree of success from time to time.

Regardless of how they are set up, the firms engaged in subdividing or land development activities must perform the basic management functions of determining objectives, planning to achieve them, organizing resources, and controlling operations. Leadership is necessary to direct, activate, and set the process into motion.

Each firm must utilize the resources available to it, that is, the abilities of people, capital, equipment, land, or other resources, in the process of producing and marketing the goods and services it provides. Its sales must be at prices in excess of costs if it is to remain in business very long.

We are concerned chiefly with subdividing and land development in this chapter and with building processes and problems in the next. In recent years, large-scale developers have tended to combine subdivision, land development, and building operations. In some cases complete communities, even entirely new towns, have been developed, including commercial and industrial structures as well as housing and community facilities. Major corporations such as U. S. Steel, Chrysler, Gulf Oil, and others have joined National Homes, Weyerhaeuser, and others that have had more traditional relationships to this field.

Types of Products

We should be careful to note, however, that whether a real estate firm is engaged in land development, building, brokerage, property management, or financing activities, it must perform production and marketing as well as financing activities. Although we refer to land development and building firms as being engaged in production activities, we use this term to refer to what they do for the community as a whole. Similarly, we refer to brokerage firms and property management firms as marketing enterprises because they perform marketing functions for the public. They must both produce and market their services, however, as well as arrange to finance their own programs.

Decision Factors

Of special importance in decisions related to land development are careful market analyses and the predictions of probable market changes based on them. Analyses of general and local business conditions often play an important part in such decisions. In addition, consideration is given to construction costs and trends, availability and cost of financing, price trends, and government policies especially as related to taxes, public improvements, environmental controls, and zoning and similar regulations. All of these factors will affect cost–return–risk relationships which are basic to decisions regarding land development.

Various types of costs are of importance in land development. These may be grouped as (1) economic, (2) social, (3) time, and (4) supersession costs. Economic costs include the costs of the labor and capital resources required to make land ready for use. Social costs include the disruptions and inconveniences that may be involved. Time costs largely relate to the waiting period required for land to "ripen" to productive uses. Supersession costs are incurred in scrapping existing improvements to make possible new land uses.

Strategic factors such as the timing of the development relative to competitive operations, the size of the effort, pricing policies, and the like will usually affect the decisions that are made. Attempts will be made to anticipate the decisions of competitors insofar as possible.

Decisions will finally be based on such matters as (1) the objectives to be accomplished by means of the project, (2) potential cost and return relationships, modified as necessary by tax considerations, (3) risk factors, (4) relationship of the project under consideration to others, and (5) the timing of the effort and the time required for it to pay out.

STAGES IN THE DEVELOPMENT PROCESS

The main activities essential to a new development include the following:

1. Analyzing market conditions (determining the need for and the proper time for the proposed development).
2. Selecting an appropriate location, perhaps taking an option on it.
3. Determining whether government regulations will prevent development or make costs prohibitive.
4. Analyzing the selected tract and developing preliminary plans and design.

5. Securing approval of government authorities as required. This may include a wide variety of requests, reports, hearings, and related efforts.
6. Purchasing and financing the selected tract. In the case of a shopping center, a leasing campaign may be carried on before financing is arranged.
7. Layout and design of the area, including locating and sizing the principal facilities and determining the relationship between public and private land uses; dividing the remaining portions of the land into parcels of such sizes and shapes as appear to be best adapted to the anticipated uses.
8. Establishing restrictions and methods for regulating land use.
9. Arranging protections against risks by means of insurance and bonds.
10. Construction of the various improvements necessary for the development.
11. Marketing the development.

While these activities may ideally follow the sequence suggested above, factors such as the developer's existing inventory of land and significant changes in markets or in economic and political conditions may require periodic alteration in the sequence of events.

Analyzing Market Conditions

Prior to undertaking a new land development project, it is essential that the general conditions of the market be understood. In addition, the subdivider or developer needs information about the potential market for the specific types of products that are being offered for sale. If the developer plans to sell lots, it is necessary to know something of the demand for lots of the type and price range under consideration. If the developer intends to subdivide and completely develop a tract of land, constructing houses, apartments, a shopping center, or other buildings on the lots, information will be needed about their salability or rentability. Hence, the real estate developer will begin by considering the need for additional real estate resources. The available supply and current price and rent ranges will be considered in light of potential demand. Land development calls for one of the specific applications of the market analysis procedures outlined in Chapter 7.

Generally, land development activity is greatest during periods of prosperity and high incomes. In periods of recession relatively little activity is undertaken. History indicates that all too frequently land is developed during boom periods more rapidly than it can be absorbed by the market. For example, at the end of the boom of the 1920's, Chicago and its suburbs had enough lots to house over a million additional persons living in detached houses. There were excess supplies of marginal lots—both developed and undeveloped—in many areas after the boom of the early 1970's. Thus, the *timing* of a new subdivision or development is of basic importance to its success.

A heavy volume of land development does not mean that all old subdivisions will be fully sold out. Many never will be developed because of poor locations, poor design, improper construction, or financial involvements, or for other reasons. Premature subdivisions have created numerous problems, not only for the subdivider but for the community at large. Careful market analyses should help to prevent such occurrences.

These analyses should include a consideration of the principal demand, supply, and price factors having a bearing on the specific project under consideration. The principal demand factors are the trends of employment and incomes of the potential customer group and the terms and availability of financing. From the standpoint of supply, the availability of competing facilities and the potential development of competing projects are of prime importance. Relative prices and rents for old and new accommodations of a similar size and type need careful consideration. Costs of development require careful study.

One should always remember in making analyses of this type that relatively long-range predictions are required. Only in exceptional cases is a subdivision completely developed and sold in the space of one or two years. In most cases the process goes on over a longer period of time. Often it is advisable to develop a tract in sections to be sure that the market will absorb the new properties. Development in sections also serves to limit front-end costs as well as to enhance the appearance of success of the developed property by reducing the number of vacant, undeveloped lots.

Selecting an Appropriate Location

Just as poor timing may result in unsuccessful developments, improper locations lead almost inevitably to developments which fail to become desirable additions to our real estate resources. The proper location of new real estate developments leads to orderly expansion. The successful development of a new area requires a careful study of the past trends of city growth and structure and the location of competing or complementary areas. The discussion in Chapters 7 and 8 are applicable to problems of this type.

Location factors of special importance in decisions relating to a new housing development typically include the following:

1. The site should be favorably located with respect to the needs of the population for the type and class of development planned.
2. The site should not require undue development costs and should be free from natural hazards.
3. Protections should be available as required. These may include zoning, or deed restrictions.
4. The site should be reasonably accessible in terms of time and cost of travel.

5. The planned development should put the properties in a favorable competitive situation relative to competing developments in terms of general attractiveness, lot sizes, parking areas, utilities and conveniences, roads and streets, and parks, schools, shopping centers and other public and community facilities.

The factors which are of major importance in the location of commercial and industrial real estate developments are: (1) available transportation facilities, (2) topography and the nature of the soil, (3) the relationship of the area to other parts of the region, and (4) the location and character of competing sites.

In most cities, as we have seen, the location of commercial and industrial developments is limited by zoning laws. Recently, however, the location of such developments at points far removed from the center of cities has often placed them beyond the control of zoning regulations. While this offers greater flexibility of operations, the developer will usually consider the relationship of a new commercial or industrial subdivision to the probable future pattern of growth, to competitive developments, and to the way in which the transportation network is likely to develop.

Determining Whether Government Regulations Can Be Met

Not only are zoning and building regulations important; environmental controls, costs of complying with sewer, road, traffic, and related requirements, real estate settlement procedures, flood control requirements, government mortgage guarantee regulations, and others must also be considered. Before proceeding, the developer should make sure that all requests can be met and that the costs of meeting them and making the necessary reports will not be excessive.

Analyzing the Selected Tract

Experienced developers make careful analyses and surveys of tracts prior to reaching decisions to purchase them. It is necessary to determine the usability and marketability of *all parts* of the area. Substantial losses can be avoided if advance consideration is given to the less desirable portions of a tract. A competent engineer or land planner should study the area and prepare layouts of the tract.

One student of the subject said:

Marketing subdivisions may be compared to marketing beef. The butcher pays so much a hundred for the carcass, and the subdivider pays so much an acre for his land. When the butcher retails, he charges according to the choiceness of the cut. He must charge enough for the porterhouse and tenderloin to take care of the waste and the cheap cuts.[1]

[1] Statement by the late Stewart Mott.

It should be noted also that the first properties marketed may have to be priced somewhat lower than those sold after the area has been partially developed. The earlier purchasers frequently require a price inducement for bearing a portion of the risk of a new project.

Costs of development must be studied with great care. Such costs vary widely. Flat land, of course, requires less preparation than rough terrain. An area which is to be densely settled requires heavy-duty streets and sidewalks and large water mains and sewers. Less densely settled areas often permit lighter design and narrower streets; sidewalks may not be needed. Power lines and other utilities, however, will need to be longer and thus more expensive in proportion to the number of people in the area.

Improvement costs should be related to traffic load, number of families per acre, and the character of the layout of lots and services. The buying power of the residents must be considered with care.

The largest elements in the improvement bill are the costs of streets and walks. Costs of sanitary sewers (and, except in areas of very low density, storm sewers) and water mains are added, as are costs of grading, draining, and landscaping, and of engineering service. The cost of gas and electric service requires advance payments, but usually is reimbursed as the service is put into use.

Factors of importance in studying both costs of development and marketability include (1) topography; (2) limitations established by zoning ordinances, land sales disclosure requirements, and other regulations; (3) accessibility to places of employment, to schools, and to shopping, amusement, and civic centers; (4) location with respect to other neighborhoods and special attractions such as golf courses; (5) taxes; (6) potential special assessments; and (7) future probable management, financing, and maintenance costs.

Purchasing and Financing the Selected Tract

The purchase of land for a new development is similar to the buying of other real estate. Options may be acquired; in some cases land may be purchased on contract; or it may be bought outright. Often the developer arranges to "take down" portions of a particular tract over a period of time. This arrangement may be helpful both to buyer and seller—in the former case to avoid tying up large blocks of funds and in the latter because of tax considerations. The usual complex legal formalities are involved as in all real estate transactions. Of course, it is especially important to the land developer that title matters be definitely settled and that as much red tape as possible be eliminated if parts of the development are to be sold.

Brokers are often commissioned by developers to find suitable tracts or to assemble land where diversity of ownership is involved. The difficulty of assembling tracts of sufficient size for economical development has been one of the main factors preventing the redevelopment of "near-in" areas.

Some real estate developments are financed by means of equities, with lending institutions taking "a piece of the action." Provision has been made by several states whereby large institutional lenders may develop and own real estate projects. Many operators rely on borrowed funds to a large degree. Construction financing usually is provided on a short-term basis but may be tied in with long-term mortgage arrangements. Mortgages may be insured by the Federal Housing Administration or guaranteed by the Veterans Administration or insured or guaranteed by private mortgage insurance companies.

Layout and Design

The decisions reached in regard to the number of lots to be laid out, the areas to be used for business purposes, land dedicated to public use, the utilities and conveniences to be installed, and the restrictions to be established all involve detailed study of numerous factors. For example, the type and extent of street improvements are limited on the one hand by minimum essentials for decent living and on the other by the amount which prospective buyers or tenants can pay over and above such minimum requirements.

Local customs, climate, and soil conditions play a large part in determining the types of roads and streets constructed. The general plan for developing the tract will determine the road and street pattern. This plan should recognize the best building sites prior to determining the street pattern.

The size and shape of the lots will be dependent on the anticipated land uses, on topographical features, such as the contour of the land, trees, ravines, lakes and streams, and the proposed price or rent scale. In earlier years many developers attempted to subdivide an area in such a way that the greatest possible number of lots would be obtained. Present-day practice dictates the division of an area into the greatest number of *readily salable lots*. Land planners and engineers have made substantial progress in solving problems of this type.

The inclusion of parks and other recreational areas in the plan of a subdivision adds greatly to the attractiveness and salability of many lots. The extent to which land in a tract will be dedicated for recreational use will be influenced, of course, by the nearness of the development to established areas of this type. Also, provision should be made for shopping center sites, schools, churches, and related facilities. In some cases special features such as lakes, golf courses, community centers or others are built into a development. (See, for example, Figs. 11–1 and 11–2.)

Factors Stressed by Type of Development

Developers of single-family homes try to balance costs, density, and attractiveness with anticipated sales prices. Consideration is usually given

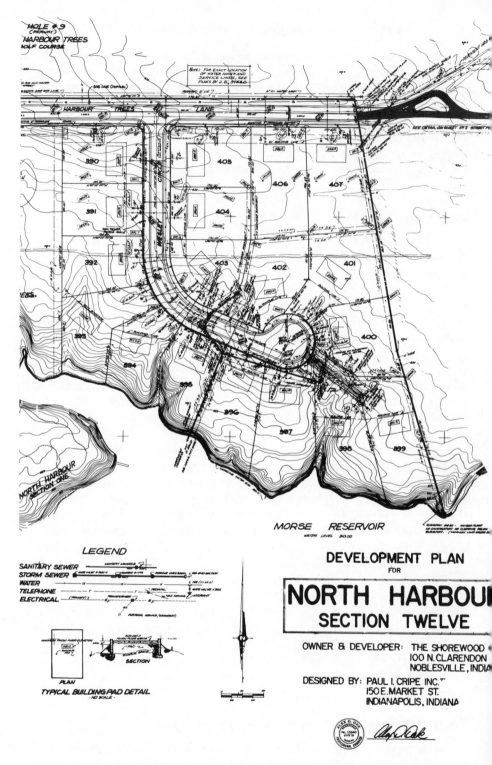

FIG. 11–1. Subdivision layout. (Courtesy Paul I. Cripe, Inc.)

294

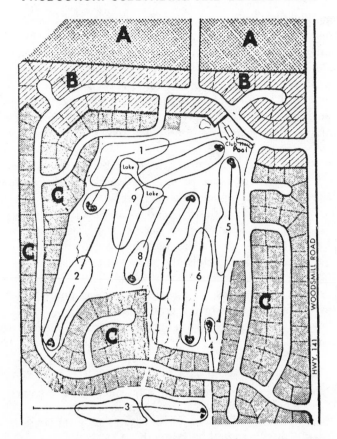

FIG. 11–2. The *Four Seasons* project in St. Louis uses 47 acres for a highly successful nine-hole golf course, complete with a club house and pool (upper right). The course is par 35 and is 2,900 yards in length. The total project has 138 acres, 130 homes, and 298 apartments. (From Urban Land Institute Technical Bulletin 57.)

to the amount of land that should be set aside for schools, commercial developments, churches, parks, and other land uses that will increase the marketability of properties in the area.

In the case of apartment developments, special attention usually is given to the design of individual units in order to provide the most desirable arrangements with the least amount of space. Efforts are made to assure privacy and security and to take advantage of favorable views.

Shopping center developers allocate available land among selling areas, parking spaces, roads, and other land uses. They plan the location of various kinds of stores (and other possible commercial uses) so as to maximize income and to assure easy access by customers, suppliers, employees, and others. Good traffic flows are important. In some cases buffers are designed in order to reduce noise and to obstruct undesirable views. The major tenants, such as stores, usually exercise great influence on the plans and designs of shopping centers.

The planning and design of office buildings should reflect potential market demand and the competitive situation. Efforts are usually made to assure flexibility in the use of space; traffic flows are of great importance. The selection and location of equipment play an important role in planning. Increasingly, emphasis is given to security, heating and cooling efficiency, lighting, the location of conference rooms, and other special uses of space.

Industrial developments are often designed by the companies that will make use of them. In the case of industrial parks, flexibility tends to be emphasized. Modules of space are planned so that there can be ready adaptation to the market for desired land uses. Special attention is usually given to flexibility of utilities, ease of access, and traffic flows. Guidelines for development by individual users usually are provided.

Special buildings such as hotels and motels present special design problems. Efforts are usually made to assure ease of access, security, and amenities such as conference rooms, restaurants, swimming pools, and overall attractiveness within the scope of the anticipated market.

The following suggestions serve as guidelines for layout of a residential development:

1. Heavy through-traffic should be discouraged.
2. Extension of major streets should be planned in advance.
3. Traffic should flow toward thoroughfares.
4. Minor streets should enter major streets at right angles.
5. Dead-end streets should be avoided. (Courts with cul-de-sacs which provide adequate turning space, however, are often desirable.)
6. Streets should fit contours of the natural terrain.
7. Short blocks are not economical.
8. Plan commercial sites where needed.
9. Provide school and church sites especially as a buffer use between commercial and residential development.
10. Parks and other community recreational facilities can be a community asset.
11. Preserve natural features of site for improved appearance and function including preservation of natural drainage ways and trees.
12. Identify the best building sites—adapt the lot lines to serve these sites.
13. Deep lots are wasteful.
14. Plan lots of adequate width.
15. Avoid sharp-angled lots.
16. Plan wider corner lots.
17. Make lot lines perpendicular to street.
18. Plan lots to face desirable views.
19. Protect lots against adjacent nonconforming uses.
20. Protect residential lots against major street traffic.

21. Provide for adequate parking.
22. Develop special features such as provision for landscaped entrances and bicycle paths to improve marketability.
23. Protect the environment—prevent soil erosion, install underground utilities, and provide sanitary sewers where feasible.

Establishing Restrictions

The establishment of restrictive covenants and plans for regulating a new development should be considered as an essential part of the developer's functions.

The types of restrictions established will depend on the extent to which zoning laws and land-planning provisions regulate land uses, as well as on the character of the new development. In some places new developments are regulated by master plans established by local planning authorities. Standards for new subdivisions and developments may be established by such authorities. Zoning laws are usually the most important method for carrying into effect the master plan of a local authority. In some cases, however, this method is inadequate. The protection afforded by suitable covenants is of primary importance in the areas which lack the benefit of adequate and effective zoning. Protective covenants are an important supplementary aid in maintaining neighborhood character and values. The extent of zoning protection is limited to governmental exercise of the police powers of maintaining and promoting public health, safety, and welfare. Protective covenants, being agreements between private parties, can go further than public regulations in meeting the needs of a particular development and in providing maximum possible protection.

Usually the developer needs to establish more specific and detailed regulations than are set up by public bodies if the orderly and stable development of the new area is to be assured. Deed restrictions are the most effective means for accomplishing this purpose. They may control land uses, lot sizes, design and size of structures, position of structures on lots, nuisances, price ranges, land coverage, architectural factors, utility easements, and related matters. Deed restrictions should provide suitable enforcement provisions, be recorded in the public land records, and be superior to the lien of any mortgage that may be on record prior to recording the protective covenants. In some cases a "home association" or "property owners' maintenance association" is organized to administer such regulations.

Protective covenants may also contain various special conditions such as regulations governing individual water supply and sewage-disposal systems, for example, requiring conformance to stated standards; protection of sites for community facilities such as parks, schools, and shopping centers; and related matters. Occupancy restrictions, of course, may not be enforced by the courts.

The FHA provides this advice:

Protective covenants should provide suitable enforcement provisions, be recorded in the public land records and be superior to the lien of any mortgage that may be on record prior to the recording of the protective covenants. The proper form of protective covenants varies in the different states. A generally acceptable and enforceable form is a written declaration by the owner of the entire tract which is recorded in land office records. Sometimes in small developments, the covenants and conditions are stated on the recorded plat. When a separate declaration is made, it is good practice to record it simultaneously with the recordation of the subdivision map.[2]

In the case of condominium developments, arrangements should be made for property owners to take over the operation of common areas and facilities after a stated percentage of the properties have been sold.

Securing Approval of Government Authorities

With few exceptions, it is necessary to secure the approval of various government agencies before land development programs may be carried out. State and local planning regulations typically require that plans for each new subdivision be approved. Detailed plats and working drawings for a proposed tract or subdivision showing the lots; position of streets; type and location of utilities; proposed restrictions and quality of streets, curbs, and sidewalks; land dedicated to public use; and related matters are presented to the proper authorities for approval. Often a public hearing is required whereby neighbors and other interested parties may express their views on the merits of the proposed development. In some cases modifications are required. Sometimes approval is denied. Tax matters must be cleared in some cases.

State governments typically require the submission of plans for provision of water and for sewage disposal in order to safeguard public health. Approval must be secured to gain access to state roads. Construction of floodways is often subject to state perusal. Some states require the submission of evidence of ability to deliver title to lots and in other ways undertake to protect the public against fraud and misrepresentation.

Federal regulation is becoming more predominant in subdivision development. A recent example is the Interstate Land Sales Full Disclosure Act which in many cases requires the preparation of a detailed property report to be disseminated to prospective lot purchasers. This report is subject to the approval of the Office of Interstate Land Sales Registration. Federal regulation also pervades subdivision development where access to federal highways is required, federal taxes have a special bearing, VA or FHA financing is desired, or urban renewal funds or other federal subsidies are required.

[2] FHA *Underwriting Manual.*

As suggested above, because of the far-reaching extent of government regulation, the developer should, at an early stage in the development process become cognizant of the various governmental agencies having jurisdiction over the proposed development and the nature of their requirements. The processing time and cost for obtaining such approvals should be programmed into the development schedule.

Arranging Protections Against Risks

Before any work is actually undertaken to install the improvements in the subdivision, various protections usually are arranged against such risks as injuries to persons or property. Usually this is done through insurance coverage under a "manufacturer's and contractor's liability" policy. Also, it is customary to arrange for performance bonds if contracts are let for such work as grading, utility installation, and the like. Such bonds provide a guarantee through an insurance company that work will be completed according to the contract that has been arranged.

This statement provides a summary:

While the provisions of contract bonds vary somewhat with different owners, they follow similar lines. First, when an owner advertises a project for bidding, he normally requires all bidders to accompany their proposals with a guarantee, usually in the form of a Bid Bond or certified check. The bid bond generally guarantees that, if awarded the contract, the principal will (1) enter into the contract and furnish the required performance and payment bonds or (2) pay the owner (up to the limit of the bid bond penalty) the difference between the principal's price and the cost of awarding the contract to the next higher bidder.

The Performance Bond guarantees to the owner that the contractor will complete the project within the scheduled time, for the agreed upon price, and in strict accordance with the plans, specifications, and contract. If the contractor fails to perform, the surety on the performance bond may undertake to finish the work or pay the owner the excess cost (up to the bond penalty) of having the work completed by another contractor.

Ordinarily, a separate Payment Bond is also given to guarantee that the contractor will discharge his bills—and often those of his subcontractors—for labor and material used in the project, although this obligation is sometimes included in the performance bond.

Construction contracts occasionally require the builder to guarantee the project, or certain portions thereof, against defective workmanship and materials for stated periods of time. Although this protection is normally afforded under the performance bond, some owners ask for a separate Maintenance Bond for the purpose.[3]

In addition to owner needs for protection against risks, government agencies having jurisdiction often require the submittal of a performance

[3] Reprinted with permission from J. Burgoon, "Surety Bonds and Underwriting," in John D. Long and Davis W. Gregg, *Property and Liability Insurance Handbook* (Homewood, Ill.: Richard D. Irwin, Inc., 1965), pp. 829–30.

bond and maintenance bond for improvements shown on the approved construction plans. These bonds are written so that the warranties run to the government agency in case of default.

Construction of the Improvements

The construction process involves the actual installation of improvements on the site. The construction of improvements in even a small subdivision can be complex, requiring the utilization and coordination of various design professionals, skilled tradespeople, material, and labor. Factors such as weather, terrain, soil conditions, costs and availability of labor and materials, and local governmental regulations make each construction project somewhat unique.

Of prime importance in the construction process is a competent construction manager or, should the size of the job warrant, a construction management team to properly plan and implement the various stages of this function. Clough makes this statement regarding the importance of proper management in construction:

In general terms, management might be described as the judicious allocation and efficient usage of resources to achieve a desired end. The resources required for the construction of a project are money, labor, equipment, materials and time. Unfortunately, the construction process is not a self-regulating mechanism, and considerable management effort is required to achieve the desired end of timely completion and economy of operation. The achievement of a favorable time–cost balance by the careful scheduling and coordination of labor, equipment, subcontractors, and the maintaining of a material supply to sustain this schedule requires endeavor and skill. The project manager must blend together with the subjective ingredients of experienced judgment and intuition into an operating procedure. Astute project management requires at least as much art as science, as much human relations as management techniques.[4]

The land developer's firm may assume performance of the construction management function. Other developers may choose to contract that responsibility to a general contractor who, in turn, would coordinate the work. In either case, the construction process must be carefully managed.

Marketing a New Development

The process of marketing a new development depends on the types of properties established and the objectives of the developer. (See Figs. 11–3 and 11–4). If the subdivider wants to sell lots directly to users, quite a different marketing program will be set up than for a large-scale housing development with sales oriented toward builders.

---

[4] Reprinted with permission from Richard H. Clough, *Construction Project Management* (New York: John Wiley & Sons, Inc., 1972), pp. 5–6.

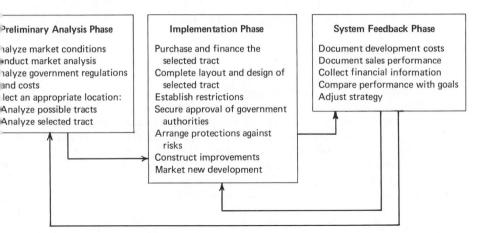

FIG. 11-3.   Essential elements of the land development process—a check list.

In the case of a subdivision, it is considered good practice to develop and market one part of the area at a time. The practice of sectionalization serves to limit risk and promote flexibility in marketing strategy. However, such sectionalization of improvement installation does not preclude the necessity of an overall integrated plan of development. Relatively few subdividers today follow the practice of simply dividing raw land and selling unimproved lots on an indiscriminate basis. Orderly development almost never results from such practices. The subdivider typically installs streets and roads and makes provision for essential utilities. Houses or other improvements may be built on the lots, either for sale or for rent.

When houses are built for sale, good practice dictates that houses be grouped rather than scattered. "Model houses" and "open houses" are often employed as selling devices. Auctions of lots sometimes are used.

Resort communities often market lots with a great deal of fanfare. They may advertise widely, make offers to transport prospects for long distances to see the development, conduct competitions, offer prizes, and use other approaches to promote sales.

If a subdivision is only partly developed and completion of the project is becoming difficult, the developer may improve the chances for success if new restrictions are placed on the land through the cooperation of the property owners. Then the area can be resubdivided into lots of proper size to fit the current market, unnecessary roads can be vacated, and, insofar as possible, objectionable features can be eliminated.

If a rental housing project is developed, the marketing process is quite different, since house services rather than the houses themselves are being sold. Marketing operations are discussed in greater detail in Chapters 13 and 14.

Preliminary Analysis Phase

Analyze market conditions
Conduct market analysis

National business activity and trends
Economy of area: basic activities, resources, and trends
Demand factors: income, employment, financial climate, population characteristics (no. of households, age distribution, social characteristics and tastes)
Supply factors: existing inventory, vacancy rates
Prices, rents, construction costs
Market area and competing sites
Conclusions as to needs, timing, strategy, and goals

Analyze government regulations and costs

Zoning   Transportation
Land planning   Fees and assessments
Environmental regulations

Select an appropriate location:
Analyze possible tracts

Physical characteristics: topography, soil types, flood plain information, utilities (sewer, water, power, telephone, gas), services (schools, transportation, recreation, fire and police protection, trash disposal), drainage, access, and other amenities
Legal characteristics: zoning and other land use constraints, building code requirements (if applicable), form of ownership, political climate for development, master land use plan, and thoroughfare plan
Economic characteristics: location factors (proximity to competing sites, adjacent land uses, accessibility), tax burdens
Raw land costs and extraordinary costs for development
Selection of most suitable tract

Analyze selected tract

Confirmation and further evaluation of factors previously listed
Preliminary land use plan and architectural plan (if applicable)
Preliminary engineering plan
Costs of development: on-site and off-site (including tap fees, etc.)
Preliminary proforma statement (hard and soft costs) and budget
Contracts with government agencies and personnel having jurisdiction and influence
Contacts with adjoining property owners and other potential remonstrators
Relationship of data to market strategy and goals previously established

FIG. 11–4. Phases of the land development process—a check list of essential elements.

Implementation Phase

Purchase and finance the selected tract

Tie up land: contingent purchase, lease (if applicable), land contract, option, or
  outright purchase
Sources:
  amounts and costs of debt funding for raw land and development costs
  amounts and costs of equity funding
Tax implications
Structure of financial package
Conformance to proforma statement and goals previously established
Obtain preliminary title binder and review
Secure financial commitment

Complete layout and design of selected tract

Engineering data: topographic mapping, boundary survey, soil tests, drainage
  data, utility capacity data
Final land planning: identification of building sites, recognition of natural
  terrain and other amenities, and layout of street, parking, and pedestrian
  access
Final construction plans and specifications: pavement, drainage, utilities, grading, landscaping, erosion control, and architectural (if applicable)
Estimate of costs and timing of costs, based on final design: relate to goals and
  proforma, establish final budget amounts

Establish restrictions

Land use restrictions supplemental to existing zoning and consistent with market-
  ing strategy
Ownership, maintenance, and rights related to common areas and easements
Enforcement of provisions

Secure approval of government authorities

Federal
State
Local
Revision of final construction plans and costs as required: compare with budgeted
  amounts

Arrange protections against risks

Performance bonding
Maintenance bonding
Liability insurance

FIG. 11–4.   Continued.

Implementation Phase (continued)

Construct improvements

> Prepare construction contracts and documents
> Prepare bid documents and bidders' list
> Evaluate bid amounts, quality of contractor, projected time of completion,
>   bonding, schedule of payments vs. goals and strategy
> Execute land purchase agreement and financing commitments (if not previously
>   done)
> Let contracts
> Monitor progress, costs, and quality of construction
> Secure government agency approvals prior to final payment

Market a new development

> Finalization of marketing strategy
> Advertising media and methods
> Financial packaging and sales models
> Establish marketing goals and means of measuring progress
> Monitor sales prospects and market

System Feedback Phase

Document development costs

> Review hard and soft costs and timing

Document sales performance

> Collect detailed reports on current and competing projects

Collect financial information

> Analyze cash flow, profit and loss statements, and related financial information

Compare performance with goals

> Match factual data against projections, goals, and strategy used to achieve them

Adjust strategy

> Align activities on current and future projects with performance data and
>   realistic projections

FIG. 11–4. Continued.

RECENT TRENDS IN LAND DEVELOPMENT

Most of the single-family homes built in the United States since the end of World War II have been constructed in new subdivisions on the periphery of existing cities or in vacant interstices between older residential communities. Developers have had the opportunity to lay out a new design of streets and a different lot size from the old pattern. Winding streets and cul-de-sacs often replaced the old rigid design of streets and lots. Planning the new subdivisions created an extensive field of activity for land planners.

Vacant land on the edge of cities becomes ripe for house building when sewers and water mains are extended from the central city or its principal built-up suburbs. Many new housing developments have been constructed in areas closely adjacent to the older settled areas and have been a mass extension of urban growth from the main urban body. Others have been located in undeveloped areas. Some redevelopment of older areas has also occurred.

Houses in high-priced residential developments sometimes have been constructed on larger lots of one or more acres, in areas separated from the concentrated urban mass by green belts. Some entire communities have been built, as in Pittsburgh, which are in open areas, and which have their own sewage-disposal system and water system. Other communities have relied on individual septic tanks, which have sometimes, under certain soil conditions, become objectionable and polluted the area. Many cities, villages, and counties in the United States have sought to regulate density of residential development by requiring minimum lot sizes.

Planned Unit Developments

Because of high land costs, efforts have been made to use land with greater intensity in residential developments but still to provide for adequate open areas and privacy. This has led to what we often refer to as "planned unit developments" (PUD). In these, townhouses and apartments are used, perhaps in a mixture with single-family detached houses but provision is made for lawns, gardens, and play areas that are carefully related to the dwellings.

Large-Scale Developments

Large-scale, carefully planned developments of 600 to 1,200 or more acres are sometimes undertaken. Such developments may include single-family units, garden and high-rise apartments, and townhouses. Provision is made for recreation areas, shopping centers, schools, and related facilities. In some cases entire cities or "new towns" are developed. An example is Columbia, Maryland, a development that includes a 14,500-acre tract of land between Baltimore and Washington, D. C. Reston, Virginia, another "new town," encompasses 7,000 acres.

PROBLEMS OF LAND DEVELOPMENT AND URBAN GROWTH

Subdividers and land developers have sometimes been criticized for lack of foresight in arranging for the orderly expansion of urban areas. Premature subdivisions, poor planning of new areas, attempts to make excessive profits, unsound financing plans, and failure to establish adequate regulations and controls have been common criticisms.

Although land developers have contributed their share to present-day problems of land utilization, governments have often failed to arrange for orderly developments and to set up a realistic framework within which competitive forces could operate.

Long-Term Planning

In recent years land use planning has been extended to cover metropolitan areas reaching beyond the traditional political boundaries. Carefully developed plans for long-term growth have been worked out for a number of localities including both urban and rural areas. In some cases zoning prescribes minimum lot sizes of from one to four acres, and this is permissible if for health or safety purposes; however, if large areas are set up as a requirement in order to limit growth, such regulations may be unconstitutional. Despite the progress that has been made, much remains to be done in this field. Indeed, too much rather than too little regulation may now be a danger.

Rising Standards

Higher standards are being followed in many subdivision developments. These include wider streets and thicker pavement design, curbs and gutters in lieu of side ditches, and requirements to provide storm sewers, sanitary sewers, and water mains. Increasing restrictions are being placed on private wells and private sewage-disposal systems.

The importance of large-scale developments to reduce costs is being stressed, as well as reduction in the scattering of developments, and the need for expansion of community facilities to keep up with land needs. Regional planning and the coordination of public facilities on a metropolitan basis are being accorded increased attention.

Public and Private Division of Labor

The improvement of land development in the future will require the very best efforts of both public and private business administration. Recognition must be given to the development of a sound division of labor between government and private enterprises. Possibly new governmental devices will have to be developed in order to provide a sound framework wihin which the private developer can operate.

On the other hand, private practices must improve. We can hardly expect this to happen unless the necessary inducements are present. Private business practices respond more definitely to promises of profits and sound investments than to preachments by public-spirited citizens. Realistic recognition of this should help city planning commissions and other public bodies in their work. Advancement in the field of land development will result chiefly from a many-sided attack on current problems by private enterprises and public agencies.

SUMMARY

The terms *subdividing* and *land development* describe the activities of those firms and individuals engaged in the production of real estate resources. Decisions at this stage have long-range importance, since the manner in which these functions are performed has considerable impact on the eventual character of the property and of the community or neighborhood of which it forms a part. Developers and builders usually are interested in immediate or early sale of the properties involved, and their outlook is essentially short-run. Users, investors, and property managers, however, typically take a longer-range view, since their interests are tied in with the development of the community and the future income-producing potential of the properties.

Although subdividers and developers are engaged in the production of real estate resources, each firm must arrange the financing of its own operations and the marketing of its own products. These products may be raw land, partially or completely developed lots, and perhaps buildings and other improvements. The timing of development and subdividing is of extreme importance in determining a project's success, and therefore should be based on careful market analysis and determination of ability to meet government regulations and their costs. "Planned unit developments" are growing in importance.

Location, timing, and costs all are important factors in the production of real estate resources. Financial institutions and other investors exercise much influence on decisions to produce real estate resources. Governmental approvals also are important, particularly with respect to building permits, zoning laws, environmental controls, interstate land sales, and insuring or guaranteeing of mortgages through FHA or VA if such arrangements are desired. Approvals also are required to insure conformity with local use and occupancy regulations and with public health requirements. The influence of the consumer of housing is highly important in developing improved standards.

QUESTIONS FOR STUDY

1. Suppose that you are planning the introduction of a proposed "Woodland Acres" subdivision. What market factors would you consider in determining whether this new subdivision might be successful?
2. What factors would be most important in determining the location of this subdivision?
3. Should you include commercial, residential, and recreational sites in the plan for the "Woodland Acres" subdivision? Explain.
4. Would you plan to include land for apartment houses as well as for single-family homes? Explain your position.
5. In your planning for the subdivision, what allowances should you make for traffic patterns? If the land is irregular in contour, how should the streets be laid out?
6. Outline the principal regulations that would help to assure the orderly development of a subdivision.
7. Why is timing so important in new land developments?
8. Make a list of the important costs involved in developing land, and describe them.
9. Are greater public controls needed over private subdivision developments? Give reasons for your position on this question. Which controls are important? Which least justified?
10. Are the interests of a land developer typically of a long-term or short-term nature with respect to a specific project? Explain.
11. What factors determine the way in which a tract of land should be subdivided into lots?
12. What are the most important items that should be included in protective covenants?
13. What is meant by a "planned unit development"?
14. Are large-scale developments likely to increase in importance?

SUGGESTED READINGS

AMERICAN INSTITUTE OF REAL ESTATE APPRAISERS. *The Appraisal of Real Estate* (6th ed.). Chicago: The Institute, 1973. Chs. 6, 7.

LONG, JOHN D., and GREGG, DAVIS W. *Property and Liability Insurance Handbook.* Homewood, Ill.: Richard D. Irwin, Inc., 1965. Chs. 53, 55, 57.

MCMAHAN, JOHN. *Property Development.* New York: McGraw-Hill Book Co., 1976. Ch. 13.

NATIONAL ASSOCIATION OF HOME BUILDERS. *Land Development Manual.* Washington, D. C.: The Association, 1974.

———. *Handbook for Subdivision Practice.* 1971.

OLIN, HAROLD B., SCHMIDT, JOHN L., and LEWIS, WALTER H. *Construction: Principles, Material and Methods.* Chicago: Institute of Financial Education, 1975. Pp. 601–13. (This is volume 3 of *Construction Lending Guide* published by The U. S. League of Savings Associations. Chicago: 1975.)

SELDIN, MAURY. *Land Investment.* Homewood, Ill.: Richard D. Irwin, Inc. (Dow Jones), 1975.

SELDIN, MAURY, and SWESNIK, RICHARD H. *Real Estate Investment Strategy.* New York: John Wiley & Sons, Inc., 1970. Ch. 4.

WILEY, ROBERT J. *Real Estate Investment—Analysis and Strategy.* New York: The Ronald Press Co., 1977. Ch. 16.

CASE 11–1

Sans Souci Estates

The purpose of this case study is to illustrate the nature of land development decisions.

The Flamingo Development Company, subdividers and builders since 1953, purchased 40 acres in the Eastwood section of a West Coast metropolitan area. The Eastwood section had its greatest development in the post-World War II years when land formerly used for growing citrus fruits was developed with low- to medium-priced homes financed by VA-guaranteed and FHA-insured mortgages. Though the heyday of Eastwood has passed, the Flamingo Development Company believes that there is a strong market in Eastwood for medium-priced conventionally financed homes.

The Flamingo Development Company decided to call the 40-acre development Sans Souci Estates. The land to the north, south, and east is almost fully developed. The houses built in the immediate post-World War II period are in a general price range of $28,000 to $30,000. The homes most recently built are larger and sell in the general price range of $38,000 to $40,500. Sans Souci Estates is about three miles from Eastwood Shopping Center, a major regional center.

The Flamingo Development Company considered three alternative land patterns:

1. A gridiron pattern with lot sizes ranging from 50 × 110 feet to 55 × 125 feet. This plan would provide for 160 lots. Total costs as follows:

A. Paving (streets, curbs, sidewalks)	$134,900	
B. Grading	34,900	
C. Sanitary sewer	69,800	
D. Storm sewer	51,200	
E. Water mains	46,500	
F. Erosion control	8,200	
Subtotal—Hard costs		$345,500
Engineering and surveying		73,500
TOTAL—Hard costs plus engineering and surveying		$419,000

2. A gridiron pattern with lot sizes ranging from 70 × 110 feet to 75 × 125 feet. This plan would provide for 120 lots with costs as follows:

A. Paving (streets, curbs, sidewalks)	$129,100	
B. Grading	33,400	
C. Sanitary sewer	66,800	
D. Storm sewer	48,900	
E. Water mains	44,500	
F. Erosion control	7,800	
Subtotal—Hard costs		$330,500
Engineering and surveying		72,000
TOTAL—Hard costs plus engineering and surveying		$402,500

3. A curvilinear street pattern with cul-de-sac. Lot sizes would range from 70 × 110 feet to 75 × 125 feet except some irregularly shaped lots of at least 7,500 square feet. This plan would provide for 120 lots.

A. Paving (streets, curbs, sidewalks)		$132,700
B. Grading		34,300
C. Sanitary sewer		68,600
D. Storm sewer		50,300
E. Water mains		45,800
F. Erosion control		8,000
Subtotal—Hard costs		$339,700
Engineering and surveying		72,000
TOTAL—Hard costs plus engineering and surveying		$411,700

Eastwood has a comprehensive zoning plan. The restrictions applicable to the Sans Souci Estates and the neighboring area provide, among other things, that:

1. No buildings or land shall be used except for the following purposes:
   a. Single-family dwellings
   b. Parks and playgrounds owned and operated by a government agency
2. No buildings shall be erected having a height in excess of two and one-half stories or 35 feet.
3. No main building shall be erected unless the yards and lot area are maintained.

The Flamingo Development Company purchased the property with a down payment of $40,000, and executed a purchase-money blanket mortgage for the balance of $160,000. The mortgage calls for payment of $40,000 or more annually plus 8 per cent interest. There is no prepayment penalty. The mortgage has a release clause providing that 10 acres will be released for each $40,000 payment on the mortgage. There is no subordination clause. The Flamingo Development Company is considering the alternative of developing the land in four units of 10 acres each, two units of 20 acres each, or one of 40 acres.

The Flamingo Development Company has, in addition to capital equipment and the $40,000 equity in the land, the sum of $100,000 in cash available for the development of Sans Souci Estates. Flamingo Development Company also has contact with a number of investors who would be willing to participate in the development on a joint-venture basis. The investors would be willing to furnish the capital and participate in 50 per cent of the profit.

Questions

1. On what basis did you think the officials of the Flamingo Development Company decided that this land was ripe for development?
2. Which of the three alternative land patterns would you choose? Explain your choice. Can you think of any more desirable ways of developing the property than those enumerated?
3. Would your choice of land patterns be any different if you were going to build instead of just subdividing? Explain.
4. How much would each lot cost under each of the three alternative arrangements?
5. How many acres would you develop at one time: 10 acres, 20 acres, or all 40 acres? How would you decide?
6. Would you add to or decrease the deed restrictions? Why?

STUDY PROJECT 11–1

Attractiveness of Low-Rise Suburban Apartment Developments

John J. Schmidt, of the U. S. League of Savings Associations, raises the following questions as to the attractiveness of low-rise suburban apartment developments.

Are the buildings attractive when viewed at a distance? Are the spaces between them in scale?

Does the project's overall design seem to take advantage of natural land features? Has the developer taken care to retain trees and other natural growth?

Are the buildings fitted into the topography, or has the topography been flattened to make way for the buildings?

Do the project's outside areas show evidence of good maintenance and housekeeping?

Is the landscaping attractive and tasteful? Or is it inadequate and poorly maintained, perhaps with bare spots that would be ugly in dry weather and muddy when it rains?

Is the space between the buildings pleasant to look at?

Are there play areas especially designed for children? Are they located where the sounds of children playing will not annoy tenants?

Are the buildings attractive when viewed close-up? Do the exterior fixtures appear of good quality?

Does the general parking plan seem practical and convenient?

Are parking facilities located relatively close to the building entrances, and is the path from the car to the building pleasant?

Is access to the units convenient, or are some tenants forced to do excessive walking and stair-climbing?

Do the building entrances provide protected stair enclosures? Especially, do stairs to upper units provide protection from rain, snow, and ice?

Are views from inside the units attractive? And do lower-level units have good ventilation and natural light?

Are so-called "private" balconies really private? Especially, are they reasonably isolated from noisy play areas?

Do all special facilities, including swimming pools and clubhouses, also show good maintenance and housekeeping?

Questions

1. Which of the factors mentioned do you consider most important?
2. Do you think additional factors might be considered in determining the attractiveness of a low-rise suburban apartment development?

12

PRODUCTION: BUILDING

RELATION OF BUILDING TO LAND DEVELOPMENT

In the preceding chapter we considered the functions and some of the problems of the land developer and subdivider. We pointed out that in many cases building and land development were integrated operations, while in others they were carried on separately. Obviously, the completed product is composed of land and buildings, hence the best results are often achieved when the processes of land development and building are integrated and there is close coordination between them.

New real estate resources are the result of at least six processes: (1) initiating, (2) planning, (3) land development, (4) building, (5) financing, and (6) marketing. As we pointed out in the preceding chapter, all of these processes except building are involved in land development if a project is undertaken solely for the purpose of marketing lots. When we include construction, however, many of these activities become more complicated.

Building Processes

The building process itself requires the performance of these principal functions: (1) *initiating;* (2) *planning,* including the design and engineering of the building (this is chiefly the responsibility of the architect in order to meet the program requirements of the developer); (3) *financing,* including construction loans and financing the sale of the final product; and (4) *construction,* including purchase of the materials and equipment, employment of labor, and assembly and installation of the materials and equipment. This is largely the work of the contractor and subcontractors and may be appropriately thought of as a fabricating or manufacturing process.

Construction Enterprises

The business firms engaged in construction range all the way from very small organizations to large companies operating on a regional, national, and even an international basis. Some major corporations are now involved in construction projects. General contractors and subcontractors are included. Lumber and building supply dealers form a part of this industry. Prefabricated house manufacturers and the manufacturers of building materials and equipment play a major role in the construction field. The firms in this industry, as in others, may be individual proprietorships, partnerships, or corporations. Syndicates may be set up for large projects.

Each of these business firms must establish its own objectives and manage its resources as effectively as possible in trying to attain its objectives. Its owners and managers must establish plans to achieve objectives, organize resources, and control operations. Leadership plays a big part in the success of enterprises in this field. Even in small construction enterprises, large amounts of money are involved. Hence, owners and managers must be able and willing to undertake big risks. This often requires courage of a high order plus good judgment and organizing ability as well as a sense of timing.

Construction Decisions

As we suggested in the preceding chapter, a number of complicated factors are involved in decisions to undertake new land development programs. Such programs frequently include building as well as land development. Primary decisions are made by the owners of the land. They may sell off the land in stages, thus helping to finance the project. Such arrangements may help them with their tax problems. Those who lend money to developers almost always play a major role in such decisions.

Since large land development and building programs typically continue over a long period of time, it becomes extremely difficult to estimate potential costs, returns, and risks with any degree of accuracy. Some developers contemplate relatively quick sale and recapture of their investment through small subdivision and building operations in which all properties are designed for sale. Long-term investments are involved in large multifamily housing developments, shopping centers, or office buildings.

Typically, the firms engaged strictly in construction have only a short-run interest in these projects. Such firms may have a general or a special contract for a construction project. Even in short-run periods many uncertainties exist. Costs may vary widely in the space of a few months. There may be sudden changes in weather conditions. Labor problems may cause expensive work stoppages. It may be impossible to get delivery of key materials. These are all parts of the risk undertaken by the building contractor who assumes responsibility for a project.

A builder may take stock in the new development as partial compensation, thereby gaining both a long- and a short-term interest in it, the length of the term depending on the type of development.

INITIATING AND PLANNING

The preliminary stages of a building operation include initiating and planning. Each of these stages will depend on the type of initiator, the size of the operation, and the care with which planning is carried out.

Types of Initiators

A real estate development may be initiated by an individual for the sole purpose of fulfilling a requirement for a place to live. The purchaser will probably buy a lot, consult an architect, arrange financing, and make arrangements with a contractor who will secure the necessary materials, equipment, and labor.

The initiator may be a builder who is undertaking a new development for the purpose of building and selling houses or building and renting houses or apartments. An industrial firm may initiate a project such as an addition to existing plant facilities or the erection of new plants. A merchant may want to build a store. A private investor may develop a shoping center or an apartment house. A carpenter may decide to build a few homes for sales. Almost anyone with savings or credit may initiate a building project.

Size of Operations

The size of the operation may range from a single house or the conversion of an old dwelling into several efficiency apartments to the development of a community or a new town. The resources available, condition of the market, risks–cost–return relationships, and objectives of the developer—all will affect the scope of the project.

New communities have been developed in many places. An entire town has been developed as a retirement community at Sun City, Arizona, by the Del Webb organization. The developers of the Irvine Ranch in California created a major city. "New towns" such as Reston and Columbia also exemplify very large-scale efforts.

During recent years, industrialized home manufacturers have become an important part of the building industry. They have been of major importance in the housing field but have also engaged in shopping centers and related developments. Mobile home manufacturers have occupied a prominent place in the residential field. Building materials and equipment manufacturers have influenced the methods of both large- and small-scale on-site builders. Through research programs they have made improvements in the use of materials and in the efficiency of building processes.

Regardless of who initiates a building project, plans must be made, financing arranged, and construction carried out. In some instances the initiator may perform all of these functions. In projects of any size, however, specialists usually perform various parts of the process.

Planning Construction

Planning is usually the work of the owner or developer and the architect/designer or engineer. The developer determines the type, price range, and quality of structure. These design parameters should be based on a thorough study of the potential market area. On the basis of this information, the architect plans the building. Architectural planning includes the following activities: (1) schematic design including preliminary sketches and estimates of probable construction costs and time; (2) design development which comprises preliminary design drawings, outline of specifications, and probable cost estimates; (3) preparation of construction documents—working drawings, specifications, and all documents necessary for bidding and construction; (4) actual construction, with the architect providing general supervision and project inspection. Interspersed within the planning function is ongoing contact with the several government agencies having jurisdiction over the design of the buildings. Feedback from these agencies often has significant impact on the final product.

The architect's preliminary sketches are diagrams of the building which give a clear picture of the proposed arrangement, the location and size of the rooms, the general appearance of the structure, the equipment to be included, and the position of the structure on the lot. Preliminary cost estimates are often made on the basis of these sketches.

After definite agreement has been reached on all points between the developer and the architect, working drawings are prepared which show the exact size and location of all walls, partitions, and rooms, the material to be used at various points, and all details of construction. Specifications are then written which supplement the drawings, establishing the quality of materials and workmanship and indicating how the work is to be executed.

FINANCING

Ordinarily contractors do not finance construction. Usually they provide only the working capital for current operations either from their own funds or from bank or individual loans. The builder and other private investors may form a pool, with profits being divided and the arrangement being dissolved at the completion of a project. In most other manufacturing processes, of course, the producer finances the operation. When construction is undertaken, however, the owner or developer and the ultimate consumer may both become involved in the financing of production.

Progress Payments

A fairly typical arrangement is that of the construction loan under which a financing institution agrees to disburse funds at various stages of the building process. These periodic payment requests are commonly known as construction draws—the developer draws a portion of the total construction loan commitment as each phase of the building project is completed. As a protection to the lender, disbursements are usually made only for work in place. As a further safeguard, the lender will often hold back a portion of the draw request for a short period of time to determine whether there are any possible defects in construction. This withholding is called retainage and commonly runs in the range of 5 to 10 per cent of the gross draw request.

Upon completion of building, the construction loan is typically supplanted by a mortgage. As an alternative, the permanent mortgage is recorded in advance of construction and payments are disbursed at various stages of construction. In some instances a commitment is given with provision for merging of the short-term construction loan with long-term financing.

Conditional Commitments

In the case of residential construction, the builder usually arranges for individual mortgages for each house and assigns the mortgage to the purchaser. Many lending institutions engage in construction financing in the hope of securing mortgages. The use of FHA "conditional commitments" to insure loans usually provides the owner or developer with sufficient credit to finance all or substantial portions of construction. Commitments from the Veterans' Administration for loan guarantees are often used in a similar manner. Some lenders may take "a piece of the action" in the case of income properties and become part owners.

Business Properties

Industrial plants are usually financed by the firms which own or intend to use them. Commercial properties may be financed by private investors or by those owning or using the properties. Insurance companies are an important source of funds. Again, there is often a fusion of construction and long-term financing. Sale and leaseback arrangements have been used widely as a method of financing commercial properties.

Equities

Some larger financial institutions now develop properties and rent them, financing the entire operation from start to finish. Or they take "a piece of the action" on a variety of bases. Major corporations may take equity positions in developments, and, of course, a broad range of individual and institutional investors may be involved.

Cumbersome Processes

Except for the latter type of arrangement, most of the financing of construction is cumbersome, chiefly because the property rather than the credit of the developer or contractor is the principal security. Laborers and subcontractors are protected by mechanics' liens, an arrangement which also reflects this situation. Thus, financial institutions can exert great influence on construction operations because of their dominant position in providing the necessary credit advances.

CONSTRUCTION: BUILDING OPERATIONS

Generally speaking, building operations fall into two main categories: (1) those accomplished by a builder-developer-contractor employing an architect or a designer either on a fee basis or as a member of the staff; and (2) those accomplished by an individual or organization with the work being let to a contractor but with an architect employed to administer the contract for the owner, as in the case of a custom-built house project. Figures 12–1 and 12–2 illustrate these two categories of building operations.

Bids

Bids are usually invited from several general contractors, although contracts may be let without competitive bidding. If bids are invited, the contract is normally awarded to the lowest bidder, unless the submitted figure is so low that there is doubt about the contractor's ability to do a satisfactory job. Bids may be taken on the following bases:

1. A fixed price for the entire project
2. Cost plus a percentage for profit (usually 10 per cent)
3. Cost plus a profit percentage, say 10 per cent, but with a maximum limit established
4. Cost plus a percentage with a maximum upper limit, with provision for dividing any savings between contractor and developer
5. Cost plus a fixed fee

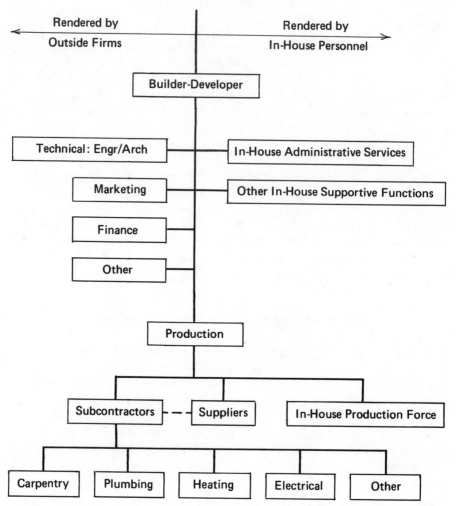

FIG. 12–1. A typical builder-developer arrangement.

Other methods may be used as well, but the above arrangements are typical. The fixed price method is used very widely. Contracts for mechanical work may be let separately with a general contract covering the rest of the project.

A single contract may be awarded to a general contractor, or various contracts may be let for specific parts of the project. If the former plan is followed, the general contractor typically parcels out certain phases of the work among subcontractors. In the case of some large projects, all of the work may be sublet. In either event, the construction process is seldom carried out by a single organization.

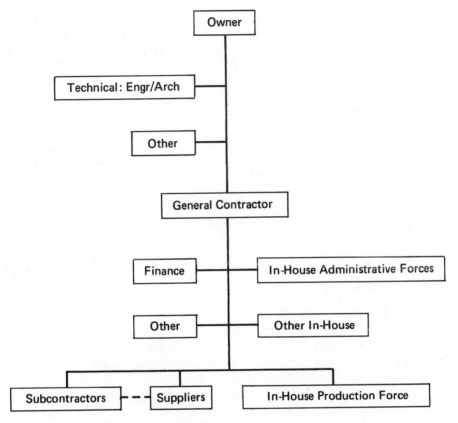

FIG. 12–2. A typical custom-house arrangement.

Division of Work

The general contractor usually reserves such work as the available equipment can handle. In addition to an overall management function, excavating, putting in foundations, masonry, carpentry, and similar work are usually the responsibility of the general contractor.

The types of work for which subcontractors may be used include roofing, plumbing, lathing, painting, tiling, heating, electricity, and structural iron work. A subcontractor may be a building supply jobber or dealer, but more frequently such suppliers sell materials to the general contractor or to one or more subcontractors. Many materials are originally processed by building supply manufacturers, who sell them directly to contractors or through supply dealers. Restrictive practices sometimes surround these operations, as we shall see in a later section.

Work Force

After all contractual agreements have been arranged and provision has been made for the required materials, the necessary labor force is hired and the actual work of construction is carried out. Many different types of labor are required even in the construction of a single-family dwelling. From twenty-five to forty-five crafts may be involved in relatively simple house-building operations. As many as eighty occupational groups may be engaged in a large-scale building project.

Because of the high degree of organization typical of building labor, the contractor and subcontractors frequently arrange for the necessary labor through a union official. Since the degree of labor organization varies from city to city, workers are sometimes hired directly. Contractors seldom maintain anything resembling a permanent work force, although a skeleton organization may move from job to job. Usually other laborers are recruited as needed for each job.

Project Scheduling

Because of the complexity of the building process, two innovative programs to manage the various phases of construction have been developed—the critical path method (CPM) and the program evaluation and review technique (PERT). These two methods, as well as several offshoots, require the identification of all the occupational groups and activities involved in the project. Knowledge of the alternative sequences of work activities and an estimate of the time required to perform each activity are essential. From this information a diagram can be prepared which illustrates the various work activities, the possible sequences of activities, and the corresponding completion times. The "critical path" or sequence requiring the least gross completion time can then be identified. The identification of the critical path thus enables the construction manager to note those items of work most critical to timely completion of the project. The computer can be used to advantage in the scheduling of large jobs utilizing these techniques.

Completion

The building process is completed when the owner or developer accepts the structure as finished and final payments including retainage have been made. The period between the letting of contracts and the completion of construction may be as short as several weeks in the case of prefabricated operations. It may cover several months or even a year or two or longer for large projects.

CONSTRUCTION: BUILDING COSTS

Except for such prefabrication of structural parts or equipment as takes place, the "manufacturing" of a building occurs at the site. Hence, costs vary with local situations.

Architects' Fees

Architects' fees usually are 6 to 8 per cent of the cost of a structure, except on very small projects where the percentage is higher. Fees vary with services performed. When an architect performs "full services" and handles the job for a client, a fee of 8 to 10 per cent may be quite reasonable. An architect is sometimes engaged on the basis of a one-time development cost plus royalties if the designs are to be repeated. A fee of 1 to 1½ per cent of cost may then be reasonable.

Local Variations in Material Costs

Building costs vary widely between localities because of differences in the local availability of materials and resulting transportation costs. Table 12–1 illustrates how material (and labor) costs vary from locality to locality. Furthermore, building costs are affected greatly by differences in climate. Not only are insulating and heating costs vastly different from one part of the country to another, but so are the requirements for foundations, glazing, roofing, and many other items.

TABLE 12–1. Selected Locality Adjustments

	General	Labor	Material
	(Use as coefficient; no unit)		
Anchorage, Alaska	1.29	1.36	1.21
Atlanta, Georgia	0.90	0.83	0.98
Chicago, Illinois	1.00	1.06	0.93
Columbia, South Carolina	0.74	0.61	0.87
Houston, Texas	0.87	0.85	0.90
Indianapolis, Indiana	0.92	0.94	0.90
Jackson, Mississippi	0.79	0.69	0.89
Los Angeles, California	1.02	1.12	0.92
Miami, Florida	0.86	0.81	0.92
Minneapolis, Minnesota	0.97	0.92	1.01
New York, New York	1.18	1.25	1.11
St. Louis, Missouri	1.00	1.01	1.00
San Francisco, California	1.12	1.16	1.08
Seattle, Washington	1.02	0.96	1.07

Note: The locality adjustments above can be used to adjust building costs in the "1976 Dodge Construction Systems Costs" for local conditions.
Source: "1976 Dodge Construction Systems Costs," McGraw-Hill Information Systems Co., New York, N. Y., and Woodard Tower Inc., Princeton, N. J., 1975, pp. 236–41.

Materials Distribution

The contractor may buy materials and supplies in several ways. Usually the channels for distributing building materials are similar to those of many other products: from manufacturer to wholesaler or jobber to retailer and then to the consumer, who in this instance, however, is represented by the contractor.

Some manufacturers maintain control of the distribution process down through the retailing level; others sell to wholesalers who distribute through their subsidiaries or sell to independent dealers. The typical lumber dealer generally handles a wide variety of materials, though usually there are separate dealers in hardware, paint, wallpaper, and similar items. Plumbing materials, linoleum, tile, heating equipment, and electric wiring often are installed by local dealers. Larger builders, however, may absorb these functions.

Although the dealer serves the contractor in numerous ways, such as maintaining inventory and frequently promoting business and helping to arrange financing, there are numerous instances of special arrangements which favor the more substantial builders or which limit in various ways the introduction of certain new products into a local market.

Labor Costs and Efficiency

All types of labor in the building trades usually receive high wages on an hourly or daily basis. Approximately half of the cost of most structures is required to pay the labor bill. Because the degree of labor organization varies widely from locality to locality, there are substantial differences in labor costs.

The actual cost of materials in place depends upon the efficiency of labor. When building is at low ebb, bricklayers tend to lay more brick than when jobs are plentiful. Some contractors subcontract all or nearly all work, putting it on a price basis; the resulting in-place costs are often low even though the weekly wages of workers on such projects are among the highest in the building trades.

Other Costs

Other expenditures typically incurred in the usual construction project include costs of construction loans; building permits; workmen's compensation; liability, unemployment, and other types of insurance; social security taxes; sales taxes; contractors' overhead and profit; and the maintenance of equipment. The payment of bonuses and incentives may represent substantial amounts. Environmental and safety regulations may result in additional costs.

CONSTRUCTION: LARGE-SCALE PRODUCTION OPERATIONS

Significant advances have been made in the application of standardization and large-scale production methods to the building industry. Three principal types of developments are tending toward the industrialization of building: (1) simplification and standardization of parts by manufacturers; (2) adaptation of factory methods to production at the site by large-scale contractors and builders; and (3) prefabrication of virtually complete structures for assembly at the site.

Two main types of industrialized components may be identified: panelized structures and modular structures. Panelized structures include wall sections, roof panels, and other panels. Modular structures comprise "three-dimensional" components such as entire factory-assembled rooms or living units.

A number of preparatory operations are now carried on away from the site with manufacturers preparing precut lumber, roof framing, stairs, prehung doors and windows, cabinets, and similar items. In addition, much equipment assembly is completed prior to delivery to the site.

Simplification and Standardization

Standardization of house plans and designs has been progressing for some time and has brought economies through reduction in costs of design and increased efficiency of labor. The standardization of plans, designs, and materials as well as more manufacturing of parts away from the site, has brought economies to nearly all types of builders.

On-Site Factory Methods

Large-scale builders now arrange for workers to move from one operation to another, organizing the work with a relatively high degree of efficiency as in a factory operation. In part, this has been made possible by the introduction of a number of labor-saving devices including power excavating, grading, and hoisting machinery; electric saws, hammers, and drills; concrete, mortar, glue, and plaster mixers; spray guns for paint; and power sanders. The introduction of some of these labor-saving devices, however, has sometimes been resisted by the unions, as has the use of precut and prefabricated materials which are delivered to the site for assembly.

Manufactured Housing

Prefabricated or manufactured housing has made significant progress. Economies of substantial proportions have been achieved both in production and distribution processes. Great progress has also been made in purchasing materials and equipment on a large scale for assembly in factories

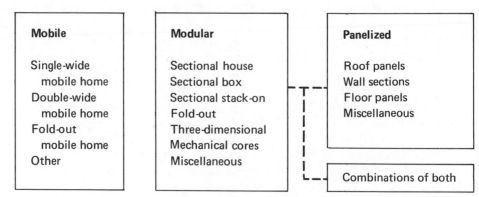

FIG. 12–3. Types of industrialized housing.

and delivery as a more or less complete package. Prefabrication has probably led to greater mechanization of traditional building processes as well, not only for houses but also for large-scale projects such as office buildings. It has also helped to stimulate the use of "modular" methods of production.

With the solution of various manufacturing problems, greater emphasis is being given to the marketing and financing of prefabricated or manufactured houses. They have gained wide acceptance. Manufactured houses including mobile homes now dominate the small-house field. Many local building codes no longer exclude prefabricated or manufactured houses. Building codes, however, create numerous problems for mobile home developments. Sometimes union rules tend to cancel the economies resulting from improved production methods.

Marketing Practices of Prefabricators and Home Manufacturers

The use of local dealer representatives is one method of marketing prefabricated homes. Similar arrangements are typical of the mobile home field. This permits local acquisition of land and the utilization of and adaptation to local labor and supply conditions. It also aids in the development of local sources of financing. Future developments in production and distribution will depend to a large extent on whether financing arrangements will meet the requirements of this industry.

Specific arrangements for local dealerships vary widely. Some manufacturers control them very closely, and others have rather informal working relationships with their dealers. Integration of manufacturers' and local dealers' activities is especially important in connection with advertising and sales promotional campaigns. Another arrangement is the company-owned dealership. The parent company in such cases controls the entire process from factory through financing and sale to the ultimate buyer.

This arrangement has some advantages but may or may not be done locally as in the case of an independent builder-dealer.

One of the major problems of local dealers or company-owned dealerships in the housing industry arises from the fact that land cannot be prefabricated. As we saw in the preceding chapter, the costs of acquiring and developing land are often very great. Sometimes the financial requirements for land development are beyond the resources of local dealers and beyond their ability to command the necessary credit through traditional channels. Hence, some house manufacturers have established special financial programs to assist local dealers.

Mobile Homes

Some builders and developers have made use of mobile homes in recent years. Many types are 14 feet wide and have a length of 60 feet or more. The limitations imposed by highway regulations for moving mobile units vary widely. In some cases two units are combined on a "double wide" basis. Some combined units contain as many as two baths and four bedrooms.

Specialized manufacturers have developed in this field including Skyline, Fleetwood, National, and others. Large-scale plants provide efficient production methods. Assembly usually includes major appliances and furniture. Thus, when delivered a unit is ready for almost immediate occupancy.

There are usually local retail outlets selling directly to the public. Mobile home park developers provide parking spaces, usually on a monthly rental basis. Frequently these developers are local people; in some cases building organizations go into this field and operate on a wide basis. Some mobile home parks are very attractive and carefully planned and developed; others leave much to be desired.

Mobile homes have been popular in part because they are classified as personal property and carry personal rather than real property taxes. Financing generally can be arranged without difficulty even in tight money periods although the rates are usually high.

BUILDING INDUSTRY TRENDS

Despite its problems the building industry has made progress in a number of directions in recent years. Of special importance are advances in (1) technology, (2) engineering and architecture, (3) management, and (4) warranty programs. Problems persist, however, in a number of areas including labor, materials distribution, and government–business relationships.

Technology

Technological advances include the development of new products, improved uses of old products, and more efficient production methods resulting from new machinery, prefabrication, and modular construction. Product changes range all the way from better heating and lighting equipment, air conditioning, and cooking and other kitchen equipment to improved uses of glass, better insulation, the use of aluminum covering for exteriors, and plastic plumbing. Technology may soon give us even better basic systems of construction, improved finishes for both interior and exterior application and such mechanical devices as automatic cleaning equipment, luminous walls, and "instant cooking." We may soon have competitive solar heating and cooling systems. Even the sewerless toilet may not be too many years away.

Engineering and Architecture

Engineering and architectural advances include improved space planning, more efficient layout of buildings, better combination of building materials, and many related developments. Even houses in the lower price ranges have been given the benefit of good architectural design and planning.

Management

Management has improved the processes of planning, organizing, and controlling operations. Longer-range planning has characterized the activities of subdividers and builders. Seasonal fluctuations have been reduced by careful scheduling of work so as to allow for colder weather operations. The increased diversity of materials and products used in construction has necessitated better managerial planning and scheduling. Many builders have been able to improve their organizational arrangements through better division of work and more effective supervision. The use of CPM, PERT, and related "critical path" methods has been widespread. Controls have improved in part because of rising costs and in part because of tax considerations. Inventory controls have been improved in the construction industry but there have been advances also in inspections, in cost accounting, and in budgeting.

An outgrowth of these improved management techniques has been the development of a contracting system called "construction management." Under this system, the owner employs a construction manager in addition to an architect at the inception of a project. The prime duties of the construction manager are twofold: (1) working with the architect and owner in the planning and design stages of the project, and (2) assuming the responsibility of carrying out the construction phases of the project. The input of the construction manager in the early stages of the project permits "value engineering"—experience-tempered planning on such areas as cost control, material specification, labor organization, governmental requirements, and job scheduling. The construction management approach may also permit "fast tracking" or starting of construction before all plans and specifications are complete, thereby hastening the progress of the job. Construction managers have typically emerged from the construction ranks although the design disciplines have contributed to this growing field of professional managers. The construction management approach has been most popular in the larger building projects.

Warranty Programs

Increased concern for the protection of the consumer has led to some innovative programs in the building industry. A recent example is the Home Owners Warranty Program (HOW) instituted by the National Association of Home Builders (NAHB). The HOW program provides a ten-year protection package for new home purchasers. Under this voluntary program, the builder purchases an insurance package from a designated private insurance company with the home purchaser as the beneficiary. The plan covers labor and materials in the early years and major structural features over the entire ten-year period. Warranty programs have also been instituted for "used" homes. One such program is endorsed by the National Association of Realtors (NAR). Judging from the early success of HOW and similar programs, it would appear that warranty programs will become a permanent feature of the building industry.

Restrictions

As competition has grown more intense, greater emphasis has been placed on improved products and methods and on cost cutting. The industry continues to suffer from restrictive building codes and labor practices, and from its dependence on the development of regional supporting facilities by government to allow for new land development. Many builders, of course, continue to follow outmoded practices. Informal agreements sometimes result in price fixing and the reduction of competition.

Because of restrictive practices, the introduction of new products and methods often is retarded. There has been some tendency to revise building codes in order to introduce greater flexibility, but many localities follow requirements that are unduly restrictive. Building operations have been limited by the slow pace of many local governments and other agencies.

Although problems persist, the building industry can take credit for significant advances in recent years. The building industry holds numerous opportunities for young people who have energy, imagination, and a willingness to pioneer. Government also has provided encouragement through such programs as providing subsidies to stimulate the use of solar energy, in the hope of alleviating fuel shortages in the future.

Labor Organizations

Building labor is highly organized in most cities. Many organizations continue to follow craft rather than industrial lines. Jurisdictional disputes are among the more difficult problems of the building industry and at least some of these would be eliminated if labor were organized on a different basis.

The attitudes of labor unions in the building trades have tended to retard the introduction of labor-saving machinery and devices. There has also been insistence that production be limited to prescribed speeds. Featherbedding rules are common. While one can hardly blame individual workers for resisting the introduction of labor-saving machinery and for not wanting to work themselves out of jobs, union leaders have often been slow to recognize that these policies are shortsighted and not in the ultimate interests of the workers. In the long run, the earnings of workers are limited by their productivity. Labor-saving devices aid in the process of increasing output per worker. If this were not the case, China and India would have the highest wage levels in the world, since they have few labor-saving devices in use and the proportion of labor to capital employed in production is high.

The building trades have succeeded in establishing high hourly or daily wage scales. In part this is an attempt to compensate for seasonal and cyclical variations in construction activity, and in part it is the result of a high degree of labor organization and the strategic position of building labor which enables it to enforce its demands.

Limitations on the number of apprentices who are trained, the relatively disorganized condition of some employers, the small scale of a number of building operations, and the policies of trade unions in resisting the introduction of labor-saving devices all help to explain the success of labor organizations. Not only are wage scales high, they are relatively inflexible downward. Even during recession periods, wage rates tend to be maintained at high levels. Productivity of workers, however, tends to increase in such periods.

It is probable that considerable benefit would result from a more flexible wage scale, for labor, for the builder, and for the consumer. It may be that some form of annual wage arrangement is the answer to these problems. The nature of employment in the building trades, however, with laborers moving from one job to another as projects are finished, is a real obstacle to the establishment of an annual wage.

Improved labor relations would be highly beneficial to the construction industry. Ordinarily the number of wage disputes is higher in this field than in most others, and the elimination of some of the lost time and the added risks which result would benefit worker and employer alike.

Materials Distribution Problems

The materials distribution system now results in highly competitive pricing. The emergence of "cash and carry" lumberyards and builder–dealer merchandising connections contribute to the intensity of competition. Because of their dominant position in many local communities, the materials dealers must be reckoned with by manufacturers and builders alike. Some dealers organize and establish more or less fixed prices and working agreements, thus reducing competition. The combination of the functions of dealer and builder in the manufactured house industry has broadened competition.

Construction materials dealers serve building contractors in a number of ways. They may help with inventory problems, with promoting business, and sometimes with short-term financing.

Government and Building

As we have suggested, the building codes of a number of cities make excessive requirements and hinder the introduction of new structural materials. In addition there are fire-prevention, elevator, and related codes, as well as occupancy regulations. Codes are seldom changed as often as necessary to keep abreast of industrial developments. Also, the administration of building codes frequently leaves something to be desired. Progress toward performance codes is being made, however, and significant improvement may be expected in the years ahead. Environmental regulations have often created problems for builders and added to costs.

Licensing laws for architects, contractors, engineers, and even workers in certain building trades are in force in a number of states. While their objectives are desirable, they often lead to restraints and virtually monopolistic practices. The property standards and minimum construction requirements set up by the Federal Housing Administration (FHA) have had desirable effects, but have also added to the regulatory problems faced by the building industry. The federal government has influenced building through improvement of financing practices as a result of the work of the Federal Home Loan Bank System, and the Federal Home Loan Mortgage Corporation ("Freddy Mac"), the FHA, the Veterans' Administration (VA), the Government National Mortgage Association ("Ginny Mae"), and the Federal National Mortgage Association ("Fanny Mae"). The Bureau of Standards has helped to develop and improve materials as well as to establish better criteria for judging the performance of materials. The Department of Commerce (especially the Bureau of the Census) and the Federal Home Loan Bank System have prepared much information about housing markets. The Department of Housing and Urban Development has attempted to stimulate innovation.

Limited progress has been made in eliminating restrictive and monopolistic practices in the building industry. Local zoning laws and city planning regulations affect building activities, and local tax burdens must be reckoned with constantly. The laws governing the sale, transfer, and marketing of new real estate developments often are not adapted to present-day requirements.

The Building Industry's Industrial Revolution

The large amount of experimentation going on in the building industry may be comparable to the experiences of other industries during the earlier phases of their industrial revolutions. As a result of this experimentation, the building industry has already taken on a quite different appearance in recent decades. This is probably the most important reason for optimism in regard to the potentialities of this field.

As Lyle C. Bryant has pointed out,

Industrial revolutions are never accomplished overnight. As we look back over industrial history, however, the striking fact is that almost every industry has had its "revolution," each heralded by a period of seething unrest and experimentation much like what we see in the building industry today.[1]

SUMMARY

The building process consists of the planning, financing, and construction of buildings upon improved land. Land development and building operations often are combined. Construction firms range in size from very small to very large builders. Construction is a risky business, involving substantial sums of money.

Almost anyone with savings or credit may initiate a building project, whether an individual desiring a residence or a large operative builder. Whether the project is a single residence or an entire community, it must be planned, financed, and constructed. Various specialized parties such as architects, contractors, and subcontractors are involved in the physical operation, while financing usually is arranged through one or another type of financial institution. Decisions about construction are made primarily

---

[1] Letter to the authors.

by property owners and developers, subject to the veto of lenders and the influence of various specialists, notably architects, engineers, and construction managers.

In recent years, the building industry has enjoyed advances in technology, engineering and architecture, management, and warranty programs. Of particular importance have been the development of simplification and standardization, the use of factory methods of production at the building site, and prefabrication of materials for assembly at the site. Materials distribution, governmental factors, and labor relations remain as critical problem areas. In labor, extensive organization of the building trades into many different craft unions, and the instability of employer–employee relationships have tended to result in jurisdictional disputes, featherbedding, and resistance to technological advance. Significant changes may be anticipated in methods of using land and carrying out construction as well as in quality and character of design.

QUESTIONS FOR STUDY

1. What are the main processes involved in the development of new real estate resources?
2. Describe the principal steps in planning for the construction of a single-family residence. Would the planning be any different in the case of an apartment building?
3. What are the two principal types of building operations in terms of the role of the architect?
4. Can you suggest ways in which the financing of building construction might be improved?
5. What is the relationship of the subcontractor to the contractor? Why does the contractor sublet parts of a contract? What is meant by construction management?
6. Why do building costs vary between regions of the country?
7. Explain the important advantages of prefabrication and modular construction; the main advantages of large-scale on-site construction.
8. Explain CPM and PERT. What are their chief advantages?
9. If you bought a mobile home, you would be getting a considerably different product than if you bought a house. Describe the differences in both the product and the transactions involved.
10. How might labor practices in the building industry be improved?
11. Would you favor the establishment of an annual wage in the building industry? Why or why not?
12. What are the principal advantages of building codes? In what ways may building codes hinder construction activities?
13. Outline the major current trends in the building industry. What are the significant changes that appear to lie ahead?

SUGGESTED READINGS

FICEK, EDMUND F., HENDERSON, T. P., and JOHNSON, ROSS H. *Real Estate Principles and Practices.* Columbus, Ohio: Charles E. Merrill Publishing Co., 1976. Ch. 18.

KRATOVIL, ROBERT. *Real Estate Law* (6th ed.). Englewood Cliffs, N. J.: Prentice-Hall, Inc., 1974. Chs. 21, 26.

MCMAHAN, JOHN. *Property Development.* New York: McGraw-Hill Book Co., 1976. Ch. 14.

STUDY PROJECT 12–1

NASA's "House of the Future"

The National Aeronautics and Space Administration (NASA) has constructed a Technology Utilization House at the NASA Langley Research Center to demonstrate technologies from the space program that are applicable to the construction industry. Features of the house include (1) solar collectors used with a heat pump and nighttime radiators to supply virtually all requirements for domestic hot water and space heating; (2) a larger than normal roof overhang on the south wall that allows the sun to enter the south-facing windows only during October through March; (3) solar cells that convert light energy into electrical energy without moving parts; (4) insulation of exterior and interior walls with a plastic foam; (5) recovery of fireplace heat to heat water and to transfer the heat to the heat storage system; (6) accurate and automatic control of the heating and cooling system; (7) a prefabricated floor that provides inexpensive insulation and is noncombustible; (8) a heat pipe that uses capillary action of a liquid in a sealed pipe to transfer heat for cooking in the kitchen, for freezing, and for defrosting foods; (9) a waste-water reuse system that reduces water consumption by collecting waste water from bathroom sinks, bathtubs, showers, and laundry equipment and recycling it for use as toilet flush water (waste from toilets goes directly to the sewer); (10) a temperature-compensating thermister in each light bulb socket that protects the light bulb against current surges and increases the life of the light bulb; (11) precast, fire-resistant walls that reduce heat loss and cut down noise transmission; (12) a microwave oven that reduces cooking time and requires less energy; (13) the use of exhaust heat from large appliances such as the refrigerator, the oven, and the clothes dryer; (14) a flat electrical conductor cable that substantially reduces copper requirements and can be easily installed or modified; (15) interior wall studs reconstituted from sawdust, thereby making use of previously discarded material and reducing the cutting of new timber; (16) an emergency lighting system for use during power failures; (17) a security system that monitors both the grounds and the interior of the house; (18) a fire system that senses combustion products before they are noticeable to occupants of the house; (19) the use of fire-retardant materials for curtains, carpets, insulation, furniture covering, flooring, etc.; (20) a tornado detector that is attached to the television and sounds an audible alarm upon the appearance of a tornado within 18 miles; (21) outside doors with self-locking hinges that automatically lock the hinge side of the doors when they are closed and prevent the removal of the closed doors even after removal of the hinge pins; (22) two domestic hot water tanks, one of which contains a heat exchanger that uses solar energy to preheat incoming water to approximately 130° F., after which the water is transferred to

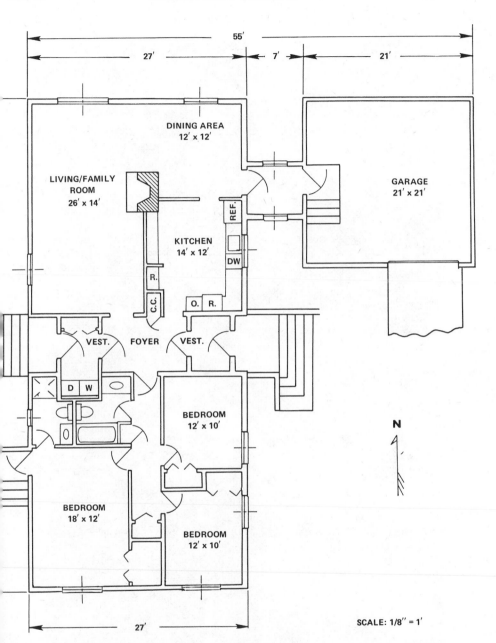

Floor plan of NASA Technology Utilization House. The enclosed living space is just over 1,600 square feet.

NASA Technology Utilization House—the "House of the Future"—at NASA Langley Research Center, Hampton, Virginia.

the other tank, where the water temperature is raised by electricity to the desired temperature; (23) exterior rolling shutters that are effective in heat control and energy saving; and (24) a skylight that brings daylight into the foyer, thereby reducing the need for artificial light during daytime hours.

Questions

1. Which features of the NASA "House of the Future" do you consider most important? Why?
2. Which of these features do you believe to be most revolutionary? Explain.

13

MARKETING: BROKERAGE
AND PROMOTION*

DECISIONS IN REAL ESTATE MARKETING

The basic decisions in regard to the marketing of real estate are made
by present and prospective property owners who must decide whether to
buy or sell, at which prices, on what terms, and at what time. Sellers and
buyers may be individuals, business firms, or governmental or institutional
agencies. The motives behind decisions to buy or not to buy, or to buy
more or less, or to sell or not to sell, or to sell more or less may arise from
a variety of sources.

Of major importance are objectives, which in turn may vary widely.
For example, the owners and managers of a business firm may decide to
buy land to allow for future expansion; individual investors may be concerned with increasing the return on their capital or with improving their
tax positions, or they may wish to secure better locations. The same objectives may motivate both purchases and sales: a business firm may sell to
another in order to move to a new location, but at the same time both firms
may thus assure themselves of space for future growth. Of course, opposing
objectives may also lead to purchases and sales.

Factors Influencing Decisions

Decisions of this type may be influenced by many factors. (1) Anticipated changes in the trend of general and local business conditions are

* We acknowledge with thanks the assistance of James H. McMullin of Real Estate
Service, Inc., Arlington, Va., in reviewing this chapter.

important; for example, differences of opinion may exist about trends of expansion or contraction or the rates at which they may occur. (2) Anticipated changes in real estate markets or in specific sectors of such markets may lead to decisions as to property purchase or sale. (3) Prospective changes in money market conditions may have a strong impact on such decisions. (4) Probabilities of change in location influences may be important—for example, belief in the rapid expansion of a new subdivision or in the future of a new shopping center may lead to decisions to buy; belief in no expansion or slow expansion may lead to decisions to sell. (5) Finally, decisions may be influenced by the available alternatives. Property owners may be forced to liquidate holdings quickly in order to meet pressing personal or business problems. Business firms may be forced to buy particular properties because they are the only properties which will allow expansion at certain locations. Pollution or energy problems may dictate sales. Sometimes speculation or fear of recession plays a part in decisions to buy or sell.

Other factors may play a part as well, including probable changes in taxes, in government, or in political conditions; anticipated changes in technology; possible population movements; international uncertainties; and the like. Often tax considerations such as depreciation allowances, capital gain possibilities, trading properties to ease tax impacts, and others are of special importance. Those we have outlined give some indication of the many factors that are likely to play a major part in decisions to buy or sell real property.

Role of Brokers and Sales People

Because the processes of buying and selling real estate are complex and the market is not well organized, the decisions of prospective buyers and sellers often are facilitated, influenced, and translated into action by brokers and sales personnel. We pay special attention to their work in this chapter, centering on such topics as the major characteristics of real estate marketing, real estate brokerage and sales organizations, listing procedures and arrangements, relationships between owners and brokers, processes and methods involved in the selling of real estate, promotion programs including advertising and public relations, sales contracts, financial factors in sales, title transfers, and various possibilities for improving the marketing of real estate. In the next chapter we will consider property management and the rental rather than the sale of real properties.

Characteristics of Real Estate Marketing

The marketing of real estate involves all of the processes of bringing together buyers, sellers, and users of real properties or property services. It frequently includes assistance in making financial arrangements to carry out sales or leases. Often provisions for the management of properties are involved as well. Buyers and sellers, lessors and lessees, of course, can negotiate directly and often do. In some cases the developer of a project may set up an internal sales force, which often works well when large projects are involved. Sometimes outside brokers are used, either independently or in cooperation with an internal sales force. Individual owners of homes sometimes perform a part of the sales function in cooperation with brokers.

Brokers play a major role in many real estate transactions, serving essentially as negotiators and counselors. They play a more important part in the marketing of real estate than do brokers and middlemen in many other fields.

Because of the nature of the real estate market there is wide room for bargaining, since prices are not set with the same precision as in many other types of markets. The original asking price by a seller of property may be much higher than any bids that can be secured. Gradually adjustments are worked out. The broker tries to find the potential user or investor who can secure maximum advantage from the property. The seller is informed of sales prices or rents for comparable space. In some cases the broker may be careful to keep the potential buyer and the seller apart until the final closing. In other cases the broker will bring them together and skillfully guide the interview.

Since it is often difficult for sellers and buyers alike to secure adequate information about property values, current prices and rents, financing arrangements, and the like, the broker performs the function of supplying such information. In addition, the broker helps to avoid errors in the complicated process of selling real property.

A popular impression is that all a real estate broker needs to start in business is a real estate license and an automobile. Some brokers enter the business with little more. Their exit may be swift. The successful broker needs adequate knowledge of the local economy, the market, and the properties available for sale. The broker must be able to inspire confidence in buyers and sellers. They must rely on the broker for much guidance and this requires confidence and trust.

Types of Customers

Many large corporations include real estate departments in their organizations for the purpose of arranging for the use and management of the properties that are needed for their operations. Such departments often work with local real estate brokers in making arrangements for the sale, purchase, leasing, or financing of real properties. The bulk of the work of brokers, however, is carried out for individuals, families, small businessmen, and small investors. Because of their knowledge of the local market, familiarity with properties, and skill in negotiating, brokers are usually able to market properties to greater advantage than those who own them. The work of brokers may range from simple transactions such as the sale of a single-family home to complicated arrangements involving the sale, financing, and leasing of large blocks of properties.

Selling Organizations

The organizations engaged in real estate brokerage include many types, ranging from one-person offices to brokerage departments of large real estate firms. Most brokerage firms operate in the local market. Some may have referral and related arrangements with others through organizations that are set up for this purpose, such as Red Carpet, Century 21, Homes for Living, or Gallery of Homes.[1]

A large real estate firm will usually have brokerage, management, leasing, insurance, mortgage, and appraising departments. Some of the more aggressive ones even have their own construction crews. In addition there may be separate departments for advertising, collections, accounting, and legal work. (See Fig. 13–1.) Both the brokerage department of a larger organization and the one-person office perform the functions of securing listings, advertising, selling properties, arranging for the closing of deals, and related activities. In the smaller organization the broker, often with the aid of a secretary or assistant, will perform all of these functions.

In larger organizations the broker will have a number of salespersons in addition to office personnel and may have specialists in charge of legal, advertising, and appraising work. The salespersons may work under the direction of the broker or a sales manager, and they may specialize in residential, business, or industrial properties.

Usually we refer to the owner of a real estate agency as a *broker,* and to those who assist in the marketing of properties as salespersons. A Realtor is a member of a local real estate board which is affiliated with the National Association of Realtors (NAR). The term *Realtor*® is copyrighted by this organization and may be used only by authorized persons. (See Appendix B.)

BROKER–OWNER RELATIONSHIPS

Whenever owners of real estate employ the services of others to assist in the sale of a property, they enter into an agency or brokerage agreement in which the property is listed for sale. The legal rules governing the relationship between owners and brokers are a special branch of the law of agency.

The relationship between owners and brokers is established by an agreement between the parties. The agreement may be oral or it may be a written contract. (See Fig. 13–2.) In a majority of states, agreements between principal and broker need not be in writing, although written

---

[1] Raymond B. Dowling and Mary Alice Hines, "Here Comes the Real Estate Franchise," *Real Estate Review,* vol. 7, no. 2 (Summer, 1977).

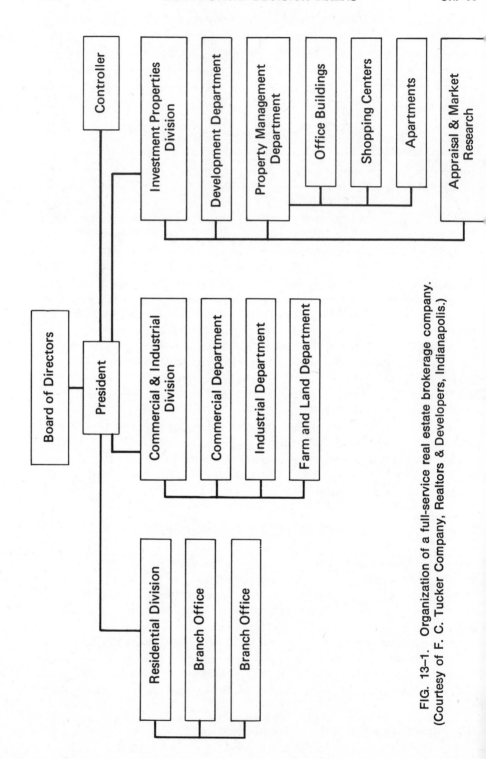

FIG. 13-1. Organization of a full-service real estate brokerage company. (Courtesy of F. C. Tucker Company, Realtors & Developers, Indianapolis.)

agreements are preferable and many states have set up definite statutes requiring that such agreements be in writing.

The authority given to a broker by an owner may be of a general or a special nature; for example, if the broker is to manage an apartment or office building for the owner, the agency will be general, but if the owner lists a piece of property with the broker for sale, the agency is usually special. Ordinarily, the duty of a broker is merely to find a purchaser who is ready, willing, and able to purchase in accordance with the terms of the listing contract.

Other authority may be given, such as the right to show the property, to put up signs, to advertise, or even to sign the contract of sale. If the agent departs from delegated authority, the owner may be liable; nevertheless, if the principal or the agent has acted in such a manner that an action would be reasonably believed to have been authorized, as interpreted by persons in the community where the agent acted, or even though the agent has exceeded delegated authority and there has been no reliance, the principal is responsible if he or she ratifies the agent's act. If the owner does not ratify, the broker may be responsible to the third party.

The broker is expected to act in good faith always and to exercise reasonable care and diligence. If higher prices are offered than are asked, the agent is obliged to indicate this fact to the owner and not to use such knowledge for personal profit. A universally accepted rule of agency is that an agent cannot serve two principals. This rule applies to brokers. Thus, a broker cannot represent both the buyer and the seller unless both know of the arrangement and consent to it. Then the broker must act with absolute impartiality.

Types of Listing Agreements

The agreements which are drawn up between an owner and a broker may be of various types, the most important being (1) open listing, (2) exclusive agency, and (3) exclusive right to sell contracts. In addition, "multiple listing" arrangements operate in many cities.

Listing agreements, when entered into, will usually include, in addition to the parties to the contract: a sufficiently accurate description of the property to make it possible to prepare a sales agreement, and the terms of the sale, including the broker's commission, the length of time for which the property is listed, and any special conditions to be fulfilled. (See Figs. 13–2 and 13–3.)

In an open listing contract the owner may employ as many brokers as desired. A time limit may or may not be set. The broker making the sale collects the commission; but the owner may sell the property, in which case no commission is paid. If a contract is drawn up in which the designated broker is the only agent of the owner, an exclusive agency agreement exists. In such cases the broker receives a commission if sale takes place

REAL ESTATE LISTING CONTRACT (EXCLUSIVE RIGHT TO SELL)

SALES PRICE $49,500.00   TYPE HOME Southern Colonial   TOTAL BEDROOMS 4   TOTAL BATHS 2

ADDRESS 37 Grand Avenue, Jackson City   JURISDICTION OF River County, Indiana

AMT OF LOAN TO BE ASSUMED $ 36,980.00   AS OF WHAT DATE June 1, TY   TAXES & INS INCLUDED: X   YEARS TO GO 23   AMOUNT PAYABLE MONTHLY $ 392.00 @ 7½%   LOAN TYPE Conv.

2nd MORTGAGE

MORTGAGE COMPANY ABC Mortgage Company

OWNER'S NAME Lawrence Williams & Carol Williams (H&W)   PHONES (HOME) 444-3217   (BUSINESS)

TENANT'S NAME   PHONES (HOME)   (BUSINESS)

POSSESSION Complete 15DAFC   DATE LISTED: June 15, TY   EXCLUSIVE FOR 120 days   DATE OF EXPIRATION Oct. 15, TY

LISTING BROKER England Realty   KEY AVAILABLE AT England Realty   PHONE

LISTING SALESMAN Mary England   HOME PHONE: HOW TO BE SHOWN by appt. only except Sun.

ENTRANCE FOYER □ CENTER HALL □		TYPE KITCHEN CABINETS ✓
LIVING ROOM SIZE 18' x 12'	FIREPLACE ■	TYPE COUNTER TOPS
DINING ROOM SIZE 14 x 12	AGE 15 yrs. AIR CONDITIONING ■	EAT-IN SIZE KITCHEN ✓
	ROOFING TOOL HOUSE □	TYPE STOVE
BEDROOM TOTAL: 4 DOWN 0 UP 4	GARAGE SIZE 2 car PATIO □	BUILT IN OVEN & RANGE ■
	SIDE DRIVE □ CIRCULAR DRIVE ■	
BATHS TOTAL: 2 DOWN 1 UP 1	PORCH □ SIDE □ REAR ■ SCREENED ■	SEPARATE STOVE INCLUDED □
DEN SIZE 10' x 12' FIREPLACE ■	FENCED YARD □ OUTDOOR GRILL □	REFRIGERATOR INCLUDED ■
FAMILY ROOM SIZE FIREPLACE □	STORM WINDOWS ■	DISHWASHER INCLUDED ✓ yes
RECREATION ROOM SIZE FIREPLACE □	STORM DOORS ■ SIDEWALKS ■	DISPOSAL INCLUDED ■
	CURBS & GUTTERS ■	
BASEMENT SIZE 34' x 26	STORM SEWERS □ ALLEY □	DOUBLE SINK ■ SINGLE SINK □
NONE □ 1/4 □ 1/3 □ 1/2 □ 3/4 □ FULL ■	WATER SUPPLY ■ city	STAINLESS STEEL ■ PORCELAIN □
UTILITY ROOM	SEWER ■ city SEPTIC □	WASHER INCLUDED ■ DRYER INCLUDED ■
TYPE HOT WATER SYSTEM: electric	TYPE GAS: NATURAL ■ BOTTLED □	LAND ASSESSMENT $
TYPE HEAT electric	WHY SELLING	IMPROVEMENTS $
EST. FUEL COST	PROPERTY DESCRIPTION	TOTAL ASSESSMENT $ 16,000.00
ATTIC □		TAX RATE $8.72/100
PULL DOWN STAIRWAY □ REGULAR STAIRWAY □ TRAP DOOR □	LOT SIZE 110' x 150'	TOTAL ANNUAL TAXES $ 1395.20
NAME OF BUILDER	LOT NO. 17 BLOCK 4 SECTION A	
SQUARE FOOTAGE 2700		
EXTERIOR OF HOUSE Brick & Frame	Rolling Hills Subdivision, Jackson City, River County, Indiana	

NAME OF SCHOOLS: ELEMENTARY: JR. HIGH:

HIGH: PAROCHIAL:

PUBLIC TRANSPORTATION: _____
NEAREST SHOPPING AREA: _____
REMARKS ___will pay no points, prefer cash or cash and consumption of present mortgage___

Date: ___June 15, TY___

In consideration of the services of ___England Realty___ (herein called "Broker") to be rendered to the undersigned (herein called "Owner"), and of the promise of Broker to make reasonable efforts to obtain a Purchaser therefor, Owner hereby lists with Broker the real estate and all improvements thereon which are described above (all herein called "the property"), and Owner hereby grants to Broker the exclusive and irrevocable right to sell such property from 12:00 Noon on ___June 15___, 19__TY__ until 12:00 Midnight on ___October 15___, 19__TY__ (herein called "period of time"), for the price of ___forty nine thousand and five hundred and no/100___ Dollars ($ _49,500.00_) or for such other price and upon such other terms (including exchange) as Owner may subsequently authorize during the period of time.

It is understood by Owner that the above sum or any other price subsequently authorized by Owner shall include a cash fee of ___7___ per cent of such price or other price which shall be payable by Owner to Broker upon consummation by any Purchaser or Purchasers of a valid contract of sale of the property during the period of time and whether or not Broker was a procuring cause of any such contract of sale.

If the property is sold or exchanged by Owner, or by Broker or by any other person to any Purchaser to whom the property was shown by Broker or any representative of Broker within sixty (60) days after the expiration of the period of time mentioned above, Owner agrees to pay to Broker a cash fee which shall be the same percentage of the purchase price as the percentage mentioned above.

Broker is hereby authorized by Owner to place a "For Sale" sign on the property and to remove all signs of other brokers or salesmen during the period of time, and Owner hereby agrees to make the property available to Broker at all reasonable hours for the purpose of showing it to prospective Purchasers.

Owner agrees to convey the property to the Purchaser by deed with the usual covenants of title and free and clear from all encumbrances, tenancies, liens (for taxes or otherwise), but subject to applicable restrictive covenants of record. Owner acknowledges receipt of a copy of this agreement.

WITNESS the following signature(s) and seal(s):

Date Signed: ___June 15, TY___

Listing Agent ___England Realty___

Address ___37 Grand Avenue___   Telephone ___444-3217___

Lawrence Williams (Owner)

Carol Williams (Owner)

FIG. 13-2. Standard listing contract. (Used by permission of Real Estate Certification Program, Indiana University.)

Exclusive Authorization to Sell

In consideration of the services of _____ John Adams _____ herein called Broker,

I hereby employ Broker, exclusively, and irrevocably, for the period beginning __May 1__ , 19 ____ and ending at midnight __July 29__ , 19 __ ,

to sell the property situated in __city of Walnut Creek__ , County of __Contra Costa__ , California, described as follows:

Lot 3, Block 6, Walnut Heights Tract recorded 1944 in Book 66 of Maps at Page 389,

Official Records of Contra Costa County; also known as 66 Magnolia Way, Walnut Creek,

California.

and I hereby grant Broker the exclusive and irrevocable right to sell said property within said time for __Thirty-Thousand and no/100__

($ __30,000.00__) Dollars and to accept a deposit thereon _____

Terms: At least $9,000 cash including deposit. Balance by buyer taking premises subject

to existing first trust deed described below; seller taking back second trust deed

against subject property securing note in maximum amount of $5,000 payable $60.67

or more monthly including 8% annual interest, with said note all due and payable in

ten years.

I hereby agree to pay Broker as commission __Six percent (6%)__ _____ of the selling price

if said property is sold during the term hereof or any extension thereof by Broker or by me or by another broker or through any other source. If said property is withdrawn from sale, transferred, or leased during the term hereof or any extension thereof, I agree to pay Broker said percent of the above listed price.

If a sale, lease or other transfer of said property is made within three (3) months after this authorization or any extension thereof terminates to parties with whom Broker negotiates during the term hereof or any extension thereof and Broker notifies me in writing of such negotiations, personally or by mail, during the term hereof or any extension thereof, then I agree to pay said commission to Broker.

Evidence of title shall be a California Land Title Association standard coverage form policy of title insurance to be paid for by __Seller__

If deposits or amounts paid on account of purchase price are forfeited, Broker shall be entitled to one-half thereof, but not to exceed the amount of the commission.

I hereby acknowledge receipt of a copy hereof.

Date ____ May 1 _____ 19 ____ *John Smith*

_____ Walnut Creek _____ , California *Eva Smith*

66 Magnolia Way

(Address of Owner)

Walnut Creek   921-1111

(City)   (Zone)   (Phone)   Owner

In consideration of the execution of the foregoing, the undersigned Broker agrees to use diligence in procuring a purchaser.

200 Main Street   *John Adams*

(Address of Broker)   Broker

Walnut Creek   921-1234

(City)   (Zone)   (Phone)

Size of parcel: __70 x 100 feet__ _____ Taxes: $ __535__ ____ per year.

Loan Information __First T/D note in original amount of $20,000 paid down to $16,000 as of__

May 1, 19 , bears annual interest at 7.2% and is payable at not less than $144 or

~~xxxxxxxxxxxxxxxx~~ more per month on principal and interest. First T/D recorded in

Book 101, at Page 55 O.R. Contra Costa County; beneficiary, Bank of Commerce, Walnut Creek

FIG. 13–3. California standard listing contract.

as a result of the efforts of anyone but the owner. A third type of agreement is provided in the exclusive-right-to-sell contract. Under such an agreement the broker is the only agent who is compensated regardless of who sells the property.

Multiple Listing

While most owners prefer to dispose of their properties as quickly as possible, they often find it difficult to decide between an open listing, which engages the interest of a large number of brokers, and an exclusive-right-to-sell agreement, which places responsibility on a specific broker and assures a reward for sales efforts. In order to secure the major advantages of both methods, many real estate boards have set up "multiple listing" systems. Where such arrangements exist, the broker with whom a property is listed automatically lists it with other members of the organization. If the listing broker sells the property, the full commission is paid; if another sells it, the commission is split on a predetermined basis between the selling broker and the one with whom the property was listed. In some cities, multiple listing systems are almost compulsory for registered brokers or those who are members of a local association or board—that is, every member of the board is required to list all properties with the organization. More generally, however, an optional system exists. The use of the multiple listing system preserves many of the advantages of the exclusive-right-to-sell contract, and at the same time extends the scope of the market by including as many brokers as possible. (See Fig. 13–4.)

Broker's Authority

Except where a broker's employment is definitely indicated as exclusive, it is assumed that a nonexclusive agreement exists. In such cases, as many listings may be made with as many brokers as the owner wishes, all being terminated in various ways, such as the destruction of the property, bankruptcy, insanity, death of either party, and mutual consent, or revocation. Thus, in most situations, the owner may revoke the broker's authority without incurring any liability, unless the revocation is effected to avoid paying a commission after the broker has introduced the owner to a prospect.

In cases where there is doubt of a right to a commission, it is necessary to show that the broker was actually employed and was the "procuring cause" of the sale; that good faith was exercised; that the broker produced the customer on the seller's terms; that the customer was ready, able, and willing to buy; that the contract was consummated within the time limits, if any were set; and that a completed transaction was brought about if the contract required it.

REALTORS ® MULTIPLE LISTING SERVICE OF NORTHERN VIRGINIA, INC.

ADDRESS: _____ ZIP _____ $ _____ PX NO. _____

Lot ____ Block ____ Subdiv. _____ CNTY. ____ GRID# ____ AREA CODE

BASEMENT	1ST FLOOR	2ND FLOOR		EQUIPMENT	No	Yes	Constr.
Size	L.R.	B.R.		Stove			Style
O.S.E.	D.R.			Refrig.			Age
Cr. Sp.	KIT.			Dishwher.			Hse. Dms.
R.R.	ESIK.			Disposal			Water
Bath	B.R.	Bath		Ex. Fan			Sewage
B.R.		3RD LEVEL		Shds./Blds.			Taxes
		B.R.		A.C. Units			Poss.
Heat	Bath	Bath		C.A.C.			Lot size
Hot Water	Ent. Way.	Firepl.		Washer			Sq. Ft.
How Shown		Fence		Dryer			Porch
				Storm Wind.			Garage
				Swim. Pool			

1st Trust $ _____ @ _____ %$ _____ PI TI mo. MTGEE _____

Known Assumption Terms _____

PLEASE (✓) EXISTING 1st TRUST IS A FHA 203 ( ) FHA 222 ( ) GI ( ) CONVT. ( ) LOAN # _____

2ND TRUST $ _____ @ _____ %$ _____ /MO DUE _____ ASSUMABLE? _____ OWTB$ _____

CASH TO ASSUME _____ CRV$ _____ FHA$ _____ CONV. _____

HIGH SCH. _____ JR.HI _____ WHY SELLING _____

ELEM. SCH. _____ PAROCH _____

REMARKS _____

DIRECTIONS FROM: _____

Owner _____ Phone:Res. _____ Bus. _____

Until: _____ Phone: _____ Listing Code: _____

OCCUPANT _____ Lister _____ Home Phone _____

Addr. _____ REALTOR® _____ Code #: _____ Bus. Phone _____

ADDRESS: _____ | FL | BR | BA | $ | PX No.

LISTING AGREEMENT FOR EXCLUSIVE LISTING

To: _____

_____REALTOR® Date_____

In consideration of the use of the services and facilities of your office, (see information on reverse) you are hereby granted the exclusive privilege for_____days from this date to sell my/our property, including kitchen stove, refrigerator and other equipment listed contained therein, located at_____

for $_____, or such other price as I/we may later agree upon, which price includes selling commission.

The property may be sold subject to an existing first deed of trust having an unpaid balance of about $_____. Minimum cash that can be considered is $_____and owner will take back second trust in the amount of $_____.

In the event of sale I/we will execute the usual sales contract customarily in use in the State of Virginia.

I/we agree to pay a commission of_____percent of the sales price of the property in cash, if during this listing period this property is sold by you or me, us or anyone else; or if you or any member of REALTORS®Multiple Listing Service produces a purchaser ready willing and able to purchase the property; or if within_____days after the expiration of the listing contract a sale is made by me to any person to whom the property has been shown during the listing period; or should I or we refuse to settle on any valid sales contract. I certify lister has shown me the advantages of the Multiple Listing Service but for personal reasons I have given them a non Multiple Listing, Private Exclusive, listing.

This exclusive right to sell will expire at midnight _____

You are hereby authorized to place your "For Sale" sign on the property and to remove all others. The entire property will be available to you for showing at all reasonable hours. The agent is not responsible for vandalism, theft, or damage of any nature whatsoever to the property. The property listed herein shall be shown and made available to all persons without regard to race, color, religion, creed, ancestry, sex or marital status. The above agreement and listing data contains the entire terms and provisions of this contract and may be used as a basis for presenting the property to prospective buyers.

I/WE HEREBY ACKNOWLEDGE THAT I/WE HAVE RECEIVED A COPY OF THIS CONTRACT AND HAVE READ THE STATEMENT ON THE REVERSE

Listing Broker/Sales Mgr._____(Seal)　Owner_____(Seal)

Sales Associate _____(Seal)　Owner_____(Seal)

RML Form #7
Revised 7/75

SEND TO REALTORS®MULTIPLE LISTING SERVICE

FIG. 13–4.　Multiple listing form.　(Courtesy Multiple Listing Service of Northern Virginia, Inc.)

Securing Listings

Real estate brokers must have listings before they can sell any property. The listings may be thought of as their merchandise, as the stock of goods on the shelves of their stores. In ordinary periods, relatively little difficulty may be encountered by brokers in securing listings. Business acquaintances, the owners of property with whom they have dealt, and former customers may provide an adequate stock of merchandise. There are times, however, when brokers must make special efforts to secure listings, especially when the market is active.

Brokers may advertise, indicating their desire for listings; they may call on or write letters to property owners who may be willing to dispose of their properties; they may canvass management firms to determine whether rental properties are for sale; they may canvass financial institutions who hold foreclosed properties or who have clients with properties for sale; and they may engage in numerous other related activities. In some cases, brokers have carried on house-to-house canvasses inquiring whether home owners are interested in selling their properties. There has been much argument among brokers as to the advisability of this doorbell ringing technique.

All the above suggests that brokers' acquaintances in the business community, their reputation for efficient service, and the quality of their advertising are of major importance in securing listings. These same factors are also of basic importance in the selling of properties once they are listed.

Some real estate firms combine brokerage with property management. In such a combination the property management activities of the firm may yield a number of listings for the brokerage department. Since the firm is serving the owners through the management of properties, the owners are very likely to ask the same firm to sell such properties as are to be placed on the market.

Terms of Listing Agreement

It is not only important for brokers to secure listings; they must also obtain them under favorable conditions. If an owner lists a property at a price which is far above the market, there is relatively little chance for the broker to market it, regardless of how much effort and money are spent. Real estate brokers often say, "A property well listed is half sold." By this they mean that the property is listed at a price and on terms which are reasonable in relation to current market conditions and that the period of the listing is long enough to allow the broker to carry out a thorough sales campaign.

Listing Policies

Brokers prefer that residential properties be listed under exclusive-right-to-sell agreements for periods of at least ninety days. In the case of special-purpose property a longer period may be desirable. Typically the broker's commission for single-family residential properties is 5 to 7 per cent of the sales price. Apartment commissions are usually in the 4 to 8 per cent range, business properties 3 to 5 per cent, and unimproved land 5 to 10 per cent. There may be some scaling down for larger properties.

Some brokers accept listings on terms that are not realistic. As a result, the properties cannot be sold; later, negotiations have to be carried on with owners and prices and terms adjusted to levels that should have been worked out originally. Experienced brokerage offices refuse to accept listings unless prices and terms are realistic. This saves the time of salespersons, eliminates renegotiations, and speeds up the turnover of property listings. Listings are sometimes accepted on almost any terms in order to prevent competitors from getting them. They are then renegotiated if possible before the end of the time involved in the original listing agreement. The first type of policy is probably to be preferred. The latter works reasonably well in a period when markets are expanding rapidly but in other periods properties listed on nonrealistic bases can waste sales effort and advertising expense, and result in painful renegotiations and general frustration.

The obtaining of listing under favorable conditions is often the primary factor in the success of a real estate brokerage organization. A broker may ask several salespersons to give an independent estimate of the price that can be secured for a property before it is listed for sale. The salesperson who calls on the owners to arrange the listing is armed with this information. Records of sales in the area in which a property is located and information about sales prices for comparable properties are usually considered before a listing is arranged. The public records may be checked to determine if possible the amount that the owner paid for the property. In these ways brokers are often able to avoid delays in the sale of property because the original asking price is too high.

THE SELLING OF REAL ESTATE

In boom periods the selling of real property may amount to little more than taking orders. When demands are high and brokerage offices have long lists of live prospects who are anxious to secure desirable space, relatively few sales problems are encountered. Such periods are relatively rare, however, and even in boom periods there may be many people who would like to buy but who are unable to meet the prices demanded by owners.

Usually, therefore, every brokerage office will maintain a list of prospects. These are secured from answers to advertisements, from acquaintances of the broker or salespersons, from tenants in buildings managed by the firm or others, from financial institutions, and from other business firms. Prospect files are kept alive by frequent analysis in order that dead cards may be eliminated and live ones substituted.

Matching Properties and Customers

The primary job of the real estate broker or salespersons is to match properties and customers. Only in the case of new construction can the property be tailor-made to fit the customers' needs, whether a residence, a store, or a factory building is involved. Matching properties and customers requires a detailed knowledge of the property on the one hand and the needs of the customer on the other. It is important to recognize that *exchange must be a mutually beneficial proposition if an enterprise system is to function.* Too often people think that in a business transaction one of the parties must gain an advantage. Or skill in selling is thought of as a series of hocus-pocus procedures and mumbo-jumbo phrases whereby customers are forced to act contrary to their wishes or best interests. Both of these ideas are subject to question.

Exchange must be mutually beneficial; both the seller and the buyer must gain or expect to gain, otherwise no exchange will take place. The buyer must want the property more than the money and the seller must want the money more than the property. The broker's job is to arrange a meeting of minds between buyer and seller, and basically that means finding a property suitable to the buyer's needs at a price that is mutually agreeable to both parties.

In some cases other factors also are involved. For example, the broker may find it necessary to help the buyer arrange for financing; legal difficulties may require solution; tax problems may complicate the seller's or the buyer's situation; it may be necessary to arrange for extensive alterations or repairs; or special arrangements may be necessary for closing the deal, such as escrow agreements and the like. In some emergencies, it may be necessary to buy or sell quickly.

Qualifications of Brokers

This brief summary of the processes involved in selling real estate suggests that brokers and salespersons need a broad knowledge of a number of subjects and a detailed knowledge of real estate and the factors which have a bearing on real estate values. A broker should be able to analyze properties in terms of their adequacy for the uses which a prospective customer may wish to make of them. Similarly, the broker should be able to analyze the customer's needs and match these with appropriate properties.

This requires a detailed knowledge of real estate financing, subdividing and land development, building activities, the local real estate market, and general and local economic trends which bear on real estate values. Brokers should know enough real estate law to recognize those situations which require competent legal advice. In addition, they need a knowledge of office organization and procedure, commercial correspondence and business communications, advertising media and methods, and related information.

Much has been said about the importance of a pleasant personality for a real estate broker. While tact, good humor, and the ability to persuade are important, there are many successful brokers who have less than the average share of these qualities. Tact and good humor cannot take the place of knowledge, judgment, imagination, organizing ability, and hard work. Even so, we should recognize that those who know how to "win friends and influence people" are more likely to succeed than those who do not have such abilities.

Selling Methods and Strategies

The right kind of salesperson has a very important place in the operations of the broker and in the whole process of marketing real estate. By the "right" kind of salesperson we mean someone who correctly analyzes properties and customers' needs, the presentation of *facts* rather than opinions about properties, and the exercise of imagination to help the customer see the possibilities of the properties under consideration.

As has been indicated, selling starts with listing. Realistic pricing and related sales terms are a primary factor in real estate sales. Following listing, a selling strategy needs to be worked out. The broker needs to think in terms of potential buyers, people who may lead to potential buyers, competitive properties, alternative plans for developing sales, the selection of the alternative offering most promise, and then action in terms of advertising, sales promotion activities, brochures, sales kits, and the like.

Basically, the selling of real properties involves exactly the same processes used in selling other types of goods and services. Specific methods vary widely, depending on the type of property being marketed, the personality of the salesperson, and the kind of customer. To a large extent selling is a psychological process about which it is difficult to generalize. Methods that are successful if employed by one salesperson will fail if used by another. Successful salespersons must study themselves as well as the property and the customer. They must determine in advance how they can best bring about a meeting of minds.

Methods which will help to bring about the sale of one type of property may be ineffective if used in connection with another. Also, the types of selling methods which will produce desired effects for one group of customers often fail if used in dealing with another group. Probably the only statement with general validity is that adequate information, carefully and honestly presented, is the most useful selling device available.

Adequacy of Information

For the real estate salesperson, adequate information about the subject property includes a knowledge of the exact location, size, and shape of the lot and detailed data about the building or buildings involved, especially with respect to such items as age, type of construction, number of stories, floor area, and potential monetary or direct returns. The salesperson should know the type of depreciation schedules that may be set up, be acquainted with the district in which the property is located, and understand the relationship of the district to the growth and structure of the city. In addition there should be familiarity with sales which have recently been made of similar types of property, the values of competing properties in the area, and the trends of prices and rents for properties of the type under consideration. All of this information has little value, however, unless the salesperson applies it to specific sales problems. Basically, this means property analysis with a view to matching the customer's requirements.

Steps in the Sale

The steps in a sale are sometimes listed as (1) attention, (2) interest, (3) belief, (4) conviction, and (5) action. In some cases a sixth, satisfaction, is added. Sometimes these steps are reduced to (1) attention, (2) interest, (3) desire, and (4) action.

Regardless of how divided, the sales process is not really a series of separate steps. It is a continuous process in which the customer's mind may have passed through the earlier steps listed above before the salesperson appears. Competent salespersons direct the interviews with the customers but only in rare cases will they undertake to dominate them. Efforts will be made to lead the customer to a final decision by suggestion, by providing additional information, and by answering objections.

Leadership in a sales interview may be lost if the salesperson fails to keep up with the customer, turns the interview into an argument, or lets it become a visit. Analysis of the customer will help to avoid such mistakes. Another cause of failure in selling is losing the confidence of the customer. Misrepresentation of facts, attempts to conceal undesirable features rather than admitting them frankly, and exaggeration lead to loss of confidence. Such simple things as failure to keep appointments may undermine confidence. Loss of confidence also results if the salesperson is unable to provide adequate information.

Ordinary courtesy and good manners are essential to the successful sales-person. Lack of consideration, overbearing attitudes, and the like may be very costly.

Every salesperson should use nontechnical language. Even business executives are not familiar with all of the technical language used in real estate transactions. The house buyer may be puzzled by such terms as *equity, elevation, cubic content, masonry construction, amortization,* and many other terms which are used commonly by those associated with real estate. The avoidance of technical language prevents confusion in the mind of the customer and facilitates the selling process.

PROMOTION

We use the term "promotion" to include all types of activities and pro-grams intended to aid the sales process. In the real estate field this will encompass advertising, open houses, displays and related efforts, and pub-lic relations programs. We emphasize particularly the areas of advertising and public relations here.

Advertising and public relations serve the dual purposes of securing list-ings of properties to sell or rent on the one hand and of facilitating the selling or renting processes on the other. In most types of enterprises advertising and public relations activities are used primarily as an aid in selling. In the real estate business such efforts also help to secure the merchandise for the broker to market. Similarly, a real estate financing in-stitution by its promotion efforts will appeal to both savers and borrowers.

Effective public relations programs require two-way communications be-tween a firm and its public. It is important for the firm to know what the public thinks of it and its programs. Then proper steps can be taken to correct undesirable impressions or to add to points of strength. In all types of promotion programs it is well to remember that ideas have wide appeal and that originality is often the key to success.[2]

Evaluation of public relations programs is extremely difficult. If coupons are used in advertising, it is possible to estimate the impact of the advertise-ments involved. In most cases, however, it is not possible to measure very closely. In a final analysis, success depends on the total volume of business generated over a period of time.

Promotion Strategy

To be effective, promotion programs should be planned with a view to furthering the objectives of the organization. Formulation of effective

---

[2] See Albert W. Frey and Jean C. Halterman, *Advertising* (4th ed.; New York: The Ronald Press Co., 1970), pp. 226–29.

programs requires careful analysis of the firm's business and its market. It is necessary also to budget carefully the resources that will be allocated to the various phases of the programs that are evolved. In short, a careful *promotion strategy* is needed. This will cover such factors as the type of programs to be undertaken, the size of the effort, relationships between programs, and relations to the competitive situation. For example, if it is anticipated that competitors will expand promotion efforts, it may be desirable to expand even more and to start sooner. Or expansion of a competitor's advertising program, for example, may be countered by a reduction in advertising effort but by expansion of direct sales programs. As is true in other fields, promotion strategy depends to a considerable extent on anticipated changes in market conditions, public attitudes, governmental influences, and programs of competitors.

The fundamental questions of *what* is to be sold, *where*, and *to whom* require analyses of the properties that are for sale or rent, the services that may be provided by the firm, and the markets in which the firm will compete. Careful market analysis, as outlined in Chapter 7, often is helpful in planning promotion programs. Different types of programs may be indicated depending on whether the market is expected to advance, decline, or continue at the same level.

Economic Soundness of Promotion and Advertising

The economic soundness of promotion programs and especially of advertising has been debated for some time. Some economists have taken a highly critical position relative to advertising and to many other forms of promotion. False and misleading advertising, of course, is harmful. All types of promotion, however, should not be condemned on this account. New products could hardly be introduced and brought to a wide market without promotional efforts. The function of informing customers and potential customers about a product is important. Some consumers appear to prefer the glamor and reassurance of advertising programs to cheaper prices.

Types of Real Estate Advertising

Real estate advertising may be classified according to purpose, media used, and the form in which it is presented. In terms of purpose, three main types may be distinguished: primary institutional, name, and specific.

Primary institutional advertising pertains to real estate in general and has for its chief purpose the creation of favorable public attitudes toward real estate, investments in real estate, or the people engaged in the real estate business. From a competitive standpoint every type of commodity is in competition with every other type for a slice of the consumer's dollar.

Institutional advertising is designed to aid real estate in this competition. Such organizations as the National Association of Realtors, local real estate boards, the American Bankers Association, the U. S. League of Savings Associations, the National Association of Mutual Savings Banks, the Mortgage Bankers Association, and the National Association of Home Builders as well as other associations of builders carry on advertising of this type.

Name advertising has for its main purpose the popularizing of the name, activities, and reputation of a specific real estate firm. Name advertising is designed to appeal to the owner who may wish to list a property for sale or rent, to the saver and borrower, to the contractor and property buyer or user. Such advertising may include "spots" on TV and radio programs, business cards in the classified advertising columns of newspapers, or the sponsoring of special publicity programs.

For example, a firm may distribute quarterly or monthly "Letters" containing comment on economic and business conditions or covering other topics. Such letters may form the basis for news releases as well.

Specific advertising pertains to individual properties and property services. Its purpose is to aid in the selling or renting of a specific property. The most widely used type is classified newspaper advertising, which usually combines name and specific appeals.

Some advertising which appears to be specific may in fact pertain to several properties. A presentation of facts about a property may be a blind advertisement which could apply to any one of several properties. Inquiries generated by the advertisement may be referred to the properties most likely to appeal to the prospect.

Major Advertising Media

The major advertising media for most Realtors® are newspapers, magazines, radio, and television. In addition, signs, posters, direct mail, streetcar or bus cards, office displays, and a miscellany of items such as blotters, matchbooks, calendars, letterheads, and others are often used.

Since the market for many types of real estate is local in nature, the newspaper fits such advertising requirements rather specifically. Newspapers reach a heterogeneous group of readers. The reading life of a newspaper is very short; usually it is read as soon as received and then discarded. The average time spent in reading it is about twenty minutes.

There are various advantages and disadvantages to advertising in morning or afternoon papers or in daily or Sunday editions. Much real estate advertising is concentrated in the classified sections of Sunday editions, since greater circulation may be provided, readers have more leisure time, and in the case of residential properties much of the "shopping" is done on weekends. The Sunday editions combine many of the advantages of the newspaper and magazine media for the real estate advertiser.

Magazines have a longer reading life than newspapers and are often read more carefully. However, some magazines are directed toward a specific local market. Products which are sold in national or regional markets are more likely to be advertised in national magazines.

Thus, industrial properties are likely to be advertised in magazines that reach various industry groups, farm properties in farm journals, and resort and recreation properties in magazines stressing outdoor activities, sports, and recreation. Advertisements relating to properties that may appeal to retired people are found in a number of magazines.

Display and classified advertising are the two main kinds which appear in newspapers and magazines. Real estate firms use classified advertising to a predominant extent, although in special cases display advertisements are used. Preferred space in a newspaper is usually considered to be the right-hand column on the right-hand page, the front or back page of a section, and the positions next to reading matter. Such spaces often command extra rates.

Other Forms of Advertising

As we have suggested Realtors® often make use of direct mail advertising, signs and posters, displays, novelties, and other types of advertising.

Direct mail advertising includes letters, folders, booklets, cards, leaflets, and the like. It is the most selective of all types of advertising. However, it is somewhat costly in terms of cost per reader, but selectivity may make such costs relatively low. Effectiveness of direct mail advertising depends on the copy used and especially on the mailing list which is prepared. In some cases direct mail is sent to persons of influence such as financial executives and others who are in a position to refer customers.

Mailing lists may be based on prospect files, names of people visiting open houses, respondents to advertisements, city directories, members of civic clubs, and the like. Mailing lists for specific purposes may be purchased.

Radio and television are among the major media, with the latter currently achieving phenomenal results for many advertisers; but both are less selective than newspapers. Television affords the additional power of demonstration. Short announcements or spots on local stations are preferable for most real estate purposes. Programs, especially on television, quickly reach prohibitive costs. Use of either or both of these media should be carefully coordinated with other advertisements for maximum effectiveness.

"For Sale" or "For Rent" signs on properties are among the oldest forms of real estate advertising. They have been generally successful. Usually they carry the broker's name, office location, and telephone number. "Sold" signs are sometimes used to attract future listings. A suburban operator north of Chicago found signs pointing to, and briefly describing, a sub-division were the most effective form of advertising.

Posters are used in connection with the sale of new developments or the renting of space in larger buildings. Car or bus cards are often used to advertise a real estate firm rather than specific properties.

Displays are not used widely in the real estate field. Some brokers display in their offices photographs of properties which they are marketing. A few use window displays. Often displays at home shows or other oc-casions are utilized. These types of advertising may be effective, but they reach limited audiences and hence may be relatively costly.

Many real estate firms use calendars as a form of name advertising. Some make use of novelties, blotters, and similar devices.

Motivation Research

In recent years, advertising specialists have given considerable attention to motivation research as a means of finding out why some advertising messages are more effective than others. Through motivation research, at-tempts are made to determine why prospective buyers react as they do to products or services or to the advertisements used in attempting to sell them. For example, are people considering the purchase of a home more interested in shelter, comfort, conveniences, or the prestige of home ownership? Why have colonial style houses had such a strong appeal over many years? Is this because many people think of a little white house in an attractive location, perhaps with a white fence around it, when they think of a home? Through motivation research, attempts are made to answer questions like this about consumer preferences.

Motivation research has revealed that the home owners of today differ in some respects from those of yesterday. Home ownership is currently viewed as an investment rather than in terms of a permanent, deeprooted family association. Although the home has kept the traditional values of thirty years ago—security, shelter, privacy, independence, pride of owner-ship, and the like—the owner tends to view a home today more as an invest-ment, a form of saving, and a means of building an equity.

Motivational research techniques are used to uncover ways to understand the ultimate consumers of real estate better and to gain a better perspective on their feelings toward the purchase of a home and the assumption of a mortgage, as well as their attitudes toward lending institutions.

Public Relations and Publicity

The term "public relations" may be used in such a broad sense as to include almost every type of activity that a firm or the members of its staff may undertake. Many public relations programs try to develop a broad understanding between the business firm and the public it serves or the public at large.

Such understanding requires that *two-way* communication be established and maintained between the firm and its public. As a result of such a program, those who operate a real estate firm should be able to determine what the public thinks of it, where its points of strength and weakness may lie, and the types of programs that will add to its strength and shore up its weaknesses.

The primary purpose of most public relations programs is to win the approval of the community and the public. This may be done in a variety of ways. In the real estate field, special attention is often given to community activities, especially those that are likely to lead to community betterment such as work on the solution of tax or other government problems, assistance in land planning or zoning programs, or help in the improvement of schools, parks, and other community facilities. Those in the real estate business usually have information and experience of a type that enables them to make real contributions to the solution of such community problems. Such efforts may bring favorable public reaction to the firm, develop close association with community leaders, and generally assist other aspects of the firm's promotion programs.

Publicity Programs

A real estate firm may be able to publicize many of its activities or those associated with it through the news columns of newspapers or radio or television news broadcasts, or in related ways. A regular program of providing news releases may be very productive if carried out with imagination and efficiency. The following events may have news value if stories are prepared properly for release:

1. The sale or lease of an unusual property
2. Announcement of a new building program
3. Special or unusual arrangements for financing sales
4. Office expansion or announcement of a new location for an office
5. Promotion of personnel
6. Firm activities designed to recognize unusual services of its personnel
7. Volume of sales or rentals for a quarter or a year
8. Personal activities of staff members, especially of a professional type, such as attending conventions, study groups, special courses, institutes, and real estate board or other trade association activities
9. Community service of officers or staff members
10. Sponsorship of home shows
11. Modernization and repair programs
12. Any activities relating to the improvement of housing or living conditions

Best results are secured if the job of preparing and releasing publicity is assigned to one member of the staff or if it is part of the broker's special activities. Whoever handles publicity must become acquainted with the editors, financial editors, or real estate editors of local papers and those who prepare and present the news program of local radio and television stations. Sometimes local and national trade association publications provide outlets for publicity releases as well.

CLOSING THE SALE

When a buyer and seller are brought together, the broker's function is not completed. The broker prepares an Offer to Purchase stipulating the terms the buyer is willing to make. The offer then is delivered to the owner for acceptance, denial, or counterproposals. If the owner agrees to all the terms of the offer, a legal contract then is entered into between the two. If the offer is made "subject to" some conditions, such as special arrangements, there is no contract until the conditions have been met. However, once such a contract has been drawn up, the broker may collect the commission even though the transaction is not completed.

After the broker has brought seller and buyer together, a purchase-and-sale agreement is usually drawn up. Of course, a sale of real estate may be made without a preliminary contract, the seller executing and delivering a deed and the buyer paying the purchase price; but in practice such transactions are rare. In some cases the agreement is a land contract or a contract for deed, which may be a method of selling real estate on the installment plan.

Options

Sometimes the buyer secures an option to purchase, which is an agreement to buy a stipulated property at a certain price within a designated period. For this option the buyer pays a certain sum, which is usually applied on the purchase price if the transaction is completed.

Exchange Agreements

In some cases exchange agreements are drawn up in which properties are traded, rather than sold for money. Exchange agreements differ little from ordinary contracts of sale; but they are double in form, and the price is paid in whole or part by property rather than money.

Auctions

Buyers and sellers may also be brought together by auction sales, which may be voluntary or involuntary. In voluntary auction sales, the terms of

REAL ESTATE SALES CONTRACT (OFFER TO PURCHASE AGREEMENT)

This AGREEMENT made as of _____ July 1 _____, 19 TY ,

among _____ George Bell and Linda Bell (H&W) _____ (herein called "Purchaser"),

and _____ Lawrence Williams & Carol Williams (H & W) _____ (herein called "Seller")

and _____ England Realty _____ (herein called "Broker"),

provides that Purchaser agrees to buy through Broker as agent for Seller, and Seller agrees to sell the following described real estate, and all improvements thereon, located in the jurisdiction of _____ Jackson City, River County, Indiana _____,

(all herein called "the property"): _____ Lot 17, Block 4, Section A, of Rolling Hills Subdivision of Jackson City, River County, Indiana _____

_____, and more commonly known as _____ 37 Grand Avenue _____

_____ Jackson City, Indiana _____ (street address).

1. The purchase price of the property is _____ forty-nine thousand and five hundred and no/100 _____

Dollars ($ 49,500.00), and such purchase price shall be paid as follows:

_____ Cash plus assumption of present mortgage _____

2. Purchaser has made a deposit of _____ two thousand and no/100 _____ Dollars ($ 2,000.00)

with Broker, receipt of which is hereby acknowledged, and such deposit shall be held by Broker in escrow until the date of settlement and then applied to the purchase price, or returned to Purchaser if the title to the property is not marketable.

3. Seller agrees to convey the property to Purchaser by Deed with the usual covenants of title and free and clear from all monetary encumbrances, tenancies, liens (for taxes or otherwise), except as may be otherwise provided above, but subject to applicable restrictive covenants of record. Seller further agrees to deliver possession of the property to Purchaser on the date of settlement and to pay the expense of preparing the deed of conveyance.

4. Settlement shall be made at _____ England Realty _____ on or before _____ August 1 _____, 19 TY , or as soon thereafter as title can be examined and necessary documents prepared, with allowance of a reasonable time for Seller to correct any defects reported by the title examiner.

5. All taxes, interest, rent, and impound escrow deposits, if any, shall be prorated as of the date of settlement.

6. All risk of loss or damage to the property by fire, windstorm, casualty, or other cause is assumed by Seller until the date of settlement.

7. Purchaser and Seller agree that Broker was the sole procuring cause of this Contract of Purchase, and Seller agrees to pay Broker for services rendered a cash fee of _____ 7 _____ per cent of the purchase price. If either Purchaser or Seller defaults under such Contract, such defaulting party shall be liable for the cash fee of Broker and any expenses incurred by the non-defaulting party in connection with this transaction.

Subject to: _____

8. Purchaser represents that an inspection satisfactory to Purchaser has been made of the property, and Purchaser agrees to accept the property in its present condition except as may be otherwise provided in the description of the property above.

9. This Contract of Purchase constitutes the entire agreement among the parties and may not be modified or changed except by written instrument executed by all of the parties, including Broker.

10. This Contract of Purchase shall be construed, interpreted, and applied according to the law of the jurisdiction of ____Indiana____ and shall be binding upon and shall inure to the benefit of the heirs, personal representatives, successors, and assigns of the parties.

All parties to this agreement acknowledge receipt of a certified copy.

WITNESS the following signatures:

Maurice Williams   Seller

Carol Williams   Seller

England Realty   Broker

George Bell   Purchaser

Linda Bell   Purchaser

Deposit Rec'd $ ___2,000.00___

Personal Check   Cash

(Cashier's Check)   Company Check

Sales Agent: Mary England

FIG. 13–5. Standard offer to purchase. (Used by permission of Real Estate Certification Program, Indiana University.)

sale are written in advance. After the property is sold to the highest bidder, the transaction becomes a private matter between the bidder and the owner. Involuntary auction sales usually result from the desire to satisfy a lien. Such sales must be public, adequate notice must be given, and various legal formalities must be satisfied.

Sales Agreements

The drawing up of a sales agreement is an important step in the selling process, since it is the first evidence of a meeting of minds between the buyer and seller. Contracts should be carefully drawn. It is always wise to arrange a written statement which contains all of the items about which the parties have agreed. (See Fig. 13–5.) Such an agreement is preliminary to a sale; if consideration is given, an option contract is formed which may bind the parties for a period of time during which various matters may be investigated. In some cases an escrow agreement is made.

Main Items in Contract for Sale

A contract for sale should cover at least the following items: (1) the parties, (2) legal description of the property, (3) the price and financial arrangements, (4) title, (5) time and place of closing, and (6) various special items. As in all other contracts, the parties must be legally competent and capable of entering into contracts. For example, the ability of a corporation to contract is indicated by its charter. In real estate contracts it is always wise to require signatures by both husband and wife in order to remove any doubts about dower rights. Also, if purchasers are to take title as *joint tenants* or *tenants in common,* it is necessary to indicate this fact. Good practice dictates that both parties to a contract should sign it in duplicate, each retaining a signed copy.

Property Description

While a property is usually designated by street and number during the early stages of a transaction, it is usually necessary to describe it more exactly in the sale contract. The description need not be as detailed as it is in the deed, but it must be accurate. Property may be located by metes and bounds, that is, with reference to certain landmarks, roads, rivers, streets, corners, or other designated points, and then described by a certain number of feet in various directions from a starting point. In most cities property may be located by a plat or subdivision map which is filed in the land records office. Lots and blocks are numbered on such a plat and descriptions can easily be made. Property may also be designated with reference to government land surveys; that is, with respect to north and south lines or *principal meridians,* east and west lines or *base lines,* townships, and sections, as outlined in Chapter 3.

Basic Financial Arrangements

The financial arrangements between the buyer and seller must be set forth exactly in the contract of sale. Of greatest importance are the following: (1) price, (2) the earnest money, (3) the amount of cash to be paid on closing, (4) existing mortgages and purchase money mortgages, and (5) miscellaneous items.

In order to guard against uncertainty, it is desirable that a complete closing statement be drawn up indicating the purchase price, the amount to be paid at the time the transaction is closed, the presence of existing mortgages and the method of their disposal, agreements regarding purchase money mortgages, and an itemized statement of any other financial arrangements which are involved.

Price and Deposit

The price of the property that is agreed to by buyer and seller is of basic importance. It is usually the primary ingredient in the transaction. Usually the purchaser is required to make a deposit at the time the contract is drawn up. This deposit is called earnest money and is used to bind the transaction. Typically, it represents at least 10 per cent of the purchase price, the amount varying according to the agreement between the parties. In case the buyer fails to perform the terms of the contract, this amount may be forfeited to the seller, who may then use it to pay any commission owed to a broker.

Money and Mortgages

The amount of money to be paid to the seller at the time the deal is closed should also be designated in the contract. Sometimes the exact form of payment is dictated. For example, a certified check may be required. It is necessary to indicate specifically the amount to be paid at the time closing takes place in order to make certain that there has been a complete understanding between the buyer and seller.

Since most real estate is mortgaged, it is necessary to make some arrangement regarding the mortgages, if any, which are in force. A recorded mortgage is an encumbrance on the property, and the purchaser takes the property subject to it. The mortgagee may proceed against the land after sale to a third person. The third person, however, does not subject any personal assets to the payment of the mortgage unless it is assumed. So it is important that the contract of sale indicate in detailed form the terms of existing mortgages.

In some cases real estate is sold subject to a *purchase money mortgage*—that is, the seller agrees to take back a mortgage for a certain part of the price. In such a mortgage the general rules governing all mortgage transactions regulate the relationship between the parties. Ordinarily such mortgages are subordinate to any existing mortgages in force. Disclosure settlement statements may be required.

Taxes and Other Matters

Various miscellaneous items governing the financial arrangements between the buyer and the seller should also be indicated. For example, taxes may be delinquent or payable at some future time, and there should be a definite agreement regarding the amounts which each party shall pay. Also, arrangements must be made regarding special assessments, rents, insurance, water charges, and other similar matters.

Title Problems

Before a piece of real estate can be transferred, it is necessary to determine the condition of the title. Because of the many uncertainties surrounding the title to a piece of property, careful investigations must be conducted before a transaction can be completed. A contract of sale usually provides that the seller shall furnish a good, merchantable title.

It may also require the furnishing of a complete abstract or summary history of the *chain of title*, which includes all deeds and other instruments of record since the original grant of land by the government. The buyer may require some form of title insurance or a certificate of title. Typically, all of these matters are indicated in the contract, together with certain defects or encumbrances which the buyer is willing to waive.

Also, the contract usually specifies the form of deed which the seller will deliver, indicating whether a warranty, quit-claim, bargain-and-sale, or other type of deed is to be given. In ordinary transactions the buyer demands a full covenant warranty deed in which the seller takes all responsibility for the validity of the title. In some cases a bargain-and-sale or special warranty deed is all that can be demanded; for example, this would be the case in purchasing from a trustee or the executor of an estate. Such a deed limits the personal liability of the seller. It is seldom used in a free conveyance, for most purchasers are unwilling to buy a title that may be valueless. Usually the party who is to draw the deed and pay the expenses is indicated in the contract; otherwise, the seller cares for these matters.

While it is necessary to indicate the time and place of closing, it is desirable to include such provisions in the contract. In addition, contracts often include clauses in regard to the payment of brokers' commissions, loss or damage by fire, limitation of the seller's liability in case of defective title, provisions allowing the purchaser to assign the contract, as well as provisions regarding fixtures and personal property, making time the essence of the contract, leases, and various other subjects.

Compliance

After the contract of sale has been signed, each party must comply with its conditions. If the property does not comply with its description or the title is not as agreed, the vendor must see that the conditions of the contract are met. A check of the property description may indicate that it does not coincide with the tract which the buyer specified. Similarly, encroachments may be discovered; that is, a building on the land may be partially located on adjoining land, or a building on adjoining land may encroach on the seller's property. Any substantial difficulty of this type may render the property unmarketable. On the other hand, slight encroachments may be of little consequence. Where one property is separated from another by a party wall, it is necessary to determine that this actually bounds the property.

Of greater difficulty, however, is the problem of determining the status of title. The buyer usually requires that a title search be made as soon as a contract of sale has been entered into so that the status of the title can be known. The seller may be required to furnish an abstract of title, a guarantee policy, or a certificate of title. An abstract will present a complete history of the property, and an attorney's opinion is provided for the buyer. However, a title company may make a search and, upon the payment of a certain amount, issue a title insurance policy. The value of certification or guarantee depends on the character of the assuring agency. Title insurance usually provides that the insuring company will indemnify the assured according to various agreements; for example, (1) the insuring company may guarantee that the *record of title* is good except for certain noted defects or (2) it may insure against unknown defects. In some states a system of title registration simplifies the process of examination of title.

When the buyer's attorney receives an abstract, the abstract is checked and the attorney advises the buyer as to the status of the title. If defects are discovered which the seller cannot or will not correct, or if no title insurance or other guarantee against loss is provided, the buyer may refuse to complete the transaction. Usually the seller is expected to provide a good, merchantable title.

Closing Statements

After all problems of the type outlined above are settled, the parties to the transaction and their lawyers meet at the time and place appointed for closing. The deed must be checked regarding description, parties, signatures, acknowledgments, and other items. Also, other instruments such as mortgages are examined. At the closing, adjustments are determined, insurance policies transferred, other details settled, and the deed is delivered to the buyer, who then pays the purchase price. The buyer is entitled to immediate possession unless otherwise specified. As soon as the transfer is completed, the buyer or the buyer's attorney records the deed and other necessary instruments.

At the time of closing a closing statement is prepared in which real estate taxes, insurance, and rents are prorated. (See Fig. 13–6.) The seller normally pays taxes and insurance up to the time of closing and receives credit for taxes or insurance paid in advance. Similarly the seller receives rents up to the time of closing and gives credit to the buyer for rents paid to the seller but accruing after the date of closing. The closing statement also shows how the commission is to be distributed. It is the final accounting of the transaction and is an important record.

Consumer Protections

The National Consumer Credit Protection Act, usually referred to as Truth in Lending Act, requires the Federal Reserve to set up governing regulations. Regulation Z requires disclosure of information to the home buyer, especially annual interest rates and finance charges. The borrower may rescind a transaction under stated conditions. Guidelines for the advertising of credit terms are provided.

The Real Estate Settlement Procedures Act requires purchasers who are typically home buyers to be provided with a booklet entitled *Settlement Costs,* which details the items that must be covered.[3] The lending institution has the primary responsibility for assuring that the borrower is provided with adequate information.

Civil Rights

Brokers are required to conform to the provisions of the Civil Rights Act of 1968 which, among other things, prohibits discrimination among buyers or renters of real estate or borrowers on real estate. This includes discriminatory refusal to sell or rent as well as refusal to negotiate to sell or rent. Also, there may not be discrimination in advertising or in any other manner.

Escrow

Sometimes an obstacle arises so that closing cannot be completed. When this occurs, if the parties do not desire to arrange another meeting, the transaction may be completed in *escrow;* that is, the purchaser may have the

---

[3] See Dept. of Housing and Urban Development, *Settlement Costs: A HUD Guide* (rev. ed.; Washington, D. C.: Government Printing Office, 1976).

	BUYER'S STATEMENT		SELLER'S STATEMENT	
	DEBIT	CREDIT	DEBIT	CREDIT
Sales Price	49,500.00			49,500.00
Deposit		2,000.00		
Sales Fee - 7%			3,465.00	
Assumed Mortgage Balance		36,951.40	36,951.40	
Taxes - In Advance- Prorated	581.35			581.35
Loan Assumption Fee - 1%	369.51			
Legal Fees - Buyer	150.00			
Legal Fees - Seller			75.00	
Recording Fees	28.00			
Credit Report	25.00			
Owner's Title Insurance			188.75	
Purchase of Seller's Escrow	965.00			965.00
Balance Due from Buyers		12,667.46		
Balance Due to Sellers			10,366.20	
	$51,618.86	$51,618.86	$51,046.35	$51,046.35

FIG. 13–6. Standard closing statement. (Used by permission of Real Estate Certification Program, Indiana University.)

papers delivered to a third person who holds them until all matters are cleared up and then delivers them to the proper parties.

Escrow arrangements allow for checking documents and related matters, provide time for the buyer to arrange financing, and generally facilitate the process of completing the transaction. Escrow companies have developed in some places to provide such services.

Enforcing the Contract

If either party to a contract fails to perform the agreement, various remedies are available to the other party. Such a failure to carry out the contract does not affect the broker's right to a commission, but it may interfere with the completion of the transaction.

If a seller has a change of mind, the buyer may follow several courses of action: (1) The buyer may sue the seller for *specific performance*. It should be noted in this connection that most real estate contracts may be specifically enforced; that is, the court may force either party to carry out the agreement exactly, but this is discretionary with the court. (2) The contract may be rescinded, and the buyer can ask for the purchase money back, together with any costs which have resulted from the contract. (3) The buyer may sue for breach of contract and damages.

On the other hand, if the purchaser refuses to carry out the buyer's part of the agreement, the seller may similarly sue for specific performance, or declare the contract void and the earnest money forfeited, or sue for damages.

Exchanges and Trade-ins

One of the areas of real estate marketing which has gained in importance is that of exchanging one property for another. The problem is particularly acute in the case of single-family homes. For example, if the buyer of a new house wishes to trade in the old house, it may be done in the same manner as an old car may be traded in on a new one. Some builders and brokers work out their own arrangements to provide for trade-ins. Much remains to be done, however, in this field.

A closely related problem arises from the increasing number of people who are required to move from one city to another because of changes in their work assignments. Some companies guarantee certain managerial employees against loss if they are required to move to conform to company programs. Usually an independent appraisal is made and if the homeowner who is forced to move finds it necessary to sell for less than the appraised value, the company makes up the difference. Networks are being developed which permit the turning in of a property in one city to a broker for sale and the purchase of a house in another city from another affiliated broker with appropriate arrangements to tie both transactions together.

SUMMARY

Basic decisions in real estate marketing are made by present and prospective property owners who are motivated by a variety of factors. Brokerage and promotion play a large part in real estate marketing due to the difficulties of bringing buyers and sellers together. Selling organizations vary in size and degree of specialization. Listing of properties for sale often is the key to successful sales; listing agreements of various types may be arranged. Multiple listing systems are expanding in popularity. Processes of selling real estate resemble those in other fields but knowledge of real estate resources is essential.

Promotion includes all types of activities and programs that help and support the sales effort. Advertising, displays, open houses, public relations programs, and related activities are all parts of promotion. Publicity programs often are used to good advantage by brokerage firms.

Upon completion of a sale, a purchase-and-sale agreement usually is drawn up pending final arrangements. Financing often is worked out by the broker. Title problems sometimes create difficulties. When all matters are worked out, a final closing statement is set up. In some cases escrow agreements are used. Contracts finally arranged may be enforced specifically or alternative arrangements may be worked out.

QUESTIONS FOR STUDY

1. Why do brokers play such an important role in the marketing of real properties?
2. What is meant by "listing"? How does a broker obtain listings?
3. How do you interpret the statement: "A property well listed is half sold"?
4. Differentiate among the various types of listing contracts employed by brokers. If you were a broker, which would you prefer? If you were a small manufacturer desiring to sell your property, which type of listing contract would you prefer? Why?
5. The ABC Corporation is transferring its local plant manager, Mr. Carson, to the home office in another state. He has to dispose of his home within 30 days, and asks you to sell it for him. Mr. Carson wants $37,500 for the property. After inspecting the property, you decide that it will not bring more than $35,000 in the current market and may have to be sold for even less in order to complete a sale within 30 days. What action would you take under these circumstances?
6. "Exchange must always be a mutually beneficial proposition." Why? Is this statement consistent with the attempt of a firm to maximize its profits? Explain.
7. Indicate ways in which the selling of real estate differs from the selling of other commodities.
8. Define "promotion" as it pertains to real estate sales. What is meant by a "promotion strategy"?
9. Prepare illustrations of the principal types of real estate advertising. Which types of advertising would be most effective for residences, investment property, industrial property?
10. Distinguish between public relations and publicity.

11. If the seller of a certain real property has a change of mind after signing a sales contract, what remedies are available to the buyer?
12. What essential items need to be covered by a contract for the sale of real estate?

SUGGESTED READINGS

CASE, FREDERICK E. *Real Estate Brokerage.* Englewood Cliffs, N. J.: Prentice-Hall, Inc., 1965. Chs. 6, 7, 9.

FREY, ALBERT, and HALTERMAN, JEAN C. *Advertising* (4th ed.). New York: The Ronald Press Co., 1970. Chs. 2, 3, 15.

HINES, MARY ALICE. *Principles and Practices of Real Estate.* Homewood, Ill.: Richard D. Irwin, Inc., 1976. Ch. 11.

LUSK, HAROLD F., HEWITT, CHARLES M., DONNELL, JOHN D., and BARNES, JAMES A. *Business Law: Principles and Cases* (Third Uniform Commercial Code Edition). Homewood, Ill.: Richard D. Irwin, Inc., 1974. Chs. 5, 18, 30.

McMAHAN, JOHN. *Property Development.* New York: McGraw-Hill Book Co., 1976. Ch. 15.

O'DONNELL, PAUL T., and MALEADY, EUGENE L. *Principles of Real Estate.* Philadelphia: W. B. Saunders Co., 1975. Chs. 10, 11, 12.

CASE 13–1

A & A Realty

A & A Realty is a partnership consisting of two partners and eight salespersons. They operate in a community of about 40,000 adjacent to a major metropolitan area and specialize in the sale of properties in the $20,000 to $50,000 class. They have been in operation since 1958 and have a membership in the local real estate board. They believe that the success of their firm is built on their selling program, the chief characteristics of which are:

1. SELECT A LOCATION. Each salesperson in the firm is assigned to a particular section of the town and is responsible for knowing about all properties which are being offered for sale in this area and all persons who might wish to purchase property in this area. Each salesperson is expected to spend a good portion of working time going from door to door in the area asking about properties which might be for sale or seeking persons who might wish to purchase properties. A & A's slogan is: "Ring doorbells, ring doorbells, ring doorbells," and they believe that this is the cornerstone for any brokerage operation.

   a. *Do you believe that the emphasis on a policy of this kind will be successful in a majority of real estate sales?*
   b. *How would you supplement such a program in order to develop sales projects?*
   c. *What kind of training would you give the salespersons who are going to do the doorbell ringing?*

2. GET TO KNOW THE NEIGHBORS. The firm urges each salesperson to get acquainted with the people in the assigned neighborhood. They believe that this is important, not only because a friendly neighbor will encourage sales, but because it will also make it easier to find prospective clients. Neighbors often know friends or relatives who would be interested in moving next door.

3. HAVING SOMETHING TO OFFER. Each salesperson is encouraged to return to the persons in the area who have had business with the firm and to offer the services of the firm to them. This includes such things as helping them to find contractors when they want to repair their houses, keeping them informed as to new city activities which might affect their neighborhood, and similar services. They believe that if the former clients come to rely on the salesperson both as a friend and as a source of valuable information, they will be willing to share information about possible future business.

d. *What other services do you believe this firm could render? How would you make such services "services" and not "nuisances"?*

4. GET LISTING IN WRITING. This firm believes that all the listings which they obtain should be exclusive listings, for the following reasons:

4.1 While listing is given to a number of agents, no one works on it.

4.2 An exclusive listing means that one office is concentrating its interest and talents on the property.

4.3 One person will be responsible for obtaining the best offer and there will be only one offer and, therefore, no confusion.

The listing contract which they use is the one advocated by their real estate board and it provides for exclusive listing.

e. *Do you believe it is necessary to get listings in writings?*
f. *Do you think this firm is correct in insisting on an exclusive listing?*
g. *What other device can be used with exclusive listings to disseminate information about the property?*
h. *Do you think that the information listed on the listing contract is sufficient, or would you want additional information about the property?*

5. USE A CHECK SHEET IN SELLING PROPERTY. When a listing has been obtained through the firm, this listing is then assigned to one of the salespersons. The information is furnished on a sheet of paper which fits into a small notebook, and the salesperson is expected to follow up on the listing until a client is obtained. On the reverse side of the notebook sheet are listed the steps which the salesperson is expected to follow in selling the property. These steps include:

5.1   Calling on any prospects developed through personal contacts.

5.2   Talking with the persons who are currently occupying the property which is to be sold.

5.3   Calling on the neighbors in person, notifying them that the property is to be offered for sale, and asking them whether there is anyone they would like to have move in. The call is then followed up with a letter within the next few days.

5.4   Arranging to place a sign on the property announcing that it is for sale.

5.5   Preparing classified advertising and arranging an insertion schedule. (This firm specializes in the use of the morning paper.)

5.6 Filing property listings with the local Realtors' ® group.

5.7 Sending a letter to other agents telling them about the property, particularly when the property has unusual characteristics which might meet someone's particular needs.

5.8 Notifying by mail the various personnel firms throughout the city,ꞌ particularly those with big companies, informing them that the property will be available in the near future.

5.9 Determining how much of a mortgage can be obtained on the property and being fully informed about any financial plans in connection with the property.

5.10 Calling the owner at least once every two weeks to deliver an update on what has been done and what is being done in order to sell the property.

5.11 After the property has been sold, sending a card to the neighbors introducing them to the new owner of the property.

6. SHOW PROPERTY TO PROSPECTIVE CLIENTS. Before a prospective client is taken to a home, the salesperson should inform the people occupying the property and arrange for an appointment. As the prospects are being taken to the property, the route should be arranged so that they will be shown the most favorable parts of the neighborhood in which they will be living. When they arrive at the house, the salesperson should first talk about the outside of the house, pointing out both the strengths and the weaknesses of the structure. (A & A has found it successful to point out the defects and let the prospects sell the salesperson on how easy it would be to remedy them. The firm emphasizes that women buy houses, and that the sales talk should be built so as to appeal to women. A & A also believes that emotions sell houses and that the sales program should be designed to emphasize those factors which would appeal to the emotions, such as beautiful fireplace, unusual views, and unusual architectural treatments inside and outside the house.)

When the firm has arranged for an appointment to show a house, A & A sends the people occupying the house a small pamphlet which shows how people living in a house can help its sale; however, this will be successful only when the people occupying the house are selling the house. Many times, the person in the house will be renting it and will not be anxious to have it sold. In this case, the salesperson must plan a program so as to have minimum interference from the occupants of the house.

i. Evaluate the strength and weakness of this program, and indicate how you would improve it.

j. What steps would you take to show a house which is occupied by persons who do not want the property to be sold?

k. Do you think a sales training program of any kind is necessary for a salesperson in this program? If so, what would you include in such a program?

7. CLOSE THE SALE. After the prospect has indicated an interest in buying the property, the salesperson is encouraged to put the prospect's offer in writing and to urge the giving of earnest money. They believe that the earnest money should be an amount equal to the commission that the firm will receive for the sale of the property. Once the offer has been written out, the firm presents the offer to the owner and lets the offer speak for itself. They urge the seller to review the offer and to try to decide whether

a sale of the property is acceptable under the terms and conditions outlined in the offer. Once the seller has agreed to sell, the firm calls in attorneys and, with the attorneys, completes the papers necessary to close the transaction.

l. What items do you think should be included in the written offer? How would you persuade a prospect to put an offer in writing? to give earnest money?

    8. SUPPLY A SALESPERSON'S HANDBOOK. The firm believes that each salesperson should be encouraged to keep a handbook containing the following information:

    8.1 Prospects
    8.2 Listings
    8.3 Payment books from savings and loan associations
    8.4 Tax rates

m. Can you think of any other items which should be included in the handbook? How would you expect the salesperson to use this handbook?

CASE 13–2

The Sale of a Home

In mid-August of this year, Fred M. Williams received word from his employer that he was to be transferred to another city in three months. In anticipation of the move, Mr. Williams and his wife, Josie R., decided at an early date to contact Barbara Friendswood, a licensed broker and owner of Friendswood Realty Co., Oakpark, Nostate, regarding the sale of their home. Ms. Friendswood had assisted the Williamses in the purchase of their current home five years earlier. On August 26 of this year Barbara Friendswood visited the home, made an estimate of its value, and filled out a listing contract which the Williamses signed, and Ms. Friendswood accepted on the same date.

The Listing. Other data pertinent to the listing of the property follow:

Address of listed property: 4750 East Buttonwood Drive, Oakpark, Nostate.

Legal description: Lot 43 in Arlington's Third Section, recorded as Instrument #1413 in Plat Book 5, pages 323 to 326 in the Office of the Recorder, Walnut County, Nostate.

Assessed value for taxes: $16,000 building; $4,000 land.

Tax rate: The present tax rate is $12.20/100. The taxes for the year are due December 31 of this year and have not been paid.

Mortgage: Mortgage balance after the August 15 payment of this year is $48,200. The mortgage is assumable and is held by the First Savings & Loan of Oakpark. The interest rate is 8 per cent. Monthly payments for principal and interest are $384.48 due on the 15th of the month. The interest is paid monthly for interest accrued from previous thirty days. A mortgage exemption has not been filed. There are no other liens or mortgages. No escrow balance exists. It is a conventional mortgage with a remaining term of 23 years.

Insurance: The existing policy is for $50,000, $480.00 premium for three years (in advance). Expiration date is December 3rd of next year.

Listing price: $68,900.

Length of listing: 90 days, commencing 12 Noon on August 26 of this year.

Brokerage commission: 7 per cent of gross sales price.

Will exchange for: No exchange.

Terms: Cash or cash and assumption of mortgage. No trade.

Possession: 30 days after final closing.

Other facts: Seller will negotiate taxes. Seller will not pay charges for FHA or VA financing. Friendswood Realty Co. is a member of the Oakpark Multi-listing Association.

The home is a two-story structure with brick veneer and colonial styling. It is located on the west side of Buttonwood Drive and is six years old. Features are: a 2½-car garage, screened-in porch, central air, gas hot water, gas heat, full basement, family room with fireplace, three baths, and four bedrooms. The home is fully carpeted. The first floor has one bedroom, family room, sitting parlor, dining room, kitchen, utility room, and one full bath. The remaining three bedrooms are on the second floor along with two full baths. The basement is unfinished.

The house is located on a wooded lot measuring 90 feet wide and 150 feet deep.

The Williamses' home is on city water and sanitary sewers. The house is fully insulated and has a garbage disposal. Built-in appliances include a dishwasher and range and oven. The water softener is leased.

The listing contract which the Williamses and Friendswood Realty Co. entered into appears as Exhibit A (pages 376–77).

The Offer To Purchase. On September 26 of this year Ted S. and Suzie B. Novice, 2302 Spillway Lane, Oakpark, made an offer on the Williams property through Joseph Field, broker for Field Real Estate, Inc., a cooperating broker and member of Oakpark Multi-listing Association. The offer is for $67,000 with assumption of the present mortgage and the seller extending the Novices a $5,000 purchase money mortgage to be paid back in equal quarterly installments over a five-year period at 7 per cent interest on the unpaid balance. The Novices give a check of $4,000 to Joseph Field as an earnest money deposit. The offer stipulates that taxes and insurance are to be prorated (the insurance policy is to be assumed) and the seller is to pay for a mechanical/structural inspection of the home. Closing is to be on or before October 13 of this year. The title policy shall be in the amount of the sales price. Said title policy shall be ordered by the seller immediately upon loan assumption approval and said policy shall be paid by the seller. The buyers request a staked survey to be provided at the sellers' expense. Acceptance of the offer must be within two days. Purchaser is to have complete possession within 15 days after closing. Liquidated damages are to be $30.00 per day.

On September 27 of this year the offer was accepted by the Williamses. The Offer to Purchase entered into by the Williamses and Novices appears as Exhibit B (pages 378–79).

The Closing.   The closing was set for October 13 of this year.   Other charges relative to the closing are as follows:

Mortgage assumption fee = ½% of mortgage balance	
Title policy	$230.00
Deed preparation	15.00
Recording of deed	4.00
Lot staking	100.00
Inspection fee (mech/struc)	30.00
Credit report	10.00

The sample closing statements for the buyers and sellers, including supporting calculations, appear as Exhibit C (pages 380–81) and Exhibit D (pages 382–83).

Questions

1. Based on the information supplied in the case study, fill out a listing contract and Offer to Purchase contract utilizing standard contract forms used in your specific locality.
2. Compare and contrast the standard contract forms used in your locality with those presented in Exhibits A and B. Cite advantages of each.
3. Prepare the sellers' and buyers' closing statements using the facts presented. How do your answers compare with those shown in Exhibits C, D, and E? How do local customs and practices affect the closing statements?
4. Assuming the sellers were not agreeable to extending a purchase money mortgage for $5,000.00 to the buyers, what other means might be available to secure the additional $5,000.00 necessary to close the sale on the Williams home? How would these alternative means of financing affect the buyers' and sellers' closing statements?
5. The sale involved both Friendswood Realty Co. and Field Real Estate, Inc. Using your local real estate board as a reference, how might the sales commission be divided in a case such as this?

REAL ESTATE LISTING CONTRACT (EXCLUSIVE RIGHT TO SELL)

SALES PRICE $68,900.00   TYPE HOME Colonial—2 story   TOTAL BEDROOMS 4   TOTAL BATHS 3

ADDRESS 4750 E. Buttonwood Dr.   JURISDICTION OF Oakpark, Walnut Co., Nostate

AMT OF LOAN TO BE ASSUMED $ 48,200.00   AS OF WHAT DATE 8/15/TY   AMOUNT PAYABLE MONTHLY $ 384.48 @ 8 %   YEARS TO GO 23   TYPE LOAN Conv.

MORTGAGE COMPANY First Savings & Loan of Oakpark   2nd MORTGAGE N/A   TAXES & INS. INCLUDED No

OWNER'S NAME Fred M. & Josie R. Williams   PHONES (HOME) N/G   (BUSINESS) N/G

TENANT'S NAME N/A   PHONES (HOME) N/G   (BUSINESS) N/G

POSSESSION 30 DAFC   DATE LISTED 8/26/TY   EXCLUSIVE FOR 90 days   DATE OF EXPIRATION Nov. 30

LISTING BROKER Friendswood Realty Co.   PHONE N/G   KEY AVAILABLE AT N/G

LISTING SALESMAN Barbara Friendswood (Broker)   HOME PHONE N/G   HOW TO BE SHOWN N/G

ENTRANCE FOYER □   CENTER HALL □   AIR CONDITIONING ☑   TYPE KITCHEN CABINETS N/G

LIVING ROOM SIZE N/G   FIREPLACE □   TOOL HOUSE □   TYPE COUNTER TOPS N/G

DINING ROOM SIZE N/G   AGE 6   ROOFING N/G   PATIO □   EAT-IN SIZE KITCHEN □

BEDROOM TOTAL: 4 DOWN 1 UP 3   GARAGE SIZE 2½ car   CIRCULAR DRIVE □   TYPE STOVE □

BATHS TOTAL: 3 DOWN 1 UP 2   SIDE DRIVE □   SCREENED ☑   BUILT-IN OVEN & RANGE ☑

DEN SIZE N/G FIREPLACE □   PORCH □ SIDE □ REAR □   OUTDOOR GRILL □   SEPARATE STOVE INCLUDED □

FAMILY ROOM SIZE N/G FIREPLACE ☑   FENCED YARD   STORM DOORS □   REFRIGERATOR INCLUDED □

RECREATION ROOM SIZE N/G FIREPLACE □   STORM WINDOWS □   SIDEWALKS □   DISHWASHER INCLUDED Yes

BASEMENT SIZE   CURBS & GUTTERS □   ALLEY □   DISPOSAL INCLUDED □

NONE □ 1/4 □ 1/3 □ 1/2 □ 3/4 □ FULL ☑   STORM SEWERS □   DOUBLE SINK □   SINGLE SINK □

UTILITY ROOM N/G   WATER SUPPLY City   SEPTIC □   STAINLESS STEEL □   PORCELAIN □

SEWER ☑   TYPE GAS: NATURAL ☑   BOTTLED □   WASHER INCLUDED □   DRYER INCLUDED □

TYPE HOT WATER SYSTEM: WHY SELLING Transfer   LAND ASSESSMENT $ 4,000.00

TYPE HEAT Gas   IMPROVEMENTS $ 16,000.00

EST. FUEL COST N/G   PROPERTY DESCRIPTION   TOTAL ASSESSMENT $ 20,000.00

ATTIC □   TAX RATE 12.20/100

PULL DOWN STAIRWAY □   REGULAR STAIRWAY □   TRAP DOOR □   LOT SIZE 90' x 150'd   TOTAL ANNUAL TAXES $ 2,440.00

NAME OF BUILDER N/G   LOT NO. 43 BLOCK N/G SECTION 3

SQUARE FOOTAGE N/G

EXTERIOR OF HOUSE Brick Veneer

NAME OF SCHOOLS: ELEMENTARY N/G   JR. HIGH N/G   HIGH: N/G   PAROCHIAL: N/G

PUBLIC TRANSPORTATION: N/G

NEAREST SHOPPING AREA: N/G

REMARKS   House fully carpeted and fully insulated

Date: 8/26/TY

In consideration of the services of **Friendswood Realty Co.** (herein called "Broker") to be rendered to the undersigned (herein called "Owner"), and of the promise of Broker to make reasonable efforts to obtain a Purchaser therefor, Owner hereby lists with Broker the real estate and all improvements thereon which are described above (all herein called "the property"), and Owner hereby grants to Broker the exclusive and irrevocable right to sell such property from 12:00 Noon on __8/26__, 19 __TY__ until 12:00 Midnight on __11/26__, 19 __TY__ (herein called "period of time"), for the price of __Sixty-eight Thousand Nine Hundred__ Dollars ($ __68,900.00__) or for such other price and upon such other terms (including exchange) as Owner may subsequently authorize during the period of time.

It is understood by Owner that the above sum or any other price subsequently authorized by Owner shall include a cash fee of __seven (7%)__ per cent of such price or other price which shall be payable by Owner to Broker upon consummation by any Purchaser or Purchasers of a valid contract of sale of the property during the period of time and whether or not Broker was a procuring cause of any such contract of sale.

If the property is sold or exchanged by Owner, or by Broker or by any other person to any Purchaser to whom the property was shown by Broker or any representative of Broker within sixty (60) days after the expiration of the period of time mentioned above, Owner agrees to pay to Broker a cash fee which shall be the same percentage of the purchase price as the percentage mentioned above.

Broker is hereby authorized by Owner to place a "For Sale" sign on the property and to remove all signs of other brokers or salesmen during the period of time, and Owner hereby agrees to make the property available to Broker at all reasonable hours for the purpose of showing it to prospective Purchasers.

Owner agrees to convey the property to the Purchaser by deed with the usual covenants of title and free and clear from all encumbrances, tenancies, liens (for taxes or otherwise), but subject to applicable restrictive covenants of record. Owner acknowledges receipt of a copy of this agreement.

WITNESS the following signature(s) and seal(s):

Date Signed: __8/26/TY__

Listing Agent   Friendswood Realty Co. by

Address __Oakpark, Nostate__   Telephone __N/G__

Fred M. William (Owner)

Josie R. Williams (Owner)

Exhibit A.

REAL ESTATE SALES CONTRACT (OFFER TO PURCHASE AGREEMENT)

This AGREEMENT made as of _____ September 27 _____, 19 __TY__,

among _____ Ted S. Novice and Suzie B. Novice _____

(herein called "Purchaser"),

and _____ Fred M. Williams and Josie R. Williams _____

(herein called "Seller").

and _____ Friendswood Realty Co. and Field Real Estate, Inc. (cooperating broker) _____ (herein called "Broker"), provides that Purchaser agrees to buy through Broker as agent for Seller, and Seller agrees to sell the following described real estate, and all improvements thereon, located in the jurisdiction of _____ Oakpark, Walnut County, Nostate _____,

(all herein called "the property"): _____ Lot 43 in Arlington's Third Section, recorded as Instrument #1413 in Plat Book 5, pages 323 to 326 in the Office of the Recorder, Walnut County, Nostate _____, and more commonly known as _____ 4750 East Buttonwood Drive, Oakpark, Nostate _____ (street address).

1. The purchase price of the property is _____ Sixty-seven thousand and no/100 _____ Dollars ($ 67,000.00), and such purchase price shall be paid as follows:

Assumption of the present mortgage with the Seller extending the Buyer a $5,000.00 purchase money mortgage to be paid back in equal quarterly installments over a 5 year period plus 7% interest on the unpaid balance.

2. Purchaser has made a deposit of _____ Four thousand and no/100 _____ Dollars ($ 4,000.00) with Broker, receipt of which is hereby acknowledged, and such deposit shall be held by Broker in escrow until the date of settlement and then applied to the purchase price, or returned to Purchaser if the title to the property is not marketable.

3. Seller agrees to convey the property to Purchaser by Deed with the usual covenants of title and free and clear from all monetary encumbrances, tenancies, liens (for taxes or otherwise), except as may be otherwise provided above, but subject to applicable restrictive covenants of record. Seller further agrees to deliver possession of the property to Purchaser on the date of settlement and to pay the expense of preparing the deed of conveyance.

4. Settlement shall be made at _____ N/G _____ October 13 _____, 19 __TY__, or as soon thereafter as title can be examined and necessary documents prepared, with allowance of a reasonable time for Seller to correct any defects reported by the title examiner.

5. All taxes, interest, rent, and impound escrow deposits, if any, shall be prorated as of the date of settlement.

6. All risk of loss or damage to the property by fire, windstorm, casualty, or other cause is assumed by Seller until the date of settlement.

7. Purchaser and Seller agree that Broker was the sole procuring cause of this Contract of Purchase, and Seller agrees to pay Broker for services rendered a cash fee of _____ 7 _____ per cent of the purchase price. If either Purchaser or Seller defaults under such Contract, such defaulting party shall be liable for the cash fee of Broker and any expenses incurred by the non-defaulting party in connection with this transaction.

Subject to: _____ Insurance is to be prorated; Seller to pay for mechanical/structural inspection; Seller shall furnish title policy in the amount of the purchase price; a staked survey shall be provided at Seller's expense; Seller shall have possession 15 DAFC; liquidated damages $30/day.

8. Purchaser represents that an inspection satisfactory to Purchaser has been made of the property, and Purchaser agrees to accept the property in its present condition except as may be otherwise provided in the description of the property above.

9. This Contract of Purchase constitutes the entire agreement among the parties and may not be modified or changed except by written instrument executed by all of the parties, including Broker.

10. This Contract of Purchase shall be construed, interpreted, and applied according to the law of the jurisdiction of _____ and shall be binding upon and shall inure to the benefit of the heirs, personal representatives, successors, and assigns of the parties.

All parties to this agreement acknowledge receipt of a certified copy.

WITNESS the following signatures:

Fred M. Williams _____ Seller

Josie R. Williams _____ Seller

Joseph Siert _____ Broker

Ted A. Novice _____ Purchaser

Susie B. Novice _____ Purchaser

Deposit Rec'd $ __4,000.00__

Personal Check   Cash

Cashier's Check   Company Check

Sales Agent:

Exhibit B.

	BUYER'S STATEMENT		SELLER'S STATEMENT	
	DEBIT	CREDIT	DEBIT	CREDIT
SALES PRICE	$67,000.00			$67,000.00
ESCROW FUNDS				
INSURANCE (PRORATED)				
(1 yrs. 1 mos. 20 days)	182.13			182.13
REAL ESTATE TAXES				
this year payable Dec. 31, TY		1,918.11	1,918.11	
MORTGAGE BALANCE		48,136.85	48,136.85	
INTEREST (PRORATED) FROM 9/15 TO 10/13		310.30	310.30	
RENT – FROM TO				
EARNEST MONEY DEPOSIT		4,000.00		
BROKER'S COMMISSION 7%			4,690.00	
DEED PREPARATION FEE			15.00	
ABSTRACT CONTINUATION OR TITLE POLICY FEE GROSS INCOME TAX STAMPS (Corporation Seller Only)			230.00	
OTHER ITEMS:				
Recording of Deed	4.00			
Credit Report	10.00			
Purchase Money Mortgage		5,000.00	5,000.00	
Mortgage Assumption Fee	240.68			

Exhibit C.

	BUYER'S STATEMENT		SELLER'S STATEMENT	
	DEBIT	CREDIT	DEBIT	CREDIT
Mechanical/Structural Insp.			30.00	
Lot Staking			100.00	
Purchase Money Mortgage				5,000.00
	$67,436.81	$59,365.26	$60,430.26	$67,182.13

BALANCE DUE SELLER $6,751.87
BALANCE DUE FROM BUYERS $8,071.55

Exhibit C.   Continued.

SETTLEMENT STATEMENT SUPPLEMENTAL CALCULATIONS

I. *Prorate Insurance*:

  A. Calculate time unused on current policy:

        October, this year   17 days
        December, next year   3 days
                            20 days total
      plus 1 month
      plus 1 year
      therefore total unused time = 1 year, 1 month, 20 days

  B. Calculate yearly, monthly, daily rates:

        $480.00 per 3 years
      or $480.00/3 = $160.00/year
      or $160.00/12 =   13.33/month
      or $ 13.33/30 =   .44/day

  C. Calculate unused insurance premium:

      $160.00/year X 1 year = $160.00
      $ 13.33/month X 1 month =   13.33
      $ .44/day X 20 days =   8.80
      TOTAL $182.13

II. *Broker's Commission*: .07 X $67,000 = $4,690.00

III. *Prorate Taxes:* This year's taxes, paid in arrears, due Dec. 31, TY

  A. Calculate time used, this year: 9 mos, 13 days

  B. Calculate monthly tax rate:

    (16,000 + 4,000) (12.20/100) 12 months = $203.33/month

  C. Calculate daily rate:

    203.33/month ÷ 30 days = $6.78/day

  D. Calculate prorated taxes due Dec. 31, TY

    $203.33/mo. X 9 mos. = 1,829.97
    $ 6.78/day X 13 days =   88.14
                       $1,918.11

Exhibit D.

IV. *Update Mortgage Balance*:

After August 15th payment, balance equals $48,200
PI = $384.48/month, interest = 8%

$48,200 X .08 =	$ 3,856.00 interest per year
$ 3,856.00 ÷ 12 months =	321.33 interest per month
$ 384.48 − $321.33 =	63.15 principal reduction with
	September 15th payment
$48,200 − $63.15 =	$48,136.85 balance after September
	15th payment

V. *Prorate Interest*:

A. Days used since September 15th payment: 29 days (count 9/15)
B. Calculate interest charges per day:

$48,136.85 mortgage balance after September 15th payment
$48,136.85 X .08 = $3,850.95 interest per year
$ 3,850.95 ÷ 12 = $ 320.91 interest per month
$ 320.91 ÷ 30 = $10.70 interest per day

C. Calculate prorated interest to day of closing: $10.70 X 29 = $310.30

VI. *Mortgage Assumption Fee*: .005 X $48,136.85 = $240.68

NOTE: Local convention dictates the following (conventions in your area may vary:)

1. The closing day is the responsibility of the seller.

2. Calculations for taxes, insurance and mortgage interest are calculated on a 30-day month; the yearly, monthly and daily rates are rounded to two places.

Exhibit D.   Continued.

STUDY PROJECT 13–1

Six Great Motivators *

Competition for savings is strong. Our public relations effort must be intensified, expanded, and made even more effective if we are to keep our place in the sun and if we are to continue approximately the same rate of growth that we have enjoyed recently.

To a very great degree, the success of these efforts will depend upon the measure of understanding we have of the basic emotions and impulses—motivational forces—that govern people. I think it can be argued that this understanding of people is the paramount consideration involved in developing our various public relations and promotional programs.

Some years ago, the advertising people gave the fancy-sounding title of "motivation research" to the job of understanding people. It is this understanding of people and why they act as they do that might be called the golden key to public relations success.

The first important motivational force that has direct influence on public relations activities is that people like to feel that they are needed. This basic desire to be needed suggests a variety of approaches as far as public relations programs are concerned.

One such approach is that people's savings are needed to build a safe future for the family. Another is that their savings are needed now so that the saver can enjoy new and wonderful products of the future. Still another approach is that savings are needed to provide the fuel of capital for the expansion and growth of our economy. And a fourth approach is that savings are needed for patriotic reasons—currently this patriotic reason is the fighting of inflation.

The second basic motivational force which can influence our public relations programs is that people like to be successful. An obvious major public relations approach here is that people who save are successful people because they have mastered the problem of putting away part of what they earn. Similarly, people like to feel that they are part of a successful, progressive enterprise, which accounts, incidentally, for the sense of proprietorship that many families display in the growth of the savings association in their community.

The third great force that should affect public relations planning is that people like a sense of physical well-being.

There are at least three considerations here that apply to public relations programs—office quarters, personnel and the dress of personnel. With respect to office quarters, the building of new buildings, the remodeling or modernization of old quarters has played a vital part in developing new business. With respect to personnel, people like warm, friendly employees to handle their affairs. As to the dress of personnel, studies have shown that people are greatly impressed by the appearance of other people; the trend toward more casual dress in recent years does not keep employees from being neatly and suitably attired.

The fourth great moving force affecting public relations programs of associations is that people like to feel secure.

The search for security has brought remarkable changes in American life. It has developed a tremendous life insurance industry; it has inspired passage of unemployment compensation and social security laws; it brought the Blue Cross and Blue Shield health insurance into being; it caused the establishment of literally thousands of private retirement and pension plans.

. . .

* From an article by William B. O'Connell, revised by the author in 1976.

There is still another element involved in the search for security, and that is the seeking of assurance that savings placed with a savings association are safe. In the past 10 years I have given a great deal of thought and study to this matter and long ago reached the conclusion that public confidence in the safety of our institutions is more vital to our prestige than anything else.

This suggests immediately the necessity of placing repeated emphasis on such factors of safety as sound and careful management, including auditing, the federal-agency insurance of savings accounts, and the assistance available through the Federal Home Loan Bank System.

The fifth great motivational "mover" is that people like to be appreciated. Look for opportunities to say "thank you" in many different ways, not only to persons when they open new accounts but on the anniversary dates of the day on which the accounts were opened. You can say "thank you," too, to persons who have shown consistency and regularity in adding to their accounts.

The sixth great mover is that people like to be informed.

This is more true today than it ever was. Our educational levels have advanced generation by generation, and today a higher percentage of youngsters go through college than went through high school 50 years ago. As a result, the hunger for knowledge and information is more active than ever before.

Questions

1. How might the "six great motivators" be applied to the public relations program of a real estate brokerage firm?
2. Compare the discussion of motivation research in this study project with that presented in Chapter 13.

14

MARKETING: PROPERTY MANAGEMENT

CHARACTERISTICS OF PROPERTY MANAGEMENT

In this chapter we consider the marketing of property services rather than the properties themselves. This general field, usually referred to as property management, has developed rapidly in recent years.

Our attention will center at the outset on several basic definitions of management and property management, the reasons for the development of this field, the requirements of property managers, the major types of management, and the **professional management organization.**

Basic Definitions

Because terms often have special meanings in different fields, we will define the ways in which the terms management, administration, and property management are used here.

The terms *management* and *administration* are used in relation to all types of organized activities. As we suggested in our discussions in the introductory chapters, we use these terms interchangeably in most situations to identify the processes of using resources effectively in the attainment of desired objectives. In this broad sense, the term *management* may be applied to all types of business and to all aspects of the real estate business.

The term *property management,* however, has come to have certain special connotations in the real estate business. Although an owner may also manage a property, the term *property management* usually is applied to situations in which someone other than the owner performs the management function. Because this type of usage has grown up in the real estate field, we tend to use the term *administration* in relation to broader managerial processes and the term *management* in the specialized sense of property management as indicated above. Although we use the term *property management* in the customary narrow sense, it will be understood that when an individual owner or a business firm manages a property, the principles and methods of the property manager may be applied.

Reasons for Property Management

The increasing complexities of many problems associated with the managing of real properties, together with the fact that some owners know relatively little about real estate principles and practices, accounts in large part for the development of this specialized branch of the real estate business. Absentee ownership, use of trustee arrangements, tax factors, technological developments, and growth of the corporate ownership of real property have contributed to the development of property management. In addition, it is often difficult for some owners to maintain favorable income–expense relationships for their properties.

Inflexible Resources

Certain conditions create special types of problems for the manager of real property. The durability of real estate necessitates managerial planning over longer periods of time than are required for many other types of business. Furthermore, real properties are economically inflexible—that is, once they are improved their uses are relatively fixed for long periods. Hence, to a large extent the manager is called upon to operate properties so as to get as large a return as possible from relatively fixed resources.

Current expenses are only slightly more flexible than the basic investment. Many important operating expenses, such as taxes, insurance, and interest charges, are usually beyond the control of the property manager. Hence, a slight decline in gross income usually means a considerably larger decline in net returns.

As we have said before, the fact that real properties are fixed in location means that the manager cannot move a property to those who desire its services; rather, they must be induced to come to it. For the same reason, the property cannot escape adverse developments affecting a city or a neighborhood or district.

Requirements of Property Managers

While property management is a specialized branch of the real estate business, a knowledge of the basic principles which explain the utilization of real estate is helpful in developing a successful operation. Thus, good management requires adequate information about the economic base and future prospects of the city in which a property is located. Knowledge of the structure of the city and its characteristics of growth and development are extremely helpful in the planning of long-range management programs. The manager should understand the forces affecting the specific districts or neighborhoods in which the managed properties are located. In addition, the manager should be familiar with the forces affecting the market for the types of real estate being managed. Market information is needed almost constantly and should be kept up to date and analyzed currently. With such knowledge, the property manager can adjust rental schedules and certain types of expenditures in accordance with changes in the market.

Apartment houses, office buildings, loft buildings, stores, and dwellings are the types of property most frequently operated under the direction of specialized property managers. Farm management has grown in importance in recent years. Some shopping centers and industrial districts are operated by management organizations. Each type of property involves special problems of management, but the general principles of management are the same for all.

Relationship of Management to Ownership

The real estate manager operates as the agent of the owner. In most respects the manager's legal position could be compared to that of the manager of the branch office of an organization. Legally, the property manager is considered a general agent and thus has the right to exercise judgment and discretion. The property manager owes the employer the duty of loyalty, and hence may not take secret commissions from suppliers or donations from tenants.

The exercise of care, diligence, and skill is expected of the property manager. Typically, such duties as the following are involved: Lease negotiations, rent collection, maintenance and repair work, keeping the property in rentable condition, hiring required personnel, arranging insurance, payment of taxes, and related activities.

The owner of the property is liable for the property manager's acts if done within designated authority; however, the property manager may not substitute personal judgment for that of the owner.

The duties of the manager include the keeping of records and the rendering of appropriate reports to the owner of the property at specified times or whenever requested. If more than one property is being managed, care must be taken to keep separate accounts and not to commingle funds.[1]

Management Contracts

Frequently, the property manager's relationship with the owner is defined by a specific contract. When such a contract is drawn up, it in-

[1] See Robert Kratovil, *Real Estate Law* (6th ed.; Englewood Cliffs, N. J.: Prentice-Hall, Inc., 1974), ch. 10.

cludes a description of the property to be managed, the length of time for which the agreement is to run, removal and cancellation provisions, the amount of compensation to be paid the manager, and the duties and powers delegated. As in all other contracts, the parties must be legally competent and all terms of the agreement must be stated definitely and exactly. Since the manager is the owner's agent, the general law of agency governs such relationships, but the use of a specific contract eliminates many special problems.

Typically, such contracts are drawn up for specific periods with provisions for renewal, the owner often reserving the right to cancel the agreement by giving the manager adequate notice of such intention. Management contracts should present a complete list of the functions to be performed by the manager and should provide for complete centralization of authority in the manager with respect to all work undertaken in connection with the property. Sometimes management contracts are set up with a trial period of three or six months.

Compensation is usually computed on the basis of a percentage of gross collections, 5 to 8 per cent being a "normal" management fee, although other arrangements are not uncommon. The amount of compensation and the manner of computing and paying it should be specified in the manager's contract.

Types of Managements

The management functions may be performed by individual agents of the owner or by a management company which operates a number of properties for many different owners. Frequently a real estate office conducting a general brokerage business will include a property management department in its organization. Some economies are effected by this arrangement, and the selling process is often facilitated if a buyer knows that the firm making the sale is willing to manage the property. While the average property management department seldom produces large revenues, it is a source of steady income, a factor of considerable importance to real estate firms during periods of limited market activity.

The Professional Management Organization

In order to perform the manifold functions required of management, various employees must be hired; where the scope of operations is broad, a complete organization must be set up. (See Fig. 14–1.) If a number of buildings are involved, superintendents may be hired for each one of sufficient size to require a full-time person. Of course, janitors must be hired and supervised, as well as other laborers, including repair and maintenance people. In larger management organizations, special functions, such as collecting rents and hearing complaints, may be delegated to specific people. Similarly, advertising may be handled by one department,

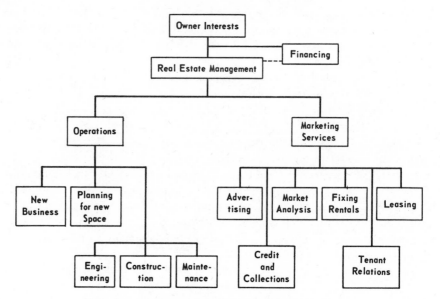

FIG. 14–1. Real estate management diagram.

tenant selection by another, and legal matters by a third department. Accounts always require special attention, and accounting departments are normally provided in all offices of any size.

The management of a property often involves certain responsibilities which cannot be departmentalized and which are on the borderline between the functions of the manager and the owners. In some cases, these are handled in part by attorneys.

PROPERTY MANAGEMENT FUNCTIONS

The functions performed by property managers include the general management processes of establishing objectives, planning to achieve them, organizing resources, and controlling operations. The property manager also performs the functions of (1) planning space, (2) marketing property services, (3) conserving the property and its surroundings, and (4) supervising the operation of the property, which will include among other things the maintenance of accurate records and accounts. The manager is expected to keep the owner informed regarding the property and its operation and to review with the owner any significant changes in policy.

In the performance of management functions, the property manager must consider the interests of three parties: the owner, the tenants, and "the party of the third part," the members of the community in which the property is located. The owner is concerned with potential changes in the value of the property and is interested especially in securing a reasonable return on the investment. Tenants are interested in the space and equipment provided, their condition and maintenance, their cost to them, and the special services and conveniences which may be provided. The community has a continuing interest in property management policies, since they will have a direct bearing on the advance or decline of the property involved and its environment.

Planning Space

If managers have adequate information about the local market, their advice to owners, architects, and builders will be of great value in planning new buildings or in modernization and repair programs. A competent manager is able to advise concerning the type of building accommodations most readily marketable, the competitive position of various types of properties in the market, and the many special requirements of prospective tenants. Also, a manager usually knows something of the most economical methods for arranging rooms, halls, and storage space.

In the case of older buildings, managers must accept the space available and utilize it as efficiently as possible. Sometimes it is possible to alter the arrangement of an older building, but whether this should be done depends on the possibilities of securing adequate return on the additional investment required.[2]

Establishing Rental Schedules

Once a building, regardless of type, is constructed, the manager must fix a rental schedule and enter the market. Fixing a rental schedule calls for an accurate knowledge of such matters as the character of competing space, rents currently charged, the nature of the potential demand, the special requirements of prospective tenants, and the various advantages and disadvantages of the location. A general level of rents is determined first, from which the manager is able to develop a rental schedule for the individual quarters. Specific rates, however, are determined on the basis of market conditions. If net income is to be maximized, rents must be adjusted carefully. For example, if rents are too low, all of the space will be rented but the total return will be less than might be realized under a higher rental schedule. On the other hand, if rents are too high, the increase in the number of vacancies will reduce income. The determination of a rental schedule for a building is one of the basic functions of a manager, and to a large extent success or failure depends on the care with which this work is done. Also, the process of adjusting rental schedules is never complete—rents must follow the market, rising when the demand for space is strong and diminishing when demand falls off. Constant analysis of all factors affecting the market is essential in the performance of this function.

[2] James C. Downs, Jr., *Principles of Real Estate Management* (11th ed.; Chicago: Institute of Real Estate Management, 1975), ch. 5.

Attracting Tenants

With the establishment of a rental schedule, it becomes necessary for the manager to secure tenants. Promotion programs as outlined in the preceding chapter may be helpful. If the building is new, it may be necessary to advertise and solicit for tenants. A new building opens with a competitive advantage, for it usually makes available all of the newest facilities. The opening of a new building is always detrimental to existing buildings, even if it is only a small structure. When a large new office or apartment building is opened, the existing structures must face stiff competition. Tenants of existing buildings are made conscious of the advantages of the new building through advertising and systematic solicitation. If special concessions are offered by the new building or if rental schedules compare favorably with those of existing structures, there will be a tendency for tenants to move from their old quarters to the new building.

The process of advertising space requires great care, for it is easy to waste funds on improperly directed advertising. If the management organization is sufficiently large, this function may be performed by a special person or department. If not, it is often wise for the manager to employ outside assistance in this work.

In established management organizations, the number of prospective tenants who will call at the office in search of accommodations is frequently large. This is especially true in the case of people seeking residential space, particularly if the management office has developed a reputation for fair dealing and courteous treatment of tenants over a period of time.

In the process of attracting tenants, the wise manager is careful to consider both short- and long-range factors. To a large extent, the condition of the market will govern the specific procedure followed—a buyer's market calls for a different program from that suitable in a seller's market. The original rental campaign continues until complete or nearly complete occupancy is achieved. Thereafter, the problem of management is to hold tenants and to meet the competition of other buildings, both old and new.

The successful manager is familiar with current vacancy rates in various types of properties in the city. There is probably no such thing as a normal vacancy, although a vacancy ratio of around 5 to 8 per cent for office buildings and 5 to 10 per cent for apartment houses is generally considered normal. A manager's own vacancy situation is always significant, since it helps to determine policy changes.

Selecting Residential Tenants. It is very important that the character of prospective tenants, especially in large apartment houses, be investigated carefully at the time a building is being opened for occupancy, since tenants give a building the reputation of being either desirable or undesirable. If a manager can secure a highly desirable group of tenants in the first instance, many renting problems will be solved for some time in the future. The following factors are of major importance in selecting residential tenants: stability, housekeeping ability, child care, living habits, tenant compatibility, and social responsibility. The housing of more than a dozen families under one roof requires exceptionally careful selection of tenants. Hence the apartment house manager often requires a signed application for a lease, accompanied by a deposit, in order to allow time for investigation. Then the actual lease is signed later.

Selecting Tenants for Office Buildings. The manager of an office building faces a number of special problems in selecting tenants. There must always be caution against certain types of tenants, especially those whose businesses might involve unethical practices. The manager must decide whether a few large tenants are preferable to a number of small ones, a specialized tenancy to a general one. Usually, property managers prefer to have enough leading firms operating in a certain line of business to create a "center," but not so many that the exodus of such a group will result in the loss of a large percentage of the tenants. In connection with the selection of commercial tenants, attention should be given to such factors as the ability, aggressiveness, and progressiveness of the firms under consideration as well as tenant reputation, service requirements, and expansion requirements.

Medical buildings, because of their particular physical requirements, are an exception. In larger cities, physicians tend to congregate in certain buildings and expect the property manager to enforce high standards in the selection of tenants.

With the expansion of its activities, the federal government has become an important customer in the market for office space. Its leasing requirements and policies differ somewhat from those of the average tenant. For example, annual rent may not exceed a fixed percentage of the fair market value of space leased, and the cost of repairs and alterations may not exceed a stated percentage of the first year's rental. Leases are made on a government form. Sometimes a 30-day cancellation clause is required in order to permit a move to governmentally owned space if it becomes available, and the time of the lease seldom runs longer than the end of the fiscal year (June 30).

Other Functions

In addition to planning space, establishing rental schedules, and attracting and selecting tenants, the property manager performs the functions of leasing space, conserving property, and supervising building operations. We will discuss each of these topics in the following sections.

LEASING PRACTICES

Property managers ordinarily arrange all leases for the space they operate. However, leases are not used for all types of property, and the extent of their use varies from one part of the country to another, depending on the statutes of various states. About 50 per cent of the management offices which operate residential buildings require tenants to sign leases for at least one year. In some states, leases for one year or longer must be in writing to be valid; in others, oral leases are valid for as long as three years. In many cases residential space is rented on a month-to-month basis, and the tenants are free to move or the owner or manager can request tenants to move if either party gives appropriate notice.[3]

Security Required

It is not customary to require the tenant to post any security when leases for residential property are signed. A lease ordinarily binds the owner and manager very effectively because the property serves as security and guarantees performance of the terms of the contract. But unless the tenant is financially responsible and has assets which can be attached if the lease is broken, it is difficult to enforce a lease of this type.

When leases run for periods of longer than a year, which is common practice in the renting of stores, loft building space, or offices, definite lease agreements are usually drawn up, with liquidated damage provisions for failure to perform the contracts. Since business firms usually possess more financial responsibility than individuals, property owners and managers have greater protection in such cases. When leases run for long periods of time, they are usually considered to involve many special problems not normally a part of the functions of property management.

Legal Relationships Established

From a legal standpoint, a lease is a transfer of possession and the right to use property to the tenant for a stipulated period, during which the tenant pays rent to the owner. At the end of the period the right of possession reverts to the owner of the fee. It is a contract containing various terms and conditions, the most important being the agreement to pay rent. To be valid, such a contract must be entered into by parties who are legally competent and it must describe the property, the term or period of the lease, the rent, and special covenants of the contracting parties completely and exactly. (See Figs. 14-2 and 14-3.)

Special problems which may be anticipated in the lease include such items as the exact dates on which the lease begins and ends, arrange-

---

[3] Subject to rent control regulations, if in force.

ments governing the agreement in case of damage to the space, such as may result from fire, termination of the lease in case of complete destruction of the building, and the relationship which shall exist between tenant and owner in case a new building is constructed.

Other points which are often included in the lease are these: (1) reservation by the manager of the right to enter upon the premises for inspection, (2) specific uses to which the property may be put, (3) restriction or regulation of subleases, (4) control of the placement of signs and other additions which may affect the appearance of the building, and (5) definition of the rights of the tenant in case of condemnation proceedings.

Rents and Concessions

The rents fixed in a lease may be of several types: (1) a flat rate for the period covered; (2) a graded or step-up rental; (3) a percentage rental varying with the amount of tenant's gross or net income; or (4) a rental which is adjusted by reappraisal of the property at certain times.[4] Also, various combinations of these types of leases may be worked out. For example, a lease on a business property might be drawn up which provides for a minimum flat rent, plus a percentage of the tenant's gross business receipts if they exceed a certain stipulated amount. In the case of long-term leases, such an arrangement is often desirable to guard against important changes in the value of money.

Concessions or special services provided by the owner may be such as to create a wide gap between the real and the nominal money rent. Thus, a rental may be set at $225 per month for an apartment, with a concession of one month's rent, which means in fact that the real charge is $206.25 per month. Managers often make such arrangements instead of cutting rents, because they believe that it will be easier, when the market warrants a return to the old level, to raise rents by eliminating concessions than by reinstating a schedule previously abandoned. The provision of special equipment, or, in some cases, the payment of moving expenses in order to get the tenant in are other examples of concessions.

Duration of Leases

Different provisions are to be found respecting the duration of the lease:

1. Tenancies for a fixed or definite term
2. Tenancies for a periodic term, subject to termination upon notice (tenancy "from month to month" or "from year to year")
3. Tenancies for an indefinite period, subject to termination with notice (tenancy at will)

Sometimes leases hold over—that is, the tenant stays after the expiration of the lease. If this happens, as a general rule the owner has the

---

[4] Reappraisal leases have seldom worked out advantageously, since it is difficult to secure an adjusted appraisal which will be acceptable to both landlord and tenant.

X 48—Form of Apartment Lease Approved by the Committee on Real Property of The Association of the Bar of the City of New York.

JULIUS BLUMBERG, INC., LAW BLANK PUBLISHERS
80 EXCHANGE PLACE AT BROADWAY, NEW YORK

Lease, made the 12th day of December 19 , between John Land 400 West 66th Street, Manhattan, New York
hereinafter called the Landlord, and

Robert Money 5000 Riverside Drive, Manhattan, New York
hereinafter called the Tenant.

WITNESSETH: The Landlord hereby leases to the Tenant, Apartment 5B on the Fifth floor, in premises, 400 West 66th Street Borough of Manhattan , City of New York, hereinafter called the building, to be used as a private dwelling apartment, and not otherwise, for a term to commence January 1st 19 and to end December 31st 19 unless sooner terminated as hereinafter provided, at the annual rent of $ 1800.00 payable in equal monthly installments of $ 150.00 each in advance on the first day of each calendar month during the term, the first of said installments to be paid on the signing of this lease.

The parties hereto further agree as follows:

1st. The Tenant will pay the rent as herein provided.

2nd. The Tenant will take good care of the leased premises, fixtures and appurtenances, and suffer no waste or injury; make all repairs to the leased premises, fixtures and appurtenances necessitated by the fault of the Tenant, his family, guests, servants, assignees or under-tenant; conform to all laws, orders and regulations of the Federal, State or Municipal governments, or of any of their departments, and regulations of the New York Board of Fire Underwriters, applicable to the leased premises, but shall not be required to make any expenditure to comply therewith unless necessitated by his fault; and save harmless the Landlord from any liability arising from injury to person or property caused by any act or omission of the Tenant, his family, guests, servants, assignees or under-tenants; repair at or before the end of the term, all injury done by the installation or removal of furniture and other property; and at the end or other expiration of the term, surrender the leased premises in as good condition as they were at the beginning of the term, reasonable wear and damage by fire or other casualty excepted.

3rd. The Tenant will not, without the Landlord's written consent, make any alteration in the leased premises and will not deface or permit the defacing of any part of the leased premises; will not do or suffer anything to be done on the leased premises which will increase the rate of fire insurance on the building; will not use any shades, awnings, window air-conditioning units or window guards, except such as shall be approved by the Landlord; will not keep or harbor any animal in the leased premises without first obtaining the written consent of the Landlord; will not permit the accumulation of waste or refuse matter; and will not assign this lease or underlet the leased premises or any part thereof without the Landlord's written consent, which consent the Landlord agrees not to withhold unreasonably.

4th. The Tenant will observe and comply with such reasonable rules as the Landlord may prescribe on written notice to the Tenant for the safety, care and cleanliness of the building, and the comfort, quiet and convenience of other occupants of the building.

5th. The Landlord shall furnish, insofar as the present facilities of Landlord provide, the following services: (a) Elevator service; (b) Hot and cold water in reasonable quantities; (c) Heat at reasonable hours during the cold seasons of the year; (d) Air-conditioning during the warm seasons of the year.

6th. The Landlord shall have the privilege of furnishing the electric current consumed at the leased premises, and current so furnished shall be paid for by the Tenant at the rates charged for similar consumption by the local public utility company. If the Landlord furnishes the Tenant with telephone service, the Tenant shall pay for each call at the rate established by the Landlord, but the Tenant shall not be precluded from obtaining telephone service direct from the telephone company. Charges for electric current and telephone service shall be deemed additional rent, and for non-payment of same the Landlord shall have the same remedies as for non-payment of the fixed rent.

7th. In case of damage by fire to the building, without the fault of the Tenant, if the damage is so extensive as to amount practically to the total destruction of the leased premises or of the building, or if the Landlord shall within a reasonable time decide to rebuild, this lease shall cease and come to an end, and the rent shall be apportioned to the time of the damage. In all other cases where the leased premises are damaged by fire without the fault of the Tenant, the Landlord shall repair the damage with reasonable dispatch, and if the damage has rendered the premises untenantable, in whole or in part, there shall be an apportionment of the rent until the damage has been repaired. In determining what constitutes reasonable dispatch consideration shall be given to delays caused by strikes, adjustment of insurance and other causes beyond the Landlord's control.

8th. If the leased premises, or any part thereof, are taken by virtue of eminent domain, this lease shall expire on the date when the same shall be so taken, and the rent shall be apportioned as of said date. No part of any award for the leased premises, however, shall belong to the Tenant.

9th. If the Tenant defaults in the performance of any of the covenants or conditions herein contained, other than the covenants to pay rent, or if any conduct of the Tenant or occupants of the leased premises shall be objectionable, the Landlord may give to the Tenant ten days' written notice thereof, and if such default has not been cured or the objectionable conduct stopped within said ten day period, then at the expiration of said ten days the Landlord may give the Tenant five days' notice of the termination of this lease, and at the expiration of said five days' notice the term of this lease shall expire, and the Tenant shall then surrender the leased premises to the Landlord, but the Tenant shall remain liable as hereinafter provided. In case of default by the Tenant in the payment of rent, or if the ten day notice above provided for shall have been given and the ten day period shall have elapsed without curing such default or stopping the objectionable conduct, and the five day notice above provided for shall have been given and the five day period shall have elapsed, or if the leased premises become vacant or deserted, the Landlord may at any time thereafter resume possession thereof by any lawful means, and remove the Tenant or other occupants and their effects, by dispossess proceedings, or otherwise, without being liable to prosecution or damages therefor, and hold the premises as if this lease had not been made. In any such case, the Landlord may at the Landlord's option relet the premises or any part thereof as agent of the Tenant or otherwise, and receive the rent therefor, applying the same first to the payment of such expenses as the Landlord may have incurred in connection with such resumption of possession and reletting, including brokerage, cleaning, repairs, and decorations, and then to the payment of rent and performance of the other covenants of the Tenant as herein provided; and the Tenant agrees, whether or not the Landlord has relet, to pay to the Landlord the rent and other sums herein agreed to be paid by the Tenant, less the proceeds of the reletting, if any, as ascertained from time to time, and the same shall be payable by the Tenant on the several rent days above specified. The Tenant hereby waives all right of redemption to which the Tenant or any person claiming under the Tenant might be entitled by any law now or hereafter in force.

10th. The failure of either party to insist in any instance on strict performance of any covenant hereof, or to exercise any option herein contained, shall not be construed as a waiver of such covenant or option in any other instance. No modification of any provision hereof and no cancellation or surrender hereof shall be valid unless in writing, and signed by the parties.

11th. If this lease is assigned by the Tenant, or the leased premises are underlet or occupied by anybody other than the Tenant, the Landlord may collect rent from the assignee, under-tenant or occupant, and apply the net amount collected to the rent herein reserved, and no such collection shall be deemed a waiver of the covenant herein against assignment and underletting, or the acceptance of such assignee, under-tenant or occupant as Tenant, or a release of the Tenant from further performance of the covenants herein contained.

12th. This lease shall be subject and subordinate at all times to the lien of existing mortgages and of mortgages which hereafter may be made a lien on the premises. Although no instrument or act on the part of the Tenant shall be necessary to effectuate such subordination, the Tenant will, nevertheless, execute and deliver such further instruments subordinating this lease to the lien of any such mortgages as may be desired by the mortgagee. The Tenant hereby appoints the Landlord his attorney in fact, irrevocably, to execute and deliver any such instrument for the Tenant. If any underlying lease to which this lease may be subject shall terminate, the Tenant shall attorn to the owner of the reversion.

13th. All improvements made by the Tenant to the leased premises which are so attached to the freehold that they cannot be removed without material injury to the premises, shall become the property of the Landlord.

14th. Any notice by either party to the other shall be in writing and shall be deemed to be duly given only if delivered personally or mailed by registered or certified mail in a postpaid envelope addressed (a) if to the Tenant, at the building in which the leased premises are located, and (b) if to the Landlord, at the address, if any, noted on the lease, or, if none, then to the building, provided, however, that if either party admit, either in writing or under oath, the receipt of notice, evidence of service in accordance herewith shall not be necessary.

15th. The Landlord shall not be liable for damage or injury to person or property occurring within the leased premises, unless caused by or resulting from the negligence of the Landlord or any of the Landlord's agents, servants or employees, in the operation or maintenance of the leased premises or the building.

FIG. 14–2a. Lease form. (Prepared by The Association of the Bar of the City of New York. Published by Julius Blumberg, Inc., New York.)

16th. If the making of repairs or improvements to the building or its appliances, or to the leased premises, other than those made at the Tenant's request or caused by the Tenant's negligence, shall render the leased premises untenantable in whole or in part, there shall be a proportionate abatement of the rent during the period of such untenantability.

17th. Interruption or curtailment of any service maintained in the building if caused by strikes, mechanical difficulties, or any other cause beyond the Landlord's control, whether similar or dissimilar to those enumerated, shall not entitle the Tenant to any claim against the Landlord or to any reduction in rent, nor shall the same constitute constructive or partial eviction, unless the Landlord shall fail to take such measures as may be reasonable in the circumstances to restore the service without undue delay.

18th. During the four months prior to the expiration of the term, applicants shall be admitted at all reasonable hours of the day to view the premises until rented; and the Landlord and the Landlord's agents shall be permitted at any time during the term to examine the leased premises at any reasonable hour; and workmen may enter at any time when authorized by the Landlord to facilitate repairs in any part of the building; and if the Tenant shall not be personally present to permit any such permissible entry into the premises, the Landlord may enter same by a master key, or forcibly, without being liable in damages therefor and without affecting the obligations of the Tenant hereunder.

19th. Neither party has made any representation or promises, except as contained herein, or in some further writing signed by the party making such representation or promise.

20th. The Landlord covenants that the Tenant, on paying the rent and performing the covenants hereof, shall and may peaceably and quietly have, hold and enjoy the leased premises for the term herein mentioned.

21st. The provisions of this lease shall bind and enure to the benefit of the Landlord and the Tenant, and their respective successors, legal representatives and assigns. The Landlord shall be released from, and the Landlord's grantee shall be liable for, all liability of Landlord hereunder accruing from and after each grant of the reversion.

22nd. The Landlord acknowledges receipt from the Tenant of $ 150.00 as security for the performance of the Tenant's obligations under this lease. To the extent that said sum shall remain unapplied to such performance after the date fixed as the end of the term or after the earlier expiration of the term pursuant to paragraphs 7th·or 8th hereof, said sum shall be returned by the Landlord to the Tenant if the Tenant shall have surrendered possession of the leased premises to the Landlord as herein provided.

IN WITNESS WHEREOF, the parties hereto have signed this instrument, the day and year above written.

In the presence of:

John Land
Landlord

Robert Money
Tenant

FIG. 14–2b.   Lease form—reverse.

option of either taking proceedings to dispossess the tenant or of assuming that the lease has been renewed for another term.

Once a lease has been drawn up and signed, it may be terminated by expiration of the agreement, by eviction of the tenant by the owner, forfeiture of the lease by the tenant, or voluntary surrender and acceptance. Each of these methods of terminating the lease, except the first, is governed by detailed legal regulations.

Express and Implied Covenants

As in the case of most real estate contracts, leases contain certain express and implied covenants, the landlord or lessor guaranteeing possession and quiet enjoyment and promising that the property will be suitable for use. The lessee guarantees to pay rent, to use the property in a stipulated fashion, and to care for the premises. In accordance with the latter agreement, the lessee is usually required to carry certain insurance for the protection of the property, although this varies with the type of property involved. In the case of business property the lessee is often required to assist in the payment of taxes if they reach a certain point. Such an agreement in a lease is called a *tax participation clause.*

LEASE
(NON-RESIDENTIAL - SHORT FORM)
CALIFORNIA REAL ESTATE ASSOCIATION STANDARD FORM
THIS IS INTENDED TO BE A LEGALLY BINDING AGREEMENT—READ IT CAREFULLY

_____, California

_____ 19_____

_____ Lessor, and

_____ Lessee,

agree as follows:

1. Lessor leases to Lessee and Lessee hires from Lessor those premises described as:_____
_____
_____

together with the following furniture and fixtures:_____
_____

(Insert "as shown on Exhibit A attached hereto" and attach the exhibit if the list is extensive.)

2. The term of this lease shall be_____
                              (years/months)

commencing _____, 19_____ and terminating _____

_____, 19_____. Any holding over by Lessee with Lessor's consent beyond the term of this lease shall be a month to month tenancy at the rental and upon the applicable terms of this lease except as specified here:_____
_____

3. Lessee is to pay rent as follows: $_____
_____
_____

The rent shall be paid at _____
or at any address designated by the Lessor in writing.

4. Lessee also agrees to pay upon execution of this lease, in addition to rent, a security deposit of
$_____. Said deposit will be returned to Lessee by Lessor or his successors upon full performance of the terms of this lease.

5. Lessee agrees to pay for all utilities except_____

which shall be paid for by Lessor.

6. Lessee has examined the premises and all furniture and fixtures contained therein, and accepts the same as being clean and in good order, condition and repair, with the following exceptions:_____
_____

7. The premises are rented for use only as_____
_____

8. Lessee shall not disturb, annoy, endanger or inconvenience other tenants of the building or neighbors, nor use the premises for any immoral or unlawful purposes, nor violate any law or ordinance, nor commit waste or nuisance upon or about the premises.

9. Lessee shall keep the premises rented for his exclusive use in good order and condition and pay for any repairs caused by his negligence or misuse or that of his invitees. Lessor shall maintain any other parts of the property and pay for repairs not caused by Lessee's negligence or misuse or that of his invitees.

10. Lessee shall not paint nor make alterations of the premises without Lessor's prior written consent.

11. This lease will terminate if the premises become uninhabitable because of dilapidation, condemnation, fire or other casualty for more than 30 days. Rent will be reduced proportionately if the premises are uninhabitable for any shorter period.

12. With Lessee's permission, which shall not unreasonably be withheld, Lessor or his agent shall be permitted to enter to inspect, to make repairs, and to show the premises to prospective tenants or purchasers. In an emergency, Landlord or his agent may enter the premises without securing prior permission from Tenant, but shall give Tenant notice of such entry immediately thereafter.

13. Lessee shall not let or sublet all or any part of the premises nor assign this lease or any interest in it without the prior written consent of Lessor. Lessor's consent thereto shall not unreasonably be withheld.

14. If Lessee abandons or vacates the premises, Lessor may at his option terminate this lease, re-enter the the premises and remove all property.

15. The prevailing party may recover from the other party his costs and attorney fees of any action brought by either party to enforce any terms of this lease or recover possession of the premises.

16. Either party may terminate this lease in the event of a violation of any provision of this lease by the other party.

17. Time is of the essence. The waiver by Lessor of any breach shall not be construed to be a continuing waiver of any subsequent breach.

Lessor: _____   Lessee: _____

Lessor: _____   Lessee: _____

FIG. 14–3. California standard lease form.

CONSERVATION OF PROPERTY

The property manager is responsible for the maintenance of the property so that its economic life may be as long as possible. This means that a regular program for making repairs and replacements must be followed.

Modernization

At times modernization will be undertaken. For example, older office buildings have frequently been able to compete effectively with new buildings because their managers have devised modernization programs giving them many of the desirable features provided by newly produced structures. The complete interior modernization of an older building represents a huge outlay, but it may be carried out on a piecemeal basis over a period of time. Thus, special attention may at one time be given to a particular floor that seems to have "gone dead," at another time to the space which is being rented to new tenants, and at still another time to that occupied by important tenants whose leases are up for renewal. When such a program is carried out over a ten- or twelve-year period, no great outlay is necessary at any one time and the program can often be financed out of increased earnings resulting from the changes themselves. The operation of office buildings has been virtually revolutionized by automatic elevators, air conditioning, increased use of electrical equipment, and improved office layout and design.

Repairs

The careful planning of repair programs over a period of time, and the proper allowance for such work in the budgetary setup of the organization, are important functions of good property management. In apartment house management it is usually safe to allocate one month's rent per year to normal repairs and decorations. Another 5 per cent of the income is usually set aside for painting, roofing, renovation of heating equipment, and other types of repairs which do not arise every year but must be paid for over varying periods of time.

People Factors

Successful conservation of a property requires that attention be given not only to the physical condition of the structure, but also to the quality of the tenants and to the properties and people in the surrounding neighborhood. Property managers frequently have real opportunities for the upgrading of an area by the careful and systematic selection of tenants as well as by following adequate maintenance and modernization programs. Neither a property nor its environment can be thought of in connection with management programs without giving careful consideration to the people living or working in the property and in the area.

Thus property managers are involved with a process of *community organization* even though they seldom think of playing such a role. Physical facilities take on meaning only in relation to people and the various interrelations among the people who may be involved. Property managers can benefit from the work of sociologists and social psychologists as well as that of engineers and architects.

SUPERVISING BUILDING OPERATIONS

The day-to-day and month-to-month operation of a building involves a multitude of activities. The competent manager constantly checks receipts and outlays in order to maintain a proper relation among different income and expense items, such as upkeep, conservation, and improvement of the property. Such a ratio will vary with conditions in the market, the age of the property, and the special objectives of the management program.

Building operation includes the jobs of collecting rent, paying insurance premiums and taxes, and purchasing and using supplies, in addition to many related activities. Valuable information on this subject and related management problems will be found in the publications of the Institute of Real Estate Management of the National Association of Realtors®.

Collecting Rents

It is necessary to collect rents in order to obtain income in the case of a leased property. While the large majority of tenants will pay promptly if asked punctually and in a proper manner, at least 10 per cent of the potential collections are likely to cause problems. Many collection systems fail because threats are made and never carried out. The making of threats is a last resort of the manager and is used as a collection device by the careful manager only after all others have failed. Informal reports from property managers indicate that the best collection procedure is simply to demand what is due at the time it is due; follow-up notices after a five-day interval often are helpful and if not heeded another notice requesting a call at the management office may be effective. Managers for the most part appear to believe it is wrong to have the tenant feel that a collector will be sent if payment is not made; rather the tenant should feel an obligation to handle the payment.

It is common knowledge that many tenants of residential properties take offense at being asked to pay their debts, regardless of how adroitly they are handled. Insofar as possible, the wise manager will try to determine whether difficulties of this kind are likely to arise before the tenant is accepted. Credit reports and careful analysis of references are useful in this connection, and in some cities real estate boards or property managers' associations maintain files of information covering a large number of tenants.

Some delinquency always will develop, since a few people follow the policy of moving every few months, to the chagrin and loss of managers and owners. An average rental loss of 5 per cent is not uncommon. Of course, the management office can create a great deal of good will by granting extensions of time for payment when they are honestly deserved. In order to grant such favors, however, it is necessary to secure a considerable amount of knowledge regarding the tenants involved.

Collections are not such a difficult problem in the case of business properties or office buildings, since the tenants are more likely to pay their obligations in a prompt and businesslike manner. Even here the collection problem sometimes becomes burdensome and must be handled firmly and tactfully, unless it is apparent that the tenant is unable to pay. Then steps are taken to obtain possession of the property without delay.

Providing Insurance

The property manager may be responsible for placing insurance and paying for it regularly. Normally, fire insurance in an amount equal to approximately 80 per cent of the replacement cost of buildings is carried (80 per cent coinsurance). Sometimes in the case of large buildings this is supplemented by use and occupancy insurance—that is, insurance against the loss of rent resulting from destruction of a building.

Public liability insurance typically is carried for all buildings. Also, boiler and plate glass insurance may be necessary; if rent collectors are employed, good practice requires that they be bonded. Insurance against theft, tornadoes, and other hazards is also carried by many management organizations. Good management often can effect substantial savings in insurance by eliminating various risks or by the use of coinsurance, thus securing the benefits of reduced insurance premiums.

Taxes and Fees

The payment of taxes and special assessments, as well as of local license and inspection fees, requires careful and prompt attention by a property manager. Where the taxes on a building appear to be out of line with those on similar structures, the management can effect savings by calling this fact to the attention of the proper tax officials. Errors are sometimes made by tax officials who may estimate the value of a building by its external appearance rather than by its earning power. This is especially true of large office buildings or apartment houses. The preparation and submission of accurate statistical materials to the proper tax officers, presenting data on earning power, is often a helpful method of attacking this problem. Problems of this type often arise in connection with older buildings which have been assessed at high values during years when their earning power was great, but for which tax adjustments were not made as income-producing ability declined.

Tenant Relations

The basic opportunity available to every property management organization for building good will arises from its numerous relationships with the tenants. Such good will is an important asset—one that can be created only over a period of time. As one management official has said, unlike brokers, property managers do not sell prospects once; they must keep them sold. The effectiveness with which this selling process is carried out is a good measure of tenant–landlord relations.

Many managers follow the practice of writing or visiting every new tenant within 30 days after occupancy in a building. This makes it clear that tenant welfare is being considered. An opportunity is provided for bringing any complaints to the attention of the manager. This is done in the belief that hunting for trouble will lead to fewer demands on the part of tenants. However, many managers do not share this view. Much depends on the type of tenant involved. Some managers write to desirable tenants who have moved from a building, thanking them for their considerate treatment of the property and for their patronage. Such letters often lead to favorable indirect advertising.

In the management of a large building, it is necessary to follow the principle of seeking the greatest good for the greatest number. Frequently, there will be tenants who will not recognize the rights of other occupants of the building and who will not take proper care of the quarters they are renting. When this happens, it is best to request the removal of such tenants as soon as possible, for they can quickly destroy much of the good will the management has built up.

Handling Complaints

Complaints and requests from desirable tenants require a sympathetic hearing, even when they are unreasonable, as is often the case. Impatient treatment of minor complaints often results in the loss of a desirable tenant. The policy of establishing general rules to which exceptions cannot be made has provided many managers with a convenient device for refusing impossible or difficult requests. General rules also help to avoid the charge that the management is playing favorites. Especially in office or apartment buildings, any special concessions are soon discovered. Tenants resent any appearance of favoritism on the part of management and are likely to demand similar concessions themselves.

In the management of office buildings special devices for creating good will are frequently employed. Among these are the provision of safety vaults, special parking accommodations, libraries and conference rooms, and even the publication of a house organ. Many such devices are beyond the resources of the average building; but every manager, by the exercise of foresight and imagination, can find many ways of cultivating the good will of tenants.

Management Records and Accounts

In order to control operations effectively, a manager needs adequate records of all transactions and accurate accounts of all operations. Probably no single aspect of property management requires more attention. Without adequate and accurate accounting methods, it is impossible for the manager to render the proper reports to the owner. Without proper accounting the owner cannot determine the success of the policies being followed and precise knowledge of the points at which savings can be effected will be lacking.

The type of accounting system which a manager will use depends in large part on the magnitude of operations, the size of the building or buildings under supervision, and the characteristics of the manager. Bookkeeping machines and the use of addressograph plates for rent bills, employees' names, and social security numbers are often justified in larger offices. Possible shortcuts, as the elimination of various forms, must always be considered from the standpoint of savings secured and effects on standard accounting procedure.

Some managers follow a policy of requiring the preparation of data periodically on the basis of unit costs—for example, rental rates per square foot or per room, cost of heating per cubic foot, annual expenses per unit, per room, or per square or cubic foot, and similar reductions of various items of income and expense to unit bases. Such records are often useful in determining efficiency of operations, but their value depends in part on the records available and the uses to which they can be put. If sufficiently extensive data are involved and they can be put to a variety of uses, access to a computer may prove to be desirable.

Reorganized buildings often have special requirements in their trust indentures calling for the allocation of a certain portion of the net income to specific accounts, such as bond retirement. Certain items such as net income, extraordinary expenses, and others are frequently defined in such indentures in a manner that does not conform to customary management or accounting procedure. This creates special problems. Again, institutional owners, such as insurance companies and banks, often require the use of accounting forms designed for general uses which do not fit the needs of specific buildings.

PROFESSIONAL MANAGEMENT ORGANIZATION

The chief professional organization in the property management field is the Institute of Real Estate Management. It was established in 1933, first as an organization of management firms but later (1938) as a professional society of qualified individuals. Membership is limited to those who can meet stated experience, educational, and ethical standards, and can successfully pass designated examinations. Those selected for membership may make use of the designation CPM (Certified Property Manager).

The Institute has done much to further the development of the property management field. It publishes *The Journal of Property Management* and various other reports and studies. It provides for a ready exchange of experience among members. It stimulates educational programs and encourages the continuing personal and professional development of its members. In addition, it helps to present the entire field in a favorable light with respect to the investing and renting public, thus performing a highly valuable public relations function.

Another nationwide organization is Building Owners and Managers Association International (BOMAI). Membership in BOMAI is primarily made up of owners and managers of office buildings. This organization provides educational programs and the means for furthering the professional development and ethical standards of its members, and publishes various reports and studies, including BOMAI's Office Building Experience Exchange Report. The official publication of BOMAI is *Skyscraper Management.*

SUMMARY

Property management refers to the performance of the managerial function with regard to real estate resources by specialized individuals or firms rather than by the owners of properties. It is increasing in scope and importance because of the growing complexity of tax, legal, and managerial factors. Although property management refers to a specialized activity, its principles and methods may be applied successfully by those who manage their own properties.

The property manager, who may be part of a brokerage firm, has the legal status of general agent for principals who are the property owners, and therefore seeks to achieve the objectives of the owners, which usually means obtaining the best possible return from the relatively fixed resources of land and buildings.

The primary functions of property management include planning space, marketing property services, conserving the property and its surroundings, and supervising the operation of the property. These functions include such activities as establishing and adjusting rental schedules; selecting tenants and collecting rents; repair, maintenance, and building operation; arranging for insurance; tenant relations; and the keeping of accounts and records. The property manager should be cognizant of developments within the community or neighborhood which affect the income-producing ability of the principal's property.

QUESTIONS FOR STUDY

1. How do you explain the growth of property management in recent years?
2. In which ways may the following factors create problems for the property manager? (a) The durability of real property. (b) The economic inflexibility of real properties. (c) Inflexibility of operating expenses. (d) Fixity of location of real property. (e) Uniqueness of each piece of real property.
3. Assume that you are managing the Hilltop Apartments, owned by the widow of the late J. Randolph Hilltop. (a) Make a list of your specific duties as manager of this property. (b) What are your obligations to Mrs. Hilltop, as owner of the property? (c) How would you expect to be compensated? (d) What factors would you consider most important in establishing the rental schedule for the building?
4. Suppose that you take over the management of an office building and find that the rents being charged there are approximately 10 per cent above the rents of comparable properties. Vacancy rates, however, have been about the same. Would you conclude that this rental schedule was too high? Why or why not?
5. Give reasons why you believe that it is or is not desirable to establish general rules for all the tenants in a building.
6. What is meant by "hunting for trouble" in connection with tenant relations? Indicate reasons why this is or is not a sound management practice.
7. Differentiate among flat-rate, graded, percentage, and reappraisal leases.
8. The small office building that you are managing has a replacement cost of $500,000. How much insurance should be carried on this building? If more than one type of insurance is necessary, list the different types and reasons why each should be carried.
9. As manager of the property in question 8 you discover that the taxes are apparently higher than taxes on similar properties. What action would you take? Is it your responsibility as property manager to take any action at all?
10. List the factors you would consider in selecting tenants for an apartment building. In what ways can careful selection of tenants help lengthen the economic life of the building?

SUGGESTED READINGS

Downs, Anthony. *Federal Housing Substitutes: How Are They Working?* Lexington, Mass.: Lexington Books, 1973.

Downs, James C., Jr. *Principles of Real Estate Management* (11th ed.). Chicago, Ill.: Institute of Real Estate Management, 1975.

Glassman, Sidney. *Tools for Creative Property Management.* Chicago, Ill.: Institute of Real Estate Management, 1974.

Hanford, Lloyd D., Sr. *The Property Management Process.* Chicago, Ill.: Institute of Real Estate Management, 1972.

Kratovil, Robert. *Real Estate Law* (6th ed.). Englewood Cliffs, N. J.: Prentice-Hall, Inc., 1974. Ch. 29.

McMahan, John. *Property Development.* New York: McGraw-Hill Book Co., 1976. Ch. 16.

The Omnibus Realty Company has decided to expand operations to include property management. The various members of the firm have recommended alternative policies and have given a brief statement of the advantages of each of the alternative policies as revealed in the following minutes of a company meeting.

Mr. Omnibus: Gentlemen, today we will consider some alternative policies for the property management department which we are planning to add to our operation. First, we will consider the question of flexibility of rents.

Mr. Maxim: If we are to maximize the income for our property owners, it will be necessary to adjust rents frequently in accordance with changes in market conditions. Also, this means changing rents for occupied apartments, not just changing rents as space becomes available.

Mr. Axim: We should not be so concerned with maximizing scheduled gross income. If we raise rents frequently we may find large vacancy and collection losses and high expenses. That is, we may expect that tenancy turnover will be quite high and maintenance expenses would rise. I, therefore, believe the policy should be only to raise rents when space becomes available or under conditions where our rents fall substantially below the prevailing market rental levels. Not only will this maximize long-run net returns but I think it leads to better tenant relations. I don't anticipate any problems because of rent differentials due to different dates of beginning occupancy.

Mr. Novis: Wouldn't the requirements for long-term leases solve this problem for us?

Mr. Omnibus: Some interesting questions have been raised. We will consider these and come back to them later. Let's now turn to the question of selection of tenants.

Mr. Maxim: Since we are trying to maximize income I see no reason to ever let an apartment stay vacant as long as there is someone willing to pay the rent. Therefore, as long as a prospective tenant seems able to pay and is of apparently good character, I think that we owe it to the property owners to immediately rent the space and thereby minimize vacancy losses.

Mr. Axim: While it is true that we do not wish to have vacancy losses, I think that if we carefully select our tenants we will have a lower turnover and thus less vacancies. This should also minimize losses since we may then select a good caliber tenant, not to mention the possibilities of minimizing repair expenses and other maintenance charges. I don't think that we need to check back to see if the ancestors of prospective tenants came over on the Mayflower, but I would at least like to see a policy of requiring an application and a deposit giving us sufficient time to check credit references and background.

Mr. Novis: Checking out the tenants seems to be a good idea, but I think that most prospective tenants would be offended if we questioned their character. Therefore, why don't we just adopt a policy of accepting tenants if they make a nice appearance?

Mr. Omnibus: Well, this brings us to the question as to whether we should require leases which will spell out the terms of our agreement.

Mr. Maxim: Since I think we should have flexible rent and therefore short-term leases or no leases at all, the question comes down to how we should spell out the terms of the agreement. We may from time to time desire to change the rules by which we operate; therefore, I would rather not commit ourselves as to terms of tenancy. The alternative of setting up general rules posted in the building and in our office, letting all tenants know what we expect and what we will do, would be sufficient. In this way we have the flexibility of changing our rules and yet the tenants can know what is expected of them by merely looking at our rules from time to time.

Mr. Axim: When we lease a space for a period, whether it is short or long, I think the terms of the tenancy should be specifically spelled out and should be held for the period. Therefore, I believe that all the essential elements of the agreement should be contained in a lease and if changes are necessary they would be made at time of renewal. In this way, the tenants having signed the lease will certainly know what is expected of them and what they may expect of us.

Mr. Novis: There are certain conditions of the lease which we will want to have written in order to be enforceable. And therefore I think that we ought to adopt a policy of requiring written leases. As for operational rules, we may desire to vary these from property to property so why not just inform the tenant whenever an issue arises? In this way, we can always adjust to the situation.

Mr. Omnibus: This brings us to the general area of tenant relations. I would like you gentlemen to render opinions on collection of rents and policies for providing maintenance and repairs.

Mr. Maxim: I think the less contact we have with the tenants the less difficulties will arise. Therefore, I would be in favor of a policy of having the tenants mail their checks to the office. With regard to repairs, when the building needs repairs, the tenants will certainly let us know. So I would not be in favor of going out and looking for things to do.

Mr. Axim: Good tenant relations in the long run can mean more income for our property owners. I think we should have considerable personal contact with our tenants. Therefore, I recommend that a representative of the office call for the rent on the due date and at that time inquire as to any needs, complaints, or recommendations on the part of the tenants. Also, preventive maintenance is important for prolonging the economic life of the property and hence the earnings of the property so I recommend periodic inspection of the property to see that it is being kept up. Deferred maintenance in the long run can be costly. While such a policy may mean a lower net income for some period, in the long run we will benefit the property as well as the tenants.

Mr. Novis: With regard to rent, I don't think people like to be reminded, so I would be in favor of having them mail their checks. As for maintenance, if we go ahead with our plans to provide our own maintenance crews we might as well keep them busy by having them go to each of the properties and do whatever they see necessary rather than waiting for someone to complain.

Questions

1. Which of the suggested policies would you recommend? Explain your reasons for each of your policy recommendations.
2. Do you agree that all arguments presented for each of the alternative policies are valid? Explain.
3. Have you made any implicit assumptions as to the type of property the property management department would be handling? If so, what are these assumptions?
4. Evaluate for Omnibus the inspection and tenant relations policies described as follows: The firm of Applegate and Smith, Property Managers, follows the practice of making an annual inspection of each property under the firm's

management to determine its general condition. The tenants are not interviewed at the time of the inspection, as tenants are prone to ask for a large amount of repair and renovation work. Mr. Smith states: "Given the slightest opportunity, most tenants will ask for almost anything; yet if they have to call at the office or write a letter asking that certain things be done, fewer complaints come in. In fact, many tenants will do minor repair jobs themselves rather than make a complaint."

15

FINANCING: METHODS AND INSTRUMENTS*

CHARACTERISTICS OF REAL ESTATE FINANCE

In this chapter and the two that follow, we consider the subject of real estate finance. This chapter deals with the methods and instruments used in the financing of real estate resources and projects; Chapter 16 with the principal institutions and agencies operating in this field; and Chapter 17 with risk analysis.

As we have pointed out repeatedly, the terms and availability of financing play a major role in decisions affecting the development, marketing, ownership, and use of real estate. For example, most purchasers of real property, whether they are business firms or individuals, must borrow a part or all of the funds needed to pay for the desired property. Similarly, most builders, land developers, and subdividers must borrow a part or all of the funds needed to finance construction and land development.

Like most other commodities that have economic value, real estate resources may be pledged as security for loans. Although the principles of finance involved are similar to those explaining other types of financing decisions and programs, the major characteristics of real properties, particularly their long life, fixed locations, lack of liquidity, and relatively limited marketability, have brought about the development of numerous special practices and policies.

Major Characteristics

Of the various characteristics of real estate finance the following are of major importance:

* We appreciate the assistance of Kenneth J. Thygerson, Chief Economist of the U. S. League of Savings Associations, and Leon Kendall, President, Mortgage Guaranty Insurance Corporation, in reviewing this chapter.

1. The terms and availability of credit in the real estate field depend in part on conditions in the general capital markets. Real estate is in competition with other types of investment opportunities for the funds with which to finance the purchase, development, or use of real estate resources. During tight money periods real estate, especially housing, has not been an effective competitor for funds.

2. Although some short-term financing is used, especially in the case of construction projects, most of the financing in the real estate field is long-term in character. Real properties and even repairs on real properties last for long periods of time and investments in them are relatively fixed.

3. Loans typically are made against the security of real properties, and mortgages or similar instruments are used to pledge the borrower's interests. The processes required to mortgage real estate are complex and technical. They vary greatly from place to place.

4. Because of the long-term nature of real estate financing, special risks are involved. These arise from changes and anticipated changes in business conditions, government programs, inflationary or deflationary forces, local economic conditions, location factors, the property itself, consumer preferences, market changes including interest rates and property values, legal factors, and administrative arrangements.

5. Real estate resources and projects may be financed by means of equity (owner's) or borrowed funds. Or leases may provide for the use of property without the necessity of financing ownership.

Equity Funds

Whenever fee ownership is to be acquired, the prospective buyer faces several alternatives. If the entire purchase price can be paid out of savings or other funds, no financing problem is involved. Conversely, when the seller is willing to sell "on contract" without down payment, no equity funds need be raised. In most cases the buyer will have available some portion of the purchase price and will borrow funds for the remainder. Sometimes the necessary down payment cannot be made from available resources and the problem of assembling sufficient equity funds must be faced.

Thus the buyer of a house may borrow against life insurance or personal assets, or use personal credit to raise funds from relatives or other sources to assemble the necessary equity funds. A business firm may borrow by pledging other real properties or other assets. It may issue securities to raise funds for this purchase and for other purposes. Or other available funds may be used.

The equity for real estate developments such as apartment houses, office buildings, and shopping centers is often secured by organizing a corporation and selling stock. In some cases, the services of architects, engineers, and builders are paid for in whole or in part by means of stock. Sometimes the owner of the land will take all or part payment in the form of stock. Although the developer's equity position is diluted by stock payments to others, less cash has to be raised when this method is used.

Partnerships, syndicates, and trusts may also be formed to provide for the assembly of equity funds for real estate developments. Estates, foundations, unions, and limited dividend corporations have also engaged in the equity financing of a number of housing projects.

In more recent years various financial institutions were given authority to make equity investments in residential income-producing housing. Such investments may represent "a piece of the action" or be owned outright, with or without mortgage financing. In addition, life insurance companies are authorized in all but a few states to make equity investments in nonresidential income properties. Under certain conditions various savings and loan associations and mutual savings banks may acquire land for development. Service corporations of savings and loan associations are gaining importance as equity investors. Some Real Estate Investment Trusts invest in equities.

Investment Decisions

The factors which play a major role in investment decisions will vary depending on whether equity or debt investments or combinations of them are under consideration. There will be differences also between individual and institutional investors. Decision factors of these types are considered at greater length in Chapter 17.

Instruments: Mortgages, Trust Deeds, Others

The borrowing of funds for the purpose of financing fee ownership of real estate is accomplished largely by the use of the mortgage, the trust deed in the nature of a mortgage, bonds, and land contracts. Other arrangements are also possible but are of less importance. Construction financing may be accomplished by a short-term loan or under various types of mortgage arrangements. Property improvements may be financed by the use of open-end mortgages or by the use of personal credit. The purchase of equipment is sometimes financed by means of a "package mortgage," as well as by the use of personal loans or installment credits. Of major importance, however, is the mortgage, and we shall give special attention to the processes of mortgage financing.

THE MORTGAGE [1]

A mortgage creates the existence of a debt and requires a pledge of property to secure it. Technically the mortgage note admits the debt and

---

[1] For a more complete discussion, see Harold F. Lusk and W. B. French, *Law of the Real Estate Business* (3rd ed.; Homewood, Ill.: Richard D. Irwin, Inc., 1975), ch. 25. See also Robert Kratovil, *Real Estate Law* (6th ed.; Englewood Cliffs, N. J.: Prentice-Hall, Inc., 1974), ch. 20.

contains an agreement to repay it in accordance with specified conditions. The mortgage pledges the property as security for the obligation. The note makes the borrower personally liable for the obligation, and the property cannot simply be abandoned to avoid payment of the debt. It is possible, however, to create a mortgage without the mortgage note; in that case the borrower has no personal liability. Or the instrument may have an exculpatory clause relieving the borrower of personal liability.

Definitions of a Mortgage

At common law a mortgage amounted to a conveyance of an estate to the mortgagee, which conveyance became void upon the performance of the terms of the mortgage. Today it is considered more in the nature of a lien upon the estate to secure the performance, normally a money payment, specified in the instrument. The term *mortgage* is commonly used to denote the instrument by which such interest in property is transferred. Any instrument or legal form which conveys an interest in property for the purpose of giving security is in effect a mortgage, regardless of its form.

Several of the terms used in the above definition require further clarification. We have already pointed out that a *deed* is an instrument that conveys title to real property. A *conveyance* is a transfer of the interest in property from one person to another. In mortgage transactions the debtor or borrower is called the *mortgagor*. The creditor or lender is called the *mortgagee*. The period for which the mortgage is made is called the *term*.

In order that a conveyance of the type required in a mortgage transaction be valid, it must be in writing, must be executed by the mortgagor with all the formality prescribed by the statutes of the particular state in which the property lies, and must be delivered to the mortgagee. The laws of the state in which the property is located govern the mortgage transaction. (See Fig. 15-1.)

Lien vs. Title Theory

In the earlier stages of the development of the law of mortgages, the actual possession of property, as well as the title to it, passed to the mortgagee or lender during the period of the loan. If the debt was not paid in full and in accordance with all of the requirements on the day it became due, all of the rights of the mortgagor or borrower were forfeited. As mortgage transactions developed, experience indicated that the possession of the property was not necessary in order to secure the lender against loss. Consequently, the law was changed to permit the mortgagor to retain possession as long as the mortgage was not in default.

At the present time some states provide that the title, as well as the possession of the property, is kept by the mortgagor, the mortgage being regarded merely as a lien and not as an actual conveyance of title. These

CONSULT YOUR LAWYER BEFORE SIGNING THIS INSTRUMENT—THIS INSTRUMENT SHOULD BE USED BY LAWYERS ONLY.

THIS MORTGAGE, made the   day of   , nineteen hundred and

BETWEEN

, the mortgagor,

and

, the mortgagee,

WITNESSETH, that to secure the payment of an indebtedness in the sum of

dollars,

lawful money of the United States, to be paid

with interest thereon to be computed from the date hereof, at the rate of   per centum
per annum, and to be paid on the   day of   19   , next ensuing and
      thereafter,

according to a certain bond,
note or obligation bearing even date herewith, the mortgagor hereby mortgages to the mortgagee

ALL that certain plot, piece or parcel of land, with the buildings and improvements thereon erected, situate,
lying and being in the

FIG. 15–1. Mortgage form. (Courtesy The Title Guarantee Company,
New York.)

TOGETHER with all right, title and interest of the mortgagor in and to the land lying in the streets and roads in front of and adjoining said premises;

TOGETHER with all fixtures, chattels and articles of personal property now or hereafter attached to or used in connection with said premises, including but not limited to furnaces, boilers, oil burners, radiators and piping, coal stokers, plumbing and bathroom fixtures, refrigeration, air conditioning and sprinkler systems, wash-tubs, sinks, gas and electric fixtures, stoves, ranges, awnings, screens, window shades, elevators, motors, dynamos, refrigerators, kitchen cabinets, incinerators, plants and shrubbery and all other equipment and machinery, appliances, fittings, and fixtures of every kind in or used in the operation of the buildings standing on said premises, together with any and all replacements thereof and additions thereto;

TOGETHER with all awards heretofore and hereafter made to the mortgagor for taking by eminent domain the whole or any part of said premises or any easement therein, including any awards for changes of grade of streets, which said awards are hereby assigned to the mortgagee, who is hereby authorized to collect and receive the proceeds of such awards and to give proper receipts and acquittances therefor, and to apply the same toward the payment of the mortgage debt, notwithstanding the fact that the amount owing thereon may not then be due and payable; and the said mortgagor hereby agrees, upon request, to make, execute and deliver any and all assignments and other instruments sufficient for the purpose of assigning said awards to the mortgagee, free, clear and discharged of any encumbrances of any kind or nature whatsoever.

AND the mortgagor covenants with the mortgagee as follows:

1. That the mortgagor will pay the indebtedness as hereinbefore provided.

2. That the mortgagor will keep the buildings on the premises insured against loss by fire for the benefit of the mortgagee; that he will assign and deliver the policies to the mortgagee; and that he will reimburse the mortgagee for any premiums paid for insurance made by the mortgagee on the mortgagor's default in so insuring the buildings or in so assigning and delivering the policies.

3. That no building on the premises shall be altered, removed or demolished without the consent of the mortgagee.

4. That the whole of said principal sum and interest shall become due at the option of the mortgagee: after default in the payment of any instalment of principal or of interest for fifteen days; or after default in the payment of any tax, water rate, sewer rent or assessment for thirty days after notice and demand; or after default after notice and demand either in assigning and delivering the policies insuring the buildings against loss by fire or in reimbursing the mortgagee for premiums paid on such insurance, as hereinbefore provided; or after default upon request in furnishing a statement of the amount due on the mortgage and whether any off-sets or defenses exist against the mortgage debt, as hereinafter provided. An assessment which has been made payable in instalments at the application of the mortgagor or lessee of the premises shall nevertheless, for the purpose of this paragraph, be deemed due and payable in its entirety on the day the first instalment becomes due or payable or a lien.

5. That the holder of this mortgage, in any action to foreclose it, shall be entitled to the appointment of a receiver.

6. That the mortgagor will pay all taxes, assessments, sewer rents or water rates, and in default thereof, the mortgagee may pay the same.

7. That the mortgagor within five days upon request in person or within ten days upon request by mail will furnish a written statement duly acknowledged of the amount due on this mortgage and whether any off-sets or defenses exist against the mortgage debt.

8. That notice and demand or request may be in writing and may be served in person or by mail.

9. That the mortgagor warrants the title to the premises.

10. That the fire insurance policies required by paragraph No. 2 above shall contain the usual extended coverage endorsement; that in addition thereto the mortgagor, within thirty days after notice and demand, will keep the premises insured against war risk and any other hazard that may reasonably be required by the mortgagee. All of the provisions of paragraphs No. 2 and No. 4 above relating to fire insurance and the provisions of Section 254 of the Real Property Law construing the same shall apply to the additional insurance required by this paragraph.

11. That in case of a foreclosure sale, said premises, or so much thereof as may be affected by this mortgage, may be sold in one parcel.

12. That if any action or proceeding be commenced (except an action to foreclose this mortgage or to collect the debt secured thereby), to which action or proceeding the mortgagee is made a party, or in which it becomes necessary to defend or uphold the lien of this mortgage, all sums paid by the mortgagee for the expense of any litigation to prosecute or defend the rights and lien created by this mortgage (including reasonable counsel fees), shall be paid by the mortgagor, together with interest thereon at the rate of six per cent. per annum, and any such sum and the interest thereon shall be a lien on said premises, prior to any right, or title to, interest in or claim upon said premises attaching or accruing subsequent to the lien of this mortgage, and shall be deemed to be secured by this mortgage. In any action or proceeding to foreclose this mortgage, or to recover or collect the debt secured thereby, the provisions of law respecting the recovering of costs, disbursements and allowances shall prevail unaffected by this covenant.

FIG. 15–1. Continued.

13. That the mortgagor hereby assigns to the mortgagee the rents, issues and profits of the premises as further security for the payment of said indebtedness, and the mortgagor grants to the mortgagee the right to enter upon and to take possession of the premises for the purpose of collecting the same and to let the premises or any part thereof, and to apply the rents, issues and profits, after payment of all necessary charges and expenses, on account of said indebtedness. This assignment and grant shall continue in effect until this mortgage is paid. The mortgagee hereby waives the right to enter upon and to take possession of said premises for the purpose of collecting said rents, issues and profits, and the mortgagor shall be entitled to collect and receive said rents, issues and profits until default under any of the covenants, conditions or agreements contained in this mortgage, and agrees to use such rents, issues and profits in payment of principal and interest becoming due on this mortgage and in payment of taxes, assessments, sewer rents, water rates and carrying charges becoming due against said premises, but such right of the mortgagor may be revoked by the mortgagee upon any default, on five days' written notice. The mortgagor will not, without the written consent of the mortgagee, receive or collect rent from any tenant of said premises or any part thereof for a period of more than one month in advance, and in the event of any default under this mortgage will pay monthly in advance to the mortgagee, or to any receiver appointed to collect said rents, issues and profits, the fair and reasonable rental value for the use and occupation of said premises or of such part thereof as may be in the possession of the mortgagor, and upon default in any such payment will vacate and surrender the possession of said premises to the mortgagee or to such receiver, and in default thereof may be evicted by summary proceedings.

14. That the whole of said principal sum and the interest shall become due at the option of the mortgagee: (a) after failure to exhibit to the mortgagee, within ten days after demand, receipts showing payment of all taxes, water rates, sewer rents and assessments; or (b) after the actual or threatened alteration, demolition or removal of any building on the premises without the written consent of the mortgagee; or (c) after the assignment of the rents of the premises or any part thereof without the written consent of the mortgagee; or (d) if the buildings on said premises are not maintained in reasonably good repair; or (e) after failure to comply with any requirement or order or notice of violation of law or ordinance issued by any governmental department claiming jurisdiction over the premises within three months from the issuance thereof; or (f) if on application of the mortgagee two or more fire insurance companies lawfully doing business in the State of New York refuse to issue policies insuring the buildings on the premises; or (g) in the event of the removal, demolition or destruction in whole or in part of any of the fixtures, chattels or articles of personal property covered hereby, unless the same are promptly replaced by similar fixtures, chattels and articles of personal property at least equal in quality and condition to those replaced, free from chattel mortgages or other encumbrances thereon and free from any reservation of title thereto; or (h) after thirty days' notice to the mortgagor, in the event of the passage of any law deducting from the value of land for the purposes of taxation any lien thereon, or changing in any way the taxation of mortgages or debts secured thereby for state or local purposes; or (i) if the mortgagor fails to keep, observe and perform any of the other covenants, conditions or agreements contained in this mortgage.

15. That the mortgagor will, in compliance with Section 13 of the Lien Law, receive the advances secured hereby and will hold the right to receive such advances as a trust fund to be applied first for the purpose of paying the cost of the improvement and will apply the same first to the payment of the cost of the improvement before using any part of the total of the same for any other purpose.

ike out this 16. se 16 if plicable. That the execution of this mortgage has been duly authorized by the board of directors of the mortgagor.

This mortgage may not be changed or terminated orally. The covenants contained in this mortgage shall run with the land and bind the mortgagor, the heirs, personal representatives, successors and assigns of the mortgagor and all subsequent owners, encumbrancers, tenants and subtenants of the premises, and shall enure to the benefit of the mortgagee, the personal representatives, successors and assigns of the mortgagee and all subsequent holders of this mortgage. The word "mortgagor" shall be construed as if it read "mortgagors" and the word "mortgagee" shall be construed as if it read "mortgagees" whenever the sense of this mortgage so requires.

IN WITNESS WHEREOF, this mortgage has been duly executed by the mortgagor.

IN PRESENCE OF:

FIG. 15–1. Continued.

STATE OF NEW YORK, COUNTY OF   ss:

On the   day of   19   , before me personally came

to me known to be the individual   described in and who executed the foregoing instrument, and acknowledged that executed the same.

STATE OF NEW YORK, COUNTY OF   ss:

On the   day of   19   , before me personally came

to me known to be the individual   described in and who executed the foregoing instrument, and acknowledged that executed the same.

STATE OF NEW YORK, COUNTY OF   ss:

On the   day of   19   , before me personally came
to me known, who, being by me duly sworn, did depose and say that   he resides at No.
                         ;

that   he is the
of
                 , the corporation described
in and which executed the foregoing instrument; that   he knows the seal of said corporation; that the seal affixed to said instrument is such corporate seal; that it was so affixed by order of the board of directors of said corporation, and that   he signed h   name thereto by like order.

STATE OF NEW YORK, COUNTY OF   ss:

On the   day of   19   , before me personally came
the subscribing witness to the foregoing instrument, with whom I am personally acquainted, who, being by me duly sworn, did depose and say that   he resides at No.
                         ;

that   he knows

                       to be the individual
described in and who executed the foregoing instrument; that   he, said subscribing witness, was present and saw   execute the same; and that   he, said witness, at the same time subscribed h   name as witness thereto.

𝔐ortgage

TITLE NO.

TO

SECTION

BLOCK

LOT

COUNTY OR TOWN

STANDARD FORM OF NEW YORK BOARD OF TITLE UNDERWRITERS

Distributed by

TITLE GUARANTEE-NEW YORK

A TICOR COMPANY

Recorded At Request of The Title Guarantee Company

RETURN BY MAIL TO:

Zip No.

FIG. 15–1.   Continued.

are called lien theory states, as contrasted with title theory states, in which the law more nearly resembles the earlier concept.

The arbitrary forfeiting of all rights in the property by the borrower in case of default on the debt worked considerable hardship on the mortgagor, particularly in those cases where the value of the property was considerably greater than the debt. This aspect of the earlier law of mortgages was also changed. At the present time, all states require that some legal steps be taken by the mortgagee after default of the debt before the property can be proceeded against for debt payment. Such legal steps are called *foreclosure*, and this may take a number of forms. There are still wide variations among the states. Usually this process provides for the public sale of the property under the foreclosure laws, with the mortgagee securing repayment from the proceeds of the sale and the mortgagor being allowed to keep any surplus which remains. If a sufficient amount is not realized, the lender may secure a deficiency judgment against the borrower. (This is not the case in all states, however.)

TYPES OF MORTGAGES

Mortgages may be classified by degree of priority, by method of repayment, financing requirements, and whether insured or not. There are blanket, package, and open-end mortgages as well as purchase money mortgages.

Degree of Priority

Any mortgage which is subordinate to a mortgage or mortgages on the same property is a junior mortgage. The degree of priority is usually indicated by referring to the instrument as a first, second, third, or—in rare cases—fourth mortgage; but the public records must always be consulted to determine which claims against the property have precedence. Also, a junior mortgage may become a senior lien if prior claims are paid. Obviously, junior mortgages typically contain more risk than senior mortgages, and consequently they usually yield a higher rate of return and are not written for long periods.

There are cases where a deed in the form of an absolute conveyance is used to transfer the title to the property. It may contain no reference to any debt or condition, indicating that it is really given as security for a debt. Such a legal instrument may be a mortgage in legal effect if it is actually given for the purpose of securing a debt and if this fact can be proved in the courts.

Method of Repayment

Various methods of repayment may be provided in a mortgage agreement. If no payments on the principal are made during the term of the mortgage, it is called a *straight term* mortgage. If repayment is made in accordance with a definite plan which requires the repayment of certain amounts at definite times so that all of the debt is retired by the end of the term, the mortgage is *amortized*. This is currently the most widely used type. If parts of the debt are repaid during the term of the mortgage and part remains to be paid when the debt falls due, it is called a *partially amortized* mortgage. Various combinations of straight term and amortized mortgages may be used; for example, a straight term mortgage may allow amortization in part or in entirety according to the terms of the instrument; or an amortized mortgage may be converted into a straight term agreement under certain conditions. In some cases mortgages "balloon out" with a big final payment at the end of the term. Frequently the balloon mortgages are used with renewal options that provide refinancing of the final payment with conventional mortgages at current rates of interest. This arrangement helps the lender to adjust to interest rate risk.

Insured, Guaranteed, and Conventional Mortgages

Mortgages that are insured by the Federal Housing Administration or guaranteed by the Veterans' Administration are usually referred to as insured or guaranteed in contrast to others which are referred to as conventional mortgages. Private systems of mortgage insurance and guaranty have grown in importance. The Mortgage Guaranty Insurance Corporation (MGIC) and Commercial Loan Insurance Corporation (CLIC) are cases in point. FHA, VA, and private mortgage insurance plans will be discussed in greater detail in the next chapter.

Mortgage insurance and guarantees have stimulated the use of high loan to value ratio and long-term mortgages and this has broadened the home ownership market. Both down payments and monthly payments are reduced through such arrangements. Apartment house financing has also been aided by mortgage insurance. Cooperative and condominium ownerships along with subsidized rent and interest plans have also been important factors in the market.

Variable and Fixed Interest Rate Mortgages

Inflationary tendencies have created special types of risks for mortgage lenders. One method of adjusting to such risks is the use of variable rate mortgages; arrangements are made for the mortgage interest rate to advance or decline with some index of changes in the cost of money such as the prime rate. Adjustments usually are made at stated intervals. Similar problems have stimulated the increased use of prepayment penalties when mortgages carry fixed interest rates. Also, shorter maturities have been introduced by some lenders who use fixed rates to allow for frequent re-adjustments of such rates. For example, in Canada many mortgages are renegotiated at three- or five-year intervals.

Flexible Payment Mortgages

Various plans have been developed to allow for flexibility in home mortgage payments. For example, payments may be related to income or there may be a gradual increase in payments over time. A reverse annuity type mortgage allows the borrower to draw back some of the equity after paying the mortgage off or paying it down to a nominal level. Provisions can also be made for paying interest only for the first five years or a similar period, to accommodate the needs of younger families.[2]

Special Financing Requirements

Special types of mortgages have developed in response to particular types of financing requirements. For example, the blanket mortgage assists in the financing of new developments, the package mortgage allows for the financing of equipment and fixtures under the mortgage, and the open-end mortgage provides for future advances to the borrower using the same instrument. Purchase money mortgages are often used in financing a new project, and wrap-around mortgages are sometimes used in refinancing properties. Each of these will be discussed briefly here.

Blanket Mortgage.   This type of mortgage "blankets" several or a number of pieces of property. It is often used in the financing of new developments. As sales are made, releases are granted to remove from the blanket mortgage the properties that are sold. For example, an individual buyer of a lot in a new subdivision development typically will make a large enough down payment to provide for the release of the lot from the blanket mortgage. In many cases the seller of the land may take back a purchase money mortgage and arrange for releases under it. Corporate mortgages may make use of blanket arrangements. Mortgages which include "after-acquired" property clauses may be thought of as in effect blanket mortgages.

The Package Mortgage.   Because of the increasing amount of equipment used in homes and the special problems arising from financing the purchase of such equipment, a number of financial institutions make use of the so-called package mortgage. Practices vary between states, but usually provision is made for financing the equipment under the mortgage which is set up to finance home purchase. The various items of equipment

---

[2] See, for example, Franco Modigliani and Donald R. Lessard (eds.), *New Mortgage Designs for Stable Housing in an Inflationary Environment* (Federal Reserve Bank of Boston, 1975), esp. pp. 47–69.

included must be designated exactly and made a part of the mortgage agreement. Usually, only equipment which has a relatively long, useful life is included in such arrangements. The Federal Housing Administration insures mortgages of this type and has developed an extensive list of equipment which is considered to be eligible for inclusion in mortgage agreements. Such items of equipment as the following are included: plumbing accessories, air-conditioning systems, awnings, blinds, cabinets and bookcases (not built in), dishwashers, fireplace accessories, floor coverings, garbage disposal units, laundering equipment, radiator covers, ranges, refrigerators, screens, storm doors, and the like.

The package mortgage, by financing equipment, makes homes easier to sell and the homeowner has one monthly payment to cover the house and the appliances. Usually, also, the package mortgage reduces costs to the homeowner.

The Open-End Mortgage. If an ordinary mortgage is set up with provisions for securing future advances to the borrower, an open-end mortgage is created. In recent years such arrangements have been made by various mortgage lenders in order to allow the borrower to secure funds for the maintenance and improvement of the mortgaged property. Some legal difficulties may arise in case other liens or judgments are placed against the property before additional funds are requested under the open-end provision. However, many mortgage lenders have adopted this type of mortgage in order to discourage the borrower from using short-term loans to finance necessary improvements to the property. Such loans may impair the borrower's ability to carry regular mortgage obligations. At the same time the improvements may be desirable to maintain the property in good condition. The use of the open-end mortgage appears to be gaining in popularity, since the borrower can obtain financing for improvements or other purposes on the basis of the terms and interest rates set up in the original mortgage.

Purchase Money Mortgage. This type of mortgage is a conventional mortgage through which the owner becomes the mortgagee rather than a financial institution or some other source of funds. The purchase money mortgage is given to the seller of a property as part payment of the purchase price and is used to consummate the sale, typically when other sources of funds are not available.

Wrap-around Mortgage. The "wrap-around" mortgage in effect surrounds an existing first mortgage. It is actually a second mortgage. The borrower usually advances an amount approximately equal to the difference between balance outstanding on the original mortgage loan and the amount agreed upon for the wrap-around arrangement. In most cases the borrower makes payments to the wrap-around mortgage lender who pays the holder of the original mortgage. It enables the borrower to expand the loan without disturbing the original arrangement.

WHEN RECORDED, PLEASE MAIL TO:

DEED OF TRUST

This Deed of Trust, made this _____ day of _____ 19_____, between

whose address is _____
(Street and Number)   (City)   (State)   (Zip)

herein called TRUSTOR,

herein called TRUSTEE, and

a California corporation, herein called BENEFICIARY.

WITNESSETH: That Trustor irrevocably GRANTS, TRANSFERS and ASSIGNS to TRUSTEE, IN TRUST, WITH POWER OF SALE, the property in the County of _____, State of California, described as:

Together with the improvements now or hereafter placed thereon and the easements, hereditaments and appurtenances thereunto belonging, including water rights benefiting said property whether represented by shares of a company or otherwise, and the rents, issues and profits therefrom, SUBJECT, HOWEVER, to the right, power and authority hereinafter given to and conferred upon Beneficiary to collect and apply such rents, issues and profits;

For the purpose of Securing: 1. Payment of the sum of $ _____ with interest thereon according to the terms of a promissory note or notes of even date herewith, made by Trustor, payable to the order of the Beneficiary and extensions or renewals thereof. 2. Payment of such additional sums, with interest thereon, as may be borrowed hereafter from the Beneficiary by the then record owner or owners of said property and evidenced by another promissory note or notes. 3. Payment, with interest thereon, of any other indebtedness or obligation of the Trustor (or of any successor in interest of the Trustor to said property) to the Beneficiary, whether created directly or acquired by assignment, whether absolute or contingent, whether matured or unmatured, whether otherwise secured or not, and whether existing at the time of the execution of this deed of trust or arising thereafter. 4. Performance of each agreement of Trustor herein contained.

FIG. 15–2a.   Deed of trust, State of California.

In consideration of the loan(s) extended to the Trustor and/or to protect the security of this Deed of Trust, Trustor agrees:

(1) To keep said property in good condition and repair; not to remove, demolish or substantially alter (except as such alteration may be required by laws, ordinances or regulations) any building or structure thereon; to complete or restore promptly and in good and workmanlike manner any building or structure which may be constructed, damaged or destroyed thereon, and to pay when due all claims for labor performed and materials furnished therefor; to comply with all laws affecting said property or requiring any alterations or improvements to be made thereon; not to commit or permit waste thereof; not to commit, suffer or permit any act upon said property in violation of law; to cultivate, irrigate, fertilize, fumigate, prune and do all other acts which from the character or use of said property may be reasonably necessary, the specific enumerations herein not excluding the general.

(2) To provide, maintain, and deliver to Beneficiary, fire, and if required by Beneficiary, other insurance satisfactory to and with loss payable to Beneficiary. If said insurance policies have not been delivered to the Beneficiary thirty days before the expiration of any of the said insurance, with evidence of the premium having been paid, the Beneficiary shall have the right, but is not obligated, to obtain said insurance on behalf of the Trustor and pay the premium thereon. Neither Trustee nor Beneficiary shall be responsible for such insurance or for the collection of any insurance monies, or for any insolvency of any insurer or insurance underwriter. The amount collected under any policy of insurance may, at the option of the Beneficiary, be applied by Beneficiary upon any obligation secured hereby and in such order as Beneficiary may determine, or said amount or any portion thereof may, at the option of the Beneficiary, either be used in replacing or restoring the improvements partially or totally destroyed to a condition satisfactory to said Beneficiary, or be released to the Trustor, in either of which events neither the Trustee nor the Beneficiary shall be obligated to see to the proper application thereof; nor shall the amount so released or used be deemed a payment on any obligation secured hereby. Such application, use, and/or release shall not cure or waive any default or notice of default hereunder or invalidate any act done pursuant to such notice. Any unexpired insurance and all returnable insurance premiums shall inure to the benefit of, and pass to, the purchaser of the property covered thereby at any trustee's sale held hereunder or at any foreclosure sale of said property.

(3) To appear in and defend any action or proceeding purporting to affect the security hereof or the rights or powers of Beneficiary or Trustee; and to pay all costs and expenses, including cost of evidence of title and attorney's fees in a reasonable sum, in any such action or proceeding in which Beneficiary or Trustee may appear, or in any action or proceeding instituted by Beneficiary or Trustee to protect or enforce the security of this Deed of Trust or the obligations secured hereby.

(4) To pay (a) at least ten days before delinquency, all taxes and assessments affecting the property, and not permit any improvement bond to issue for any special assessments for public improvements, all assessments upon water company stock, and all rents, assessments and charges for water appurtenant to or used in connection with the property; (b) when due, all encumbrances charges and liens on the property or any part thereof, which appear to be prior or superior hereto, with interest; and (c) all costs, fees and expenses of this trust.

(5) That should Trustor fail to make any payment or to do any act as herein provided, then Beneficiary or Trustee. but without obligation so to do and without notice to or demand upon Trustor and without releasing Trustor from any obligation hereof, may: (a) make or do the same in such manner and to such extent as either may deem necessary to protect the security hereof, Beneficiary or Trustee being authorized to enter upon said property for such purpose; (b) appear in, commence or defend any action or proceeding purporting to affect the security hereof or the rights or powers of Beneficiary or Trustee; (c) pay, purchase, contest or compromise any encumbrance, charge or lien which in the judgment of either appears to be prior or superior hereto; and (d) in exercising any such powers, or in enforcing this Deed of Trust by judicial foreclosure, pay necessary expenses, employ counsel and pay his reasonable fees.

(6) That if an impound account is provided for by agreement between the Trustor and the Beneficiary, and/or if such an account is permitted under California statutes, the undersigned Trustor agrees to pay to Beneficiary such sums as are required to maintain a reserve for payment of charges for taxes, assessments and fire and extended coverage insurance premiums with respect to the property as reasonably estimated by Beneficiary. Such payments shall be made, at Beneficiary's demand, no more often than monthly and shall be in amounts sufficient to maintain the reserve at all times at an amount equal to the sum of the accounts determined by:

a. dividing the estimated amount of each such charge next due by the number of months which elapse between successive dates for the

b. multiplying the result of (a) by the number of months elapsed since one month prior to the last due date for such charge. ("Due date" shall mean the delinquency date with respect to each installment of taxes and assessments and the policy expiration date with respect to insurance: each installment of property taxes and items collected therewith shall be treated as a separate charge for purposes of determining consecutive due dates.)

In consideration of its administration of such reserve, Beneficiary may invest and use all funds in such reserve and will not be obligated to pay any interest to the Trustor except as otherwise required by law. The trustor agrees that the Beneficiary may treat such funds as general assets of the Beneficiary and it need not segregate or separately deposit such reserve, unless otherwise required by law. Beneficiary agrees only to apply funds in such reserve towards payment of such charges when payable, any excess of any such charges over amount paid to reserve by Trustor to be paid to Beneficiary by Trustor on demand in advance of the due date for such charge, or if Beneficiary shall elect to advance all or any part of such excess then Trustor shall reimburse Beneficiary for the same on demand. In the event a notice of default is recorded under the terms of this Deed of Trust securing the obligation of this loan, Beneficiary may, at its option and without prior notice, apply any balance in any such reserve to reduction of the obligations secured hereby in such manner as it shall determine and such application shall not be deemed to waive or cure the default. Failure to make any payment to reserve or to reimburse Beneficiary for any advance made by it, as provided in this paragraph, shall constitute a default under this Deed of Trust.

(7) To pay immediately and without demand all sums expended by Beneficiary or Trustee pursuant to the provisions hereof, with interest from date of expenditure at the rate specified in the obligation secured hereby.

(8) That if the loan secured hereby or any part thereof is being obtained for the purpose of construction of improvements on said property, Trustor also agrees, anything in this Deed to the contrary notwithstanding: (a) to complete same in accordance with plans and specifications satisfactory to Beneficiary; (b) to allow Beneficiary to inspect said property at all times during construction; (c) to replace any work or materials unsatisfactory to Beneficiary, within fifteen (15) calendar days after written notice from Beneficiary of such fact, which notice may be given to the Trustor by registered mail, sent to his last known address, or by personal service of the same; (d) that work shall not cease on the construction of such improvements for any reason whatsoever for a period of fifteen (15) calendar days. The Trustee, upon presentation to it of an affidavit signed by Beneficiary, setting forth facts showing a default by Trustor under this paragraph, is authorized to accept as true and conclusive all facts and statements therein, and to act thereon hereunder.

(9) That any award of damage made in connection with the condemnation for public use of or injury to the property or any part thereof is hereby assigned and shall be paid to Beneficiary, who may apply or release such monies received therefor in the same manner and with the same effects as above provided for the disposition of proceeds of fire or other insurance, and Trustor will execute such further assignment of any such award as Beneficiary or Trustee requires.

(10) That the acceptance by Beneficiary of any payment less than the amount then due shall be deemed an acceptance on account only and shall not constitute a waiver of the obligation of Trustor to pay the entire sum then due or of Beneficiary's right either to require prompt payment of all sums then due or to declare default. The acceptance of any sum secured hereby after its due date shall not constitute a waiver of the right of Beneficiary either to require prompt payment when due of all other sums so secured or to declare default for failure so to pay, and no waiver of any default shall be a waiver of any preceding or succeeding default of any kind, nor shall the consent to any transaction or occurrence be a consent to, or a waiver of the right to require a consent to, any other transaction or occurrence whether or not similar in nature.

(11) That at any time, or from time to time, without liability therefore and without notice, upon written request of Beneficiary and presentation of this Deed of Trust and the note or notes secured hereby for endorsement, and without affecting the personal liability of any person for payment of the obligation secured hereby or the effect of this Deed of Trust upon the remainder of said property in securing the full amount of the indebtedness then or thereafter secured hereby Trustee may: Reconvey any part of said property; consent in writing to the making of any map or plat thereof; join in granting any easement thereon; or join in any extension agreement or any agreement subordinating the lien or charge hereof.

FIG. 15-2a.   Continued.

(12) That upon written request of Beneficiary stating that all sums secured hereby have been paid, and upon surrender of this Deed of Trust and said note to Trustee for cancellation and retention and upon payment of its fees, Trustee shall reconvey, without warranty, the property then held hereunder. The recitals in such reconveyance of any matters or facts shall be conclusive proof of the truthfulness thereof. The grantee in such reconveyance may be described as "the person or persons legally entitled thereto." Five years after issuance of such full reconveyance, Trustee may destroy said note and this Deed (unless directed in such request to retain them). Such request and reconveyance shall operate as a reassignment of the rents, issues and profits hereinafter assigned to Beneficiary.

(13) That as additional security, Trustor hereby gives to and confers upon Beneficiary the right, power and authority, during the continuance of these Trusts, to collect the rents, royalties, issues and profits of said property, reserving unto Trustor the right, prior to any default by Trustor in payment of any obligation secured hereby or in performance of any agreement hereunder, to collect and retain such rents, royalties, issues and profits as, but not before they become due and payable. Upon any such default, Beneficiary may at any time without notice, either in person, by agent, or by a receiver to be appointed by a court, and without regard to the adequacy of any security for the obligations hereby secured, (a) enter upon and take possession of said property or any part thereof, and (b) with or without taking possession, in his own name sue for or otherwise collect such rents, royalties, issues and profits, including those past due and unpaid, and apply the same less costs and expenses of operation and collection, including reasonable attorney's fees, upon any obligations secured hereby, and in such order as Beneficiary may determine. The entering upon and taking possession of said property, the collection of such rents, royalties, issues and profits and the application thereof as aforesaid shall not cure or waive any default or notice of default hereunder or invalidate any act done pursuant to such notice.

(14) That upon default by Trustor in payment of any obligation secured hereby or in performance of any agreement hereunder, or upon default under any prior lien or encumbrance on all or part of said property, Beneficiary may declare all sums secured hereby immediately due and payable. Such declaration may be accomplished by delivery to Trustee of written declaration of default and demand for sale and of written notice of default and of election to cause to be sold said property, which notice Trustee shall cause to be filed for record, or, at its option, Beneficiary may record a written notice of default and initiate proceedings for judicial foreclosure on said property. In connection with any demand for sale, Beneficiary also shall deposit with Trustee this Deed, said note and all documents evidencing expenditures secured hereby.

(15) That after the lapse of such time as may then be required by law following the recordation of said notice of default, and notice of sale having been given as then required by law, Trustee, without demand on Trustor, shall sell said property at the time and place fixed by it in said notice of sale, either as a whole or in separate parcels, and in such order as it may determine, at public auction to the highest bidder for cash in lawful money of the United States, payable at time of sale. Trustee may postpone sale of all or any portion of said property by public announcement at such time and place of sale, and from time to time thereafter may postpone such sale by public announcement at the time fixed by the preceding postponement. Trustee shall deliver to such purchaser its deed conveying the property so sold, but without any covenant or warranty, express or implied. The recitals in such deed of any matters or facts shall be conclusive proof of the truthfulness thereof. Any person, including Trustor, Trustee, or Beneficiary may purchase at such sale. After deducting all costs, fees and expenses of Trustee and of this Trust, including costs of evidence of title in connection with sale, Trustee shall apply the proceeds of sale to payment of: (a) all sums expended under the terms hereof, not then repaid, with accrued interest at the rate specified in the obligation secured hereby; (b) all other sums then secured hereby; and (c) the remainder, if any, to the person or persons legally entitled thereto.

(16) That Trustee and Beneficiary, and each of them, shall be entitled to enforce payment and/or performance of any obligations secured hereby and to exercise all rights and powers under this Deed of Trust or under any other agreement or any laws now or hereafter in force, notwithstanding some or all of the obligations secured hereby are now or shall hereafter be otherwise secured, whether by mortgage, deed of trust, pledge, lien assignment or otherwise. Neither the acceptance of this Deed of Trust nor its enforcement whether by court action or pursuant to the power of sale or other powers herein contained, shall prejudice or in any manner affect Trustee's or Beneficiary's right to realize upon or enforce any other security now or hereafter held by Trustee or Beneficiary, it being agreed that Trustee and Beneficiary, and each of them shall be entitled to enforce this Deed of Trust and any other security now or hereafter held by Beneficiary or Trustee in such order and manner as they or either of them may in their uncontrolled discretion determine.

Beneficiary from time to time and with or without notice may release any person now or hereafter liable for the performance of such obligation, extend the time for payment or performance, accept additional security, and alter, substitute or release any security.

(18) That if this Deed or any note secured hereby provides for any charge for prepayment of any obligation secured hereby, Trustor agrees to pay such charge if any such obligation be paid prior to the due date thereof, notwithstanding that all sums or obligations secured hereby shall have become immediately due and payable by reason of any provision herein contained.

(19) That no remedy hereby given to Beneficiary or Trustee is exclusive of any other remedy hereunder or under any present or future law.

(20) That Beneficiary may, from time to time, by instrument in writing, substitute a successor or successors to any Trustee named herein or acting hereunder, which instrument, executed and acknowledged by Beneficiary and recorded in the office of the recorder of the county or counties where said property is situated, shall be conclusive proof of proper substitution of such successor Trustee or Trustees, who shall without conveyance from the Trustee predecessor, succeed to all its title, estate, rights, powers and duties. Said instrument must contain the name of the original Trustor, Trustee and Beneficiary hereunder, the book and page where this Deed is recorded, and the name and address of the new Trustee. If notice of default shall have been recorded, this power of substitution cannot be exercised until after the costs, fees and expenses of the then acting Trustee shall have been paid to such Trustee who shall endorse receipt thereof upon such instrument of substitution. The procedure herein provided for substitution of Trustee shall be exclusive of all other provisions for substitution, statutory or otherwise.

(21) That Trustor waives the right to assert at any time statute of limitations as a bar to any action brought to enforce any obligation hereby secured

(22) That this Deed shall inure to and bind their heirs, legatees, devisees, administrators, executors, successors, and assigns of the parties hereto. All obligations of Trustor hereunder are joint and several. The term "Beneficiary" shall mean the owner and holder, including pledgees of the indebtedness secured hereby, whether or not named as Beneficiary herein, and whether by operation of law or otherwise. Whenever used, the singular number shall include the plural, the plural the singular, and the use of any gender shall include all genders.

(23) That Trustee accepts this Trust when this Deed, duly executed and acknowledged, is made a public record as provided by law. Trustee is not obligated to notify any party hereto of pending sale under any other Deed of Trust or of any action or proceeding in which Trustor, Beneficiary or Trustee shall be a party unless brought by Trustee. The Trustee shall not be obligated to perform any act required of the Trustee hereunder unless the Trustee is requested in writing and is reasonably indemnified against loss, cost, liability and expense.

(24) To pay $15 for each statement requested by Trustor, or on his behalf, which contains only information that is among the matters specified in Chapter 1561, California Statutes 1961, and to pay the reasonable charges of Beneficiary for any other service rendered Trustor, or on his behalf, connected with this Deed of Trust or the loan secured hereby including, without limiting the generality of the foregoing; the delivery to an escrow holder of a request for full or partial reconveyance of this Deed of Trust; transmitting to an escrow holder monies secured hereby; changing its records pertaining to this Deed of Trust and the loan secured hereby to show a new owner of said property; replacing an existing policy of fire insurance or other casualty insurance held by Beneficiary hereunder, with another such policy. Any such charge shall be secured hereby and Trustor agrees to pay the same, together with interest from the date of such charge at the rate specified in the obligation secured hereby, immediately and without demand.

FIG. 15-2a. Continued.

(25) Trustor agrees that if the Trustor shall sell, contract to sell, convey, alienate, or further encumber said property, or any part thereof, or any interest therein, or shall be divested of his title or any interest therein in any manner or way, whether voluntary or involuntary, except for transfers of title exempted from this clause by regulation or statute, all obligations secured hereby, irrespective of the maturity date expressed in any note evidencing the same, at the option of the Beneficiary and without demand or notice, shall immediately become due and payable. This provision shall not accelerate any of the obligations secured hereby solely because the real property described herein has become subject to a junior encumbrance or lien, provided that said real property contains at least one, but not more than four, housing units. The Trustor will provide to the Beneficiary an exact duplicate copy of any contract providing for the conveyance of any interest in the aforesaid property or any deed of trust or similar instrument creating a lien or encumbrance on said property immediately upon the execution of any such contract, deed or other instrument. The undersigned Trustor requests that a copy of any Notice of Default and of any Notice of Sale hereunder be mailed to him at his address hereinbefore set forth.

STATE OF CALIFORNIA, County of _____ ss.

On _____ before me, the undersigned, a Notary Public in and for said County and State, personally appeared _____

known to me to be the person_____ whose name_____ subscribed to the within instrument and acknowledges that_____ executed the same. Witness my hand and official seal

Order No._____ Escrow No._____

Request for full reconveyance
To be used only when note has been paid.

TO _____

Dated _____

The undersigned is the legal owner and holder of all indebtedness secured by the within Deed of Trust. All sums secured by said Deed of Trust have been fully paid and satisfied; and you are hereby requested and directed, on payment to you of any sums owing to you under the terms of said Deed of Trust, to cancel all evidences of indebtedness secured by said Deed of Trust and delivered to you herewith together with said Deed of Trust, and to reconvey, without warranty, to the parties designated by the terms of said Deed of Trust, the estate now held by you under the same.

Mail Reconveyance to:

By _____

By _____

Do not lose or destroy this Deed of Trust OR THE NOTE(S). Both must be delivered to the Trustee for cancellation and retention before reconveyance will be made.

FIG. 15–2a. Continued.

Mortgage Elements

Two basic elements must be present in order for a mortgage to exist: a *debt* and a *pledge of property to secure the debt.* (See Fig. 15–1.) If either of these elements is lacking, no mortgage agreement exists. The debt may have been incurred prior to making the agreement or simultaneously with it, or it may come into existence after the date of the agreement. A mortgage which is given to secure a debt already in existence is subject to prior mortgages and liens, even though these are not recorded. This is due to the fact that the lender did not rely upon mortgage security at the time the loan was made. Hence, the law holds that the lender has not been injured by any failure to record such prior claims and will not offer protection against them.

If a mortgage is given to secure advances to be made in the future, the amount of such loans need not be stated in the mortgage and may be at the option of the mortgagee. However, it is customary to fix a maximum amount in such an agreement. There is no question regarding the validity of such mortgages, but the rights of subsequent mortgagees and others who secure claims against the property differ widely from one state to another.[3]

Ownership Interest

Anyone who desires to mortgage a piece of property must actually possess a stated interest in the property being offered as security. In general, any interest in real property which can be sold or assigned can be mortgaged. But, as we have already pointed out, the interests that one may own in real property are many and varied. Thus, the mortgagee must always be certain that the mortgagor actually possesses the title to the property being offered for sale.[4] The title may be clouded and the owner may not be aware of it. Taxes, special assessments, prior mortgages, mechanics' liens, attachments, judgments, or court orders may leave little actual ownership for the borrower to mortgage. Similarly, private or public restrictions may so limit the use of a property that it is incapable of earning the type of return which is expected of it. Rights of dower and curtesy, easements, reservations, encroachments, prior liens, and rights of tenants are all possible claims that

---

[3] In general, the law states that the making of such advances is optional with the mortgagee, and if those who hold junior liens against the collateral notify the mortgagee of their claims and direct the mortgagee not to make further advances, such advances will be inferior to the junior claims.

[4] Under certain circumstances a mortgage will be held to convey an interest which the mortgagor or borrower did not own at the time the agreement was made. For example, the mortgage might contain a provision by which the mortgagor stated and guaranteed good title to the property. If the mortgagor did not have such title and later acquired it, the law will hold that such title actually passed to the mortgagee or lender at the time the agreement was made. This is permitted because it would be unjust to allow the borrower a self-benefit through a personal wrong.

SINGLE FAMILY DWELLING

Loan No._____

$ _____ California _____ 19___

FOR VALUE RECEIVED, in installments as herein stated, the undersigned jointly and severally promise(s) to pay to _____ a California corporation, or order, at its principal office in _____ California, or at any other place designated by the holder, the principal sum of _____ DOLLARS,

with interest from the date hereof on the unpaid principal at the rate of _____ per cent per annum: Principal and interest payable in monthly installments of $ _____ on the _____ day of each calendar month, beginning _____ 19___ and continuing monthly thereafter until _____ at which time all unpaid principal together with interest due thereon shall become due and payable.

Each installment payment shall be applied first to interest then due and the balance, if any, shall be applied in reduction of principal. Should default be made in the payment of any installment when due, or in the performance of any agreement in the Deed of Trust securing the payment of this note, the holder hereof may, at its option, declare any portion or the entire amount of principal and interest immediately due and payable.

Principal and interest are payable in lawful money of the United States. Should interest not be paid when due, at the option of the holder, it shall be added to the unpaid principal and thereafter bear like interest as the principal.

The undersigned agrees with the promisee named above, that in the event that any payment hereunder is not made when due, the holder of this note will suffer substantial damage by reason of the holder's internal collection expenses in attempting to collect such payment, and by reason of loss of use of the money which would otherwise have been received, which damages are extremely difficult or impracticable of ascertainment. The undersigned, therefore, agrees to pay to any holder of this note with respect to each payment which is not made when due, a late charge of $ _____

The foregoing notwithstanding, if the State of California shall enact a statute modifying authorized maximum late charges chargeable by savings and loan associations, the undersigned and the promisee agree that the undersigned shall pay a late charge each time such charges are due as provided above, at the maximum rate authorized by such statute in lieu of the foregoing late charge.

In addition to such agreed late charge, the undersigned agrees to pay reasonable attorneys' costs and fees and all out-of-pocket expenses of the holder paid to others, including title, recording, filing, trustee and other costs or fees, which may be incurred in connec-

The Deed of Trust securing this note contains the following agreement by trustor: "Trustor agrees that if the Trustor shall sell, contract to sell, convey, alienate, or further encumber said property, or any part thereof, or any interest therein, or shall be divested of his title or any interest therein in any manner or way, whether voluntary or involuntary, except for transfers of title exempted from this clause by regulation or statute, all obligations secured hereby, irrespective of the maturity date expressed in any note evidencing the same, at the option of the Beneficiary and without demand or notice, shall immediately become due and payable. This provision shall not accelerate any of the obligations secured hereby solely because the real property described herein has become subject to a junior encumbrance or lien, provided that said real property contains at least one, but not more than four, housing units. The Trustor will provide to the Beneficiary an exact duplicate copy of any contract providing for the conveyance of any interest in the aforesaid property or any deed of trust or similar instrument creating a lien or encumbrance on said property immediately upon the execution of any such contract, deed or other instrument.

Each of such options may be exercised separately, or may be exercised concurrently with any other option or options. Failure to exercise any option shall not constitute a waiver of the right of the holder hereof to exercise such option in the event of any subsequent default.

The undersigned and endorsers hereof hereby jointly and severally waive demand, presentment for payment, protest, notice of nonpayment and notice of dishonor.

"The undersigned shall have the privilege of prepaying the principal of this note either in full or in part at any time; provided, however, if such prepayment occurs within 5 years of the date hereof, that when the aggregate amount of prepayments in any 12-month period exceeds 20% of the original principal amount of this note, the undersigned agrees to pay 180 days interest on such amount prepaid in excess of said 20%, notwithstanding that all obligations herein shall have become due and payable by reason of any provision contained herein or in the deed of trust securing this note."

This note is secured by a Deed of Trust of even date herewith to   as Trustee.

DO NOT DESTROY THIS NOTE:
When paid, this note, with the Deed of Trust Securing same must be surrendered to Trustee for cancellation and retention before reconveyance will be made.

FIG. 15–2b.   Promissory note to accompany deed of trust, State of California.

may interfere with the setting up of a satisfactory mortgage agreement. Such matters must always be determined by a competent lawyer or title company.

Property Description

A careful and accurate description of the property is of major importance, since this eliminates uncertainties regarding the location or extent of the property which is mortgaged. Usually it is sufficient to describe the property by referring to it in the way in which it is described in the deed or as the number of a lot shown on a recorded map, but personal investigation and inspection help to avoid mistakes and misunderstanding. Surveys by competent engineers should be made whenever questions arise which are likely to create future problems.

In general, the property should be designated with accuracy and the amount of the debt, the terms of repayment, the exact conditions under which the conveyance is made, and any special promises or agreements that are a part of the contract should be indicated.

Strict Foreclosure

The legal steps that must be taken by the mortgagee or lender for the purpose of having the property applied to the payment of a defaulted debt are called *foreclosure*. Legally there is a distinction between *strict foreclosure* and *foreclosure by sale*, although the latter method has come to be used so generally that most people have this in mind when they speak of the process of foreclosure.

One of the early developments of the law of mortgages relieved the borrower from forfeiting the property through failure to pay within the time set, provided payment was made within a reasonable time thereafter. The time was determined by a court of equity. This process made it necessary for the mortgagee to institute a court action in order to determine that a reasonable time had elapsed. In case sufficient time had been allowed, the mortgagee was able to secure a decree foreclosing or terminating all rights and interests of the mortgagor in the property. Such an action by a court constitutes strict foreclosure. The decree given by the court under strict foreclosure proceedings does not order a sale of the property but confirms the absolute title to it in the mortgagee or lender.

Strict foreclosure is still used in many states, but is permitted only under special circumstances. For example, this method may be proper in cases where the value of the property does not exceed the debt and the mortgagor does not contest the action. It is also proper in cases where the mortgage is in the form of an absolute deed without any written condition or agreement to reconvey. As we have indicated, however, the method most generally used in this country to collect a defaulted mortgage debt is fore-closure by sale. There is considerable variation from state to state in regard to the methods and practices followed.

In most states the mortgagee has several remedies from which the one best suited to the purpose may be chosen. Where there is no prohibition by statute, all remedies may be pursued concurrently or successively. The mortgagee may sue for judgment on the note, which can be collected out of other property owned by the debtor, and at the same time start foreclosure proceedings. In some states a judgment for the debt may be taken in the foreclosure action and will stand against the debtor to the extent that it exceeds the amount realized from the foreclosure sale. In other states separate court action must be brought to make up any deficiency.

Foreclosure by Sale

The two methods of foreclosure by sale most commonly used are (1) foreclosure under power of sale contained in a mortgage or deed of trust, and (2) foreclosure by court action resulting in a decree of sale.

If the mortgage instrument expressly authorizes the mortgagee or trustee to sell the property in the event of default, the laws of many states permit this to be done so long as the procedure prescribed by statute is followed. Whether the mortgagor has the right to redeem the property within a certain period after sale depends entirely upon the laws of the state in which the property is located. Some states allow no redemption after a sale of this type. Others provide that the mortgagor may redeem the property within a certain period after sale if the costs of the sale and the full amount of the debt are first paid.

Many states require that all foreclosure sales must result from court action even though mortgages and deeds of trust contain powers of sale. Under this arrangement a suit is brought by the mortgagee against the mortgagor and all parties who have acquired an interest in the property subsequent to the mortgage.

The law provides that the rights of no person shall be affected by a decree unless that person is before the court. Because of this regulation, it is important for the mortgagee to search the record carefully in order that all persons who have acquired rights in the property may be made parties to the proceedings and properly served with summonses or otherwise brought before the court.

Usually the decree directs the sheriff to sell the property to the highest bidder after public notices of the time and place of sale as prescribed by statute. The purchaser at the sale may receive a deed from the sheriff conveying an absolute title, or may receive merely a sheriff's certificate which will become a conveyance of the title within a specified period if the property is not redeemed within that time.

Redemption

The interest of the mortgagor in the property prior to foreclosure is frequently called the *equity of redemption*. This should not be confused with the *statutory right of redemption*, which is a legal privilege recognized in certain states. In some states the mortgagor, and frequently junior lien holders as well, are given the right to redeem the title upon payment of the redemption price within a certain time after the foreclosure sale. This redemption period ranges from six months in some states to two years in others. Some states allow the mortgagor to retain possession of the property during the redemption period, while other give possession to the purchaser and allow retention of the property unless it is actually redeemed within the time allowed.

In some cases a mortgagor is unable to pay a debt but is willing to convey the property to the mortgagee in order to satisfy the claim. By doing this the mortgagor is relieved (if the mortgagee agrees) of personal liability, the danger of future deficiency judgments, and the unpleasant publicity frequently associated with foreclosure proceedings. Such a proposal is often agreeable to the mortgagee, for it provides relief from the expenses and delays connected with foreclosure proceedings. Under some conditions, the lender may even pay the borrower a sum of money for title to the property. However, a deed of this type must be considered carefully by the mortgagee before it is accepted because its validity depends upon the intention of the parties involved and on other special circumstances. Also, obligations to others may be assumed with this title.

TRUST DEED AND OTHER FINANCING ARRANGEMENTS

In addition to a mortgage, a trust deed, mortgage bonds, a land contract, and a lease with option to purchase may be used in financing real property.

The trust deed in the nature of a mortgage [5] is an instrument which provides for the conveyance of title to a third party who holds it *in trust* as security for the payment of an obligation by a borrower. The creditor is called the *beneficiary*, the *legal holder*, or the *mortgagee*. The party holding the title for the period of the loan is called the *trustee*. The trustee, then, is holding the stakes, with instructions to reconvey title to the debtor when the debt is repaid, or to sell the property in event of default. Sales proceeds are applied to the payment of the debt, with any surplus remaining payable to the borrower. In some states, this instrument has virtually supplanted the mortgage, and it is commonly used the country over in trans-

---

[5] The trust created for holding a trust deed in the nature of a mortgage should not be confused with the "naked" or "dry" trust. The latter is created solely to hold title to property and is not associated with any debt. In fact, it performs no functions other than to hold title for the convenience of the transferor. The "naked" trust is common in Illinois and a few other states.

actions involving substantial amounts of funds. In a number of states, the trust deed can be foreclosed by trustee's sale without any court proceedings. However, in most states, the trust deed is virtually identical to the mortgage and is legally considered as such.

Mortgage Bonds

When several persons or a group of persons lend money on the security of a property, mortgage bonds may be issued. A customary procedure is to give a mortgage or a trust deed to a trustee, who holds it for the benefit of the bondholders. In such cases, the mortgage is accompanied by a trust agreement, which sets forth in detail the rights of the bondholders in the security and the duties of the trustee. For example, a corporation may wish to borrow an amount which is greater than any one person wishes to lend. In such a case the corporation may convey its property to a trustee and provide for the issuance of bonds against it. Such bonds can then be sold to the public generally and the debt distributed among a great many persons. In cases of this type, the trustee acts on behalf of all of the bondholders. If foreclosure and sale become necessary, the trustee pays over to each bondholder a proportionate share of the proceeds.

Some savings and loan associations have from time to time issued mortgage-backed bonds which allow them to attract long-term funds at fixed rates.

Land Contract

The land contract, or contract for a deed, is a written agreement by which a property is sold to a buyer who agrees to pay in installments the established price with interest over a specified period of years. Generally a down payment is required, although the amount is usually nominal, 10 per cent or less of the purchase price being common. Under the land contract, the seller retains title until the agreed payments have been made by the purchaser. Frequently, however, the agreement provides that when the installment payments have reached a specified percentage of the purchase price (for example, one half), the seller will give a deed or transfer title under a regular mortgage as security for the remaining payments. The most appealing factor to the purchaser is probably the simplicity of arrangement. Buyers can sometimes secure property under land contract where the down payment necessary under a conventional mortgage would obviate the transaction. Retention of title makes it relatively easy for the seller in most states to avoid the cumbersomeness of conventional mortgage procedure in enforcing the terms of the contract. The land contract, however, poses certain dangers for the unwary purchaser. Generally the contract is not recorded; hence the purchasers may lose their protection, and the equitable interest, as well as use and occupancy upon default. It is also possible that the seller may lose, through foreclosures of prior liens, the right to convey title before the purchaser is in a position to demand it.

Various state laws apply to land contracts. In some states the seller is considered to be the owner until complete payment is made much like installment sales contracts. Other states consider the land contract to be much like a mortgage.

Lease With Option To Purchase

This arrangement may be thought of as a type of land contract. The prospective buyers can get use of the property and protect occupancy in case they decide to buy. Usually the lease payments become the down payment and the arrangement can become a more typical land contract.

Disclosure

Federal legislation, especially the Real Estate Settlement Procedures Act, requires lenders to make certain that borrowers, particularly on homes, are clearly aware of their rights and obligations. The Department of Housing and Urban Development provides a booklet for this purpose entitled "Settlement Costs" which includes recommended forms to use in connection with home loans.[6]

CONSTRUCTION FINANCING

Individuals and firms engaging in the development of real estate, whether the task be road building or house building, rarely have sufficient funds to carry a job to completion without some form of financing. Personal or company capital is supplemented with loans, advances from purchasers, and credit from material suppliers and subcontractors. The various sources of financing can be combined in many ways, and, of course, not all of them are used in every building venture.

Construction financing varies according to the requirements and characteristics of the participants in a particular building project. In the same construction job, the originator or sponsor and subcontractors may require financing for themselves, but may also provide financing for others. For example, an individual or firm for whom a structure is being built might obtain a loan to finance the project and also make personal advances to the builder who in turn operates between advances on a commercial line of credit and credit from subcontractors and material suppliers.

Interim and Long-Term Financing

The most common type of construction financing is the construction loan granted to the originator or sponsor of the building project in which

[6] See Dept. of Housing and Urban Development, *Settlement Costs: A HUD Guide* (Washington, D. C.: Government Printing Office, 1976).

the proceeds of the loan are disbursed as construction progresses. A construction loan may be either one or a series of short-term notes which are drawn at intervals during the construction and refinanced when the project is completed, or a single long-term loan in which the principal is advanced in installments. Thus, construction financing may be either interim financing or an integral part of long-term financing.

A short-term construction loan is not necessarily a mortgage loan, although the long-term loans are nearly always secured by a mortgage on the real estate being improved. Established building firms frequently obtain construction financing through an unsecured line of credit, just as other types of firms borrow on their general credit. Individuals or companies having special structures custom-built for them, such as residences or stores or factory buildings, typically have to pledge the property being developed in order to obtain construction funds.

Disbursement Schedules

Many different construction-loan disbursement schedules are in use. They are not influenced by whether the loan is long- or short-term. Some systems permit payouts as certain phases of the project are completed; for example, 25 per cent of the loan is paid out when the foundation is completed, 25 per cent when the structure is under roof and rough plumbing and wiring are installed, 35 per cent when the structure is completed and ready for occupancy, and 15 per cent after the period for filing mechanics' liens has elapsed. Other payout systems permit the borrower to draw loan funds in amounts equal to a certain percentage of the cost of the work completed for which payment has not already been made. The final balance of the loan is disbursed upon completion. In some cases there is a retainage of a percentage of funds to make certain that all bills are paid and all requirements are met. Some systems simply require the builder to submit all bills to the lender, who in turn pays them and gives the builder the balance of the loan account upon completion. The Federal Housing Administration and the Veterans' Administration require three inspections during construction on residential units which are to be eligible for insurance or guaranties, so the payouts on FHA and VA projects are usually related to the required inspections.

Regulations and Policies of Lenders

Whether construction financing is interim financing or a part of a long-term loan depends on regulations and on the policies of the lender granting the loan. The financial and operating characteristics of the borrower, of course, will be a factor of importance. National banks and federally chartered savings and loan associations are permitted to grant loans for construction purposes without regard to mortgage security. Construction may also be financed with ordinary mortgage loans in which the principal is advanced during construction.

Some lenders and some borrowers are not interested in long-term mortgage financing. Commercial banks are often willing to finance building operations as a commercial venture but do not care to invest in long-term mortgage loans. Other lenders may be willing to finance construction on a short-term basis so that they can temporarily avoid committing funds on a long-term basis. Building firms engaging in custom construction are often not concerned with long-term financing but only with financing the project during the construction period. Real estate investment trusts have played an active role in construction financing.

Suppliers and Subcontractors

Material suppliers and subcontractors participate in construction financing by granting credit to builders and owners while a project is being brought to completion. Credit from suppliers and subcontractors can be used either to supplement or to replace construction loans.

Standby Arrangements

Various types of standby arrangements may be used in connection with construction loans. For example, a standby commitment for permanent financing may be necessary to facilitate construction financing. If money markets ease, the developer may let the standby commitment expire and secure financing from other sources.

USE OF LEASES IN LIEU OF FINANCING

As we indicated previously, property users in some instances employ leases to avoid the financing problems arising from fee ownership. In some cases the line of demarcation between certain forms of leasing agreements and various mortgage agreements is barely discernible, although from a strictly legal standpoint distinctions do exist. Many business firms implement leases in acquiring the use of various types of properties. Leasing has been used to an increasing extent by chain store organizations. Industrial and public utility firms have also made use of such arrangements. Probably the most important reason for this development has been the need of business firms while they are expanding to conserve capital for current uses rather than to commit it to long-term fixed uses. Rising prices and high income taxes may also contribute to the need for current capital. Under leasing arrangements no fixed debts are created and no debt is reflected upon the financial statements of a firm. Thus it may sometimes be referred to as "off balance sheet" financing. There are some income tax advantages in the leasing arrangement, since rent is considered a business expense while repayment of the principal of a mortgage is not. Interest on a mortgage, however, is considered a business expense.

Types of Leases

A number of types of leases are in use, ranging from the ordinary short-term lease, in which a business firm or individual rents an existing property and pays periodic rentals for the duration of the lease, to long-term leases including ground leases. Under long-term amortized leases, a business firm may arrange to have a site purchased and improvements constructed for it by an individual or a company for lease back to the firm. Under this type of arrangement, the rentals will often completely amortize the investment and also provide a return to the lessor. At the end of such a period, title to the property vests in the lessee. In this instance the lease is almost identical, from an economic standpoint, with the purchase of a property with a 100 per cent loan amortized in a given period. In legal terms, of course, this is not the case.

Different types of business organizations follow various arrangements in regard to leases. For example, a grocery chain organization ordinarily will not lease an outlet in an outlying shopping center for more than five or ten years. However, arrangements are usually made for renewal at the option of the chain store organization. Some department and variety stores have leased outlets in so-called "100 per cent" retail locations for 30 years or longer; but even in such locations, shorter terms are used with increasing frequency. Leases for long terms often include provisions for payments based upon a percentage of the dollar volume of business. This arrangement is commonly called a *percentage lease*. Sometimes there are *graded* or *step-up leases*, with the rental moving from one level to another in accordance with the specific agreements that have been made. When the lessor has the responsibility for taxes, insurance, and property maintenance, the arrangement is called a *gross lease*, in contrast to a *net lease*, in which the lessee assumes that responsibility.

The Buy–Build–Sell Lease. Sometimes a property which is needed by a business organization is not available at the time and in the location desired. In such instances business firms may buy land in the desired location, build the type of structure and other improvements that are needed, and then sell the property to individual or institutional investors, arranging to lease it back after the sale. This is known as a *buy–build–sell lease*. Such plans provide properties of exactly the type desired, and only temporary financing needs to be obtained by the business organization wishing to use the property. Safeway Stores pioneered this type of arrangment.

In some cases arrangements are made whereby the property may be repurchased by prearrangement. Usually this prearrangement is called a *rejectable offer*. The lessee states that the lease is to be cancelled and offers to repurchase on the basis of the original arrangement. If the offer to repurchase is not accepted by the lessor, the lease is cancelled.

The Sale–Leaseback Arrangement. The buy–build–sell lease outlined above is a specialized type of the sale–leaseback arrangement, which is more commonly associated with the sale of existing properties with arrangements for leasing them back. Such arrangements enable a business firm to raise funds for working capital purposes without surrendering the use of the property which has been owned up to that point. Many of the early sale–leaseback arrangements were made with educational institutions, foundations, and charitable organizations, which enjoyed tax exemptions. However, changes in the revenue laws have provided for the taxation of such organizations at full corporate rates on rentals received from properties that were leased to the extent that borrowed funds were used.

Life insurance companies have acquired the right to invest in income properties, and they have been one of the more important sources of funds for arrangements of this type. More recently, pension funds have played an important role in this field. Many of the earlier sale–leaseback arrangements contained options to repurchase; but because questions were raised regarding the tax status of such arrangements, repurchase agreements are not currently being used to any great extent. Renewal provisions, however, are almost always used.

The Long-Term Ground Lease. The ground lease system dates back to English and colonial procedures. Ground leases once played an important part in the development of business properties, and are still employed in a few localities, particularly in Pennsylvania, Hawaii, and Maryland, as a means for real estate financing. The long-term ground lease usually runs for 99 years and may be renewable forever. It applies only to the land, and arrangements are usually required for improving the land within a specified period of time. Such improvements then serve as security for the lease and insure continued occupancy by the tenant. These leases are almost always "net" in form. Because of difficulties that arose with arrangements of this type during the depression years, most business firms have tended to prefer package deals that secure both land and building under a single long-term lease.

DEBT–EQUITY COMBINATIONS

Inflationary tendencies with their high interest rates brought increased use of a variety of debt–equity combinations in real estate finance. These "piece of the action" types of plans include percentages of gross or net income, joint ventures, and other types of arrangements. It is quite often referred to as "participation" by the lender.

Percentage of Gross Income

Under this plan the lender gets an added return over and above the interest on the mortgage on the basis of a percentage—usually 2 to 4 per cent—of the gross income. Closely related is an arrangement which provides for a percentage of the gross income after a specified dollar volume is reached. No added "kicker" is available to the lender until the property achieves a degree of success. Typically the participation is on the basis of 20 to 30 per cent of the gross above the target volume.

Percentage of Net Income

Although a variety of arrangements are possible a typical one is a purchase–leaseback of the underlying land with a percentage of net income tied into the ground lease along with a lease–hold mortgage on the improvements. Often there are arrangements which allow no prepayment for a period—usually 10 to 12 years or provide for a substantial prepayment penalty. Arrangements of this type often allow the lender to participate to the extent of 25 to 50 per cent of the net income after debt service.

Joint Ventures

Many different types of joint ventures have been worked out. Typically the developer has no money in the venture but provides for management, construction, marketing, and promotion. The lender provides all of the money required. The developer and the lender then may share on a predetermined basis—usually 50 per cent—in the net proceeds after debt service.

Other Arrangements

Many types of plans have been developed and are in the process of development to provide new combinations of debt and equity financing. For example, efforts are being made to develop a plan whereby the lender on a single-family home will participate in the gains which may result if the property is sold. If the owner sells the house and realizes a $1,000 gain, the lender would get some participation, this amount based on a predetermined percentage.

SUMMARY

Because of the high unit value of real properties, most people in the real estate field rely heavily on borrowed funds to accomplish the development, construction, or purchase of real estate. Thus, the terms and availability of financing are important factors in real estate decisions.

Like many other economic goods, real estate may be pledged as security for borrowed funds. Because of fixity of location, long life, and limited marketability of real estate, special practices and instruments have been developed for use in the financing of real properties.

This chapter emphasizes financing through use of mortgages and related instruments like trust deeds in the nature of a mortgage, bonds, and land contracts. Mortgages, which are evidences of debt and pledges of property as security, are classified by degree of priority; method of repayment; insured, guaranteed, and conventional types; variable and fixed interest rates; flexible payment; and special financing requirements including blanket, package, open-end, and purchase money mortgages.

The most common course of action in the event of default on a mortgage is foreclosure by sale. Most states make allowance for the interest of the mortgagor by establishing redemption provisions.

Various types of leases may be employed by users of real estate resources who do not care to undertake the financial responsibility of ownership.

Debt–equity combinations are also used. Of special importance are percentage-of-income arrangements and joint ventures.

QUESTIONS FOR STUDY

1. How are the terms and availability of real estate credit related to conditions in the general capital markets?
2. Over the past year assume that conditions in the mortgage markets, particularly for single-family homes, have been highly competitive. Business expansion is increasing the demand for funds for plant and equipment expenditures. What effect do you believe this is likely to have on the home mortgage market? Explain your position.
3. List the chief sources of equity funds for investment in real estate.
4. Differentiate between each of the following pairs: (a) A first mortgage and a second mortgage. (b) A senior mortgage and a junior mortgage. (c) A conventional mortgage and an insured or guaranteed mortgage. (d) An amortized mortgage and a straight term mortgage. (e) An open-end mortgage and a package mortgage. (f) A fixed and variable interest rate. (g) A fixed and flexible payment mortgage.
5. Indicate the various types of action available to mortgagees in the event of default on a mortgage.
6. Describe the process of financing a construction project.
7. Explain the difference between the buy–build–sell lease and the sale–lease-back arrangement.
8. Why do some firms prefer leasing arrangements to the alternative of financing ownership of the real estate resources they employ?
9. Which of the various types of lease arrangements would you prefer, and in each case give reasons to explain your preference, if you were: (a) A real estate manager for a chain of grocery stores? (b) A property manager for a shopping center? (c) A physician leasing office space? (d) A general manager of a small, single-plant manufacturing firm?
10. In purchasing a new house for your family residence, would you prefer to assume a "conventional" mortgage or an "insured" mortgage? Why? Explain the relative advantages and disadvantages of each.
11. Why are debt–equity combinations growing in importance?

SUGGESTED READINGS

LUSK, HAROLD, and FRENCH, WILLIAM B. *Law of the Real Estate Business* (3rd ed.). Homewood, Ill.: Richard D. Irwin, Inc., 1975. Ch. 9.

KRATOVIL, ROBERT. *Real Estate Law* (6th ed.). Englewood Cliffs, N. J.: Prentice-Hall, Inc., 1974. Chs. 19–23, incl.

McMAHAN, JOHN. *Property Development.* New York: McGraw-Hill Book Co., 1976. Ch. 11.

WILEY, ROBERT J. *Real Estate Investment—Analysis and Strategy.* New York: The Ronald Press Co., 1977. Ch. 9.

CASE 15–1

Boysun v. Boysun *

This was an action by Mike E. Boysun (plaintiff) against John C. Boysun and Tillie Boysun, his wife (defendants), to quiet title to certain land. Judgment for Mike E. Boysun, and John C. and Tillie Boysun appealed. Judgment affirmed.

John C. and Tillie Boysun owned a farm which was mortgaged for $4,400. They were in default on their payments and delinquent in the payment of their taxes, and the mortgagee was threatening to foreclose.

John was unable to borrow money to pay the mortgage. Mike offered to purchase the land subject to the encumbrances. He stated at the time that it was worth no more than the encumbrances. John and Tillie executed a quit-claim deed conveying the farm to Mike. Mike orally agreed to reconvey the farm to John or to convey it to a purchaser if John found one. Thereafter John and his family moved to another state. Mike worked the farm in 1953 and 1954 and paid the taxes from 1951 through 1958.

In the early part of 1954 John told Mike that he had a purchaser who would pay $11,000 for the farm but Mike wished to keep the farm. Thereafter, Mike sent money to John, and the amount sent plus the amount Mike paid to discharge the encumbrances on the farm amounted to $11,000. John and Tillie claim that the quitclaim deed was to secure a loan and asked the court to hold it to be a mortgage. John claimed that the money Mike sent him was a loan.

James T. Harrison, Chief Justice. The ultimate question of whether a transaction was intended by the parties to be a mortgage or a sale rests on the intention of the parties at the time of the execution of the instrument, and to establish this intention the courts will examine the surrounding circumstances.

It has been repeatedly held that the evidence to prove that a deed, absolute on its face, was intended to be a mortgage must be clear and convincing. However, this rule is subject to some modification in situations where there is an option to repurchase or a conditional sale. The general rule is that if there is doubt whether a sale or a mortgage was intended, the court will be inclined to resolve the doubt in favor of the mortgage.

John and Tillie in this action rely heavily on the *Murray* case. In that case this court listed a number of facts and circumstances which, if present, tend to confirm the view that the transaction was a mortgage and not a sale. These factors are as follows:

* 368 P.2d 439 (Sup. Ct. Mont. 1962). See Harold F. Lusk, Charles M. Hewitt, John D. Donnell, and James A. Barnes, *Business Law: Principles and Cases* (3rd Uniform Commercial Code Edition; Homewood, Ill.: Richard D. Irwin, Inc., 1974), pp. 947–49.

(*a*) The transaction in its inception had for its purpose a loan, not a sale.

(*b*) The grantor was in financial distress at the time of the transaction.

(*c*) The price which the grantee claims he paid for the property appears to have been grossly inadequate.

(*d*) According to grantee's own theory, the transaction did not amount to an absolute sale, but to a conditional sale; that is, a sale with an option to grantor to repurchase.

John and Tillie list the four factors and allege that they are all present in the instant case. We have some difficulty with this assertion. The third principle relied on in the *Murray* case is based on the inadequacy of the price the vendor received for his property. The adequacy of consideration must be tested by conditions existing at the time of the transaction.

In *Titus* v. *Wallick,* the court held that in order for evidence of a disparity between the consideration for a deed and the value of the land to be of weight, it is essential that there be a satisfactory showing of such disparity.

There is no evidence in the record to support John and Tillie's allegation of a disparity between the purchase price and the value of the land at the time of sale. The only statement as to the value of the land at the time the deed was executed was the testimony of Mike Boysun. He stated the reason he would not loan money against the property was because it was not worth any more than what was against it.

In addition to the above-stated facts there are two elements present in the instant case which were not present in the *Murray* case. A deed, though absolute on its face, will be construed as a mortgage whenever it is shown that the instrument was intended to secure a debt. However, a debt must be shown to exist between the parties, as a mortgage is a mere incident of the debt.

In the *Murray* case there was testimony in the record that the parties intended the money paid to be a loan and that a debt was created between the parties. In the instant case, Mike Boysun testified that the agreement between the parties was that any time John paid the money spent by Mike on the property he was to get the property back. John's testimony supports this theory that he received an option to repurchase. His testimony indicates that he felt no obligation to pay any money back to Mike, but rather he had an option to do so if desired.

John and Tillie place considerable emphasis on the fact that Mike Boysun while testifying stated that John had a year or two to redeem the property. They cite this to show that a mortgage was intended. We feel little weight should be given to such statements made by a layman, especially in a situation such as the present wherein it is evident from the legal tangle of the parties that they knew little, if anything, about the law.

The second factor which is present in the instant case, which is absent from the *Murray* case, is the preponderant and inescapable fact that the option to repurchase was exercised. The testimony of two disinterested witnesses established the fact that in the Spring of 1954, John Boysun exercised his option to repurchase. In addition to exercising his option the testimony in the record establishes that he received his option price.

Questions

1. What is the nature of a mortgage under common law? In a title theory state? In a lien theory state? Which type state do you believe Montana is?
2. What are the four factors which, under Montana law, determine that a transaction is a mortgage and not a sale? Which ones are met in this case? Which are not met?

3. Does Mike's payment of $11,000 abrogate John's right to repurchase? Why or why not?

STUDY PROJECT 15–1

Mortgage Reforms *

For the last 40 years, the United States has relied almost exclusively on the long-term, fixed-rate, fully amortized mortgage as the sole instrument for financing single-family housing. This instrument worked very well during the first 30 years of its life when interest rates were relatively stable and inflation was not a serious problem. However, the wild swings in interest rates and housing construction and the inflation of the last 10 years have illustrated all too well the inadequacies of such an instrument as the sole means of financing housing.

The defects of the conventional mortgage in today's economic environment are numerous, including the facts that:

1. Mortgage lenders must charge high interest rates to new borrowers in order to offset their loss on the low-yield loans still on their books. In effect, new borrowers are forced to subsidize old borrowers who are lucky enough to have low interest rate loans.

2. Many potential borrowers are priced out of the housing market altogether, either because they lack the required down payment or because they cannot afford the required monthly payments. The latter problem is particularly serious because the amount of house a family can purchase depends upon its current income—even though the home will be occupied well into the future, when a typical family's income will be much higher.

3. Potential borrowers are forced to pay an inflation premium that reflects the lender's estimate of the future rate of inflation. This can be an especially excessive burden on potential borrowers during periods of unstable prices and uncertainty regarding the future pattern of inflation.

4. Thrift institutions are prevented from paying competitive rates for deposits because their portfolio yields are locked into fixed interest rate loans.

The net result is that the conventional mortgage does not fit the needs of either the borrower or the lender very well in an inflationary economy. Consequently, some lenders, such as commercial banks and insurance companies, have virtually withdrawn from the single-family mortgage market.

This paper presents several alternative instruments as illustrations of changes that could be made to make mortgages more responsive to the needs of individual borrowers. The intent is not to drive the conventional mortgage out of existence, but rather to create a whole smorgasbord of mortgage loan instruments that would be available to meet the requirements of individual homebuyers.

It should be emphasized that federally chartered savings and loan associations could issue these mortgage instruments under present Federal laws. However, the Federal Home Loan Bank Board would have to issue regulations authorizing them. In contrast, Federal legislation would be required before national banks could issue some of the instruments. Similarly, some States would have to adopt either legislative or regulatory changes before State-chartered banks, savings and loan associations, and mutual savings banks could issue some of the mortgages.

Alternative Mortgage Instruments. In order to be effective, any new mortgage document must provide more benefits to both borrowers and lenders than the present conventional mortgage. From the borrower's standpoint, desirable

---

* From David L. Smith, "Reforming the Mortgage Instrument," *FHLBB Journal* (May, 1976), pp. 2–9. Reproduced by permission.

characteristics include: (1) the ability to choose a particular ratio of mortgage payments to family income; (2) a low level of uncertainty about the cost of the mortgage; and (3) relative short-run stability in the ratio of payments to income.

Ideally, a borrower should be able to select a mortgage payment-to-income ratio that will vary over the life of the loan according to his particular needs. For example, one family might desire to have the ratio rise over time, another might select a declining ratio, and a third might select a stable ratio. Families should not be expected to enter into long-term contracts that contain a high degree of uncertainty about the payment-to-income ratio. Finally, although the long-run trend of the payment-to-income ratio may be either up or down, the ratio should be relatively stable in the short run.

Thus, the borrower's major interest lies in his ability to select a mortgage with a relatively stable payment-to-income ratio that can be tailored to fit his individual circumstances.

The mortgage lender's needs, however, are quite different. The major mortgage lenders—savings and loan associations and mutual savings banks—finance their long-term mortgages with relatively short-term deposits. This maturity mismatch causes serious problems for thrift institutions when short-term interest rates rise sharply, because thrifts cannot pay competitive rates for deposits due to the fact that they are locked in to long-term mortgages. (At present, Regulation Q interest rate ceilings also prevent thrifts from paying competitive rates for deposits.) Therefore, the most desirable characteristic for a mortgage instrument—from the lender's standpoint—is the ability to provide a short-term rate of return commensurate with money market instruments. Such an instrument would be equivalent to a series of rollover short-term instruments and would enable thrift institutions to compete effectively for funds through all phases of the credit cycle, assuming that Regulation Q is modified.

At first glance, the interests of borrower and lender appear to clash head-on. The borrower desires stability in the payment-to-income ratio and the lender desires short-term yield variability. The solution to this apparent dilemma lies in the nature of the mortgage itself. Interest rates are used to determine both mortgage payments and mortgage interest. However, it it not necessary that payments and interest be determined by employing the same interest rate. In fact, a wide range of mortgage instruments are possible if one interest rate is used to calculate the mortgage payment and another interest rate is used to calculate the borrower's interest obligation. In addition, other mortgage instruments are possible if the outstanding balance is allowed to increase during the early years of the loan.

The alternative mortgage instruments described in this article cover a wide range of possibilities and would provide varying degrees of benefits to borrowers and/or lenders. It must be emphasized that not all of the instruments are equally beneficial to both borrowers and lenders, nor do they all contain all of the desirable characteristics just outlined.

The Conventional Mortgage. The conventional mortgage uses the same interest rate to calculate both payments and interest owed. The primary advantage of this mortgage, from the borrower's point of view, is the fact that the monthly payment is fixed for the life of the loan. However, since family income tends to rise over time, the payment-to-income ratio falls, thereby forcing the family to devote relatively more of its income to housing in the early years of the loan. Another advantage, and a major reason for its introduction in the first place, is that the loan will be completely paid off at maturity—usually 30 years.

A major defect of the conventional level payment mortgage in an inflationary environment is that it imposes an uneven cash flow burden on the average borrower. The burden is heaviest in the early years of the loan and declines each year as inflation raises the borrower's income. This phenomenon is often referred to as the inflationary gap between what families currently can afford in monthly payments and the actual amount the market requires them to pay.

The net result is that the use of conventional mortgages in an inflationary environment reduces the demand for housing by inducing potential buyers—especially young families—to scale down their demands in terms of quantity and/or quality or to forego acquisition until their income or financial assets have risen to the point where they can afford housing.

Another defect of the conventional mortgage is the high cost imposed on a homeowner when he gives up an old, low-interest mortgage in order to buy a new house. Many families are simply unable to afford the added costs associated with such a move. Other families—for example, those transferred to another city—not only must give up the low-interest mortgage, but must finance much more expensive homes because of the general inflation of house prices.[1]

Graduated Payment Mortgages. A graduated payment mortgage also uses the same interest rate to calculate both payments and interest owed, but the monthly payments start out at a low level and gradually increase (for example, at 5 per cent a year) until they rise above the level at which a standard conventional mortgage would have been written.[2] This type of mortgage directly attacks the problem caused by the conventional mortgage when the amount of house a family can buy depends upon its current income. Thus, the graduated payment mortgage would be particularly attractive to the young family buying its first home because the income requirements to support a conventional mortgage could be reduced significantly. In effect, a graduated payment mortgage would enable a family to raise its housing standard to a level that would average out more accurately with its expected lifetime income.

The major differences between a graduated payment mortgage and a conventional mortgage are that:

1. The payments rise over time, rather than remaining fixed over the life of the loan; and

2. The payments in the early years of the loan are not sufficient to amortize the loan so that the family would, in effect, be borrowing the difference between its payments and the current interest due and paying off these amounts in later years.

A $30,000 conventional mortgage at 9 percent would require an annual income of $16,400.[3] A graduated payment mortgage—that also yielded 9 per cent to the lender—could enable a family with an income of $12,000 to afford the same mortgage. If the mortgage payments rose 5 per cent annually, 10 years would elapse

---

[1] For a more detailed discussion of the problems of the conventional mortgage instrument, see Donald Lessard and Franco Modigliani, "Inflation and the Housing Market: Problems and Potential Solutions," in Modigliani and Lessard, editors, *New Mortgage Designs for Stable Housing in an Inflationary Environment* (Boston: Federal Reserve Bank of Boston, January 1975), pp. 13–45, and William Poole, "Housing Finance Under Inflationary Conditions," in *Ways to Moderate Fluctuations in Housing Construction* (Washington: Board of Governors of the Federal Reserve System, December 1972), pp. 355–76.

[2] The rate of increase in the payments does not have to be fixed for the life of the loan—it could be adjusted to fit individual circumstances. For example, it could rise at 5 per cent annually for 10 years, remain level for 10 years, and then decline for the remaining ten. Or, to fit the needs of older borrowers who expect to retire in a few years, the payments could start out higher than for a conventional loan and then gradually decline.

[3] Assuming a 30-year mortgage at 9 per cent, with property taxes and insurance of $100 per month, where total housing expenses (principal, interest, taxes, and insurance) do not exceed 25 per cent of family income.

before the monthly payments reached the same level as a conventional mortgage for the same house. Thus, a family with an annual income of $12,000 that had good reason to expect its income to grow by at least 5 per cent a year could afford a $30,000 graduated payment mortgage, whereas it would not be able to afford a $30,000 conventional mortgage.

A major drawback of the graduated payment mortgage is that a family's income may not increase in line with the rate of increase in the payments. Another disadvantage of this mortgage is that it does not help to solve the thrift institutions' mismatch of long-term mortgages financed by short-term deposits. In fact, the lender's yield on a graduated payment mortgage would be slightly below that on a conventional mortgage in the early years because of the former's negative amortization feature.

Flexible Payment Mortgages. The Federal Home Loan Bank Board recently authorized federally chartered savings and loan associations to issue a form of graduated payment mortgage called the flexible payment mortgage. This instrument permits interest-only payments for the first 5 years (no negative amortization is allowed), at which time the payments are increased to a fully amortized basis for the remaining term.[4] For example, a $30,000 conventional 30-year mortgage at 9 per cent would require monthly payments of $242. With a flexible payment mortgage, the monthly payments would be $225 for the first 5 years and would rise to $252 in the sixth year.

As in the case of the graduated payment mortgage, an important advantage of the flexible payment mortgage is that it reduces the income required to support a given mortgage, thereby permitting a family to afford a mortgage for which it otherwise might not have qualified. As already noted, a borrower obtaining a $30,000 conventional mortgage at 9 per cent would need an annual income of $16,400. However, if the same borrower were offered a 9 per cent, 30-year flexible payment mortgage, his annual income would need to be only $15,600. If the borrower had good reason to expect his income to rise to at least $17,000 by the end of the fifth year, he would benefit from a flexible payment mortgage.

Use of a flexible payment mortgage also would permit the borrower to purchase a larger house than he could with a conventional loan. For example, if the borrower had an annual income of $16,400 and had $3,000 for a down payment, he would just qualify for a $30,000 conventional mortgage and, thus, could purchase a $33,000 home. With a flexible payment mortgage, the borrower could maintain the same ratio of payments to income and obtain a loan for $32,300. Thus, he could purchase a $35,300 home—7 per cent more than with a conventional mortgage.

Although flexible payment mortgages do offer some benefits to the borrower, they are very limited in terms of the reduced income requirements for a larger mortgage than can be afforded. This limitation is due to the restriction that prohibits negative amortization. In addition, the flexible payment mortgage fails to offer any benefits to the lender, because it is a fixed interest rate instrument that does not have any cash flow from amortization during the first five years of the loan.

Charts 1 and 2 compare conventional, graduated payment and flexible payment mortgages in terms of the monthly payments and the outstanding balance on a $30,000, 30-year mortgage at 9 per cent. It must be noted that the graduated payment mortgage involves negative amortization in the early years of the loan.

---

[4] See Henry J. Cassidy and Josephine M. McElhone, "The Flexible Payment Mortgage," *FHLBB Journal*, August 1974, pp. 7–11. See also, Maurice D. Weinrobe, "Whatever Happened to the Flexible Payment Mortgage," *FHLBB Journal*, December 1975, pp. 16–21.

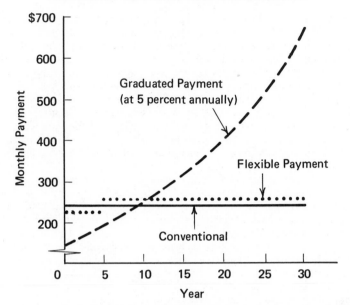

CHART 1.   Monthly payments on $30,000, 30-year mortgages at 9 per cent interest.

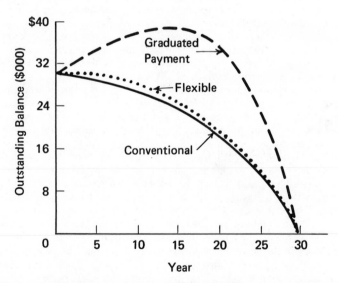

CHART 2.   Outstanding balance on $30,000, 30-year mortgages at 9 per cent interest.

Thus, sale of the home could require the borrower to repay the lender more than the original amount of the loan. This situation could present problems if the value of the property does not increase as fast as the outstanding balance of the loan.

The Variable Rate Mortgage. The standard variable rate mortgage also uses the same interest rate to calculate both mortgage payments and interest owed. However, the interest rate is tied to some reference rate that fluctuates over the life of the contract. Changes in the interest rate may be affected by any one of three methods. First, it could be a variable payment loan, wherein maturity is fixed and changes in interest rate are reflected in the monthly payment. Second, it could be a variable maturity loan, under which the monthly payment would be fixed, but the maturity would be adjusted to reflect changing interest rates. Third, changes could be made in both the maturity and the payment in order to minimize the variability in the payment-to-income ratio. All of these methods would tie the interest rate to a reference index that would be some market interest rate.[5]

Variable payment mortgages have recently gained prominence in California with seven State-chartered savings and loan associations and two commercial banks presently offering the instrument. Restrictions may be placed on both the frequency and magnitude in changes in the index. In the case of California, State-chartered savings and loan associations are required by law to implement index changes no more frequently than semiannually, use the weighted average cost of funds to savings and loan associations in California, and implement changes only if the index moves at least 10, but not more than 25, basis points. Decreases are mandatory, but increases are optional. Finally, there is an absolute ceiling of 250 basis points over the original contract rate.[6]

A significant advantage of variable rate mortgages is that changes in interest rates are reflected in changes in all outstanding variable rate loans, so that the burden of interest rate shifts is not entirely borne by new borrowers. Thus, variable rate mortgages should eventually result in lower average rates for new loans because lenders will not be forced to charge new borrowers high interest rates so that, in effect, they subsidize borrowers who have below market loans. Several California lenders also have provided that variable rate mortgages may be assumed by new buyers so that the seller is guaranteed that financing is available if the prospective buyer meets the lender's credit standards.

In addition, several California lenders have provided an open-end line of credit on variable rate mortgages by which additional funds may be advanced to the borrower—at the mortgage rate—for any purpose. Thus, the mortgage can be used to borrow on the equity for such purposes as vacations, home modernization, college financing, etc.

The principal problem with the variable payment mortgage is that, while it meets the lender's needs, it fails to provide the borrower with a stable payment-to-income ratio. This problem can be reduced by limiting the amount of change in any given period or by using a less volatile reference index. For example, the cost-of-funds index used in California is relatively stable in the short run. However, use of a stable index fails to provide the mortgage lender with the short-term yield volatility needed to compete for short-term funds.

The Dual-Rate Variable Rate Mortgage. The dual-rate variable rate mortgage attempts to provide the borrower with a relatively stable payment-to-income ratio while simultaneously providing the lender with a short-term yield by using

---

[5] Another form of a variable rate mortgage is a renegotiated loan, under which the maturity is fixed, but the interest rate and the monthly payment are renegotiated periodically, say every 5 years. This type of loan is often referred to as the Canadian roll-over loan. See Donald R. Lessard, "Roll-over Mortgages in Canada," Modigliani and Lessard, editors, *New Mortgage Designs for Stable Housing in an Inflationary Environment* (Boston: Federal Reserve Bank of Boston, January 1975), pp. 131–41.

[6] For a discussion of the California experience, see Mark J. Riedy, "VRM's in California: The Early Experience," *FHLBB Journal,* March 1976, pp. 14–16.

two distinct rates—one to compute interest on the outstanding balance and one to compute the monthly payment.

With this instrument, a short-term interest rate would be used to compute interest on the outstanding balance, but a long-term interest rate would be used to compute the monthly payment. In effect, the dual-rate VRM would enable the lending institution to earn a rate adequate to keep its deposit rate competitive with other short-term market instruments, while simultaneously providing the borrower with a relatively smooth path of monthly payments. Thus, the dual-rate VRM would be more beneficial to both borrowers and lenders than the standard variable rate mortgage, especially the version now used in California.[7]

Charts 3 and 4 compare the monthly payments and outstanding balance for a $30,000 mortgage issued in 1960 for a conventional loan at 6 per cent, a standard variable rate mortgage using the 1-year U. S. Treasury bill rate as the reference index and a dual-rate variable rate mortgage using the 1-year U. S. Treasury bill rate as the rate to determine the interest owed, and the 3- to 5-year U. S. Treasury bond rate to calculate the payment.

As shown in Chart 3, the dual-rate VRM produces a more stable path of payments than does the standard variable rate mortgage.

Graduated Payment Variable Rate Mortgage. This instrument combines the features of the graduated payment mortgage that are beneficial to the borrower with the features of the standard variable rate mortgage that are beneficial to the lender, so that the result is an instrument that provides significant benefits to both borrowers and lenders.

The graduated payment VRM would enable the borrower to select an initial payment (and, thus, an initial payment-to-income ratio) and also the rate at which the payments would increase (or decrease) over time. The lender would calculate the amount of interest owed by using a reference index, such as the interest rate on 1-year U. S. Treasury bills.

Charts 5 and 6 illustrate how a graduated payment variable rate mortgage issued in 1960 would have compared with the dual-rate VRM described above. The graduated VRM provides the borrower with the advantages of a low start payment and certainty about the future payments. However, the payments do reach a relatively high level after the 10th year. This type of mortgage might be very attractive to the young family buying its first home—particularly if the buyer did not expect to live in it more than 10 years.

The dual VRM does have a low start feature and involves more uncertainty about the path of payments, but the payments do not rise to abnormally high levels. This type of instrument might be very attractive to somewhat older families that were not overly concerned with relatively modest changes in mortgage payments—particularly if it expected to live in the house for a long time.

The essential point is that different families have different needs and expectations and should be able to select mortgage instruments that fit their particular circumstances, rather than have to use any one instrument.

Reverse Annuity Mortgages. Senior citizen homeowners often face the reverse problem of young families in that their incomes are relatively low and that, although they may own their homes free and clear, they must move in order to utilize their equities. Under a reverse annuity mortgage, the lender would pay the borrower a fixed annuity, based on a percentage of the value of the property. The annuitant would not be required to repay the loan until his demise, at which time the loan would be paid through probate. In effect, a reverse annuity mort-

[7] For a more complete discussion of the dual-rate VRM, see Richard A. Cohn and Stanley Fischer, "Alternative Mortgage Design," in Modigliani and Lessard, editors, *New Mortgage Designs for Stable Housing in an Inflationary Environment* (Boston: Federal Reserve Bank of Boston, January 1975), pp. 47–74.

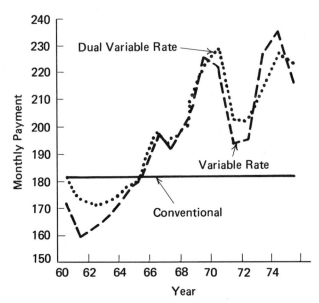

CHART 3.   Monthly payments on $30,000, 30-year mortgages.

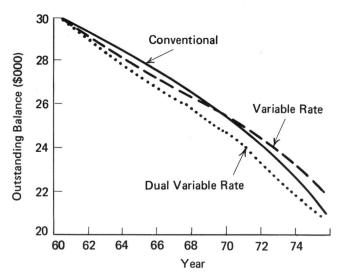

CHART 4.   Outstanding balance on $30,000, 30-year mortgages.

gage would enable a retired couple to draw on the equity of their home by increasing their loan balance each month. No cash payment of interest would be involved, as the increase in the loan balance each month would represent the cash advanced, plus interest on the outstanding balance.

For example, assume a retired couple had a $37,500 house and wanted additional money to supplement retirement income. With a reverse annuity mortgage, the mortgage lender could make monthly payments of $167 to the couple for 10

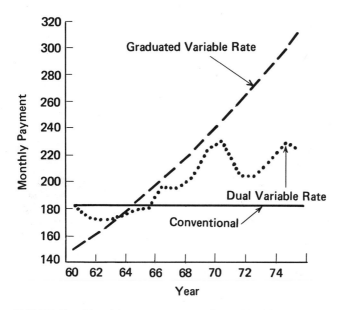

CHART 5.   Monthly payments of $30,000, 30-year mortgages.

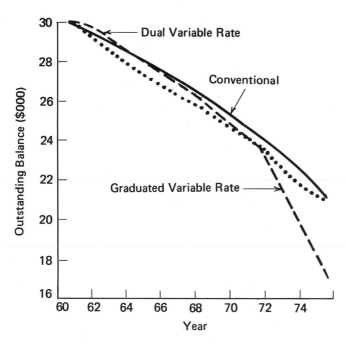

CHART 6.   Outstanding balance on $30,000, 30-year mortgages.

years. At the end of 10 years, the couple would have been advanced $20,040 and would owe the lender a total of $29,960.[8] In effect, the couple would be able to live in their home while simultaneously drawing down their equity in it. The interest owed to the lender would represent rent of $83 per month for the 10-year period; i.e., $9,920 divided by 120 months.

would be used to pay the lender for the money extended. If the couple lived be-

If the annuitants die before maturity of the annuity, the proceeds of the estate yond the 10-year period, they could sell their home and move to other living quarters. If they wished to remain in the house, and if the house had appreciated in value, a new reverse annuity could be issued, based on the current market value of the house. Finally, the couple could enter into a sale–leaseback arrangement with the lender so that they could continue to live in the home for the rest of their lives. In this case, the lender could let the couple live in the house for a nominal lease (equal to the taxes) and take the risk that the house will appreciate in value.

The Deferred Interest Loan. With a deferred interest mortgage, the borrower would receive a significantly lower initial interest rate and, thus, lower initial mortgage payments. In return, the lender would receive the deferred interest plus a fee upon resale of the house. In the event the house is not sold within 5 years, the mortgage could be refinanced as a conventional loan, with the deferred interest and the fee coming from the borrower's equity in the home.

Such a mortgage instrument might be very attractive to families that did not expect to live in a house for more than 5 years because it would offer them a choice between two different payments for the same house, or a choice between two different houses, each with the same initial monthly payments.

For example, if a prospective borrower wished to purchase a $33,000 house with a $30,000 mortgage, a conventional loan at 9 per cent interest for 30 years would require monthly payments of $242. With a deferred interest loan at 7 per cent for the first 5 years, the monthly payments would be $200. Assuming that the fee was three points on the value of the mortgage ($900) and that the home was sold at the end of the fifth year, the borrower would pay the lender the deferred interest ($3,000) plus the $900 out of his equity in the home.

The deferred interest loan would also enable the borrower to choose a more expensive home rather than reduce his monthly payments. Instead of purchasing the $33,000 home with a conventional mortgage, assume that the borrower chooses to purchase a $39,300 home with a $36,300 deferred interest loan at 7 per cent. Again, assume that the house is sold at the end of the fifth year. The borrower would owe the lender $4,800 ($3,700 is deferred interest, plus a $1,100 fee) out of his equity in the home. Assuming that the value of both houses rose 5 per cent annually, the borrower's net equity would be only $3,002 less with the more expensive home than with the $33,000 home financed conventionally and sold at the same time—but the borrower would have had the benefit of living in the better home for 5 years at a cost of only $50 per month; i.e., $3,002 divided by 60 months.

Table 1 illustrates how a deferred interest loan would compare with a conventional loan and provide the borrower with a choice between two different payments for the same house, or a choice between two different houses, each at the same initial payment. Both examples assume that the borrower chooses to remain in the house for the full 30-year term and, thus, the deferred interest loan is converted to a conventional loan at the end of the fifth year. In the event that the

[8] Assuming a fixed interest rate of 9 per cent. This type of loan could be either on a fixed or variable interest rate basis.

TABLE 1.   Comparison of a Conventional and a Deferred Interest Loan

Item	Choice No. 1—Two Ways to Finance a $33,000 House With Different Initial Payments		Choice No. 2—Two Different Houses With the Same Initial Payment	
	Conventional	Deferred Interest	Conventional	Deferred Interest
Original price	$33,000	$33,000	$33,000	$39,300
Down payment	3,000	3,000	3,000	3,000
Loan amount	30,000	30,000	30,000	36,300
Interest rate	9%	7%	9%	7%
Monthly payment	$242	$200	$242	$242
Annual income required	$16,400	$14,400	$16,400	$16,400
Refinance at end of 5 years:				
Appreciated value after 5 years (assuming 5 per cent annual increase)		$42,117		$50,158
Outstanding balance		28,230		28,230
Equity		13,887		21,928
Deferred interest due		3,000		3,700
Loan fee		900		1,100
Net equity		9,987		17,128
New loan amount		32,130		33,030
Term (years)		30		30
Interest rate		9%		9%
Monthly payment		$258		$266
Annual income required		17,185		17,600
Required increase in income per year		3.6%		1.4%
Sell house at end of 5 years:				
Appreciated value	$42,117	$42,117	$42,117	$50,158
Capital gain	9,117	9,117	9,117	10,858
Broker's fee (6 per cent)	2,527	2,527	2,527	3,010
Deferred interest due		3,000		3,700
Loan fee		900		1,100
Net capital gain	6,590	2,690	6,590	3,048
Amortization	1,230	1,770	1,230	1,770
Net equity	7,820	4,460	7,820	4,818

house is sold before the fifth year, the deferred interest loan would simply be repaid.

A different version of the deferred interest loan is the contingent appreciation participation (CAP)[9] mortgage that also would provide the borrower with a significantly lower initial interest rate. In return, the lender would be permitted to share in the appreciated value of single-family homes.

In contrast to the deferred interest loan, where the deferred interest plus the fee would be independent of any appreciation in the value of the house, the CAP

[9] See Bernard N. Freedman, "Contingent Participation Mortgages on Single Family Homes," in *Ways to Moderate Fluctuations in Housing Construction* (Washington: Board of Governors of the Federal Reserve System, December 1972), pp. 160–176.

mortgage would provide that the lender share in any capital appreciation according to some specified formula. For example, if the basic CAP factor were fixed at one-fifth and the lender provided a mortgage equal to 90 per cent of the value of the property, the lender's eventual share in any net gain realized on resale would equal one-fifth of 90 per cent, or 18 per cent.

The basic mechanics of the CAP loan are summarized in Table 2. In this case, a $33,000 home is financed with a $30,000 CAP loan and sold after 5 years with an average rate of appreciation in the value of the house of 5 per cent. At the time of sale, the borrower would pay the lender 18 per cent of his capital gain, or $1,641. In return, the borrower would have received a CAP loan with an 8-per cent interest rate, instead of a conventional loan at 9 per cent. Thus, the borrower's monthly payments would have been $220, instead of $242.

TABLE 2. Comparison of a Conventional and a Contingent
Appreciation Participation Mortgage

Item	Conventional	Contingent-Participation
Original sales price	$33,000	$33,000
Down payment	3,000	3,000
Loan amount	30,000	30,000
Term (years)	30	30
Interest rate	9%	8%
Monthly payment	$242	$220
Annual income required	$16,400	$15,400
House sold after 5 years:		
Appreciated value (assuming 5 per cent appreciation)	$42,117	$42,117
Capital gain	9,117	9,117
Broker's fee (6 per cent)	2,527	2,527
CAP fee (18 per cent of $9,117)		1,641
Net capital gain	6,590	4,949
Amortization	1,230	1,470
Net equity	7,820	6,419

A major advantage of the CAP loan is its flexibility because the borrower could obtain an even lower interest, say 7 per cent, if he were willing to provide the lender with a larger proportion of his eventual capital appreciation.

Additional Mortgage Contract Features. In addition to providing for financing of the house, any new mortgage contract should also contain a number of additional features specifically designed to aid the borrower. These features should include:

1. Using the equity in the house as collateral for additional credit. Given the fact that much of the wealth of American families is tied up in their homes, the mortgage loan should be used to extend additional credit at the current mortgage interest rate. As previously noted, the mortgage would function as an open line of credit and provide funds for a new automobile, college education, a vacation, etc.

2. A skip payment provision in the event the borrower loses his job or becomes disabled.

3. A provision that any form of variable rate mortgage can be assumed by a new borrower. In effect, the due on sale clause that provides that the loan is due and payable upon resale could be eliminated from mortgage contracts.

Summing up, the conventional fixed-rate level payment mortgage should be supplemented with new mortgage contracts that can be tailor-made to fit the needs and expectations of individual borrowers. No one or two or three mortgage instruments can possibly meet all of the diverse needs of individual borrowers and simultaneously meet the needs of mortgage lenders. The mortgage and housing markets of the United States would be best served if borrowers were free to choose from a whole smorgasbord of mortgage instruments.

Questions

1. What are the major defects of the conventional mortgage under current conditions?
2. Which types of mortgages should a borrower be able to choose?
3. List the major differences between the conventional and the graduated payment mortgage.
4. What is meant by a dual-rate variable rate mortgage?
5. Explain reverse annuity mortgages.

16

FINANCING: INSTITUTIONS AND AGENCIES*

TYPES OF INSTITUTIONS

In the preceding chapter we considered some of the more widely used methods and instruments of real estate finance. We turn now to a review of the principal institutions and agencies operating in this field: savings and loan associations, commercial and mutual savings banks, and life insurance companies. We also consider briefly individual lenders; mortgage bankers, brokers, and companies; pension funds; real estate investment trusts; and other sources of funds for real estate projects and programs.

Stock or Mutual Institutions

The principal institutions engaged in real estate finance are organized either on a stock or on a mutual basis. Thus there are stock and mutual life insurace companies, mutual and stock savings and loan associations, and mutual savings banks; commercial banks typically are organized as stock companies. Virtually all of the institutions in this field are organized as corporations, but in the case of mutuals ownership rests with members—that is, policyholders in the case of mutual life insurance companies, members in the case of mutual savings and loan associations, credit unions, and mutual savings banks.

Federal or State Charter

Regardless of how they are organized, financial institutions typically must secure special federal or state charters in order to do business. Thus, they are granted a preferential position. This is not true, of course, of

* The authors thank Kenneth J. Thygerson, Chief Economist of the U. S. League of Savings Associations, and Leon Kendall, President, Mortgage Guarantee Insurance Corporation, for reviewing this chapter.

individual investors and certain mortgage and investment companies that are also real estate lenders.

Public and Quasi-Public Agencies

Financial institutions are influenced in their decisions and programs by public and quasi-public agencies and policies to a greater extent than most other business organizations. Thus financial institutions in the real estate field are influenced by Federal Reserve and Treasury monetary and fiscal policies just as are all financial institutions. In addition, there are a number of agencies that affect real estate financing programs rather directly, particularly in the housing field. These include the Federal Home Loan Bank System and its subsidiary The Federal Home Loan Mortgage Corporation; the Veterans' Administration; and the Department of Housing and Urban Development, which includes the Federal Housing Administration, the Government National Mortgage Association, and others. The Federal National Mortgage Association operates on a quasi-private basis. Also, the Federal Land Banks, the Farmers Home Administration, and several other agencies are important in the financing of farms and rural housing.

Savings and Loan Associations

Savings and loan associations, referred to in various parts of the country as homestead associations, building and loan associations, savings associations, and cooperative banks, are one of the most important sources of funds for real estate financing, especially in the field of housing and home ownership. These institutions typically make well over half of the nonfarm home mortgages and hold about the same proportion of the total mortgage debt on one- to four-family nonfarm homes. They also engage in construction financing and make modernization and repair loans.

These institutions specialize in residential mortgage financing. Most of their loans are made on the security of single-family houses, although they also finance multi-unit residential structures both for rental and ownership under condominium arrangements, and, to a more limited extent, smaller commercial, industrial, and institutional properties. They have authority to invest to a certain extent in the obligations of municipalities and to make loans to finance college education. Besides mortgages, their investments typically are limited to United States government bonds and home improvement loans. In some cases they may own and develop subdivisions. They may also finance mobile homes and vacation homes as well as certain types of home equipment. Some state-chartered institutions may make consumer loans.

Savings and Loan Development

Originally patterned somewhat after the building societies of England, the early organizations of this type started as small mutual benefit societies, typically being dissolved whenever all members had acquired homes. This terminating arrangement was supplemented gradually by other plans, until today there is no necessary relationship between the members of the associations who save and those who borrow. In terms of actual operating procedures, however, savings and loan associations now more nearly resemble mutual savings banks than the old mutual benefit societies from which they developed. Some states provide for stock or guaranteed stock types of organization, as well as mutuals. Federal charters for stock associations were granted on a limited basis.

The growth of savings and loan associations was encouraged considerably by the establishment of the Federal Home Loan Bank System in 1932 and the system of federally chartered institutions in the following year. In addition, the establishment of the Federal Savings and Loan Insurance Corporation, with the insurance of savings accounts, was of major importance to the growth of these associations. Their growth has been rapid, total assets rising from $8.7 billion in 1945 to around $400 billion in 1977.[1] There are around 5,000 savings and loan associations in operation. Of these, about two-fifths have federal charters; the remainder have state charters. However, the federally chartered institutions hold more than half of total assets. Most savings and loan associations qualify for insurance of savers' accounts through the facilities of the Federal Savings and Loan Insurance Corporation.

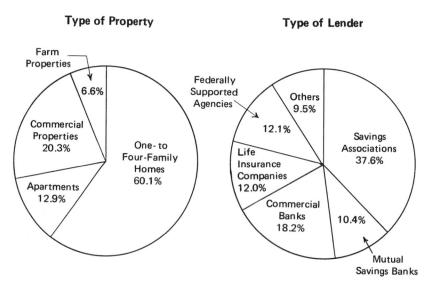

FIG. 16–1. Total mortgage loans outstanding, year-end 1975. (*Source:* Federal Reserve Board.)

[1] For detailed information, see *Savings and Loan Fact Book* (annual) (Chicago: U. S. League of Savings Associations).

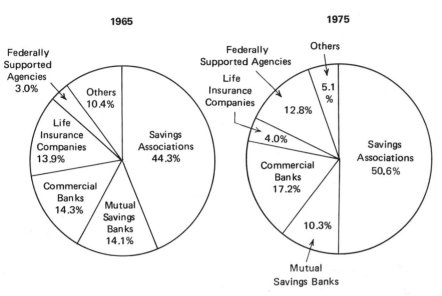

FIG. 16–2. Mortgage loans outstanding on one- to four-family nonfarm homes, by type of lender, year-end 1965 and 1975. (*Source:* Federal Home Loan Bank Board; Federal Reserve Board.)

Savings and loan associations generally emphasize local areas in their lending operations. They were early pioneers in the development of the amortized mortgage. They may buy mortgages originated in other areas or sell local mortgages to lenders elsewhere. These associations, however, pride themselves on being local thrift and home-financing institutions. Many of them have attained large size, with a number in the multibillion-dollar category. The general trend is toward a smaller number of associations of larger than current average size.

In most states branch operations are authorized. Generally these are states in which banks also have authority to establish branches. A few associations operate over entire regions, such as Farm and Home Savings and Loan Association of Nevada, Missouri, with branches in Texas and the Pacific First Federal of Tacoma, Washington, with branches throughout Washington and Oregon. In addition, some savings and loan holding companies operate across state lines.

Mutual Savings Banks

Although savings and loan associations have developed throughout the country, mutual savings banks have been concentrated largely in the New England and Middle Atlantic states. These banks are especially important in Massachusetts, New York, and Connecticut, with more than one-third of all mutual savings banks in the country being in Massachusetts.

They are also important in a few widely scattered cities such as Philadelphia, Minneapolis, and Seattle. Most of these banks are old and firmly established institutions with a long record of experience in real estate investments covering, in some cases, more than a century. Real estate investments ordinarily represent a considerable proportion of their total assets. Mutual savings banks, with their emphasis on thrift, have been well adapted to the requirements of real estate financing, since time deposits represent a large proportion of their total deposits. These institutions hold about 13 per cent of the total mortgage debt on one- to four-family nonfarm homes.

Commercial Banks

Commercial banks have always been an important source of funds for real estate financing. Banks have always been regulated rather closely in regard to mortgage lending, the principal limitations being on the ratio of the loan to the appraised value of the property and/or the term of the loan.

National banks may lend on housing on fairly liberal terms. However, if the mortgages are guaranteed by the Veterans' Administration or insured by the FHA, or by private mortgage insurors, other restrictions do not apply.

State banks are also regulated with respect to their mortgage practices. As a practical matter, state laws do not vary so widely with respect to mortgage practices as was once the case. The activities of the federal government have tended to iron out many variations.

Mortgage lending, however, is relatively less important for commercial banks than for some of the other types of lending institutions. Typically, the mortgage lending activities of a bank are carried on by its mortgage loan department. The size and complexity of such a department varies with the volume of business.

The importance of commercial banks in real estate financing is greater than would be indicated by their direct mortgage investments. They play a significant role in the short-term financing of building operations, where permanent financing is often assumed by some other type of lending institution upon completion of construction. Commercial banks also extend credit to other financial institutions, which then supply long-term real estate credit. Thus, commercial banks in such instances finance the mortgage inventories of other institutions. In some cases they engage in "warehousing" operations, holding mortgages for short terms under agreements with other lenders to repurchase them. Also, many banks acquire mortgages on real estate security in the exercise of trust functions; these loans do not appear on the banks' records of assets. Trust funds are sometimes invested in junior mortgages. In terms of direct investments, the real estate mortgage portfolios of commercial banks have tended to increase. Also, bank holding companies often own mortgage banking or brokerage companies.

Life Insurance Companies

Life insurance companies are one of the important sources of real estate mortgage credit. While some life insurance companies prefer to finance larger projects, the operations of some of them have been extended into the field of small-property financing as well.[2]

In general, insurance companies have been attracted to larger real estate projects, in some cases taking "a piece of the action," in others limiting their financing to mortgages. Often their loans are made through local mortgage brokers or correspondents who act as their representatives. In some cases the insurance companies make loans through their own representatives who are direct employees of the companies which they represent. Many insurance companies buy mortgages, leaving the servicing to be done by local brokers or originators of mortgages who receive a commission for this work.

Mortgage Banking

Mortgage brokers and mortgage companies perform mortgage banking functions, financing a variety of activities. Typically they channel funds from large institutional investors to owners and users of properties.

A mortgage company typically is organized as a closely held, private corporation. It originates and services residential mortgage loans for institutional investors. It has a comparatively small capital investment relative to its volume of business. Commercial bank credit is used extensively to finance operations and mortgage inventory. Mortgages are usually held only for short periods of time between closing mortgage loans and their delivery to ultimate investors.

Mortgage brokers often represent an insurance company or other financial institution. Mortgage companies may deal with a number of institutions and agencies. Many are owned by bank holding companies. Usually these organizations place funds of lenders or originate mortgages and sell them, retaining a servicing fee. Servicing includes collecting interest and principal payments and often the disbursement of funds for taxes and insurance on the mortgaged properties.

In some cases, mortgage companies deal in second mortgages and other junior liens, often originating such loans and selling them to private investors.

Mortgage companies have helped to channel funds between short- and long-term capital markets and have facilitated the movement of funds be-

---

[2] For detailed information about the lending activities of life insurance companies, see *Life Insurance Fact Book* (annual) (New York: Institute of Life Insurance). See also Phillip E. Kidd, *Mortgage Banking 1963–72: A Financial Intermediary in Transition,* unpublished doctoral dissertation, American University, 1976.

tween primary and secondary mortgage markets. In some ways their operations resemble those of bond dealers.

SPECIAL SOURCES OF FUNDS

Among the various sources of funds for real estate financing are pension funds, real estate investment corporations, syndicates, real estate investment trusts, individuals, and others. We will consider each of these briefly.

Pension Funds

In recent years various pension funds have become a source of support for the financing of real estate projects. Usually such funds are administered under a trust arrangement. Their principal purpose is to finance retirement programs for participants. Such trusts may be administered by an official of the company or union under which the program is operated. In some cases, funds of this type are administered by insurance companies under appropriate annuity contracts. In such cases, of course, the funds are invested by the insurance companies. Often commercial banks administer pension funds for the companies involved.

While the bulk of the investments of pension funds has tended to center in government and corporate bonds, mortgage investments have been growing in importance. Usually mortgages are purchased that have been originated by banks, mortgage companies, and other lenders. Mortgage investments of pension funds have tended to be concentrated in FHA insured and VA guaranteed loans. Pension funds have invested in mortgages through mortgage-backed securities, for example, FHLMC-guaranteed participating certificates.

Real Estate Investment Corporations and Syndicates

Real estate investment corporations are well known among the intermediaries that have developed to allow investors to channel funds into the real estate market. The real estate investment corporation and the syndicate are fairly widely used. The real estate investment corporation may be a builder and developer or may be a corporation that has a special interest in the real estate field and offers its securities to the public for purchase.

Syndicates are limited partnerships in which the principal participants are usually the general partners and have unlimited liability, but provision is made for limited partners who may receive and share proportionately in profits but have no voice in day-to-day operations. Their liability is limited to their investment.

Real Estate Investment Trusts

Real estate investment trusts have a long history, having been started more than 100 years ago in Massachusetts. The development occurred because Massachusetts law did not allow corporations to hold real estate for investment purposes, but trusts were permitted to make such investments. The early trusts were closely held but subsequently offered shares of beneficial interest to the public. They expanded beyond the New England area and prospered until a Supreme Court decision in 1935 determined that they should be taxed as regular corporations, thus removing an earlier tax advantage. Federal regulations subsequently gave real estate investment trusts an advantage equal to that of the regular investment company or mutual fund. The development of rules and regulations provided that the trusts should comply with detailed regulation by the Treasury Department and they became in essence closed-end investment trusts with major investments in real estate and mortgages.

To qualify for preferred tax treatment, the real estate investment trusts must: (1) pay out 90 per cent of their net income to shareholders; (2) have at least 100 shareholders; (3) permit no more than 50 per cent (in value) of their outstanding stock to be owned by or for five or fewer individuals (they should not be merchants of real estate); (4) 75 per cent of gross income must come from real property interests. Many real estate investment trusts with heavy investments in construction loans and mortgages suffered losses in the recession of 1973–75. Equity trusts typically had a better experience.[3]

Credit Unions

Credit unions may be chartered either by the various states or by the federal government. Federal credit unions were authorized to make home mortgage loans in 1977.[4] Such loans may be made on principal residences for terms up to 30 years. Some state-chartered credit unions may also make home mortgage loans. Provisions vary widely from state to state.

Individuals

The lending practices of private individuals vary so widely that only the most general statements can be made about them. Often private individuals take greater risks than could be accepted by lending institutions. Sometimes noneconomic considerations govern the actions of private individuals, as in the case of a father who sells his son a house and takes back a mortgage on generous terms. Regardless of their methods, or the motives

---

[3] See John McMahan, *Property Development* (New York: McGraw-Hill Book Co., 1976).

[4] See Public Law 95–22.

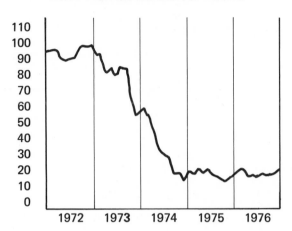

Source: All REITs traded on the New York Stock Exchange, American Stock Exchange, and the national o-t-c market. For July, 1976, 160 REITs were included.

Explanatory Note: The index is calculated in the same way as most published indexes, with appropriate adjustments being made as new trusts are added or existing trusts are deleted or suspended.

The addition of large numbers of new stocks to any stock price index adds a significant amount of inertia to the index which may lead to incorrect interpretations of the movements of the index. In order to minimize this problem for the NAREIT index, January, 1972, was selected as the initial date of the index instead of an earlier date.

FIG. 16–3. NAREIT stock price index (January, 1976 = 100). (*Source: REIT Fact Book, 1976, p. 37.*)

behind their actions, private individuals are an important source of funds for real estate financing. This is especially true of junior financing arrangements, particularly in the residential field.

Non-Financial Institutions

Foundations, colleges, universities, and other non-financial institutions often invest in real estate mortgages. Some institutions of this type have invested large amounts of money in this manner. In addition, cooperative societies and cooperative credit unions have some importance in this field.

State and Local Governments

State and local governments have not occupied a place of major importance in the provision of funds for real estate financing in this country until recently. Several states have made special provisions for home loans for veterans or other special groups. Provision has been made for local public housing authorities, redevelopment activities, and similar arrangements by state and local governments. Loans and subsidies of various types are made to local authorities by federal agencies for various purposes such as redevelopment, slum clearance, and public housing programs.

Various state housing agencies have been set up. Usually these are sub-sidized by the federal government through permission to issue tax-exempt securities. The proceeds can then be used for housing purposes.

THE FEDERAL GOVERNMENT AND REAL ESTATE FINANCE

In some degree, the federal government has had an interest in real estate finance from the time of its establishment. Early programs for the disposition of the public domain included many financing problems. The Homestead Act included financial features. Other programs might be cited as well.

The enactment of the Federal Farm Loan Act in 1916 marked the beginning of the government's present activities in the financing of farms. Although the United States Housing Corporation operated during World War I, it was subsequently liquidated; present federal programs in the housing field date largely from the early 1930's. World War II, the Korean War, the war in Indo-China, and extensive defense programs have all influenced federal programs in the housing field.

It is not our intention to review all of the federal activities in housing and related areas, but rather to concentrate on those that have a primary bearing on real estate finance.[5]

General Monetary and Credit Policies

Financial institutions and other lenders in the real estate field are in-fluenced greatly by general money market conditions and by Federal Reserve policies. The Federal Reserve may influence the availability of funds by pur-suing policies designed to produce varying degrees of easy or tight money market conditions. The impact of such policies often is uneven as between different money markets and financial institutions.[6] Mortgage interest rates typically respond rather slowly to general money market changes. Insured and guaranteed loans typically have carried fixed interest rates, thus neces-sitating the use of discounts or premiums to adjust to market changes. Usury laws present special problems in many states. Therefore, when yields on government and corporate bonds rise, there is a tendency for

---

[5] We do not cover, for example, the activities of the PWA Housing Division, the Resettlement Administration, various activities of the WPA, TVA, and the U. S. Hous-ing Authority. Also, we do not include discussions of war housing programs or those of the National Housing Agency, the RFC, or the RFC Mortgage Company. And although the history of the HOLC (Home Owners' Loan Corporation) is highly interest-ing and was a most successful operation of the Federal Home Loan Bank Board, it is more of historical than current interest and will not be included here. See Study Project 16–1.

[6] See Arthur Burns's statement which appears as a study project at the end of this chapter. See also Edward E. Edwards and Arthur M. Weimer, *Cyclical Fluctuations in Residential Construction* (Bloomington, Ind.: Business and Real Estate Trends, Inc., 1967).

funds to move out of the mortgage market into such investments; when bond yields decline, funds tend to move back into the mortgage market. The mortgage market is not a good competitor for funds when interest rates are high.

Because the Treasury Department is such a large user of funds, the policies followed in borrowing either for new purposes or to refinance older bond issues, including interest rates offered, maturities of bonds, and the like, are bound to affect money markets generally and the mortgage market as well. Thus, those who lend funds to finance real estate projects attempt to anticipate changes in money markets and in Federal Reserve and related monetary policies. The impact of such changes is felt rather directly by financial institutions and through them by borrowers.

Federal Agencies

The various federal programs are coordinated by a number of agencies. We will review some of them here including the Federal Home Loan Bank System, the Veterans' Administration as it pertains to VA loans, the Department of Housing and Urban Development, including the Federal Housing Administration, the Goverment National Mortgage Association, and other agencies. We will also consider the Federal National Mortgage Association.

Federal Home Loan Bank System

The Federal Home Loan Bank Act was passed in 1932 and has had important consequences for urban real estate finance. This Act set up a system of twelve regional banks administered under a board of directors and allowed membership to various state- and federally chartered financial institutions, other than commercial banks, which engaged in long-term home financing and conformed to certain requirements. The large majority of the membership in the ensuing years was comprised of savings and loan associations. The various Federal Home Loan Banks, which in a sense serve as reserve banks in their regions for their members, may make loans directly to their member institutions but not directly to private investors. While the government subscribed to a substantial block of the stock of these banks originally, provisions were set up for the retirement of these subscriptions over a period of years through the purchase of stock by member institutions. Since 1951, the capital stock of the Federal Home Loan Banks has been owned entirely by their member institutions.

Membership in the Federal Home Loan Bank System consists primarily of savings and loan associations plus a few savings banks and a handful of insurance companies. Of the savings and loan association members there is an almost equal division between federally chartered and state-chartered institutions.

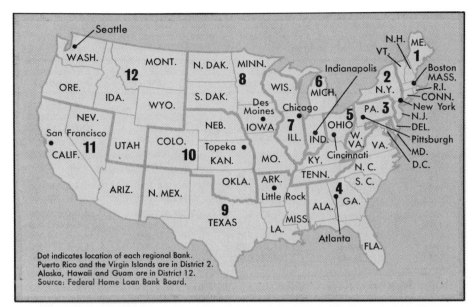

FIG 16-4. Federal Home Loan Bank Districts. (*Source:* Federal Home Loan Bank Board.)

The main idea back of the establishment for the Federal Home Loan Bank system was the forming of a central pool of funds which might be used for mortgage purposes and which would tend toward the development of a national mortgage market.[7] It was patterned somewhat after the central mortgage financing institutions of Europe, such as the Swedish Town Mortgage System. The stated objectives of the system were to relieve financial strains on home owners and financial institutions during emergencies, to assist in the support of home construction, and to strengthen the institutions specializing in the financing of home ownership.

Federal Savings and Loan Associations

As a part of the Home Owner's Loan Act of 1933, provision was made for a system of Federal Savings and Loan Associations. Such associations are incorporated under federal law, being chartered by the Federal Home Loan Bank Board either as new associations or as converted state-chartered institutions. They are required to become members of the Federal Home Loan Bank System. The basic purpose of this legislation was to meet a need in many communities for more adequate home financing facilities by providing for local institutions throughout the country which would operate under a uniform plan incorporating the best operating principles

[7] See, for example, Gary L. Baxter, *Recommendations for Improving the Effectiveness of the Credit Policies of the Federal Home Loan Bank System,* Indiana University doctoral dissertation, 1975.

and practices of savings institutions specializing in home financing. These federal institutions have access to funds, in addition to those provided by their own members, by borrowing from the Federal Home Loan Bank of their region either on their own unsecured notes or on the security of mortgages or from other sources.

Federal Savings and Loan Insurance Corporation

Provision was made in 1934 for the insurance of the savings and investment accounts in saving and loan associations by Title IV of the National Housing Act. Under this legislation, savers' and investors' accounts were insured at first up to $5,000 and later up to $40,000. Membership in the Federal Savings and Loan Insurance Corporation (FSLIC) is compulsory for federally chartered institutions and is optional for state-chartered institutions. Members of the FSLIC hold over 97 per cent of the assets of the industry.

Federal Home Loan Mortgage Corporation

The Federal Home Loan Mortgage Corporation (FHLMC) was established in 1970 to serve as a secondary mortgage market facility. It operates under the direction of the Federal Home Loan Bank Board. The FHLMC (often referred to as "Freddie Mac" or "the Mortgage Corporation") provides for a secondary market for conventional mortgages, including both conventional whole mortgage loans and participations in conventional loans, as well as FHA and VA loans. The FHLMC operates both as a buyer and seller of mortgages.

Veterans' Administration Loans

Under the Servicemen's Readjustment Act of 1944, the Veterans' Administration was authorized to guarantee veterans' loans secured by real property. Subsequent amendments included veterans of later service. Varying arrangements were made from time to time as to amounts and terms of the loan guarantees. A financial institution may be guaranteed against loss on loans to honorably discharged veterans up to a stated percentage of a property's value but not beyond stated amounts and terms.

Mortgage loans of this type are made by all types of financial institutions as well as by private lenders. Interest rates have been fixed at various levels.

Mortgage lenders often prefer loans guaranteed by the Veterans' Administration to those insured by the FHA because in case of default, and after all reasonable efforts to make adjustments have been exhausted, the lender may file a claim for the full amount of the guaranty to be paid in cash by the Veterans' Administration.

Experience with VA loans has been highly favorable. Sometimes interest rates are set at levels below those dictated in the competitive market and this has resulted in substantial discounts. The Government National Mortgage Association and the FNMA may help to provide a market at such times.

Department of Housing and Urban Development

In 1965 Congress authorized the establishment of the Department of Housing and Urban Development (HUD).[8] It includes the Federal Housing Administration, The Government National Mortgage Association, and various public housing and urban renewal programs.

The Housing and Home Finance Agency (HHFA) was established in 1947 for the purpose of coordinating various federal activities in the housing field. The Federal Home Loan Bank System, which was a part of this agency originally, was subsequently restored to its position as an independent agency. The HHFA and its constituent agencies became the basic elements in the Department of Housing and Urban Development.

The Federal Housing Administration

The Federal Housing Administration was set up by authority of the National Housing Act of 1934. While the original provisions of this Act have been modified by subsequent legislation, the main functions of this agency have followed a rather uniform pattern. Basically, FHA is an insurance agency of the government, insuring lending institutions against loss in the financing of mortgages and loans made in accordance with the requirements of law and the administrative regulations of the FHA. Programs of the FHA have been altered from time to time to meet changing conditions, including property improvement loan insurance, home mortgage insurance on one-to-four-family dwellings, the insurance of mortgages on rental housing projects, mobile homes, and related programs. Special arrangements have been made to facilitate the construction of housing in problem areas. Provisions have also been made for the insurance of mortgages on cooperative housing, mortgages on publicly owned housing, farm housing, and for the insurance of loans for other purposes.

The traditional role of the FHA was modified in recent years with the agency becoming responsible for various interest rate subsidy and rent supplement programs. Problems arose and a moratorium was placed on various programs. As a result, there was some reduction in all types of FHA program activities.

The Federal National Mortgage Association

In the National Housing Act of 1934 provision was made for the establishment of national mortgage associations to serve as a secondary mortgage market. Until 1938, no national mortgage associations had been estab-

---

[8] Public Law 89–174, 89th Congress, September 9, 1965 (79 Stat. 667).

lished; hence the Federal National Mortgage Association (FNMA) was set up in that year as a subsidiary of the Reconstruction Finance Corporation (RFC), with funds provided by the RFC Mortgage Company. The FNMA ("Fanny Mae") provided a market for insured mortgages and enabled institutions to sell their mortgages, retaining the servicing fee.

The FNMA was made the sole possible national mortgage association in 1948. The Housing Act of 1948 authorized the FNMA to purchase not only mortgages on one- to four-family houses insured by FHA but also FHA-insured mortgages on rental property and mortgages guaranteed by the Veterans' Administration.

In 1968 the FNMA was converted into a private corporation. Since that time it has been engaged primarily in secondary mortgage market operations. Of special importance have been its weekly auctions. These provide for weekly announcements of commitments available and approved sellers may submit bids, including price and terms. Sellers provide for servicing. FNMA has been authorized to deal in conventional as well as government insured and guaranteed mortgages. Lenders selling mortgages to this agency are required to conform to its regulations. From time to time, FNMA may sell mortgages as well as buy them. FNMA has been described as "a private corporation with a public purpose."

Government National Mortgage Association

The Housing and Urban Development Act of 1968 established the Government National Mortgage Association (usually referred to as "Ginny Mae") as a part of the Department of Housing and Urban Development to administer the various special assistance programs that had formerly been a part of FNMA's operations. Among its more important functions, GNMA issues various guarantees of securities that are backed by mortgage loans. Various management and liquidation functions are performed by GNMA as well.

GNMA is a wholly owned corporate instrumentality of the U. S. Government, operating within the Department of Housing and Urban Development. GNMA and FNMA have from time to time worked together on loan purchases under the so-called Tandem Programs. GNMA may issue a commitment to purchase a mortgage at a fixed price. After acquiring it, GNMA sells it to FNMA at the prevailing market price, absorbing any discount from the price paid to the seller.

The Tandem Plan may also involve purchases of below-market interest rate conventional mortgages by GNMA operating through FNMA or FHLMC as agents. The lower rate is passed on to the borrower. When loans are closed they are delivered to either FNMA or FHLMC with the discount absorbed by GNMA.

As has been indicated, GNMA issues guarantees of certain securities backed by mortgages. Such guarantees bear the full faith and credit of the U. S. Government. Guarantees are made as to the payment of the principal and interest on securities which are based on or backed by a pool of FHA, VA, or Farmers Home Administration mortgages.

Federal Farm Programs

Various federal programs for the provision of assistance in financing farms and farm homes and other buildings have been carried on since the enactment of the Federal Farm Loan Act of 1916. Under this Act, the federal land banks were established to provide financial assistance for farmers by means of loans made through national farm loan associations for periods of five to forty years on the basis of first mortgages on farms. The borrower is required to purchase a limited amount of stock in the Land Bank that makes the loan.

Joint stock land banks were also set up in 1916 but were discontinued in 1933. At that time, the Federal Farm Mortgage Corporation was established to administer Land Bank Commissioner loans. These were discontinued in 1947. The Farm Security Administration was set up in 1937 and subsequently was replaced by the Farmers Home Administration. Direct loans are provided through this organization to farmers for acquiring ownership and for constructing and repairing homes and other buildings but only in case financing cannot be arranged through other sources. The Farmers Home Administration also provides for the insurance of certain farm mortgages.

A program for the financing of low- and moderate-income housing in smaller cities and towns has developed rather rapidly. To qualify for a home loan it is necessary to show that credit could not be obtained from private sources. The real estate must be located in a town with a population of not more than 20,000. In addition to direct loans, a loan guarantee program for privately made loans secured by residential and also by commercial and industrial properties was established to encourage private mortgage credit to take the place of direct lending by the Farmers Home Administration.

Other Federal Programs

Federal programs have included several arrangements for the financing of public housing and urban renewal projects. Various rent supplement and below-market interest rate programs have been introduced. The National Housing Partnerships concept was designed to attract capital from a variety of sources into the housing field. It makes use of the limited partnership arrangement.

In addition a variety of grants are available for demolition projects. Rehabilitation loans and grants are provided under specified conditions. College housing loans and various loans and programs help to provide housing for senior citizens. Programs have also been introduced to help develop new towns and new planned communities through loans to developers, although the volume of activity has varied greatly.

SUMMARY

This chapter described the nature of the more important institutions and agencies operating in the field of real estate finance. Particular attention was directed to the activities of commercial and mutual savings banks, savings and loan associations, and life insurance companies. Individual lenders, mortgage bankers, brokers, and companies, real estate investment trusts, and pension funds also may be important suppliers of funds.

Financial institutions are subject to extensive regulation and control by governmental agencies. To some extent this results from the partial-monopoly nature of financial institutions which must obtain special permission in order to operate. Much governmental influence is indirect, resulting from the effect of Federal Reserve and Treasury policies on the supply of funds and the level of interest rates.

Government activity in the housing field has led to the establishment of a number of agencies, all of which influence or regulate private real estate decisions to some extent. These agencies include the Federal Home Loan Bank System, the Veterans' Administration, and the Department of Housing and Urban Development, with its component parts.

The programs and policies of private financial institutions and of governmental agencies are important factors in determining decisions in the real estate field. These institutions and agencies influence, among other factors, the availability of real estate credit, the desirability of alternative investments, and the methods by which real estate is financed.

QUESTIONS FOR STUDY

1. Who are the principal borrowers in the real estate mortgage market? Who are the principal lenders?
2. Describe the functions performed by mortgage brokers in the financing of real estate. How important are these functions?
3. Which financial institutions are most important in real estate finance? What reasons can you give to explain their importance?
4. Describe the purpose and primary operations of the Department of Housing and Urban Development.
5. Explain the roles played by insurance companies, savings and loan associations, mutual savings banks, and commercial banks in the financing of real estate. Do commercial banks have any particular advantages or disadvantages as compared with other institutions engaged in real estate finance? Explain.

6. Describe the Federal National Mortgage Association, the Government National Mortgage Association, and the Federal Home Loan Mortgage Corporation.
7. Which of the financial institutions involved in the real estate field are likely to enjoy most rapid growth in the next decade? Why?
8. Explain the relationship between Federal Reserve policies and the availability of mortgage funds. How is the supply of mortgage credit related to general money market conditions?
9. In what way can the operations of the Treasury Department affect the terms and availability of mortgage funds?
10. Describe the structure and organization of the Federal Home Loan Bank System. How do its activities influence the financing of real estate?
11. Do you think the federal government will play a larger or smaller role in the area of real estate finance in the years ahead? Are there likely to be marked differences between urban and rural real estate in this regard?

SUGGESTED READINGS

EDWARDS, EDWARD E., and WEIMER, ARTHUR M. *Cyclical Fluctuations in Residential Construction.* Bloomington, Ind.: Business and Real Estate Trends, Inc., 1968.

HINES, MARY ALICE. *Principles and Practices in Real Estate.* Homewood, Ill.: Richard D. Irwin, Inc., 1976. Chs. 19 and 20.

HOAGLAND, HENRY E., and STONE, LEO D. *Real Estate Finance* (5th ed.). Homewood, Ill.: Richard D. Irwin, Inc., 1974. Chs. 11–15, 23–29.

MAISEL, SHERMAN J. *Financing Real Estate: Principles and Practices.* New York: McGraw-Hill Book Co., 1965. Chs. i–v.

SMITH, HALBERT C., TSCHAPPAT, CARL J., and RACSTER, RONALD L. *Real Estate and Urban Development* (rev. ed.). Homewood, Ill.: Richard D. Irwin, Inc., 1977. Ch. 14.

UNGER, MAURICE A. *Real Estate Principles and Practices.* Cincinnati, Ohio: Southwestern Publishing Co., 1974. Chs. 15 and 16.

STUDY PROJECT 16–1

The Federal Government and Private Mortgages *

The beginning of the federal government's concern with the mortgage market lay in a period of deep economic depression. A main purpose was to create instruments that would promote, if not inflation, at least "reflation"—instruments that would help clear depression-choked markets and assist the recovery and expansion of the economy. The ensuing history is like the story of the water-carrying broom of the Sorcerer's Apprentice—once a seemingly good thing was started, there was no stopping short of disaster.

The beginning—now more than forty years ago—was beguilingly innocent. As the government ventured into the new territory of urban mortgage credit (it had

---

* From Miles L. Colean, "The Federal Government's Impact on the Private Mortgage Market," *The MGIC Newsletter* (January 1975). Reproduced by permission of Mortgage Guaranty Insurance Corporation.

already moved deeply into that of farm credit), the objective was assistance to the **private** residential mortgage market—to revive it, reform it, restore public confidence in it, and expand it. The chosen means were there, all established before 1935:

1. The Federal Home Loan Bank System and its governing Federal Home Loan Bank Board, created to revive and strengthen private thrift institutions, especially federally chartered savings and loan associations.

2. The Federal Savings and Loan Insurance Corporation, designed to give S & L accounts a protection similar to that of bank accounts through the Federal Deposit Insurance Corporation.

3. The Home Owner's Loan Corporation, strictly an emergency instrumentality, formed to rescue basically solvent home borrowers and home lenders from their current illiquidity.

4. The RFC Mortgage Company, a subsidiary of the Reconstruction Finance Corporation, having a purpose similar to the HOLC in respect to mortgages on income-producing urban property.

5. Finally, the Federal Housing Administration with a dual purpose of (a) inducing banks and other financial institutions to make unsecured loans for home repair and improvement and (b) of creating a system of mortgage insurance for residential property that would further aid reform and expansion, by diminishing risk on mortgage loans with low downpayments, extended maturities, and regular amortization.

All these institutions were expected to be ultimately self-supporting and all did repay government advances for initial set-up and operation. None of them involved actual subsidy except the FHA home repair operation, which at first required no insurance premium. Of the strictly emergency institutions, the HOLC and the RFC Mortgage Company were liquidated without loss to the government, while the FHA repair loan insurance was subsequently continued on a self-supporting basis through the institution of an insurance premium.

Thus, aside from a later and rather off-hand attention to what proved to be a costly but ineffective subsidized public housing operation, the New Deal had put its emphasis on the strengthening of private institutions and the broadening of private markets. Its monuments were the Federal Home Loan Bank System and the FHA Mortgage Insurance System, both independent establishments and both without cost to the government.

Both served the purposes for which they were designed. By the advent of World War II, private home mortgage activity had been reestablished on a sounder and broader basis than ever before. More lending institutions were participating in it than ever before, serving a wider economic and geographic range of borrowers. A steadily increasing number of new houses was being built, but under the shelter of ample mortgage credit on easy terms, the cost of new homes steadily rose.

What was good obviously might be made better. The recession of 1937 brought demands for still more credit on even more liberal terms. FHA mortgage insurance was seen to be a made-to-order means for this purpose. Downpayments on insured loans were reduced; maturities were extended; maximum mortgage amounts were increased; and, amid the now ample supply of credit, interest rates were lowered. The government-owned Federal National Mortgage Association was chartered to provide a supplemental outlet mainly for mortgages created by mortgage companies, which had become major originators of FHA insured mortgage loans. A formula for meeting curtailment of building or covering of increase in building cost had been discovered.

Post-War Years Witness Broadening Government Role. World War II brought vast changes, all to the diminution of reliance on private mortgage originators and investors. The government agencies, including the Public Housing Authority, were incongruously lumped into a National Housing Agency. Direct federal lending for new construction, which had largely been resisted and constrained in the pre-war period, was much expanded. And, most significant, a centralized decision-making by government in matters relating to the location, price, and financing of housing was firmly established as a key feature of government policy.

After WWII, the focus on privately directed private mortgage activity that had mainly characterized the New Deal was never fully restored. If there were no longer the necessity for concentrating on defense workers, then it was veterans, college students, old people, families of "low and moderate income" that must be given special treatment. (Note that before the war, it was "low" income that was stressed for special treatment. The addition of "moderate" was a response of expanding government encroachment, reacting to government induced postwar inflation.)

The war-time National Housing Agency was succeeded by a peace-time Housing and Home Finance Agency and later by a new cabinet Department of Housing and Urban Development. From this ominously increasing centralization of authority the Home Loan Bank System was rescued in 1955, thanks to the political wallop of the savings and loan groups; but the FHA, despite the persistent efforts at restoration of its former status, remained a captive and the main instrument of centralized policy.

The Housing Act of 1949 was a watershed. Focus now clearly shifted from the private market, which, not fulfilling the Utopian fantasy of new houses for every element of the population, was considered to have failed in its responsibility. The public housing operation was expanded. Special forms of mortgage insurance were invented to succor disadvantaged sectors of demand. FNMA was reorganized to more effectively support the special insurance programs, characteristically at submarket interest rates in times of restricted credit or faltering building activity.

Yet this was not enough to still the growing impatience with the operation of the private market, to fulfill the new concepts of government responsibility, and to meet the insatiable demands of the building industry.

The Act of 1968 introduced out-and-out subsidy into the FHA system in the form of partial payment by government of interest on insured loans or of rents in apartments financed with insured loans. The Government National Mortgage Association was created to assure a market for the subsidized loans and otherwise to support the special forms of FHA insurance. As the subsidized activity was more and more vigorously promoted, the original private market orientation of FHA was badly clouded and its basic self-supporting, private market activity precipitously declined until at present its continuance as an instrumentality of the private market is in doubt.

Back when the 1949 legislative tide was first clearly encroaching on the original purposes of FHA, the author of this sad tale asked one of the promulgators of the new dispensation why, with all the effort to redirect FHA activity to meet preconceived purposes, the Home Loan Bank System was left untouched. The answer was, "Give us time." Although the restored independence of the System in 1955 was a setback, the "time" has now obviously come. Earmarked advances are now available from the Federal Home Loan Banks for special classes of loans. The Federal Home Loan Mortgage Corporation, formed ostensibly to provide savings and loan associations with a duplicate of FNMA fashioned to their own purposes, was authorized to offer these institutions a source of subsidized credit. Both innovations strongly suggest that the Home Loan Bank System may at last be headed in the same direction as FHA.

Inflation One of the Primary Factors. What are the causes of this long accelerating progression away from a mortgage system organized around privately oriented and privately supported institutions? There are several. One is the delusions of the liberal mind seeking easy and appealing answers to difficult and sometimes unanswerable social questions. Another is the insistence of the home-building industry on maintaining an uninterrupted and contiually expanding supply of credit irrespective of conditions in the housing market, or the stage of an economic cycle, or the credit demands of other elements in the economy. Along with this, all too often is the complicity of mortgage institutions that welcome government relief when their own activity is curtailed or their solvency threatened by monetary restraint.

But entwined with it all is the inflation that has been the endemic postwar disease. With only slight interruptions, prices have risen throughout the postwar period until at last they have advanced beyond the ability of personal income to keep ahead. The mortgage credit formula that was effective in increasing the use of credit when credit was stagnant and industrial capacity was idle has become a dangerous contributor to inflation at a time when credit is increased faster than the ability to produce. The housing market has been overstimulated. Consequent increases in prices and interest rates have choked production. And yet, the only remedy offered is the old and inappropriate one of more credit to stimulate more building in a congested market.

An important cause of the over-expansion of credit has been the efforts of government to meet pressures on the financial market created by its own policies. The supportive agencies—the Federal Home Loan Banks, FHLMC, FNMA, and GNMA (among others)—all depending on borrowed funds, have created demands in competition with all other claimants for funds, including state and local governments, private corporations and individuals, as well as the Treasury itself.

The resulting pressures push up interest rates and draw funds from private mortgage institutions, which, mainly because of legal or regulatory barriers, are unable to meet the rate competition.

The greater the scope of the government credit programs and the time over which they are pursued, the greater will be the upward push on interest rates and prices and the less will be the ability of private credit institutions to function in their accustomed roles. Government intervention in the credit markets thus has perverse effects, which may well exceed its benefits. It tends to defeat its own purpose and to intensify the problem it seeks to cure.

Nevertheless, the predilection of government under such circumstances is to seek new and more extensive forms of intervention to compensate for those that have fallen short of the objective. Unfortunately this predilection is often shared by leaders in the private activities most to suffer from its effects. Thus the call, even on the part of private credit institutions (as well as that of builders) for interest rate subsidies, for tax exemption of interest on savings, for tax exemption for home mortgage payments, and for other costly devices to ease the burdens to which previous rescue efforts have contributed.

The Price of Government Involvement. Each step in this apparently unalterable progression deprives private institutions and private entrepreneurs of some measure of their freedom of action. Subsidy, of whatever nature, takes its toll. It has its price in the substitution of government decisions for private decisions as to where, for what, to whom, and within what other limitations loans are to be made. That has been increasingly the consequence of the long erosion of the FHA system. It will as surely be the result of the special funds and other features being offered or sought for by thrift institutions.

The shift from private to government decision-making is a disruptive affair. First, timing is likely to be bad, as witness how in the past the impact of special, low interest rate funds provided through FNMA tended to come after the excuse for them had passed. Witness now how the allocation of the special funds for mortgages has been made on the basis of what areas had previously been most active—a method sure to restimulate already congested markets and to leave little aid for those where demand may have been sluggish.

More serious, however, than the results of miscalculated government policies is the deprivation to the public of the flexibility and breadth of action possible through unhampered private institutional operations. Government programs tend to be rigid and their flexibility to decrease as the involvement of government increases. Government programs are characteristically complex and costly and frustrating to deal with, and their complexity increases as original shortcomings come to light or the almost inevitable abuses begin to develop. And the end is lower production and more inflation.

One thing is certain: as government interventions in the market expand, private institutions are weakened. As the range of government decision widens, and as the dependence on government increases, private institutions, to the extent that they can exist at all, become mere agents of government to carry out government policy. What this means in loss of the freedom of decision that the private market permits, in the scope of decision that the private market seeks, and in the simplicity of action the private market can provide has never been calculated. Perhaps it cannot be calculated. But we shall be able to measure the full extent and cost of it, if it is allowed to happen. And, if present trends persist, it is most likely to happen.

Comment

What can be done about increasing government encroachment in home mortgage markets? Our author has a constructive suggestion: fight inflation. More specifically, fight government programs that require either the Treasury or a government agency to borrow money to finance home building. That cure is strong medicine, but the argument for it is equally strong.

Hidden in the author's presentation is an altogether different approach. Let's think for a moment of his brief account of the HOLC and the RFC Mortgage Corporation. Here were two successful programs, aimed at solving a current problem rather than putting the federal government in the home mortgage business on a permanent basis. Why not look upon our present difficulties—the inability of thrift institutions to compete effectively for new savings dollars—in the same way? Why not think now in terms of an emergency program, one that will phase itself out.

The HOLC, as our author points out, was designed in part to rescue home mortgage lenders submerged in portfolios of delinquent loans—assets that at market value were worth less than par. Today our thrift institutions are again submerged in loans that, while not delinquent, are nevertheless worth less than par. If these loans could be transferred to an emergency agency, the thrift institutions might quickly recover and return home finance to the private sector.

Transferring mortgages to an agency of this type would not necessitate any raising of funds in money and capital markets. The agency could pay for the mortgages with non-marketable bonds, to be held by the thrift institution, which would continue to service the mortgages. Bond interest would be payable monthly, either at a fixed or a variable rate.

Under such a program the mortgages would be guaranteed by the thrift institution, with the agency having the right of offset against any delinquent loans. Thus no bureaucracy would be needed to appraise properties or to pass on personal credit or to do anything else other than obtain necessary appropriations to meet the difference between bond interest and interest earned on the mortgages.

Miles Colean likely would object to these appropriations as additional subsidies, which they are, but if they restore private lending they should eliminate the need for further subsidies and for further encroachment of government into home mortgage markets.

—EDWARD E. EDWARDS
Consulting Editor

Questions

1. In which principal ways has the federal government influenced the private mortgage market?
2. What has been the role of inflation in expanding the influence of government in the mortgage market?
3. Do you agree or disagree with Professor Edwards' suggestion?

STUDY PROJECT 16–2

The Mortgage Corporation *

As early as the 1950s, a need for a secondary market in conventional residential mortgages was being discussed by American thrift institutions and their organizations.

In the 1960s, this concern was translated into specific legislative proposals by the organizations and industry leaders. The proposals drew the favorable attention of Sen. John Sparkman (D–Ala.), and his housing subcommittee of the Senate Committee on Banking, Housing and Urban Affairs. And in 1970, the subcommittee's bill, S3685, resulted in the Emergency Home Financing Act of 1970. Title III of the act as amended is known as The Federal Home Loan Mortgage Corporation Act.

At first, The Mortgage Corporation was limited by the same uncertainties that had prevented the spontaneous development of a secondary market in conventional home mortgages. Mortgage documents varied from region to region and state lending and foreclosure laws differed substantially. Thus, in addition to the difficulty of finding a buyer when you wanted to sell or a seller when you wanted to buy, mortgage quality was extremely difficult to assess.

Together with the Federal National Mortgage Association and the industry, we helped to develop and win adoption of uniform loan documents.

Then we put together a computer matrix for assisting in the underwriting of the loans. Today, every mortgage being considered for purchase by The Mortgage Corporation is screened by this computer program for its adherence to the standards of Mortgage Corporation quality. The computer system "flags" anomalous or questionable loans which are then examined by a human underwriter before acceptance or rejection.

This automation of our underwriting activity enabled us to build prodigious productivity while still maintaining a quality of mortgages that has established the industry standard.

The original financing of The Mortgage Corporation was through nonvoting capital stock, issued to the 12 Federal Home Loan Banks for a total of $100 million as of December 31, 1973. We also issued nearly $1.9 billion in bonds guaranteed by GNMA and backed by FHA and VA mortgages conveyed to the Federal Home Loan Mortgage Corporation Trust. At first, as in the industry at large,

---

* Adapted from a speech, "Mortgage Corporation: A Gleam Becomes a Galvanizer," by Victor H. Indiek, President, Federal Home Loan Mortgage Corporation.

our secondary market activities were confined to such government-backed mortgages. Then we moved into buying participations in mortgages, leaving a share of each risk in the hands of the mortgage originators. In 1972, we began buying conventional whole loans.

In 1971, we introduced our Mortgage Participation Certificate and, in 1975, our Guaranteed Mortgage Certificate. We now rely almost entirely on these two instruments to fund our current activities.

Periodically, The Mortgage Corporation assembles groups of from 2,000 to 5,000 mortgages each with an original principal balance of about $100 million. Each Mortgage Participation Certificate (PC) represents an undivided interest in such a group of conventional mortgages individually underwritten and previously purchased by The Mortgage Corporation. To date, nearly $2 billion in PCs have been sold to more than 1,000 different investors. Although anyone may invest in PCs (they come in denominations ranging from $100,000 to $1 million), most of the investors in them have been thrift institutions. That's because PCs, which pass through interest and principal payments monthly from the underlying mortgages, qualify as mortgage investments for the purpose of certain tax and other regulations and laws applicable to thrift institutions.

At first, each PC group contained mortgages purchased from a single seller-servicer. So each was a small group. In 1973, we changed the system to make the groups sufficiently large that occasional mortgage prepayments would have only a minor effect on the monthly payment of principal to PC holders.

We offered those early PCs in a periodic special sales. In 1974, that system, which we concluded failed to offer PC investors sufficient access to the PC program, was changed. Now PCs are sold on each business day through The Mortgage Corporation's five regional offices in Arlington, Va., Atlanta, Chicago, Dallas, and Los Angeles.

Last year, we acted to make the PC even more flexible. We added a variety of settlment date opportunities to aid PC buyers in the management of their funds. A system of increasingly higher yields for delayed settlement programs was adopted, as were progressive front-end fees for delayed settlements. These fees range from .25 per cent for mandatory deliveries in 30–59 days to a full 1 per cent for delivery in 120–150 days at the option of The Mortgage Corporation. Current yield quotes for each program are available daily from the Mortgage Corporation's regional offices.

We also took another step last year to assist PC buyers. The Mortgage Corporation established a secondary market in PCs.

As long as a PC holder has held PCs for 60 days, we will offer to buy up to $5 million in those PCs on any one day from any one holder. The price we offer is determined by the certificate rate of the PCs, market conditions at the time, and the level of our inventory in repurchased PCs.

We think that the current unprecedented interest by the market in PCs as mortgage-related investments is due in part to our repurchase program. It provides a new liquidity in PCs that may meet a need of some investors. Since the formal repurchase program in PCs was established last June, investors have sold $36.6 million in PCs back to The Mortgage Corporation. We have resold $35.6 million of these.

The Guaranteed Mortgage Certificate (GMC) is unlike the PC in one essential way. It provides convenience usually associated only with bonds while maintaining the high yield and safety of a mortgage-related instrument. GMCs pay interest semiannually and principal annually. The final payment date of a GMC is 30 years from its date of issue, but any certificate holder may, at the holder's option, require The Mortgage Corporation to repurchase the certificate at par on a stated date prior to maturity. For the GMC issued August 1976, the certificate holders, may at their option, require The Mortgage Corporation to repurchase their certificates twenty years after issuance. The maximum average weighted life of a GMC so repurchased is 10.2 years. If the option were not exercised, the maximum average weighted life would be 10.9 years. Because of these features, GMCs do not qualify as mortgage investments for federal regulatory or tax purposes.

GMCs are sold in fully registered form in initial principal amounts of $100,000, $500,00 and $1 million. The first two issues of GMC's, totalling $500,000, were in 1975. In February 1976, $200 million in GMCs were issued at 8.55 per cent, and in August 1976, $200 million were issued at a certificate rate of 8.375 per cent. Subsequent issues are contemplated, depending upon the volume of mortgages available for sale and on market conditions.

There are times when investors other than traditional mortgage investors, desiring a monthly return on their investments, could find the PC a useful investment. Equally, there are times when even a savings and loan association, with an ample portfolio of mortgage investments, might well opt for GMC purchases. Mainly, though, we think PCs serve the industry well as a mechanism for transferring funds from areas oversupplied with mortgage money to those in need of it. GMC's, we think, perform their greatest service by attracting into the mortgage market capital-market funds that might otherwise never be available for conventional residential mortgage financing.

The Mortgage Corporation's mission of building a secondary market for conventional mortgages is likely to be a continuing challenge for many years to come. Our programs of purchasing mortgages, of selling mortgages through our PCs and GMCs, and of standing as an example to the industry are demanding upon our resources and our expertise. Still, we continue to seek innovations for the future that will bring even more liquidity to the one money market that may mean more, more directly, to more people than any other.

That's what we do best and we intend to keep on doing our best at it.

Questions

1. How was the Federal Home Loan Mortgage Corporation financed originally?
2. How does The Mortgage Corporation use the Mortgage Participation Certificate?
3. How does the Guaranteed Mortgage Certificate differ from the Mortgage Participation Certificate?
4. How does The Mortgage Corporation plan to continue to build a secondary market for conventional mortgages?

STUDY PROJECT 16–3

The Federal Reserve System *

Industrial nations, including our own, nowadays rely heavily on monetary policy to promote expansion of production and employment, to limit any decline that may occur in overall economic activity, or to blunt the forces of inflation.

There are two major reasons for the emphasis on monetary policy. In the first place, manipulation of governmental expenditures has proved to be a rather clumsy device for dealing with rapidly changing economic developments. Secondly, the process of reaching a consensus on needed tax changes usually turns out to be complex and time-consuming. Experience has thus taught us that altera-

---

* From Arthur F. Burns, "The Independence of the Federal Reserve System." Dr. Burns provided this statement for use in this text. It is based on comments on a speech.

tions of fiscal policy, once undertaken, frequently have a large part of their economic effect too late to be of much value in moderating fluctuations in business activity.

Fortunately, monetary policy is relatively free of these shortcomings. Flexibility is the great virtue of instruments of monetary and credit policy. Changes in the course of monetary policy can be made promptly and—if need be—frequently. Under our scheme of governmental organization, the Federal Reserve can make the hard decisions that might be avoided by decision makers subject to the day-to-day pressures of political life.

The founders of the Federal Reserve System were well aware of the dangers that would inhere in the creation of a monetary authority subservient to the Executive Branch of government—and thus subject to political manipulation. Carter Glass, Chairman of the House Banking and Currency Committee when the Federal Reserve Act was passed in 1913, reported that the Committee regarded the Federal Reserve Board "as a distinctly nonpartisan organization whose functions are to be wholly divorced from politics." That view was fully shared by President Woodrow Wilson, who was extremely careful to avoid any suggestion of interference with the newly created monetary authority, thereby setting a precedent that has been usually followed by succeeding Presidents.

In the years that followed creation of the Federal Reserve System, experience —particularly during the Great Depression—suggested that the degree of independence assigned to the monetary authority was insufficient. The Banking Acts of 1933 and 1935 sought to rectify this and other defects in the financial structure.

In particular, the Secretary of the Treasury and the Comptroller of the Currency, who originally were *ex officio* members of the Board, were relieved of this responsibility.

Our system of monetary management, I believe, is working in the way the founders of the Federal Reserve intended. Nonetheless, there are now, as there have been over the years, some well-meaning individuals in our country who believe that the authority of the Federal Reserve to make decisions about the course of monetary policy should be circumscribed. The specific proposals that have been put forth over the years differ greatly, but they usually have had one feature in common—namely, control by the Executive Branch of government over the monetary authority.

A move in this direction would be unwise and even dangerous. It is encouraging to find that, despite occasional outbursts of temper, a majority of the Congress share this belief. I doubt that the American people would want to see the power to create money lodged in the presidency—which may mean that it would in fact be exercised by political aides in the White House. Such a step would create a potential for political mischief or abuse on a large scale than we have yet seen. Certainly, if the spending propensities of Federal officials were given freer rein, the inflationary tendency that weakend our economy over much of the past decade would in all likelihood be aggravated.

The need for a strong monetary authority to discipline the inflationary tendency inherent in modern economies is evident from the historical experience of the nations around the world. Among the major industrial countries, West Germany and the United States appear to have achieved the greatest success—albeit woefully insufficient success—in resisting inflationary pressures in the period since World War II. It is no accident that both countries have strong central banks. In some other countries, where the monetary authority is dominated by the Executive or the legislature, inflationary financial policies have brought economic chaos and even extinguished political freedom.

It is, of course, essential that the monetary authority observe the spirit as well as the letter of our laws. In our democratic society the independence of a governmental agency can never be absolute. The Federal Reserve System is thus subject not only to the provisions of the Federal Reserve Act, but also to the Employment Act and numerous other statutes. The original design of the Federal Reserve System recognized this duty by requiring the Federal Reserve to account for its stewardship to the Congress. The oversight responsibilities of the Congress for the conduct of the monetary authority do not, however, require congressional involvement in the details of implementing monetary policy. The technical complexities of adjusting monetary or credit instruments to the needs of a modern industrial economy are far too great to be dealt with by a large deliberative body. At the same time, there is a significant role for the Congress in setting forth the economic and financial objectives that the monetary authority is expected to observe and honor.

Over the past year, the Congress has been exercising its vital oversight function through a new and more systematic procedure, spelled out in House Concurrent Resolution No. 133. That resolution requires the Federal Reserve to report to the Congress at quarterly intervals on the course of monetary policy, and to project ranges of growth in the major monetary and credit aggregates for the year ahead.

We at the Federal Reserve regard the dialogue between the monetary authority and the Congress stimulated by the Concurrent Resolution as constructive. It has given the Congress a better opportunity to express its views on the appropriateness of our actions. It has also provided us at the Federal Reserve with an opportunity to explain fully the reasons for our actions, and to communicate to the Congress and to the public at large our firm intention to adhere to a course of monetary policy that is consistent not only with continued economic expansion at a satisfactory rate, but also with further gradual unwinding of inflationary tendencies.

Such a course of policy, I believe, is the only option open to us if we as a nation are to have any hope of regaining price stability and maintaining a robust economy. Our country is passing through a fateful stage in its history. Economic, social, and political trends of the past several decades have released powerful forces of inflation that threaten the vitality of our economy and the freedom of our people.

Defeating the forces of inflation requires determined action. Greater discipline is needed in our fiscal affairs, and structural reforms are required to improve the functioning of our labor and product markets. But all such reforms would come to naught in the absence of a prudent course of monetary policy. At this critical time in our history, any interference with the ability of the Federal Reserve to stick to a moderate rate of monetary expansion could have grave consequences for the economic and political future of our country.

Questions

1. Do you agree that the power to create money should not be lodged in the Presidency? Explain.
2. Is an independent Federal Reserve essential to a healthy mortgage market? Why or why not?

17

FINANCING: RISK ANALYSIS*

IMPORTANCE OF MORTGAGE CREDIT

Although we may ordinarily think of finance as a matter of borrowing and lending, it is important to recognize that nearly all types of real estate decisions have important financial aspects. Decisions to buy, build, lease, sell, improve, and use real estate all involve financial considerations. Thus, the administration of real estate finance is almost as broad a field as real estate administration in general.

Financing Property Use

One way to narrow the analysis of real estate finance is to center attention primarily on two ways of viewing the subject: (1) how to finance the use of real property, and (2) how to invest in real estate without responsibility for the use of it.[1] In connection with the first point, the arrangements that are made may range from complete equity ownership on the one hand to leasing arrangements on the other. Some type of mortgage arrangement, however, is the most widely used method of financing the use of real estate.

Investment Without Responsibility for Use

In connection with the second point made above, a wide variety of methods of investing in real estate may be employed without being responsible for its use, including complete equity ownership of leased property, various equity and debt combinations of leased property, savings and

* The authors appreciate the assistance of Kenneth J. Thygerson, Chief Economist of the U. S. League of Savings Associations, and Leon Kendall, President, Mortgage Guarantee Insurance Corporation, in reviewing this chapter.

[1] Suggested by Edward E. Edwards, Fred T. Greene Professor Emeritus of Finance, Indiana University.

loan accounts, Federal Home Loan Bank obligations, and others. Again, however, various types of mortgages represent the most widely used methods of investing in real estate without incurring responsibility for the use of the real estate.

Equity Investments

As we have suggested, real estate investments may range from equities to mortgages; a variety of combinations of equity and debt interests may be arranged. As we pointed out in Chapter 15, many kinds of methods and instruments are available to facilitate real estate investments including leases which may be used as a means of financing the use of property.

Equities may range from 100 per cent of the investment in a piece of real estate to a thin 1 or 2 per cent. Equities may be combined with debt financing in many ways. Debt investors may take "a piece of the action." General and limited partnerships may be set up; these in turn may be combined with various forms of debt investments. For example, percentage leases may be used under various arrangements. Many other types of combinations may be worked out as well. The popularity of different arrangements will vary with money market conditions, investor preferences, general economic trends, and other things.

Investment Decisions

Although both equity and debt investors will be concerned with estimating risks and returns there will be significant differences in the priorities and emphasis which will be given to these and related decision factors. For example, equity investors may consider both financial and nonfinancial risks and rewards. Home owners may be especially concerned with the nonfinancial aspects of their investment decisions, for example. Individual investors may place a high priority on cash flow. In judging investment opportunities, they may select from a variety of alternatives using the "indifference value" of cash flows, total returns, degrees of risk, and related factors as guides.

Both debt and equity investors, of course, will give careful consideration to the present value of the future returns and benefits that may be anticipated from an investment. The discount rate will play a major role in such decisions.

In estimating the degree of certainty and uncertainty which will be faced, investors may use a variety of ways of undertaking to assess the future. They make think in terms of probabilities. They may assume various attitudes toward risk and make estimates as to the extent to which various types of risks may be acceptable. The decisions of investors in such cases may be analyzed in terms of utility curves. Investment decision models may be developed. Illustrations of these types of decision factors are presented in Study Project 17–1 at the end of this chapter.

Mortgages

Since we cannot cover the entire range of methods of financing the use of real estate or investing in it, we will center our attention in this discussion on mortgage credit and the administration of mortgage risk. In mortgage transactions, we always have a borrower and a lender. Their decisions will be influenced by the objectives they hope to achieve, anticipated relationships between costs and returns, degree of risk involved, and the alternative arrangements that may be available.

Risks and Returns. The mortgage lender is concerned with the soundness of the projects being financed and the conditions under which the risks are carried. The lender's decision to advance funds will be affected by estimates of the income prospects of the borrower, the market trends likely to affect the property, and the return on the investment relative to the risk involved, probable yield on other investments, interest rate risk, and purchasing power risk. When general and local prospects appear to be favorable, the lender will tend to be more liberal in financing arrangements than when the outlook is more uncertain. At times virtually no credit may be available for mortgage financing because lenders are much more interested in liquidity than in yield.

The borrower's decision to use mortgage credit will turn primarily on estimates of the return that can be earned on the borrowed funds relative to their cost and the risks involved. In some cases, of course, the borrower may borrow to protect an earlier position.

Public Interest. Problems of mortgage financing are important to the public as well as to borrowers and lenders. The public at large is interested in the proportion of savings going into real estate projects and in the efficiency with which such savings are used. Mortgage lending plays a major role in channeling savings into real estate projects.

LENDING POLICIES AND PRACTICES

The lender is primarily concerned with the repayment of the loan with interest over a number of years. While liberal financing terms facilitate the programs of the developer, broker, owner, or user of property, conservative financing terms may prevent them from undertaking unsound ventures. In many respects a lender with a long-range point of view thus serves as a stabilizing force in the real estate market.

Lender Conflicts

The lender, however, faces numerous conflicts in policies. Ultraconservative practices usually limit earnings. Liberal financing may lead to numerous foreclosure problems. The overoptimism of a boom period may lead to extension of credit on terms that are too liberal for the life of the mortgages that are made. Such overoptimism, moreover, may cause booms to run greater extremes than would otherwise be the case, as in the early 1970's. By contrast, highly conservative practices in boom periods may limit developments which are needed for the orderly progress of the community. Also, ultraconservative practices during the depths of a recession may prolong the agony of such a period.

New Financing vs. Old

The mortgage lender who is financing new real estate projects is helping to create competition for properties which stand as security for mortgages that have already been made. If a new type of construction is being featured by a builder, the mortgage lender who supplies financing may find that such properties are not marketable if foreclosure becomes necessary. Or, if successful, such projects may produce properties that cause rapid obsolescence of properties that the lender is already looking to as security for mortgages. On the other hand, if the mortgage lender fails to finance a progressive builder, a good market for investment funds may be lost.

The mortgage lender, who tends to object to government regulation during prosperous times, cannot object too strongly because it may be necessary to rely on the support of the government when the cold wind of a recession paralyzes operations. Also, government policies are among the primary factors in the creation of inflationary or deflationary tendencies in the economy.

Key Role of Lender

The mortgage lender, whether a banker, a savings and loan association official, a representative of an insurance company, or a private investor, thus provides an interesting study of contrasts and conflicts. Lenders' policies often contrast sharply with those of others in the real estate field. Personal objectives and policies are often in serious conflict with one another. Yet, as one of the key figures in the real estate business, the lender's decisions have important long- and short-range effects, both on real estate in general and on the success or failure of specific projects for the development, marketing, ownership, and use of real properties.

Management Problems of Lenders

Like other business firms, the owners and managers of the institutions engaged in real estate finance must determine objectives, develop plans to achieve such objectives, organize resources effectively, and control operations to assure conformity with plans. Of special importance in the successful management of such institutions is the care with which the risks involved in mortgage financing are estimated and the effectiveness of the programs to carry these risks.

The various institutions engaged in mortgage finance have essentially the same management problems. (See Figs. 17–1 and 17–2.). It is necessary to attract savings at costs that permit successful lending operations. The required personnel must be selected, hired, trained, and organized into an effective work team. Proper locations must be selected and developed for the place or places of business. It is necessary to generate the required loan volume, and more specifically to select the risks to be underwritten. After loans have been made, they must be serviced, and all mortgage loans as a group, or the *portfolio,* must be administered in a manner that makes the total loan program successful. The decisions and programs undertaken in order to accomplish these things will be influenced by anticipated changes in business conditions, money markets, real estate activity, and government policies. Of special importance are anticipated changes in interest rates and the price level.

Like the managers of other types of business activities, the managers of mortgage lending institutions have the general problem of securing the required resources on sufficiently favorable terms to carry on the programs believed to be essential in achieving selected objectives. In our discussions here, attention will center primarily in the management of the risks that are involved in mortgage financing.

RISKS IN LENDING

The individuals and institutions engaged in lending funds on the basis of real estate mortgages assume various types of risks. The successful administration of these risks is a complicated process. Although individual investors who finance real estate projects may make their decisions on informal bases in regard to the risks they assume, institutional lenders have developed rather definite procedures for arriving at decisions and for carrying them out.

The following steps typically are involved. After an application for a mortgage loan is made, a preliminary analysis is undertaken. If the results are favorable, the property to be pledged as security for the loan is appraised. The credit status of the borrower is determined. Final decisions are then reached, often by a loan committee. Once the loan becomes a part of the portfolio of the institution, it must be serviced throughout the period of its life. That is, interest and amortization payments are collected, and taxes and insurance payments are arranged.

Sometimes the loans are refinanced, and this may be a source of risk. If refinancing occurs early in the life of the loan, the costs of serving the mortgage may exceed returns. Hence, some mortgage loans contain prepayment penalties. Refinancing usually results if competitive conditions change. Thus, it is desirable that loans be well adapted to the needs and financial ability of the borrower on rates and terms that are likely to be competitive at least for a reasonable period of time. For example, some

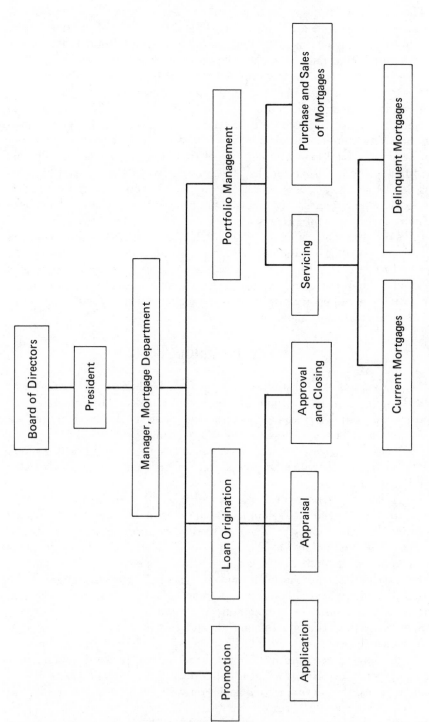

FIG. 17–1. Mortgage lending organization.

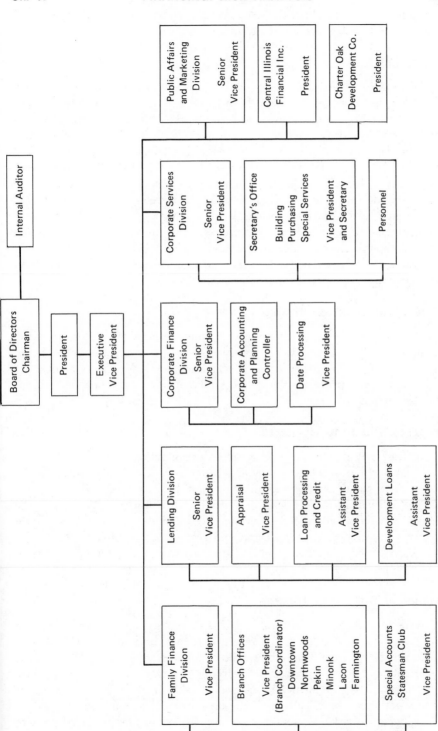

FIG. 17–2. Organization chart, First Federal Savings of Peoria, Illinois. Reproduced by permission.

mortgages provide for variable interest rates. In some cases equity interests are combined with mortgage lending.

Sources of Risks

The risks involved in mortgage financing vary widely from one project to another, but they tend to arise from essentially the same sources. These sources affect both the borrower and the lender. Both must assume various risks. The borrower may lose the property and the income it may bring, plus (in some cases) other resources as well. The lender may lose yield on the funds advanced and may even lose all or part of the principal amount. The borrower has to decide how much can be paid for borrowed funds in relation to the return expected from using them, recognizing the risks that are assumed in pledging the property. The lender has the problem of adjusting risks to the cost of funds and the return secured as a result of lending them. Although we pay special attention to the risks of the lender in this discussion, it is important to note that the risks of both the borrower and the lender arise from the same general sources.

Interest Rate and Purchasing Power Risk

Both the borrower and lender face the uncertainties of interest rate risk. Arrangements may be made for shifting this risk to borrower or lender or for sharing or pooling or insuring it. Similarly, both face risks of changes in the purchasing power of the dollar. Inflation favors the borrower, deflation the lender.

Borrower and Property Risks

The borrower may be unable to meet the obligation under the mortgage loan. This will bring losses, of course, and may also bring losses to the lender. The yield on the investment may be impaired. The property pledged as security for the loan may decline in value, and as a result the amount realized from its sale may not be adequate to cover the unpaid balance of the loan plus foreclosure and related costs. Finally, the lender runs the risk that the other assets of the borrower may not be adequate to make up the difference.

Estimating Risks and Returns

The lender thus has the problem of estimating the risk involved in a mortgage loan in relation to the return that may be realized. If risks are considered to be high, it may be possible to make adjustments by charging higher interest rates, arranging for variable interest rates, taking "a piece of the action," that is, participating in ownership in some way, lending for a short period of time (although in some cases this may increase rather than reduce the risk), or lending a relatively small amount in relation to the value of the property. In some cases, of course, the risks may be considered too great to make adjustments to them. Also, some lenders have fairly standardized lending plans and will only select those loans that fit these plans, rejecting others which might be acceptable under proper conditions by other lenders.

In order to estimate the borrower and property risks involved, most lenders analyze (1) the borrower, (2) the property, (3) the market, (4) legal rules and regulations, and (5) problems of administering the loan.

Insurance of Risks

Some risks can be insured. General mortgage risks can be transferred to public agencies such as FHA or VA or to private mortgage insurance companies such as MGIC, IMI, PMI, CMI, and others. The hazards of fire, windstorm, public liability, and similar uncertainties can be transferred to a major extent to appropriate insurance companies. Certain hazards in defects to title to property may be shifted to a title insurance company. Credit life insurance may be used to help meet the risk of the borrower's death or disability. Even interest rate risk might be insured if the necessary plans were available. Almost all other types of risks, however, must be assumed by the lender in advancing funds on the basis of real estate security unless mortgage insurance or guarantees (public or private) are used. Thus, the risks of the lender on real estate security are numerous and complex.

LINES OF DEFENSE

Against these various types of risk there are several lines of defense. The first of these is the borrower's income-producing ability. If this is sufficient, the pledge of property need not be used. If not, or if the original borrower sells the property to a less desirable credit risk, the property becomes the second line of defense. In some cases a foreclosure of the property does not recompense the lender for the entire amount of the advance. Such conditions frequently arise where property is foreclosed during periods of depression. The mortgagee may then sue the borrower and receive a deficiency judgment, the value of which depends on the borrower's assets. (Its value varies also from state to state.)

The deficiency judgment forms the third line of defense. In cases where the borrower's assets are sufficient, such deficiency judgment is valuable security, since it cannot be evaded except by bankruptcy. Of course, if a deed is given in lieu of foreclosure, the third line of defense is not available to the lender. We should remember, also, that forced sales usually occur during depression periods when deficiency judgments are most likely to be valueless.

High levels of economic activity both nationally and locally often help in carrying mortgage risks. Recognition must be given, however, to the effect of inflation or deflation on long-term mortgage loans. In the 1960's and 1970's inflation proved to be the major problem. The late 1970's and early 1980's are in the process of writing their history and mortgage lenders, borrowers, governmental agencies, and the public at large will find it necessary to adjust to the effect of changes in interest rates and the value of the dollar. Lines of defense against these risks are in the process of being developed.

Borrower Risks

All lenders of money are vitally interested in the individuals or companies that obligate themselves to repay a loan, even though a property is offered as security. Although individuals and companies may borrow for various purposes, two main groups may be designated: (1) individuals wishing to finance the ownership of homes, and (2) individuals and companies financing real estate projects for business and income-producing purposes.

Analysis of risks arising in connection with the first group of borrowers requires that attention be given to the borrower's personal fortune, income, the type of work in which the borrower is engaged, future prospects for economic advance or decline, health, number of dependents, and the extent of various obligations or potential obligations of a personal and business nature. Certain personal characteristics require consideration, including reputation for fair dealing and prompt payment of obligations, and ability to manage personal affairs.

Analysis of risks arising in connection with the second group of borrowers designated above necessitates a consideration of the financial status of the person or company involved, and the income-producing ability of the project which is to be financed. If the borrower is a corporation, the lender has no recourse to the incomes or assets of individuals, and hence attention must be directed to the condition and earning capacity of the company and the economic soundness of the project.

Property Risks

Analysis of the uncertainties arising in connection with the pledge of a specific parcel of real estate as security for a mortgage requires a consideration of all the factors likely to affect its value during the period of the loan. In addition, it is necessary for the mortgagee to consider such questions as: (1) the value of the property in relation to the amount of the loan requested; (2) the property's economic life, structural soundness, and durability in relation to the term of the loan; (3) its inherent income-producing ability in relation to the amount of the loan, plus interest and servicing charges; and (4) its present and prospective competitive position in the market. Basically, the lender tries to make certain that the market value of the property will exceed the unpaid balance of the loan throughout the life of the mortgage.

The economic life of a property is a function of its location, design, structural soundness, and marketability. Analysis of the income-producing ability of a property requires a consideration of its adaptability to the uses to which it is put and the potential demand for the type of services it is yielding in relation to the probable future supply likely to become available. An estimate of potential income-producing ability, however, is of little value unless considered in connection with the amount of the loan plus interest and servicing charges during the period of the financing contract. Like so many other problems of this type, it is difficult to consider a single factor except in relationship to others. For example, property changes will affect the borrower. A sudden decline in a property's value may cause the borrower to sell or to abandon any interest in it.

Market Risks

Since investments in real estate typically are not liquid, the degree of marketability is an important risk element. For example, special-purpose buildings are generally not so easy to market as other types, and hence involve a greater amount of uncertainty. Similarly, expensive residences are often hard to sell for amounts that even approximate the original investments in them. Also, their degree of marketability is usually limited, especially in small cities. The competitive position of the property in the market at the time and under probable future market conditions is of primary importance in the analysis of mortgage risk.

Sudden declines in markets have a profound effect on mortgages made just prior to such changes. Such mortgages have not been *seasoned*—that is, reduced in amount owed by amortization payments. When a borrower has reduced the principal on a high loan—value loan only slightly, there may be an inclination to abandon the property if the amount still due on the mortgage is greater than the current market price of the property. Thus, greater risks of loss appear to be concentrated in the early years of the life of a mortgage. We should note, however, that a period of inflation could help the borrower to achieve a strong position even if the loan is not reduced at all. Also, the type of property may have a great deal of bearing on risk. For example, a 30 per cent loan on a vacant lot might go into default while an 80 or 90 per cent loan on a well-built and properly located house that the borrower wanted to keep as a home might prove to be highly successful.

Legal Risks

We have pointed out that the laws regulating real estate finance are much more complex and involved than those regulating many other types of transactions. For example, the lender must determine whether the borrower is capable of mortgaging the property, whether there is actual ownership or such interest in it as is claimed, and the extent of all preceding claims outstanding against it. In some cases zoning laws or deed restrictions may limit the uses to which a property may be put and seriously impair its earning power. In some parts of the country foreclosure laws are very favorable to the borrower and foreclosure costs are high. In others, such laws favor the lender. Risks may arise from rent control laws, condominium conversion moratoriums, and possible changes in tax laws—both those affecting properties directly or their owners through income tax changes.

Administrative Risks

In drawing up a loan agreement, the lender assumes various risks of an administrative nature. Allowances for such risks can be made in numerous ways, no one of which is completely separated from the others. The ratio of loan to value, the interest rate, the term of the loan, the method of repayment, and the amount of initial or continuing servicing charges must be adjusted to each other in specific situations if allowances for administrative risks are to be made.

Loan–Value Ratios

Traditionally, a low loan–value ratio was believed to be sufficient protection against most risks. However, difficulties often arise because values are frequently overestimated. For example, a loan–value ratio of 60 per cent might afford little protection to a lender if the transaction were entered into during a boom period when the value of the property was estimated at a high figure. Shrinkage of value might soon result in a loan–value ratio of 100 or even 110 per cent or more.

Again, a low loan–value ratio might bring about a situation in which the borrower was forced to resort to second- or third-mortgage financing, the costs of which might be high enough to impair ability to meet the obligations of all the mortgages; or the borrower might refinance the mortgage at an early date, with the result that the mortgage would not have earned enough to pay the cost of putting it on the books. Similarly, a low loan–value ratio might afford slight protection against various uncertainties if the loan had an extremely long term, during which no repayments of principal were made, but during which the property depreciated rapidly. By contrast, inflation might move up a property's value.

Other Adjustments

The interest rate must also be considered in relation to other factors and with respect to the possibilities of price level changes during the term of the loan. For example, provisions which allow the interest rate to fluctuate with general price level changes reduce such risks. Variable interest rates are used by a growing number of mortgage lenders. Some mortgages are renegotiated every three to five years although written for 25 or 30 years.

The term of the loan represents similar problems. Unless the term is considered in relation to the method of repayment, it has little significance. Risks may be guarded against to some extent by the plan of repayment. Thus a 20-year loan on an amortized basis may contain less risk than a 10-year straight term loan, depending on the rate of amortization. It should be noted in this connection that an amortization plan which provides for large payments during the earlier years of a loan usually contains less risk than one providing for a uniform rate of repayment or one requiring larger payments during the later years of the term, or a so-called "balloon" payment at the end. On the other hand, some mortgages with lower early payments succeed because they fit the income pattern of the borrower. Some mortgages provide for the payment of interest only for the first five years. Also, a lender may think that liberal loans are justified during boom periods if they are amortized. Hence risks may be increased simply because there is a device for meeting them.

Again, conservative appraisals, in the minds of some lenders, may be balanced by liberal loans, or high interest rates by longer-term loans. Thus every device for reducing risk may become a risk element itself if the administration of a mortgage lending program is weak.

Amortized mortgages are not sound risks simply because they are amortized. Like other risk elements, amortization must be adjusted to all of the facts bearing on the probable success of the mortgage arrangement. Further, it is always necessary to bear in mind that real estate credit is of a long-term character, and therefore a financing transaction may fail because the loan agreement was not adjusted to the longer-range risk factors in a specific situation, such as purchasing power risk, income level changes, or others.

Portfolio Management

Obviously the risks assumed in one mortgage loan may offset in part the risks assumed in another. There is thus somewhat less total risk in an entire loan portfolio than in all of the loans individually. Typically, all of the loans made will not go into default at one time. Loans made at an earlier period that have been partially amortized may help to carry the risks of recently made loans. Variable interest rate mortgages may be balanced against fixed rate loans. Insured and guaranteed mortgages may be balanced against those that are not insured or guaranteed.

Nevertheless, the management of the mortgage loan portfolio requires constant attention. In some cases it may be desirable to sell loans in order to meet current demands or to improve yield on the entire portfolio. In other cases buying loans may be indicated. These processes have been facilitated by the use of FNMA, FHLMC, and GNMA. Sometimes geographic spreading of risks may dictate the sale or purchase of loans, especially if the institution may only originate loans in a given area.

In some cases it may be advisable to undertake the financing of new developments by providing construction loans in the interest of securing from such activities a volume of mortgage loans that may remain in the portfolio for a long time.

A mortgage loan portfolio cannot be managed without regard to the overall programs of the institution. For example, provision of adequate liquidity may at times necessitate the sacrifice of yield by shifting funds from mortgages to government bonds or other securities that have the desired liquidity. In some cases considerations of this type may dictate the distribution of loans among conventional, insured, and guaranteed mortgages.

Anticipated changes in money market conditions, in real estate activity, or in government policies or programs may also influence the decisions taken in the management of a mortgage loan portfolio. For example, if money markets are expected to become tight with rising interest rates, lending volume may be restricted in the hope of securing higher yields later.

Secondary Market for Home Mortgage Loans

When financial institutions and other investors buy and sell mortgages, the processes are carried on in what is referred to as the secondary market for home mortgage loans. Transactions can occur informally or on a more organized basis. For example, there has developed an Automated Mortgage Market Information Network (AMMINET) to facilitate transactions. There are regular opportunities for purchases and sales with FNMA, GNMA, or FHLMC and this sector of the market has grown in importance.

The volume of activity in the secondary home mortgage market expanded rapidly in the 1970's. More than 80 per cent of this volume was made up of mortgages on 1–4-family homes with the remainder on apartment house loans. Although FHA-insured and VA-guaranteed loans dominated the secondary market for many years, transactions in conventional home mortgages advanced rapidly in the 1970's. Also, loans insured by the Farmers Home Administration gained an increasing share of this market.[2]

[2] See Arnold H. Diamond, "Secondary Market for Home Mortgage Loans," paper presented at the 5th Annual Mid-year Meeting of the American Real Estate and Urban Economics Association in cooperation with the Federal Home Loan Bank Board, Washington, D. C., May 24, 1977. See also another paper at the same meeting: Dennis J. Jacob and Kenneth J. Thygerson, "The Federal Sector Mortgage Market: Impact on Specialized Mortgage Lenders."

Defense Against Interest Rate and Purchasing Power Risk

As has been suggested above, variable interest rates may be set up to shift the risk of interest rate advances to the borrower. Such practices seem likely to increase in the years ahead. They may be coupled with repayment penalties attached to fixed interest rate mortgages in order to shift a major share of the risk of declining interest rates to borrowers.

It may be that new devices may be developed for handling interest rate risk. For example, since neither the borrower nor the lender has much if any control over conditions, it may be desirable to establish a program for insuring interest rate risk, at least on home mortgages. Whether such a program could be developed successfully remains to be seen. Professor Edward E. Edwards has recommended that such an effort be undertaken.[3]

Defenses against purchasing power risk to date are largely of the type that relate the value of the principal of a mortgage to price level changes. Thus, if the amount due on a mortgage varied with changes in the consumer price index, for example, or some other price index, the lender would be able to shift purchasing power risk to the borrower in the event of inflation, but would be assuming greater risk in the event of deflation. It is sometimes argued that the lender gains from inflation as well as deflation under present mortgage arrangements which typically do not make provision for price level changes. Thus, it is contended that if prices rise the value of the property which stands as security rises and hence the risk that the loan will not be repaid is reduced. Even if the dollars repaid are worth less, the risks have been reduced. On the other hand if price levels decline, the lender is repaid in dollars of higher value, hence stands to gain as well. It is doubtful, however, that the reduction in risk in case of price level advances compensates for the loss of purchasing power in the dollars used to repay the loan.

If inflation persists and becomes a growing problem we are likely to see increased efforts to adjust to risks of price level advances. Some efforts along these lines have been made in various South American countries and in Israel.[4] Other countries have experimented with bonds that change in value with price level changes.

---

[3] Privately circulated memoranda, 1975–76. See also Committee on Banking, Currency and Housing, House of Representatives, 94th Congress, First Session, *Financial Institutions and the National Economy* (Washington, D. C.: Government Printing Office, 1975).

[4] See Franco Modigliani and Donald R. Lessard, Eds., *New Mortgage Decisions for Stable Housing in an Inflationary Environment* (Boston: Federal Reserve Bank of Boston, 1975).

SUMMARY

Primary decisions in real estate finance are made by borrowers and lenders. Although their objectives differ, both borrowers and lenders assume risks, and need to administer their financial programs so as to carry such risks.

The borrower runs the risk of losing the property and the direct or monetary income it produces, and perhaps other losses as well. The borrower's decision concerns the estimate of the return that can be earned on borrowed funds and whether this exceeds the costs, with appropriate allowance for risks.

Lenders must assume several special risks. The lender may lose all or part of the principal sum, as well as the interest income. There is the danger that the borrower will not be able to meet the obligation, that the mortgaged property may decline in value and not be adequate to cover the unpaid balance, and that the borrower may not have sufficient assets to make up the deficiency. The lender is concerned with the return on the investment relative to the risk involved and the returns on alternative investments. Once the loan is made, the lender's primary interest is in the repayment of the principal amount, with interest, within the specified time.

The risks assumed by both borrowers and lenders arise from the same general sources. These sources are the income-producing ability or other resources of the borrower, the value and income-producing ability of the property, and the uncertainties of market conditions. Legal and administrative risks are important. Inflation and deflation will have major effects on borrowers and lenders with interest rate and purchasing power risks of prime concern.

Financial institutions engaging in real estate finance have the problem of attracting the savings of individuals and business firms on terms that will permit profitable lending. They also have the problems of managing mortgage portfolios as well as the usual types of management problems common to most business enterprises.

QUESTIONS FOR STUDY

1. List the principal sources of risk to lenders in the financing of real estate. Can these risks be avoided? Explain.
2. List the factors you would consider in evaluating an individual borrower. Which factors would you consider most important?
3. Would the same factors be important in analyzing a commercial borrower? Explain any additional factors that should be considered in the case of the commercial borrower.
4. Which government economic stabilization policies are of major importance to a mortgage lender? Why?

5. Which type of risk is represented by each of the following, and how does it apply? (a) Loan–value ratio, (b) term of the loan in relation to the life of the property, (c) the interest rate, (d) the rate of amortization, and (c) the borrower.

6. If real estate values decline sharply, can any adjustments be made to prevent a mortgage from going into foreclosure? Please comment.

7. Give reasons why most real estate transactions involve small equity and heavy reliance on borrowed funds. Is this a desirable state of affairs? Explain.

8. What is meant by a "seasoned mortgage"? Explain any differences in risk between seasoned and unseasoned mortgages.

9. Outline the possible conflicts of interest involved in the leading policies of financial institutions in the real estate field. How may these conflicts be resolved?

10. What are the principal ways in which lenders can adjust to differences in risk as between alternative lending opportunities?

11. Suggest some of the different forms that legal risks may take.

12. If a financial institution pursues a policy of conservative lending but makes liberal appraisals, would you consider this an inconsistent policy? Why or why not? What reasons could you advance in defense of such a policy?

13. What is the reasoning behind use of the loan–value ratio as a protection against risk?

14. Explain what is meant by interest rate risk. By purchasing power risk. How may adjustments be made for such risks?

SUGGESTED READINGS

EDWARDS, EDWARD E., and WEIMER, ARTHUR M. *Cyclical Fluctuations in Residential Construction.* Bloomington, Ind.: Business and Real Estate Trends, Inc., 1968.

FEDERAL HOUSING ADMINISTRATION. *Underwriting Handbook* (rev. ed.). Washington, D. C.: Government Printing Office.

FICEK, EDMUND F., HENDERSON, THOMAS P., and JOHNSON, ROSS H. *Real Estate Principles and Practices.* Columbus, Ohio: Charles E. Merrill Publishing Co., 1976. Ch. 7.

HOAGLAND, HENRY E., and STONE, LEO D. *Real Estate Finance* (5th ed.). Homewood, Ill.: Richard D. Irwin, Inc., 1973. Chs. 8 and 9.

MAISEL, SHERMAN J. *Financing Real Estate: Principles and Practices.* New York: McGraw-Hill Book Co., 1965. Chs. 6–11.

————, and RULACK, STEVEN E. *Real Estate Investment and Finance.* New York: McGraw-Hill Book Co., 1976.

SELDIN, MAURY, and SWESNIK, RICHARD H. *Real Estate Investment Strategy.* New York: John Wiley & Sons, 1970.

UNGER, MAURICE H. *Real Estate Principles and Practices.* Chicago: South-Western Publishing Co., 1974. Chs. 6, 14, 15, and 16.

WENDT, PAUL F., and CERF, ALAN R. *Real Estate Investment, Analysis and Taxation.* New York: McGraw-Hill Book Co., 1969. Ch. 10.

WILEY, ROBERT J. *Real Estate Investment—Analysis and Strategy.* New York: The Ronald Press Co., 1977. Ch. 7.

CASE 17-1

A Mortgage Loan Application

John J. and Mary E. Smith are building a house in suburban Indianapolis, just outside Noblesville, Indiana, and would like to mortgage it with the Railroadmen's Federal Savings and Loan Association. As a member of Railroadmen's Federal loan committee, you must evaluate the mortgage loan application (pages 502–505). The following questions, among others, must be answered.

Questions

1. Describe the nature and extent of the interest rate and purchasing power risks to Railroadmen's Federal.
2. How would you evaluate borrower risk in this case?
3. The surrounding houses range in value from $20,000 to $25,000. Does this represent property risk?
4. Would you make this loan without mortgage insurance or guarantee? Would you make it at all?

STUDY PROJECT 17-1

Contemporary Decision Theory and Real Estate Investment *

Decision theory is a familiar term in the progressive business world; its application in investment decision making is commonplace—except in the area of real estate investment.[1]

This paper will not explain why real estate appraisal and investment literature is almost void of such esoteric terms as: time value of money, probabilities, or utility functions—all of which are used extensively in modern investment decision theory. Rather, this paper will attempt to bring real estate investment decision making up to date; it will focus on the relevance and usefulness of modern business decision theory and the concepts on which it is built in relation to this process.

A model will be used to illustrate exactly how investment decision making can be applied to a specific real estate investment decision. A conscious and orderly application of rational decision making can replace—and improve upon—the typical process which involves the largely subconscious and intuitive employment of much the same components.

Financial Rewards. Modern decision theory recognizes that investment decisions in real life are made on the basis of considerations which often go beyond or may be inconsistent with, the maximizing of financial rewards. Real estate investments illustrate this to the extent to which they reflect goals of prestige, personal pride, or the satisfaction of land ownership. For example, how does one express the various degrees of pride in real estate ownership, a pride reflecting an attitude which enters into the decisions of many individual investors? How

---

* By Richard U. Ratcliff and Bernhard Schwab. By permission, from *The Appraisal Journal,* April 1970. The opinions expressed herein are those of the authors and do not necessarily carry the endorsement of the American Institute of Real Estate Appraisers.

[1] See D. B. Hertz, "Risk Analysis in Capital Investment," *Harvard Business Review,* January–February, 1964; Grayson C. Jackson, *Decisions Under Uncertainty: Drilling Decisions by Gas and Oil Operators,* Boston: Harvard University—Division of Research, 1960; Smith Barney & Co., "Investment Decision Making: New Perspectives and Methods," 1968.

does one reflect the unreasoned biases such as preferences for certain forms of architecture and distates for other?

In addition, there are other types of considerations which are subject to quantification but are so complex that few investors make the attempt. Investment decisions are thus, not the simple maximizing decisions of classical economics; they involve many incommensurables as well as many subjective elements. Each investor, whether a person or a corporation, reflects in his investment decision a very complex mixture of: goals, values systems, biases, degrees of analytical ability, stocks of applicable knowledge, and financial situations, etc. A clear picture of the financial implications of an investment decision enables one to assess the amount of money required to satisfy such non-monetary desires as pride of ownership and prestige, thereby clarifying the investor's thinking regarding a particular property.

There are innumerable measures of financial performances such as the accountant's net income, taxable income or yield on investment. However, *cash flow*, i.e., the dollars remaining in the hands of the investor after he has met all prior claims of: operating expenses, financial obligations—usually lease and mortgage payments in the case of real estate—and income taxes will serve as the most practical basis for investment in our model for real estate investment decision making. Spendable cash on hand is an understandable concept and plays a major and often exclusive role in investment decision making.

Judging Investment Opportunities. Before an investment decision can be made, the investor must determine—for each alternative investment opportunity —the capital amount which he would equate with its prospective financial rewards (cash flow), i.e., he must determine the capital *"indifference value"* of the prospective financial rewards. The investor must select, from alternative investment opportunities, that choice for which the cost of acquisition bears the most favorable relationship to its indifference value. For example, if the investor determines that the capital sum indifference values of three alternative investments are $10,000, $50,000, and $100,000, he may: (1) disregard the first because the seller of the first property is asking $25,000; and (2) not consider the last option if he has only $50,000 capital available. However, if the owner of the $100,000 property is willing to sell for $50,000, the investor could acquire the property at one-half its worth to him.

Present Value of Future Returns. All benefits from a prospective real estate investment are generally viewed as future benefits. Trained appraisers and financial analysts know the theory and practice of expressing these future benefits in terms of the present value, i.e., value at the time of the investment decision. A $1,000 sum in hand today is worth more to its possessor than a perfectly reliable promise of $1,000 five years from today. At 6% interest compounded annually, the $1,000 held today would grow substantially in 5 years to a total of $1,338. From another viewpoint, $747 in hand today could grow—through investment at 6% and the operation of compound interest—to $1,000 in five years. It is thus a matter of financial indifference whether I have $747 in hand or a reliable promise to pay $1,000 in 5 years—assuming the workings of compound interest at 6%. In any form of investment decision, the time-value of money should be considered; equal weight should not be accorded to a dollar expected to be received a year from now and to a dollar which will not be available for five years.

Discount Rate. In analyzing an investment in terms of the cash flow which it generates, the cash flow is determined by: (1) the periodic cash flows over the terms of ownership; and (2) the net proceeds from the liquidation of the investment at the end of the holding period. The indifference value of these future rewards—expressed as the total capital presently in hand—is then determined. This requires the utilization of a conversion ratio, i.e., a discount rate

RESIDENTIAL LOAN APPLICATION   **RAILROADMEN'S FEDERAL SAVINGS AND LOAN ASSOCIATION OF INDIANAPOLIS**

MORTGAGE APPLIED FOR	[X] Conventional [ ] FHA [ ] VA	Amount $30,000.00	Interest Rate 8.50 %	No. of Months 360	Monthly Payment Principal & Interest $ 230.68	Escrow/Impounds (to be collected monthly) [X] Taxes [X] Hazard Ins. [ ] Mtg. Ins.

Prepayment Option

SUBJECT PROPERTY

Property Street Address 3220 Ridge Road	City Indianapolis	County Marion	State Ind.	Zip 46222	No. Units 1

Legal Description (Attach description if necessary)   Year Built

Purpose of Loan:	[X] Purchase	[ ] Construction-Permanent	[ ] Construction	[ ] Refinance	[ ] Other (Explain)

Complete this line if Construction-Permanent or Construction Loan

Lot Value Data — Year Acquired — Original Cost $ — Present Value (a) $ — Cost of Imps. (b) $ — Total (a + b) $

Complete this line if a Refinance Loan

Year Acquired — Original Cost $ — Amt. Existing Liens $ — Purpose of Refinance — Describe Improvements [ ] made [ ] to be made   Cost: $

Title Will Be Held In What Name(s)
John J. Smith and Mary E. Smith

Manner In Which Title Will Be Held
Entireties

Source of Down Payment and Settlement Charges
Cash and Sale of Home

ENTER TOTAL AS PURCHASE PRICE IN DETAILS OF PURCHASE.

This application is designed to be completed by the borrower(s) with the lender's assistance. The Co-Borrower Section and all other Co-Borrower questions must be completed and the appropriate box(es) checked if [ ] another person will be jointly obligated with the Borrower on the loan, or [ ] the Borrower is relying on income from alimony, child support or separate maintenance or on the income or assets of another person as a basis for repayment of the loan, or [ ] the Borrower is married and resides, or the property is located, in a community property state.

BORROWER

Name John J. Smith			Age 32	School Yrs 16

Present Address   No. Years 2   [X] Own [ ] Rent
Street 5870 W. 14th Street
City/State/Zip Indianapolis, Indiana 46224
Former address if less than 2 years at present address
Street
City/State/Zip
Years at former address   [ ] Own [ ] Rent

Marital Status	[X] Married [ ] Separated [ ] Unmarried (incl. single, divorced, widowed)	DEPENDENTS OTHER THAN LISTED BY CO-BORROWER NO 1 AGES 2

Name and Address of Employer
A. C. Pharmaceutical Co.
9 W. Jackson St.
Indianapolis, Indiana 46204

Years employed in this line of work or profession? 5 years
Years on this job 5
[ ] Self Employed*

Position/Title
Process Operator

Type of Business
Pharmaceutical

Social Security Number***   Home Phone   Business Phone

CO-BORROWER

Name Mary E. Smith			Age 30	School Yrs 12

Present Address   No. Years 2   [X] Own [ ] Rent
Street 5870 W. 14th Street
City/State/Zip Indianapolis, Indiana 46224
Former address if less than 2 years at present address
Street
City/State/Zip
Years at former address   [ ] Own [ ] Rent

Marital Status	[X] Married [ ] Separated [ ] Unmarried (incl. single, divorced, widowed)	DEPENDENTS OTHER THAN LISTED BY BORROWER NO AGES

Name and Address of Employer
N/A

Years employed in this line of work or profession? years
Years on this job years
[ ] Self Employed*

Position/Title

Type of Business

Social Security Number***   Home Phone   Business Phone

GROSS MONTHLY INCOME

Item	Borrower	Co-Borrower	Total
Base Empl. Income	$1,333.33	$	$1,333.33
Overtime			
Bonuses			
Commissions			
Dividends/Interest			
Net Rental Income			
Other† (Before completing, see notice under Describe Other Income below.)			
Total	$1,333.33	$	$1,333.33

MONTHLY HOUSING EXPENSE**

	PRESENT $	PROPOSED $
Rent		
First Mortgage (P&I)	144.30	$ 230.68
Other Financing (P&I)		
Hazard Insurance	12.00	18.32
Real Estate Taxes	32.70	50.00
Mortgage Insurance		
Homeowner Assn. Dues		
Other		
Total Monthly Pmt.	$189.00	$ 299.00
Utilities	70.00	100.00
Total	$259.00	$ 399.00

DETAILS OF PURCHASE

a. Purchase Price	$ 40,000.00
b. Total Closing Costs (Est.)	452.00
c. Prepaid Escrows (Est.)	
d. Total (a + b + c)	$40,452.00
e. Amount This Mortgage	(30,000.00)
f. Other Financing	( )
g. Present Equity in Lot	( )
h. Amount of Cash Deposit	(1,000.00)
i. Closing Costs Paid by Seller	( )
j. Cash Reqd. For Closing (Est.)	$ 9,452.00

DESCRIBE OTHER INCOME

NOTICE:† Alimony, child support, or separate maintenance income need not be revealed if the Borrower or Co-Borrower does not choose to have it considered as a basis for repaying this loan.

B—Borrower C—Co-Borrower	Monthly Amount
	$

IF EMPLOYED IN CURRENT POSITION FOR LESS THAN TWO YEARS COMPLETE THE FOLLOWING

B/C	Previous Employer/School	City/State	Type of Business	Position/Title	Dates From/To	Monthly Income
						$

THESE QUESTIONS APPLY TO BOTH BORROWER AND CO-BORROWER

	Borrower Yes or No	Co-Borrower Yes or No
If a "yes" answer is given to a question in this column, explain on an attached sheet.		
Have you any outstanding judgments? In the last 14 years, have you been declared bankrupt?	No	No
Have you had property foreclosed upon or given title or deed in lieu thereof?	No	No
Are you a co-maker or endorser on a note?	No	No
Are you a party in a law suit?	No	No
Are you obligated to pay alimony, child support, or separate maintenance?	No	No
Is any part of the down payment borrowed?	No	No

	Borrower Yes or No	Co-Borrower Yes or No
Do you have health and accident insurance?	Yes	Yes
Do you have major medical coverage?	Yes	Yes
Do you intend to occupy this property?	Yes	Yes
Will this property be your primary residence?	Yes	Yes
Have you previously owned a home?	Yes	Yes
Sales Price of previously owned home?	$ 25,000	$ 25,000

*FHLMC requires self employed to furnish signed copies of one or more most recent Federal Tax Returns or audited Profit and Loss Statements. FNMA requires business credit report, signed Federal Income Tax returns for last two years, and, if available, audited P/L plus balance sheet for same period.
**All Present Monthly Housing Expenses of Borrower and Co-Borrower should be listed on a combined basis.
***Neither FHLMC nor FNMA requires this information.

FHLMC 65 Rev. 3/77

FNMA 1003. Rev. 3/77

Mortgage loan application.

STATEMENT OF ASSETS AND LIABILITIES

This Statement and any applicable supporting schedules may be completed jointly by both married and unmarried co-borrowers if their assets and liabilities are sufficiently joined so that the Statement can be meaningfully and fairly presented on a combined basis; otherwise separate Statements and Schedules are required (FHLMC 65A/FNMA 1003A). If the co-borrower section was completed about a spouse, this statement and supporting schedules must be completed about that spouse also.

☐ Completed Jointly   ☐ Not Completed Jointly

ASSETS

Description	Cash or Market Value
Cash Deposit Toward Purchase Held By T. & L. Realty Co.	$ 1,000.00
Checking and Savings Accounts (Show Names of Institutions/Acct. Nos.) Central National Bank 91 41 1925	500.00
Central National Bank 13 00125 6	6,500.00
Stocks and Bonds (No./Description) Series E. Bonds	300.00
Life Insurance Net Cash Value Face Amount ($ 30,000.00	400.00
SUBTOTAL LIQUID ASSETS	$ 8,700.00
Real Estate Owned (Enter Market Value from Schedule of Real Estate Owned)	25,000.00
Vested Interest in Retirement Fund	
Net Worth of Business Owned (ATTACH FINANCIAL STATEMENT)	
Automobiles (Make and Year) 1977 Buick	6,000.00
Furniture and Personal Property	12,000.00
Other Assets (Itemize)	
TOTAL ASSETS	A $51,700.00

LIABILITIES AND PLEDGED ASSETS

Indicate by (*) those liabilities or pledged assets which will be satisfied upon sale of real estate owned or upon refinancing of subject property.

Creditors' Name, Address and Account Number	Acct. Name If Not Borrower's	Mo. Pmt. and Mos. left to pay	Unpaid Balance
Installment Debts (include "revolving" charge accts)		$ Pmt./Mos.	$
T & T Department Store		20.00/15	300.00
		/	
		/	
		/	
		/	
Automobile Loans			
Third Bank & Trust Co.		108.00/30	3,240.00
Real Estate Loans			
Railroadmen's Fed. Sav. and Loan Association			18,500.00
Other Debts Including Stock Pledges		/	
Alimony, Child Support and Separate Maintenance Payments Owed To		/	
TOTAL MONTHLY PAYMENTS		$	
NET WORTH (A minus B) $ 29,660.00		TOTAL LIABILITIES	B $22,040.00

Address of Property (Indicate S if Sold, PS if Pending Sale or R if Rental being held for income)		Type of Property	Present Market Value	Amount of Mortgages & Liens	Gross Rental Income	Mortgage Payments	Taxes, Ins. Maintenance and Misc.	Net Rental Income
5870 W. 14th Street	PS	SF	$25,000.00	$18,500.00	$	$144.30	$114.70	$
TOTALS ➤			$	$	$	$	$	$

LIST PREVIOUS CREDIT REFERENCES

B—Borrower C—Co-Borrower	Creditor's Name and Address	Account Number	Purpose	Highest Balance	Date Paid
B	Central National Bank	11-0103-2	Auto	$ 3,800.00	4/75
	200 W. 1st Street				

List any additional names under which credit has previously been received _____

AGREEMENT: The undersigned applies for the loan indicated in this application to be secured by a first mortgage or deed of trust on the property described herein, and represents that the property will not be used for any illegal or restricted purpose, and that all statements made in this application are true and are made for the purpose of obtaining the loan. Verification may be obtained from any source named in this application. The original or a copy of this application will be retained by the lender, even if the loan is not granted.

Settlement booklet received   JJS

I/we fully understand that it is a federal crime punishable by fine or imprisonment, or both, to knowingly make any false statements concerning any of the above facts as applicable under the provisions of Title 18 United States Code, Section 1014.

_____ Date 5/20/77   *Mary E. Smith*   Date 5/20/77
Borrower's Signature   Co-Borrower's Signature

VOLUNTARY INFORMATION FOR GOVERNMENT MONITORING PURPOSES

If this loan is for purchase or construction of a home, the following information is requested by the Federal Government to monitor this lender's compliance with Equal Credit Opportunity and Fair Housing Laws. The law provides that a lender may neither discriminate on the basis of this information nor on whether or not it is furnished. Furnishing this information is optional. If you do not wish to furnish the following information, please initial below.

BORROWER: I do not wish to furnish this information (initials)   JJS | **CO-BORROWER:** I do not wish to furnish this information (initials)   MES

RACE/	☐ American Indian, Alaskan Native	☐ Asian, Pacific Islander		**RACE/**	☐ American Indian, Alaskan Native	☐ Asian, Pacific Islander
NATIONAL ORIGIN	☐ Black	☐ Hispanic	☐ White	**NATIONAL ORIGIN**	☐ Black	☐ Hispanic	☐ White

SEX ☐ Female ☐ Male   ☐ Other (specify)   **SEX** ☐ Female ☐ Male   ☐ Other (specify)

FOR LENDER'S USE ONLY

(FNMA REQUIREMENT ONLY) This application was taken by   D. R. Brown   , in a face to face interview with the prospective borrower.

LOAN COMMITTEE ACTION

Amount $ 30,000.00   Rate 8½   % years   30   std.   X   reg. _____   Credit Report approved   5/23/77   by   DBW

Subject to the following conditions:

RAILROADMEN'S FEDERAL SAVINGS AND LOAN ASSOCIATION OF INDIANAPOLIS   , a full time employee of

Date   5/23/77   Chairman   R. T. Goodman

Mortgage loan application—reverse side.

which mathematically equates the expected future returns and the present in-difference value. In an intuitive and subjective investment decision, the investor would move directly from the rewards to the capital amount without using arithmetic. However, our objective approach to investment decisions involves a series of steps employing quantitative judgments.

The discount rate is an essential link between future benefits and present or investment value and must be determined before the investor can proceed with the actual analysis. This is a subjective decision which does not entail considerations of risk and uncertainty. These considerations are taken into account at another point in the decision making calculations. The discount rate should reflect the investor's personal time preference for money. Utilizing the "alternative opportunity rate," i.e., the average annual rate of profit per dollar invested expected from alternative investment opportunities, is a simple but insufficient substitute.

For example, consider a man of 65 on the verge of retirement who is contemplating the purchase of a small apartment structure as an investment. He expects to hold it for about 10 years and then sell it before his death. He has made forecasts of the property's cash productivity over the next 10 years and an estimate of its liquidation value at the end of this period. He intends to live off the income for a time and then liquidate the investment to simplify estate problems at the time of his death. One can see the complexities of selecting a discount rate which will convert these forecasts into a capital sum which he will accept as a fair exchange for the prospective rewards from the investment. It should be noted that alternate investment opportunities taken alone are not the sole or final determinants of the discount rate.

Non-Monetary Considerations. In actual situations, non-monetary considerations enter into the time value of money. Not all the benefits of ownership can be measured in dollar returns; some investors find satisfaction from the prestige of property ownership or a traditional sense of security just in owning real estate. This type of psychic income enters into the time value of money; and, when dollar returns are supplemented by intangible rewards, the discount rate applied to the dollar income will tend to be lower. Another factor is the relationship between (1) the time pattern of the cash flow and (2) the financial needs and investment objectives of the investor. For example, a doctor with substantial income will attach a lower time value to the cash flow during the years in which his professional income continues, and a high value to the returns after his retirement.

Where intangibles are not involved, the return on an alternative riskless investment is probably the best basis for establishing the time value of money or discount rate. The investor can decide the capital amount which he would equate with a guaranteed annuity of $10,000 per year for 10 years (or some other amount in the general range of the annual cash flow expected from the property and for the expected period of holding). Table 1 sets forth the discount rates which equate annuities of $1 per year and the indifference values as present lump sums. Thus, an indifference value of $56,500 related to an annuity of $10,000 for 10 years indicates a discount rate of about 12%.

Certainty and Uncertainty. Investment decisions are never based on *any* certainty, e.g., on guaranteed financial rewards. All business decisions require forecasts or predictions of outcomes which are necessarily based on inadequate information and unpredictable circumstances. The degrees of uncertainty range from almost reliable predictions (such as the return on government bonds) to highly speculative outcomes which are often characteristic of mining stock.

In real estate investment, the future financial rewards which require prediction are: (1) the periodic cash flow over the term of ownership, and (2) the net

TABLE 1. Indifference Values for Annuities of $1 per Year
at Various Discount Rates

Discount Rate as a Percent

Annuity in years	6	7	8	9	10	11	12
1	0.94	0.93	0.93	0.92	0.91	0.90	0.89
2	1.83	1.81	1.78	1.76	1.74	1.71	1.69
3	2.67	2.62	2.58	2.53	2.49	2.44	2.40
4	3.46	3.39	3.31	3.24	3.17	3.10	3.04
5	4.21	4.10	3.99	3.89	3.79	3.69	3.60
6	4.92	4.76	4.62	4.49	4.35	4.23	4.11
7	5.58	5.39	5.21	5.03	4.87	4.71	4.56
8	6.21	5.97	5.75	5.53	5.33	5.15	4.97
9	6.80	6.51	6.25	5.99	5.76	5.54	5.33
10	7.36	7.02	6.71	6.42	6.14	5.89	5.65

1. Present Value of $1 per annum. Values for other terms and discount rates can be secured by reference to any standard set of compound interest tables.

proceeds from the liquidation of the investment at the end of the holding period. The investor—with limited information and often limited understanding—makes his own best possible predictions. He will have some judgment, explicit or intuitive, on the odds (or chances) that the actuality will be higher than his prediction, or that it will be lower; and his feeling regarding the degree of uncertainty with respect to his prediction will influence his investment decision. Statisticians have technical and more precise concepts for expressing these common-sense and universally used judgments to describe the possible variability of a prediction. These must be explained because our investment decision model will require that the investor convert his judgments on uncertainty into quantitative terms.

Statisticians often express probabilities of some event occurring in terms of the number of chances out of 100, or some variation of this expression. For example, in predicting the future selling price of property, one might say that there is a 10 out of 100 chance that it will sell for more than $55,000 and a 20 out of 100 chance that it might bring less than $45,000. If there is some basis for judging the odds all up and down the line of possible selling prices, we could derive a curve like Figure 1a where the vertical scale is the odds expressed in terms of the number of chances out of 100 and the horizontal scale is the range of possible selling prices. For certain kinds of properties like a fairly new tract house or standard design where there is ample market information and plenty of recent "comparables," the predicted range of possible selling prices will be narrow and the curve will look like Curve A in Figure 2, which reflects the fact that the forecast can come very close to what the property will actually bring because the person making the forecast is well-informed and skilled in analyzing the real estate market. But for other kinds of property such as an expensive luxury home with few comparables and a style of architecture which will not appeal to many buyers but which might appeal greatly to a few, Curve B in Figure 2 will reflect the fact that the forecaster cannot be very certain of his prediction and that the actual selling price might fall

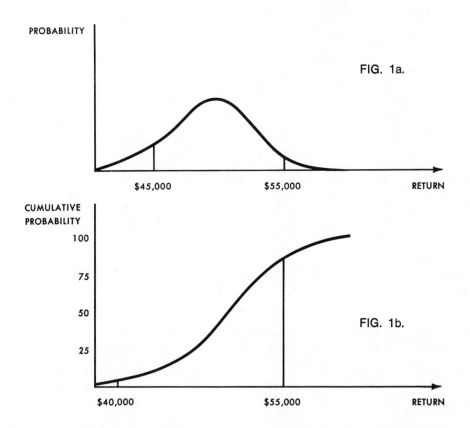

anywhere within a rather wide range of values. In both Curves A and B, the vertical height of the curve at various points along the value scale indicates the forecaster's best judgment of the odds that the actual selling price will fall upon that value. More precisely, such curves give the probability of the selling price falling within a certain range, this probability simply being proportional to the area under the curve within that range.

It is often convenient to use another form of expression for the same predictions which are the basis for Curves A and B in Figure 2. Figure 1b uses the same basic predictions and the same scales of odds and dollars, but shows the odds in cumulative form, i.e., at each point along the selling price scale, the height of the curve is the sum of the odds or chances at all lower prices up to that point. Thus at $40,000, this sum can be read on the odds scale at 10, which means that there are 10 chances out of 100 that the property will sell for $40,000 or less. The curve also tells us that there are 90 chances out of 100 that it will sell for $55,000 or less which means that there is a 10 out of 100 chance that it will bring more than $55,000. It is a commonplace that actual investors think in these terms of the chances that a property will bring more or less than a certain price, but it is also true that they rarely express these expectations in just this form. To do so infers a degree of precision of prediction which most practical men would say is impossible and unrealistic. On the other

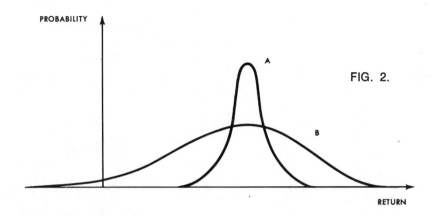

FIG. 2.

hand, it seems clear that an educated guess will generally be better than no explicit judgment at all. Certainly one of the reasons why investors do not attempt to express the expected odds in actual numbers, is that they would not know how to incorporate this judgment in their investment calculation. Our model will offer this opportunity.

Attitude Toward Risk. In the evaluation of investments whose returns are subject to uncertainty, the investor's attitude toward risk plays an important role; this attitude is clarified through quantitative expression. Investors are conditioned by the risk characteristics of the benefits expected to flow from the investment. Some investors place a high value on certainty; others will accept various degrees of uncertainty or risk of loss, depending on the offsetting possibilities of large gains.

Consider two investment propositions, A and B, which are described by the probability curves shown in Figure 2. Both propositions may yield the same average return; however, proposition B involves considerably more uncertainty than proposition A—it represents a greater gamble, with a possible potential for large gains but also for large losses. Thus, while the most probable expected returns may be equal for both propositions, the investor may prefer one proposition over the other. A conservative investor, being averse to risk, may reject proposition B and accept proposition A—even if proposition B should yield a somewhat higher expected return than proposition A. The ranking of investment alternatives will generally be significantly influenced by the investor's attitude toward risk; i.e., by the relative values which he places on positive cash flow and on losses.

The investor's attitude towards positive cash flow or losses can be represented graphically by deriving a "utility curve" as shown in Figure 3. In this graph, the vertical distance between the curve and the horizontal line is a measure of the value placed on a given investment outcome (gain to the right or loss to the left). It follows from Figure 3 that the positive value placed on the gain of the first $20,000 is greater than the value placed on the gain of an additional $20,000. In other words, the value placed on a gain of $40,000 is less than twice the value on a gain of $2,000. Furthermore, the negative value or disutility placed on a loss of $20,000 is as large as the positive value placed on a gain of $35,000—i.e., a 50% chance of making a profit of $35,000 would be offset by a 50% chance of losing $20,000. Similarly, a 50% chance of making a profit of $100,000 would be offset by a 50% chance of losing $24,000.

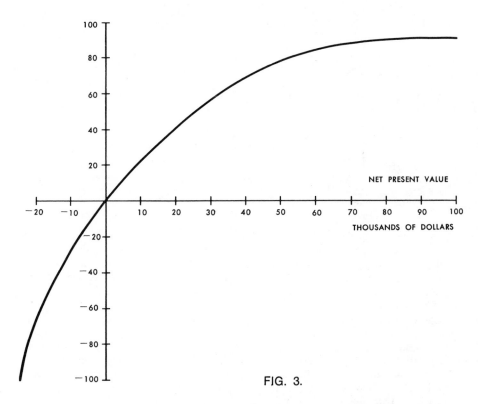

FIG. 3.

Derived Utility Table (from Figure 3)

Net Present Value (Thousands of Dollars)	−25	−20	−15	−10	5	15	25	40	60	80	100
Investor's Utility	−100	−65	−45	−25	12	32	50	70	85	90	92

The Figure 4 curves illustrate various possible utility functions. Figure 4a represents the most liberal position where almost equal values are assigned to gains and losses. Figure 4c represents the most conservative position—the highest degree of risk aversion (the negative value on the loss of a given amount far exceeds the positive value placed on a gain of the same amount).

Thus, before being able to make intelligent and consistent investment decisions, the investor has to ask himself consciously the values which he places on possible gains and losses. The majority of real estate investors will: (1) most likely have a utility curve somewhat averse to risk (following the general curvature as shown in Figures 4b and 4c); and (2) place higher negative values on losses than positive values on commensurate gains. Few investors would undertake an investment with a 50% chance of a loss of $100,000, even if there is a 50% probability of making a profit of $10,000. Most investors will prefer investment proposition A over proposition B in Figure 2. Again, the investor's particular utility curve may vary over time—e.g., the negative value

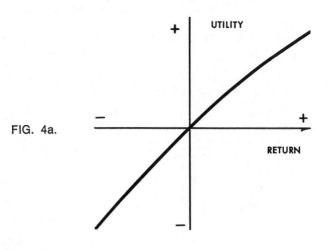

FIG. 4a.

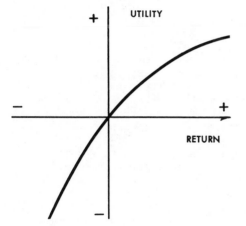

FIG. 4c.

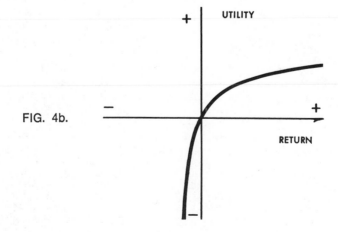

FIG. 4b.

placed on losses is likely to depend on his general financial position and prospects—and, hence, will be revised periodically.[2]

Real Estate Investment Decision Model.   All considerations which enter into
investment decisions can not be translated in quantitative terms; however, those
elements which can be identified have been identified. A model combining
these selected quantities into a final investment decision has been developed; the
investor must supply the following inputs:

1. A forecast of the most probable periodic returns as cash flows from the
   property and a forecast of the net cash proceeds from liquidation at the
   end of a period of ownership.
2. A qualification of this forecast in terms of a probability distribution. Three
   forecasts of cash flow and liquidation proceeds, each at a different level of
   probability, must be made.
3. The selection of a discount rate representing the investor's time preference
   of money.
4. An expression of the investor's personal utility curve.

A standardized format has been developed which could be used by any investor when evaluating property investments. This format is presented in
connection with the investment analysis example which follows; the entries and
calculations for a hypothetical investment analysis are presented. While the
general concepts are applicable to a variety of investment situations, this format
was designed for investment decisions related to income-producing real property.

Overall Structure. Considering the uncertain nature of investment, three
probability levels have been selected for evaluation. Each level is in the form
of an after-tax discounted cash flow forecast and reflects a different chance of
realization. Rather than utilizing a continuous probability distribution, these
discrete points were evaluated in correspondence to three probability levels.
The three points evaluated are: (1) "Low" (L); (2) "Most Probable" (MP);
and (3) "High" (H).[3] These probability points were arbitrarily chosen so that
the estimated probability of doing either worse than the pessimistic point (L) or
better than the optimistic point (H) is 10%, as shown in Figure 5. At the midpoint the probability is 80% or the most probable (MP) outcome.

The three probability points provide a basis for establishing an expected
utility for each probability level. The total expected utility to the investor for
the property under evaluation is then the sum of the expected utilities for each
of the three probability levels. From the expected utilities at the three levels,
the final step is to derive the "cash indifference acquisition price," which is the
maximum amount which the investor would be willing to bid for the property
under the estimates and assumptions made.

A Standardized Investment Analysis Format.   The proposed standardized
investment analysis format can be applied to any income property. The example income property is a three story, frame apartment building in the final

---

[2] For a detailed description on how an investor may derive his utility function, see
the excellent article by R. O. Swalm, "Utility Theory—Insights into Risk Taking,"
Harvard Business Review, November–December, 1966. Some standard textbooks on
modern decision theory which may be useful in this context are G. Hadley, *Introduction
to Probability and Statistical Decision Making: New Perspectives and Methods* (San
Francisco: Holden Day, 1967); and I. Horowitz, *An Introduction to Quantitative Business Analysis* (New York: McGraw-Hill Book Co., 1965).

[3] The number of points to be evaluated can be increased if additional accuracy is desired; thus, for particularly risky propositions with wide fluctuations of possible returns,
one may decide to use five rather than three probability levels.

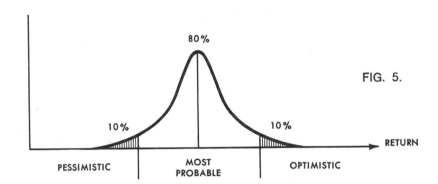

FIG. 5.

stages of construction. The apartment contains nine studio and fifteen single-bedroom suites and is similar in construction, style and attributes to other apartments located in the same general area. The area is in transition; old single-family residences are rapidly being replaced by low-rise apartment blocks (a process which has gained momentum during the past five years). Although favorably located with respect to the central business district, shopping facilities, transportation arteries, and a popular recreation area, the apartment building will be subject to increasing competition both from within the area and from rapidly growing competitive areas.

Case Study and Format Description. Each of the in-put estimates and calculations require a detailed explanation.

Section A—Basic Parameters

Item (a). Property identification—Schwabcliff Gardens

Item (b). Probability levels
> (1) High (H) = 10 out of 100 (.10)
> (2) Most Probable (MP) = 80 out of 100 (.80)
> (3) Low (L) = 10 out of 100 (.10)

Item (c). Depreciation method. The double declining balance method based on a 5% straight line rate was selected from among the methods permitted for income tax calculation.

Item (d). Marginal tax rate—50%. This is the marginal tax rate of the investor on total income from all sources used to measure benefit from tax loss, if any, on the income property investment. It is assumed that the investor is incorporated and has a large source of other income not related to the investment under analysis. Therefore, the investor's marginal tax rate is 50% on all of the property income (other than capital gains which are taxed at the maximum rate of 25%). Similarly, losses on the property provide tax benefits which are offset at the marginal tax rate against other income in the same year in which the loss occurs.

Item (e). Discount rate—6%. This rate reflects the time value of money to the investor. This discount rate reflects a safe rate of return which can be obtained by this investor in riskless investments such as government securities.

Section B—Initial Acquisition of Property. The following entries can be established prior to acquisition of the property and are thus subject to little uncertainty.

TABLE 2. Probability Level—Low

Year	1	2	3	4	5	6	7	8	9	10
Discount factors at 6.0%	.943	.890	.840	.792	.747	.705	.665	.627	.592	.558
(6) Gross income (full occupancy)	38,880	38,880	38,400	37,600	37,200	36,600	35,800	35,000	34,200	33,400
(7) Occupancy rate	.70	.90	.94	.94	.94	.92	.92	.90	.90	.90
(8) Effective gross income	27,220	34,990	36,100	35,340	34,970	33,670	32,940	31,500	30,780	30,060
(9) Operating expenses	14,750	15,500	16,000	16,200	16,400	16,600	16,800	17,000	17,250	17,500
(10) Interest on mortgage	17,480	17,160	16,800	16,400	15,990	15,530	15,020	14,460	13,850	13,180
(11) Book value of building	205,000	184,500	166,050	149,450	134,500	121,050	108,950	98,050	88,250	79,420
(12) Depreciation allowance	20,500	18,450	16,610	13,450	14,950	12,110	10,890	9,810	8,820	7,940
(13) Taxable income	−25,510	−16,120	−13,310	−12,210	−10,870	−10,570	−9,770	−9,770	−9,140	−8,560
(14) Taxes	—	—	—	—	—	—	—	—	—	—
(15) Benefit of tax shield	12,750	8,060	6,650	6,100	5,430	5,280	4,880	4,880	4,570	4,280
(16) Annual mortgage principal	3,400	3,720	4,080	4,480	4,890	5,360	5,860	6,420	7,030	7,700
(17) Mortgage principal payments (cumulative)	3,400	7,120	11,200	15,680	20,570	25,930	31,790	38,210	45,240	52,940
(18) Unpaid mortgage principal	180,600	176,880	172,800	168,320	163,430	158,080	152,210	145,790	138,760	131,060
(19) Cash flow after taxes	4,350	6,670	5,880	4,370	3,130	1,470	150	−1,490	−2,780	−4,040
(20) Discounted cash flow after taxes	4,100	5,940	4,940	3,460	2,340	1,040	90	−930	−1,650	−2,250
(21) Discounted cash flow after taxes (cumulative)	4,100	10,040	14,980	18,440	20,780	21,820	21,910	20,980	19,330	17,080

Line 1. Estimated acquisition price	$275,000
Line 2. Initial mortgage debt	$184,000
Interest rate—9½%	
Term—20 years	
Amortization—constant annual payments on	
interest and principal	
Line 3. Initial equity	$ 91,000
Line 4. Depreciation base (estimated value of building)	$205,000
Line 5. Estimated land value	70,000

Line 1: Estimated acquisition price. The investor must make an initial assumption as to the most probable acquisition price of the property; it is required: (1) as a basis for a derived assumption on mortgage financing; and (2) on the initial depreciation base for the analysis which follows. In the case of an existing property this price will be based on the tasking price; it will reflect the investor's estimate of how this price may be modified in the bargaining process. For a proposed project not yet in existence, the price of acquisition would be the sum of the acquisition price of the land plus estimated costs of the improvements. The results of this analysis will be a value which will show through comparison whether the initial estimate of the cost of acquisition represents a favorable overall investment opportunity.

Line 2: Initial mortgage debt. This input is the total amount of mortgage debt which can be raised for this property, given the above estimated acquisition price.

Line 3: Initial equity. The difference between lines 1 and 2.

Line 4: Depreciation base. Estimated value for building.

Line 5: Estimated value for land. The difference between line 1 (estimated acquisition price) and line 4 (estimated value of building).

Section C—Operating Costs and Revenues (see Tables 2, 3 and 4). At this point the analyst must estimate the number of years which the investor expects to retain property ownership before sale and liquidation of his investment. A ten-year period has been used in the case example.

One set of forecasts and calculations is required for each of the three selected probability levels. The projections for the Low (L) level represent estimates of productivity factors with only a 10 out of 100 probability of a lower actuality; at the other end of the scale, the High (H) projections are estimated to have only 10 out of 100 chances of being exceeded. The Most Probable (MP) projections are estimated to have an 80 out of 100 chance of being realized. In the case at hand, for example, the low projections of gross income reflect the possibility of a decline in income due to increasing competition which may depress rental rates. The rent-up period may be extended and the ultimate level of occupancy could continue at an unfavorable ratio. Operating expenses are projected to start at a high point and to increase substantially during the ten-year period. Note that the mortgage interest, the principal repayments and the allowances for depreciation are the same for each probability level. In this example, the projections of gross income, occupancy rates and operating expenses thus determine the differences in after-tax cash flows obtained at the three levels of probability.

The total accumulated discounted after-tax cash flow from operations appears on line 21 in year 10. This figure is carried forward to Section E of the analysis and added to the discounted cash flow from the sale of the property in order to obtain the total discounted return from the investment.

Line 6: Gross income with full occupancy. Assume 100% occupancy and derive the gross income for each year of the assumed holding period.

TABLE 3. Probability Level—Most Probable

Year	1	2	3	4	5	6	7	8	9	10
Discount factors at 6.0%	.943	.890	.840	.792	.747	.705	.665	.627	.592	.558
(6) Gross income (full occupancy)	38,880	39,600	40,800	42,000	43,200	43,800	43,800	44,400	44,400	45,000
(7) Occupancy rate	.75	.90	.98	.98	.98	.97	.96	.95	.95	.95
(8) Effective gross income	29,160	35,640	39,980	41,160	42,340	42,490	42,050	42,180	42,180	42,750
(9) Operating expenses	14,000	14,750	15,000	15,000	15,000	15,500	15,500	15,500	16,000	16,000
(10) Interest on mortgage	17,480	17,160	16,800	16,400	15,990	15,530	15,020	14,460	13,850	13,180
(11) Book value of building	205,000	184,500	166,050	149,450	134,500	121,050	108,950	98,050	88,250	79,420
(12) Depreciation allowance	20,500	18,450	16,610	14,950	13,450	12,110	10,890	9,810	8,820	7,940
(13) Taxable income	−22,820	−14,720	−8,430	−5,190	−2,100	−650	640	2,410	3,510	7,880
(14) Taxes	—	—	—	—	—	—	320	1,200	1,750	3,940
(15) Benefit of tax shield	11,410	7,360	4,210	2,590	1,050	320	—	—	—	—
(16) Annual mortgage principal	3,400	3,720	4,080	4,480	4,890	5,360	5,860	6,420	7,030	7,700
(17) Mortgage principal payments (cumulative)	3,400	7,120	11,200	15,680	20,570	25,930	31,790	38,210	45,240	52,940
(18) Unpaid mortgage principal	180,600	176,880	172,800	168,320	163,430	158,080	152,210	145,790	138,760	131,060
(19) Cash flow after taxes	5,690	7,370	8,320	7,880	7,510	6,430	5,350	4,590	3,540	4,180
(20) Discounted cash flow after taxes	5,370	6,560	6,990	6,240	5,610	4,530	3,560	2,880	2,090	2,330
(21) Discounted cash flow after taxes (cumulative)	5,370	11,930	18,920	25,160	30,770	35,300	38,860	41,740	43,830	46,160

TABLE 4.　Probability Level—High

Year	1	2	3	4	5	6	7	8	9	10
Discount factors at 6.0%	.943	.890	.840	.792	.747	.705	.665	.627	.592	.558
(6) Gross income (full occupancy)	38,880	40,200	42,000	43,200	45,000	45,600	46,200	46,800	47,400	48,000
(7) Occupancy rate	.90	.98	.99	.99	.99	.99	.98	.98	.98	.97
(8) Effective gross income	34,990	39,400	41,580	42,770	44,550	45,040	45,280	45,860	46,450	46,560
(9) Operating expenses	12,500	12,800	13,000	13,000	13,000	13,150	13,500	13,500	14,000	14,000
(10) Interest on mortgage	17,480	17,160	16,800	16,400	15,990	15,530	15,020	14,460	13,850	13,180
(11) Book value of building	205,000	184,500	166,050	149,450	134,500	121,050	108,950	98,050	88,250	79,420
(12) Depreciation allowance	20,500	18,450	16,610	14,950	13,450	12,110	10,890	9,810	8,820	7,940
(13) Taxable income	-15,490	-9,010	-4,830	-1,580	2,110	4,250	5,870	8,090	9,780	11,440
(14) Taxes	—	—	—	—	1,050	2,120	2,930	4,040	4,890	5,720
(15) Benefit of tax shield	7,740	4,500	2,410	790	—	—	—	—	—	—
(16) Annual mortgage principal	3,400	3,720	4,080	4,480	4,890	5,360	5,860	6,420	7,030	7,700
(17) Mortgage principal payments (cumulative)	3,400	7,120	11,200	15,680	20,570	25,930	31,790	38,210	45,240	52,940
(18) Unpaid mortgage principal	180,600	176,880	172,800	168,320	163,430	158,080	152,210	145,790	138,760	131,060
(19) Cash flow after taxes	9,360	10,230	10,120	9,680	9,610	8,870	7,960	7,430	6,680	5,960
(20) Discounted cash flow after taxes	8,830	9,100	8,500	7,670	7,180	6,250	5,290	4,660	3,950	3,320
(21) Discounted cash flow after taxes (cumulative)	8,830	17,930	26,430	34,100	41,280	47,530	52,820	57,480	61,430	64,750

Line 7: Occupancy rate. Estimate the actual occupancy rate for eace year (in per cent).

Line 8: Effective gross income. Line 6 multiplied by line 7.

Line 9: Operating expenses. Estimate of total annual expenses incurred in operating the property.

Line 10: Interest on mortgage for each year.

Line 11: Book value of building at beginning of each year. Initial building value less accumulated depreciation allowances.

Line 12: Depreciation allowance. This is based on the book value derived from line 11 and the depreciation method as specified in Section A.

Line 13: Taxable income. Line 8 (effective gross income) minus line 9 (operating expenses), line 10 (interest on mortgage), and line 12 (depreciation allowance).

Line 14: Taxes. Based on line 13 and the investor's marginal income tax rate as specified in Section A, if the taxable income is positive.

Line 15: Benefit of tax shield if taxable income is negative. A negative value in line 13 can benefit the investor—it enables him to offset such negative income against taxable income from other sources. Enter the savings in tax derived from reductions of other taxable income using the marginal tax rate from Section A.

Line 16: Annual principal payments on mortgage.

Line 17: Principal payments on mortgage (cumulative). For each year, the sum of all previous annual entries from line 16 (example: entry for year 3 equals sum of entries for years 1, 2, and 3 from line 16). This gives the total amount of mortgage principal repaid up to the current year.

Line 18: Remaining principal on mortgage. Line 2 (initial mortgage debt) minus line 17 (total amount of mortgage principal repaid up to that year).

Line 19: Annual cash flow after taxes. Sum of line 13 (taxable income), line 15 (benefit of tax shield if taxable income is negative), plus line 12 (depreciation allowance) minus line 16 (principal payments on mortgage), and minus line 14 (taxes).

Line 20: Annual discounted cash flow after taxes. Yearly entries on line 19 are multiplied by the discount factors, i.e., the present values of $1 at the selection discount rate which are to be entered for each year.

Line 21: Discounted cash flow after taxes (cumulative). For each year, the sum of all previous annual entries from line 20—this gives the total discounted cash flow accumulated at the end of that year.

  Section D—Investment Liquidation. The selling price of the property at the end of the assumed holding period is estimated for each of the three probability levels. (See Table 5) Capital gains—as defined under U. S. tax law—are determined and the maximum tax rate of 25% is applied; the capital gains tax is then deducted from the selling price. Finally, the principal outstanding on the mortgage is deducted to determine the net cash flow to the investor on the sale of the property. The resulting cash flow is then discounted to present value figures. Under Canadian tax laws, the excess depreciation or capital cost allowance must be recaptured at the investor's marginal tax rate and the capital gains (excess of selling price over initial purchase price) are non-taxable. In order to use this analysis in Canada, some minor changes in format are thus required in this section of the analysis.

Line 22: The estimated selling price of the property. Expected market value at the end of the assumed holding period.

Line 23: Book value of the property. At the end of the assumed holding period —line 5 (initial value of land) plus line 11 (depreciated book value of building).

TABLE 5

	L	MP	H
Line 22: Estimated selling price	245,000	295,000	325,000
Line 23: Book value of property	149,420	149,420	149,420
Line 24: Capital gains	95,580	145,580	175,580
Line 25: Taxes on capital gains	23,890	36,390	43,890
Line 26: Net to seller	90,050	127,550	150,050
Line 27: Discounted net to seller	50,250	71,170	83,730
(Discount factor =.558..the present value of $1 in 10 years at 6%)			

Line 24: Capital gains. Line 22 (estimated selling price of property) minus line 23 (terminal book value of property).

Line 25: Taxes on capital gains. Case example assumes U. S. tax laws.

Line 26: Net proceeds to seller. Line 22 (estimated selling price of property) minus line 25 (taxes on capital gains) and line 18 (remaining principal on mortgage).

Line 27: Discounted net to seller. The entry on line 26 is multiplied by the discount factor.

Section E—Utility Calculation (see table 6). Each investor has a unique utility function which reflects his attitude toward risk. The first step in this section is thus to quantify this individual utility function in the form presented in Figure 3 (including its derived table). The investor's attitude is expressed as a series of points which represent the relative utilities of dollar gains and losses. These points are plotted according to: (1) a horizontal dollar scale of gains and losses, and (2) a vertical scale of relative utilities and disutilities—as in Figure 3. They are then connected to form a curve from which a utility table can be derived from readings along the curve. This curve and table are essential before the utility

TABLE 6

	L	MP	H
Line 28: Total discounted return (21+27)	67,330	117,330	148,480
Line 29: Initial equity (from line 3)	91,000	91,000	91,000
Line 30: Total return to initial equity (28÷29)	.74	1.29	1.63
Line 31: Difference: total return—initial equity (28−29)	−23,670	26,330	57,480
Line 32: Utility factor (from utility table)	−90	52	83
Line 33: Percent probability	.10	.80	.10
Line 34: Expected utility (32×33)	−9.0	41.6	8.3
Line 35: Total expected utility for this property (L 34 + MP 34 + H 34)			40.9

calculation step can be completed. The curve and table in Figure 3 represent the utility function of our hypothetical investor.

Entered on line 28 are (1) the total discounted return for each of the three probability levels which represents the total appropriate cumulative discounted cash flow from operations (Section C, Line 21) and (2) the discounted net to seller at liquidation (Section D, Line 27). These returns are related to the initial equity as (1) a ratio in Line 30, and (2) a dollar difference in Line 31—for each probability level. By referring to the utility table in Figure 3, these dollar differences are converted to utility factors (Line 32). Each utility factor must be weighted (Line 33) according to the chances of achieving each level in order to derive the expected utility for each of the three levels (Line 34). The sum of the three weighted utilities (40.9 in this example), represents the total expected utility for this property according to: (1) the productivity predictions at the three levels of probability and (2) the utility function defined by the investor.

Line 28: Total discounted return from investment. This gives the cumulative total net return, appropriately discounted, derived as the sum of line 21 (discounted cash flow after taxes, cumulative), and line 27 (discounted net to seller from investment liquidation).

Line 29: Initial equity. Same entry as in line 3.

Line 30: Ratio of total return to initial equity. The present value of the cumulative net return as a percentage of initial equity (line 28 divided by line 29).

Line 31: Difference—Total return less initial equity. The amount by which the total cumulative discounted return to equity differs from the initial equity. (Line 28 minus line 29).

Line 32: Utility factor. Derived by reading from the table, based on Figure 3, the utility value corresponding to the dollar difference derived in line 21 (excess or deficit on recapture of initial equity).

Line 33: Percent probability for this probability level. 10% for L (Low) and H (High), 80% for MP (Most Probable) probability levels, as established in Section A.

Line 34: Expected utility at each probability level. Line 33 (percent probability) times line 32 (utility factor).

Line 35: Total expected utility for this property. Sum of expected utilities for each probability level (L, MP, H) from line 34.

Section F—Summary Evaluation

Line 36: Total adjusted difference—$19,000; dollar equivalent of line 35, from Figure 7.

Line 37: Cash indifference value—$294,900; line 1 plus 35.

The final step is to convert the total expected utility for the property to a dollar figure by referring to the derived utility curve. The utility measure of 40.9 from Line 35 can be converted to about $19,000; this amount represents the excess in discounted return to the investor over the initial equity under the assumptions of productivity, probability and utility.

The cash indifference value (line 37) is the initially assumed acquisition price of the property plus the $19,000 premium which the investor would be justified in paying under the assumptions. Had the total expected utility for the property been a negative figure, the investor's cash indifference value would have been less than the initial acquisition price; the investment thus would probably not be made at or above the acquisition price. In any case, the cash indifference value provides the investor with a point of reference which reflects his own estimates and notions of productivity, risk and utility; it is a "value to the investor" against which (1) he may judge the seller's asking price and (2) which will guide him in his negotiations.

The result of this investment analysis is, in part, a function of initial estimates of: (1) the acquisition price, (2) financing pattern, and (3) depreciation base. If the Cash Indifference Value is substantially different from the assumed Acquisition Price, the analyst may re-work the analysis utilizing new assumptions on financing and the depreciation base which conform more closely to the calculated Cash Indifference Value. Mortgage lenders and tax authorities often base their value decisions closer to the calculated Cash Indifference Value than to the originally assumed Acquisition Price.

Conclusions. In every field of human decision making technological progress has been largely a matter of reducing uncertainty; certainty can rarely be assured. The X-ray plate and the electro-cardiogram require the skilled interpretation of the physician and are not positive indicators which eliminate uncertainty. The analytical model presented here is no more than a small step toward reducing uncertainty in judgments on real estate investments. It requires explicit consideration of components in the decision making process which are treated intuitively and often sub-consciously by the analyst. Though the variables are not capable of exact measurement, if recognized and thoughtfully considered, they may be given relative numerical expression. The final decision benefits by this kind of narrowing of uncertainty, though much uncertainty remains.

Application. A similar formal investment evaluation scheme was recently introduced in a manufacturing enterprise by one of the authors. Within three two-hour training sessions, a reasonable operating knowledge of the procedures —including the underlying business theories of discounted cash flow, probability, and utility—was conveyed to the decision makers. Once the method was instituted, the necessity for thinking propositions through in all their ramifications and consequences, and the availability of quantitative results, served to stimulate and guide the investors' resourcefulness in the search for better alternatives; it generated consideration of alternative financing arrangements, alternative locations, and other alternative solutions.

This investment evaluation procedure was first introduced in 1967 in a company with only $1 million sales per year. Since that time, it has been successfully adopted by the parent company, a diversified medium-sized enterprise, for corporate evaluation of divisional projects. There is no reason why these concepts and procedures which have proven themselves in investment evaluation in a manufacturing context should not prove equally beneficial to investors in the real estate sector by providing a systematic framework to guide experience and judgment in an increasingly complex and competitive decision making environment.

Questions

1. What are the principal factors which investors typically consider in making judgments regarding real estate investment opportunities?
2. How can non-monetary factors be given consideration in real estate investment decisions?
3. How can the probability of events occurring in the future be expressed in a way which will aid investment decisions?
4. What is meant by cumulative probability?
5. How may attitudes toward risk affect investment decisions?
6. What is meant by a "utility curve"?
7. Do you believe the analysis followed in the case study reflects useful approaches to real estate investment decisions?

IV

Special Properties and Problems

The final section of the book discusses various special properties and problems. Chapter 18 reviews housing trends and related topics. Several interesting study projects help to point up the discussions in this chapter. One deals with the status of urban renewal. Another reviews some of the possibilities of house building in the 1980's. Chapter 19 considers various types of business real estate, including stores, shopping centers, office buildings, industrial properties, and special-purpose properties. Case studies present some interesting aspects of financing an office building, and some of the problems related to industrial location.

Farms, ranches, forests, recreational land, and other rural real estate are considered in Chapter 20. A short study project on farm management is included. This is followed by a discussion of international real estate trends. A case study on a corporate location problem abroad points up some of the discussion in this chapter.

The final chapter, entitled "Toward Improved Real Estate Administration," is itself almost a study project since it raises various questions and possibilities regarding real estate decisions and resources in the years ahead.

18

HOUSING TRENDS
AND PROBLEMS

HOUSING NEEDS AND WANTS

Housing problems reflect the needs and wants of people for housing, relative to its availability. Needs result from population growth as well as from changes in age distribution. Needs arise also from the movement of people from place to place. Although population is always a basic factor in housing needs and wants, incomes are essential in translating needs and wants into effective demands. Thus, people will get the housing they are willing to pay for either directly or through subsidies or other arrangements. Effective demands will reflect the percentage of income which people are willing to spend for housing relative to other things. Decisions on housing expenditures are affected by the priorities which people assign to various needs, the availability of funds and their cost, the technology available for use by the housing industry, the effectiveness with which housing can be marketed and managed, and other factors.

Estimates of population changes and potential housing needs have been lowered in recent years.[1] Population estimates for the year 2000 had ranged as high as 340 million. More recent estimates, however, place this figure at around 245 to 260 million. The increase from around 214 million in

[1] See, for example, the report of the President's Committee on Urban Housing, *A Decent Home* (Washington, D. C.: Government Printing Office, 1968), which projected the need for 26 million new or rehabilitated housing units for the period 1968 to 1978. See also Robert C. Turner, *Economic Growth: The Outlook for Ten and Twenty-five Years* (Bloomington, Ind.: Committee for Futures Studies, 1975), and Study Project 5–1, on page 137. See also Joseph A. Pechman (ed.), *The 1978 Budget: Setting National Priorities* (Washington, D. C.: The Brookings Institution, 1977), especially Richard P. Nathan and Paul R. Dommell, "The Cities," pp. 283–316.

1976 to 245 million obviously would translate into lower housing requirements than an increase to 260 million or to something over 300 million. Lower long-term population estimates influence the thinking of investors in residential real estate as well as builders, city planners, and others.

Population Growth

It now appears that zero population growth (ZPG) may be reached during the 1990's.[2] The labor force, however, will continue to grow throughout the rest of the century because of the high number of births in the 1950's and 1960's.

Because of the changing age distribution of the population, the types of goods and services needed by young adults are likely to be in relatively strong demand into the 1980's. Thereafter there may be some changes in the needs for housing, automobiles, furniture, appliances, and related items. Population trends are already shifting housing demands from larger to smaller dwelling units. Because of family size and energy problems, smaller automobile models have become more popular than formerly.

Age Distribution

During the 1980's the age groups under 13 will tend to decline in numbers as will the 14–17 age group. The 18–24 age group will tend to hold steady; there will be slight gains in the 25–34 age group. The 35–44 age group will register gains and the 45–54 age group will increase slightly. The older age groups will tend to increase, although at slower rates.

Population Movements

Americans have always been a mobile people and they continue to follow this pattern. We have pointed out that on the average approximately one out of five families moves each year and it has been estimated that, in the group moving, one out of five moves from one area or region to another.

In recent years the principal population movements have been from farms and rural areas to cities and from the central parts of the cities to suburban and outlying areas. There have also been movements to the South and West.

Currently, however, the movement from the farms and rural areas has virtually stopped. Indeed, there has been some movement in the opposite direction. The outward movement from the center of cities not only to the suburbs but into the surrounding countryside seems likely to continue. Even though efforts have been made to induce people to move back to the central city, it seems probable that trends will continue to be outward. Some moves back to the central city have occurred and more may take place, particularly if central cities can be revitalized.

[2] Turner, *op. cit.*

Movements to the South and Southwest have persisted but at slower rates than formerly. Population changes and shifts tend to spell additional needs for housing in new locations. (See Figs. 18–1 and 18–2.)

Living Standards

Past trends suggest not only that people will need more housing in the future but that they will want housing of higher quality Whether they will be able to afford better housing, however, is not clear. Costs have advanced. rapidly in terms of both construction and current operations. Technology may help.

Quality of housing may improve; for example, more than two-thirds of new housing is built with more than one bath; almost all new dwelling units have air conditioning; and better designs, insulation, and quality of materials are generally in evidence.

High costs of energy have had an effect on housing location and demands. Environmental problems have influenced zoning and building codes, and hence housing development.

It is possible that people may deliberately reduce their standards of living, perhaps hoping that this will help to solve some of our social and environmental problems. It is doubtful that the number who may do this will be sufficiently large to affect long-term trends, but the possibility should be recognized.

Another possibility (but not a strong probability) is that people will

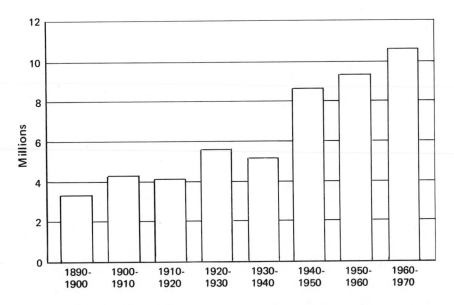

FIG. 18–1. Population change for ten-year periods: 1890 to 1970.

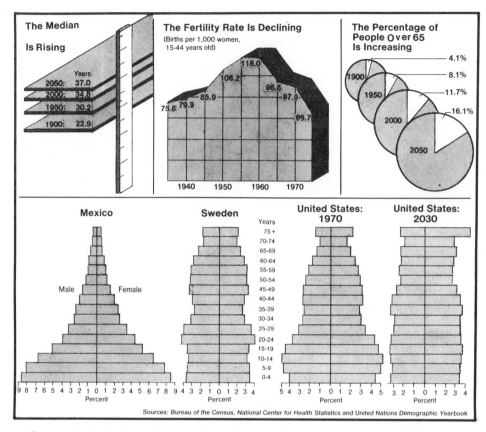

Top graphs depict United States population trends. Those on bottom show differences between countries having high and low growth rates. In Mexico, with growing population, younger rate ranges predominate. Sweden, with low growth, shows balance between young and old. The U. S. in 1970 had pattern similar to Mexico's, except that the birth rate dropped. By the year 2030, the U. S. may show a population profile similar to Sweden's.

FIG. 18–2. New population trends. (*Source: The New York Times,* February 6, 1977.)

prefer to spend more of their incomes on other things and less on housing than in the past. For example, production efficiencies and cost reductions in other areas might have such a result; or people may change their value scales in ways that favor other things relative to housing.

Land Use Policy

Increased restrictions on land use are debated widely as a major issue of public policy. Restrictions tend to add to land costs. Justification is usually based on dangers of overcrowding and hence damage to the environment.

The Continental United States has a density of only 70 people per square mile compared to 600 in the United Kingdom, 650 in West Germany, and 250 in France. Thus environmental dangers usually arise from sources other than overcrowding.[3] Even so, these issues will be under consideration in the foreseeable future and may have a heavy bearing on housing location and costs.

Housing Standards

From a public policy standpoint people may determine that no one should have a lower housing standard than a predefined level. To a degree housing codes do this now; but many are not enforced. In the future standards for minimal housing may be raised and enforcement may become more rigorous. People may also wish to have a large portion of their tax dollars allocated to provide better housing for those in lower income groups; as a result those in higher income brackets may have relatively less to spend for housing or other things.

It is not possible to estimate very exactly the trend of developments in housing; some possibilities are suggested by the above discussion but we should recognize that events may unfold in entirely different ways.

Future Consumer Wants

What kinds of housing will consumers want in the future? How will such wants be determined?

Consumer opinion surveys and similar types of investigations can determine with reasonable accuracy which types of properties and property services appear to be most popular currently and in the near future. Greatest contributions to improving products, however, have usually been made by those who are able to anticipate the wants of the people, often before they themselves were aware of them. People did not know whether they wanted color television before it was made available; when it became available, it was difficult to determine how much people would be willing to pay for it.

Much the same thing is true of housing. If the original pioneers in the prefabricated housing industry, for example, had asked people if they wanted such a product, in all probability few prefabricated houses would have been produced. Such pioneers in new building methods, designs, and marketing practices, however, have found a widespread acceptance of their products once they were made available at attractive prices.

An interesting analogy may be drawn from the automobile field. Market studies often brought striking similarity of styles and types. As a result, however, foreign cars began to find a market here and they in turn have influenced domestic styles and types.

[3] See, for example, B. Bruce Briggs, "Land Use and The Environment" in *No Land is an Island* (San Francisco: Institute for Contemporary Studies, 1975).

FACTORS IN POTENTIAL HOUSING DEMAND

Housing demand is primarily a reflection of (1) incomes and income prospects, (2) terms and availability of financing plus anticipated changes in financial terms, (3) preferences of consumers for housing or for other goods and services or for savings and (4) cost and price factors, including materials, labor, land, financing, energy, the environment, and others. Also, population forces play a role in establishing overall housing needs as we suggested above.

The demand for housing involves more than the desire and willingness to pay for shelter, comfort, and privacy. It includes prestige and status factors, particularly in the case of home ownership. Prestige factors, however, may also be of importance in regard to rental housing, especially in the higher rental ranges.

It is important to recognize the interrelationships between housing demand factors. For example, incomes and income prospects may be indicative of a strong demand for housing but may be offset by unfavorable financing terms or by high costs and prices. High energy costs have had a decided effect on housing demands. Recent and projected population growth suggests that housing needs will be high in the 1980's. If incomes do not expand, however, or if building costs advance rapidly or if financing is not available on favorable terms, or if energy and environmental costs are usually high, there may be little expansion in housing demand despite the pressures of population. Or again, people may prefer to spend more or less on travel, automobiles, amusements, education, or other things than on housing. Public policy may bring efforts to revitalize older areas of our cities and to conserve the existing housing supply rather than to add greatly to this supply.

Impact of Income on Demand

Of major importance to an understanding of changes in the demand for housing is the trend of personal incomes, both in monetary and in real terms. In 1950, for example, income per capita after taxes, measured in terms of 1972 dollars, was $2,386. By 1960, it increased to $2,697 (again in terms of 1972 dollars). In 1970, per-capita disposable (after-tax) income was $3,348 in current dollars or $3,619 in 1972 dollars. Rising incomes have tended to emphasize qualitative factors in housing demands. In 1975 the comparable figures were $5,040 in current dollars and $4,012 in 1972 dollars.

As income levels move upward, the luxury and qualitative aspects of housing tend to increase in importance. Conversely, as incomes decline, the utilitarian aspects of housing demand tend to increase in relative importance.

When real incomes are high and tending to go higher, the demand for all types of residential real estate, with the possible exception of that renting at very low levels, must be considered in terms of its luxury aspects. In a sense, of course, nearly all housing as we know it today is a luxury. All of the people in the country could be provided with shelter in barracks or mobile homes for a fraction of the investment that is represented by our current housing supply and for a small fraction of the annual costs of the housing services that we enjoy. When incomes are high, however, quality factors gain in importance.

Competition Between New and Old Housing

During periods when demand is unusually strong and before building programs can add appreciably to the available supply, the prices of older houses and the rents for older apartments move up along with the prices and rents for newer accommodations. As the number of dwelling units increases, however, older houses begin to lose out in competition with newer, more modern structures. Hence the prices and rents of older properties level out and begin to move downward before newer properties are affected.

Eventually, if there are great additions to supply or if real incomes begin to move downward, some of the older properties may be able to compete more effectively as consumers try to reduce their living expenses. Often older properties are not encumbered with heavy carrying charges and gain in relative competitive position. As newer properties are refinanced or other adjustments are made to cyclical changes, they will move into a more favorable competitive position relative to older structures.

When incomes are high and consumers stress the qualitative and luxury aspects of housing, the rate at which dwelling units grow obsolete increases. Hence there is a tendency for older houses to lose out in their competition with newer accommodations. Considerable emphasis at such times is placed on modernization and repair programs for older properties. Indeed, recent years have seen an upsurge in the popularity of programs to renovate older and larger houses.

Filtering

Most of us occupy housing that someone has used before; some of this housing is owned, some rented. The term "filtering" or "filtering down" has been applied to the process of moving dwelling units from higher to lower income users, much as automobiles filter or move from those who own them as new cars and those who own them later on.

The filtering process has not worked as well in housing as in the automobile market, in part because surplus supplies are needed for the process to work and in part because the housing market has a number of barriers to open competition that interfere with the easy movement of dwelling units from one user to another. Of major importance among such barriers is fixity of location, of course; in addition, zoning and deed restrictions play a part.

Filtering works better in some parts of the housing market than in others.[4] It works best in the middle price and rent ranges, fairly well in the higher ranges. It works only to a limited extent in the lower price and rent ranges.

Doubling Up

The sharing of dwellings by families, or doubling up, often is widespread during periods of housing shortages or in recessions. It is a commonplace practice among many in lower income groups. Even in prosperous periods and in cases where there is no economic necessity, some families double up for a variety of reasons. A young married couple may live with in-laws until an apartment or house is located. Three or four single persons may share an apartment. An elderly couple may live with a son or daughter in order to help look after children so both of the young people may work. Or there may be doubling up in order to look after those who are ill or incapacitated. For the most part, however, economic reasons are primarily responsible for doubling up.

Income Subsidies

Housing demand results not only from what people spend for housing out of their own incomes but also from what government does with tax dollars. The tax dollars may have both a direct impact as in the case of direct subsidies or an indirect one as in the case of tax exemptions. For example, funds expended for public housing add to housing demands, for practical purposes almost as directly as funds expended by private citizens from their after-tax incomes. Similarly, rent supplement programs add to housing demand; this is also true of interest supplement programs.

On the other hand there are some indirect subsidies that also tend to stimulate housing demand. For example, a home owner pays no income tax on the indirect income, that is, the value of the house services derived from occupying the house. If there is a mortgage on the house the owner can deduct interest charges when computing federal income tax. By contrast a tenant cannot deduct rental payments although this may be reflected in rents following the owners' deduction.

Thus, when we try to estimate the impact of income on housing demand we need to consider not only direct incomes but the impact of subsidies and related adjustments as well.

Impact of Economic Policies

Government policies have a considerable influence on how we spend our incomes in general but especially in the housing field. The impact of economic stabilization efforts through the medium of monetary and credit

[4] See George E. Moody, *Housing Characteristics and The Filtering Process: An Empirical Analysis of Bloomington, Indiana and Pueblo, Colorado* (Bloomington: Indiana University, 1976), unpublished doctoral dissertation.

policies has been usually heavy in the housing field. Tight money policies leading to higher interest rates soon price most of those who want home mortgages out of the market. Home financing institutions like savings and loan associations with a large inventory of lower interest rate mortgages cannot compete for funds because they cannot pay the higher rates that the market sets under such conditions. As a result housing carries an unusually heavy burden in such stabilization periods.

Economic policies which lead to inflationary tendencies increase desires for home ownership relative to renting. The opposite tends to be true under deflationary conditions. We should note also that inflationary expectations usually lead to high interest rates and these tend to have a depressing effect on housing markets even though interest in ownership may be high.

Prospective home owners prefer to enter the market when interest rates are favorable in the hope that they will be protected against future price and interest rate advances. Variable interest rates and flexible payment mortgages, however, may become more common and add some elements of stability to these markets.

Policies which attempt to hold down costs favor housing relative to other goods and services because of the relatively high levels of costs of land development and building. On the other hand policies that may tend to undermine ownership such as rent controls tend to be unfavorable for the housing field.

Policies that favor housing, such as special financing arrangements of the FHA or VA type or those of the Federal Home Loan Bank Board or GNMA, tend to stimulate housing demand in comparison to the demand for other things. Elimination of such restrictions as usury laws would have a favorable effect as would greater flexibility in building codes.

Other policy areas might be discussed as well; for example, the entire field of property taxation relative to the taxation of other things is important. Our discussion, however, is intended to suggest the types of factors that may affect future housing demand rather than to present an exhaustive discussion of all of the forces involved.

Financing

Since few home buyers have the funds to pay for a house when it is bought, financing terms and conditions play an important role, especially in the demand for single-family homes or for apartments under cooperative or condominium arrangements. Thus when down payments are low, terms of mortgages are long, and interest rates and costs are low, a tremendous stimulus is given to the demand for owner-occupied homes. Buyers use small amounts of their own funds and a major amount of a financial institution's or other lender's funds to make the purchase.

When money markets are tight and funds for home financing are not readily available, the demand for owner-occupied homes declines more or less sharply, even though incomes may continue to be high. At such times the demand for rented living accommodations may increase. Builders may wish to shift to the construction of apartment houses. Financing of residential income properties may lose out to other fields as interest rates rise. Promoters and developers will expand their operations when financing terms are favorable. At times they may be able to operate by using equities. Then lenders may get "a piece of the action," that is, an equity participation under such arrangements.

Savings and loan associations play a major role in the home financing market as we have seen. They specialize in this type of business and do not tend to move into and out of the home mortgage market as conditions in the other financial markets change. Insurance companies and savings and commercial banks, which enjoy broader investment powers, tend to shift their activities between the various capital markets as yields and investment opportunities change.

There are widespread differences of opinion as to the relative desirability of using specialized financial institutions to channel funds into housing investments. Some contend that all financial institutions should have the same broad investment powers, allowing people to compete for the funds they want. Others favor specialized institutions, contending that mortgages seldom have been strong competitors for funds under high interest rate conditions and hence that housing, along with small business and small municipalities, soon gets priced out of the market under highly competitive conditions. Some have argued for the earmarking of specific percentages of the assets of specialized institutions for investment in housing; this has been suggested especially for pension funds, which to date have had limited investments in this field.

Also there are a variety of issues in regard to the extent of financial subsidy that should be provided. Rent and interest rate subsidies (for example, the Section 235 and 236 programs) represent one approach. There are arguments that special incentives toward saving, such as tax incentives, would be a better approach to a subsidy arrangement than direct housing assistance. It is argued that if savings were plentiful, interest rates would be reasonable and housing could compete for funds in the open market.

FACTORS IN POTENTIAL HOUSING SUPPLY

The supply of housing has been accumulating for many years. It now includes over 70 million dwelling units. A large proportion are single-family homes but there are many doubles, duplexes, small apartment houses, large apartment houses and complexes, town houses, row houses, and other types. This supply of dwelling units includes vacation cabins and cottages. It includes slum dwellings and exclusive residences, simple dwellings or deluxe living quarters. The diversity of dwellings as to type, age, condition, location, quality, architectural style, construction materials, and other classifications is very great.

This country has been described as a nation in which we agree to disagree. We allow for a wide variety of values, interests, priorities, objectives, life styles, and preferences. There are few areas where this is more in evidence than in housing. Some people spend far beyond their means on housing, preferring to achieve some sort of balance by cutting down in other areas; others spend far less than they could afford on housing, preferring expenditures on automobiles, travel, entertainment, or other things. Some get housing for little or nothing, as in public housing projects; military personnel or government officials are able to occupy official residences. In some cases subsidies are used. For example, public policy may require the conservation of older neighborhoods and older dwelling units by the use of subsidies.

Thus, we make use of our existing housing supply in many ways. It is used with great intensity as in cases of slum housing where many people occupy small spaces in order to reduce the cost per person or where two or more families double up for economic or personal reasons. Other dwelling units stand idle for many months out of the year because the owner has another home or is traveling extensively or is too ill to occupy the space.

Repairs and Maintenance

All housing deteriorates over time or is damaged by use to a greater or lesser degree. Carefully planned repair and maintenance programs prolong the life of existing properties and add to their utility and attractiveness. Repairs and maintenance are encouraged by special financing arrangements, in some cases making it possible to do this under existing mortgages Title I programs under the FHA provide for the guarantee of loans made for repair and maintenance purposes. Special inducements may be provided to encourage insulation and energy conservation. Many savings and loan associations have special financing plans for modernization and repair programs. As our dwelling units have become increasingly mechanized, the costs of maintaining equipment of many types have gone up and its condition is of major importance to the enjoyment of the dwelling unit. Heating and air conditioning units, electrical and gas systems, disposals, dryers and dehumidifiers, vacuum cleaners, refrigerators, radio and TV sets, and many other things all call for almost constant repair and attention along with the basic structural parts of the dwelling unit.

Redlining

There are growing efforts to conserve older neighborhoods and older houses. For example, legislation against "redlining" has been enacted.[5]

[5] See Michael Angelasto and David Listokin, "Redlining in perspective—an evaluation of strategies to deal with the urban financing dilemma," paper presented at meeting of The American Real Estate and Urban Economics Assn. in cooperation with The Federal Home Loan Bank Board, Washington, D. C., May 21, 1976.

This is designed to prevent the practice of eliminating older areas from those eligible for mortgage loans on the part of home financing institutions. Managers of such institutions are caught in a dilemma between protecting the safety of their savers' deposits on the one hand and responding to the needs of older neighborhoods on the other.

Questions may be raised about a variety of redlining practices. For example, do city governments redline by limiting municipal services to older areas? Or do professional people redline by refusing to provide their services to older neighborhoods for various reasons?

Block Grants

Federal financial assistance to communities for the purpose of preventing deterioration of neighborhoods, especially in the older areas of the cities, assumed new proportions with the emergence of the community development block grant. This program was a part of the Housing and Community Development Act of 1974, later modified somewhat by the Housing and Community Development Act of 1977. In lieu of specific categorical programs, under the block grant approach cities could formulate their own development plans and programs and then (often within certain requirements) secure a block grant to help support them.

Reductions in Supply

Each year a small percentage of the existing supply of dwelling units is lost through fire, windstorm, earthquake, flood, accident, or deliberate demolition. Some residential structures are demolished because they are no longer fit for use, others because they are in the way of a new road or street or renewal project or other improvement. There are many dwellings which undoubtedly should be demolished and would be if an adequate supply of other housing were available. The percentage of demolitions varies from year to year and, of course, varies considerably from place to place, reflecting differences in local conditions. The growing number of abandoned houses, especially in city centers, may step up the demolition rate.[6] Vandalism has forced demolition in some cases.

Changes are occurring almost continuously in the quality of our housing supply. Physical depreciation goes on day by day and year by year. Newer and better housing units bring obsolescence to those in the existing supply. To some extent these tendencies are counteracted by remodeling, repair, and modernization programs. Changes are turning some neighborhoods into slums at the same time that renewal and related programs are rescuing others. Thus, despite the appearance of permanence of the housing supply, it is undergoing constant change.

---

[6] See also George Sternlieb, "The Abandoned Building as a Clue to the Future of the American City," for the U. S. Senate Subcommittee on Housing and Urban Affairs of the Banking and Currency Committee, 1970.

Additions to Housing Supply

Each year we add to our supply of housing. Although some estimates of needs indicate production requirements that would average around 2.3 to 2.5 million new or rehabilitated dwelling units annually, we have only on occasion approached such a volume In peak years with housing starts nearing the 2 million level and if mobile homes are added, we have not been greatly below such totals. Even at a 2 million level, annual additions to the supply would represent less than 3 per cent of the total.

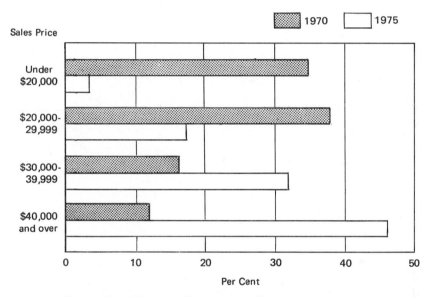

Source: Bureau of the Census and Department of Housing and Urban Development.

FIG. 18–3. New single-family homes sold, by sales price (percentage distribution). (*Source: Savings & Loan Fact Book,* 1976.)

Additions to the housing supply annually range from deluxe single-family homes to smaller homes, doubles, duplexes, garden apartments, high-rise apartment complexes, vacation homes, and others. Mobile homes now are a significant factor in our annual additions to the housing supply. Public housing developments account for a small percentage of additions to the housing supply. New units may be subsidized in varying degrees, some being financed by government directly, some through government assistance, others through private financial arrangements. Some new housing is located in the central city, some in suburban and outlying areas, others in the open countryside. Some new housing is built by conventional methods, some is of manufactured, prefabricated, or modular construction, and as we have suggested some is provided as mobile homes.

Mobile Homes

A very large percentage of the mobile homes are "mobile" only at the time they are delivered to the site. Few are ever moved. Many are located in attractive parks, some on golf courses or lakes; some, however, are found in less attractive locations. We should distinguish between mobile homes of this type and the "travel trailers," which are designed to move readily, being towed by a car or truck. Mobile home production has exceeded 400,000 per year on occasion.[7] Travel trailers, though popular, seldom have reached more than 20 per cent of this level. There are also house cars, land yachts, and self-propelled and largely self-contained vacation homes that go by a variety of names. These types are gaining in popularity but are as yet a small factor in the overall supply of housing.

Modular Housing

The term modular housing has been used in a variety of ways. In some cases it is used to designate units that resemble mobile homes but that may be assembled in a variety of ways from "double wide" to large-scale arrangements. Early hopes for housing of this type have not generally been realized. Technological advances will be needed for further progress in this area.

Production Problems

As we have seen in our earlier discussions, the production processes involved in the construction of buildings have improved over time but still have a long way to go if costs are to be brought into line with those in other fields. HUD's "Operation Breakthrough" was an effort to stimulate innovation in the housing field and especially in the production of new housing, but met with only limited success.

Efforts have been made to provide federal and other support for "new towns" on the theory that very large-scale operations would lead to economies in production. Except for a few cases, however, experience in this area has not been encouraging.

We have considered various production problems in our discussions in Chapters 11 and 12. All we wish to add here is the observation that improved production processes will mean much to our future housing supply. Any improvements that will provide more house for less cost will help housing in its competition for a slice of the consumer's dollar. Such improvements may range from architectural, engineering, and structural to land planning and zoning to finance, marketing, and government regulations. The National Association of Home Builders, for example, has developed a warranty system under which builders are able to assure basic

[7] See Harold A. Dickinson, "A Promising Future for the Mobile Home," *Real Estate Review,* vol. 6, no. 1 (Spring 1976).

performance of structures for specified periods or provide insurance to pay for deficiencies. The National Association of Realtors has worked on a similar program for existing homes.

Much has been said about restrictive building codes and much needs to be done in this area. National performance standards would be extremely helpful. But there are restrictions in many other areas including finance, entry into building trades, marketing practices, environmental standards, energy limitations, and others.

Marketing Changes

There is increasing recognition that land development holds the key to most successful house-building operations and to stable future residential neighborhoods. It may be that greater gains in the future will be made in the areas of land development and marketing than in any other phase of housing.

The combination of land development, building, and marketing has been helpful to both conventional builders and prefabricators. The careful coordination of these activities, plus assistance provided for the local dealer by the manufacturer of prefabricated homes in land assembly and planning. market analysis, scheduling of building programs, and financing, have been of major importance in the success of prefabrication.

There continues to be great need for the simplification of real estate transfers. This would benefit especially the residential market, with its numerous small transactions and its relatively uninformed buyers and sellers, especially in the owned-home field. With the great progress that has been made in other areas, it is to be hoped that the transfer of title, insurance of title, abstracting. and the many other phases of the process of property transfer may be simplified in future years. The Real Estate Settlement Procedures Act as amended in 1976 provides for orderly processing of transactions.

Other marketing developments of importance include the increased role being played by property managers, the development of programs for trading-in houses, and the improvement of transfers between cities for the many people required to move from place to place because of job relocations each year. The development of real estate broker networks like "Gallery of Homes" and "Century 21" has been helpful in this area.

As we indicated earlier, more and more residential properties are being managed by professional property managers. The success of the property manager in increasing returns on investments in residential properties has led to a substantial expansion of this type of activity. The growing complexity of business practices, particularly with respect to government regulation and taxation, also explains the increasing importance of this phase of residential real estate marketing. In some cases failure of condominium developments may be attributed to a considerable degree to ineffective management of the properties.

Trade-in Problems

Difficulties have been encountered in developing an effective system for trading-in used houses. Although builders and brokers have made valiant efforts in this area, much remains to be done. Some business firms have made special efforts to facilitate the transfer of executive personnel from one part of the country to another. Financial institutions have experimented in this area as well. To date, however, there are few places where one can trade-in a house with anything approximating the ease with which one trades-in a car.

One phase of the problem pertains to the local market. Those buying and selling houses or condominiums in the same city have a better chance of working out a trade-in arrangement than those moving from one city to another, which is the second phase of the problem.

Consumer Protections

The consumer movement has had its impact in the real estate field. There has been much legislation, such as Truth-in-Lending, Truth-in-Advertising, the Real Estate Settlement Procedures Act, "redlining" legislation, anti-discrimination legislation, and others. In general, consumers have been given added protection although at some cost in terms of bureaucratic procedures and various delays.

In most cases consumers are dealt with fairly but, as in every line of business, a very small percentage of those involved try to take advantage of the lack of knowledge or inexperience of consumers. This small percentage requires regulation and, of course, this imposes the regulations on all.

USER PREFERENCES

Some of the users of housing prefer to own it, others to rent it. Some like single-family detached homes, other like town houses, either owned under a condominium arrangement or rented. Some like more than one house—second homes have gained in popularity. Some prefer to live in the suburbs, others near in, still others in the open countryside.

Home Ownership

Preferences for owner-occupied homes are usually a result of moderate to higher incomes along with easy financing and some tax advantages. In 1920, owner-occupied homes represented 45.6 per cent of nonfarm dwellings. Prosperous conditions in the 1920's brought this to 47.8 per cent by 1930. The depression reduced owner-occupied homes to 43.6 per cent of the nonfarm dwelling units by 1940, a slightly lower percentage than in 1920. The prosperity of the 1940's (and controlled rents, which limited access to rental properties) resulted in the most rapid gain of home owner-ship for any decade in our history; by 1950, 55 per cent of the nonfarm dwellings were occupied by owners. By 1960 this proportion had advanced to nearly 62 per cent, by 1970 to nearly 63 per cent, and by 1975 to 64.6 per cent.

A decline in incomes or in income prospects tends to slow down the trend toward home ownership. When incomes move downward, consumers are reluctant to take on the long-range obligations that are involved in home ownership. Also, they may prefer not to be tied too closely to one area, since greater economic opportunities may develop elsewhere. During peri-ods of recession most people attach great importance to the liquidity of their investments.

For most families, home ownership is advantageous when prices are rising since the investment involved is hedged against inflation and against rising costs of operation. Indeed, home ownership is one of the main ways by which a family of moderate means may to some degree protect itself against inflationary developments.

In a period of declining incomes the opposite is true; and consumers tend to favor rented rather than owned space, since rents tend to decline while the major costs of home ownership, such as taxes and mortgage pay-ments, do not usually go down.

TABLE 18–1.   Home Ownership by Decades

Years	Occupied Units	Owner-Occupied Units	Percentage Owned
1930	29,905,000	14,280,000	47.8
1940	34,855,000	15,196,000	43.6
1950	42,826,000	23,560,000	55.0
1960	53,024,000	32,797,000	61.9
1970	63,417,000	39,862,000	62.9

Sources: Bureau of the Census, 1970 Census of Population; United States League of Savings Associations, Savings and Loan Fact Book (Chicago: The League, annual).

Home ownership tends to be more common in the smaller urban places than in large metropolitan communities. Less than half of the families own their homes in metropolitan communities, while over two-thirds are home owners in small towns and rural areas. There is some variation between large cities as well, however, with Detroit ranking much higher in terms of home ownership than New York. The lower percentage of home ownership in New York and Chicago than in other cities probably is due to the availability of a large number of rental apartments in these larger cities.

Home ownership tends to be higher among older than younger families. Only a small percentage of the families headed by persons 25 years of age or less are home owners, while over two-thirds of the families headed by persons 65 and over fall in this group.

According to a study conducted by the U. S. League of Savings Associations, the average age of the buyer of the typical single-family house who uses savings and loan financing is about 41 years. Of the heads of households buying homes and using conventional mortgage financing provided by savings and loan associations, 14 per cent are under 30 years of age, 16 per cent between 30 and 35, 17 per cent between 35 and 40, 17 per cent between 40 and 45, 15 per cent between 45 and 50, and 10 per cent between 50 and 55. Thereafter, the percentages of buyers drops sharply, with only 11 per cent over 55 years of age.

Relative income affects home ownership, with more concentration in the higher brackets than in the lower-income levels. Home ownership varies somewhat with occupation; managerial and self-employed rank higher, and unskilled and service personnel lower than the average for all groups. Whether this is simply a reflection of incomes or whether occupation also has a bearing is not definite.

The bulk of owner-occupied homes are single-family, detached structures. In doubles, duplexes, and structures with three or four dwelling units, owners often occupy one unit and rent out the remaining space. Only a small percentage of the structures with five or more units are owner-occupied. Most of these are condominiums or cooperatively owned apartment buildings. The trend toward the ownership of individual apartments has been rising, despite a variety of problems, especially in the higher price ranges, since the condominium arrangement has become more generally available.

Rental Housing

Construction of rental housing expands in boom periods and declines in recessions. In 1970, 55.6 per cent of the new houses were one-family homes, 3.3 per cent two-family, and 41.2 per cent three- or more family units. In 1975 the trend was back toward single-family homes.

The majority of apartment house developments are of the garden type —one- to three-story buildings—but there is a substantial supply of high-rise, elevator apartments in many communities.

The threat of rent control has tended to discourage the development of apartment house projects. This, plus rising taxes, construction costs, and energy problems has impeded the development of multifamily housing. Some rental units have been converted to condominiums.

Garden apartments tend to employ the same general construction and materials as single-family dwellings. As in the case of town houses, garden-type apartments may be rented or sold directly or through a condominium arrangement. High-rise, elevator apartment buildings usually have concrete or steel-frame structures. Many are of the luxury type. They may be rented or sold through cooperative or condominium arrangements.[8]

Condominiums and Cooperatives

Cooperatives and condominiums are similar in that they both involve an ownership concept. In a cooperative the occupant acquires ownership by purchasing shares in a corporation that owns the building. Ownership of such shares offers a preferred position as against nonshareholders. The owner may be required to offer shares to the corporation in case of a desire to sell, and typically approval will be required for improvements and changes.

The condominium provides for the individual ownership of a specific apartment together with ownership of an undivided interest in the land and other parts of the structure and land area in common with other owners. Thus, owners have the same general ownership rights in an apartment that they might have in a single-family home, except that the ownership of land, hallways, lobbies, garages, swimming pools, and similar improvements is shared. The buyer has a deed to the apartment and can mortgage, sell, or bequeath it. This form of ownership has increased the attractiveness of apartments to a number of families. However, in many cases there have been problems arising out of the difficulty of getting agreement among the owners as to the maintenance of the properties and a variety of other types of difficulties.[9]

Second Homes

There has been somewhat of a trend toward "second homes." Many American families own a second home, just as they own a second car. In many families, especially large ones, a second home is an economical means of providing family vacations in favorite recreation spots. In some cases a vacation home is a "second" at the time of purchase but is intended eventually to serve as a retirement home.

The size and cost of a second home may vary widely, but wealth is no requisite. Low-cost, do-it-yourself, or premanufactured units are often chosen. In some cases, the cost of a land site in popular recreation areas may exceed construction costs.

While lake cottages, beach bungalows, and more elegant summer homes have been on the American scene for years, many vacation homes are built with the same year-round facilities that are found in permanent residences.

---

[8] John J. Dee, *An Analysis of the Return–Risk Structure of Apartment House Investments* (Bloomington: Indiana University, 1974), doctoral dissertation.

[9] Arthur E. Warner, *Condominium: Concept, Control, Consumer Acceptance* (Columbia: Center for Real Estate and Urban Economics, Univ. of South Carolina, 1976). Major problems are identified as adequacy of disclosure, recreation leases, use of deposit monies, "sweetheart contracts," representation and promotion material, and tenant displacement.

For some people second homes have proved to be sound investments. Arrangements are sometimes made to rent them to others when not being used. This not only provides added income but also depreciation often can be offset against income. If located in rapidly expanding areas some second homes have gone up in value.

Location Preferences

As we suggested in the introductory discussions in this chapter, people are likely to continue to move about in search of desirable locations.

Some people will continue in suburban and outlying locations. Indeed, these are currently the most popular locations. Others will be encouraged to continue to live near the center of cities rather than moving out. Efforts to conserve older neighborhoods and older houses may be a factor in location selection.

The location of economic opportunities will be of major importance in location preferences. Some types of jobs, especially those in highly skilled and specialized occupations, undoubtedly will expand in or near city centers. Such opportunities will attract skilled workers and specialists. Many types of jobs will continue to be decentralized and this means that many types of workers also will continue to move outward.

SUMMARY

The housing needs and wants of our people will reflect population growth, changes in age distribution, and movement of the people from place to place. Much will depend on the priorities people assign to housing, both for themselves and for the general housing standards they believe should be established and enforced. Consumer wants may change over time especially as new housing services and products and new products and services in other areas are developed.

Major factor in translating housing needs and wants into potential housing demand include income trends and expectations, the competition between new and used houses and the possibilities for greater filtering, the extent of doubling up, and the use of income and related subsidies. In addition, housing demand will be influenced greatly by general economic policies and especially the impact of future money and credit policies. Financing will continue to play a major role in potential housing demand, reflecting inflationary or deflationary factors and money market conditions including the general availability of capital and the intensity of competition for funds.

The potential housing supply will reflect the repair and maintenance of the existing supply, demolitions and other reductions in supply, and the rate of house building. Mobile homes may be an important factor in future housing supply. Improved production and marketing methods could be of major importance.

The future housing of our people will reflect preferences for home ownership of various types including condominium and cooperative arrangements. Rental housing may gain in popularity if costs continue to advance and property taxes rise. Second homes have grown in importance. Location preferences continue to favor outlying locations.

QUESTIONS FOR STUDY

1. What are the principal factors in determining housing needs and wants? How do they translate into effective demands? Do you anticipate major changes in the 1980's relative to the 1970's?
2. Do you think a growing number of people will undertake to reduce their living standards? Is housing more likely to be affected than other sectors by any such movement?
3. Do you think people will favor housing relative to other things in the expenditures of their future incomes? Why or why not?
4. Explain the filtering process. To what extend does it work or fail to work? Is it likely to be more effective in the future?
5. How important are income subsidies likely to be in future housing policies?
6. Why will financing continue to be such an important factor in future housing demand? Would savings incentives be preferable to income subsidies as a way of assuring adequate funds for housing? Explain.
7. How important are specialized financial institutions in providing funds for housing finance?
8. How do you account for the wide diversity of housing in this country?
9. Why are dwelling units lost from the housing supply each year? How important are repair and modernization programs?
10. What is "redlining?"
11. Will mobile homes be an important part of the future housing supply? Explain. Is house quality likely to improve if the number of housing starts annually is increased? Why or why not?
12. What is the outlook for improved production processes in housing? In which areas are advances most likely to be made?
13. Which improvements are needed in house marketing? Why are trade-in problems so important?
14. Is home ownership likely to be as popular in the future as in the past? Why or why not?
15. How important are condominiums and cooperatives likely to be in the future?
16. How do you account for the growing interest in second homes?
17. What are likely to be the preferences of people in regard to the location of their housing in the future? Explain.

SUGGESTED READINGS

EDWARDS, EDWARD E., and WEIMER, ARTHUR M. *Cyclical Fluctuations in Residential Construction.* Bloomington, Ind.: Business and Real Estate Trends, Inc., 1968.

HINES, MARY ALICE. *Principles and Practices of Real Estate.* Homewood, Ill.: Richard D. Irwin, Inc., 1976. Ch. 23.

McMAHAN, JOHN. *Property Development.* New York: McGraw-Hill Book Co., 1967. Ch. 7.

WILEY, ROBERT J. *Real Estate Investment—Analysis and Strategy.* New York: The Ronald Press Co., 1977. Ch. 13.

STUDY PROJECT 18–1

A Survey of Urban Renewal *

With his signing of the Housing and Community Development Act of 1974, President Ford essentially signed a death warrant for the major part of the urban renewal program. Section 116(a) of that legislation states that after January 1, 1975, with the exception of previously committed programs and projects, no new grants or loans would be made under title I of the Housing Act of 1949, the major urban renewal legislation. Thus, we now have an opportunity to evaluate a costly and controversial twenty-five-year program whose major costs and benefits have already been incurred. Urban renewal projects entailed what was initially a novel relationship both between local and federal governments and the public and private sectors. Since this model has been used to ameliorate other national problems, it is also useful to evaluate the strengths, weaknesses and incentives in the urban renewal program.

History of Urban Renewal. The National Housing Act of 1949 authorized urban renewal, initially labeled "urban redevelopment," as a new form of government intervention in the housing market. The act also authorized the construction of a large amount of public housing, but its funding was insufficient ever to attain the construction goal. The major intent of the act was to achieve "the goal of a decent home and suitable living environment for every American family." While this is certainly a laudable objective, the vagueness of the legislation coupled with pressures from various interest groups led to controversial subsidiary goals. Modifications of the initial legislation were frequent: there were approximately half a dozen major amendments to the act.

The immediate impact of the 1949 legislation was to decrease substantially the cost of urban renewal projects from the point of view of local governments. However, like most joint national and local government programs, the federal funds for urban renewal came with requirements and restrictions on their disbursement. A specific procedure had to be followed to obtain any financial aid from the federal government.

As the initial step, localities were required to develop a "workable program" designed to analyze comprehensively the overall problems which the renewal project was intended to solve. In theory, the workable program would also evaluate techniques other than redevelopment, such as zoning, housing, and building and health codes. However, primarily because of the large federal subsidies for redevelopment, most plans concluded that renewal projects were the optimal methods of achieving the goals.

The next step in the process was general approval of the workable program by the Department of Housing and Urban Development (HUD). The agency stead it simply determined whether the plan met certain constraints, such as ade-

---

* From Bruce L. Jaffee, "What Happened to Urban Renewal?" *Business Horizons* (February, 1977), pp. 81–91. Reproduced by permission.

did not evaluate the suitability of the project in achieving national goals. Inquate comprehensiveness and consistency, and it appraised the technical feasibility of the project and the relocation program.

The lack of emphasis on determining the priority of the projects in terms of national goals had the advantage of leading to decentralized control and diversity among the projects throughout the country. However, decentralization induced projects maximizing local goals which may have conflicted with programs in other communities. Furthermore, these local objectives may have been inconsistent with the maximization of social welfare for the country as a whole.

Once preliminary approval from HUD was obtained, the next step was the designation of a local urban renewal agency, officially called the "local public agency" or LPA. This organization could be either an existing or, more frequently, a new governmental body. The LPA would then develop a specific urban renewal plan and seek approval from HUD. Provided the proposal met certain general guidelines, it would be approved by HUD on essentially a first come, first served basis.

Upon final approval from HUD, the LPA began to acquire property throughout the urban renewal area. "Fair value" would be paid for the property, and existing tenants were relocated on the basis of a specific plan required by HUD. Once the property was purchased, the next step was the clearance of the site and the construction of improvements, such as the rerouting of streets, the installation of sewers and street lights, and the development of public facilities such as parks and schools.

The final part of the direct governmental involvement in the project was the sale of the land to one or more public or private redevelopers. These groups were usually restricted to following a specific construction or land use plan after they purchased the site.

The roles of the federal government in this process were to: (1) approve the urban renewal plan; (2) lend working capital for planning, surveys, and acquisition of property; (3) compensate those existing tenants who required relocation because of the project; and, most important, (4) finance up to two-thirds of the "net project cost," the total expenditure of the LPA net of the revenue from the land sold to the redevelopers. This last item required the largest amount of government funds. During its existence, urban renewal was one of the more financially significant programs of the federal government at the domestic level. Total federal grants to specific projects totaled approximately $10 billion.[1] In addition to this substantial federal contribution, the private sector contributed large resources to urban renewal projects. Its expenditures for site acquisition and construction of buildings were typically several times larger than the direct governmental expenditure.

While the urban renewal program consisted of several different types of activities, urban renewal projects comprised 76.0% of the total federal grants approved from January 1, 1950 to June 30, 1974, the approximate end of funding for those projects. Furthermore, the neighborhood development programs, which are similar to urban renewal projects, accounted for 20.4% of the remainder. As of June 30, 1974, there were 2,102 urban renewal projects, of which 1,016 were completed, 1,073 were underway, and 13 were in the planning stage.[2]

Although urban renewal was a decentralized program, the federal funds were not randomly scattered throughout the country. In fact, the accompanying table shows that only seven states received 54% of all the federal assistance.

[1] U. S. Department of Housing and Urban Development, *Urban Renewal Directory* (GPO, June 30, 1974), Table 1.
[2] *Urban Renewal Directory.*

States Receiving More Than $500 Million in Approved Grants
for Urban Renewal Projects

State	Localities	Projects	Grants Approved (in thousands)
California	39	71	$654,862
Connecticut	38	85	573,595
Massachusetts	32	83	677,011
New Jersey	55	122	550,141
New York	81	169	1,234,568
Ohio	34	76	506,774
Pennsylvania	150	317	1,156,340
National totals *	*992*	*2,102*	*$9,989,361*

* Includes the District of Columbia, Guam, Puerto Rico and the Virgin Islands.
Source: U. S. Department of Housing and Urban Development, *1974 Statistical Yearbook,* Table 15, p. 18.

Goals of Urban Renewal. In order to evaluate the success of the urban renewal program, its goals must be understood. This is difficult, since the objectives are several, vaguely formulated, and frequently conflicting. However, three broad goals of urban renewal seem to be enhancement of the productivity of urban land, reduction of the social costs of slums, and improvement of the economic condition of the community. Each of these will be discussed in turn.

Efficiency of Land Use. The argument that urban renewal can increase the productivity of land is based on the concept of market failure. It has been maintained that central city land markets have been slow to adjust to major changes in the economic structure of the economy. The widespread use of automobiles and trucks, the decreased reliance on rail transportation, and the switch to continuous, one-story production in manufacturing are only a few of the factors which drastically reduced many of the advantages of sites in inner cities. Although decentralization of employment and housing has occurred throughout this century, the trend has accelerated in the last thirty years.

Some observers allege that the central city land markets would quickly adjust to these changed conditions if it were not for the dispersed ownership pattern of property and the design of public services such as streets and utilities. This property ownership pattern makes it expensive to assemble the large parcels of land needed for new buildings. Costly negotiations have to be conducted with a large number of property owners. Furthermore, the existing owners may have considerable market power because of the all or nothing nature of the land assembly process. In the limiting case, the last seller can "hold out" for all the expected excess profits from the project. This possibility may deter private developers from attempting land acquisition unless the process can be conducted in secret. It frequently will be more profitable to obtain large sites in industrial parks or in suburban and rural areas where land ownership is usually much more concentrated.

The existing structure of public services may be a second barrier to the redesign by the private sector of city sites. Small city blocks, narrow streets, limited space for large trucks, and the pattern of utility lines severely constrain major changes in the existing pattern of land use. Only if the public sector assists in the project can this constraint be overcome.

While these barriers point to a need for government interference through the power of eminent domain and the restructuring of some public services, they are a poor basis for the large subsidies which were the most crucial aspect of urban renewal. Furthermore, they are a weak argument for national as opposed to local subsidies since most benefits, if not all, accrue to the local economy. In addition, the net cost of any such subsidy should be small since limited government programs to correct inefficiencies in the urban land market should lead to increased land values. Thus, it is necessary to analyze the other objectives of urban renewal to find a justification for the subsidy from the federal government.

Problem of Blight and Slums. The elimination of blight and slums was the most well-known, and most controversial, goal of the urban renewal program. Slums have been graphically described as "groups of dwellings which are not considered to be decent, safe, or sanitary. They are likely to be dilapidated, overcrowded, filthy, vermin-infested fire traps." Slum dwellings are certainly low quality housing, but they are usually the least expensive living quarters in an urban area. It has been maintained that increases in the income of the poor will lead gradually and indirectly to the reduction of slums. However, urban renewal projects attempted to eliminate slums more directly. Government intervention was justified on three grounds:

Even with moderate increases in income for the poor, slums will remain because of what are called neighborhood effect or improvement externalities.

The profitability of the production and provision of slum dwellings rests on market biases which are either ethically disapproved or the inadvertent result of public policies.

The existence of slums creates social costs.

The neighborhood improvement externality is based on the observation that quality, and therefore price, of dwelling units is partly determined by the characteristics of the surrounding area. If nearby homes, schools and stores deteriorate in quality, the value of a dwelling unit will decline even if there are no changes in its own structural condition. This interdependency discourages individual improvements in a slum neighborhood. The upgrading of one structure will produce positive benefits in terms of higher values to the surrounding buildings. These externalities occur at no cost to those who receive them. Thus, it is to their advantage to let neighbors undertake improvements while they do nothing. Since all owners in the neighborhood will be in the same position, the net effect will be no improvements at all, even if higher values could be attained if all buildings were improved. Governmental intervention can either require everyone to make the improvements or, as in urban renewal, concentrate ownership so that the number of "free riders" is reduced, or even eliminated, in the case of a single owner of all the property in the area.

Correction of biases in the slum housing market was a second justification for government action through urban renewal programs. Although there is some evidence that ownership of slum property is not especially profitable, serious market imperfections still may exist.[3] Since residents of slums are predominantly members of minority groups, discrimination is likely to constrain their flexibility in the housing market. The net effect is a demand with a relatively low price elasticity and a market characterized by considerable price discrimination. On the supply side, the federal income tax laws encourage the use of accelerated depreciation by the owners of slum housing. When this depreciation is faster than the actual economic deterioration of the structure, it increases the profitability of slum ownership and the frequency with which the property is sold and re-

[3] Michael A. Stegman, *Housing Investment in the Inner City: The Dynamics of Decline* (Cambridge, Mass.: MIT Press, 1972).

purchased. But it is not true that rapid depreciation encourages neglect and low levels of maintenance. In fact, the reverse is more likely to be true. The profitability of using accelerated depreciation ultimately rests on the sale of the dwelling at more than its depreciated cost. This increase will generally be taxed at the relatively low tax rate for capital gains. Lack of maintenance will be reflected in a lower market price and thus a smaller profit and capital gain from the sale. Furthermore, if rapid depreciation actually increases the profitability of slum ownership, it will also encourage an increase in supply because it is a relatively easy market to enter. The net effect will be lower prices and rents for slum dwellings.

A stronger case for supply-side biases in the provision of slums can be made in the areas of property taxation and credit markets. The property tax discourages the upgrading of slum property by heavily taxing the improvements. It has been estimated that the property tax in many major cities in the United States is equivalent to an annual excise tax of between 25 and 35%.[4] The only other major commodities which have such high excise tax rates are tobacco and alcohol, products whose consumption society generally seems to want to discourage.

The reluctance of lenders to make loans in slum areas also discourages improvements and home ownership. Investments in deteriorating neighborhoods are risky because of the relatively high probability of declines in market values. Potential lenders are also aware that the value of any improvements in a single structure may not be fully capitalized in its market value because of the neighborhood improvement externality discussed above. Yet these observations can become a self-fulfilling prophecy. If low-cost funds are unavailable for investment in a slum or near slum area, it is virtually guaranteed that the neighborhood will decline. To the extent it is known that some financial institutions demarcate certain areas as off limits for its loans (the so-called "red-lining" practice), other investors will find it in their best interests to follow the same strategy, and the credit market will be rapidly closed for that area. This externality can be overcome either by an agreement among all lenders to make loans in the area simultaneously, or, more likely, by a government program such as urban renewal which initially grants government loans and subsidies to the area and concentrates the ownership pattern so that the neighborhood improvement externality is muted or eliminated.

Recent federal legislation, the Home Mortgage Disclosure Act of 1975, may also affect the credit externality. The act, effective June 28, 1976, requires certain loan information to be published by census tract. Although it is too soon to evaluate the impact of this law, the disclosure provisions may reduce the magnitude of the credit externality through moral suasion resulting from publicizing the lending policies of financial institutions.

A third justification for government action to reduce or eliminate slums rests on the social costs which slums produce. Slum dwellings are frequently fire traps and a menace to health. Furthermore, the neighborhood and the inherent poverty are frequently associated with high levels of crime and personality and social adjustment problems. These characteristics of slum living, regardless of their cause, have affected the population at large. Taxes have been raised to provide at least some of the public and social services required by the residents of slums. In addition, social costs are incurred indirectly throughout the whole community, as evidenced by the costs and fear of crime, deterioration in the quality of education, reduced worker morale and productivity, and loss of community-wide

[4] Federal Reserve Bank of Boston, *New England Economic Review* (May/June 1975), p. 6.

spirit and identification. These problems are extremely difficult to measure, but they are likely to be significant and should not be ignored. It is very doubtful, moreover, that urban renewal projects were effective in reducing the magnitude of these social costs; in fact, the projects may have actully aggravated these problems.

Improving Central City Finances. The first two broad goals of urban renewal may indirectly lead to transfers of resources from one group to another. The third objective of urban renewal attempts explicitly to redistribute income from the nation as a whole to communities with urban renewal programs. This transfer is inherent in the subsidy formula where the federal government paid approximately two-thirds of the total costs of the projects. While there is still considerable controversy over the efficacy of urban renewal from a national point of view, most projects were undoubtedly worthwhile from a local perspective since most of the benefits accrued locally while the community incurred only about one-third of the direct costs.

Urban renewal was also designed to improve the financial position of the community indirectly. If slum problems were actually ameliorated, the cost of public services could be reduced. If property tax assessments in the renewal area increased as a result of the project without offsetting declines elsewhere in the community, the tax base would be improved. Data indicate that at least in the renewal area, the assessed value of taxable land and structures increased. Before redevelopment this figure was estimated to be $320 million. After the completion of the projects, the total was estimated to have risen to $1,001 million, a 213% increase.[5]

Land Use Succession. Some benefits of urban renewal are tangible and easy to observe. New, modern, aesthetically pleasing buildings are likely to replace old, drab, dilapidated structures in the renewal area. However, the fact that the renewal required a government subsidy suggests the original land uses may have generated higher property values than the post-renewal pattern of land use. In the private or free market, reconstruction will not occur unless

$$V_o + D_o + C_n < V_n$$

where V_o is the value of the land and structure in their original uses, D_o is the cost of demolishing the old structure, C_n is the cost of constructing a new building, and V_n is the value of the land and its new structure. Thus, only if the increased value is large enough to pay for the demolition and new construction, will there be major changes in land use. With rising costs of demolition and new construction, old land uses are apt to remain even if they do not superficially appear to be the most productive.

Urban renewal is based partly on the premise that land uses adjust very slowly to changes in the optimal long-run productivity of sites. That is, although V_n may ultimately exceed V_o by an amount large enough to pay for D_o and C_n, the adjustment process is inefficiently slow, so that current values of V_n may be considerably below its long-run equilibrium value. To speed up the transition process, the federal government, through urban renewal, offered a subsidy equal to approximately two-thirds of the difference between $(V_o + D_o)$ and $(V_n - C_n)$ and allowed the sale of the property at the current value of $(V_n - C_n)$. This basis for a subsidy rests on the controversial proposition that real estate markets are inefficient and government agencies are more adept at determining future land uses than the private market. Although this hypothesis is difficult to prove or refute, real estate experts frequently maintain that there is a high level of

[5] U. S. Department of Housing and Urban Development, *1974 Statistical Yearbook* (GPO), Table 21, p. 24.

competition in land markets, information is good and widely disseminated, and current market values adjust quickly to expected changes.

A stronger case for government subsidy is that it will generate positive externalities in the renewal area. In particular, after redevelopment is completed the area is likely to have less crime, more social activities, an improved level of health and sanitation, and a lower level of pollution. While these are real benefits, it is also necessary to consider, as is infrequently done, whether these goals could be achieved at a lower cost by a different program. Similarly, it is useful to at least pose the question of whether higher returns could be attained by investing the funds elsewhere in the community. These are difficult alternatives to evaluate, but few government programs, including urban renewal, even explicitly attempt to solve these problems. The requirements for environmental impact statements under the National Environmental Policy Act is one notable exception.

The Effect on Housing. The most serious criticisms of urban renewal deal with the effect of the program on those displaced because of the project. Those affected, primarily the poor and minorities, gradually became more organized and vocal in their opposition. They characterized the program, with considerable justification, as "Negro removal" rather than urban renewal. This opposition led to major modifications in the direction and characteristics of the program and ultimately was a major cause of its demise.

During its relatively long life, urban renewal had a negative effect on housing, especially for those with low incomes. More housing units were demolished than were constructed. Furthermore, most of the units were designed, and priced, for occupancy by middle and upper income groups. The poor, original residents were forced to move and compete for a reduced supply of low-cost housing. The net effect was frequently an increase in housing costs for the poor and the transfer of the slums from the renewal areas to other locations in the community.

These problems were partly mitigated during the life of the urban renewal program. In later years a larger proportion of the new housing was earmarked for occupancy by low income residents, and funds for relocation were increased. However, because of the long lags in completing projects, few of the original residents actually returned to their redeveloped neighborhoods. The more recent projects also reduced the emphasis on residential slums and housing. The renewal areas were frequently dominated by what were considered to be low valued commercial and industrial properties. New construction emphasized public buildings and private and governmental office buildings. As evidence of the emphasis on government-owned buildings, only 47% of the total land value for all projects completed by June 30, 1973 was taxable property; the figure was 77% before redevelopment was started.[6]

In addition to usually causing the original residents of the redevelopment area to select less preferred housing or business alternatives, urban renewal also led to a loss of accumulated knowledge about the neighborhood. An outsider may find few amenities in a dilapidated and low income area. However, the existing workers and residents, who are frequently uneducated, poor or disabled, may consider their familiarity with the neighborhood to be of some value. They know the locations of friends, stores, mass transit stops, churches, schools and other public facilities. A forced relocation may lead to a total loss of this information. Its reacquisition may be especially costly for those in new surroundings with severely limited incomes, mobility and adaptability. Furthermore, the move itself is likely to be accompanied by considerable fear and trepidation. Even those who remain in the general area of the redevelopment project are likely to bear some of these costs. There will be considerable upheaval in the neighborhood, with many fa-

[6] *1974 Statistical Yearbook.*

miliar commercial establishments and public facilities either closing or moving, and the loss of neighborhood cohesion, however tenuous it may have been. Urban renewal did little to compensate for these social and psychological costs of redevelopment and relocation. It was assumed that the renewal areas were so deteriorated, and fear and alienation were so rampant, that these costs were low and those relocated quickly became accustomed to and approved of their new neighborhoods. Sociologists and psychologists have found the magnitude of those costs to vary both among families and projects.

The Effect on Equity. It is an exaggeration to say that urban renewal led to benefits for the middle and upper income classes and imposed costs on the poor, but the program did have some adverse distributional impacts. An objective of some projects was to attract higher income residents into the renewal area. It was hoped these people would provide income and racial stability to the area and generate demands for what were considered to be high quality activities such as theaters, shops, parks and restaurants. Because of these social benefits it was alleged that it was acceptable to direct the urban renewal subsidy toward housing for these groups. But these subsidies were opposed on the grounds that middle and upper income individuals and families can live anywhere. The poor, because of low income, discrimination and restricted mobility, are primarily limited to central cities. Thus, it is argued that it is more equitable, and possibly less expensive, to subsidize the poor to suburbanize than to "bribe" higher income groups to move back into the city.

A second controversial distributional effect is the benefit received by owners of downtown property in or near the renewal project. To the extent that urban renewal attempts to hasten the transition of land from one use to another, the LPA will pay more for land and property than they ultimately will be worth. Unless familiarity with the neighborhood and goodwill were especially valued by the owner, the payments from the authority were frequently more than the market value. The owners of real estate adjacent to the redevelopment area almost always benefited from the project. Instead of experiencing declining land and property values because of their proximity to a deteriorating area, they received gains because of the increased economic activity generated by the project. Regardless of whether or not these equity effects are socially acceptable, some consideration should be given to alternative, and possibly more efficient, methods of hastening the transition of property from one use to another.

Current Community Development. In recent years the construction phase of urban renewal projects has gradually faded away, but the impacts still linger and will affect the pattern of urban land use for decades. With the passage of the Housing and Community Development Act of 1974, which in effect repealed title I of the Housing Act of 1949, attention has turned toward alternative methods of achieving at least some of the objectives of urban renewal.

The approach taken by the Nixon and Ford administrations stressed "block" grants for local development and subsidized mortgage rates and housing rents to upgrade housing for low and middle income families. The 1974 legislation eliminated ten major community development programs, of which urban renewal had received the most funding. Each of these programs were categorical in the sense that a community could receive funds only if its development plan fell into at least one of the jurisdictional boxes covered by the programs. It was argued this approach led to costly and time-consuming administration. In addition, it biased local projects toward those which would receive federal subsidies, even if other programs would have been more productive investments from a national point of view.

Both the executive and congressional branches agreed there should be a major overhaul and consolidation of urban renewal and related programs, but they disagreed about the amount of flexibility local communities should have in spending their federal grants. The administration wanted to extend the revenue sharing concept of few spending restrictions to the community development area. The bill which was enacted, however, outlines what are alleged to be specific objectives for the program and contains procedures to ensure that federal funds will be used to meet these goals.

Nonetheless, the Housing and Community Development Act of 1974 allows eligible communities to spend their federal grants with considerably more discretion than before. The major priorities of the block grants are to:

Eliminate blight and slums and prevent the deterioration of property
Eliminate conditions detrimental to health, safety and public welfare
Conserve and increase the supply of housing
Expand and improve the quality and quantity of public services
Achieve a better use of land and other resources
Enlarge the diversity and vitality of neighborhoods
Restore and preserve urban property which has exceptional historic, architectural, or aesthetic value.

Some of these goals are so vague and broad it is difficult to view them as serious restraints to the local selection of programs.

Funds for community development grants are distributed to communities which submit plans meeting standards administered by HUD. The amount of money received by the applicants is based on a formula which includes total population, housing overcrowding, and the extent of poverty as some of its criteria. The last category, poverty, is relatively heavily weighted. Under this comprehensive program, $1.855 billion was appropriated in fiscal year 1975. Approximately $2.780 billion was appropriated in fiscal year 1976, and President Ford requested $3.248 billion in his proposed budget for fiscal year 1977.[7]

Presidents Nixon and Ford have generally abandoned the traditional technique of directly subsidizing the construction of new housing for those with low or moderate incomes. With the exception of housing for the elderly, large-scale housing developments supported by the government have been curtailed. Instead, recent administrations have advocated programs which provide subsidies to eligible home owners or renters. Those enacted in recent years are usually called the section 235, section 236, section 8, and Tandem Plan programs. Each essentially lowers the cost of either homeownership or apartment rental. The primary beneficiaries have been families at or slightly above the poverty level of income. The most destitute groups have continued to rely on traditional public housing programs.

These new initiatives to improve housing for at least moderate income households have been controversial. First, they have not provided as many housing units as their sponsors had predicted. Second, the programs have been plagued with scandal and temporary suspensions, making planning difficult and leaving the future direction of the programs in considerable doubt. A third area of controversy is the efficacy of the program in enabling the poor to leave slum neighborhoods.

Alternatives to Urban Renewal. The following four methods are suggested as alternatives for accomplishing the goals of urban renewal.

Reduce residential slums by increasing the demand for housing either by a rent subsidy program for the poor, possibly using the section 236 and section 8 legislation as models, or by a general income transfer program. Any rent subsidy

[7] *The Budget of the United States Government, Fiscal Year 1977,* Appendix, p. 413.

should not be restricted to slum dwellers. Otherwise it would penalize households with the same income as slum residents which have undertaken the financial burden of living in higher quality housing outside of slum areas.

Economists generally prefer an income transfer program to an equally costly program tied to the consumption of a particular good or service. They argue that the former program will be more effective in increasing the overall welfare of the recipients, since the income can be spent in whatever proportions will maximize their overall standard of living. A specific subsidy, on the other hand, biases consumption in a direction which may not be highly valued by some recipients. Nonetheless, these subsidies are frequently justified by the paternalistic view that the poor do not recognize what is in their best interest in the long-run. Furthermore, a specific housing subsidy would induce a greater increase in the quantity of housing than would a general income subsidy.

Rent subsidies, unlike redevelopment projects, do not lead to forced dislocation of a large number of households or to significant neighborhood upheaval. These are probably the most important justifications for demand subsidies as a substitute for urban renewal. However, slums are not likely to be eliminated from an area, and market imperfections will undoubtedly remain. Furthermore, rent subsidies are not effective in solving the problems of nonresidential slums. The focus is on subsidizing poor households rather than particular land uses and local governments. However, the financial condition of central cities is likely to improve indirectly as a result of subsidies. At least some of the additional spending will lead to an improvement in housing quality, thus increasing assessed values.

Increase the supply of housing through construction subsidies, such as charging interest rates below the market level. If the construction subsidy is general, slum dwellers will be aided only indirectly, since those purchasing new homes sell their old ones to those who in turn "filter down" their homes. However, the aid would be more direct if the general subsidy were coupled with spot rehabilitation and some public investment in the slum area. The more heavily the construction subsidies are concentrated at the low quality levels of the housing stock and in or near slum areas, the greater will be the decrease in slum occupancy. However, such concentration is difficult to obtain. It violates the usual profit incentives of builders. Unlike the record of major redevelopment, however, construction subsidies will increrase the overall supply of housing and tend to reduce housing prices.

Ameliorate the imperfections in the housing market. As discussed earlier, improvement of the quality of slums by the private market is inhibited by the dependency of the value of individual structures on the condition of neighboring buildings. The government could reduce these externalities by guaranteeing loans for improving slum units or designating a specific area as a renewal zone in order to attract private funds.

Stricter enforcement of building codes is unlikely to have a significant overall effect on the quality of structures in slums. The required improvements are likely to lead to higher rents, thus worsening the financial position of slum residents. It would, however, be worthwhile to institute a building rating scheme whereby independent inspectors would examine the quality of structures. They would assign a grade to the apartment and structure and require that it be posted in a conspicuous place. Renters could then evaluate the quality of apartments and better determine whether the lower quality is compensated by lower rents. Such a rating scheme could lead to significant improvements in the functioning of the housing market in slum areas.

Probably the most insidious imperfection in housing is discrimination. Although it has been made illegal by both state and federal legislation, the problem still remains. Its impact is felt not only through higher prices, but also in the longer and more costly search costs which minorities require to find suitable housing.

Substitute rehabilitation for massive redevelopment. Government participation in the rehabilitation process is likely to reduce the risk of default on private rehabilitation loans, the high processing costs for small loans, and the credit neighborhood effect. The resources needed to achieve a particular level of structural improvement will be less under rehabilitation than redevelopment. Furthermore, neighborhoods are kept intact. However, rehabilitation only partially approaches the problems urban renewal attempted to solve. Rehabilitation is an inadequate solution to serious dilapidation and precludes the possibility of major changes in land use. There are no subsidies to attract middle class residents to the area, and the program is likely to have high administrative costs.

Urban renewal has passed away, but its legacy lives on. During its long and controversial history, it has had a major impact on the pattern of land use in virtually every major community in the country. Its goals were so ambitious, and some groups gained so much, that it will undoubtedly be rediscovered in future years and transmuted into new, grandiose legislation.

Questions

1. The National Housing Act of 1949 stated that its purpose was to achieve "the goal of a decent home and suitable living environment for every American family." Is this an acceptable objective of American housing policy?
2. What was meant by a "workable" program in connection with urban renewal projects?
3. The broad goals of urban renewal appear to be: (a) enhancement of the productivity of urban land, (b) reduction of the social costs of slums, and (c) improvement of the economic condition of the community. To what extent were these goals achieved?
4. Why were the major aspects of the urban renewal program not extended in the Housing and Community Development Act of 1974?
5. What appear to be the principal directions of Federal programs in the areas of housing and urban development?
6. Outline the major alternatives to urban renewal.

STUDY PROJECT 18–2

Future Prospects for House Building *

The rate of population growth has dropped dramatically in the past fifteen years, and will soon approach zero. The costs of land and construction have risen so much that most Americans are now priced out of the new house market. Vigorous economic growth and rising incomes in the United States are coming to an end. Therefore, the future prospects for residential construction are poor indeed.

There is an element of truth in each of these premises. But it does not necessarily follow that residential construction is a declining industry, especially in the next decade or so. In fact, demographic, economic and technological influences all suggest a far brighter future.

* From Robert C. Turner, "House Building in the 1980's," *The MGIC Newsletter* (August 1976). Reproduced by permission of Mortgage Guaranty Insurance Corporation.

Demographic Influences. The annual rate of population growth has declined from 1.7–1.8 per cent in the 1950's to less than half that figure. However, two important facts emerge from an analysis of population data.

First, the decline is the result of a sharp drop in the birth rate, not of an increase in the death rate. The sharp drop, however, followed a boom in the birth rate, and in the number of babies born, from 1946–61. What has happened is that we are experiencing a big decline in the number of children, but a continuing increase in the number of adults. For example, the Bureau of the Census estimates that the population 25 years of age and over—that portion of the population that is "adult" in the sense that it either already occupies a housing unit or is likely to be in the market for housing—will be as follows:

	Millions
1975	119.6
1980	130.1
1985	141.7
1990	152.2

This is an increase of 32.6 million persons in 15 years, compared with an increase of only 19.6 million in the 15 years from 1960–75.

Second, what counts in determining the demand for housing is not total population, or even adult population, but the number of households. For many years there has been a tendency for elderly people to continue to occupy a residential unit, rather than to move in with their children. Also, in more recent years, there has been a marked increase in the number of non-elderly "live-alones" and households with children headed by a single parent. The rising divorce rate has contributed to this effect.

The Census Bureau makes three projections of annual household formation to 1990, the difference in the projections depending on the relative weight given to long-term trends versus recent experience. Their projections of the average annual increase in number of households are:

	High (A)	Medium (B)	Low (C)
		(in thousands)	
1975–80	1,637	1,534	1,329
1980–85	1,701	1,566	1,299
1985–90	1,572	1,416	1,106

These figures compare with an average annual increase during 1960–75 of 1,245 thousand. Thus, if projections A or B prove to be correct, annual household formation will substantially exceed that of the past 15 years. And even accepting projection C, the same will be true until the mid-1980's.

The projections do not measure probable total demand for housing because they do not allow for demolitions, conversions, mergers of existing units, or changes in vacancy rates (including "statistical" vacancies arising from ownership of second and third homes by a single household). However, demographic influences alone will mean a strong real demand for housing for at least 10, and perhaps 15 years.

On the other hand, there will be fewer children per family. Average household size will decline also because of the increase in the number of live-alones and childless elderly persons. The Census Bureau estimates that average household size will decline from 3.14 in 1970 to 2.40–2.80 in 1990. The range reflects alternative assumptions as to both household formation and the fertility rate.

The actual figure is likely to be much closer to the lower than to the upper end of the ranges shown.

In dollar terms, this decline in average household size may serve as an offsetting influence to the increase in the number of households. Demographic influences alone (that is, making no allowance for rising incomes) would indicate smaller residential units: one or two instead of three or four bedroom houses; fewer "family" or "recreation" rooms; also less laundry equipment, freezers, and other multi-child-family oriented appliances, together with the space needed for them. Smaller households may also lead to a decrease in the number of bathrooms and, coupled with rising land costs, will tend to decrease yard space or eliminate it entirely. Mobile homes will be adequate to the needs of an increasing percentage of households. Therefore, although the number of housing units built, including mobile homes, will probably rise, the cost per unit (in constant dollars) will probably decline.

Nevertheless, the basic total demand for housing, measured in dollars of constant purchasing power, should trend upward by 32 to 40 per cent from 1975 to 1985, followed by a moderate decline during 1985–90. Even 1990 (trend value) should be a far better year than 1975 or, for that matter, 1976.

Economic Influences. The pace of total economic growth in the next two decades or so will probably slow down. Part of this slowdown will be because of the decline in the number of new entrants into the labor force after the early 1980's, when the lean baby crop of the 1960's and 1970's reaches working age. Part of it, however, will be due to a lesser rate of rise in output per manhour (labor productivity). The chief reasons for this decreased rate of rise are gradually increased natural resource problems (and prices), especially energy; increased costs of environmental improvements; and the increasing cost of scientific and technological research.

Even allowing for these factors, real incomes per employed person should rise by 2.0 to 2.5 per cent a year over the next decade or so, and incomes per family by a slightly higher percentage because of the increased number of workers per family.

Doomsday is *not* just around the corner, as some would have us believe. No stoppage of the growth in real incomes in the United States should occur for at least 25 and probably 50 years—assuming, of course, the absence of war or other international catastrophe. This means that, if the rising costs of construction relative to other costs can be stopped, consumers will be in a better income position to buy housing than they have been in the past.

The most important single cause of the rising relative costs of residential construction has been the rise in mortgage interest rates, which have increase 68 per cent in the past 10 years. The basic cause of the rise in mortgage interest rates is the change in the anticipated inflation rate. It is brave man who would forecast interest rates 10 and 15 years from now. But most economists expect no comparable increase in the next 10 years, and perhaps some decline.

Further, people are coming to realize that a house is about the best inflation hedge there is. Not in all localities, to be sure, but on the average, yes. A 9 per cent mortgage interest rate is not "high" if house and land prices are going to rise by 6 per cent or more a year. Also, in a period of inflation—if it is kept from escalating—incomes catch up with prices and mortgage payments. The introduction of gradually increasing, rather than constant, annual mortgage payments would reflect this fact and be a big help to the housing industry.

My net conclusion, therefore, is that unless inflation gets out of hand, it will not serve as a significant barrier to further increases in residential construction. This conclusion is reinforced by prospective further inceases in real incomes per family.

Technological Influences. Modern technology has only begun to affect the housing industry. The reasons for this are many, but two stand out. First, obsolete building codes have stifled innovation and increased costs unnecessarily. Fortunately, building codes are being updated in many cities. An increasing number of states are enacting legislation exempting factory-built homes from local building codes.

Second, in the past single-family house building has been a small-scale operation, conducted by contractors who could not afford to do much technological research. More recently, large companies are entering the industry, companies that can afford to do research. The prefabricated house has been around for a long time and will continue to supply a substantial percentage of the market. But the wave of the future is likely to be modular unit construction.

Houses assembled on site, by local contractors, from large modular units can meet the buyer's desire for a degree of individuality in design, yield units of a wide range of sizes, and reduce costs significantly by using less costly labor. Further, because on-site construction time is much shorter, savings in costs from tied-up capital are reduced and house-buyer needs can be met more quickly. Technological research by large companies should yield better materials, improved durability of such things as plumbing and exterior finish, and lower maintenance costs.

Another technological development in the offing is design to make maximum use of solar heat. Complete heating and air conditioning by solar energy is probably several decades in the future, except in a few areas where the sun shines most of the time. But the use of solar radiation as an intermittant, supplemental source of energy is already close to being a practical reality for new houses. By the mid-1980's, most new housing units, except those where the sun rarely shines, will be designed to make maximum use of the sun's energy.

Still another technological development that will affect house construction indirectly is the recent explosion in communications technology—audio, visual, and data communication. Already, many large corporations are decentralizing their operations, from the congested high-cost metropolis to exurbia and smaller cities, because adequate communication is so easy that it is not necessary to locate all officers and other employees in one place. Nor will it be necessary to locate offices of companies engaged in the same or related businesses in one city, let alone one area of one city. The New York Stock Exchange, for example, in ten years will probably be an electronic network rather than a place where traders meet.

It is only one step further to locate people's offices in their homes, so that no commuting at all is required. The decentralization of business operations made possible by communications technology will play a major role in the location of housing, with people living where they want to live for non-occupational reasons, and where land costs are lower.

In summary, the future of the home construction industry is far from poor, at least for 10 or 15 years. But major technological changes are in prospect. Those in the industry, both manufacturers and contractors, who take advantage of these changes will prosper. Those who do not will face a shrinking market.

Comment

Professor Turner may be too pessimistic in assuming that smaller households will lead to smaller, cheaper houses. While it is true that less space and fewer facilities will be needed, it should also be true that families will have more freedom to own the kind of house or houses they really want. Whether a family spends its income on housing or something else will depend to a large extent on the relative attractiveness of spending it on housing, and that should be a tremendous challenge to the building industry.

Demographic factors appear to be the most important determinants of housing demand when birth rate, household formation, family size, age distribution and other variables are changing significantly. But a stable, high income population can—and likely will if that is ever achieved—generate a large demand, too. Housing in such a society will be a luxury good, even more so than it is today, and the demand for it will depend on competing opportunities for the spending of family income. Changes in taste, technology, employment opportunities, where and how people want to spend their vacations and their retirement, and other non-demographic factors can become the determining elements.

In view of the longer-run prospects for housing demand, some of the things that are happening in the housing markets today seem quite inconsistent. For example, the idea of the "family home"—one in which the family would live from early marriage until death or retirement, and perhaps take that long to pay for—does not seem to fit. Newly married couples, even if the marriage will eventually end in divorce, as so many marriages do, are likely to live in several different houses or apartments. Home ownership, financed with a 25 or 30 year mortgage, hardly suits that life style, yet that is what the market mainly offers.

Whether home ownership rather than renting, or leasing with option to buy, or other means of acquiring the use of housing is so much in the public interest that it must be heavily subsidized needs to be studied. While it is doubtful that present laws (under which the income from owner-occupied houses is not taxed, but interest and property taxes are deductible from taxable income) will soon be changed, both the good and bad effects of such treatment should be researched and the results publicized.

For most home buyers the subsidy in the tax structure does them—and the homebuilding industry—less good than would the further modification of the now ill-advised laws and regulations requiring equal monthly payments and regulations requiring equal monthly payments on home mortgages. Only with low initial but steadily increasing payments can a home buyer keep his housing costs consistent with his income in an inflationary economy. However, making it easier for families to rent may be a better objective for public policy than making it easier for them to buy.

For a nation like Professor Turner suggests we are becoming there should be a well organized and efficient rental market for all types of housing accommodations. It is highly doubtful that such a market will ever develop if owning continues to be so heavily subsidized.

—EDWARD E. EDWARDS
Consulting Editor

Questions

1. If the rate of population growth is approaching zero, how can Professor Turner argue that there will be an increase in housing demand in the 1980's?
2. What is likely to be the effect on housing demand of fewer children per family? Explain.
3. What are Professor Turner's expectations in regard to the rate of economic growth? Real incomes? Construction costs? Technological influences on housing?
4. Do you agree with Professor Turner's or Professor Edwards' point of view in regard to whether smaller households will lead to smaller, cheaper houses?
5. Do you agree with Professor Edwards regarding inconsistencies in present arrangements for owning or renting housing? Explain.

19

COMMERCIAL AND
INDUSTRIAL PROPERTIES

BUSINESS REAL ESTATE DECISIONS

The markets for commercial and industrial real estate may be thought of as regional in most cases, but they may be national and even international in extent. Thus decisions related to commercial and industrial real estate are affected by many forces from local to international developments.

Scope of Markets

The leasing of a retail store is likely to involve virtually a national market if the tenant prospects are chain organizations. The extent of the interest of chain organizations in purchasing or leasing the store, however, will depend on local conditions, on the strength of the local market, and on the competitive position of the property under consideration in that market. Space in an office building may be leased by organizations operating on a regional or national basis, but their interest in a specific space will be influenced greatly by local market factors. Much the same thing is true of the market for industrial real estate.

Owners and Users

Decisions to purchase or lease commercial and industrial real estate are generated by prospects for returns from the use of the properties that fit the needs of particular firms or persons. The users of such real estate may own or rent. Investors may purchase for lease to users. Builders, promoters, and speculators may develop new properties for lease or sale to business firms. Decisions to buy or lease commercial and industrial real estate depend in part on the present level and future prospects of general business conditions, on the relative prosperity of the particular line of business activity involved, and on real estate market conditions. As in the case of residential real estate, income and income prospects, plus the terms and availability of financing, play a major role in determining the strength of demand.

Administration of Business Real Estate

In some business firms the decisions relating to real estate are made by one or another of the top officials. Only an occasional decision of importance is necessary. Between such decisions, real estate involves largely housekeeping activities that are parceled out to one of the operating divisions of the company.

For many business firms, real estate is of sufficient importance to call for full-time management direction and a specialized staff. This is notably true in chain store organizations, firms in the rubber industry and in petroleum, organic chemicals, and paper products. Of course, for firms in the construction field or in land development and subdividing, real estate is of basic importance to top management. Lumbering companies, public utilities and other energy companies, railroads, and various other transportation lines pay special attention to real estate functions.

In many companies the real estate manager reports to the vice president and treasurer. Some treasurers or assistant treasurers perform the required real estate functions in addition to other duties. In a few instances there is a vice president for real estate because of its importance in the company's program.

HISTORICAL CHANGES IN RETAILING

The department store originated in Paris and was introduced into the United States in the 1860's by Marshall Field in Chicago, Wanamaker in Philadelphia, and Stewart in New York. With the development of mass transportation—horse-drawn streetcars in the 1860's; cable cars, elevated lines, and electric surface cars in the 1890's; and subways in the early years of the twentieth century—downtown locations increased significantly in importance. All the various types of transportation converged in the central business district and created high land values at central locations such as State and Madison streets in Chicago, 34th Street and Sixth Avenue in New York, and Broad and Market streets in Philadelphia. Department stores sought out such locations, expanding both laterally and vertically. Macy's in New York, Hudson's in Detroit, and Marshall Field's in Chicago developed into huge establishments.

Decentralization

Department stores continued to play a major role in retailing despite the decentralization of retail activity. Such stores became the chief magnets for regional shopping centers just as had been the case in downtown business districts.

The decentralization of retailing activities started after World War I. It was characterized at first by the rise of outlying centers at streetcar intersections or streetcar transfer corners, subway stations, and suburban railroad stations. Downtown areas were not affected very much except in the larger cities.

The automobile brought further decentralization, extending the process. This process of decentralization, however, proceeded at a leisurely rate. There were 27 million cars in the United States as early as 1929 but they had only little impact on the pattern of retail distribution. For example, the Country Club Plaza in Kansas City, built in 1920, was the first large shopping center that did not depend on mass transportation but relied on private automobiles. Some other centers of this type began to make their appearance, but it was not until after World War II that the shopping center became a major force in the retailing pattern.

Early Shopping Centers

Early centers of this type included Silver Spring in the Washington, D.C., area, Cameron Village in Raleigh, North Carolina, and Utica Square in Tulsa, Oklahoma. These were built on vacant tracts of land near the center of the city and at the edge of built-up areas.

As the highway network around cities expanded, opportunities for shopping centers multiplied rapidly. Northland in Detroit, Old Orchard in Chicago, North Shore north of Boston, Southdale in Minneapolis, and many others were built on large tracts of land on or near expressways in trade areas with a large total population and income, but often there were relatively few families in the immediate vicinity.

Mall-Type Centers

The first of the mall-type centers with stores in the center of a large tract surrounded by parking was Northgate in Seattle. It was designed by John Graham and opened in 1950. The first types were open malls. The closed, heated and air-conditioned malls which have become very popular were first developed in the late 1950's and early 1960's. Examples include Ward Parkway in Kansas City (1958), Cherry Hill in New Jersey (1961), and Sharpstown in Houston (1961).

CENTRAL BUSINESS DISTRICT

In the central retail district are located the largest department stores and the greatest concentration of stores selling women's and men's apparel, shoes, and jewelry, as well as variety stores. These stores are usually grouped together in a few blocks, within walking distance of each other in what is known as the "100 per cent" retail location.

The central business district often includes the central office building area or the financial district of a city, so that the office workers contribute to retail sales. It often serves also as the entertainment and cultural center. In the central business district there may also be located state, city, county, or federal office buildings and the courts. In the larger centers, international offices, both private and governmental, are often found as well.

Location

This concentrated business district is usually located at the converging point of mass transportation lines leading to all parts of the metropolitan area, such as State and Madison streets in Chicago, 34th Street and Sixth Avenue in New York City, and 8th and Market streets in Philadelphia. In smaller cities this center is often located at the intersection of the two principal traffic arteries.

Convenience and Competition

The basic reason for the concentration of stores in fashion goods lines is the desire of shoppers to compare styles and fashions as to quality and price. It has been found that competing stores in apparel lines sell more merchandise per square foot when they are grouped together than when they are isolated. It is thus not merely the convenience and accessibility of the central business district to residents of the entire metropolitan area, but its ability to offer a complete range of styles and fashions that causes the volume of sales to reach high levels in these central areas. This is largely what prompts business decisions to locate there. Department stores cannot thrive on neighborhood. trade because they cannot afford to offer a sufficiently large stock of merchandise to such a limited market. Such stores usually operate successfully, however, in the larger outlying shopping centers. Indeed, many super-regional and regional shopping centers now rival the central business district in range of customer choices.

Volume

The store managers who bid for space in the central business district and pay high rents for a position in the "100 per cent" location do so because of the opportunity to obtain a high volume of sales. They would locate in side streets or in outlying neighborhoods if their volume of business would be as great as on "Main Street." In fact, as we have said, some types of stores, like supermarkets, can do a record volume of business in neighborhood centers and do not need to pay the premium for central business locations. Other types of stores, like furniture stores, with a low volume of sales per square foot, are located on the fringe of the central business districts where rents are lower, or on the upper floors of buildings in central business districts. Many are found in outlying locations.

Department Stores

Large department stores, which consist in effect of many stores under one roof, continue to be a feature of central business districts although some have experienced lower business volume. These stores frequently occupy whole blocks, such as Macy's in New York, Marshall Field's in Chicago, and Hudson's in Detroit. The largest stores may have 2 million square feet of floor area in a single building and generate huge annual sales totals.

Space Arrangements

Department stores usually own the land and building occupied by the store, or lease required space on a long-term basis. The department store is a specialized building and can usually be used only by another department store. Chain department store organizations have grown in importance; for example, Allied Stores operate many stores, each under an individual firm name, and have huge aggregate sales of around $1 billion. This organization has bought independent stores in many cities. Many department stores operate branches, which are usually located in the same metropolitan area; thus they can obtain the benefit of advertising in the local media and use the same warehousing facilities. Other chain department stores include the May Company, Macy's, Lazarus Federated Department Stores, Lord & Taylor, and others.

The sale or purchase of department stores as real estate does not occur frequently. The usual transaction is the purchase of the store with its land and buildings, fixtures, stock of goods, and good will by a national chain department store organization such as Allied or Federated Stores.

Nearby Locations

Department stores typically generated demands for nearby space on the part of specialty apparel, shoe, and variety stores. Such firms often seek locations near a department store, which attracts customers from all over the metropolitan area by its advertising.

National chain organizations have discovered, from analyzing their own sales experience, the conditions under which they can thrive best. When they are selling merchandise in a certain price range, they seek locations where shoppers in that income group congregate. They know which types of stores complement each other. Many chain stores prefer to locate between two of the largest department stores.

Regional and Super-regional Shopping Centers

Regional and super-regional shopping centers are generally comparable to the central business district of most metropolitan areas. A wide selection of merchandise is available, particularly in women's and men's clothing, shoes, books, restaurants, services, and recreational facilities.

FIG. 19–1. Lenox Square, Atlanta. (By permission.)

Early regional shopping centers typically started with one or two major department stores located on an open mall surrounded by parking areas. Usually they required 70–100 acres of land. Owners of a department store in this earlier period usually preferred to have a shopping center to themselves. Subsequently it was found that there were advantages in locating several major department stores in the same center. Added sales were generated.

In a typical arrangement a major department store would be located at each end of the shopping center with two at the center. Open malls were often enclosed when additional department stores were located in a center. In some cases extra parking was provided by double-decking parts of the parking area or by providing parking garages. Thus regional centers in many instances developed into what we now refer to as super-regional centers. Typically a super-regional center has three or four major department stores and draws on a wide trading area.

In smaller cities, especially if they are a long way from a major metropolitan area, there is a tendency to develop mini malls or smaller regional centers typically including one or two small department stores with supplementary stores sufficient to serve the needs of that particular area.

Community Center

The community center usually has a junior department store as its principal tenant. This main store typically has 40,000 square feet, more or less.

TABLE 19–1.   Median Gross Leasable Areas

	Square Feet
Beauty shop	1,200
Supermarket	20,000
Medical and dental	880
Drugs	7,305
Cleaners and dyers	1,600
Barber shop	620
Ladies' ready-to-wear	2,000
Restaurant without liquor	2,305
Real estate	949
Cards and gifts	1,800
Coin laundries	1,470
Liquor and wine	2,400
Banks	2,594
Variety store	7,500
Ladies' specialty	1,660
Hardware	5,400
Service station	1,745
Yard goods	3,003
Radio-TV	2,100
Ice cream parlor	1,109
	67,640

Source: Adapted from *Dollars and Cents of Shopping Centers* (Washington, D. C.: Urban Land Institute, 1975).

The center typically has from 80,000 to 275,000 square feet. Supermarkets, drugstores, variety stores, and some apparel stores are found in such a center. According to the Urban Land Institute these centers have a median size of 153,500 square feet of gross leasable area.[1] (See Table 19–1.)

Neighborhood Center

The neighborhood center has supermarkets, drug stores, beauty and barber shops, cleaners, and other local convenience stores. Various combinations may be found. Usually a neighborhood center will range from 25,000 to 100,000 square feet.

The Discount Center

In recent years the discount house has played a growing role in the retailing field. Such stores as Zayre's, K-Mart (Kresge), Woolco (Woolworth), and others are important in this connection. They are self-service stores: the customers wait on themselves, pay cash, and take the merchandise away in their own cars or pay a delivery charge. These stores are often large units with 100,000 square feet or more of store area on 10 or

[1] Urban Land Institute, *Dollars and Cents of Shopping Centers: 1975* (6th Ed.) (Washington, D. C.: The Institute, 1975), p. 106. See also subsequent editions (issued at three-year intervals).

more acres and carry a number of lines of merchandise. Variety stores also have moved into the discount area. Discount centers usually have a supermarket along with a discount store.

Supermarkets

The recent trend toward the large supermarket with a free parking lot has caused hundreds of isolated locations to develop. These stores seek locations with enough vacant land to afford free parking for their customers, and they may select an area where there are no other stores in order to secure such a tract. Such stores can do a record volume of business without supplementary establishments. They may, however, be combined with other stores in a neighborhood or discount center.

Franchising

Although franchises have been used for a long time, the concept has been expanded, especially to retailing activities, in recent years. Examples include motels such as Howard Johnson's, Marriott and Holiday Inns, drive-in eating places such as McDonald's and Denny's restaurants, auto and trailer rentals, building products and services, and others. In general, franchising tries to combine a national effort with local ownership and initiative. Real estate brokers have been involved in franchising through the selection of desirable locations for various types of outlets; in some cases they help to arrange for construction and local financing.

Specialty Centers

A new type of shopping center has been developing in some of the larger metropolitan areas such as San Francisco, Chicago, and Salt Lake City. In some cases these are in part tourist attractions. Typically they include combinations of boutiques, artists' shops, gourmet food stores, and restaurants which are likely to attract customers from both the local and more distant areas. Sometimes these are developed in older buildings such as former car barns or industrial buildings.[2]

Parking

Free automobile parking for the shoppers is the indispensable requirement for the shopping center. The amount of land that should be set aside for parking varies according to the population of shoppers who come on mass transportation lines and the number who live within walking distance. For centers in which most of the shoppers come by private automobile, a 4-to-1 ratio between parking and mall areas and net selling area is considered sufficient. It is not necessary to take care of the peak load of

[2] See, for example, Naomi Weinberg, "The Story of Trolley Square," *Real Estate Review* (Fall, 1976). New York University.

Christmas shoppers, as parking areas used for this peak load would be idle eleven months of the year.

The necessity of providing a large parking area means that even a small neighborhood center should have 5 acres of land, and a super-regional shopping center 100 acres or more. A developer planning a shopping center usually has to find this amount of land under one ownership or in a few ownerships, because no power of condemnation is involved and prohibitive prices may have to be paid in acquiring a number of separate parcels. Since around 80 per cent of the land must be made available for free parking, an extra-high land cost makes such projects unprofitable.

Location

Some developers have located their centers at major highway intersections. This creates a problem of traffic congestion, because the shoppers' traffic is added to that of the other traffic. It is desirable that the shopping center location be on a major thoroughfare such as a radial highway and near a circumferential highway going around the periphery of the city. It is not necessary or even desirable that a center be located at a cloverleaf intersection, if it is somewhere near the point of traffic interchange. Frequently, the ideal location is not available because it is already filled in with houses, so the largest available tract under one ownership is selected. Traffic volume on existing highways must be considered in planning a shopping center. The problem of crossing any heavy streams of traffic must also be studied.

The location must have a sufficient number of families and buying power within a reasonable driving-time distance to support it, with allowances for competing centers of the same type. The trade area cannot be measured entirely in terms of driving-time distance in all directions, however, because shoppers will often drive halfway across a state in rural areas to reach a regional center, while they will not come from a downtown area only a few miles away.

The location of new shopping centers has been influenced considerably by the federal highway program, with its provision for limited-access roads between major cities and belt highways around cities. Instead of building shopping centers on the edges of the old cities, as in the early postwar developments, new centers tend to be located at central points accessible from a number of large and small cities.

Guarantees and Percentages

Department stores are the major magnets which attract customers to regional or super-regional shopping centers. Consequently, shopping center developers are usually willing to sell or lease land to such department stores at or near their original cost.

Nearly all shopping centers make use of percentage leases; hence their owners enjoy an attractive hedge against inflation. The main dangers to the owners arise from increases in real estate taxes since they typically are able to arrange for long-term financing and to transfer operating and related costs to the tenants.

In some cases major department store owners such as J. L. Hudson. Marshall Field, Allied Stores, Federated Stores, Sears, Roebuck and J. C. Penny have bought the land for a center and have leased it to other department stores and smaller tenants.

The percentages charged under percentage leases cover a wide range from 1 to 1½ per cent for chain groceries, 1½ to 2½ per cent for larger discount stores, 2½ to 3 per cent for department stores, 5 to 9 per cent for restaurants, 8 to 10 per cent for art shops, 40 to 60 per cent for storage garages, and 70 per cent or more for parking lots and garages.[3]

Percentage leases in high-volume stores must yield enough to cover not only interest, depreciation, and real estate taxes on the building, but also a return on high land value The land value is determined by capitalizing the amount that remains after deducting the annual charges on the building and real estate taxes on the land.

Retail store leases are usually executed for a term of ten years or more if a new building is being constructed for the tenant. Shorter terms may be employed for stores already in existence. These leases often provide for an option to renew on the part of the tenant.

Shopping center leases often provide for a minimum guarantee as well as a rental based on percentage of sales. Rents paid above the minimum guarantee are often referred to as overage rents. The minimum guarantees of strong tenants such as national chain organizations are the chief factor in providing security for mortgage loans. A high minimum, however, is often obtained at the sacrifice of a lower percentage of sales.

Percentage leases are sometimes on a sliding scale, with the percentage declining after a certain volume of sales is reached. In negotiating the leases the prospective tenant often asks for extras in the form of special store fronts, air conditioning, mezzanine floors, finished basements, and sometimes even the store fixtures. Consequently the real estate broker negotiating the lease must have a thorough knowledge of every element of construction and equipment costs. In some cases the tenant provides everything except the shell of the structure.

National chain stores frequently offer the store owner a percentage which is fixed on a national basis. Extra percentages, however, may be obtained in centers which provide special features, such as special air conditioning, underground delivery facilities, or expensive store fronts.

For certain types of stores, such as barbershops or small businesses that do not keep detailed books, the rental may be set on a fixed monthly basis

---

[3] See the December 1976 issue of *Buildings, The Construction and Building Management Journal.*

plus a cost-of-living adjustment rather than on a percentage of sales. The Consumer's Price Index issued by the Bureau of Labor Statistics is one of the more frequently used indices.

Future Retailing Trends

Outlying centers will undoubtedly continue to play the major role in the shopping center field. Improvements in mass transportation may revitalize some downtown areas and add growth potential to the retail establishments located there. New downtown developments that combine hotels, stores, offices, and apartments in one aggregate, like Atwater Park Plaza in Montreal, Penn Square in Philadelphia, Water Tower Place in Chicago, and others, provide highly attractive retail opportunities. (See Fig. 19–2.)

The Retail Brokerage Field

Shopping centers undoubtedly will be a major field for commercial brokerage and lending activity in the future. All the tenants are granted joint rights in the parking area of shopping centers and, as a result, a single store cannot readily be sold. However, the leasing of stores in these centers and the management of the centers has become an important field of real estate endeavor. Tenants who move to outlying centers often are supplanted by others who find advantages in central locations.

Lease Information

Prospective lessors or lessees of space often rely on brokers for information to guide their decisions. Brokers who specialize in commercial leases hence must secure all the information available regarding the terms of leases in the areas in which they are operating. These leases are usually recorded, but the rentals paid are not always revealed in the recorded instruments. Representatives of insurance companies and other brokers usually have knowledge of leases in which they have participated and can exchange information.

OFFICE BUILDINGS

The modern office building evolved as a result of the need for bringing business executives, brokers, lawyers, investors, and others within walking distance of each other so that they could meet quickly in face-to-face contact.

Early Development

The early office buildings, prior to 1880, did not exceed six stories in height, except in a few rare instances. Taller buildings were not practical

FIG. 19–2. Water Tower Place, a full-block $160-million urban center located on Chicago's North Michigan Avenue. The 74-story complex includes a 600,000-sq.-ft. atrium shopping mall on eight levels, Ritz-Carlton Hotel, 260 luxury condominium residences, a stage theater and four motion picture theaters as well as 200,000 sq. ft. of corporate and professional offices. (Reproduced by permission of Urban Investment and Development Co.)

because the walls of a solid masonry building would be so thick at the base that they would absorb most of the ground floor rentable area. The invention of the steel-frame skyscraper in Chicago resulted in the construction of the Home Insurance Building in 1884. The development of the hydraulic and then the electric elevator contributed further to the development of the modern skyscraper. The early office buildings in Chicago, such as the Tacoma Building, the Capitol Building, and the Masonic Temple, built in 1889–90, did not exceed 16 to 22 stories in height. After 1923, a revision of the zoning ordinance in Chicago permitted higher towers. New York City had the tallest office buildings for many years—the Empire State Building has 102 stories, the Chrysler Building 73 stories, and the World Trade Center over a hundred stories. Chicago challenged New York, however, with the John Hancock Building, The First National Bank Building, Marina City, and finally the Sears Tower which is now the tallest of all. (See Fig. 19–3). Many other cities have developed major offices buildings as well.

Supply of Office Space

Most of the larger office buildings that have ever been erected in this country are still in existence. The office building supply is a result of an accretion to a large, existing stock of building space. Office buildings have been built in a series of waves. Periods of overbuilding in which more office building space was constructed than could be absorbed were followed by years of complete cessation of office building. Office building in Chicago reached peaks in the early 1890's, from 1910 to 1914, from 1923 to 1930 and in the early 1970's. Office building in New York City followed a cyclical pattern which was somewhat different from that in Chicago. The middle 1970's have seen another period of waiting for demands to catch up with supplies.

Overbuilding Problems

After periods of overbuilding of office space, office rents and net incomes tend to decline and may remain depressed for long periods, even if general business conditions are good. There was practically no office building construction in Chicago after the Field Building was completed in 1930 until the Prudential Insurance Building was constructed in 1953. It required a period of twenty-three years to absorb the excess supply of vacant space that was created during the 1920's.

Office Rentals

The rent for modern office building space normally includes heat, cooling, cleaning service, janitor service, electricity, and water. Consequently the increasing cost of these services has compelled property managers to secure higher rents for space in new buildings. Because of the cost of these

FIG. 19–3. The Sears Tower, Chicago—at present, the world's tallest office building. (Photo courtesy of Sears, Roebuck & Co.)

services, office building net income tends to decline rapidly when vacancies increase.

The office buildings erected in earlier years still constitute a significant proportion of the existing supply. Some of these buildings were sold at foreclosure and refinanced with lower mortgages. Consequently these buildings have been able to carry the interest on the refinanced mortgages as well as operating costs and still rent for relatively modest amounts. New buildings erected at current costs must in most cities secure much higher rentals. Consequently new office buildings must be able to compete with office buildings constructed at much lower cost levels. Their many attractive new features often enable them to compete to advantage.

Office Building Occupancy

Some office buildings are designed for use by a major corporation or government agency. Most office buildings, however, are erected for multiple-tenant occupancy. This means that a number of small offices are rented to a variety of tenants on every floor. In this type of occupancy the building manager must provide all services. Public hallways cannot be rented. When an entire floor is rented to a single company, however, all the floor area will produce an income.

Office buildings located in central business districts frequently contain retail stores on the ground floor. In financial districts, banks often occupy the ground floor of an office building which they own, and rent the space in the upper floors. In a few cases, such as the Terminal Building in Cleveland and the Carew Tower in Cincinnati, a hotel and department store are combined with the office building. In St. Louis, large department stores typically occupy the lower floors of office buildings, with offices on the upper floors. The Merchandise Mart of Chicago has offices on the five lower floors and manufacturers' representatives occupy the space on the upper floors. In office buildings on such main retail streets as State Street in Chicago there are numerous dentists' and doctors' offices. In other buildings, retail stores are found on upper floors, intermingled with offices. These office buildings with mixed types of uses involve special problems of management.

Types of Office Building Locations

Office building districts may be concentrated, as in the Chicago Loop, or scattered in a number of sub-office building locations, as in New York. More recently offices have developed in suburban areas. In the course of time, office building districts tend to move. In Chicago the office building area of around 1890 was located at the south end of the Loop. Later new office buildings were developed on North Michigan Avenue. In New York there was a movement away from the downtown Wall Street areas to the uptown areas. Construction in the Wall Street financial district has revived in recent years.

Some office buildings have been developed in outlying locations, thus stimulating further the suburban trend. In some cases, office buildings are developed in conjunction with larger regional shopping centers, Northland in Detroit, Lenox Square in Atlanta, and Ward Parkway in Kansas City being cases in point. Of special importance in such locations are medical and dental clinics, real estate offices, and the home offices of various corporations. Parking is of growing importance. A one-to-one ratio of parking space to office space is considered adequate and often necessary to get financing. Redevelopment programs have been important factors in office building development in such cities as Pittsburgh and Philadelphia. In nearly all cities new office buildings tend to be located in the direction of high-income areas; for example, to the northwest in Washington, D. C., to the north in New York City, to the west in Houston, and to the northwest in Los Angeles.

Advantages of Various Office Building Locations

Tenants seek offices at points of maximum convenience from the standpoint of their own particular lines of business. Brokers typically want offices near the Stock Exchange, lawyers near the courts or title companies, insurance people near the insurance company offices, and the like. Specialized office building districts tend to develop, such as the financial district on LaSalle Street in Chicago, the fire and casualty insurance center in New York, and the advertising, radio, and television center in uptown New York. Convenient transportation to residential areas is also important. The midtown area of New York has the advantages of the major terminals with their suburban trains and the subways; the Loop in Chicago is at the point where suburban railroads, elevated lines, buses, and subways converge.

Demand for Office Space

The amount of office space needed varies in different cities. On the average, about 2 square feet of office space per capita will serve the needs of the residents of an area. More is needed for regional, national, and international centers. New York's requirements may be over 15 feet per capita (excluding North Jersey), Chicago, 7 to 8 feet, and so on. The demand for office space reflects the general level of business activity and conditions in special lines of business.

Ownership and Management of Office Buildings

Tall office buildings are the outstanding landmarks of most American cities. Because of the prestige attached to their ownership, banks, savings associations, large insurance companies, and other financial institutions often own the buildings in which they occupy quarters. In the 1920's, office buildings were often financed by bond issues, with the equity retained by promoters. When these mortgages were foreclosed, new investment groups bought control, usually by acquiring the bonds far below par value. Recent office building construction has been financed largely by loans from insurance companies and not by sales of bonds to the public. The equity has often been retained by the builder or developer. In some cases, the lender takes an equity position or "a piece of the action."

The manager of an office building attempts to set rates for space that allow for differences in the desirability of various areas in the building. The most desirable space is that with direct outside light on floors at elevator express stops. An ideal depth for most offices is 40 feet, which allows for a 20-foot reception area space and 20 feet for interior offices.

In selecting tenants, preference will usually be given to companies of outstanding prestige that may attract other desirable tenants to the building. It is necessary to consider the needs for expansion and, if possible, to have sufficient leeway to be able to meet the potential needs of desirable tenants.

The office building manager has the job not only of selecting tenants but also of employing service workers and supervising maintenance and repairs. Building managers' associations exchange information on operating experience, study relationships with building employee unions, and cooperate on other problems affecting the industry. The Building Owners and Managers Association plays a role of special importance.

Insurance Company Experience

Some organizations, for example insurance companies, maintain large office buildings for their own use. Here face-to-face contacts with other companies are not important and there is no need for them to be near other office buildings. The large insurance companies in New York—the Metropolitan Life Insurance Company, the New York Life, the Equitable, and the Mutual—maintain central offices. The Prudential and John Hancock office buildings in Chicago derive advantages from their central location.

In other cases, however, insurance companies, such as those in Hartford, Connecticut, have located their offices away from the central business district. In Houston, Texas, the Prudential Insurance Company developed a twenty-story office building that is located on a 26-acre tract opposite the Shamrock Hotel, five miles from downtown Houston. The large ground area permits ample free parking and a large outdoor swimming pool. Most of the workers live in the vicinity of the office building.

INDUSTRIAL REAL ESTATE

The market for industrial real estate is affected by factors substantially different from those which have a primary bearing on the markets for retail or office space. While the trend of demand for retail space has moved outward from the center of the city, and that for office space has moved outward to some extent, the demand for central locations for such uses remains stronger than in the case of industrial real estate. The most desirable sites for factories, in nearly all instances, are no longer found near the center of metropolitan areas but in outlying suburban or even in rural locations along railroad lines or highways, or near sources of raw materials.

Central and Outlying Locations

At one time industrial uses also competed for central locations, since only in such areas could the combination of factors involving rail or water transportation, nearness to sources of power, and nearness to workers' homes be found. With the development of truck transportation and belt lines, power transmission over wider areas, and the general use of automobiles by workers, industry has moved outward from city centers.

In general, industries seek sites that are not congested and are easily accessible for materials and workers. Emphasis is placed on relatively low land costs and attempts are made to minimize tax burdens. Single-story factory buildings, permitting continuity of operations on the same level, emphasize the need for low-priced land. Industries engaged in heavy manufacturing or those with highly specialized requirements usually own the space they use. Others often lease or make use of the sale–leaseback device.

Industrial Parks and Districts

Of special importance in the market for industrial real estate are industrial parks and districts. (See Fig. 19–4.) Such developments as the Central Manufacturing District and the Clearing Industrial District in Chicago, the Trinity Industrial District of Dallas, and the Bergen County Terminal in New Jersey are typical. Organizations of this type provide industrial facilities with rail service, financing arrangements, fire and police protection, heat, light, gas, water, and other services. Space is available for purchase or rent on varying bases. The Trinity Industrial District of Dallas is located within five minutes of the downtown area on property that was reclaimed from flood land. Levees were built and channels straightened so that industrial locations could be provided. Many industrial parks are located in suburban areas, however, where cheap land and low tax rates provide advantages. In many instances, industrial parks serve best the needs of the lighter industries, since heavy industry often requires special-purpose construction and equipment.

Trends in Industrial Construction

With greater specialization, emphasis has been given to the development of facilities which serve the needs of specific industries. Some plants

FIG. 19–4. An industrial district near O'Hare Field, near Chicago. (Photo courtesy of Trammel Crow Co. and Richard A. Rauch of Rauch & Co.)

are referred to as "controlled conditions plants," providing ideal operating and working conditions with control of light, temperature, humidity, and noise.

Many plants are designed so that the interior arrangements may be as flexible as possible. Larger bays are being used, typically running up to 100 feet, in contrast to 50 to 60 feet in older plants. Building heights are being raised in order to allow for conveyor operations; greater emphasis is given to low-cost maintenance; and the exteriors of plants are being given greater attention, with carefully maintained grounds, landscaping, neat lawns, and recreational areas.

Wholesale and Storage Warehouses

Wholesale and storage warehouses are often located near central-city areas. As a result of the direct delivery of merchandise from the manufacturer to the retailer, the wholesale function has declined. Large warehouses once stored merchandise near the Loop of Chicago and the downtown areas of other cities. Now frequent door-to-door deliveries are made by trucks from factories to stores. Cold storage warehouses still remain near central business districts, and department stores and other stores still maintain warehouses for distribution of goods within the metropolitan area.

The Merchandise Mart in Chicago, once designed for wholesale use, is now highly successful as a headquarters for manufacturers' representatives. For example, one entire floor may be devoted to furniture, another to women's apparel, and so on. The Furniture Mart is the leading furniture wholesale market. Buyers meet there especially at certain seasons.

The supply of central warehouse and storage space probably is adequate for most future needs because many factories have moved away from the multi-story buildings to outlying one-story plants. Space in such multi-story buildings often is well designed for warehouse or storage use.

Demand for Industrial Space

Decisions affecting real estate in the industrial field tend to reflect general company policies with respect to expansion programs, preferences in regard to adjoining or new locations in the same or in other cities, the use of branch operations, and the like. Tax burdens, freight rates, labor relations, local government attitudes, transportation facilities, power, water supply, pollution problems, and related factors all have a bearing. Typically, an industrial organization is not interested in local economic conditions to the same degree as a retail establishment. Indeed, some industries seek out locally depressed areas in order to take advantage of an available labor supply. The regional movement of industry to the South, for example, has been influenced to a degree by labor market conditions.

SELECTION OF INDUSTRIAL LOCATIONS

As a general rule, processing plants which increase the bulk of products, or make fragile or perishable products, prefer to be near their customers; plants which reduce the bulk of products, or make less perishable goods, do not regard nearness to the consumer as particularly vital. Since a very large portion of all material going into factory production has already been processed by another factory, the supplier groups tend to locate near the industries which they serve. As a result there is a heavy concentration of industry on the New York–Chicago axis. There is more production of this type within 100 miles of New York than in the eight southeastern states, and within 100 miles of Chicago than in all of the western states excepting those on the Pacific Coast.

Selection Factors

In selecting a factory location, business managers typically analyze (1) the general region in which the factory is to be built, (2) the particular city within the region, (3) the selected area within the metropolitan region, and (4) the specific site. The basic purpose of selecting the location is, of course, to find the site in which the industry can operate to maximum advantage, where production costs will be lowest, and the costs of marketing at a minimum.

The Region

Many types of industries can operate to greatest advantage only in definite regions. However, these regions may be rather broad in extent. Thus, the steel industry must be situated at the most economical meeting place of coal and iron ore. The steel industries in Chicago, Pittsburgh, and Cleveland are based on the accessibility to coal by rail or river and to the iron ore of the Mesabi Range, which is available by cheap water transportation on the Great Lakes. The increasing dependence on imported iron ore caused the building of the Fairless Steel Works on the Delaware River near Trenton and the doubling of the capacity of the Bethlehem Steel Plant at Baltimore.

Many steel-using industries find it necessary to locate near the primary steel plants. Industries refining bulky materials must also be located near the source of supply. Thus, the concentration plant of the Kennecott Copper Corporation's Utah mine is located at Bingham Canyon at the source of supply, because the copper-bearing rock has only 1 per cent copper and it would be uneconomical to transport this bulky material great distances.

Proximity to markets is also an important consideration in factory location. Many industries are located in the northeastern part of the United States because of the nearness to the great concentrations of urban population in that region.

The electronics industry and related activities have been less directly tied to raw materials and markets than some of the older industries. Also, research and development programs of various firms often are located in favorable environments such as university towns or in pleasant climates. We should note too that political factors may play a part in the location of various defense and similar types of installations.

The Specific City Within the Region

It sometimes happens that the maximum advantages of location in a region can be obtained in only one specific city. Thus, industries depending upon ocean shipments must be located near ports, such as New York, Baltimore, New Orleans, or San Francisco. Where it is important to be at the center of the railroad network, the Chicago area is often preferred. In other cases, the specific industry must be located near others of the same type or near complementary industries. Women's ready-to-wear manufacturers find it desirable to be in or near the New York fashion center, because styles change quickly. Manufacturers of cameras prefer to be near Rochester, New York. The leading automobile firms obtain advantages by being close to the automobile-parts manufacturers in Detroit.

In many cases, however, an industry could be located to almost equal advantage in any of five, six, or more cities. The decision as to which city is selected is often governed by the availability of a site or factory building, by the preference of the factory manager for a certain city as a place of residence, by the promotional activities of the local chamber of commerce, by the tax situation, by the characteristics of the labor supply, or by the railroad, trucking, and other transportation facilities of a given city.

The General Area Within the Metropolitan Region

As we have indicated, new plants are now more frequently located in outlying and suburban areas than in the central districts as was formerly the case. The chief cause of this has been the growing preference for the one-story industrial building as compared with the multi-story type. The one-story plant requires extensive ground areas which usually cannot be found in central locations. Factory operations can be carried on in these single-story buildings at a substantial saving in cost compared with the same factory processes in factories with several floor levels. The advantages of one-story factory buildings located in suburban or rural areas include the following:

1. The factory process is continuous without the necessity of interrupting manufacturing operations at each floor level.

2. There is no waste space for elevators or ramps and no cost of elevator operation.
3. Heavy machinery can be installed in any part of the building.
4. Railroad freight cars and trucks can enter the plant directly, which results in a saving in handling costs.
5. Overhead cranes can be installed and the plant can be equipped with conveyors for moving goods in process through the building.
6. The one-story plant is far more flexible and can be more easily expanded to meet the growth of any particular department. If there is ample ground area and the building is constructed with curtain walls, any part of the building can be pushed out to meet the needs of growth.
7. The factory grounds usually include ample areas for the parking of the workers' cars.
8. There is more room for recreation areas on the grounds and it is easier to provide cafeterias and special conveniences within the buildings.
9. The cost of one-story buildings is often less per square foot than the multi-story type.
10. The land cost is lower in outlying locations than in central areas.
11. Real estate taxes are usually lower in suburban or rural tracts.
12. Because of widespread automobile ownership, workers prefer to work in pleasant modern factories with ample parking areas rather than in congested central-city areas. Workers can reach these locations more quickly on the highways encircling the metropolitan areas than the central districts with their heavy traffic.
13. Suburban and rural locations are more convenient for interstate trucks, which are widely used. Downtown traffic congestion can be avoided. Suburban plants also are more conveniently located with respect to outlying railroad belt lines.
14. Industrial districts in which a group of factories can obtain advantages by operating as neighbors also can be created more easily in suburban or rural locations than in downtown areas.
15. Outlying areas often present fewer environmental problems.

The Specific Site

Having narrowed the choice down to one specific city and to a general area within the metropolitan area of that city, it is necessary to select the exact site. The following factors will be weighed by plant managers in this process:

1. In reviewing all the sites, it is necessary to find those that are zoned for industry and which will permit the location of the specific type of industrial plant proposed. If not actually zoned, opinions can be secured from zoning authorities as to what zoning is possible. Environmental regulations often are a factor of importance.
2. It is often desirable to have a location with direct access to a railroad from which a railroad siding could be constructed into the site

at reasonable cost. It is often desirable also to be near a major highway for truck transportation.

3. Sites with bus transportation to the homes of the workers may be preferred, as some auxiliary transportation often is desirable even though most of the workers have cars.

4. The site should have sewer and water connections, particularly in the case of a small industry. Some large industries install their own sewage-disposal plants and develop their own water supply. In the case of such industries the availability of a source of water is important. It is also necessary to ascertain how sewage and factory wastes can be discharged without contributing to pollution problems.

5. Tracts of sufficient size for the type of operation under consideration must be selected. Consideration is often given to room for expansion. An area under one or at most two ownerships must usually be found.

6. When there are a number of different local municipalities or townships in the metropolitan area, the sites in the one which will do most to facilitate the location of the new industry usually are preferred.

7. The factory should be located on a site most convenient to the homes of the present workers or to the areas where most of the future labor supply may be located.

8. Access to power lines is necessary. Other energy factors may require consideration.

9. If all other advantages are equal, the site which can be obtained at the lowest price will usually be purchased.

SUMMARY

The market for business real estate may be regional, national, or even international in scope.

Real estate administration may occupy various positions in the organization of a firm, depending upon the importance of real estate to the firm's operations. Major real estate decisions usually are made at top levels of management.

Large department stores, central offices, and financial institutions usually form the nuclei of the central district. Space in the central business district usually is leased for long periods, and percentage leases with a fixed minimum rent, or sometimes a sliding scale, are commonly used. Key tenants may be given special rent concessions because of their ability to attract other firms to the building or area.

Outlying shopping centers have become a dominant force in retailing, ranging from super-regional centers to smaller neighborhood outlets. Parking space is an essential feature of the larger centers, and a 4-to-1 ratio of parking to store space is common. This greatly increases the amount of land needed by retail establishments.

The modern skyscraper office building serves the desire of the executives of business firms to be located within easy access of each other. The skyscraper was made possible by the advent of steel-frame construction and the electric elevator. Office buildings historically have been built in waves; when overbuilding occurred, rents have been depressed for long periods, regardless of the trend of general business conditions. The supply of office space is relatively fixed in the short run. High occupancy rates typically are needed to make office buildings a financial success. Demand for office space depends to a considerable extent on the level of general business activity.

Improved transportation has allowed more decentralization of industry, and manufacturing firms now tend to seek uncongested sites readily accessible for suppliers and employees. Thus, they can make use of locations where land prices and tax burdens are lower. Some areas have seen the development of industrial parks or districts. Industrial location depends also on such important factors as the nature of the product, the location of raw materials and markets, and the supply of power and of labor. A growing preference for one-story buildings has increased the demand for land in outlying locations for industrial purposes.

QUESTIONS FOR STUDY

1. How do the markets for commercial and industrial real estate differ from residential real estate markets?
2. Where do you think the real estate function should be placed in the firm's organization? Explain. To what extent will this depend on the nature of the firm's business?
3. Describe typical leasing agreements for retail operations.
4. What is meant by a "100 per cent" retail location?
5. Why has the large department store been an important inhabitant of the central business district? Will this be true in the future? Explain.
6. Define and describe each of the principal types of shopping centers.
7. How do you explain the popularity of large, centrally located office buildings?
8. Have office buildings tended to be decentralized in the manner that has characterized residential and retail developments? Why or why not?
9. Describe the major factors determining rentals of office space.
10. Explain the advantages and disadvantages of: (a) single-tenant versus multiple-tenant office buildings. (b) specialized-tenant versus generalized-tenant occupancy of office buildings.
11. What are the principal characteristics of the market for industrial real estate?
12. Describe the main characteristics of industrial parks and districts.
13. Indicate the main factors involved in selecting a site for an industrial location of: (a) the general region, (b) the choice among cities, (c) the site within a specific city.

SUGGESTED READINGS

HINES, MARY ALICE. *Principles and Practices of Real Estate.* Homewood, Ill.: Richard D. Irwin, Inc., 1976. Ch. 18.

HOOVER, EDGAR M. *Location of Economic Activity.* New York: McGraw-Hill Book Co., 1948.

HOYT, HOMER. *According to Hoyt* (2nd ed.). Washington, D. C.: Hoyt, 1970. Sec. XI.

KINNARD, WILLIAM N., and MESSNER, STEPHEN D. *Industrial Real Estate* (2nd ed.). Washington, D. C.: Society of Industrial Realtors, 1971.

McMAHAN, JOHN. *Property Development.* New York: McGraw-Hill Book Co., 1976. Chs. 8 and 9.

WENDT, PAUL F., and CERF, ALAN R. *Real Estate Investment, Analysis and Taxation.* New York: McGraw-Hill Book Co., Inc., 1969. Chs. 7–9.

WILEY, ROBERT J. *Real Estate Investment—Analysis and Strategy.* New York: The Ronald Press Co., 1977. Chs. 14 and 15.

CASE 19–1

Western Federal Savings and Loan Association of Denver *

Since January 1962, Western Federal Savings and Loan Association of Denver has owned and occupied its modern, first-class, 26-story home office building in the heart of downtown Denver's financial district (see opposite). For many years now the Association has been the largest Savings and Loan Association in the Rocky Mountain West and currently the Association has assets of nearly a billion dollars.

The Association normally invests the greatest portion of its resources in high-quality long-term mortgage loans on single- and multi-family dwellings. In addition the Association regularly invests a portion of its resources in long-term mortgage loans on commercial real estate and is actively engaged in the short-term mortgage lending market through its construction loan activities.

Chartered as a United States Corporation, the Association is a mutual institution and, therefore, has no stock ownership. In addition the Association must operate within the regulations provided by the Federal Home Loan Bank System. Until recently, these regulations have permitted investment in real estate only when the real property was to be occupied fully or in part by the Association as home or branch office quarters. The Association, because of this limitation, has not speculated in real estate investments or other specialized land banking. However, since 1950 the Association has owned the real estate occupied by its home office and branch offices. These real estate investments have been very successful.

This success has encouraged management to consider additional real estate investment in the anticipation that their eventual sale will contribute to the surplus of the Association.

Some key statistics concerning the home office building are:

1. Original cost:
   a. Land $1,000,000
   b. Building $6,000,000 $7,000,000
2. Estimated market value: $9,000,000

* Material used by permission of Western Savings and Loan Association.

Western Savings Building.

3. Estimated loan available:
   a. Amount $6,300,000
   b. Term   25 yrs
   c. Interest rate   8½%

Some key operational statistics include:

1. Total square footage of rental space   112,000 sq. ft.
2. Current vacancy ratio   –
3. Current rent schedule:
   a. Plaza levels through 14th floor   7.50/sq. ft.
   b. 15th floor through 19th floor   7.00/sq. ft.
   c. 20th floor through 24th floor   8.90/sq. ft.
4. Current return on investment:
   $349,180 on $7,000,000 invested capital   4.99%
5. Rent escalation clause:
   1½¢/sq. ft. for every 1¢/hr of wage increase for Building
   Service Employees in the City of Denver

Because the Association owns its 26-story home office building free and clear, numerous offers have been received to either sell the building and lease it back or to mortgage the building. These offers present three interesting and challenging basic alternatives to the Association:

1. Should the building be sold and leased back?
   The value of the property could be seriously impaired by new office buildings in downtown Denver.
2. Should the building be mortgaged?
   Presuming that the Association could borrow at 8½ to 9½ per cent and then either invest in fixed-dollar investment with a return greater than 8½ to 9½ per cent or invest in shorter-term loans or construction loans with even higher yields, such a move could provide the Association with reasonable long-term capital cost.
3. Should the Association leave the *status quo?*
   Recognizing that the Association has made a good real estate investment, that the return on invested capital is at 4.99 per cent, and that the benefits of future depreciation and/or cost appreciation would continue to accrue, the Association assumes little risk by leaving the *status quo.*

Questions

1. If Western Federal earns 8½ to 9½ per cent on mortgage loans, how does its office building look as an investment?
2. What is a good capitalization rate for income on the building? Justify your answer.
3. Using the capitalization rate from question 2, what is the value of the building?
4. How does that value compare to the estimated market value?
5. If you were a potential buyer, what rate of return would you want on your investment? What would you be willing to pay for the building?
6. Assume you are Western Federal's real estate officer. What is your recommendation to the board of directors?

CASE 19–2

A B Chemical Company

The A B Chemical Company manufactures a variety of pharmaceutical products at plants located at Maynard, Kansas, and Center City, Kansas. Early in 1976 a new product was being developed which would be marketed through a dual distribution system including direct sales to large customers and sales through distributors and warehouses to smaller customers. This product would be manufactured at a new location. A general statement of the requirements of the plant is described below.

The site cannot be chosen solely on the basis of meeting the requirements for the initial production. Company plans, while not specific in terms of precise products to be manufactured in the future, nevertheless contemplate growth and the introduction of new products into the new plant facility. Accordingly, the plant site selected must also contemplate the possibility of future substantial growth.

A decision was made to select the optimum location for the proposed new facility, bearing in mind the need not only of the immediate contemplated plant, but also possible future growth and development of the plant. It was decided to employ The Fantus Company of Chicago, location consultants, to conduct a search and study encompassing the entire United States. During the research the consulting company did not reveal the company name.

Some of the basic requirements for a suitable site were supplied to Fantus. These were as follows:

Labor: 150 people (start with 50). Community must have supply of high caliber trainable workers available. Company will train. Need a few skilled tradesmen.

Freight: Truck and rail. Rail potential 300 cars per year inbound plus part of outbound. Balance of shipments primarily full truckload throughout country. Require good truck service.

Utilities: Power: 6,000 KW, 90–95% P.F., 4,250,000 KWH per month. Loop feed or dual source desirable.

Fuel: 11,250 MFC per month of natural gas (peak load, 1 hour per day, 4 times average load, balance of load stable 24 hours per day). Oil can be used instead of gas.

Water: Sanitary use, maximum 500,000 gallons per month. Process uses 5,000 gallons per minute, continuous. Company will develop cooling water system, but water with a maximum summer temperature of 60° F must be available in this quantity.

Sewer: Company will treat effluent.

Site: 50–100 acres. Rail service available. Power and gas available (gas may be omitted). Water not exceeding 60° C maximum summer temperature available. Must be located on or near (with pipeline easement) a river with an average flow of at least 6,000 cubic feet per second. Prefer 2–5 miles from populated area.

Defining the Area. *Many factors operate to control the location of the proposed plant.* Among the most important cost factors are utility costs, transportation costs, labor costs, and taxes. Furthermore, many significant operating conditions had to be considered in the selection of the site and in the selection of a general area of location. Among these important operating conditions are labor attitude, productivity, quality of transportation service, accessibility of the area, living conditions, educational facilities, etc. The desire to construct certain proposed manufacturing buildings of open design would direct the search toward the south central states. Also, the desirability of TVA power was an important factor.

Certain factors operate more restrictively than others in the proposed location project. The factors which operate most restrictively to determine the area within which the plant may be located are the availability of streams with the required 6,000 cubic feet per second average flow and a minimum flow in excess of 300 cubic feet per second, the availability of 5,000 or more gallons per minute of water with a temperature never exceeding 60° F, and the cost of the very substantial quantity of electric power required. Another factor, which does not define the area as sharply, but which nevertheless indicates the general area of maximum interest, is that of transportation costs.

After completing their investigation, four sites were described:

1. Alderson, Alabama
2. Toptown, Tennessee
3. Warrentown, Kentucky
4. Travel City, Kentucky

For various reasons the consulting company selected the site at Alderson, Alabama, as the optimum location for the plant. Executives of the company examined the four sites but took no action.

Subsequently, the consulting company recommended a fifth site at Marchwood, Kentucky, which the company decided more closely satisfied their requirements; however, in inspecting other possible sites in surrounding counties, they found an area around Monterey, Kentucky, which they felt would best meet the requirements. After this decision was made, the Monterey Industrial Development Foundation obtained options on parcels of land selected by the company forming a tract of 188 acres about one mile north of Monterey. The options were assigned to the company and the purchase closed.

Developments Within the Company During the Search for and Selection of a Site. Successes of the research and development laboratories of the company during the time that the site search was being conducted resulted in increased production yields which deferred the decision to initiate construction and at the same time required the company to reappraise the site requirements. Because of increased complexity of products to be produced, it was decided that the site would have to be in a location providing for easy and quick communication between the proposed new plant and the research and development laboratories at Center City. The market estimates became more optimistic, and it was decided that the site would have to be considerably larger than originally determined. The revised specifications for the site called for a location within 1 or 1½ hours travel time from the research and development laboratories and in excess of 250 acres.

Notification to Monterey Community of the New Requirements of the Company. Representatives of the company visited the Monterey Industrial Development Foundation and explained to them the new requirements for a site and offered to grant the Foundation an option to purchase the Monterey site at its cost price without any of the costs which the company had incurred in investigating the site as well as offering to assist the Foundation in finding another industry that might be interested in locating on the Monterey site.

Search for a New Site. Action was initiated to immediately locate a satisfactory site in Kansas to meet the new specifications. The company conducted a study of all river areas with known ground water deposits within an approximate radius of 100 miles of Center City, and each possible site was thoroughly examined without revealing the company name. Extensive use was made of industrial development corporations, chambers of commerce, railroad companies, Realtors®, and the director of industrial development of the State of Kansas. In addition, considerable "raw" searching was undertaken.

Early in the investigation it was determined that the Northtown, Kansas, Industrial Development Corporation, a small group of local businessmen, had acquired 46 acres five miles north of Northtown, Kansas, in the hope of attracting an industry. Upon examining this area it was found that the land surrounding this tract, if it could be assembled, would produce a tract of satisfactory size and upon further investigation was found that all other conditions prevailing in the area met reasonably well every specification for a site. The parcels for which purchase options were desired were outlined to the Northtown Industrial Development Corporation, and with their cooperation action was taken to obtain options as quickly as possible. This was accomplished, and when the parcels were assembled they created a tract of approximately 750 acres which has since been purchased by the company. The company name was not revealed to the Northtown Industrial Development Corporation until the last option was under negotiation.

While negotiations for options were under way, investigations were undertaken by the company to determine that all conditions pertaining to the site would satisfy the company needs. These investigations included:

1. Determination that the railroad company would agree to a spur track and would grant easements for culverts through the railroad right of way for effluent pipes.
2. Determination of availability of electrical service.
3. Investigation of county zoning regulations.
4. Determination that access to the state highway would be granted.
5. Review of existing tenant leases.
6. Review of existing utility easements.
7. Determination of the availability of natural gas.
8. Review of schooling and housing in general area.
9. Review of hospital facilities in general area.
10. Determination of the requirements by State Board of Health on discharge of treated effluent into river.
11. Official survey of all tracts of land.
12. Ground water pumping tests.
13. Soil resistance tests.
14. Procurement of aerial photographs from U. S. Department of Agriculture.
15. Review of history of flooding of Walnut River and effect of upstream flood reservoirs.

Complications in Closing the Purchase. Some of the complications which developed were:

1. Land swaps where the sellers requested the company to purchase designated property and swap that property for the property required.
2. Mineral rights leases previously granted by the seller had to be transferred to the purchaser.
3. One seller was granted a life residency in the farm house on the property purchased.
4. One seller requested purchase payments to be made over a period of three years to spread taxes.

Ground-breaking took place on the site five months and nine days from the date the assignment was given to find a new site.

Questions

1. Why was location close to Center City so important?
2. Which factors were of major importance in the final site selection?
3. Why were rural or semi-rural locations considered over urban locations?
4. Why would a place like Northtown, Kansas, be a better plant site than someplace in Center City, Kansas, where the problem of travel time would be virtually eliminated?

20

FARMS, RANCHES, FORESTS, AND RECREATIONAL LAND *

TYPES OF RURAL REAL ESTATE

The line between "rural" and "urban" cannot be drawn easily. The Bureau of the Census refers to urbanized areas as cities of 50,000 people or more and their built-up suburbs but also includes within the urban population persons who live in places of 2,500 inhabitants or more.

The people in places with 2,500 inhabitants or more live on 1.53 per cent of the U. S. land area. Urban land needs will tend to increase somewhat by the year 2000. The changes from rural to urban land uses, however, are not likely to occur as rapidly in the years ahead as in the past. This will be especially true in the northern, middle, and eastern regions of the country.

Rural Land Use

Land not used for urban purposes includes farm and ranch land such as that used for crops, pasture, and grazing as well as nonproductive farm land. Also included are commercial forest land, land used for recreation, transportation, wildlife refuges, and reservoirs, and other types.

Types Selected for Discussion

We center our attention on land uses that we believe have special significance for real estate purposes. More or less arbitrarily, we have selected farms and ranches for primary consideration. We also present a summary

---

* We appreciate the assistance of Royal Shupp of the U. S. Dept. of Agriculture and Professor Robert C. Suter of Purdue University in reviewing this chapter.

discussion of land used for forestry and for rural, or rather, nonurban, recreation. Nonurban land that is used for residential purposes (urban nonfarm) is growing in importance and was considered in Chapter 18.

THE MARKET FOR FARMS

Agriculture has been going through a revolution characterized in general by a shift toward a business and managerial type of operation with increasingly heavy investments per farm. Scientific and technological advances have been back of these changes including improved feeds and fertilizers, more effective plant and animal breeding, better agricultural implements and power, improved roads and trucks, and related developments. There have been marketing as well as production changes; contract farming has increased in importance as have the efforts of various farm cooperatives. Government programs including various controls and supports have played a somewhat less important role than in the past.

Special Characteristics

Agriculture, with individual units varying through a wide range of productivity, size, and capital requirements, presents a real estate market with its own peculiar problems and characteristics. To lump all farms together into a single farm real estate market is no more correct than to lump all factories or all retail stores together.

As in the case of other types of real estate, there is no organized market for farmland. Systems for grading and classifying farmland leave much to be desired. Furthermore, the principal buyers of farmland usually are found in the immediate locality. In some instances farms are purchased by outside investors. In recent years foreign investors have increased their interest in farms.

Soil productivity, the condition of buildings and other improvements, accessibility to roads, schools, churches, electric power lines, and shopping centers, as well as community ties, family sentiment, and the like all have a bearing on the market for farms. Many of the factors are subjective in nature. Location plays a role of growing importance in determining farmland values.

Farmland is usually sold by the acre and is ordinarily priced in terms of so many dollars per acre with the value of farm buildings and other improvements included in such a price.

Farm Brokers

Farm real estate brokers usually operate within a single community and seldom cover an area that extends much beyond several counties. Some real estate brokers specialize in farmland, and may include professional farm appraisal and management as a part of their activities.

The practices followed by farm brokers differ little from those followed by the real estate brokers in urban communities. As in the case of urban real estate, income plus the terms and availability of financing are of major importance in determining the intensity of demand for farm real estate; during inflationary periods demand may rise from efforts to secure a hedge against inflation.

Supply

Despite growing demands for agricultural products, the number of farms has declined from 3.9 million in 1960 to 2.8 million in 1974.[1] At the same time, the average size of farms has increased. Farms with a thousand acres or more (less than 4 per cent of the total) account for approximately half of all farmland. The top 3 per cent of the farms account for more farm production than the bottom 78 per cent.

About 15 million people lived on farms in 1960, 10 million in 1970, and 9.3 million in 1974. Not all of the people who live on farms derive their main incomes from agriculture; many are industrial workers who farm part-time or retired persons or others not primarily dependent on agriculture.

Size of Farms

The size of farms is usually measured in terms of acres of land. The acre is not an entirely satisfactory unit of measurement, since it includes the surface area only. It does not reflect the quality of farmland, and quality varies widely. Standards have been developed for grading the quality of agricultural land but additional progress is needed. In terms of acres the average size of farms in this country has been increasing, rising from slightly over 200 to over 300 acres in the past 10 years. The basic reason for this is the increased mechanization of agricultural production. In all probability, many farmers could utilize more acres than they do now. It appears that the farmers' ability to farm more acres has increased more rapidly than the ability to acquire land.

At the present time, however, it is not a simple matter to extend the acreage which a particular farmer has under cultivation. Farmland may usually be purchased in 40-, 80-, or 160-acre multiples in the midwest and west. For example, a farmer may wish to add twenty-five acres of land to a farm. Such a block of land, however, is not likely to be available. A purchaser may have to buy an entire farm, including a set of farm buildings for which there could be little or no use. As a result of this situation, many farmers have expanded their scale of operations, not by adding more land, but by using more capital. Often the availability of improved and larger farm power and machinery virtually forces an expansion in the size of an

---

[1] See *A New U. S. Farm Policy for Changing World Food Needs* (New York: Committee for Economic Development, 1974).

operation. It is probable that the acreage of land in the average farm will continue to rise in future years.

Demand for Farms

The demand for farm real estate in the case of commercial farms, like the demand for most other types of capital goods, is a derived demand. It is derived from the demand for the goods or services in the production of which the capital goods are used. Thus, an understanding of the demand for farm products is basic to understanding the demand for such farms themselves. In cases where farms are used primarily for residential rather than commercial purposes, demand would be similar to the demand for other residential real estate. It may be helpful to divide farms according to the purposes for which they are used, such as: (1) commercial, (2) residential, (3) part-time, or (4) subsistence.[2]

The income-producing ability of farms depends on the production of crops and livestock and on the market for these products. Of course, farms are sometimes bought for essentially noneconomic reasons, such as the wish to pursue a rural way of life, sentimental attachments to a particular farm or locality, the desire to follow a hobby, such as the raising of a special breed of cattle or the conducting of special experiments, and for similar reasons. Thus, the demand for farms may arise from their ability to produce economic returns or from other motivations.

Factors Affecting Demand

The supply of farm products varies with weather, technology, and market conditions; the demand for them reflects income and population changes. The greatest fluctuations have occurred as a result of the shifting demands during war periods. In addition, however, the consumers of farm products adapt their purchases to their income situations. When incomes are high the demand for farm products is strong, particularly the demand for foods of higher quality. When incomes are low the demand for such foods as bread and potatoes does not tend to decline greatly, but the demands for foods of higher quality tend to move downward. Under high standards of living the demand for many types of food partakes of the nature of a luxury demand, with the result that substantial downward adjustments may be anticipated whenever incomes decline.

International demand for U. S. farm products has increased rapidly in recent years and foreign markets have provided an increasingly important outlet for American agricultural products. This has had both advantages and disadvantages—broader markets but also unpredictable variations in these markets. Special problems have been generated by countries that trade on a statewide basis.

[2] Classification suggested by Prof. Robert C. Suter, Purdue University.

Investors in Farms

Other sources of demand for farms should be mentioned. One of these is the investor in the higher income tax brackets who may try to buy run-down farms, spend heavily for development purposes, and then sell the farms for a capital gain or continue to hold them.

Many investors buy farms as a long-term hedge against possible future inflation. Of course, there are always investors who buy land near settled areas in the hope of sale for urban rather than rural purposes. Whenever the yield on government bonds and similar investments moves downward, the interest of investors in farms tend to advance and vice versa.

The interest of investors from abroad in U. S. farms has been increasing. In part this reflects the strength of U. S. farm investments and in part, instabilities in the home countries of foreign investors.

Farmland Tenure

A system of farmland tenure may be defined as the sum total of the various arrangements by which land is owned, rented, leased, used, controlled, and transferred. All nations have struggled with the problem of devising satisfactory rules, laws, and other arrangements for controlling these matters. For example, feudalism was a system of agricultural land tenure. There have been many other systems as well. The land practices followed in this country from Revolutionary times have had the objective of widespread ownership of farms by those who operate them. By 1975 only about a quarter of all farm operators in the United States were tenants. About three-fifths of farm operators were full owners, and the remainder were part owners. The latter group owned part of the land they operated and rented some additional land.

FACTORS AFFECTING RURAL LAND VALUES

Like other real property, the value of rural real estate depends upon its ability to produce monetary or direct use income. The value of a producing farm is derived by capitalizing the anticipated future net income.

Potential Urban Uses

Suburban land on the fringe of cities often derives its value from the anticipated urban use. Consequently, its present value is based on the value of urban land uses, discounted by the length of time it will take for such land to be utilized in that way. When sewer or water mains are extended into such areas, the price of land advances rapidly.

Costs and Returns

The level of net farm earnings depends upon relationships between prices received by farmers and production costs, which will be affected by the quality of farm management, technological developments in production, changes in the efficiency of marketing agricultural products, real estate taxes, financing charges, government programs, and related factors.

The principal physical factors affecting the value of farmland are soil productivity, rainfall, and the length of the growing season. Other factors include buildings and other improvements available, location and accessibility to markets, schools, churches, shopping centers, and power lines. Buildings and other improvements are more important for some types of farming, such as dairy and poultry farming, than for other types, such as cattle ranches.

Low-Yield Crops

The value of farmland depends also upon its suitability for different types of crops (see Fig. 20–1). The cheapest land is found in arid or semiarid regions. Its uses are limited to grazing. The value of such land may be related to the number of acres required to support one steer and the value added in the increased weight of the steer, minus labor and feeding costs. Other low-grade rural land includes that used for the production of pulpwood. Such a crop can be produced in around seven years where there is a long growing season. A slightly higher type of land is permanent pasture in areas with abundant rainfall. In Florida, for example, there are areas of this type which will support one steer per acre.

Higher Yields

Such rural land uses contrast with the rich farmland of the Middle West and California. The rich Midwest land, in an area provided with adequate summer rainfall and a growing season long enough to mature corn, produces high yields. Much of the land in this region is sufficiently level to permit the widespread use of tractors, harvesters, and similar mechanical equipment. Rainfall diminishes in the areas west of Iowa in the Dakotas, Nebraska, and Kansas. Wheat is the principal crop in these regions, as it is in Canada. The 20-inch rainfall line is an important one.

Specialty Crops

The highest farmland values result from specialty crops, especially citrus fruits. Oranges and grapefruit can be raised only in a subtropical climate where the temperature does not fall below 25 degrees or if it falls below such levels does so only for short intervals. Some cool weather is required, however, for the production of the best quality of fruit. Consequently,

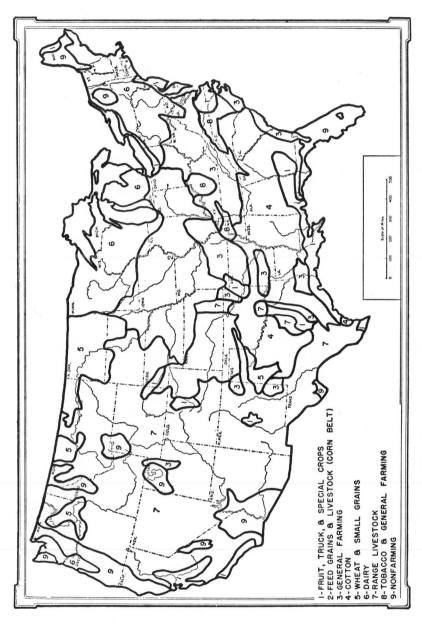

FIG. 20–1. Agricultural products of the United States.

1-FRUIT, TRUCK, & SPECIAL CROPS
2-FEED GRAINS & LIVESTOCK (CORN BELT)
3-GENERAL FARMING
4-COTTON
5-WHEAT & SMALL GRAINS
6-DAIRY
7-RANGE LIVESTOCK
8-TOBACCO & GENERAL FARMING
9-NONFARMING

commercial citrus fruits cannot be produced to any extent in the tropics. Citrus groves require eighteen to twenty years before they reach the full bearing stage. However, they have a bearing life of many years. Because of the long life and heavy capital investment required, extended periods of overproduction and low prices result when too many orchards are developed. Of special interest in connection with the growing of citrus fruits is the use of frozen concentrates, which permits the absorption of a much larger supply than formerly.

Apple orchards, peach orchards, grape vineyards, pecan groves, tung groves, and walnut groves share some of the characteristics of citrus farming, but each has its own peculiarities. Among these are greater annual fluctuations in yields and a shorter bearing life.

Orchard crops cannot be changed quickly. The owner is committed to a long-term investment and to annual operating costs regardless of market conditions.

Cotton. Cotton requires a longer growing season than corn, but a shorter one than various types of orchards. Cotton has long been one of the principal crops of the southern states, although its relative importance has diminished in more recent years.

Tobacco. At the present time, tobacco acreage is limited by government control. Consequently the right to use specified acreage for tobacco production adds to the values of the land involved. The value of the allotment tends to be added to the value of the land in making appraisals. The inventory or cost approach and others may be used. Tobacco is raised in a number of states, largely in Kentucky, Virginia, and the Carolinas.

Timberland. Timberland is valued on the basis of the estimated value of board feet of standing timber of saw-log size. Its value tends to fluctuate with the price of lumber. Scientific forestry has been practiced to an increasing extent in the United States. The adoption of sustained-yield management methods holds promise of adding to the value of timberlands.

Farm Valuation Factors

In summary, the valuation of an individual farm requires consideration of (1) the fertility of the soil; (2) climatic factors, especially rainfall and the length of the growing season; (3) topography; (4) the amount of land under cultivation and the amount used for woodland or grazing; (5) accessibility to hard roads; (6) character of the houses, barns, and other improvements; (7) quotas allowed for raising certain crops; and (8) specific location possibilities for conversion to urban uses.

Appraising Farms

Although many rules of thumb are followed by farmers, real estate brokers, and investors in estimating the value of farms, more refined techniques of appraisal have been developed in recent years (see Fig. 20–2). The steps in a farm appraisal may be outlined as follows:

1. The legal descriptions are checked against the farm boundaries. Aerial photographs are being used to an increasing extent in this process. They are often available in the county offices of the U. S. Department of Agriculture. Also, the Department's Soil Conservation Service may provide maps showing soil types and characteristics.
2. An inventory of the soil and farm improvements is made. Soil tubes and augurs are used to estimate the soil's characteristics. Estimates are made of the remaining useful life of the buildings and their current condition.
3. An estimate is made of the landowner's income from the farm. Estimates are based on prices for the crops produced on the farm. A schedule of annual expenses is established, including building depreciation.
4. The estimated net income is capitalized at a rate which reflects the going rate for investments of this type.
5. Adjustments are made as required to fit the specific situation, giving added value to farms that are especially well located and deducting for improvements that need to be made immediately.
6. Sale prices of similar farms in the community are determined from county records, newspaper files, and real estate brokers and appraisers. Comparisons are made with the farm being appraised and an estimated value is derived by correlating the value as determined by the income, capitalization, sales comparison, and inventory or cost methods.

FARM FINANCING

Capital Requirements

Total assets of American agriculture were estimated at $502.6 billion on January 1, 1975. About 84 per cent of this represented equity capital.

The value of all farm real estate in 1970 was estimated at $371.4 billion. This was over two-thirds of total farm assets. Outstanding against this was an estimated real estate debt of $46.3 billion. This means that farmers have around an 88 per cent equity in their land.

The rate of capital turnover in agriculture is typically slow. Although at times farmers have a capital turnover (length of time required for receipts to equal total capital invested) of 3 to 4 years, the normal length of time is more likely to be 6 to 8 years in the Midwest. Time required varies with type of farm, level of prices, and related factors. Dairy and poultry farmers turn their capital over more quickly than cattle farmers, for example.

Name of Applicant _____

IMPROVEMENTS

No. and Kind	Rooms	Baths	Square Footage or Dimensions	Type of Construction	Condition and Basic Description of Improvement and Alternate Usage if Applicable	Contributory Values
Dwelling Year Built 19___ (50)					(51)	$ _____
						$
						$
						$
						$
						$
						$

Value of Merchantable Timber & Pulpwood $_____   (53)   Total Contributory Value of Improvements   (52) $

602

LAND

Normal Use	Acres	Type and Quality of Soil; Topography; Crop Adaptability; Ease and Economy of Operation Any Other Important Features
(54) Woods		
(55) Pasture		
(56) Crop		
Other		
(58) TOTAL		

Number of acres irrigated: (57) _____

FIG. 20–2. Appraiser's report.

MARKET COMPARISON GRID

For each comparison item (1 thru 5) indicate a plus (+) if *subject* is *better*; a minus (−) if *comparable* is *better*; a zero (0) if *comparison* item is *equal*. Use a minimum of three sales. Adjust items on a per acre basis. Indication of dollar adjustments optional for items 1 thru 5.

Sale	No.	*Distance & Direction	No. of Acres	Bare Land Price Per Acre	(1) Location	(2) Size & Shape	(3) Soils & Topography	(4) Time	(5) Other	Indicate Per Acre Value of Subject
Sale				$						$
Sale				$						$
Sale				$						$
Sale				$						$
Sale				$						$

*From Subject Property

Based on the indications of value by the above sales, the present market value of the subject land is estimated to be $ _____ per acre × total acres =

$ _____
Total Land Value

AV "as is" (62) $ _____   PMV "as is" (63) $ _____

This property _____ satisfactory security subject to the following requirements being fulfilled:
(is − is not)

With the foregoing requirements being fulfilled the AV "as will be" (60) $ _____   PMV "as will be" (61) $ _____

Consideration has been given to total taxes, O&M, and B&I charges of $ _____ per acre and project debt liability of $ _____ against this land.

Any shortage in the acreage of this farm that may be developed upon examination of the title and verification of the plat which does not exceed _____ percent of the total acreage shown in my report and which is not caused by the exclusion of a specified part of the property will not affect my estimate of the appraised value.

REMARKS: (A) Briefly describe any unusual feature or features that would better describe the subject property.

(B) Briefly describe the area in which the property is located.

THIS SECTION APPLICABLE IF THE PMV OF THE LAND EXCEEDS TWO TIMES BASE FARM VALUE.

Procedure for Establishing Appraised Value for Subject Property:

Area Base Farm Value	$ _____	Per Acre
	x _____ 2	
	$ _____	Maximum AV Per Acre
	x _____	Total Acres of Subject
	$ _____	Total AV of Land
Plus	$ _____	Contributory Value of Improvements
	$ _____	Total Appraised Value (Insert this figure in line item number 62 on reverse side)

Date Appraised (64) _____   _____ Appraiser   (65) _____ Code

FIG. 20–2. Continued.

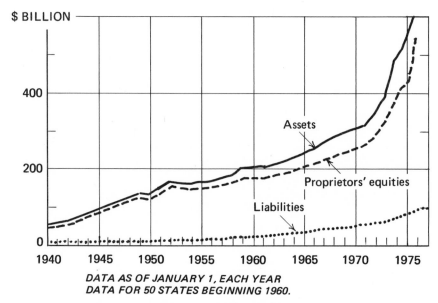

DATA AS OF JANUARY 1, EACH YEAR
DATA FOR 50 STATES BEGINNING 1960.

FIG. 20–3. Balance sheet of the farming sector. (*Source:* U. S. Dept. of Agriculture.)

TABLE 20–1. Balance Sheet of the Farming Sector, 1975

Item	January 1, 1960	January 1, 1970	January 1, 1975
	(Billions of Dollars)		
Assets			
Physical assets:			
Real estate	130.6	206.9	371.1
Non-real estate	45.3	76.5	119.7
Financial assets	18.1	22.8	29.8
Total	204.0	306.2	520.6
Claims			
Real estate debt	12.0	29.2	46.3
Non-real estate	12.8	23.8	35.5
Equities	179.2	253.1	438.8
Total	204.0	306.1	520.6

Source: Dept. of Agriculture, Economic Research Service, *Balance Sheet of the Farming Sector.*

Sources of Funds

As in the case of other real estate uses, the purchase of fee ownership with the use of both equity and debt funds, plus the leasing of properties, constitute the major methods of acquiring rights to use farm real estate. Funds for the financing of farms are made available by institutional lenders,

TABLE 20–2.   Real Estate Farm Debt Outstanding January 1, Selected Years

Year	Federal Land Banks [1]	Farmers Home Admin. [2]	Life Insurance Co's. [3]	Commercial Banks [2]	Individuals and Others [4]	Total
	(Millions of dollars)					
1965	3,687	1,285	4,288	2,417	7,218	18,894
1970	6,671	2,280	5,734	3,545	10,953	29,183
1975	13,402	3,212	6,297	5,966	17,408	46,288
	Percent increase					
1965–75	263.5	150.0	47.3	146.8	141.2	145.1

[1] Includes data for joint stock land banks and Federal Farm Mortgage Corporation.

[2] Farmers Home Administration loans prior to 1973 were revised so that all of their insured loans were included with direct loans in the FmHA total rather than being included with commercial banks or others.

[3] Life Insurance Institute Tally sheet.

[4] Estimated by ERS, USDA.

Source: Dept. of Agriculture, Economic Research Service, *Balance Sheet of the Farming Sector.*

such as commercial banks and insurance companies, by individuals (especially retired farmers), by cooperative credit agencies, and by the government. Much land is sold on contract with the seller financing the arrangement or at least the earlier stages of it.[3] During prosperous periods, banks and insurance companies are of major importance as sources of farm credit. During periods of depression and low farm incomes, the major burden of financing shifts to government agencies or to government guaranteed loans.

Of the $46.3 billion farm mortgage debt outstanding at the beginning of 1975, life insurance companies held about a sixth, banks a seventh, federal land banks a fourth, Farmers Home Administration a small percentage, and individuals and others around two-fifths. In recent years Federal Land Banks and individuals and others have increased in relative importance.

GOVERNMENT PROGRAMS

For many years we have had a system of government supports of the prices of farm products. Details of the system have varied from time to time, but have been modified to reflect changing conditions. For example, international conditions and consumer interests have brought program changes.

Basis of Support

Three basic questions are involved in a system of government support of farm prices: first, which prices shall be supported; second, on what level;

[3] Robert C. Suter, Philip J. Scaletta, and C. J. Thomas, "The Installment Land Contract: Legal Provisions and Economic Implications," Lafayette, Ind.: Purdue University, *Economic and Marketing Information* (May 28, 1971).

and third, by what means. Government supports have tended to be on a selective rather than on a uniform basis. Originally, only the so-called basic products—wheat, corn, cotton, rice, and peanuts—were supported. From time to time others have been added to the list and some have been dropped.

Supports

The basic principle determining the level at which prices are supported has been the concept of "parity." Parity is defined as the ratio which prevailed between farm prices and nonfarm prices during the period 1909 to 1914. This period is considered to be one in which a "normal" ratio between these two sets of prices prevailed. Several methods have been used to maintain parity, the most important being the "loan and storage" system. For example, farmers store wheat at an approved storage facility and offer the stored wheat as collateral for a nonrecourse loan from the government on the basis of the support price. If the farmers see fit, they may repay the loan, redeem the wheat, and sell it on the open market. If not, the government takes the wheat as payment for the loan and the transactions is concluded. In fact, such a loan is a sort of conditional sale to the government at a "pegged" minimum price. Other methods which the government has used to support prices include outright purchase in the open market, subsidized exports, market quotas, acreage restrictions, and soil bank programs.

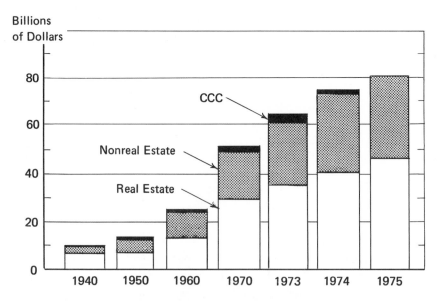

FIG. 20–4. Farm debt, loans outstanding January 1. (*Source:* Dept. of Agriculture, *Balance Sheet of the Farming Sector*, 1975.)

FARM TRENDS

In all probability, the trend toward larger and fewer farms will continue as farm management improves and as technology advances, thus making possible increased use of machinery and improved seeds and fertilizers. Larger farms are likely to take on to an increasing extent many of the characteristics of large-scale manufacturing operations. Although some prefer a return to organic agriculture, present requirements for food could not be met with such methods. There has been growing interest in small-scale subsistence farming in some quarters.

Bigger Farms—More Machines

Larger farms and more machinery will require increasing capital investment per farm and for agriculture as a whole. Managerial requirements will increase.

Some smaller farms may be absorbed by larger commercial farms. Others may be used for reforestation and recreational purposes. A growing number of people are being attracted to small farms as rural homes and as a means of escaping major food costs.

Highways

The federal highway program has had significant effects on farming. Many farms were brought closer to markets. Some farm families now live in suburban homes and commute to farm operations. This is especially true of crop farming, as in the case of the wheatlands of Kansas.

Ownership

The number of owner-operated farms may tend downward as farms grow in size. Because of the interest of investors, farm tenants may have increasing opportunities to become owners.

Science and Technology

The long-term impact of scientific and technological research on farming may be very great. It may be that in the not-too-distant future many of our food requirements will be produced in the laboratory and factory.

Conservation

Federal programs in rural areas to conserve our soil and water resources should have a significant impact on the environment for this and future generations. The Soil Conservation Service of the U. S. Department of Agriculture, for example, provides free consulting services for farmers and others in the areas of drainage and erosion control, animal waste treatment, and crop improvement through soil management. Another federal agency, the Agricultural Stabilization and Conservation Service (ASCS) provides for cost-sharing programs with farmers who install improvements which provide long-term conservation benefits.

TIMBERLAND

A considerable portion of land in the United States is covered with timber. Not only is this a source of lumber, but also of a great many by-products such as turpentine, resin, and camphor. Timberland produces both human and animal foods, such as nuts, acorns, and wild fruit. It acts as a watershed, helps to support wildlife, and also provides certain recreational resources.

Types of Land

At least three different types of land may be used for forests: (1) land where forests now exist and which is well adapted to the continuation of such use, (2) land where forests previously existed and which is better adapted to the growing of trees than to any other use, and (3) land which was previously in cultivation and might have been kept in cultivation if proper protective measures had been taken in time, but which now can be best utilized for the growing of trees.

Sustained Yield Management

Land which is now in timber and for which this is its proper use can best be kept in such use by sustained yield management. This means that the timber should be managed in such a way that it will yield a relatively uniform crop year after year, or at least at frequent intervals rather than only a single crop once every generation, half century, or longer. For many years most of our timberland has been "mined" rather than cropped. Sustained yield management involves selective cutting, taking only the mature trees for commercial lumber production. It also involves the cutting of malformed, diseased, and "weed" trees to give appropriate room, light, and plant food to the more desirable types. By this general process a forester can improve the quality of timber in much the same manner that a livestock breeder improves the quality of herd. Frequently the returns from the lower-grade products are sufficient to cover labor costs incurred in the process of sustained yield management. The trees that are cut, of course, must be replaced either by planting seedlings grown in nursery plots or by resetting certain trees which have been left standing for the purpose.

Yield Management Problems

Adequate replacement can rarely be achieved if the woodland is grazed by domestic livestock. Cattle and hogs, especially the latter, destroy al-

most all young growth in a forest. In addition there is the need to protect timber from fire, which is the ever threatening enemy of woodland.
Much progress in the field of fire prevention and protection has been made
in recent decades, but highly destructive forest fires continue to occur.

There are those who believe it is better to cut larger tracts and reforest
them rather than to follow sustained yield management programs. Much
depends on the characteristics of the forest, the terrain, and the location.

Reforestation

Where cutover land has not proved to be suitable for agricultural use,
programs for reforestation may be undertaken. In the northern parts of
the country, unfortunately, a period of fifty to one hundred years is often
required for the growing of trees from the seedling to the saw-log stage.
Because of the long waiting period, interest on the investment, taxes, and
risks from many sources, programs of this type are not always attractive to
private persons or business firms. In the South, particularly along the
lower Atlantic and Gulf coastal plains, where the growing season is long
and the rainfall is heavier, the rate of tree growth is sufficiently rapid to be
attractive to private developers and investors. In this area trees may grow
to sufficient size for commercial lumber products in twenty to thirty years.
There is also some possibility of income from turpentine and other naval
stores in the meantime. Tax arrangements have been favorable to developments of this kind.

RECREATIONAL LAND

Factors which impart recreational values to rural land include the following: (1) favorable climate, for example, cools summers, mild winters, large
percentage of sunny days, snow for skiing, and the like; (2) scenic beauty;
for example, bodies of water, mountains, and forests; (3) a relative abundance of wildlife, with opportunities for hunting, fishing, nature study, and
photography; (4) facilities for water sports, including swimming, boating,
and related activities; (5) historic or antiquarian interests, such as battle-
fields, relics of pioneer settlements, and others. If located near large population centers the value of recreational land will tend to be well supported.

Seasons

Obviously a tract of land does not need all these characteristics to have
recreational value; any one of them alone may be sufficient to merit some
degree of recreational use of land. Rarely are all of the characteristics listed
above found in combination, but it is not unusual to find several of them
available at a given site. New England, the northern lake regions, and parts
of the Rocky Mountains attract people because of their cool summers.
Florida, the Gulf coast, and parts of Texas, New Mexico, Arizona, and Cali-

fornia attract people because of their relatively warm winters. The Adirondacks, the White Mountains, and various regions in the Rockies appeal to smaller numbers of more active people for camping and for winter sports.

Hunting and Fishing

Traditionally, hunting and fishing have been the most common forms of recreational use of rural land. Private and public hunting preserves have been developed. Lakes and streams have been stocked with fish in recent years. It is estimated that more people go fishing than engage in any other form of recreation.

Vacations

The attractiveness òf lakes, streams, and ocean beaches for water sports is closely related to the almost universal search for favorable climates. More and more people have been taking regular vacations. To a large degree these are concentrated in the summer months, but winter vacations are growing more popular. As a result, the incomes of winter resorts have tended to expand. Interstate highways and jet aircraft are changing somewhat the pattern of preferences for various resort areas.

Historic Interest

Almost all of us, to some extent, are interested in our history. The Bicentennial celebration renewed national awareness of events and historical sites. Old battlegrounds, ghost towns, relics of early settlements, and similar landmarks have a wide appeal. While this country lacks the old castles and other romantic ruins of Europe, we have a rich heritage from both Indian and early American culture.

Parks

The use of rural land for parks has been growing in importance. Some of the large national parks and forests, such as Yellowstone and Glacier National parks, are famous throughout the world. In recent years a number of states have developed systems of state parks. Those of Indiana, such as Brown County, Turkey Run, and McCormicks's Creek, are cases in point. In addition the private development of parks has progressed. Usually such parks are located in accessible areas and tied in with such sports as hunting, fishing, horseback riding, and related activities.

Growing Importance of Recreation

With the growth of population, higher incomes, and increased leisure time, the demands for recreational facilities of all types have tended to expand. Outdoor recreation has attracted great numbers of people in recent years. This is due in large part to the increased mobility of our people. Widespread ownership of automobiles; favorable airline, bus, and boat fares; improved highways; and more widespread and longer vacations have all contributed to the growing interest in outdoor recreation. Furthermore, there are more retired people who have both leisure and independent incomes.

In all probability such factors as a mobile population, good incomes, and leisure time will continue to operate in the years ahead. Consequently, recreational activities, especially outdoor activities, seem likely to grow in importance.

SUMMARY

Rural real estate includes land in use for farms and ranches, forestry, recreation, nonfarm residences, and other uses. Of these, agriculture is the most important.

The income-producing ability of most rural real estate is influenced by natural resources and characteristics of the land as well as climate and location. The market for rural real estate is largely localized, and not highly organized. Most rural real estate is sold by the acre, and prices are quoted in dollars per acre. Some brokers who deal in rural real estate also offer farm management services.

The demand for agricultural land for commercial purposes is a derived demand, depending upon the demand for and prices of farm products. Some demand reflects the interest of investors in the income tax advantages of farm ownership and development, and some reflects the speculative hope that the land may be required for urban expansion in the future. Some rural land is used for recreational purposes and for part-time farming.

A recent trend, reinforced by technological improvements, is toward fewer farms, and these of larger unit size. The higher capital requirements for modern farming tend to make entry into farming more difficult. The interest of investors both at home and abroad may be helpful to young farmers.

Timberland represents an important sector of rural real estate. Sustained yield management and tax advantages have tended to attract investors into timberland in recent years.

Recreation of all types appears to be a growing influence in American life. Demands for outdoor recreational facilities are growing; this indicates a substantial expansion in the use of various lands for recreational purposes.

QUESTIONS FOR STUDY

1. Explain why agriculture has shifted toward managerial-type operations. What effect has this had on land uses and values?
2. How does the market for farms differ from the market for other types of real estate? Why?
3. Explain why the demand for commercial farms is a derived demand.

4. Do practices of farm real estate brokers differ from those in urban areas? Explain.

5. Explain the major factors that determine the value of rural land. Which of these is most important? Why?

6. Explain how farm operations can be expanded by using capital instead of additional land.

7. What factors explain the increasing average unit size of farms? What advantages do you see in this trend? Explain any disadvantages.

8. Why might investors not directly interested in farming desire to own farm property?

9. Compare and contrast the financing of farm and residential real estate. Identify and define the financing agencies that are most important in rural real estate.

10. What is your evaluation of farm price-support programs? How do these programs affect the income-producing ability of rural real estate? How do they relate to foreign markets for farm products? What is their effect on the values of rural real estate?

11. What are the major determinants of demand in the market for timberland? What are the major determinants of supply?

12. What is sustained yield management?

13. Is the amount of land devoted to recreational activities likely to increase or decrease in the years ahead? Why?

SUGGESTED READINGS

COMMITTEE FOR ECONOMIC DEVELOPMENT. *A New U.S. Farm Policy for Changing World Needs.* A Statement on National Policy, by the Research and Policy Committee. New York: October 1974.

ECONOMIC RESEARCH SERVICE, U. S. DEPARTMENT OF AGRICULTURE. *The Balance Sheet of the Farming Sector.* Washington, D. C.: Government Printing Office, current.

KAHN, SANDERS A., and CASE, FREDERICK E. *Real Estate Appraisal and Investment* (2nd ed.). New York: The Ronald Press Co., 1977. Ch. 28.

SUTER, ROBERT C. *Appraisal of Farm Real Estate.* Danville, Ill.: The Interstate Printers and Publications, Inc., 1974. Ch. 2.

STUDY PROJECT 20–1

Farm Management

Professor Robert C. Suter of Purdue University describes farm management in this way:

Farm Management is the science of the organization and operation of a farm for purposes of maximum efficiency and continuous profits. It is the business end of farming.

The functions of management are three:

1. To organize or coordinate the factors of production—land, labor and capital. This is essentially farm planning . . . enterprise selection, or farm organization.
2. To supervise the operation of the business after it has been set up or developed. This is essentially concerned with the factors affecting profits in farming, refinements in the farm plan, and selection of the most economical production practices.
3. To anticipate and, if possible, determine the future, especially the economics that may prevail with certain cost reducing technologies. This is essentially an economist's job . . . , one of prediction of technical innovation, and future prices and profits.

Questions

1. How does this description of farm management compare with business management in general? With real property management? With the management of a real estate firm?
2. Are the functions of farm management likely to become more specialized or to grow increasingly similar to management in the urban real estate field? Explain.
3. Is farm management likely to become of greater or lesser importance in the field of agriculture? Explain your estimate.

21

INTERNATIONAL
REAL ESTATE TRENDS*

WORLD URBANIZATION AND REAL ESTATE

The growth of cities at a more rapid rate than the surrounding rural areas is a worldwide phenomenon. London was the only metropolitan area approaching a population of one million in 1800; now there are around 150 metropolitan areas in the world with a million or more residents. The number of cities with a population of 100,000 or more increased from 36 in the year 1800 to over a thousand in 1970. The total urban population of the world increased from 45–50 million in 1800 to over a billion in a little over a century and a half. If the present population explosion continues, urban population may increase to around 3 billion by the year 2000. (See Table 21–1.)

This growth of cities is the consequence of a transition from a society dominated by agriculture to one with an increasing development of manufacturing, which began in England and then successively took hold in Germany, the United States, Japan, the Soviet Union, and Red China. Industrialization is progressing in India, Brazil, Mexico, and many other countries.

Relative Importance of Real Estate as an Investment

In many foreign nations real estate is a larger medium of investment than all other investments combined. In addition to large investment opportunities in real estate, the U. S. offers many attractive stocks and bonds to those who prefer this type of investment. Similar opportunities do not

---

* We appreciate the assistance of Richard A. Rauch, President, Rauch & Co., Chicago, in reviewing this chapter.

TABLE 21-1. Population, Mid-1974, and Average Growth Rates, 1960-1974 and 1965-1974
(Countries With Populations of One Million or More)

Country	Number (000)	Growth rates (%) 1960-74	Growth rates (%) 1965-74
China, People's Republic of	809,251	1.6	1.7
India	595,586	2.3	2.3
USSR	252,060	1.1	1.0
United States	211,890	1.1	1.0
Indonesia	128,400	2.1	2.3
Japan	109,670	1.1	1.2
Brazil	103,981	2.9	2.9
Bangladesh	76,200	2.5	2.3
Nigeria	73,044	2.5	2.5
Pakistan	67,213	2.9	2.9
Germany, Federal Republic of	62,040	0.8	0.6
Mexico	57,899	3.4	3.5
United Kingdom	55,970	0.5	0.4
Italy	55,410	0.7	0.7
France	52,510	1.0	0.8
Viet Nam, Socialist Republic of	44,155	2.7	2.7
Philippines	41,433	3.0	3.0
Thailand	40,780	3.1	3.1
Turkey	39,167	2.5	2.6
Egypt, Arab Republic of	36,350	2.5	2.4
Spain	35,109	1.1	1.1
Poland	33,690	0.9	0.8
Korea, Republic of	33,459	2.1	1.8
Iran	33,100	3.2	3.2
Burma	29,521	2.2	2.2
Ethiopia	27,240	2.2	2.5
South Africa	24,940	2.2	2.5
Argentina	24,646	1.5	1.5
Zaire	24,071	2.7	2.7
Colombia	23,125	2.9	2.8
Canada	22,480	1.6	1.4
Yugoslavia	21,155	1.0	0.9
Romania	21,029	1.0	1.2
German Democratic Republic	16,920	0.0	-0.1
Afghanistan	16,311	2.2	2.2
Morocco	16,291	2.4	2.4
China, Republic of	15,710	2.9	2.7
Korea, Democratic People's Republic of	15,443	2.8	2.8
Sudan	15,227	2.2	2.2
Algeria	15,215	3.2	3.3
Peru	14,953	2.9	2.9
Czechoslovakia	14,690	0.5	0.4
Tanzania[1]	14,351	2.9	2.8
Netherlands, The	13,540	1.2	1.1
Sri Lanka	13,393	2.2	2.0

Country	Number (000)	Growth rates (%) 1960-74	Growth rates (%) 1965-74
Australia	13,340	1.9	1.8
Kenya	12,910	3.2	3.4
Nepal	12,320	2.6	2.2
Malaysia	11,702	2.6	2.6
Venezuela	11,632	3.3	3.3
Uganda	11,186	2.9	3.1
Iraq	10,770	3.2	3.3
Hungary	10,460	0.3	0.3
Chile	10,408	2.2	1.9
Belgium	9,770	0.5	0.3
Ghana	9,610	2.6	2.6
Cuba	9,090	2.0	1.8
Mozambique	9,030	2.0	2.2
Greece	9,020	0.6	0.5
Portugal	9,014	0.0	-0.1
Bulgaria	8,676	0.7	0.6
Madagascar	8,560	2.7	2.8
Sweden	8,160	0.7	0.6
Saudi Arabia	8,008	1.8	1.8
Cambodia	7,725	2.5	2.7
Austria	7,550	0.5	0.5
Syrian Arab Republic	7,177	3.3	3.3
Cameroon	7,120	2.0	2.0
Ecuador	6,952	3.4	3.4
Switzerland	6,440	1.2	1.1
Ivory Coast	6,387	3.6	4.0
Yemen Arab Republic	6,379	2.4	2.4
Rhodesia	6,100	3.4	3.5
Angola	6,050	1.4	1.4
Upper Volta	5,760	2.0	1.9
Mali	5,560	2.2	2.1
Bolivia	5,470	2.6	2.6
Tunisia	5,460	2.2	2.3
Guinea	5,390	2.8	2.8
Guatemala	5,284	2.3	2.1
Denmark	5,050	0.7	0.7
Malawi	4,958	2.6	2.6
Senegal	4,869	2.6	2.7
Zambia	4,781	2.9	2.9
Finland	4,690	0.4	0.3
Dominican Republic	4,562	2.9	2.9
Haiti	4,514	1.6	1.6
Niger	4,480	2.7	2.7
Hong Kong	4,249	2.2	1.9
Rwanda	4,058	3.3	2.9

Country	Number (000)	Growth rates (%) 1960-74	Growth rates (%) 1965-74
Norway	3,990	0.8	0.8
Chad	3,952	1.8	2.0
El Salvador	3,887	3.4	3.4
Burundi	3,655	2.0	2.0
Israel	3,359	3.3	3.1
Lao People's Democratic Republic	3,260	2.4	2.4
Somalia	3,100	2.4	2.4
Ireland	3,090	0.6	0.8
Lebanon	3,065	2.7	2.8
New Zealand	3,030	1.6	1.5
Puerto Rico	3,030	1.7	1.8
Benin, People's Republic of	3,027	2.7	2.7
Sierra Leone	2,911	2.2	2.3
Honduras	2,806	2.7	2.7
Uruguay	2,754	0.5	0.4
Papua New Guinea	2,650	2.4	2.4
Jordan	2,620	3.3	3.4
Paraguay	2,484	2.6	2.6
Libyan Arab Republic	2,352	3.9	4.2
Albania	2,350	2.7	2.6
Singapore	2,219	2.1	1.8
Togo	2,176	2.7	2.7
Nicaragua	2,041	2.7	2.7
Jamaica	2,008	1.7	1.7
Costa Rica	1,921	3.1	2.9
Central African Empire	1,748	2.2	2.2
Yemen, People's Democratic Republic of	1,632	3.1	2.9
Panama	1,618	3.1	3.1
Liberia	1,500	3.3	3.3
Mongolia	1,396	2.7	2.8
Congo, People's Republic of the	1,300	2.5	2.3
Mauritania	1,290	2.1	2.5
Lesotho	1,191	2.2	2.2
Bhutan	1,150	2.3	2.3
Trinidad and Tobago	1,070	1.6	0.9

[1] Mainland Tanzania.

Source: World Bank Atlas 1976, p. 4.

always exist in undeveloped nations. In many nations, land has been the chief medium of investment because of the lack of industries offering their securities on the market.

Investments by Nationals of Other Countries in American Real Estate

There is a recent trend toward investment by people from other countries in income properties in the United States. These investments are prompted by a variety of motives: (1) the relative safety of real estate investments in the U. S.; (2) the desire to locate production facilities near the American markets; (3) the lower cost of production facilities in the U. S. than in some countries; (4) fear of either confiscation in their home lands or discriminatory taxes on their own real estate; and (5) possibility of tax advantages in investing outside their own nations.[1]

American brokers are familiar with the problems involved in securing real estate investments from other nations, and their motives for investing here. They understand how to get authority from governments to transfer funds, foreign exchange rates and practices, and financing and property management.

Foreign investors have made large investments in United States planned shopping centers, office buildings, and apartments. In addition to income property, thousands of lots in Florida resort developments have been sold to people from abroad. The Mideast has been an important source of such investors.

The Multinational Corporation

The growing numbers of business firms that operate on an international basis have given added dimensions to the international nature of real estate markets and ownership. Many companies not only export goods and services or operate licensing arrangements but also establish branch offices and in many cases manufacturing and distribution facilities abroad. Indeed, some of the larger multinational companies have extensive power and influence.

The land and buildings required for operations may be leased or owned. Partnership arrangements with the nationals of local countries may be considered more desirable than sole ownership by the multinational corporation. Some countries place limits on investments from abroad. Sometimes the ownership of real estate is limited to local people.

As has been pointed out:

As American investments abroad have expanded, some countries have placed limits on them. These limits are imposed for a variety of reasons such as nationalism, a fear of dominance by U. S. investments and the desire to maintain

---

[1] Letter to A. M. Weimer from Richard A. Rauch, President, Rauch & Co., Chicago.

opportunities for local investment. To an increasing extent American companies are sharing investment opportunities with the citizens of other countries.[2]

Investments abroad, including real estate, have been stimulated by such institutions as the International Monetary Fund, the International Bank for Reconstruction and Development, the North Atlantic Treaty Organization (NATO), The General Agreement on Tariffs and Trade (GATT), The European Common Market, The European Free Trade Association (EFTA) and the Organization of American States (OAS). The World Court at The Hague has helped to settle international problems. Other important institutions for U. S. business include The Export–Import Bank, Development Loan Fund, and The Agency for International Development (AID).

Some countries offer tax concessions such as "tax holidays" to attract investments from abroad; some serve as tax havens. In some cases special market and investment protections are provided. Even so, the risks often are great.

Ground Plans of Foreign and American Cities

Aerial views of foreign cities often disclose an irregular street pattern, with densely packed buildings, which gives the appearance of a giant organism. On the other hand, most American cities were built on a rectangular pattern. The newer suburbs of American cities, built during the automobile age, reveal a pattern of curving streets which distinguishes them from the rigidly straight lines of the old cities based on streetcar transportation. Washington, D. C., is an example of a city planned from its inception with radial streets intersecting the rectangular street pattern.

Latin American cities have followed the design laid down by the Spaniards and the Portuguese, in which the central plaza is bordered by square blocks. In Brasilia, a planner's ideal has been realized by the creation of super blocks of 2,500 population with an elementary school at the center and with four super blocks constituting a community large enough for a high school. In Brasilia there is a rigid separation between government buildings and office areas and the residential areas, and there are no grade intersections at street crossings. Other planned capital cities are Canberra, in Australia, and Islambad, the capital of Pakistan.

OWNERSHIP

The discussion of real estate decisions set forth in this text have application chiefly to nations in which (1) real properties may be privately owned, (2) there is little fear of total or partial confiscation of private property by the state, and (3) inflationary tendencies are limited.

[2] Arthur M. Weimer, David Bowen, and John D. Long, *Introduction to Business: A Management Approach* (5th ed.; Homewood, Ill.: Richard D. Irwin, Inc., 1974), pp. 493–94.

U. S. Ownership

The laws of property in the United States were first developed by the English common law, and the real estate principles observed in the United States are almost equally applicable in England and the British dominions of Canada and Australia, and in nations where English laws and principles were established as in South Africa.

Of course, private real estate ownership in the United States is subject to public control of various types such as zoning, building regulations, financing arrangements, real estate taxes, and rent control. Nevertheless, the United States is the outstanding example of a nation of private property ownership by millions of individuals, business firms, and independent institutions. The United States possesses the advantage, not only of a wide distribution of ownerships of all types of property, but also of a division of ownership into tolerably efficient economic units. There are few large tracts under one ownership except in grazing areas; on the other hand, there are few individually owned farms too small to be operated by machinery.

Communist Ownership

At the opposite pole are Soviet Russia and Communist China, where the state owns practically all of the land and where private ownership is limited to the right to use and occupy a single house or a small garden. It is obvious that the freedom to buy and sell buildings or vacant lands at prices determined by bargaining between a buyer and seller in an open market cannot exist where the right to buy or sell is denied. Movements of the buyer and seller are regulated; prices of all building materials are controlled by the state regardless of cost. The state, by its own fiat, determines where new industries, apartment developments, and new cities shall be located. In Russia rents bear no relationship to cost of construction. Consequently American principles of real estate value and real estate decision processes could not be applied to the Soviet Union without great modification.

Mixed Types

Between the private ownership of the United States and the state ownership of Russia, there are numerous mixed types. In a number of countries there has been expropriation of large land holdings and redistribution among small farmers. In present-day Finland and in Sweden the state owns large tracts of land for control purposes.

Surveys and Recording of Deeds

The transferability of real property and the ability to value parcels of real estate in the market depend upon accurate land surveys which identify each parcel, and help to assure protection for the title. As we pointed out in Chapter 3, in the United States, government land surveys established the base boundary lines for areas west of the Alleghenies, dividing most of this vast area into square-mile tracts. Deeds to lands are recorded in the county courthouses, so that the names of titleholders are a matter of public record. Title guarantee companies, or lawyers examining the abstracts showing the chain of title, or the Torrens system, can assure purchasers that they are securing a merchantable title to the land described in the deed or that title is faulty.

In contrast to this, in some of the new nations of Africa, there are no accurate land surveys. The land, as in pre-Columbian North America, is owned by the tribe.

In many nations of Europe, land in small strips has been owned by the same family for generations and is constantly subdivided further by inheritance. In some village economies, as was the case in Czarist Russia, the village elders redistribute the land among the villagers at stated intervals.

DANGERS TO OWNERSHIP

As we have suggested there are many dangers to private ownership including fear of invasion, confiscation, and inflation.

Fear of Invasion

People who live near international borders that may be crossed by invading forces often try to invest in more peaceful parts of the world. As one U. S. broker pointed out: "One of my German investors lives in Hamburg, West Germany, only 60 miles from the Russian divisions which are on the frontier with East German army units. He said that in a few days a Red armored force could seal off the Continent. . . ."[3]

Fear of Confiscation

Any nation which has enjoyed protection of private property rights may fear that a change of government will reduce the value of real estate by (1) outright confiscation, (2) condemnation at a low price, (3) rapid increase of real estate taxes, or (4) special advances in wages of building workers and operators. Activity in the real estate market will be virtually suspended if any of these occurs.

Inflation

A relatively stable currency has been important to the ownership and use of real estate in the United States. Although our dollar has lost value,

[3] Letter from Richard Rauch, *op. cit.*

long-term financing continues to be possible. Insurance companies, banks, and savings and loan institutions have been willing to make loans repayable thirty years or longer in the future in terms of fixed dollars. Whether this will continue to be true if inflationary tendencies continue is an open question.

In some countries inflation has discouraged long-term financing and has brought interest rates to five per cent *per month* or higher. The desire to invest in real estate is then strong, in order to have an inflation hedge. Often it is necessary to pay cash, however, without the benefit of long-term financing.

REAL ESTATE MARKET DIFFERENCES

Among the major factors which help to account for differences between the real estate markets in the U. S. and those of other countries are: (1) income distribution, (2) transportation and especially differences in the ownership of automobiles, (3) land use patterns including operation of the sector theory, prevalence of shopping centers, high-rise office buildings, and soil qualities, and (4) differences in real estate and appraisal practices. We will consider these topics briefly here. We should note, however, that there are trends in a number of countries that suggest movement in the direction of U. S. real estate market operations and practices.

Income Distribution

The relatively high per-capita incomes and the large middle class in the U. S. help to explain the differences between the scope and magnitude of the real estate market in this country and in other parts of the world. Figures published by the World Bank [4] provide comparisons of GNP per capita. (These figures, it should be noted, differ from per-capita income or disposable income.) Per-capita GNP at market prices for 1975 are presented in Table 21–2, which also shows average annual growth rates for the periods 1960–1974 and 1965–1974. For example, GNP per capita in the U. S. is reported at $6,670; Canada $6,190; Federal Republic of Germany $6,260; France $5,440; Australia $5,330; Japan $4,070; United Kingdom $3,590; Mexico $1,090; Brazil $920; India $140; and the Socialist Republic of Viet Nam $150.

The relatively high incomes in the U. S. make it possible for a large portion of the families to buy automobiles, single-family homes or condominiums, and a wide variety of equipment and conveniences. In 1975 there were almost 40 million owner-occupied dwelling units in the U. S. or 62.9 per cent of the total, as we have noted. The construction, financing, and marketing of new housing units at an annual rate sometimes approxi-

---

[4] Population, per capita product, and growth rates (New York: The World Bank, 1976).

TABLE 21-2. Per-Capita Gross National Product at Market Prices—Amount, 1974, and Average Annual Growth Rates, 1960–1974 and 1965–1974 (Countries with Populations of One Million or More; GNP per Capita Rounded to Nearest U. S. $10)

Country	GNP per capita Amount (US$)	Growth rates (%) 1960-74	Growth rates (%) 1965-74
Switzerland	7,870	2.9	2.9
Sweden	7,240	3.2	2.8
United States	6,670	2.9	2.4
Denmark	6,430	3.8	3.4
Germany, Federal Republic of	6,260	3.7	3.9
Canada	6,190	3.7	3.5
Norway	5,860	3.7	3.4
Belgium	5,670	4.5	4.9
France	5,440	4.4	4.8
Australia	5,330	3.2	3.4
Netherlands, The	5,250	4.0	4.1
Finland	4,700	4.6	5.2
Libyan Arab Republic	4,440	12.5	6.5
Austria	4,410	4.4	5.0
New Zealand	4,310	2.1	1.8
Japan	4,070	8.8	8.5
German Democratic Republic[1,2]	3,950	3.1	3.0
United Kingdom	3,590	2.3	2.2
Israel[1,2]	3,460	5.3	5.8
Czechoslovakia[1,2]	3,330	2.4	2.5
Saudi Arabia	2,830	8.4	9.2
Italy	2,820	4.2	4.0
Poland[1,2]	2,510	4.0	4.5
Spain	2,490	5.8	5.4
USSR[1,2]	2,380	3.8	3.4
Ireland	2,320	3.6	3.6
Singapore	2,240	7.6	10.0
Puerto Rico	2,230	5.3	4.7
Hungary[1,2]	2,180	3.2	2.9
Greece	2,090	6.8	6.5
Venezuela	1,960	2.4	2.2
Bulgaria[1,2]	1,780	4.5	3.5
Trinidad and Tobago	1,700	2.1	2.2
Portugal	1,630	7.4	7.6
Hong Kong	1,610	6.6	5.4
Argentina	1,520	2.8	2.9
Yugoslavia	1,310	4.9	5.4
Iran	1,250	6.7	7.7
South Africa	1,210	2.9	2.5
Jamaica	1,190	3.6	4.5
Uruguay	1,190	0.5	0.8
Iraq	1,110	4.0	4.8
Romania[3]	1,100	n.a.	8.0
Mexico[3]	1,090	3.3	2.8
Lebanon[4]	1,070	3.1	3.7

Country	GNP per capita Amount (US$)	Growth rates (%) 1960-74	Growth rates (%) 1965-74
Panama	1,000	4.1	3.7
Brazil	920	4.0	6.3
Costa Rica	840	2.9	3.7
Chile	830	1.7	1.3
China, Republic of	810	6.5	6.9
Turkey	750	3.9	4.3
Peru	740	2.0	1.8
Algeria	730	1.3	4.5
Angola	710	3.7	3.2
Cuba[1,2]	710	-0.9	-0.6
Malaysia	680	3.9	3.8
Nicaragua	670	3.0	1.5
Dominican Republic	650	3.1	5.5
Tunisia[5]	650	3.9	5.4
Mongolia[1,2]	610	0.8	1.8
Guatemala	580	3.3	3.8
Syrian Arab Republic	560	4.0	4.2
Albania[1,2]	530	4.4	5.0
Zambia	520	2.3	1.0
Rhodesia	520	1.9	3.5
Paraguay	510	2.0	2.5
Colombia	500	2.6	3.4
Ecuador	480	2.4	2.1
Korea, Republic of	480	7.3	8.7
Papua New Guinea	470	4.2	4.1
Congo, People's Republic of the	470	2.8	4.0
Ivory Coast	460	3.5	2.7
Jordan	430	0.9	-2.5
Morocco	430	1.8	2.8
Ghana	430	-0.2	0.3
El Salvador	410	1.8	1.0
Liberia	390	2.2	4.1
Korea, Democratic People's Republic of[1,2]	390	4.4	3.5
Mozambique[1]	340	2.8	3.5
Honduras	340	1.6	2.2
Senegal	330	-1.1	-0.9
Philippines	330	2.4	2.7
Thailand	310	4.6	4.3
China, People's Republic of[1,2]	300	5.2	4.6
Mauritania	290	3.8	1.3
Nigeria	280	2.9	6.0
Egypt, Arab Republic of	280	1.5	1.0
Bolivia	280	2.5	2.2
Cameroon	250	4.4	2.8
Togo	250	4.4	2.8

Country	GNP per capita Amount (US$)	Growth rates (%) 1960-74	Growth rates (%) 1965-74
Uganda	240	1.8	0.7
Sudan[1]	230	1.7	4.3
Yemen, People's Democratic Republic of[1,6]	220	n.a.	-4.3
Central African Empire	210	0.4	0.8
Kenya	200	3.2	3.5
Sierra Leone[7]	190	1.6	1.4
Madagascar	180	0.1	0.3
Yemen Arab Republic[1]	180	n.a.	n.a.
Indonesia	170	2.4	4.1
Haiti	170	-0.1	0.7
Tanzania[8]	160	2.6	2.3
Zaire	150	2.6	2.9
Viet Nam, Socialist Republic of[1,2]	150	0.3	-0.8
India	150	1.1	1.3
Lesotho[1]	140	4.2	3.7
Sri Lanka	130	2.1	2.0
Pakistan	130	3.4	2.5
Malawi	130	3.9	4.7
Benin, People's Republic of[1]	120	0.7	0.8
Guinea	120	0.0	0.1
Niger	120	-1.8	-3.8
Afghanistan	110	0.5	1.1
Nepal	100	0.4	0.0
Ethiopia	100	2.2	1.5
Chad	100	-1.2	-1.5
Bangladesh	100	-0.5	-1.9
Burma	100	0.7	0.8
Burundi[1]	90	-1.3	-1.3
Somalia[1]	90	-0.3	1.1
Upper Volta	90	-0.1	-0.5
Rwanda[1]	80	-0.2	1.4
Mali	80	0.9	0.4
Cambodia[1,4]	70	-2.7	-6.2
Bhutan[1]	70	-0.3	0.2
Lao People's Democratic Republic[1,4]	70	1.8	2.0

[1] Estimates of GNP per capita and its growth rate are tentative.
[2] For estimation of GNP per capita, see Technical Note, page 22.
[3] Estimate of GNP per capita does not reflect the significant devaluation of the peso in August 1976.
[4] GNP per capita estimated on the 1972-74 base period.
[5] GNP per capita growth rate relates to 1961-74.
[6] GNP per capita growth rate relates to 1969-74.
[7] GNP per capita growth rate relates to 1964-74.
[8] Mainland Tanzania.

Source: Same as Table 21-1, p. 5.

mating 2 million units provides the basis for an active real estate market.

In countries where incomes are low and where there is a small middle class, the possibilities for an active real estate market are much more limited. Often there is a wide gulf between the relatively small number of wealthy families and the great majority of people, many of whom are very poor. With a small middle class, ownership concentrated in the wealthy, and many people living on small rural plots of land, market transfers of real estate tend to be quite limited. Most property is passed on through inheritance with few other types of transfers.

Ownership of Automobiles

The relatively high incomes of families in the United States make possible the almost universal ownership of automobiles. In 1974, there were 105 million privately owned automobiles and cabs in the United States, plus 25 million trucks and buses. The widespread ownership of a private means of transportation has had a far-reaching effect on the growth of suburbs, at a substantial distance from the central business district, and it has brought about the creation of shopping centers and a widespread dispersal of factories and office buildings to the periphery of cities.

In 1973, while the United States had 2.1 persons per automobile, Canada had 2.8 and the United Kingdom 4.1. (See Table 21–3.) In that year

TABLE 21–3. Worldwide Automobile Registrations, 1973

	Cars	Trucks and Buses	Total Vehicles	Population Per Car
World	233,966,318	62,560,878	296,527,196	15
United States	101,762,477	23,658,399	125,420,876	2.1
Canada	7,823,000	1,797,400	9,620,400	2.8
Mexico	1,613,981	657,640	2,271,621	34
Argentina	2,010,000	890,000	2,900,000	12
Brazil	4,021,365	1,370,114	5,391,479	26
United Kingdom	13,497,000	1,985,000	15,482,000	4.1
Italy	13,424,118	1,083,659	14,507,777	4.1
France	14,550,000	2,250,000	16,800,000	3.6
West Germany	17,036,474	1,347,053	18,383,527	3.6
East Germany	1,400,390	476,165	1,876,555	12
Poland	780,900	391,500	1,172,400	42
USSR	1,815,000	5,060,000	6,875,000	138
India	778,529	510,572	1,289,101	738
Japan	14,473,630	10,525,651	24,999,281	7.5

Source: 1975 Automobile Facts & Figures, Motor Vehicle Manufacturers Association of the United States, Inc., pp. 26–27.

European nations had from 3.6 in France and West Germany to 4.1 in Italy; in Poland there were 42 persons per automobile, in East Germany 12, and in the USSR 138. Argentina had 12 persons per automobile, Japan 7.5, Mexico 34, and Brazil 26. Most Asiatic and African nations still have only a small number of automobiles in relation to the population. The number of automobiles has recently shown marked gains in Europe and South America.

Mass Transit Lines

Where only a small proportion of the population owns private automobiles, the predominant form of transportation is by bus or train. In some great cities like London, Paris, Berlin, Moscow, Tokyo, and Buenos Aires, there are subways in addition to buses and trains. Since mass transit lines cannot operate economically to thinly settled single-family housing areas, the majority of dwelling units in the great cities of Asia, Latin America, and Continental Europe are in apartment buildings, which are concentrated in bands along mass transit lines or bus lines, or in suburban clusters served by mass transit as in Moscow and Helsinki. Apartment units are also cheaper to build than single-family houses, and occupy far less ground area.

Mass transit lines leading to the center of the city also sustain the central business district. There has been less decentralization of cities abroad than in the U. S. although it is developing in Western Europe. In most cities outside the United States, the central areas contain the chief attractions of urban life—the parks, palaces, museums, ancient monuments, national capitols, as well as hotels, theaters, and restaurants. The Parthenon on the Acropolis is near the center of Athens; the Arc de Triomphe, the Louvre, and Notre Dame are at the center of Paris; Buckingham Palace, Westminster Abbey, the Houses of Parliament, and St. Paul's are in the center of London. The Ginza district of Tokyo—its shopping and amusement district—attracts throngs at night. The principal cathedrals, museums, capitols, and monuments of Bogotá, Lima, Buenos Aires, Rio de Janeiro, and Quito, as well as the tallest office buildings and the leading stores face or are located near the central plaza. In these foreign cities the central areas are continually rebuilt and renewed.

Sector Theory

The rise of the middle class in many nations and the increased ownership of the automobile will make it possible for more and more families to live in homes on the periphery of cities. This has already taken place in Latin America. Wealthy families have tended to move from patio-type dwellings on the central plazas to homes or apartments on the outer fringe of one sector of the city, as in Bogotá, Lima, La Paz, Quito, Santiago, Buenos Aires, Montevideo, Rio de Janeiro, and Caracas.

Shopping Centers

The increased ownership of automobiles leads to the establishment of outlying shopping centers with free automobile parking. Canada and Australia already have many shopping centers similar to those in the United States. There is a limited number of these shopping centers in other nations such as the Amstel Center in Amsterdam, Rosebank in Cape Town, South Africa, and others in Europe. Sears, Roebuck has a number of stores in Latin America in midtown locations but most of these are solitary stores.

The practice of making leases, not only with minimum guaranteed rent but also with rents based on a percentage of sales, seems to be increasing. Some rents are related to a cost of living index. Difficulties may be experienced in some countries in securing commercial zoning for a sufficient area of land to provide for shopping centers.

High-Rise Office Buildings

New tall office buildings have broken the old skylines in London, Paris, and Milan, as well as in Rio de Janeiro and Mexico City. Thus, the uniform height of buildings, so long maintained, is giving way to the irregular skyline typical of American cities. In some cases height limitations have been reestablished.

Soil Qualities

In all parts of the world are found agricultural areas in which the composition of soils, rainfall, length of the growing season, and suitability for crops are similar to some areas in the United States, and they are measured and defined by soil scientists as in the United States. Differences in the values of crop lands or grazing lands in other nations compared to the United States would result from lower labor costs and from import restrictions or tariff duties of the other nations buying the crops.

Appraisals and Real Estate Valuations

Where the titles to real estate are not jeopardized by confiscation, the value of real estate properties based on comparable sales, reproduction cost, and net income would be computed in a similar manner to that in the United States. The formula would be the same, but the figures in it would be different. Thus, in Johannesburg, South Africa, elevator office building costs of construction would be substantially lower than in the United States.

Rent control abroad has the same depressing effect on values as in the United States. In Brazil, France, and other nations where rent control is applied to existing apartments, new apartments have been built and sold on a condominium basis.

SUMMARY

World urbanization represents one of the significant developments of recent years. This reflects the increased industrialization of many parts of the world. With this has come a growing interest in real estate, notably in urban and urban-related areas. In recent years international investments in real estate have risen in importance. In many foreign countries real estate is a relatively more important medium of investment than in the United States because of the relatively greater importance of the securities market in this country. Investments of other nationals in the United States have tended to rise as have U. S. investments abroad. Differential yields on investments, differences in tax treatment, and the desire for a spreading of risks are all factors in these processes. The multinational corporations have increased international real estate activity.

The private ownership of real estate varies greatly among the countries of the world, as does the legal system which regulates such ownership. Fear of invasion and confiscation are important factors in stimulating foreign investment on the part of many nationals. A closely related factor is the fear of inflation. The ownership of real property is influenced greatly by the distribution of income that prevails in particular countries. The large middle class in the United States is a significant factor in widespread real estate ownership.

Trends toward suburban developments are less extensive abroad, even in Western Europe, than in the United States, because of the lower per-capita ownership of automobiles. This situation, however, is changing especially in Western Europe. As a result, there is likely to be an expansion of shopping centers in such countries.

QUESTIONS FOR STUDY

1. Why does real estate tend to be a relatively more important form of investment in foreign countries than in the United States?
2. Contrast the typical ground plan of U. S. and foreign cities. What factors account for the principal differences?
3. Why are investors from other countries acquiring interests in income-producing property in the U. S.?
4. How does the expanding role of the multinational corporation affect the international real estate market?
5. How does the fear of invasion and confiscation affect the ownership of real estate? The trend of land values?
6. How is inflation likely to affect real estate ownership and investment? How important is a stable currency for real estate investors? Explain.
7. In which ways may income distribution affect real estate markets?
8. As mass automobile ownership extends to countries other than the U. S., what changes in city structure would you anticipate for those countries?
9. What types of real estate market changes are created by automobiles in foreign countries? What effects will they have on real estate values?
10. Contrast real estate appraisals in the U. S. and abroad.
11. Assume you are going to Europe to promote investments in U. S. real estate. Outline a promotional approach, including the advantages of such investments.

12. Assume you are a foreign investor considering U. S. real estate. What disadvantages do you see in investing in U. S. real estate? Do they outweigh the advantages? Which factors do you think will be most significant in making your final decision?

SUGGESTED READINGS

HINES, MARY ALICE. *Principles and Practices of Real Estate.* Homewood, Ill.: Richard D. Irwin, Inc., 1976. Ch. 24.

HOYT, HOMER. *According to Hoyt* (2nd ed.). Washington, D. C.: Hoyt, 1970. Pp. 306–58.

UNITED NATIONS. *Demographic Year Book.* New York: United Nations.

The Worldmark Encyclopedia of the Nations. New York: Worldmark Press and Harper & Row, 1962.

CASE 21–1

The Edwards–Arthur Company

Edwards–Arthur, a U. S. manufacturer of pharmaceuticals and nutritional products has a pharmaceutical plant located in the Federal District of Mexico City (the equivalent of the District of Columbia in the U. S.). In addition, it has a contract manufacturer, Carrioca, for processing its powdered milk formulas for Latin American distribution.

In the past, company procedure for foreign distribution has been decided on a volume basis. First, the product is exported through a foreign distributor; as volume increases, the company establishes its own warehouse and distribution system; a further increase usually warrants a foreign contract manufacturer; and finally, more volume coupled with prosperous prospects for the future calls for the establishment of an Edwards–Arthur plant in the foreign country.

From the start, Edwards–Arthur has had its own equipment and process supervisors in the Carrioca powdered milk formula plant. Carrioca had always been a producer of butter and cheese and the quality control for these products has been far below that required for nutritional products. Recently, several problems with the Carrioca operation have become more pressing.

Raw milk is now coming from distances as far away as 300 miles. This means exceedingly higher transportation costs due to the large percentage of water in raw milk. Also, the Carrioca plant has become excessively crowded, resulting in loss of efficiency of both operating personnel and management, and a lower quality products as well. Lastly, Jones Foods has been negotiating with Carrioca in an effort to gain control of the facility.

The above problems have forced Edwards–Arthur management to consider looking elsewhere. Actually there were two alternatives open to them: (1) locate a new plant in Mexico; (2) find another contract manufacturer.

A search for a new third-party manufacturer revealed that there was only one possible contractor in Mexico who could do this type of work. This company was approached several times with the purpose of investigating possibilities for the manufacturing of Edwards–Arthur products but there appeared to be little interest in doing this type of work.

After careful consideration of all factors involved, the best alternative appeared to be the construction of a company-owned plant. This seemed to be the only permanent solution to the manufacturing of formula milk products. It would take care of long-term requirements. Proper location of the plant would permit Edwards–Arthur to obtain good quality of milk at lower prices. Adequate designs and equipment would improve efficiency, lower manufacturing costs, and improve quality of finished products. This would also place Edwards–Arthur in a better competitive position.

With a company-owned plant, management would also have the necessary flexibility to produce products or formulas that might be required by market conditions. This would be difficult to attain with a third-party manufacturing agreement.

Government sales, which are an important part of formula products sales (approximately 37 per cent), can be better protected if Edwards–Arthur manufactures its products in its own plant. Government institutions must follow the established policy of buying all their requirements directly from manufacturers, avoiding purchases from intermediaries or suppliers that do not manufacture their own products. In the past, Edwards–Arthur has been in serious danger of losing formula products sales to the Government for that particular reason. The company had been forced to exhibit proofs that it really had an investment in the former Carrioca plant and also that it was actually supervising the manufacturing processes and being responsible for them. The fact that Edwards–Arthur would manufacture the milk products in its own new plant would undoubtedly represent a very strong promotional advantage over the present situation.

There have always been doubts in some physicians' and consumers' minds about the quality of the Edwards–Arthur milks, being made by a butter and cheese manufacturer whose products usually do not require the same careful processes. Quite naturally, competition has recognized this fact and has attempted to exploit it.

The present two milk formula products producers in Mexico are North and South; both have their own plants. North has three big modern plants spread around selected milk sheds in the country and South has only one plant but it is presently starting the construction of a new modern and efficient plant at the same location.

Actually, there were several additional factors which caused the decision to build the new facility to be made: (1) the resturn on investment was calculated to be 36 per cent, (2) projected sales for the market area served were favorable, (3) the Mexican Government's attitude toward the new plant was favorable since it penalized products produced in non-Mexican plants due to the fact it has been pushing for economic development, (4) there would be no problem of disposal of butter fat and other by-products, (5) the powdered milk sales contributed 60 per cent to the Mexican profits on only 30 per cent of gross sales (the gross Mexican sales were $5 million and net profits were $625,000).

The Real Estate Decision. The real estate decision was divided into two parts:

1. Should the plant be located in the Federal District or outside?
2. If located outside, where?

A decision to locate outside the Federal District was based on (1) the fact that transportation costs would be lower for powdered milk than liquid milk, and (2) the Mexican Government's attitude toward the outside location was more favorable.

Several areas, all within a 200- to 300-mile radius of Mexico City, were considered for the site. Based on milk shed studies of the number and quality of the cattle, engineering studies, and the assistance of Mexican Agriculture Department officials, loaned by the Mexican Government, three possible locations were found. These areas and their attributes are listed below. (Abbreviations have been used for simplicity's sake).

1. *D.C.*—320 miles from Federal District; good grazing and quality cattle but smaller supply than needed; high Government approval; equal construction costs of the other two; population of 150,000 with a small junior college; truck transportation but no rail service.
2. *T*—Good herds and co-ops; 1 other milk plant in area. Oversupply exists; 280 miles from Mexico City. Population of 90,000 with a higher education institution; Government only lukewarm on approval; adequate rail service to Mexico City already exists.
3. *S.L.P.*—Good cattle, low labor supply, low educational level due to no higher educational institution in area. Population of 70,000, truck transportation, no rail service; high government approval; and nearest to Mexico City at 200 miles.

It was believed that the Mexican Government would guarantee the number and quality of cattle, give free land for the plant location, provide assurance of a substantially fixed price agreement for 3 years with the farmers, and develop rail service for the area within 3 years if sites 1 or 3 were chosen. Some assistance could also be expected if site 2 were chosen, but its form and extent were unknown.

Costs and Financing. The new plant is estimated to cost $1.5 million and the old equipment at the Carrioca plant would bring $250,000 in salvage price. The venture would be financed mostly from borrowed capital from local Mexican banks because (1) it provides a hedge against the possible devaluations of the peso, (2) the interest (11 per cent) is deductible against high Mexican tax levels, and (3) progressive profit-sharing laws in Mexico limit the amount of profits to be taken.

Questions

1. Which location should be chosen? Why?
2. Why was it decided to finance the plant through Mexican sources rather than using American sources or equity funds even though the interest rate is 11 per cent?

22

TOWARD IMPROVED
REAL ESTATE
ADMINISTRATION

SOCIAL, POLITICAL, AND ECONOMIC PRIORITIES

The role of real estate resources and real estate administration in the American economy during the remaining years of the twentieth century will depend to a considerable extent on our general social, political, and economic priorities. Our priorities have tended to change over time. How are they likely to change in the future? For example, how will our priorities affect inflationary or deflationary tendencies? Domestic or international programs? Economic expansion and stability? Energy development? Transportation? Environmental programs? Saving or spending patterns? Public or private investment? Equality or excellence?

How will changes in our priorities affect real estate administration? Real estate resources? Housing? Urban and suburban life? Rural life? The real estate business?

The economic and social policies and arrangements that are set up to give effect to our priorities will greatly influence the role of real estate in our society. Will we continue to rely as much as in the past on market competition as a form of social control? Will we rely to as great an extent as formerly on monetary and credit policies for economic stabilization purposes? Will fiscal policies and more direct forms of control be used to a greater extent than in the past? Which tax systems will be favored? Will our system of incentives be altered? For example, to what extent will profits be redefined?

The future role of real estate resources and the real estate business will depend to a considerable extent on the quality of administration in both th private and public sectors and for business generally as well as for real estate. Are the owners and users of real estate likely to be better administrators than in the past? Will the real estate business be operated more efficiently? Will the operations and administration of government agencies, especially those directly related to the real estate sector, be improved?

We will undertake to consider these questions and others related to them in this final chapter, which almost takes the form of a Study Project.

Will General Priorities Change?

Changes in priorities are almost continuously taking place. Among the priorities that are being debated are: the relative emphasis to give to military and defense purposes on the one hand and nondefense programs on the other, international and domestic programs, energy, environmental priorities, and others. Questions have been raised as to whether economic growth should be slowed down in order to reduce environmental problems. Some have undertaken deliberately to reduce their living standards in the hope of reducing pressures on the environment—for example, by using bicycles instead of motorbikes and small cars. Special efforts have been made to conserve electricity, in some cases giving up air conditioning except under extreme conditions. Can we continue to enjoy economic prosperity and at the same time solve our environmental and energy problems?

Will people continue to reduce rates of population growth? We are near Zero Population Growth on the basis of births but not if immigration is included. Total population, however, will increase somewhat because of the larger number of women of childbearing age.

The Changing Social Contract

It has been suggested that the relationships between business and our society as a whole are undergoing changes, that the "social contract" between business and society is being redefined. For example:

Today it is clear that the terms of the contract between society and business are, in fact, changing in substantial and important ways. Business is being asked to assume broader responsbilities to society than ever before and to serve a wider range of human values. Business enterprises, in effect, are being asked to contribute more to the quality of American life than just supplying quantities of goods and services. Inasmuch as business exists to serve society, its future will depend on the quality of management's response to the changing expectations of the public.[1]

In a similar vein Ian Wilson of General Electric has said recently: "As a microcosm of society, a corporation must reflect all of that society's shared values—social, moral, political and legal as well as economic." Carl Madden of American University, formerly of the U. S. Chamber of Com-

---

[1] Research and Policy Committee, Committee for Economic Development, *Social Responsibilities of Business Corporations* (New York: The Committee, 1971), p. 16.

merce, points out: "In the coming years . . . the business corporation that is successful will be forced to adapt its own values and goals to the changing values of society." Are these accurate descriptions of desired relationships between business and society? Is the "social contract" between business and society being more or less constantly redefined?

Goals

The goals of our society have been outlined as follows:

Elimination of poverty and provision of good health care.
Equal opportunity for each person to realize his or her full potential regardless of race, sex, or creed.
Education and training for a fully productive and rewarding participation in modern society.
Ample jobs and career opportunities in all parts of society.
Livable communities with decent housing, safe streets, a clean and pleasant environment, efficient transportation, good cultural and educational opportunities and a prevailing mood of civility among people.[2]

Does this statement adequately spell out our major goals? More specifically, does it do so with respect to our communities and housing? Are we changing our priorities both generally and in the real estate sector? Are we likely to put higher priorities on elimination of slums? On higher quality of housing? Or will we accept less in housing to protect our environment and reduce demand on energy sources?

What are the implications of these questions for real estate resources and real estate administration?

POLICIES AND ARRANGEMENTS

As suggested above, the social, political, and economic policies and arrangements that are set up to attain the objectives and priorities of our society will have an important bearing on the future of real estate resources and real estate administration. Such policies and arrangements will determine the extent to which we make use of competition as a form of social control or use more direct controls, the degree of reliance on monetary and credit policies for economic stabilization purposes, the use of fiscal policies for such ends, the use of selective and direct controls, changes in incentives, and many others.

Competition as a Form of Social Control

Since real estate markets do not function as effectively as markets in many other areas, there are questions as to whether the real estate sector would fare better under arrangements which would continue to rely

[2] *Ibid.*, p. 13.

heavily on competition as a form of social control or under more direct types of controls. In general those in the real estate field have continued to prefer competitive arrangements and they are likely to continue to do so. At the same time they have welcomed modifications such as special subsidies and inducements which channeled greater support to the real estate sector. Examples include special depreciation allowances, rent and interest rate subsidies, controls on rates paid on savings, tax exemption under certain conditions, and others. Which directions are likely to be followed in the future? As our society grows more complex are we likely to rely to a greater or lesser extent on competition as a control device?

Monetary vs. Fiscal or Other Controls

The heavy reliance on monetary and credit policies as major instruments in restraining inflation has often had unfavorable effects on the financing of real estate. Would shifts away from such policies be beneficial to the real estate sector? Would this mean greater reliance on fiscal policy? Would more direct controls such as regulation of wages and prices be required?

Stimulation of Housing, Savings and Capital Formation, Other Real Estate Related Areas

Any programs which will help to stimulate housing directly would appear to be favorable to the housing sector relative to other areas of the economy. Subsidies, tax advantages, improvements of roads and other transportation facilities, better traffic controls, and related developments would all be helpful. On the other hand, restrictions on development, whether because of environmental, energy, or other considerations, may create disadvantages for the real estate sector relative to others. Much depends on whether housing is going down or up relative to our range of priorities.

Programs that will channel investments into public facilities will tend to favor real estate because of the great interdependence between public and private real property. Improvements in environmental conditions may help real estate relatively more than other sectors. The same is true for transportation systems, public parks, water systems, utilities, and others. Similarly, improvements in public services contribute especially to the real estate sector. On the other hand, energy shortages and high energy costs probably have a relatively greater impact on the real estate sector than on others.

Are we likely to see more public investment in the future? Which types of public investments would be most helpful to the real estate sector?

Programs which would stimulate saving undoubtedly would benefit housing and to some extent the real estate sector in general. This would be especially true if the increased savings were channeled into this sector.

Any significant increase in the total capital available, however, would seem likely to aid the housing and the real estate sector relative to others because of this sector's limited ability to compete for funds under tight money market conditions. Many small businesses and small municipalities also have limited ability in this area and improvement for them would seem likely to be beneficial to the real estate sector as well. Are we now a capital-short economy? Are we likely to need special incentives to increase saving and the rate of capital formation? What form might such incentives take?

Incentives and Taxes

Changes in incentives would have a greater or lesser impact in the real estate field depending on which incentives were changed or in what direction. We have already mentioned savings incentives. What about profits? Society defines profits. Income tax laws spell out what may be counted as costs, depreciation rates, losses that may be carried forward or back, and other things. Real estate investments traditionally have been favored in the depreciation field; this has been notably true of housing. Modifications would change incentives.

Our tax laws have some responsibility for slum and other deteriorated areas since in most jurisdictions we tax improvements on the land more heavily than the land itself. Thus, there are fewer incentives for improving our stores, office buildings, factories, and houses than would be the case if our property tax system were structured differently. Are we likely to change our tax laws and to change them in a way that will favor real estate?

Because of the importance of incentives for all of us, any changes in our system of incentives could have widespread effects. Should our incentives be modified? Should we give greater incentives in the housing sector than in others? In the real estate field in general? Should small business be favored relative to big business? Should special tax incentives be given to small business to attract people in such enterprises? If so this would undoubtedly favor real estate since many of the enterprises in this field are relatively small operations.

Equality of Economic Opportunity

The public school system has been one of the means we have relied upon to assure reasonable equality of economic opportunity in our system. Despite many efforts to assure a reasonably equal chance to all citizens, however, discriminatory practices have persisted. The impact of such practices may have been somewhat greater in the real estate field, especially in housing, than in others. Efforts to break down barriers to opportunities are receiving widespread support. What effect will such efforts have in the future?

FUTURE ROLE OF REAL ESTATE RESOURCES

What part will real estate resources play in the future of this country? Will their role be of greater or lesser importance than it has been in the past?

Needs

Answers to these questions depend in part on our priorities and on the arrangements for carrying such priorities into effect, as we have pointed out. Answers will depend also on the number of people, their incomes, their locations, and their changing standards; for example, how much of their incomes they wish to spend for real estate resources and services in relation to other things.

Answers will reflect in part the relative cost of providing real estate resources and services in comparison to the costs of other goods and services. This will vary with the rate at which technological advances are made in the real estate field in comparison to advances in other areas and on the quality of the decisions determining the effectiveness with which resources are managed in the real estate field and in other fields.

Demands for space will increase in the years ahead. The main question is how much, as we have suggested. The location of economic opportunities and, hence, the location of the homes of people will change. Thus, there may be a surplus of real properties in some places at the same time that there are shortages in others.

Also, our expectations tend to expand. The pioneer family was at first content with a single-room log cabin without modern conveniences, but even their expectations soon rose and this process has continued to date.

Supplies

Because we add only a small percentage to the total supply of real estate resources each year, much depends on the efficiency with which existing resources are used. This in turn will vary with conservation and renewal programs. For some period of time, increased real estate requirements could be met by more intensive use of existing properties. Over a longer period, the destruction and deterioration of a portion of the available supply would require the provision of some new facilities even with a static population with static incomes and standards. Every year some real estate resources are taken out of use as a result of demolition, fires, windstorms, or other causes. Also, some properties pass out of use through obsolescence.

We have been adding new housing facilities at a rate of about 3 per cent of the total supply per year. Even if we moved this rate up to 4 per cent per year or more we would add only at a slow rate to our present housing supply. Much the same thing may be said of the development of commercial and industrial real estate.

Decisions as to the rate of building or the conservation and renewal of older properties will be made in part by private individuals and the executives of business firms and in part by public officials reflecting the points of view of the electorate. As we have seen, if real estate resources are taxed on a more favorable basis than is now the case, for example, this will have an important effect on their future role; if people wish to add to or reduce various subsidies to real estate, it will affect the rate of development or redevelopment of these resources. Programs such as urban homesteading, for example, may be expanded. Improvements may be made in financing the renovation of older properties.

Types of Properties

In a discussion of this type, distinction should be made among various types of properties. Changing technology and transportation patterns will undoubtedly alter the types of industrial real estate that will be most useful in the future. Recent rates of technological change suggest that industrial real estate resources may tend to grow obsolete rather rapidly in the years ahead. To a significant degree the same statement applies also to commercial real estate. The advent of regional and super-regional shopping centers, supermarkets and discount houses, franchising, and other arrangements has already brought rapid obsolescence to many commercial real estate resources. Obviously, new developments in the future will have similar effects.

The shopping habits and preferences of people in recent years have tended to favor outlying as against downtown locations. The continuation of this trend will have important effects in the future; a reversal of this trend, or a partial reversal, would affect demands for various types of commercial real estate.

Residential real estate resources have undergone important changes in recent years, as we have seen in our previous discussions. The preference for single-family suburban living has persisted. Some people are tending to prefer downtown or "near-in" locations for their regular residences, but are combining such living arrangements with nearby weekend cottages and other retreats.

There has been growing interest in multiple-use buildings. For example, some buildings now combine retail stores and shops, residences, offices, recreational facilities, and other uses. Are developments of this type likely to increase? If so, are they likely to be found in outlying as well as downtown locations?

Rural land uses have undergone rapid changes, as we have seen in Chapter 20. Farmers are now living and working in an increasingly interdependent world.

Power can be transmitted over wider areas than formerly. The federal highway program has brought a redistribution of both rural and urban land uses. Pipelines, new waterway developments, supersonic jet aircraft, and changes which we cannot as yet foresee will continue to bring shifts in land uses and in the intensity of land uses, both rural and urban.

Development Methods and Costs

As we suggested in earlier discussions, significant advances have been made in building, subdividing, and land development. Costs have advanced substantially, however, and in general have risen more than in other fields. If the methods of land development can be improved, and if we can continue to develop new products and processes, there undoubtedly will be continued expansion of real estate resources. Our preference for new resources may continue but we are likely to give increased emphasis to the conservation, renewal, or redevelopment of older resources.

While it is never possible to anticipate with great exactness the ways in which various areas should be developed, increased research and study undoubtedly will lead to the development of improved planning and better zoning in the years ahead. Unless improved, some zoning programs may be abandoned. Expanded research and development programs may prove useful in the public policy areas as well as in the managerial and technological fields. Indeed, the invention of new social, political, and economic relationships would appear to be essential to enable various agencies of local and state government to function with sufficient effectiveness to meet future requirements.

Conservation and Renewal

As we have pointed out, the real estate resources required in the future will be provided in part by the continued use of the resources now available. The effectiveness of such use will reflect the care with which these resources are used and managed, and on programs for redeveloping, rehabilitating, or renewing properties, neighborhoods, and districts—in short, programs that will lengthen their economic life.

Good housekeeping, both on a private and public basis, will be important in this connection. Programs which protect and improve the physical environment are likely to play a larger role. Energy conservation will be a significant factor. The development and enforcement of higher standards of land use and building occupancy will also play a part, as will the impact of tax burdens, land planning programs, and the like.

Historically it has been more expeditious to use up our forests, minerals, and similar resources as we needed them than to conserve them for future use. In part this resulted from the abundance of natural resources available and the continued discovery of new resources. In part this point of view represented a faith in the continuation of scientific and technological advances which provided substitutes for many natural resources. For example, weather control and the production of agricultural products in laboratories in future years, both distinct possibilities, could change greatly our interest in conserving the fertility of agricultural lands.

Even in the case of urban real estate resources it has often been more convenient and probably more economical to develop new areas on the periphery of cities or to establish new towns than to conserve, renew, or redevelop older areas. Also, the automobile and improved roads and streets reduced dependence on specific locations and increased greatly the amount of land area that could be used effectively for urban purposes. With energy shortages this may change.

The way in which a given piece of urban real estate is used, however, may have a considerable impact on other real properties, as we have pointed out. This is especially true of adjacent or nearby properties. Thus, we often find it necessary to clear or redevelop a slum area in order to prevent the deterioration of properties in a nearby area.

The renewal problems of the downtown area are especially complex. The present functioning heart of the city can in some cases be supplanted by reliance on other downtown areas, particularly if larger interurbias emerge; outlying business centers may absorb many of the functions typically performed by the downtown center. But in many cities it will be necessary to conserve, renew, and redevelop the downtown area.

Redlining

The problems relating to "redlining" may become more difficult. Although redlining usually refers to the practice of lenders to refuse to lend in certain areas, the issue is far more complex than this suggests. For example, do city governments in effect redline? Do schools redline? Do professional people? Stores? Service establishments?

IMPROVEMENTS IN ADMINISTRATION

How may real estate administration be improved in the years ahead and thus increase the efficiency with which our real estate resources are used? Direct answers to this question would be hard to present but some suggestions can be made as to areas of probable improvement.

One possibility is the improvement of management and administration in general. Real estate administration is not separated from other areas of administration. The same general concepts apply in real estate as in other fields. As our knowledge of decision making and implementing increases, real state administration will benefit along with other fields. University schools of business and various other areas of specialization in our universities, notably the behavioral sciences, have been giving increasing attention to the improvement of management processes. As we improve our capacity to plan, organize, and control, we may make use of such developments in real estate. Special adaptations may be required, of course, since decisions and programs for implementing decisions in the real estate field must be related to fixed sites, to long-term commitments, to large fixed investments, to special market conditions, and to other factors that pertain to the localized nature of real property income.

A second possibility for improved administration in the real estate field may arise from better administration of real estate by the owners and users of real estate—business firms, individuals and families, and various agencies and institutions. For example, many business firms are paying increased attention to the effective use of the real estate resources that are available to them. Private consumers of real estate and especially home buyers and owners are growing more sophisticated with respect to their use of real estate and their investments in it. At one time the objective of the home buyer appeared to be the achievement of debt-free home ownership. Today home owners tend to view their equity in a home as they do other types of investment. They often borrow against their equity to finance a variety of family needs.

A third area from which improvements in administration may come is the real estate business itself. Business firms in the real estate field may be managed more effectively. Improvements may be made in the processes of land development and building, real estate marketing, or the financing of real estate ownership and use.

For example, we may see the emergence of more franchising in real estate marketing, flexible payment mortgages of various types, and increased use of leases with options to purchase.

Improved government administration may be a fourth field for improvement. The types of laws and regulations in force are very important, of course, but the effectiveness with which they are administered also means much. What are the prospects for improved public administration, especially as it relates to the real estate sector?

R & D

Improvements in the various areas listed above may come about in part from research and development efforts. The real estate sector seems to make relatively less effort in this direction than most other fields. More efforts may be forthcoming. Government has helped with various programs. Improvements may arise from new insights developed by people in business or by students of business administration. Or improvements may come from sources that we cannot now foresee. The universities and independent research agencies may make important contributions. Business executives and private individuals may point the way to improvements. Also, trade associations and other organizations, as well as government agencies, may contribute to improvements in a number of ways.

Long-Range Planning

In connection with the implementation of managerial decisions, increasing emphasis has been given to long-range planning as one of the more important tools of management. Planning is of special importance in the administration of real estate resources because of their long economic life and the large investments that are represented.

New planning techniques have emerged. Model building and simulations have been used increasingly. The computer has contributed to such developments. The scenario technique, that is, developing a scenario or a series of scenarios of anticipated future events, has come in for more widespread use. The Delphi technique, apparently named for the Delphic oracle of antiquity, provides for drawing on the opinions of a number of experts. The more frequently mentioned are then resubmitted to the same group for further analysis and response and the process is repeated until a consensus or near consensus emerges.

Every business establishment, institution, and family is controlled to some degree by the real estate resources it uses. Thus, careful planning in order to anticipate future real estate requirements is highly important for business administration in general, but it acquires special significance in connection with real estate resources. For example, the growth of many business firms has been severely limited by the failure to anticipate space, equipment, and location needs.

Business managers and private individuals have tended to rely heavily on architects and engineers for assistance in planning the development or redevelopment of real estate resources. Such specialists, however, are able to do this type of planning effectively only as the owners and users of real property can outline realistically their potential needs for space and facilities. This is a planning responsibility of business management that is coming to be recognized to an increasing degree. Long-range planning for the development and use of real estate resources probably will be facilitated by improved projections of long-term economic trends as well as by better projections of the future potential of specific industries, localities, and areas.

Individuals and families are giving more attention to their real estate requirements over time. Typically, however, they do not have the degree of control over their locations nor can they translate future plans into action with the same degree of effectiveness as the owners and managers of business firms. To some extent this is true also of government agencies, since programs of government may change rapidly with shifts from one administration to another or with changes in the preferences of the electorate in regard to various programs.

Organization of Resources

Marked improvement has been made in the ability of business managers to organize resources and operations. Managers have been giving real estate resources increasing attention, as we have seen. Many firms are establishing real estate departments or paying greater attention to allocating responsibility for real estate decisions. The proper mix of real estate and other resources in the organization of a business firm's operations is not always easy to determine. It appears that improvements are being made; and there is little question of the increasing concern of business firms about the role of real estate resources in influencing the effectiveness with which other types of resources may be utilized.

The relationship of real estate resources to others in the business firm depends to a considerable extent on whether the firm is primarily engaged in manufacturing, marketing, or service activities. It is probable that more changes will be forthcoming in the service lines than others, in part because greater advances have already been made in the manufacturing and marketing fields.

Control of Operations

Significant improvements have been made in control processes in many lines of business. There has been more widespread use of budgeting in management planning and control operations. Cost accounting has contributed much to improved controls. High-speed computing equipment has broadened the types of records and controls that are feasible. Increased attention has been given to the establishment of realistic standards as a basis for measuring performance.

In the real estate field, rapidly changing values have required that careful controls be imposed to adjust for insurance requirements, tax obligations, and refinancing possibilities. More careful controls of modernization and repair programs have also been stressed in order to preserve property values.

Leadership and Entrepreneurial Ability

Future leadership will come in part from those now engaged in business administration or in one or another part of the real estate business. Such leadership will come also from younger people, many of whom are now preparing themselves for careers in the business world.

In the business world, leadership and entrepreneurial abilities often are combined. The distinction is far from easy to make. One may be a leader without being an entrepreneur. But effective leaders often have "entrepreneurial minds." They have the capacity to think creatively, to innovate, to develop new ideas and concepts, and to apply them in the solution of problems. In this respect the entrepreneur and the artist may have much in common.

Traditionally, economists have also associated entrepreneurship with risk taking. Whether this is an essential requirement may be open to question. The entrepreneurial mind may be found among public officials as well as private business people. Indeed, the close relationship between public and private programs in the real estate field suggests that leadership and creative talents of a high order will be required in the public agencies related to real estate in the years ahead.

Efficiency of Real Estate Firms

It is probable that those who develop, finance, and market real estate are as capable, work as hard, manage as carefully, and in general try to operate as efficiently as those in other fields of business. Although the numerous small organizations that are typical of this field may result in some inefficiencies and lack of coordination, there are many other fields in which enterprises are also small and not closely coordinated. Consider many of the service lines, for example.

It may be that such inefficiencies as exist are due to the nature of the commodity in which the real estate business deals and the institutional framework surrounding its operations. The long life of real properties, the fact that they represent relatively large economic units, and their fixity of location create special problems, as we have noted. Could larger enterprises deal with these problems more efficiently? The mere fact of size, of course, is no guarantee of efficiency. A large builder may be able to do more in the way of applying sound principles of land planning and reap some of the economies of large-scale operations from a project. There is always the danger, however, of overexpansion, to which the smaller operator may be less susceptible.

With respect to real estate marketing, several questions may be raised. Is there any basic difference between selling real properties or their services and selling groceries? Are the arguments against large-scale operations in the real estate brokerage field comparable to the arguments of the small, independent retailer against the chain stores? Franchising and related arrangements such as Red Carpet, Homes for Living, Gallery of Homes, and Century 21 may be pointing the way to future developments in real estate marketing.

Suppose we consider also the internal organization of our real estate enterprises. It has been suggested that the small brokerage offices, for example, cannot provide much for their employees in the way of training programs, opportunities for promotion, or provisions for retirement and the like. On the other hand, the independence of these smaller enterprises may offer great incentives through opportunities for achieving ownership of a small concern, and this may in large measure counterbalance the personnel programs and "fringe benefits" of larger organizations. If the owners and operators of small business firms were accorded special tax treatment, the appeal of the small enterprise might be increased. For example, if the owners of small business firms could pay low taxes on, say, the first $50,000 of annual income, or if they were given tax advantages until they had accumulated capital of say, a half million dollars, then managerial talent might move to small business firms rather than to the larger corporations.

There are also other advantages in the organization of a small establishment. Small organizations are more flexible, less cumbersome, and more easily adapted to changes in market requirements.

We should note that a number of techniques have improved in recent years. Appraising is an area in which real advances have been made; the same thing may be said of financial risk analysis. Improved operations have resulted from better secondary mortgage markets. The development of private mortgage insurance has contributed to progress in real estate finance.

The educational programs of a number of universities and colleges have contributed to improved practices. Special mention should be made of the institutes, short courses, and correspondence study programs sponsored by a number of the trade associations and professional organizations in this field.

Yet, much remains to be done. When we compare many real estate enterprises with those in other fields, the differences are not always in favor of the former.

Users of Real Estate and Consumerism

As we have suggested, business firms have been making significant improvements in their management of the real estate resources they own and use. Further improvements may be made. Governmental and institutional users of real estate may make further advances in the administration of their real estate resources.

The individuals and families owning and using real estate resources often are unable to bring their management problems the degree of knowledge and experience that can be provided by business firms. There is little doubt, however, that home buyers and owners have become more knowledgeable about real estate matters in recent years.

Tenants and home buyers have often felt that they were not treated fairly. This has resulted in various consumer protection laws. Among these are the Truth in Lending Act (TIL), The Real Estate Settlement Procedures Act (RESPA),[3] The Home Mortgage Disclosure Act, The Equal Credit Opportunity Act, and others. Also, some rent control laws have been enacted. Tenant unions have been formed in some places. Some consumer protection laws have been helpful. Rent controls usually make matters worse except for very short-run periods. Much remains to be done in the area of landlord–tenant relations.

Government–Business Relationships

Do we need changes in our system of legal arrangements for the ownership, transfer of title, and mortgaging of real properties? A number of forms and processes that had their origin in medieval times are still in use, even though it is difficult in many instances to justify them by the require-

---

[3] See Dept. of Housing and Urban Development, *Real Estate Settlement Procedures Act Special Information Booklet* (Washington, D. C.: Government Printing Office, 1976).

ments and standards of the modern market. If it is possible to buy the stocks or bonds of a corporation located in another part of the country by making a telephone call, why must we be burdened by the legal formalities and processes that are a part of every real property transfer? Could legislation improve these conditions? Is the real estate business carrying a part of the legal profession on its back because of these cumbersome legal formalities?

The processes of searching titles and of bringing abstracts up to date are difficult and time-consuming. Would it not be possible, by the more widespread use of either private title insurance or the Torrens system, to simplify these processes? Why should we not have a system of title insurance which insures against all defects in titles rather than against unknown defects only? Or is this more properly a government function?

The desirability of various land planning and zoning regulations has been increasingly questioned. What forms of regulation would be more desirable in this area? Could we do without zoning, for example?

While we recognize that taxation is always a point of friction between government and business establishments, do the facts of the situation call for a substantial revision of real property taxation? Should real estate taxes be frozen at current levels? Should taxes be used as a device for promoting developments which are considered to be in the public interest?

To what extent is government responsible for the improvement of business practices? Undoubtedly the activities of the Federal Home Loan Bank System have been helpful although there are complaints of over-regulation from many in the industry. In the field of agriculture, government has assumed far-reaching responsibilities for the improvement of farm practices. Should it assume similar responsibilities in the real estate field? Do we need an extension service for real estate and other small businesses similar to the programs in the field of agriculture?

How should the Department of Housing and Urban Development help us cope with some of the rapidly expanding problems of the urban community and the impact of these problems on our real estate resources? Are new types of mortgages and mortgage insurance programs likely to emerge? Will we develop programs for insuring interest rate risk? Purchasing power risk? Is it desirable to have competing government systems of real estate finance? Despite some of the arguments for greater centralization of such agencies, there appear to be real advantages in competition, even among government agencies.

Will the trend toward increasingly detailed regulation of business practices continue? The problems of complying with various government regulations have become quite complex and costly in many instances. Many people in business, and especially the real estate business, have been discouraged not only by the volume of regulations but also by the bureaucratic procedures that have characterized their administration. Are recent trends in these areas likely to continue or will conditions improve?

SUMMARY

In this final chapter we have raised a number of questions about future trends of development and about the possibilities for future improvements in real estate administration. Changes in our general objectives and priorities, of course, will have major significance for the real estate sector. The policies and arrangements that are set up to give effect to the desired priorities will also have a profound influence on the future role of real estate resources. The needs of the people will reflect their general priorities; the resources provided will depend on the relative importance assigned to them, development methods and costs, taxes and incentives, and conservation and renewal programs.

Improvements in the administration of real estate resources and real estate firms will come from research and development efforts, increased knowledge of administration, improvements in long-range planning, better organization of resources, and more effective control of operations. Leadership and entrepreneurial ability will play a role in improved real estate administration. Much will depend on improved efficiency of real estate firms and on the care with which business, governmental, and institutional users of real estate and individuals and families manage their real estate resources. Improvements in a number of government–business relationships may also prove to be helpful.

This final chapter has raised many questions, suggested only a few answers. Since it is largely in the form of a concluding study project, no study projects are given at the end of this chapter.

QUESTIONS FOR STUDY

1. Outline the social and economic priorities that you believe will be most important in the next ten years. Do you believe these will be likely to change significantly by the end of the century?
2. Which policies and arrangements for carrying priorities into effect seem most likely to be changed in the next five to ten years? How may such changes affect the real estate sector?
3. Do you think there will be significant changes in incentives?
4. Which major factors will determine the needs for real estate resources? The ability of our system to supply such needs?
5. How may research and development efforts contribute to the future supply and utilization of real estate resources? To improvements in the real estate business?
6. Outline recent developments in the field of long-range planning. Which of these will be of greatest importance in the real estate field?
7. How may improvement in the organization and control of real estate resources lead to advances in this area?
8. Outline the contributions that seem likely to come from entrepreneurship in the real estate sector.

9. Will real estate firms become more efficient? Why or why not?
10. Give examples of changes that may occur in real estate marketing and finance.
11. List major improvements that may be developed in government–business relationships in the real estate sector. Are advances likely to be made in the administration of public agencies comparable to those in the private area?

SUGGESTED READINGS

BIRCH, DAVID L. *The Economic Future of City and Suburb.* New York: Committee for Economic Development (CED), 1970. *Social Responsibilities of Business.* New York: CED, 1971.

KAHN, HERMAN. *The Next 200 Years.* New York: Wm. Morrow & Co., 1976.

KAHN, HERMAN, and BRIGGS, BRUCE. *Things to Come.* New York: The Macmillan Co., 1973.

LONG, NORTON. *The Unwalled City.* New York: Basic Books, 1972.

MCMAHAN, JOHN. "Tomorrow's Changing Demand for Real Estate," *Real Estate Review,* Winter, 1977.

TOFFLER, ALVIN. *Future Shock.* New York: Random House, 1970.

TOYNBEE, ARNOLD. *Cities on the Move.* New York: Oxford University Press, 1970. Chaps. 1 & 10.

Appendixes

A

GLOSSARY *

abstract of title. A historical summary of the conveyances, transfers, and other facts relied on as evidence of title; a summary of the documents having a bearing on the history of the title to a property.

acceleration clause. A clause in trust deeds or mortgages giving lenders the right to call all sums owing them to be immediately due and payable upon the occurrence of a certain specified event, such as a sale, demolition, default, and so forth.

accessibility. Relative difficulty of reaching real property and ease of entrance to it.

acre. A unit of land measure containing 43,560 square feet.

ad valorem. According to value.

ad valorem tax. A tax varying with the value of the property.

administration. The superintending of the execution, use, or conduct of a business, activity, or resource.

administration of real estate resources. The efficient utilization of real estate resources in the achievement of desired results, usually in combination with other resources.

advance. In a construction loan, a periodic transfer of funds from the lender to the borrower during the process of construction.

adverse possession. The open and notorious possession of real property as a claim to title. Thus, a method of acquiring title.

advertising real estate. The act of informing the public with the intent to induce some desired impression, feeling, or action relative to real estate. Public announcements and messages, the purposes of which are to aid directly or indirectly in the sale of real properties or property services.

    institutional advertising. Advertising that pertains to real estate in general and has for its purpose the creation of favorable public attitudes toward real estate, investments in real estate, or the people engaged in the real estate business.

* For a more complete coverage of real estate terms, see Byrl N. Boyce (Ed.), The American Institute of Real Estate Appraisers and The Society of Residential Appraisers, *Real Estate Appraisal Terminology* (Cambridge, Mass.: Ballinger Publishing Co., 1975).

name advertising. Advertising that has for its main purpose the popularizing of the name, activities, and reputation of a specific real estate firm.

specific advertising. Advertising that pertains to individual properties and
property services. Its purpose is to aid in the selling or renting of a
specific property.

aesthetic value. Increased worth due to pleasing views, attractive layout, design,
architectural treatment, and related factors.

agent. One who acts for and has the authority to represent another who is
known as a principal.

air rights. Rights in real property to use the space above the surface of the real
estate without precluding the use of its surface area for some other purpose.

allodial tenure. A system of ownership of real property where ownership may
be complete except for rights held by government. Allodial tenure is in
contrast to feudal tenure.

amenities, amenity return. Pleasant satisfactions that are received through
using rights in real property but that are not received in the form of money.

American Bankers Association. A trade association of commercial bankers.

American Institute of Real Estate Appraisers. A professional association of real
estate appraisers. *See* **appraiser,** *MAI* (*Member Appraisal Institute*).

American Society of Real Estate Counselors. A professional organization whose
members provide advice to the public. Members use the designation CRE.

amortization. The process of payment of a debt or obligation by a series of
payments over time. Generally the payments are in equal amounts that include principal and interest; and generally the payments are made at uniform intervals of time.

amortized mortgage. A mortgage in which repayment is made in accordance
with a definite plan that requires the repayment of certain amounts at definite times so that all the debt is released by the end of the term. *See*
amortization.

anchor tenant. The tenant with major drawing power.

appraisal, valuation. An estimate of value. In real estate, an estimate of value
of specific rights in a specific parcel of real estate as of a specific date for a
specific purpose.

appraisal report. A report, usually written, of the appraised value, together
with the pertinent information regarding the property appraised and the
evidence and analysis leading to the reported value estimate.

appraiser. One who is in the business of making appraisals on the basis of a
fee or salary or in conjunction with some other compensated service.

MAI (*Member Appraisal Institute*). A professional designation of an appraiser who is a member of the American Institute of Real Estate Appraisers, an association affiliated with the National Association of Realtors.
Also, designated members of the Society of Real Estate Appraisers.

appurtenance. Property that is an accessory to or incidental to other property
to which it is annexed.

assessment. The valuation of a property for the purpose of levying a tax; the
tax so levied.

special assessment. An assessment levied for specific purposes such as providing streets, sewers, sidewalks, and the like. An assessment related to
benefit derived by the taxes.

assignment. Transfer of an interest in an instrument such as a bond, mortgage, lease, option or land contract, in writing.

assumption of a mortgage. Agreement by the grantee of real property that is encumbered by a mortgage that he or she, the grantee, will pay such a mortgage; the assumption of a personal liability under an existing mortgage.

axial growth. City growth that takes the form of prongs or finger-like extensions moving out along main transportation routes.

balloon mortgage payment. *See* **mortgage,** *balloon mortgage payment.*

base line. *See* **legal description, land description.**

basic employment, urban growth employment. Employment in establishments that receive their income from outside the community. Basic employment is in contrast to nonbasic employment.

basic income. Income commanded from outside the community.

bill of sale. An executed written instrument given to pass title of personal property.

blanket mortgage. *See* **mortgage,** *blanket mortgage.*

blight. Decay; withering away, as of a neighborhood.

broker. An agent who negotiates for the sale, leasing, management, or financing of a property or of property rights on a commission basis that is contingent on success.

  farm broker. A broker who deals with farm properties. Farm brokers operate in localized and regional areas.

builder. One who undertakes the improvement of land by erecting structures; one who undertakes the production of real estate resources by improving land through the erection of structures.

  custom builder. A builder who builds for a specific owner.

  operative builder, speculative builder. A builder who builds for sale to the public rather than for a specific owner.

building codes. Government regulations that specify minimum construction standards for the purpose of maintaining public health and safety.

building permit. Authorization or permission by local government for the erection, alteration, or remodeling of improvements within its jurisdiction.

bundle of rights. The assortment of rights in real property. *See* **estate; property.**

business–government relations. The collection of laws, codes, regulations, and contracts between business and government, within the framework of which business operates.

buy–sell agreement. Contract typically between lenders, with one buying the other's interest in a construction loan and becoming the permanent lender.

buyer's market. *See* **market,** *buyer's market.*

CBD. *See* **central business district.**

CPM (*Certified Property Manager*). *See* **under Institute of Real Estate Management.**

capital gain. Income that is a result of sale of an asset and not from the general course of business. Capital gains are taxed at a lower rate than ordinary income.

capital market. *See* **market,** *capital market.*

capitalization. The process of reflecting future income in present value; the discounting of the future income stream to arrive at a present value.

capitalization in perpetuity. Capitalization without limit of time; perpetual.

capitalization rate. The rate at which income is discounted.

split rates. Use of different capitalization rates for land and buildings in the income approach to value.

cash flow. Flow of cash into or out of an investment. The net income from a property before depreciation and other noncash expenses. May be used on both before- and after-tax basis.

cash throw-off. Net operating income less the yearly debt service. Sometimes referred to as before-tax cash flow.

central business district. The "downtown" section of a city where the downtown shopping area and office district are located.

central city. Sometimes used to refer to the "downtown" center; also a city that is the center of a larger geographic trade area for which it performs certain market and service functions.

chattel mortgage. A loan secured by personal property.

chattels. Personal property; personalty.

closing statement. A listing of the debits and credits of the buyer and seller to a real estate transaction for the financial settlement of the transaction.

cloudy title. *See* **title,** *cloudy title.*

cluster housing. An arrangement of housing units which places them close together yet provides for large recreational areas, or "common areas" which are owned by all the neighbors.

coercive regulations. *See* **regulations,** *coercive regulations.*

commercial properties. Properties intended for use by all types of retail and wholesale stores, office buildings, hotels, and service establishments.

commitment. For a mortgage, a promise or statement by the lender of the terms and conditions under which the loan will be made.

conditional commitment. A statement that mortgage funds will be provided or guaranteed if certain conditions are met which enables an owner or developer to finance construction or ownership.

firm commitment. Written notification from a financial institution that it will lend money and the terms on which it will do so for each specific case.

common law. Rules based on usage; judge-made law in contrast to legislative or constitutional law.

common property. *See* **property,** *common property.*

community property. In certain states, the property jointly owned by husband and wife.

condemnation. The process of forcing a sale under eminent domain. Also, condemnation of unsafe structures.

conditional sales contract. *See* **land contract.**

condominium. A form of property ownership providing for individual ownership of a specific apartment or other space not necessarily on ground level together with an undivided interest in the land or other parts of the structure in common with other owners.

confiscation. The seizing of property without compensation, usually by unfriendly governments.

conformity. In real estate, the blending of an improvement with the surroundings or the essentially similar use of land in relation to its surroundings; the appearance and use of real estate that is harmonious with the surrounding real estate.

construction loan. A loan to finance the improvement of real estate.

contract. An agreement between two or more persons that is legally enforceable; a written evidence of such an agreement.

contract for deed. See **land contract, contract for deed.**

conservation. The process of saving resources from use or of using them in such a way that they will not be depleted.

consideration. Anything of value given to induce one entering into a contract; money, trust deeds, services, etc. Consideration is essential to an enforceable contract.

constant. The percentage of the original balance of a loan which is represented by the sum of the *principal and interest* payments for a year, which is needed to fully amortize the loan. For example, a 6 per cent loan amortized over 20 years has a constant of approximately 8½ per cent. Annual payments necessary to amortize a $10,000 loan over 20 years would be about $850. ($850 ÷ $10,000 = .085)

contractor, general contractor. One who supervises the improvement of land by erection of structures or other improvements; one who has the responsibility for such improvement but does not necessarily initiate the process as is done by a builder.

conversion. A change in the use of real estate without destruction of the improvements; a change in the use of real estate by altering improvements.

conveyance. Transfer of an interest in real property from one person to another person.

cooperative ownership. A form of apartment ownership. Occupant acquires ownership by purchasing shares in a corporation but typically must consult the corporation for such actions as sale or improvement.

corner influence table. A statistical table, sometimes used in real estate appraisal, that attempts to reflect the added value of a lot located on a corner.

corporeal rights. Possessory rights in real property.

cost. That which is, was, or would be given up to obtain property (or other things).

replacement cost. The cost of replacing real estate improvements with an alternative of like utility but that is not necessarily an exact replica.

reproduction cost. The cost of replacing real estate improvements with an exact replica.

cost approach to value, summation approach. Valuation approached by estimating the cost of providing a substitute for that which is being valued.

covenant, restrictive covenant. A contract between private persons usually to regulate land use or relating to land use.

credit union. A state- or federally chartered mutual financial association with a common bond.

cul-de-sac. A dead-end street that widens at the end to form a circular area sufficient to enable an auto to make a U turn.

curtesy. The life estate of the husband in the real estate owned by his wife.

custom builder. See **builder,** *custom builder.*

cycle. See **cyclical fluctuation.**

cyclical fluctuation. Variations around a trend in activity that recur from time to time; fluctuations remaining after removal of trend and seasonal factors.

data plant. A file of information on real properties maintained usually by an appraiser, mortgage lender, and the like.

dealer-builder. A builder who erects structures from prefabricated components, usually as a local representative of a prefabricated house manufacturer.

deed. An instrument conveying title to real property.

> *deed of trust.* See **trust deed.**

> *grant deed.* A deed in which the seller warrants that he or she has not previously passed title.

> *quitclaim deed.* An instrument transferring only such title as the seller may possess.

> *warranty deed.* A deed in which the seller warrants that title is "good and merchantable."

deed restrictions. Limitations placed upon the use of real property in the writing of a deed.

default. Failure to fulfill a duty or promise or to discharge contractual obligation.

defective title. See **title,** *defective title.*

deferred annuity. An income stream beginning at some future date.

deficiency judgment. A judgment for that part of a debt secured that was not liquidated by the proceeds from the sale of foreclosed real property.

demand. The set of conditions indicating how much of a good or service will be bought at various prices.

demographic. Pertaining to the structure of population; e.g., size, density, statistical characteristics.

depletion. See **depreciation,** *depletion.*

deposit, earnest money. A sum of money or other consideration tendered in conjunction with an offer to purchase rights in real property.

depreciation. Loss in property value due to any cause.

> *accelerated depreciation.* Methods of reflecting depreciation (such as double declining balance and sum-of-the-year's-digits) that enable the owner of an asset to take more depreciation in the early years of the asset's life.

> *contingent depreciation.* Loss in property value because of expectations of a decline in property services.

> *depletion.* The exhaustion of a resource such as the removal of a mineral deposit.

> *economic obsolescence.* Loss in property value from events outside the property that unfavorably affect income or income potentials.

> *functional depreciation, functional obsolescence.* Loss in property value because of a loss in ability of the physical property to provide services as compared with alternatives.

> *physical depreciation.* Loss in property value due to wearing away or deterioration.

depth table. A technique for real estate appraisal using statistical tables based on the theory that added depth increases the value of land.

developer. One who undertakes the preparation of land for income production, the construction of buildings and other improvements, and the making available of completed properties.

direct subsidy. See **subsidy,** *direct subsidy.*

discount house. Any of a number of stores whose function it is to sell in quantity at lower than usual retail prices.

disposable income. That portion of income that a household has to spend on personal consumption, i.e., after tax income.

district. A city area that has a land use different from adjacent land uses, e.g., commercial, industrial, and residential. *See* **neighborhood.**

double, duplex. Two dwelling units under one roof. A double usually means dwelling units side by side; a duplex, one dwelling unit above the other.

double taxation. *See* **taxation,** *double taxation.*

doubling up. The occupation of one dwelling unit by two or more families.

dower. The life estate of a wife in the real estate owned by her husband.

drainage. The running off of water from the surface of land.

earnest money. *See* **deposit.**

easement. The right to make limited use of real property owned by another; a right to use property without taking possession.

economic base. The major economic support of a community; economic activities that enable it to compete effectively with others.

economic base analysis. A technique for analyzing the major economic supports of a community; analysis as a means of predicting population, income, or other variables having an effect on real estate value or land utilization.

economic goods. Goods that have scarcity and utility; goods that provide desired services but that are not in sufficient abundance to be free.

economics. The branch of organized study dealing with the social organization for the utilization of resources in the attainment of objectives that the society or community sets for itself.

economy. Getting as much as possible of what one wants by the use of the means available.

effective age. A statement regarding the amount of depreciation that has occurred on a property. The amount is stated in terms of the number of years that would ordinarily be associated when compared with buildings of known ages.

effective gross income. Estimated total income minus allowance for vacancy and other income loss.

eminent domain. The right of government to take private property for public use with just compensation.

enabling act. *See* **zoning,** *enabling act.*

encroachment. An improvement on a parcel of land that intrudes on or invades a contiguous parcel of land.

encumbrance. A claim against a property such as a debt secured by a mortgage.

entrepreneur. One who undertakes business activities, accepting all risks and responsibilities.

    real estate entrepreneur. One who undertakes real estate risks and responsibilities, i.e., builder, developer, broker, leasing agent, etc.

equality of economic opportunity. A state of affairs in which all people have equal chances for the same jobs at equal pay regardless of race, creed, color, or sex.

equity. In finance, the value of the interest of an owner of property exclusive of the encumbrances on that property; also, justice.

equity kicker. An interest in the equity of a property as an incentive to provide, usually, financing.

equity of redemption. *See* **redemption,** *equity of redemption.*

erosion. The wearing away of a ground surface.

escheat. The reversion of private property to the state.

escrow. An instrument in the hands of a third party that is held for delivery until certain acts are performed or conditions fulfilled; the arrangement for the handling of such instruments.

estate. The degree, quantity, nature, and extent of an interest in real property.

    estates in expectancy. A classification of estates by time of enjoyment when possession will be at some future time. *See* **remainder; reversion.**

    estate in possession. A classification of estates by time of enjoyment when possession is present. *See* **corporeal rights.**

    estates in severalty. Ownership in a single individual; a classification of estates by number of owners where the number is one.

    freehold estate. A nonleasehold estate such as a fee simple estate, fee tail estate, and life estate.

    fee simple estate. The most complete form of estate ownership; the "totality of rights" in real property.

    fee tail estate. An estate or a limited estate in which transfer of the property is restricted in that the property must pass to the descendants of the owner. Originally used to insure the passing of land in a direct ancestral line.

    life estate. An estate that has a duration of the life of an individual. *See* **curtesy; dower.**

    joint estates. A classification of estates by number of owners where the number is two or more. *See* **tenancy,** *joint tenancy, tenancy in common.*

    nonfreehold estate, leasehold estate. The rights of tenants as distinguished from those of a freeholder. Includes estate for years, estate at will, and estate at sufferance.

    estate at sufferance. Rights of a tenant in real property after the expiration of a lease if the tenant holds over without special permission.

    estate at will. Rights of a tenant in real property that may be terminated by either landlord or tenant.

    estate for years. Rights of a tenant in real property for a definite period of time.

estate taxation. *See* **taxation,** *estate taxation.*

eviction. The taking possession of real property from one in possession.

exclusive agency listing. *See* **listing,** *exclusive agency listing.*

exclusive right-to-sell listing. *See* **listing,** *exclusive right-to-sell listing.*

exculpatory clause. Provision to relieve or absolve those who sign contracts or leases from personal obligation; also may relieve landlords of liability for personal injury to tenants as well as for property damage.

execute. To complete, to perform; e.g., to execute a deed.

Farm and Land Institute. Organization to support professional effort and studies in agricultural real estate and land for development.

Farmers Home Administration (FmHA). A federal agency for assisting the financing of rural housing.

featherbedding rules. Rules that preserve outmoded and inefficient work methods.

Federal Deposit Insurance Corporation (FDIC). Agency of the federal government that insures deposits at commercial banks and savings banks.

Federal Home Loan Bank (FHLB). A District bank of the Federal Home Loan Bank System that lends only to member financial institutions such as savings and loan associations.

Federal Home Loan Bank Board (FHLBB). The administrative agency that charters federal savings and loan associations and exercises regulatory authority over members of the Federal Home Loan Bank System.

Federal Home Loan Bank System. The Federal Home Loan Bank Board and the network of Federal Home Loan Banks and member financial institutions.

Federal Home Loan Mortgage Corporation. An agency supervised by the Federal Home Loan Bank Board for largely secondary mortgage market operations. Sometimes referred to as "Freddie Mac" or "the Mortgage Corporation."

Federal Housing Administration (FHA). An agency of the federal government that insures mortgage loans.

Federal National Mortgage Association (FNMA). An independent agency that buys and sells FHA-insured, VA-guaranteed, and conventional mortgage loans. Sometimes referred to as "Fannie Mae."

federal savings and loan association. A savings and loan association with a federal charter issued by the Federal Home Loan Bank Board. A federally chartered savings and loan association stands in contrast to a state-chartered savings and loan association.

Federal Savings and Loan Insurance Corporation. An agency of the federal government that insures savers' accounts at savings and loan associations.

farm broker. *See* **broker,** *farm broker.*

fee simple estate. *See* **estate,** *fee simple estate.*

fee tail estate. *See* **estate,** *fee tail estate.*

feudal tenure. A system of ownership of real property where ownership rests with a sovereign but where lesser interests are granted in return for loyalty or service. Contrast to allodial tenure.

feuds. Grants of land.

fidelity bond. A bond posted as security for the discharge of an obligation of personal services.

filtering down. In housing, the process of passing the use of real estate to successively lower income groups as the real estate produces less income.

financial institutions. Organizations that deal in money or claims to money and serve the function of channeling money from those who wish to lend to those who wish to borrow. Such organizations include commercial banks, savings and loan associations, savings banks, credit unions, and insurance companies.

fiscal controls. Efforts to control the level of economic activity by manipulation of the amount of federal tax and spending programs and the amount of surplus or deficit.

fixity of location. The characteristic of real estate that subjects it to the influence of its surroundings and prohibits it from escaping from such influence.

flow of funds. An accounting method (used primarily by the Federal Reserve) to describe the sources and uses of the nation's funds in a given period of time.

foreclosure. The legal steps required by law to be taken by the mortgagee after the default of a debt before the property can be proceeded against for payment of the debt.

　　foreclosure by sale. Foreclosure either under court action resulting in a decree of sale or under power of sale contained in a mortgage or trust deed.

strict foreclosure. Action by a court that, after determination that sufficient time has elapsed for a mortgagor to pay a mortgage past due, terminates all rights and interest of the mortgagor in the real property.

franchise. A specific privilege conferred by government or, in the case of an exclusive dealership, conferred by a business firm.

freehold estate. *See* **estate,** *freehold estate.*

functional plan. The special arrangement of real estate improvements as it relates to property services.

garden apartment. An apartment development; usually a two- or three-story walk-up in a pleasant setting.

graduated lease. Lease with provision for a stated rent for an initial period followed by an increase in rent or a decrease in subsequent periods.

grant. A transfer of real property by written instrument as in a deed.

private grant. The transfer of real property from one person to another.

public grant. A government grant of real property to a private party; a transfer of real property from government to a person.

grantee. One who receives a transfer of real property by deed.

grantor. One who transfers real property by deed.

gridiron pattern, gridiron plan. A layout of streets that resembles a gridiron; a system of subdivision with blocks of uniform length and width and streets that intersect at right angles.

gross income multiplier. A technique for estimating real estate value based on some factor (multiplier) times the gross income derived from the property in the past.

gross national product (GNP). The total value of all goods and services produced in the economy in any given period; also, the accounting method used to list the major income and expenditure (product) accounts of the nation.

ground lease. A lease granting right to use and occupancy of land.

guaranteed mortgage. A mortgage in which a party other than the borrower assures payment in the event of default by a mortgagor, e.g., Veterans' Administration guaranteed mortgages.

heuristics. The process of arriving at a decision through imagination or inspiration.

highest and best use. The utilization of real property to its greatest economic advantage; the use that provides the highest land value; the use of land that provides a net income stream to the land that when capitalized provides the highest land value.

homes associations. *See* **property owners' association.**

Home Owners Loan Corporation. An agency of the federal government that refinanced mortgages in default in the early 1930's.

homestead (right of), homestead exemption. The interest of the head of a family in an owned residence that is exempt from the claims of creditors.

improved value. The difference between the income-producing ability of a property in its current condition and the amount required to pay a competitive return on the investment in the property.

improvement. That which is erected or constructed upon land to release the income-earning potential of the land; buildings or appurtenances on land.

overimprovement. An improvement of real estate in excess of that justifiable to release the earning power of land.

underimprovement. An improvement insufficient to release the earning power of land.

incentive. Spur, motive, special reward, such as extra payment for reaching or exceeding a standard of performance, or for performing in a certain way.

incorporeal rights. Nonpossessory rights in real estate.

indirect subsidies. See subsidy, indirect subsidy.

inducive regulations. See regulations, inducive regulations.

industrial districts. Areas in which the primary or major improvements to land are in the nature of factory, warehouse, or related property.

industrial park. An area in which the land is developed specifically for use for industrial purposes. Usually a controlled development designed for specific types of industrial buildings with provision for streets, utilities, etc.

inheritance taxation. See taxation, inheritance taxation.

input–output analysis. A technique for analysis of an economy through description of the production and purchases of specific sectors of the economy.

Institute of Real Estate Management. A professional organization of property managers.

CPM (Certified Property Manager). Official designation for members.

insured mortgage. A mortgage in which a party other than the borrower, in return for the payment of a premium, assures payment in the event of default by a mortgagor, e.g., FHA-insured mortgages.

intangible assets. Rights in such properties as franchises, trademarks, patents, copyrights, good will, and similar items.

interest rate risk. The risk of loss due to changes in the interest rate, earnings, or the value of a property may be affected as a result of changes in prevailing interest rates in the money market. When interest rates go up or down properties are generally capitalized at higher or lower rates.

interurbia. A contiguous urban development larger than a city or metropolitan area.

intestate. Legal designation of a person who has died without leaving a valid will.

joint estates. See estate, joint estates.

joint tenancy. A joint estate with the right of survivorship.

joint venture. An arrangement under which two or more individuals or businesses will go together on a single project as partners.

judgment. The acknowledgment or award of a claim through a court of law; an obligation or debt under a court decree; also, the decree.

junior mortgage. A mortgage having claim ranking below that of another mortgage.

jurisdictional disputes. As between two labor unions or trade unions, a disagreement as to which union's members shall perform certain services.

land. In a physical sense, the earth's surface; may include the minerals below the surface and the air above the surface.

land contract, contract for deed. A written agreement by which real property is sold to a buyer who agrees to pay in installments the established price, with interest, over a specified period of years, with title remaining with the seller until the purchase price or some portion of the purchase price is paid.

land description. *See* **legal description.**

land economics. The branch of general economics that deals with the social organization for the utilization of land resources in the attainment of the objectives that the society or community sets for itself.

land planning. The designing of land area uses, road networks, and layout for utilities to achieve efficient utilization of real estate resources.

law. A generalization from experience that applies almost universally. A demonstrated relationship between cause and effect. Also, in a legal sense, an established rule or standard of conduct or action that is enforceable by government.

common law. *See* **common law.**

license law. A law that regulates the practices of real estate brokers and salesmen.

real estate law. The body of laws relating to real estate; generally evolved from the English common law but now including regulations such as zoning, building codes, etc.

leadership. The vital motivating force that inspires and directs an organization toward the achievement of its objectives.

lease. A transfer of possession and the right to use property to a tenant for a stipulated period, during which the tenant pays rent to the owner; the contract containing the terms and conditions of such an agreement.

graded or step-up lease. A lease with a rental payment that increases to specified amounts at specified periods of time.

ground lease. A lease for vacant land upon which the tenant may erect improvements.

index lease. A lease in which the rental payment varies in accordance with variation of an agreed-upon index of prices or costs.

lease with option to purchase. A lease in which the lessee has the right to purchase the real property for a stipulated price at or within a stipulated time.

leasehold, leasehold estate. An estate held under a lease.

net lease. A lease in which the tenant pays certain agreed-upon property expenses such as taxes or maintenance.

percentage lease. A lease in which the rental is based on a percentage of the lessee's sales income.

reappraisal lease. A lease in which an arrangement is made for determination of the amount of rent at some future period by independent appraisers.

tax participation clause (in a lease). An agreement in a lease where the lessee agrees to pay all or a stated portion of any increase in real estate taxes.

leasehold estate. *See* **estate,** *nonfreehold estate.*

legal description, land description. A means of identifying the exact boundaries of land by metes and bounds, by a plat, or by township and range survey system.

metes and bounds. "Metes" refers to measures; "bounds," to direction. Metes and bounds descriptions are means of describing land by measurement and direction from a known point or marker on land.

plat. A recorded map of land that identifies a parcel by a number or other designation in a subdivision.

township and range survey system. A system of legal description of land with a township as the basic unit of measurement; sometimes referred to as rectangular survey system or quadrangular survey.

base line. A parallel that serves as a reference for other parallels.

meridians. North–south lines of survey 6 miles apart.

parallel. East–west lines of survey 6 miles apart.

principal meridian. A meridian that serves as a reference for other meridians.

range. A north–south row of townships; the 6-mile strip of land between meridians.

section. A 1-mile square in a township.

tier. An east–west row of townships; the 6-mile strip of land between parallels.

township. A 6-mile square of land bounded by parallels and meridians, and composed of 36 sections.

lessee. The tenant under a lease; one who receives possession and use of real estate for a period of time in return for the payment of rent.

lessor. The landlord under a lease; one who grants permission and use of real estate for a specified period for a specified rent.

license law. Law that regulates the practices of real estate broker and salesmen.

lien. A claim against a property; the right to have the property of another sold to satisfy a debt.

lien theory of mortgage. The mortgage arrangement whereby title to mortgaged property vests in the borrower, with the lender having a lien against the property.

life estate. *See* **estate,** *life estate.*

limited partnership. An arrangement with two classes of partners—general and limited. The latter have little voice in management and no liability beyond their investments in the enterprise.

liquid assets. Things that can be converted immediately into cash.

listing. An agreement or contract between a principal and an agent providing that the agent will receive a commission for finding a buyer who is ready, willing, and able to purchase a particular property under terms specified by the agreement.

exclusive agency listing. A listing contract providing that the agent shall receive a commission if the property is sold as a result of the efforts of that agent or any other agent, but not as a result of the efforts of the principal; the contract further provides that the agent will receive a commission if a buyer is secured under the terms of the contract.

exclusive right-to-sell listing. A listing contract providing that the agent shall receive a commission if the property is sold irrespective of whether as a result of the efforts of that agent or another agent or the principal; the contract also provides that the agent shall receive a commission if a buyer is produced under the terms of the contract.

multiple listing. A listing that in addition to employing the agent, provides for the services of other agents who have agreed among themselves that they will cooperate in finding a purchaser for the property.

open listing. A listing contract providing that the agent shall receive a commission if the property is sold as a result of the efforts of that agent or if the agent produces a buyer under the terms of the contract before the property is sold.

localization of income. Income production at fixed locations; i.e., from real estate, which has a fixed and unique location.

location. Position of land and improvements in relation to other land and improvements and to local or general economic activity.

location quotient. An analytic technique using proportionality comparisons as, for example, the comparison of the percentage of an activity in a city with the percentage of the same activity in the nation.

loft building. An open floor, multistory building usually used for light manufacturing or warehousing.

lot. A specific plot of land.

MAI (Member Appraisal Institute). *See under* **appraiser.**

map. A representation of some feature on the earth's surface such as physical features or boundary lines and the like. *See* **plat, plat map; Sanborn insurance maps; time interval maps; topographical map.**

market. A set of arrangements for bringing buyers and sellers together through the price mechanism.

buyer's market. A market in which buyers can fulfill their desires at lower prices and on more advantageous terms than those prevailing earlier; a market characterized by many properties available and few potential users demanding them at prevailing prices.

capital market. The activities of all lenders and borrowers of equity and long-term debt funds.

market analysis. A study of the supply, demand, and price forces at work in a particular market; also, the process of studying supply, demand, and prices in a particular market, e.g., the real estate market.

money market. A market for funds.

seller's market. A market in which potential sellers can sell at prices higher than those prevailing in an immediately preceding period; a market characterized by very few properties available and a large number of users and potential users demanding them at prevailing prices.

meridian. *See* **legal description,** *township and range survey system.*

metes and bounds. A system of land description; "metes" refers to measures, "bounds" to direction. *See* **legal description,** *metes and bounds.*

model house. A house used for exhibition in order to sell other houses.

modular construction. Prefabrication in three dimensions; i.e., entire rooms of houses or apartments are built in the factory and shipped to their eventual location where very little on-site labor is required.

modular planning. The designing of structures using a designated size minimum dimension of length and width such as 4 feet.

monetary controls. Efforts by the Federal Reserve to influence the level of economic activity by regulating the availability of money and the rate of interest.

money market. *See* **market,** money market.

mortgage. The pledge of real property to secure a debt; the conveyance of real property as security for a debt; the instrument that is evidence of the pledge or conveyance.

assumption of mortgage. *See* **assumption of a mortgage.**

balloon mortgage payment. A large payment during the terms of a mortgage, often at the end.

blanket mortgage. A mortgage that has two or more properties pledged or conveyed as security for a debt, usually for subdividing and improvement purposes.

flexible payment mortgage. One that may be repaid in ways that vary from a set pattern.

junior mortgage. A second or third mortgage one that, in the event of liquidation, will not be paid off until after the senior mortgage.

mortgage bonds. Evidences of debt secured by a mortgage in favor of individual parties as a group, usually with the mortgage held by a third party in trust for the mortgage bond creditors.

mortgage broker. An agent who, for a commission, brings a mortgagor and mortgagee together.

mortgage company. A firm that, for a fee, brings mortgagor and mortgagee together or that acquires mortgages for the purpose of resale.

open-end mortgage. A mortgage with provisions for future advances to the borrower without the necessity of writing a new mortgage.

package mortgage. A mortgage in which the collateral is not limited to real property but includes personal property in the nature of household equipment.

purchase money mortgage. A mortgage that is given in part payment of the purchase price, in contrast to a mortgage that is given as security for repayment of funds.

subject to mortgage. Grantee takes title but is not responsible for mortgage beyond the value of his or her equity in the property. No deficiency judgment.

variable rate mortgage. Mortgage with an interest rate that changes with a designated index.

wraparound mortgage. A second mortgage, the face amount of which is equal to the unpaid balance of the first and second mortgages with the debt service handled by special arrangements.

Mortgage Bankers Association. A trade association of firms engaged in mortgage banking activities.

mortgagee. The creditor or lender under a mortgage.

mortgagor. The debtor or borrower under a mortgage.

motivation research. Analysis of consumers in an attempt to determine why prospective buyers react as they do to products or services or to advertisements used in attempting to sell to them.

multifamily structure. A dwelling for (usually) five or more household units.

multiple listing. *See* **listing,** *multiple listing.*

mutual saving bank. A financial institution in which the depositors are the owners. Mutual savings banks are a primary source of home mortgage funds.

National Association of Home Builders. A national trade association of house and apartment builders.

National Association of Mutual Savings Banks. A national trade association whose members are mutual savings banks.

National Association of Realtors®. A national real estate trade association. Includes such organizations as American Institute of Real Estate Appraisers, Institute of Farm Brokers, Institute of Real Estate Management, and others.

national income accounting. Statistical technique used in developing gross national product calculations; *see* **gross national product (GNP).**

national wealth statistics. Accounting technique for measuring the size and composition of wealth of the economic system and the changes in them.

neighborhood. A small area within a city that may be differentiated from adjacent areas, e.g., an area with homes of the same price range or people of the same income bracket. *See* **district.**

neighborhood life cycle. The succession of periods of growth, maturity, and decline that most neighborhoods tend to go through.

nonbasic employment, secondary employment, urban service employment. Usually refers to employment in establishments that receive their income from within the community. Contrast to basic employment.

nonbasic income. Usually refers to income that comes from within the community.

nonfreehold estate. *See* **estate,** *nonfreehold estate.*

obsolescence. Loss in property value because of the existence of a less costly alternative that provides comparable or more desirable property services.

open house. A house that is available for inspection by potential purchasers without appointments.

open listing. *See* **listing,** *open listing.*

operative builder. *See* **builder,** *operative builder.*

opinion of title. *See* **title,** *opinion of title.*

option (to purchase real estate). The right to purchase property at a stipulated price and under stipulated terms within a period of time; the instrument that is evidence of such a right.

ordinance. A public regulation such as a law (usually local laws).

orientation. The position of a structure on a site and its general relationship to its surroundings.

overbuilding. The building of more structures of a particular type than can be absorbed by the market at prevailing prices.

overimprovement. *See* **improvement,** *overimprovement.*

ownership of real property. The holding of rights or interests in real estate. *See* **estate,** *fee simple estate.*

PUD. *See* **planned unit development.**

package mortgage. *See* **mortgage,** *package mortgage.*

parallel. *See* **legal description,** *township and range survey system.*

parcel of real estate. A particular piece of land and its improvements.

parity. Equality; often used to refer to an equivalence between farmers' current purchasing power and their purchasing power at a selected base period maintained by government support of commodity prices.

parking lot. A parcel of real estate used for the storage of automobiles. Usually about 300 square feet per auto is required for parking space and aisles.

partially amortized mortgage. A combination of an amortized mortgage and a term mortgage (straight-term mortgage).

percentage lease. *See* **lease.**

perpetuity. Without limitation as to time, perpetual; as in capitalization in perpetuity.

personal property. The exclusive right to exercise control over personalty; all property objects other than real estate.

personalty. All property other than realty; chattels.

planned unit development (PUD). A design for an area which provides for intensive use of land often through a combination of private and common areas with arrangements for sharing responsibilities for the common areas. Typically, zoning boards consider the entire development and allow its arrangements to be substituted for traditional patterns. An example is a residential "cluster" development.

planning. The process of formulating a program in advance to achieve desired results.

> *long-range planning.* Planning for a period of years in the future. This type of planning is used as a framework for shorter-range planning.

plat, plat map. A map that shows boundary lines of parcels of real estate, usually of an area that has been subdivided into a number of lots. *See* **legal description,** *plat.*

plat book. A book containing a series of plat maps.

plottage. The extent to which value is increased when two or more lots are combined in a single ownership or use.

police power. The authority for governmental regulations necessary to safeguard the public health, morals, and safety and to promote the general welfare.

prefabrication. The process of manufacturing component parts of a structure in a factory for later assembly on-site.

present value. *See* **capitalization.**

price. That amount of money at which property is offered for sale or is exchanged for at a sale; value in terms of money.

principal. One who has another act for him or her; one who is represented by an agent. Also, the amount of a debt.

priority. A preferential rating; especially one that allocates scarce resources.

private property. *See* **property,** *private property.*

probate. The proof or act of proving at a court that a last will and testament is actually the last will and testament of a deceased person.

property. The exclusive right to exercise control over economic goods. *See* **personal property; real property.**

> *common property.* Ownership of a parcel of land by a number of people who hold their interests by virtue of ownership of adjoining parcels.
>
> *private property.* Property held by individuals or by groups of individuals except when such a group constitutes a public organization.
>
> *public property.* Property held by government.

property brief. A folder that presents pertinent information about a property.

property management. The operation of real property including the leasing of space, collection of rents, selection of tenants, and the repair and renovation of the buildings and grounds.

property owners' association, property owners' maintenance association. Organizations with the purpose of administering private regulations affecting land uses.

property services. The benefits accruing from the use of property.

property taxation. *See* **taxation,** *property taxation.*

proprietorship. A business that is run by its owner as an individual rather than as a corporation.

public housing. Housing owned by a governmental body.

public property. *See* **property,** *public property.*

purchase money mortgage. *See* **mortgage.**

purchase on contract. The purchase of property on installments with title remaining with the seller. *See* **land contract.**

purchasing power risk. Risk that the value of an investment will decline due to inflation (decline in the purchasing power of the dollar).

quadrangular survey system or rectangular survey. *See* **legal description, township and range survey system.**

R&D. *See* **research and development.**

range. *See* **legal description,** *township and range survey system.*

real estate. In a physical sense, land with or without buildings or improvements; in a legal sense, the rights in such physical objects.

real estate administration. *See* **administration of real estate resources.**

real estate appraisal. *See* **appraisal.**

real estate broker. An agent who negotiates the sale of real property or real property services for a commission that is contingent on success.

real estate business. The business that deals in rights to income or income potentials at fixed locations. It is concerned with production, marketing, and financing of these rights.

real estate developing. The process of preparing land for use, constructing buildings and other improvements, and making the completed properties available.

real estate financing. The channeling of savings into the production and use of real estate; facilitating the production and use of real estate through borrowed or equity funds. Also, the area of study dealing with the foregoing.

real estate investment corporation. A corporation that sells its securities to the public and has a special interest in real estate or is a builder or developer of real estate.

real estate investment trust. A trust established in a form similar to that of an investment or mutual fund for the purpose of allowing investors to channel funds into the real estate market in conformance with certain requirements for tax purposes.

real estate marketing. The process of putting real properties and their services into the hands of consumers. Brokerage and property management are the two main subdivisions of real estate marketing.

real estate operator. An individual engaged in the real estate business acting for himself or herself rather than as an agent.

real estate syndicate. A partnership organized for participation in a real estate venture. Partners may be limited or unlimited in their liability.

real property. The exclusive right to exercise control over real estate; a parcel of real estate.

real property taxation. *See* **taxation,** *real property taxation.*

Realtor®. A member of a local real estate board that is affiliated with the National Association of Realtors®.

Realtors National Marketing Institute. An organization of Realtors® designed to advance marketing methods and techniques.

realty. The property objects of land and all things permanently attached to it.

recapture. Usually a provision for assuring return of investment. It may be accomplished by inclusion in the capitalization rate in the income approach to valuation.

recorder. *See* **registrar of deeds.**

recording acts, registry laws. Laws that provide for the recording of instruments affecting title as a matter of public record and that preserve such evidence and give notice of their existence and content; laws providing that the recording of an instrument informs all who deal in real property of the transaction and that unless the instrument is recorded, a prospective purchaser without actual notice of its existence is protected against it.

rectangular survey. *See* **legal description.**

redemption. The regaining of title to real property after a foreclosure sale.

equity of redemption. The interest of the mortgagor in real property prior to foreclosure.

statutory right of redemption. The right under law of the mortgagor to redeem title to real property after a foreclosure sale.

redevelopment. Typically the process of clearance and reconstruction of blighted areas.

regional analysis. When applied to real estate, pertaining mainly to local economies and the surrounding area; for other purposes, the area of a "region" may be defined more broadly.

registrar of deeds, recorder. Officer in charge of a land records office.

registry laws. *See* **recording acts.**

regulations. Rules for controlling activities or procedures.

coercive regulations. Regulations which provide penalties for noncompliance.

inducive regulations. Regulations which provide incentive for compliance.

rehabilitation. The removal of blight by repair and renovation rather than by destruction of improvements.

remainder. The right of a person to interests that mature at the end of another estate; a classification of estates by time of enjoyment.

contingent remainder. An interest that will become a remainder only if some condition is fulfilled.

renewal. The process of redevelopment or rehabilitation in cities; often used in relation to rebuilding or restoration of blighted areas.

rent. The return on land or real property.

rent controls. The legal provision for a maximum rental payment for the use of real property.

rent multiplier. A factor or number used to estimate value by multiplying the rent. A rent multiplier may be either a gross rent multiplier or a net rent multiplier.

replacement cost. *See* **cost.**

reproduction cost. *See* **cost.**

research and development. The process of developing new products or new methods.

reserve for replacements. An allowance provided for the replacement of such items of equipment as appliances, elevators, carpeting, etc.

reversion. The residue of an estate left with the grantor that entitles him or her to possession after the end of another estate; a classification of estates by time of enjoyment.

rod. A unit of linear measure representing a length of 5½ yards.

SMSA. *See* **standard metropolitan statistical area.**

sale-leaseback. An arrangement that provides for a simultaneous transfer of ownership and execution of lease–the grantor becomes the lessee and the grantee the lessor.

sales kit. A file of information about the properties a broker has for sale.

Sanborn insurance maps. Maps showing locations of individual structures in many cities. Developed for underwriting insurance.

search of title. *See* **title,** *search of title.*

seasonal fluctuations. Variations in economic activity that recur at about the same time each year.

seasoned mortgage. A mortgage in which the principal has been reduced through amortization.

secondary employment. *See* **nonbasic employment.**

secondary income. *See* **nonbasic income.**

section. *See* **legal description,** *township and range survey system.*

sector theory. A theory of city growth that considers the city as a circle with wedge-shaped sectors pointing to the center. Sectors maintain this character as outward development occurs.

secular trend. *See* **trend.**

seller's market. *See* **market,** *seller's market.*

senior mortgage. A mortgage having a claim ranking above that of another mortgage.

shopping center. A planned shopping area, usually in outlying locations. Typically stores are surrounded by parking areas.

> *mall-type shopping center.* A shopping center in which the stores face inward upon an enclosed walkway rather than fronting on the parking lot, so that the shoppers can stay inside one building while they visit various stores.

> *super-regional shopping center.* A large shopping center with 250,000 to 1,000,000 square feet of store area, serving 200,000 or more people.

single-family home. A dwelling intended for occupancy by one household only.

site. A parcel of real estate that is improved or suitable for improvement.

situs. Location.

slum clearance. The removal of blighted improvements by destruction of the improvements. *See* **redevelopment; rehabilitation; renewal.**

Society of Industrial Realtors®. An association of Realtors® who specialize in industrial real estate. Members use the designation SIR.

Society of Real Estate Appraisers. A professional association of real estate appraisers.

"snob zoning." *See* **zoning.**

social contract. (business) A broad term relating to the laws and customs that have evolved to regulate relationships between business and society, indicating the rights and duties of each.

special assessment. *See* **assessment,** *special assessment.*

specific performance, specifically enforceable. The requirement that a party must perform as agreed under a contract in contrast to compensation or damages in lieu of performance; the arrangement whereby courts may force either party to a real estate contract to carry out an agreement exactly.

spot zoning. *See* **zoning,** *spot-zoning.*

standard metropolitan statistical area. A city or cities and their suburbs that constitute a single metropolitan area for statistical purposes. SMSA's must have a minimum population of 50,000.

standby commitment. A lender's agreement to provide a loan on stated conditions at a future date.

Statute of Frauds. Legislation providing that all agreements affecting title to real estate must be in writing to be enforceable.

statutory right of redemption. *See* **redemption,** *statutory right of redemption.*

straight-term mortgage. A mortgage in which repayment of principal is in one lump sum at maturity.

subcontractor. A contractor who contracts from another, usually a general contractor. A subcontractor usually is concerned only with one particular part of the improvement of real estate such as plumbing, masonry, carpentry, and the like.

subdivision. An area of land divided into parcels or lots generally of a size suitable for residential use.

subsidy. In real estate, a grant by government that eases the financial burden of holding, using, or improving real property.
> *direct subsidy.* A subsidy which is of direct, visible benefit to the recipient, such as a cash grant.
> *indirect subsidy.* A subsidy whose benefit is felt indirectly; e.g., tariffs or farm price supports may affect the land values in a particular area.

suburb. A development of real estate in areas peripheral to the central area of a city.

supermarket. A 20,000- to 40,000-square-foot grocery store that is often free-standing.

supersession costs. Costs incurred in scrapping existing improvements in order to make possible new land uses.

supply. Amount available for sale.

survey. A measurement of land to determine boundaries or points of location on land; the process of determining, or the map that shows, the exact dimension and location of a site and possibly such things as levels of the land by contour lines, boundaries and their relationship to natural formations, and the location of streets, sewers, water, and gas and electric lines.

sustained yield management. Selective harvesting of slow-growing crops such as trees to provide for a relatively stable yield every year rather than one large yield or irregular harvesting.

syndication. An arrangement whereby a group of individuals or legal entities combine to carry out a venture. Often the limited partnership is used as a structural form.

tax lien. A claim against property arising out of nonpayment of taxes; the claim may be sold by the taxing authority.

tax participation clause. *See* **lease.**

tax title. *See* **title,** *tax title.*

taxation. The right of government to payment for the support of activities in which it engages.

> *double taxation.* In real estate, the taxation of the property as an asset and the taxation of the property income the owner receives.
>
> *estate taxation.* Taxation imposed by government on property passed by will or descent.
>
> *inheritance taxation.* Taxation imposed on property received through inheritance.
>
> *property taxation.* Taxation imposed upon owners of property.
>
> *real property taxation.* Taxation imposed upon the owners of real property.

taxing district. The geographical area over which a taxing authority levies taxes.

tenancy. An interest in real property; the right to possession and use of real property.

> *at will.* By agreement of the parties, with no specified termination date.
>
> *joint tenancy.* A joint estate that provides for the right of survivorship; a joint estate in which the interest of joint tenants passes to the surviving joint tenant or tenants.
>
> *periodic tenancy.* The rights to use and occupancy under a lease that is renewed from period to period.
>
> *tenancy by entirety.* An estate held by husband and wife where both are viewed as one person under common law, which thus provides for the right of survivorship.
>
> *tenancy in common.* A joint estate in which each tenant in common (co-owner) may dispose of an interest by devise or descent.

tenure. The act, right, manner or term of holding something.

> *farmland tenure.* The sum total of the various agreements by which land is owned, rented, leased, used, controlled, and transferred.

term mortgage. *See* **straight-term mortgage.**

tier. *See* **legal description,** *township and range survey system.*

tilt-up construction. A method of building in which concrete wall sections are cast horizontally and then tilted or lifted into position.

time interval maps. A series of maps that show land use or some other feature as of different dates.

title. Proof or evidence of ownership or ownership rights.

> *abstract of title, abstract.* A historical summary of the conveyances, transfers, and other facts relied on as evidence of title; a summary of the documents having a bearing on the history of the title to a property.
>
> *cloudy title.* A title that would be impaired if an outstanding claim proved to be valid.
>
> *defective title.* A title that would be impaired if an outstanding claim proved to be valid and where such a claim could be shown to be valid.
>
> *opinion of title.* The statement, usually of an attorney, as to whether a title is believed to be clear or defective.
>
> *search of title.* A study of the history of the title to a property.

tax title. The title to real property acquired through a forced sale for taxes; an interest in real property that will become ownership if the defaulting taxpayer does not redeem the property.

title by descent. Title acquired by the laws of succession; title acquired by an heir in the absence of a will.

title by devise. Title received through a will.

title insurance. Insurance that a title is clear or clear except for defects noted; a policy of insurance that indemnifies the insured for loss occasioned by unknown defects of title.

title theory of mortgage. The mortgage arrangement whereby title to mortgaged real property vests in the lender.

topographical map. A map that shows the slope and contour of land; a map of the physical features of a parcel of real estate or an area of land.

topography. Contour and slope of land and such things as gullies, streams, knolls, and ravines.

Torrens system. A system of land title registration in which the state assures title.

township. *See* **legal description,** *township and range survey system.*

trade area. That geographical area from which purchasers of particular goods and services will ordinarily be drawn.

trade association. A voluntary organization of individuals or firms in a common area of economic activity; the organization has for its purpose the promotion of certain aspects of the common area of activity.

trade-up. *See* **filtering down.**

traffic count. The number of people and/or vehicles moving past a designated location during a stated period of time.

trend. A prevailing tendency of behavior of some observable phenomenon such as economic activity over time; a tendency that is exhibited over a long period of time despite intermittent fluctuations.

trust deed. An instrument that is evidence of the pledge of real property as security for a debt where the title to the real property is held by a third party in trust while the debtor repays the debt to the lender; the debtor is known as the *trustor;* the lender is known as the *beneficiary,* the third party is known as the trustee.

United States League of Savings Associations. A trade association of savings and loan associations.

urban growth employment. *See* **basic employment.**

urban plant. The community facilities that enable the community to function as a unit; e.g., the system of streets, sewers, water mains, parks, playgrounds, and the like.

urban renewal. *See* **renewal.**

urban service employment. *See* **nonbasic employment.**

urban size ratchet. The theory that once a town reaches a certain size, it will continue to grow of its own accord.

useful life. The period of time during which a structure may reasonably be expected to perform the functions for which it was designed.

user of real estate. One who has the use of property rights whether it be through ownership, lease, easement, or license.

valuation. *See* appraisal.

value of property. The usefulness of the property relative to its scarcity.

Veterans' Administration (VA). An agency of the federal government that, among other activities, guarantees loans made to veterans.

warehouse. A property used for storage of wares, goods, and merchandise.

wood frame construction. Walls and partition formed by wood framing of studs and other supports.

wraparound mortgage. *See* mortgage.

yield. Annual percentage return on capital.

zoning. Government regulation of land use; regulation by local government under police power of such matters as height, bulk, and use of buildings and of land.

    enabling act. A state statute necessary to provide a legal base for zoning codes.

    "snob zoning." Zoning regulations that require large lots, etc., as a method of excluding those in low-income groups.

    spot zoning. A case in which the zoning code allows pockets of nonconforming uses or where such pockets are allowed by variances.

    zoning variance. A legal exception to the zoning generally obtained through the zoning board or city council.

B

CODE OF ETHICS, NATIONAL ASSOCIATION OF REALTORS ®

Preamble . . .

Under all is the land. Upon its wise utilization and widely allocated ownership depend the survival and growth of free institutions and of our civilization. The REALTOR® should recognize that the interests of the nation and its citizens require the highest and best use of the land and the widest distribution of land ownership. They require the creation of adequate housing, the building of functioning cities, the development of productive industries and farms, and the preservation of a healthful environment.

Such interests impose obligations beyond those of ordinary commerce. They impose grave social responsibility and a patriotic duty to which the REALTOR® should dedicate himself, and for which he should be diligent in preparing himself. The REALTOR®, therefore, is zealous to maintain and improve the standards of his calling and shares with his fellow-REALTORS® a common responsibility for its integrity and honor. The term REALTOR® has come to connote competency, fairness, and high integrity resulting from adherence to a lofty ideal of moral conduct in business relations. No inducement of profit and no instruction from clients ever can justify departure from this ideal.

In the interpretation of his obligation, a REALTOR® can take no safer guide than that which has been handed down through the centuries, embodied in the Golden Rule, "Whatsoever ye would that men should do to you, do ye so to them."

Accepting this standard as his own, every REALTOR® pledges himself to observe its spirit in all of his activities and to conduct his business in accordance with the tenets set forth below.

Article 1. The REALTOR® should keep himself informed on matters affecting real estate in his community, the state, and nation so that he may be able to contribute responsibly to public thinking on such matters.

Article 2. In justice to those who place their interests in his care, the REALTOR® should endeavor always to be informed regarding laws, proposed legislation, governmental regulations, public policies, and current market conditions in order to be in a position to advise his clients properly.

Article 3. It is the duty of the REALTOR® to protect the public against fraud, misrepresentation, and unethical practices in real estate transactions. He should endeavor to eliminate in his community any practices which could be damaging to the public or bring discredit to the real estate profession. The REALTOR® should assist the governmental agency charged with regulating the practices of brokers and salesmen in his state.

Article 4. The REALTOR® should seek no unfair advantage over other REALTORS® and should conduct his business so as to avoid controversies with other REALTORS®.

Article 5. In the best interests of society, of his associates, and his own business, the REALTOR® should willingly share with other REALTORS® the lessons of his experience and study for the benefit of the public, and should be loyal to the Board of REALTORS® of his community and active in its work.

Article 6. To prevent dissension and misunderstanding and to assure better service to the owner, the REALTOR® should urge the exclusive listing of property unless contrary to the best interest of the owner.

Article 7. In accepting employment as an agent, the REALTOR® pledges himself to protect and promote the interests of the client. This obligation of absolute fidelity to the client's interests is primary, but it does not relieve the REALTOR® of the obligation to treat fairly all parties to the transaction.

Article 8. The REALTOR® shall not accept compensation from more than one party, even if permitted by law, without the full knowledge of all parties to the transaction.

Article 9. The REALTOR® shall avoid exaggeration, misrepresentation, or concealment of pertinent facts. He has an affirmative obligation to discover adverse factors that a reasonably competent and diligent investigation would disclose.

Article 10. The REALTOR® shall not deny equal professional services to any person for reasons of race, creed, sex, or country of national origin. The REALTOR® shall not be a party to any plan or agreement to discriminate against a person or persons on the basis of race, creed, sex, or country of national origin.

Article 11. A REALTOR® is expected to provide a level of competent service in keeping with the Standards of Practice in those fields in which the REALTOR® customarily engages.

The REALTOR® shall not undertake to provide specialized professional services concerning a type of property or service that is outside his field of competence unless he engages the assistance of one who is competent on such types of property or service, or unless the facts are fully disclosed to the client. Any person engaged to provide such assistance shall be so identified to the client and his contribution to the assignment should be set forth.

The REALTOR® shall refer to the Standards of Practice of the National Association as to the degree of competence that a client has a right to expect the REALTOR® to possess, taking into consideration the complexity of the problem, the availability of expert assistance, and the opportunities for experience available to the REALTOR®.

Article 12.   The REALTOR® shall not undertake to provide professional services concerning a property or its value where he has a present or contemplated interest unless such interest is specifically disclosed to all affected parties.

Article 13.   The REALTOR® shall not acquire an interest in or buy for himself, any member of his immediate family, his firm or any member thereof, or any entity in which he has a substantial ownership interest, property listed with him, without making the true position known to the listing owner. In selling property owned by himself, or in which he has any interest, the REALTOR® shall reveal the facts of his ownership or interest to the purchaser.

Article 14.   In the event of a controversy between REALTORS® associated with different firms, arising out of their relationship as REALTORS®, the REALTORS® shall submit the dispute to arbitration in accordance with the regulations of their board or boards rather than litigate the matter.

Article 15.   If a REALTOR® is charged with unethical practice or is asked to present evidence in any disciplinary proceeding or investigation, he shall place all pertinent facts before the proper tribunal of the member board or affiliated institute, society, or council of which he is a member.

Article 16.   When acting as agent, the REALTOR® shall not accept any commission, rebate, or profit on expenditures made for his principal-owner, without the principal's knowledge and consent.

Article 17.   The REALTOR® shall not engage in activities that constitute the unauthorized practice of law and shall recommend that legal counsel be obtained when the interest of any party to the transaction requires it.

Article 18.   The REALTOR® shall keep in a special account in an appropriate financial institution, separated from his own funds, monies coming into his possession in trust for other persons, such as escrows, trust funds, clients' monies, and other like items.

Article 19.   The REALTOR® shall be careful at all times to present a true picture in his advertising and representations to the public. He shall neither advertise without disclosing his name nor permit any person associated with him to use individual names or telephone numbers, unless such person's connection with the REALTOR® is obvious in the advertisement.

Article 20.   The REALTOR®, for the protection of all parties, shall see that financial obligations and commitments regarding real estate transactions are in writing, expressing the exact agreement of the parties. A copy of each agreement shall be furnished to each party upon his signing such agreement.

Article 21.   The REALTOR® shall not engage in any practice or take any action inconsistent with the agency of another REALTOR®.

Article 22.   In the sale of property which is exclusively listed with a REALTOR®, the REALTOR® shall utilize the services of other brokers upon mutually agreed upon terms when it is in the best interests of the client.

Negotiations concerning property which is listed exclusively shall be carried on with the listing broker, not with the owner, except with the consent of the listing broker.

Article 23. The REALTOR® shall not publicly disparage the business practice of a competitor nor volunteer an opinion of a competitor's transaction. If his opinion is sought and if the REALTOR® deems it appropriate to respond, such opinion shall be rendered with strict professional integrity and courtesy.

Article 24. The REALTOR® shall not directly or indirectly solicit the services or affiliation of an employee or independent contractor in the organization of another REALTOR® without prior notice to said REALTOR®.

Where the word REALTOR® is used in this Code and Preamble, it shall be deemed to include REALTOR®-ASSOCIATE. Pronouns shall be considered to include REALTORS® and REALTOR®-ASSOCIATES of both genders.

C

INTEREST AND ANNUITY TABLES *

In the calculation of present and future values, the following tables are useful. For each rate used, the six functions of $1 are shown in Columns 1–6. The seventh column on each page is a constant † table calculated on a monthly basis. The columns provide the following functions:

1. Amount of $1 — The amount to which $1 will grow in a given period of time, including the accumulation of interest at a given rate; sometimes called the future worth of $1.

2. Amount of $1 per Period — The amount to which a series of $1 installments will grow in a given number of periods with interest at a given rate; sometimes called the future worth of $1 per period.

3. Sinking Fund Factor — The fraction of $1 which must be deposited periodically in order to grow to $1 in a given period of time, including the accumulation of interest at a given rate; sometimes called the amortization rate.

4. Present Worth of $1 — The present value of $1 to be collected in the future, discounted for a given period of time at a given rate of interest; sometimes called the reversion factor.

5. Present Worth of $1 per Period — The present value of a series of future $1 payments for a given period of time, discounted at a given rate of interest; sometimes called the Inwood Coefficient or Inwood Factor.

6. Partial Payment — The level periodic payment required for both principal and interest on a loan of $1 for a given period of time, with interest at a given rate; also known as the installment to amortize $1, or mortgage requirement, or annuity worth $1 today, and the constant calculated as one payment per year.

7. Annual Constant — The annual constant is related to the partial payment. The difference is that it is computed with *monthly* rather than yearly compounding, using a monthly effective interest rate. For example, the annual constant for a 20-year loan at a nominal rate of 9 per cent to be serviced with level monthly payments would be based on an effective interest rate of .0075 per cent ($\frac{1}{12}$ of the nominal rate) and a term of 240 months. The arithmetic of computing the annual constant is the same as the arithmetic used for computing the partial payment function except that interest is compounded at $\frac{1}{12}$ the rate for 12 times as many intervals. Column 7 in the following tables is, therefore, always slightly less than the corresponding partial payment in Column 6.

* Used with permission of American Institute of Real Estate Appraisers, Chicago.

† A constant is the annual or monthly level payment to amortize a mortgage and pay the interest due on the balance on an annual basis calculated as follows:

Annual Payments ÷ Beginning Mortgage Balance, illustrated as:
$10,000 ÷ $100,000 = 10% Constant

Column 6 reports the yearly payment to repay $1 with interest. Column 7 is the annual constant based on *monthly* payments.

4% RATE I

YEARS	1 AMOUNT OF $1 The amount to which $1 will grow with compound interest	2 AMOUNT OF $1 PER YEAR The amount to which $1 per year will grow with compound interest	3 SINKING FUND FACTOR The amount per year which will grow with compound interest to $1	4 PRESENT WORTH OF $1 What $1 due in the future is worth today	5 PRESENT WORTH OF $1 PER YEAR What $1 payable yearly is worth today	6 PARTIAL PAYMENT The yearly installment to repay $1 with interest	ANNUAL CONSTANT FOR MONTHLY PAYT LOAN Annual debt service per $1 of loan (Divide by 12 to obtain monthly payment)	YEARS
1	1.040 000	1.000 000	1.000 000	.961 538	.961 538	1.040 000	1.021 7989	1
2	1.081 600	2.040 000	.490 196	.924 556	1.886 095	.530 196	.521 0991	2
3	1.124 864	3.121 600	.320 349	.888 996	2.775 091	.360 349	.354 2878	3
4	1.169 859	4.246 464	.235 490	.854 804	3.629 895	.275 490	.270 9487	4
5	1.216 653	5.416 323	.184 627	.821 927	4.451 822	.224 627	.220 9983	5
6	1.265 319	6.632 975	.150 762	.790 315	5.242 137	.190 762	.187 7422	6
7	1.315 932	7.898 294	.126 610	.759 918	6.002 055	.166 610	.164 0257	7
8	1.368 569	9.214 226	.108 528	.730 690	6.732 745	.148 528	.146 2713	8
9	1.423 312	10.582 795	.094 493	.702 587	7.435 332	.134 493	.132 4916	9
10	1.480 244	12.006 107	.083 291	.675 564	8.110 896	.123 291	.121 4942	10
11	1.539 454	13.486 351	.074 149	.649 581	8.760 477	.114 149	.112 5201	11
12	1.601 032	15.025 805	.066 552	.624 597	9.385 074	.106 552	.105 0634	12
13	1.665 074	16.626 838	.060 144	.600 574	9.985 648	.100 144	.098 7739	13
14	1.731 676	18.291 911	.054 669	.577 475	10.563 123	.094 669	.093 4015	14
15	1.800 944	20.023 588	.049 941	.555 265	11.118 387	.089 941	.088 7626	15
16	1.872 981	21.824 531	.045 820	.533 908	11.652 296	.085 820	.084 7195	16
17	1.947 900	23.697 512	.042 199	.513 373	12.165 669	.082 199	.081 1672	17
18	2.025 817	25.645 413	.038 993	.493 628	12.659 297	.078 993	.078 0237	18
19	2.106 849	27.671 229	.036 139	.474 642	13.133 939	.076 139	.075 2244	19
20	2.191 123	29.778 079	.033 582	.456 387	13.590 326	.073 582	.072 7176	20
21	2.278 768	31.969 202	.031 280	.438 834	14.029 160	.071 280	.070 4615	21
22	2.369 919	34.247 970	.029 199	.421 955	14.451 115	.069 199	.068 4217	22
23	2.464 716	36.617 889	.027 309	.405 726	14.856 842	.067 309	.066 5701	23
24	2.563 304	39.082 604	.025 587	.390 121	15.246 963	.065 587	.064 8829	24
25	2.665 836	41.645 908	.024 012	.375 117	15.622 080	.064 012	.063 3404	25
26	2.772 470	44.311 745	.022 567	.360 689	15.982 769	.062 567	.061 9259	26
27	2.883 369	47.084 214	.021 239	.346 817	16.329 586	.061 239	.060 6250	27
28	2.998 703	49.967 583	.020 013	.333 477	16.663 063	.060 013	.059 4255	28
29	3.118 651	52.966 286	.018 880	.320 651	16.983 715	.058 880	.058 3168	29
30	3.243 398	56.084 938	.017 830	.308 319	17.292 033	.057 830	.057 2898	30

4% RATE I

n	$S^n = (1+I)^n$	$S_{\overline{n}|} = \dfrac{S^n - 1}{I}$	$\dfrac{1}{S_{\overline{n}|}} = \dfrac{I}{S^n - 1}$	$V^n = \dfrac{1}{S^n}$	$a_{\overline{n}|} = \dfrac{1 - 1/S^n}{I}$	$\dfrac{1}{a_{\overline{n}|}} = \dfrac{I}{1 - 1/S^n}$	$f = \dfrac{I}{1 - 1/S^{12n}}$	n
31	3.373 133	59.328 335	.016 855	.296 460	17.588 494	.056 855	.056 3366	31
32	3.508 059	62.701 469	.015 949	.285 058	17.873 551	.055 949	.055 4500	32
33	3.648 381	66.209 527	.015 104	.274 094	18.147 646	.055 104	.054 6241	33
34	3.794 316	69.857 909	.014 315	.263 552	18.411 198	.054 315	.053 8533	34
35	3.946 089	73.652 225	.013 577	.253 415	18.664 613	.053 577	.053 1330	35
36	4.103 933	77.598 314	.012 887	.243 669	18.908 282	.052 887	.052 4587	36
37	4.268 090	81.702 246	.012 240	.234 297	19.142 579	.052 240	.051 8268	37
38	4.438 813	85.970 336	.011 632	.225 285	19.367 864	.051 632	.051 2338	38
39	4.616 366	90.409 150	.011 061	.216 621	19.584 485	.051 061	.050 6767	39
40	4.801 021	95.025 516	.010 523	.208 289	19.792 774	.050 523	.050 1526	40
41	4.993 061	99.826 536	.010 017	.200 278	19.993 052	.050 017	.049 6592	41
42	5.192 784	104.819 598	.009 540	.192 575	20.185 627	.049 540	.049 1942	42
43	5.400 495	110.012 382	.009 090	.185 168	20.370 795	.049 090	.048 7555	43
44	5.616 515	115.412 877	.008 665	.178 046	20.548 841	.048 665	.048 3412	44
45	5.841 176	121.029 392	.008 262	.171 198	20.720 040	.048 262	.047 9498	45
46	6.074 823	126.870 568	.007 882	.164 614	20.884 654	.047 882	.047 5796	46
47	6.317 816	132.945 390	.007 522	.158 283	21.042 936	.047 522	.047 2293	47
48	6.570 528	139.263 206	.007 181	.152 195	21.195 131	.047 181	.046 8975	48
49	6.833 349	145.833 734	.006 857	.146 341	21.341 472	.046 857	.046 5830	49
50	7.106 683	152.667 084	.006 550	.140 713	21.482 185	.046 550	.046 2848	50
51	7.390 951	159.773 767	.006 259	.135 301	21.617 485	.046 259	.046 0019	51
52	7.686 589	167.164 718	.005 982	.130 097	21.747 582	.045 982	.045 7333	52
53	7.994 052	174.851 306	.005 719	.125 093	21.872 675	.045 719	.045 4781	53
54	8.313 814	182.845 359	.005 469	.120 282	21.992 957	.045 469	.045 2356	54
55	8.646 367	191.159 173	.005 231	.115 656	22.108 612	.045 231	.045 0050	55
56	8.992 222	199.805 540	.005 005	.111 207	22.219 819	.045 005	.044 7856	56
57	9.351 910	208.797 762	.004 789	.106 930	22.326 749	.044 789	.044 5768	57
58	9.725 987	218.149 672	.004 584	.102 817	22.429 567	.044 584	.044 3780	58
59	10.115 026	227.875 659	.004 388	.098 863	22.528 430	.044 388	.044 1887	59
60	10.519 627	237.990 685	.004 202	.095 060	22.623 490	.044 202	.044 0083	60

$S = 1 + I$

$S = 1 + I/12$

5% RATE I

YEARS	1 AMOUNT OF $1 The amount to which $1 will grow with compound interest	2 AMOUNT OF $1 PER YEAR The amount to which $1 per year will grow with compound interest	3 SINKING FUND FACTOR The amount per year which will grow with compound interest to $1	4 PRESENT WORTH OF $1 What $1 due in the future is worth today	5 PRESENT WORTH OF $1 PER YEAR What $1 payable yearly is worth today	6 PARTIAL PAYMENT The yearly installment to repay $1 with interest	ANNUAL CONSTANT FOR MONTHLY PAY'T LOAN Annual debt service per $1 of loan (Divide by 12 to obtain monthly payment)	YEARS
1	1.050 000	1.000 000	1.000 000	.952 381	.952 381	1.050 000	1.027 2898	1
2	1.102 500	2.050 000	.487 805	.907 029	1.859 410	.537 805	.526 4567	2
3	1.157 625	3.152 500	.317 209	.863 838	2.723 248	.367 209	.359 6508	3
4	1.215 506	4.310 125	.232 012	.822 702	3.545 951	.282 012	.276 3515	4
5	1.276 282	5.525 631	.180 975	.783 526	4.329 477	.230 975	.226 4548	5
6	1.340 096	6.801 913	.147 017	.746 215	5.075 692	.197 017	.193 2592	6
7	1.407 100	8.142 008	.122 820	.710 681	5.786 373	.172 820	.169 6069	7
8	1.477 455	9.549 109	.104 722	.676 839	6.463 213	.154 722	.151 9190	8
9	1.551 328	11.026 564	.090 690	.644 609	7.107 822	.140 690	.138 2073	9
10	1.628 895	12.577 893	.079 505	.613 913	7.721 735	.129 505	.127 2786	10
11	1.710 339	14.206 787	.070 389	.584 679	8.306 414	.120 389	.118 3739	11
12	1.795 856	15.917 127	.062 825	.556 837	8.863 252	.112 825	.110 9868	12
13	1.885 649	17.712 983	.056 456	.530 321	9.393 573	.106 456	.104 7672	13
14	1.979 932	19.598 632	.051 024	.505 068	9.898 641	.101 024	.099 4645	14
15	2.078 928	21.578 564	.046 342	.481 017	10.379 658	.096 342	.094 8952	15
16	2.182 875	23.657 492	.042 270	.458 112	10.837 770	.092 270	.090 9217	16
17	2.292 018	25.840 366	.038 699	.436 297	11.274 066	.088 699	.087 4386	17
18	2.406 619	28.132 385	.035 546	.415 521	11.689 587	.085 546	.084 3641	18
19	2.526 950	30.539 004	.032 745	.395 734	12.085 321	.082 745	.081 6333	19
20	2.653 298	33.065 954	.030 243	.376 889	12.462 210	.080 243	.079 1947	20
21	2.785 963	35.719 252	.027 996	.358 942	12.821 153	.077 996	.077 0062	21
22	2.925 261	38.505 214	.025 971	.341 850	13.163 003	.075 971	.075 0337	22
23	3.071 524	41.430 475	.024 137	.325 571	13.488 642	.074 137	.073 2487	23
24	3.225 100	44.501 999	.022 471	.310 068	13.798 642	.072 471	.071 6277	24
25	3.386 355	47.727 099	.020 952	.295 303	14.093 945	.070 952	.070 1508	25
26	3.555 673	51.113 454	.019 564	.281 241	14.375 185	.069 564	.068 8012	26
27	3.733 456	54.669 126	.018 292	.267 848	14.643 034	.068 292	.067 5647	27
28	3.920 129	58.402 583	.017 123	.255 094	14.898 127	.067 123	.066 4289	28
29	4.116 136	62.322 712	.016 046	.242 946	15.141 074	.066 046	.065 3832	29
30	4.321 942	66.438 848	.015 051	.231 377	15.372 451	.065 051	.064 4186	30

5% RATE I

n	$f = \dfrac{I}{1-1/S^{12n}}$	$\dfrac{1}{a_{\overline{n}\|}} = \dfrac{I}{1-1/S^n}$	$a_{\overline{n}\|} = \dfrac{1-1/S^n}{I}$	$V^n = \dfrac{1}{S^n}$	$\dfrac{1}{s_{\overline{n}\|}} = \dfrac{I}{S^n-1}$	$s_{\overline{n}\|} = \dfrac{S^n-1}{I}$	$S^n = (1+I)^n$	n
31	.063 5270	.064 132	15.592 811	.220 359	.014 132	70.760 790	4.538 039	31
32	.062 7013	.063 280	15.802 677	.209 866	.013 280	75.298 829	4.764 941	32
33	.061 9356	.062 490	16.002 549	.199 873	.012 490	80.063 771	5.003 189	33
34	.061 2242	.061 755	16.192 904	.190 355	.011 755	85.066 959	5.253 348	34
35	.060 5625	.061 072	16.374 194	.181 290	.011 072	90.320 307	5.516 015	35
36	.059 9462	.060 434	16.546 852	.172 657	.010 434	95.836 323	5.791 816	36
37	.059 3713	.059 840	16.711 287	.164 436	.009 840	101.628 139	6.081 407	37
38	.058 8346	.059 284	16.867 893	.156 605	.009 284	107.709 546	6.385 477	38
39	.058 3330	.058 765	17.017 041	.149 148	.008 765	114.095 023	6.704 751	39
40	.057 8636	.058 278	17.159 086	.142 046	.008 278	120.799 774	7.039 989	40
41	.057 4240	.057 822	17.294 368	.135 282	.007 822	127.839 763	7.391 988	41
42	.057 0120	.057 395	17.423 208	.128 840	.007 395	135.231 751	7.761 588	42
43	.056 6255	.056 993	17.545 912	.122 704	.006 993	142.993 339	8.149 667	43
44	.056 2626	.056 616	17.662 773	.116 861	.006 616	151.143 006	8.557 150	44
45	.055 9217	.056 262	17.774 070	.111 297	.006 262	159.700 156	8.985 008	45
46	.055 6012	.055 928	17.880 066	.105 997	.005 928	168.685 164	9.434 258	46
47	.055 2997	.055 614	17.981 016	.100 949	.005 614	178.119 422	9.905 971	47
48	.055 0159	.055 318	18.077 158	.096 142	.005 318	188.025 393	10.401 270	48
49	.054 7486	.055 040	18.168 722	.091 564	.005 040	198.426 663	10.921 333	49
50	.054 4967	.054 777	18.255 925	.087 204	.004 777	209.347 996	11.467 400	50
51	.054 2591	.054 529	18.338 977	.083 051	.004 529	220.815 396	12.040 770	51
52	.054 0351	.054 294	18.418 073	.079 096	.004 294	232.856 165	12.642 808	52
53	.053 8237	.054 073	18.493 403	.075 330	.004 073	245.498 974	13.274 949	53
54	.053 6241	.053 864	18.565 146	.071 743	.003 864	258.773 922	13.938 696	54
55	.053 4356	.053 667	18.633 472	.068 326	.003 667	272.712 618	14.635 631	55
56	.053 2575	.053 480	18.698 545	.065 073	.003 480	287.348 249	15.367 412	56
57	.053 0891	.053 303	18.760 519	.061 974	.003 303	302.715 662	16.135 783	57
58	.052 9300	.053 136	18.819 542	.059 023	.003 136	318.851 445	16.942 572	58
59	.052 7794	.052 978	18.875 754	.056 212	.002 978	335.794 017	17.789 701	59
60	.052 6370	.052 828	18.929 290	.053 536	.002 828	353.583 718	18.679 186	60

$S = 1 + I/12$

$S = 1 + I$

6% RATE I

YEARS	1 AMOUNT OF $1 — The amount to which $1 will grow with compound interest	2 AMOUNT OF $1 PER YEAR — The amount to which $1 per year will grow with compound interest	3 SINKING FUND FACTOR — The amount per year which will grow with compound interest to $1	4 PRESENT WORTH OF $1 — What $1 due in the future is worth today	5 PRESENT WORTH OF $1 PER YEAR — What $1 payable yearly is worth today	6 PARTIAL PAYMENT — The yearly installment to repay $1 with interest	ANNUAL CONSTANT FOR MONTHLY PAYT LOAN — Annual debt service per $1 of loan (Divide by 12 to obtain monthly payment)	YEARS
1	1.060 000	1.000 000	1.000 000	.943 396	.943 396	1.060 000	1.032 7972	1
2	1.123 600	2.060 000	.485 437	.889 996	1.833 393	.545 437	.531 8473	2
3	1.191 016	3.183 600	.314 110	.839 619	2.673 012	.374 110	.365 0632	3
4	1.262 477	4.374 616	.228 591	.792 094	3.465 106	.288 591	.281 8203	4
5	1.338 226	5.637 093	.177 396	.747 258	4.212 364	.237 396	.231 9936	5
6	1.418 519	6.975 319	.143 363	.704 961	4.917 324	.203 363	.198 8747	6
7	1.503 630	8.393 838	.119 135	.665 057	5.582 381	.179 135	.175 3027	7
8	1.593 848	9.897 468	.101 036	.627 412	6.209 794	.161 036	.157 6972	8
9	1.689 479	11.491 316	.087 022	.591 898	6.801 692	.147 022	.144 0690	9
10	1.790 848	13.180 795	.075 868	.558 395	7.360 087	.135 868	.133 2246	10
11	1.898 299	14.971 643	.066 793	.526 788	7.886 875	.126 793	.124 4044	11
12	2.012 196	16.869 941	.059 277	.496 969	8.383 844	.119 277	.117 1020	12
13	2.132 928	18.882 138	.052 960	.468 839	8.852 683	.112 960	.110 9668	13
14	2.260 904	21.015 066	.047 585	.442 301	9.294 984	.107 585	.105 7483	14
15	2.396 558	23.275 970	.042 963	.417 265	9.712 249	.102 963	.101 2628	15
16	2.540 352	25.672 528	.038 952	.393 646	10.105 895	.098 952	.097 3725	16
17	2.692 773	28.212 880	.035 445	.371 364	10.477 260	.095 445	.093 9721	17
18	2.854 339	30.905 653	.032 357	.350 344	10.827 603	.092 357	.090 9795	18
19	3.025 600	33.759 992	.029 621	.330 513	11.158 116	.089 621	.088 3300	19
20	3.207 135	36.785 591	.027 185	.311 805	11.469 921	.087 185	.085 9717	20
21	3.399 564	39.992 727	.025 005	.294 155	11.764 077	.085 005	.083 8628	21
22	3.603 537	43.392 290	.023 046	.277 505	12.041 582	.083 046	.081 9689	22
23	3.819 750	46.995 828	.021 278	.261 797	12.303 379	.081 278	.080 2617	23
24	4.048 935	50.815 577	.019 679	.246 979	12.550 358	.079 679	.078 7174	24
25	4.291 871	54.864 512	.018 227	.232 999	12.783 356	.078 227	.077 3162	25
26	4.549 383	59.156 383	.016 904	.219 810	13.003 166	.076 904	.076 0412	26
27	4.822 346	63.705 766	.015 697	.207 368	13.210 534	.075 697	.074 8782	27
28	5.111 687	68.528 112	.014 593	.195 630	13.406 164	.074 593	.073 8149	28
29	5.418 388	73.639 798	.013 580	.184 557	13.590 721	.073 580	.072 8406	29
30	5.743 491	79.058 186	.012 649	.174 110	13.764 831	.072 649	.071 9461	30

6% RATE I

n	$S^n=(1+I)^n$	$S_{\overline{n}|}=\dfrac{S^n-1}{I}$	$\dfrac{1}{S_{\overline{n}|}}=\dfrac{I}{S^n-1}$	$V^n=\dfrac{1}{S^n}$	$a_{\overline{n}|}=\dfrac{1-1/S^n}{I}$	$\dfrac{1}{a_{\overline{n}|}}=\dfrac{I}{1-1/S^n}$	$f=\dfrac{I}{1-1/S^{12n}}$
31	6.088 101	84.801 677	.011 792	.164 255	13.929 086	.071 792	.071 1234
32	6.453 387	90.889 778	.011 002	.154 957	14.084 043	.071 002	.070 3656
33	6.840 590	97.343 165	.010 273	.146 186	14.230 230	.070 273	.069 6664
34	7.251 025	104.183 755	.009 598	.137 912	14.368 141	.069 598	.069 0204
35	7.686 087	111.434 780	.008 974	.130 105	14.498 246	.068 974	.068 4228
36	8.147 252	119.120 867	.008 395	.122 741	14.620 987	.068 395	.067 8693
37	8.636 087	127.268 119	.007 857	.115 793	14.736 780	.067 857	.067 3561
38	9.154 252	135.904 206	.007 358	.109 239	14.846 019	.067 358	.066 8797
39	9.703 507	145.058 458	.006 894	.103 056	14.949 075	.066 894	.066 4372
40	10.285 718	154.761 966	.006 462	.097 222	15.046 297	.066 462	.066 0256
41	10.902 861	165.047 684	.006 059	.091 719	15.138 016	.066 059	.065 6427
42	11.557 033	175.950 545	.005 683	.086 527	15.224 543	.065 683	.065 2860
43	12.250 455	187.507 577	.005 333	.081 630	15.306 173	.065 333	.064 9535
44	12.985 482	199.758 032	.005 006	.077 009	15.383 182	.065 006	.064 6435
45	13.764 611	212.743 514	.004 700	.072 650	15.455 832	.064 700	.064 3541
46	14.590 487	226.508 125	.004 415	.068 538	15.524 370	.064 415	.064 0840
47	15.465 917	241.098 612	.004 148	.064 658	15.589 028	.064 148	.063 8316
48	16.393 872	256.564 529	.003 898	.060 998	15.650 027	.063 898	.063 5956
49	17.377 504	272.958 401	.003 664	.057 546	15.707 572	.063 664	.063 3750
50	18.420 154	290.335 905	.003 444	.054 288	15.761 861	.063 444	.063 1686
51	19.525 364	308.756 059	.003 239	.051 215	15.813 076	.063 239	.062 9754
52	20.696 885	328.281 422	.003 046	.048 316	15.861 393	.063 046	.062 7945
53	21.938 698	348.978 308	.002 866	.045 582	15.906 974	.062 866	.062 6250
54	23.255 020	370.917 006	.002 696	.043 001	15.949 976	.062 696	.062 4663
55	24.650 322	394.172 027	.002 537	.040 567	15.990 543	.062 537	.062 3174
56	26.129 341	418.822 348	.002 388	.038 271	16.028 814	.062 388	.062 1779
57	27.697 101	444.951 689	.002 247	.036 105	16.064 919	.062 247	.062 0471
58	29.358 927	472.648 790	.002 116	.034 061	16.098 980	.062 116	.061 9243
59	31.120 463	502.007 718	.001 992	.032 133	16.131 113	.061 992	.061 8092
60	32.987 691	533.128 181	.001 876	.030 314	16.161 428	.061 876	.061 7011

$S=1+I$

$S=1+I/12$

7% RATE I

YEARS	1 AMOUNT OF $1 — The amount to which $1 will grow with compound interest	2 AMOUNT OF $1 PER YEAR — The amount to which $1 per year will grow with compound interest	3 SINKING FUND FACTOR — The amount per year which will grow with compound interest to $1	4 PRESENT WORTH OF $1 — What $1 due in the future is worth today	5 PRESENT WORTH OF $1 PER YEAR — What $1 payable yearly is worth today	6 PARTIAL PAYMENT — The yearly installment to repay $1 with interest	ANNUAL CONSTANT FOR MONTHLY PAY'T LOAN — Annual debt service per $1 of loan (Divide by 12 to obtain monthly payment)	YEARS
1	1.070 000	1.000 000	1.000 000	.934 579	.934 579	1.070 000	1.038 3210	1
2	1.144 900	2.070 000	.483 092	.873 439	1.808 018	.553 092	.537 2709	2
3	1.225 043	3.214 900	.311 052	.816 298	2.624 316	.381 052	.370 5252	3
4	1.310 796	4.439 943	.225 228	.762 895	3.387 211	.295 228	.287 3549	4
5	1.402 552	5.750 739	.173 891	.712 986	4.100 197	.243 891	.237 6144	5
6	1.500 730	7.153 291	.139 796	.666 342	4.766 540	.209 796	.204 5881	6
7	1.605 781	8.654 021	.115 553	.622 750	5.389 289	.185 553	.181 1122	7
8	1.718 186	10.259 803	.097 468	.582 009	5.971 299	.167 468	.163 6046	8
9	1.838 459	11.977 989	.083 486	.543 934	6.515 232	.153 486	.150 0753	9
10	1.967 151	13.816 448	.072 378	.508 349	7.023 582	.142 378	.139 3302	10
11	2.104 852	15.783 599	.063 357	.475 093	7.498 674	.133 357	.130 6092	11
12	2.252 192	17.888 451	.055 902	.444 012	7.942 686	.125 902	.123 4057	12
13	2.409 845	20.140 643	.049 651	.414 964	8.357 651	.119 651	.117 3689	13
14	2.578 534	22.550 488	.044 345	.387 817	8.745 468	.114 345	.112 2481	14
15	2.759 032	25.129 022	.039 795	.362 446	9.107 914	.109 795	.107 8594	15
16	2.952 164	27.888 054	.035 858	.338 735	9.446 649	.105 858	.104 0650	16
17	3.158 815	30.840 217	.032 425	.316 574	9.763 223	.102 425	.100 7593	17
18	3.379 932	33.999 033	.029 413	.295 864	10.059 087	.099 413	.097 8603	18
19	3.616 528	37.378 965	.026 753	.276 508	10.335 595	.096 753	.095 3031	19
20	3.869 684	40.995 492	.024 393	.258 419	10.594 014	.094 393	.093 0359	20
21	4.140 562	44.865 177	.022 289	.241 513	10.835 527	.092 289	.091 0166	21
22	4.430 402	49.005 739	.020 406	.225 713	11.061 240	.090 406	.089 2109	22
23	4.740 530	53.436 141	.018 714	.210 947	11.272 187	.088 714	.087 5903	23
24	5.072 367	58.176 671	.017 189	.197 147	11.469 334	.087 189	.086 1311	24
25	5.427 433	63.249 038	.015 811	.184 249	11.653 583	.085 811	.084 8135	25
26	5.807 353	68.676 470	.014 561	.172 195	11.825 779	.084 561	.083 6205	26
27	6.213 868	74.483 823	.013 426	.160 930	11.986 709	.083 426	.082 5378	27
28	6.648 838	80.697 691	.012 392	.150 402	12.137 111	.082 392	.081 5530	28
29	7.114 257	87.346 529	.011 449	.140 563	12.277 674	.081 449	.080 6556	29
30	7.612 255	94.460 786	.010 586	.131 367	12.409 041	.080 586	.079 8363	30

7% RATE I

n	$f=\dfrac{I}{1-1/S^{12n}}$	$\dfrac{1}{a_{\overline{n}}}=\dfrac{I}{1-1/S^{n}}$	$a_{\overline{n}}=\dfrac{1-1/S^{n}}{I}$	$V^{n}=\dfrac{1}{S^{n}}$	$\dfrac{1}{s_{\overline{n}}}=\dfrac{I}{S^{n}-1}$	$s_{\overline{n}}=\dfrac{S^{n}-1}{I}$	$S^{n}=(1+I)^{n}$	n
31	.079 0871	.079 797	12.531 814	.122 773	.009 797	102.073 041	8.145 113	31
32	.078 4009	.079 073	12.646 555	.114 741	.009 073	110.218 154	8.715 271	32
33	.077 7717	.078 408	12.753 790	.107 235	.008 408	118.933 425	9.325 340	33
34	.077 1939	.077 797	12.854 009	.100 219	.007 797	128.258 765	9.978 114	34
35	.076 6628	.077 234	12.947 672	.093 663	.007 234	138.236 878	10.676 581	35
36	.076 1740	.076 715	13.035 208	.087 535	.006 715	148.913 460	11.423 942	36
37	.075 7237	.076 237	13.117 017	.081 809	.006 237	160.337 402	12.223 618	37
38	.075 3086	.075 795	13.193 473	.076 457	.005 795	172.561 020	13.079 271	38
39	.074 9255	.075 387	13.264 928	.071 455	.005 387	185.640 292	13.994 820	39
40	.074 5718	.075 009	13.331 709	.066 780	.005 009	199.635 112	14.974 458	40
41	.074 2449	.074 660	13.394 120	.062 412	.004 660	214.609 570	16.022 670	41
42	.073 9426	.074 336	13.452 449	.058 329	.004 336	230.632 240	17.144 257	42
43	.073 6629	.074 036	13.506 962	.054 513	.004 036	247.776 496	18.344 355	43
44	.073 4039	.073 758	13.557 908	.050 946	.003 758	266.120 851	19.628 460	44
45	.073 1641	.073 500	13.605 522	.047 613	.003 500	285.749 311	21.002 452	45
46	.072 9418	.073 260	13.650 020	.044 499	.003 260	306.751 763	22.472 623	46
47	.072 7357	.073 037	13.691 608	.041 587	.003 037	329.224 386	24.045 707	47
48	.072 5446	.072 831	13.730 474	.038 867	.002 831	353.270 093	25.728 907	48
49	.072 3672	.072 639	13.766 799	.036 324	.002 639	378.999 000	27.529 930	49
50	.072 2026	.072 460	13.800 746	.033 948	.002 460	406.528 929	29.457 025	50
51	.072 0498	.072 294	13.832 473	.031 727	.002 294	435.985 955	31.519 017	51
52	.071 9078	.072 139	13.862 124	.029 651	.002 139	467.504 971	33.725 348	52
53	.071 7759	.071 995	13.889 836	.027 711	.001 995	501.230 319	36.086 122	53
54	.071 6534	.071 861	13.915 735	.025 899	.001 861	537.316 442	38.612 151	54
55	.071 5395	.071 736	13.939 939	.024 204	.001 736	575.928 593	41.315 001	55
56	.071 4336	.071 620	13.962 560	.022 621	.001 620	617.243 594	44.207 052	56
57	.071 3351	.071 512	13.983 701	.021 141	.001 512	661.450 646	47.301 545	57
58	.071 2435	.071 411	14.003 458	.019 758	.001 411	708.752 191	50.612 653	58
59	.071 1582	.071 317	14.021 924	.018 465	.001 317	759.364 844	54.155 539	59
60	.071 0790	.071 229	14.039 181	.017 257	.001 229	813.520 383	57.946 427	60

$$S=1+I/12$$

$$S=1+I$$

7½% RATE I

YEARS	1 AMOUNT OF $1 — The amount to which $1 will grow with compound interest	2 AMOUNT OF $1 PER YEAR — The amount to which $1 per year will grow with compound interest	3 SINKING FUND FACTOR — The amount per year which will grow with compound interest to $1	4 PRESENT WORTH OF $1 — What $1 due in the future is worth today	5 PRESENT WORTH OF $1 PER YEAR — What $1 payable yearly is worth today	6 PARTIAL PAYMENT — The yearly installment to repay $1 with interest	ANNUAL CONSTANT FOR MONTHLY PAYT LOAN — Annual debt service per $1 of loan (Divide by 12 to obtain monthly payment)	YEARS
1	1.075 000	1.000 000	1.000 000	.930 233	.930 233	1.075 000	1.041 0890	1
2	1.155 625	2.075 000	.481 928	.865 333	1.795 565	.556 928	.539 9951	2
3	1.242 297	3.230 625	.309 538	.804 961	2.600 526	.384 538	.373 2746	3
4	1.335 469	4.472 922	.223 568	.748 801	3.349 326	.298 568	.290 1468	4
5	1.435 629	5.808 391	.172 165	.696 559	4.045 885	.247 165	.240 4554	5
6	1.543 302	7.244 020	.138 045	.647 962	4.693 846	.213 045	.207 4813	6
7	1.659 049	8.787 322	.113 800	.602 755	5.296 601	.188 800	.184 0593	7
8	1.783 478	10.446 371	.095 727	.560 702	5.857 304	.170 727	.166 6064	8
9	1.917 239	12.229 849	.081 767	.521 583	6.378 887	.156 767	.153 1322	9
10	2.061 032	14.147 087	.070 686	.485 194	6.864 081	.145 686	.142 4421	10
11	2.215 609	16.208 119	.061 697	.451 343	7.315 424	.136 697	.133 7761	11
12	2.381 780	18.423 728	.054 278	.419 854	7.735 278	.129 278	.126 6272	12
13	2.560 413	20.805 508	.048 064	.390 562	8.125 840	.123 064	.120 6445	13
14	2.752 444	23.365 921	.042 797	.363 313	8.489 154	.117 797	.115 5772	14
15	2.958 877	26.118 365	.038 287	.337 966	8.827 120	.113 287	.111 2415	15
16	3.180 793	29.077 242	.034 391	.314 387	9.141 507	.109 391	.107 4993	16
17	3.419 353	32.258 035	.031 000	.292 453	9.433 960	.106 000	.104 2451	17
18	3.675 804	35.677 388	.028 029	.272 049	9.706 009	.103 029	.101 3968	18
19	3.951 489	39.353 192	.025 411	.253 069	9.959 078	.100 411	.098 8895	19
20	4.247 851	43.304 681	.023 092	.235 413	10.194 491	.098 092	.096 6712	20
21	4.566 440	47.552 532	.021 029	.218 989	10.413 480	.096 029	.094 6999	21
22	4.908 923	52.118 972	.019 187	.203 711	10.617 191	.094 187	.092 9412	22
23	5.277 092	57.027 895	.017 535	.189 498	10.806 689	.092 535	.091 3667	23
24	5.672 874	62.304 987	.016 050	.176 277	10.982 967	.091 050	.089 9526	24
25	6.098 340	67.977 862	.014 711	.163 979	11.146 946	.089 711	.088 6789	25
26	6.555 715	74.076 201	.013 500	.152 539	11.299 485	.088 500	.087 5289	26
27	7.047 394	80.631 916	.012 402	.141 896	11.441 381	.087 402	.086 4881	27
28	7.575 948	87.679 310	.011 405	.131 997	11.573 378	.086 405	.085 5441	28
29	8.144 144	95.255 258	.010 498	.122 788	11.696 165	.085 498	.084 6864	29
30	8.754 955	103.399 403	.009 671	.114 221	11.810 386	.084 671	.083 9057	30

7½% RATE I

n	$S^n=(1+I)^n$	$S_{\overline{n}\|}=\dfrac{S^n-1}{I}$	$\dfrac{1}{S_{\overline{n}\|}}=\dfrac{I}{S^n-1}$	$V^n=\dfrac{1}{S^n}$	$a_{\overline{n}\|}=\dfrac{1-1/S^n}{I}$	$\dfrac{1}{a_{\overline{n}\|}}=\dfrac{I}{1-1/S^n}$	$f=\dfrac{I}{1-1/S^{12n}}$	n
31	9.411 577	112.154 358	.008 916	.106 252	11.916 638	.083 916	.083 1941	31
32	10.117 445	121.565 935	.008 226	.098 839	12.015 478	.083 226	.082 5444	32
33	10.876 253	131.683 380	.007 594	.091 943	12.107 421	.082 594	.081 9505	33
34	11.691 972	142.559 633	.007 015	.085 529	12.192 950	.082 015	.081 4070	34
35	12.568 870	154.251 606	.006 483	.079 562	12.272 511	.081 483	.080 9091	35
36	13.511 536	166.820 476	.005 994	.074 011	12.346 522	.080 994	.080 4525	36
37	14.524 901	180.332 012	.005 545	.068 847	12.415 370	.080 545	.080 0333	37
38	15.614 268	194.856 913	.005 132	.064 044	12.479 414	.080 132	.079 6482	38
39	16.785 339	210.471 181	.004 751	.059 576	12.538 989	.079 751	.079 2942	39
40	18.044 239	227.256 520	.004 400	.055 419	12.594 409	.079 400	.078 9685	40
41	19.397 557	245.300 759	.004 077	.051 553	12.645 962	.079 077	.078 6686	41
42	20.852 374	264.698 315	.003 778	.047 956	12.693 918	.078 778	.078 3924	42
43	22.416 302	285.550 689	.003 502	.044 610	12.738 528	.078 502	.078 1378	43
44	24.097 524	307.966 991	.003 247	.041 498	12.780 026	.078 247	.077 9030	44
45	25.904 839	332.064 515	.003 011	.038 603	12.818 629	.078 011	.077 6863	45
46	27.847 702	357.969 354	.002 794	.035 910	12.854 539	.077 794	.077 4864	46
47	29.936 279	385.817 055	.002 592	.033 404	12.887 943	.077 592	.077 3018	47
48	32.181 500	415.753 334	.002 405	.031 074	12.919 017	.077 405	.077 1313	48
49	34.595 113	447.934 835	.002 232	.028 906	12.947 922	.077 232	.076 9737	49
50	37.189 746	482.529 947	.002 072	.026 889	12.974 812	.077 072	.076 8280	50
51	39.978 977	519.719 693	.001 924	.025 013	12.999 825	.076 924	.076 6934	51
52	42.977 400	559.698 670	.001 787	.023 268	13.023 093	.076 787	.076 5688	52
53	46.200 705	602.676 070	.001 659	.021 645	13.044 737	.076 659	.076 4536	53
54	49.665 758	646.876 776	.001 541	.020 135	13.064 872	.076 541	.076 3470	54
55	53.390 690	698.542 534	.001 432	.018 730	13.083 602	.076 432	.076 2484	55
56	57.394 992	751.933 224	.001 330	.017 423	13.101 025	.076 330	.076 1570	56
57	61.699 616	809.328 216	.001 236	.016 208	13.117 233	.076 236	.076 0725	57
58	66.327 087	871.027 832	.001 148	.015 077	13.132 309	.076 148	.075 9942	58
59	71.301 619	937.354 919	.001 067	.014 025	13.146 334	.076 067	.075 9217	59
60	76.649 240	1008.656 538	.000 991	.013 046	13.159 381	.075 991	.075 8546	60

$S=1+I$

$S=1+I/12$

8% RATE I

YEARS	1 AMOUNT OF $1 — The amount to which $1 will grow with compound interest	2 AMOUNT OF $1 PER YEAR — The amount to which $1 per year will grow with compound interest	3 SINKING FUND FACTOR — The amount per year which will grow with compound interest to $1	4 PRESENT WORTH OF $1 — What $1 due in the future is worth today	5 PRESENT WORTH OF $1 PER YEAR — What $1 payable yearly is worth today	6 PARTIAL PAYMENT — The yearly installment to repay $1 with interest	ANNUAL CONSTANT FOR MONTHLY PAYT LOAN — Annual debt service per $1 of loan (Divide by 12 to obtain monthly payment)	YEARS
1	1.080 000	1.000 000	1.000 000	.925 926	.925 926	1.080 000	1.043 8611	1
2	1.166 400	2.080 000	.480 769	.857 339	1.783 265	.560 769	.542 7275	2
3	1.259 712	3.246 400	.308 034	.793 832	2.577 097	.388 034	.376 0364	3
4	1.360 489	4.506 112	.221 921	.735 030	3.312 127	.301 921	.292 9551	4
5	1.469 328	5.866 601	.170 456	.680 583	3.992 710	.250 456	.243 3167	5
6	1.586 874	7.335 929	.136 315	.630 170	4.622 880	.216 315	.210 3989	6
7	1.713 824	8.922 803	.112 072	.583 490	5.206 370	.192 072	.187 0346	7
8	1.850 930	10.636 628	.094 015	.540 269	5.746 639	.174 015	.169 6402	8
9	1.999 005	12.487 558	.080 080	.500 249	6.246 888	.160 080	.155 2246	9
10	2.158 925	14.486 562	.069 029	.463 193	6.710 081	.149 029	.145 5931	10
11	2.331 639	16.645 487	.060 076	.428 883	7.138 964	.140 076	.136 9854	11
12	2.518 170	18.977 126	.052 695	.397 114	7.536 078	.132 695	.129 8943	12
13	2.719 624	21.495 297	.046 522	.367 698	7.903 776	.126 522	.123 9689	13
14	2.937 194	24.214 920	.041 297	.340 461	8.244 237	.121 297	.118 9582	14
15	3.172 169	27.152 114	.036 830	.315 242	8.559 479	.116 830	.114 6783	15
16	3.425 943	30.324 283	.032 977	.291 890	8.851 369	.112 977	.110 9910	16
17	3.700 018	33.750 226	.029 629	.270 269	9.121 638	.109 629	.107 7908	17
18	3.996 019	37.450 244	.026 702	.250 249	9.371 887	.106 702	.104 9955	18
19	4.315 701	41.446 263	.024 128	.231 712	9.603 599	.104 128	.102 5402	19
20	4.660 957	45.761 964	.021 852	.214 548	9.818 147	.101 852	.100 3728	20
21	5.033 834	50.422 921	.019 832	.198 656	10.016 803	.099 832	.098 4514	21
22	5.436 540	55.456 755	.018 032	.183 941	10.200 744	.098 032	.096 7413	22
23	5.871 464	60.893 296	.016 422	.170 315	10.371 059	.096 422	.095 2143	23
24	6.341 181	66.764 759	.014 978	.157 699	10.528 758	.094 978	.093 8465	24
25	6.848 475	73.105 940	.013 679	.146 018	10.674 776	.093 679	.092 6179	25
26	7.396 353	79.954 415	.012 507	.135 202	10.809 978	.092 507	.091 5118	26
27	7.988 061	87.350 768	.011 448	.125 187	10.935 165	.091 448	.090 5136	27
28	8.627 106	95.338 830	.010 489	.115 914	11.051 078	.090 489	.089 6110	28
29	9.317 275	103.965 936	.009 619	.107 328	11.158 406	.089 619	.088 7935	29
30	10.062 657	113.283 211	.008 827	.099 377	11.257 783	.088 827	.088 0517	30

8% RATE I

n	$S^n=(1+I)^n$	$S_{\overline{n}|}=\dfrac{S^n-1}{I}$	$\dfrac{1}{S_{\overline{n}|}}=\dfrac{I}{S^n-1}$	$V^n=\dfrac{1}{S^n}$	$a_{\overline{n}|}=\dfrac{1-1/S^n}{I}$	$\dfrac{1}{a_{\overline{n}|}}=\dfrac{I}{1-1/S^n}$	$f=\dfrac{I}{1-1/S^{12n}}$
31	10.867 669	123.345 868	.008 107	.092 016	11.349 799	.088 107	.087 3778
32	11.737 083	134.213 537	.007 451	.085 200	11.434 999	.087 451	.086 7645
33	12.676 050	145.950 620	.006 852	.078 889	11.513 888	.086 852	.086 2059
34	13.690 134	158.626 670	.006 304	.073 045	11.586 934	.086 304	.085 6964
35	14.785 344	172.316 804	.005 803	.067 635	11.654 568	.085 803	.085 2313
36	15.968 172	187.102 148	.005 345	.062 625	11.717 193	.085 345	.084 8063
37	17.245 626	203.070 320	.004 924	.057 986	11.775 179	.084 924	.084 4176
38	18.625 276	220.315 945	.004 539	.053 690	11.828 869	.084 539	.084 0619
39	20.115 298	238.941 221	.004 185	.049 713	11.878 582	.084 185	.083 7360
40	21.724 521	259.056 519	.003 860	.046 031	11.924 613	.083 860	.083 4374
41	23.462 482	280.781 040	.003 561	.042 621	11.967 235	.083 561	.083 1635
42	25.339 482	304.243 523	.003 287	.039 464	12.006 699	.083 287	.082 9123
43	27.366 640	329.583 005	.003 034	.036 541	12.043 240	.083 034	.082 6816
44	29.555 972	356.949 646	.002 802	.033 834	12.077 074	.082 802	.082 4697
45	31.920 449	386.505 617	.002 587	.031 328	12.108 402	.082 587	.082 2751
46	34.474 085	418.426 067	.002 390	.029 007	12.137 409	.082 390	.082 0962
47	37.232 012	452.900 152	.002 208	.026 859	12.164 267	.082 208	.081 9316
48	40.210 573	490.132 164	.002 040	.024 869	12.189 136	.082 040	.081 7803
49	43.427 419	530.342 737	.001 886	.023 027	12.212 163	.081 886	.081 6411
50	46.901 613	573.770 156	.001 743	.021 321	12.233 485	.081 743	.081 5129
51	50.653 742	620.671 769	.001 611	.019 742	12.253 227	.081 611	.081 3949
52	54.706 041	671.325 510	.001 490	.018 280	12.271 506	.081 490	.081 2863
53	59.082 524	726.031 551	.001 377	.016 925	12.288 432	.081 377	.081 1863
54	63.809 126	785.114 075	.001 274	.015 672	12.304 103	.081 274	.081 0941
55	68.913 856	848.923 201	.001 178	.014 511	12.318 614	.081 178	.081 0092
56	74.426 965	917.837 058	.001 090	.013 436	12.332 050	.081 090	.080 9310
57	80.381 122	992.264 022	.001 008	.012 441	12.344 491	.081 008	.080 8588
58	86.811 612	1072.645 144	.000 932	.011 519	12.356 010	.080 932	.080 7924
59	93.756 540	1159.456 755	.000 862	.010 666	12.366 676	.080 862	.080 7311
60	101.257 064	1253.213 296	.000 798	.009 876	12.376 552	.080 798	.080 6746

$S=1+I$ $\qquad$ $S=1+I/12$

8½% RATE I

YEARS	1 AMOUNT OF $1 — The amount to which $1 will grow with compound interest	2 AMOUNT OF $1 PER YEAR — The amount to which $1 per year will grow with compound interest	3 SINKING FUND FACTOR — The amount per year which will grow with compound interest to $1	4 PRESENT WORTH OF $1 — What $1 due in the future is worth today	5 PRESENT WORTH OF $1 PER YEAR — What $1 payable yearly is worth today	6 PARTIAL PAYMENT — The yearly installment to repay $1 with interest	ANNUAL CONSTANT FOR MONTHLY PAYT LOAN — Annual debt service per $1 of loan (Divide by 12 to obtain monthly payment)	YEARS
1	1.085 000	1.000 000	1.000 000	.921 659	.921 659	1.085 000	1.046 6374	1
2	1.177 225	2.085 000	.479 616	.849 455	1.771 114	.564 616	.545 4681	2
3	1.277 289	3.262 225	.306 539	.782 908	2.554 022	.391 539	.378 8104	3
4	1.385 859	4.539 514	.220 288	.721 574	3.275 597	.305 288	.295 7796	4
5	1.503 657	5.925 373	.168 766	.665 045	3.940 642	.253 766	.246 1984	5
6	1.631 468	7.429 030	.134 607	.612 945	4.553 587	.219 607	.213 3406	6
7	1.770 142	9.060 497	.110 369	.564 926	5.118 514	.195 369	.190 0378	7
8	1.920 604	10.830 639	.092 331	.520 669	5.639 183	.177 331	.172 7055	8
9	2.083 856	12.751 244	.078 424	.479 880	6.119 063	.163 424	.159 3522	9
10	2.260 983	14.835 099	.067 408	.442 285	6.561 348	.152 408	.148 7828	10
11	2.453 167	17.096 083	.058 493	.407 636	6.968 984	.143 493	.140 2367	11
12	2.661 686	19.549 250	.051 153	.375 702	7.344 686	.136 153	.133 2067	12
13	2.887 930	22.210 936	.045 023	.346 269	7.690 955	.130 023	.127 3415	13
14	3.133 404	25.098 866	.039 842	.319 142	8.010 097	.124 842	.122 3902	14
15	3.399 743	28.232 269	.035 420	.294 140	8.304 237	.120 420	.118 1687	15
16	3.688 721	31.632 012	.031 614	.271 097	8.575 333	.116 614	.114 5389	16
17	4.002 262	35.320 733	.028 312	.249 859	8.825 192	.113 312	.111 3951	17
18	4.342 455	39.322 995	.025 430	.230 285	9.055 476	.110 430	.108 6549	18
19	4.711 563	43.665 450	.022 901	.212 244	9.267 720	.107 901	.106 2535	19
20	5.112 046	48.377 013	.020 671	.195 616	9.463 337	.105 671	.104 1388	20
21	5.546 570	53.489 059	.018 695	.180 292	9.643 628	.103 695	.102 2687	21
22	6.018 028	59.035 629	.016 939	.166 167	9.809 796	.101 939	.100 6087	22
23	6.529 561	65.053 658	.015 372	.153 150	9.962 945	.100 372	.099 1304	23
24	7.084 574	71.583 219	.013 970	.141 152	10.104 097	.098 970	.097 8099	24
25	7.686 762	78.667 792	.012 712	.130 094	10.234 191	.097 712	.096 6273	25
26	8.340 137	86.354 555	.011 580	.119 902	10.354 093	.096 580	.095 5656	26
27	9.049 049	94.694 692	.010 560	.110 509	10.464 602	.095 560	.094 6105	27
28	9.818 218	103.743 741	.009 639	.101 851	10.566 453	.094 639	.093 7497	28
29	10.652 766	113.561 959	.008 806	.093 872	10.660 326	.093 806	.092 9725	29
30	11.558 252	124.214 725	.008 051	.086 518	10.746 844	.093 051	.092 2696	30

8½% RATE I

n	$f=\dfrac{I}{1-1/S^{12n}}$	$\dfrac{1}{a_{\overline{n}|}}=\dfrac{I}{1-1/S^n}$	$a_{\overline{n}|}=\dfrac{1-1/S^n}{I}$	$V^n=\dfrac{1}{S^n}$	$\dfrac{1}{S_{\overline{n}|}}=\dfrac{I}{S^n-1}$	$S_{\overline{n}|}=\dfrac{S^n-1}{I}$	$S^n=(1+I)^n$	n
31	.091 6332	.092 365	10.826 584	.079 740	.007 365	135.772 977	12.540 703	31
32	.091 0561	.091 742	10.900 078	.073 493	.006 742	148.313 680	13.606 663	32
33	.090 5322	.091 176	10.967 813	.067 736	.006 176	161.920 343	14.763 229	33
34	.090 0542	.090 660	11.030 243	.062 429	.005 660	176.683 572	16.018 104	34
35	.089 6233	.090 189	11.087 781	.057 539	.005 189	192.701 675	17.379 642	35
36	.089 2291	.089 760	11.140 812	.053 031	.004 760	210.081 318	18.856 912	36
37	.088 8700	.089 368	11.189 689	.048 876	.004 368	228.938 230	20.459 750	37
38	.088 5426	.089 010	11.234 736	.045 047	.004 010	249.397 979	22.198 828	38
39	.088 2439	.088 682	11.276 255	.041 518	.003 682	271.596 808	24.085 729	39
40	.087 9713	.088 382	11.314 520	.038 266	.003 382	295.682 536	26.133 016	40
41	.087 7223	.088 107	11.349 788	.035 268	.003 107	321.815 552	28.354 322	41
42	.087 4947	.087 856	11.382 293	.032 505	.002 856	350.169 874	30.764 439	42
43	.087 2864	.087 625	11.412 252	.029 959	.002 625	380.934 313	33.379 417	43
44	.087 0964	.087 414	11.439 864	.027 612	.002 414	414.313 730	36.216 667	44
45	.086 9223	.087 220	11.465 312	.025 448	.002 220	450.530 397	39.295 084	45
46	.086 7629	.087 042	11.488 767	.023 455	.002 042	489.825 480	42.635 166	46
47	.086 6170	.086 878	11.510 384	.021 617	.001 878	532.460 646	46.259 155	47
48	.086 4834	.086 728	11.530 308	.019 924	.001 728	578.719 801	50.191 183	48
49	.086 3610	.086 590	11.548 671	.018 363	.001 590	628.910 984	54.457 434	49
50	.086 2488	.086 463	11.565 595	.016 924	.001 463	683.368 418	59.086 316	50
51	.086 1461	.086 347	11.581 194	.015 599	.001 347	742.454 733	64.108 652	51
52	.086 0518	.086 240	11.595 570	.014 377	.001 240	806.563 386	69.557 888	52
53	.085 9654	.086 141	11.608 821	.013 250	.001 141	876.121 273	75.470 308	53
54	.085 8862	.086 051	11.621 033	.012 212	.001 051	951.591 582	81.885 284	54
55	.085 8136	.085 968	11.632 288	.011 255	.000 968	1033.476 866	88.845 534	55
56	.085 7469	.085 891	11.642 662	.010 374	.000 891	1122.322 400	96.397 404	56
57	.085 6858	.085 821	11.652 223	.009 561	.000 821	1218.719 804	104.591 183	57
58	.085 6297	.085 756	11.661 035	.008 812	.000 756	1323.310 987	113.481 434	58
59	.085 5782	.085 696	11.669 157	.008 122	.000 696	1436.792 421	123.127 356	59
60	.085 5309	.085 641	11.676 642	.007 485	.000 641	1559.919 777	133.593 181	60

$S=1+I/12$ $S=1+I$

9% RATE I

YEARS	1 AMOUNT OF $1 — The amount to which $1 will grow with compound interest	2 AMOUNT OF $1 PER YEAR — The amount to which $1 per year will grow with compound interest	3 SINKING FUND FACTOR — The amount per year which will grow with compound interest to $1	4 PRESENT WORTH OF $1 — What $1 due in the future is worth today	5 PRESENT WORTH OF $1 PER YEAR — What $1 payable yearly is worth today	6 PARTIAL PAYMENT — The yearly installment to repay $1 with interest	ANNUAL CONSTANT FOR MONTHLY PAYT LOAN — Annual debt service per $1 of loan (Divide by 12 to obtain monthly payment)	YEARS
1	1.090 000	1.000 000	1.000 000	.917 431	.917 431	1.090 000	1.049 4177	1
2	1.188 100	2.090 000	.478 469	.841 680	1.759 111	.568 469	.548 2169	2
3	1.295 029	3.278 100	.305 055	.772 183	2.531 295	.395 055	.381 5968	3
4	1.411 582	4.573 129	.218 669	.708 425	3.239 720	.308 669	.298 6205	4
5	1.538 624	5.984 711	.167 092	.649 931	3.889 651	.257 092	.249 1003	5
6	1.677 100	7.523 335	.132 920	.596 267	4.485 919	.222 920	.216 3064	6
7	1.828 039	9.200 435	.108 691	.547 034	5.032 953	.198 691	.193 0689	7
8	1.992 563	11.028 474	.090 674	.501 866	5.534 819	.180 674	.175 8024	8
9	2.171 893	13.021 036	.076 799	.460 428	5.995 247	.166 799	.162 5149	9
10	2.367 364	15.192 930	.065 820	.422 411	6.417 658	.155 820	.152 0109	10
11	2.580 426	17.560 293	.056 947	.387 533	6.805 191	.146 947	.143 5296	11
12	2.812 665	20.140 720	.049 651	.355 535	7.160 725	.139 651	.136 5637	12
13	3.065 805	22.953 385	.043 567	.326 179	7.486 904	.133 567	.130 7617	13
14	3.341 727	26.019 189	.038 433	.299 246	7.786 150	.128 433	.125 8725	14
15	3.642 482	29.360 916	.034 059	.274 538	8.060 688	.124 059	.121 7120	15
16	3.970 306	33.003 399	.030 300	.251 870	8.312 558	.120 300	.118 1419	16
17	4.327 633	36.973 705	.027 046	.231 073	8.543 631	.117 046	.115 0565	17
18	4.717 120	41.301 338	.024 212	.211 994	8.755 625	.114 212	.112 3734	18
19	5.141 661	46.018 458	.021 730	.194 490	8.950 115	.111 730	.110 0276	19
20	5.604 411	51.160 120	.019 546	.178 431	9.128 546	.109 546	.107 9671	20
21	6.108 808	56.764 530	.017 617	.163 698	9.292 244	.107 617	.106 1497	21
22	6.658 600	62.873 338	.015 905	.150 182	9.442 425	.105 905	.104 5409	22
23	7.257 874	69.531 939	.014 382	.137 781	9.580 207	.104 382	.103 1122	23
24	7.911 083	76.789 813	.013 023	.126 405	9.706 612	.103 023	.101 8397	24
25	8.623 081	84.700 896	.011 806	.115 968	9.822 580	.101 806	.100 7036	25
26	9.399 158	93.323 977	.010 715	.106 393	9.928 972	.100 715	.099 6868	26
27	10.245 082	102.723 135	.009 735	.097 608	10.026 580	.099 735	.098 7750	27
28	11.167 140	112.968 217	.008 852	.089 548	10.116 128	.098 852	.097 9560	28
29	12.172 182	124.135 356	.008 056	.082 155	10.198 283	.098 056	.097 2189	29
30	13.267 678	136.307 539	.007 336	.075 371	10.273 654	.097 336	.096 5547	30

n	$S^n=(1+I)^n$	$S_{\overline{n}}=\dfrac{S^n-1}{I}$	$\dfrac{1}{S_{\overline{n}}}=\dfrac{I}{S^n-1}$	$V^n=\dfrac{1}{S^n}$	$a_{\overline{n}}=\dfrac{1-1/S^n}{I}$	$\dfrac{1}{a_{\overline{n}}}=\dfrac{I}{1-1/S^n}$	$f=\dfrac{I}{1-1/S^{12n}}$
31	14.461 770	149.575 217	.006 686	.069 148	10.342 802	.096 686	.095 9554
32	15.763 329	164.036 987	.006 096	.063 438	10.406 240	.096 096	.095 4139
33	17.182 028	179.800 315	.005 562	.058 200	10.464 441	.095 562	.094 9242
34	18.728 411	196.982 344	.005 077	.053 395	10.517 835	.095 077	.094 4809
35	20.413 968	215.710 755	.004 636	.048 986	10.566 821	.094 636	.094 0792
36	22.251 225	236.124 723	.004 235	.044 941	10.611 763	.094 235	.093 7149
37	24.253 835	258.375 948	.003 870	.041 231	10.652 993	.093 870	.093 3843
38	26.436 680	282.629 783	.003 538	.037 826	10.690 820	.093 538	.093 0841
39	28.815 982	309.066 463	.003 236	.034 703	10.725 523	.093 236	.092 8114
40	31.409 420	337.882 445	.002 960	.031 838	10.757 360	.092 960	.092 5634
41	34.236 268	369.291 865	.002 708	.029 209	10.786 569	.092 708	.092 3378
42	37.317 532	403.528 133	.002 478	.026 797	10.813 366	.092 478	.092 1326
43	40.676 110	440.845 665	.002 268	.024 584	10.837 950	.092 268	.091 9457
44	44.336 960	481.521 775	.002 077	.022 555	10.860 505	.092 077	.091 7756
45	48.327 286	525.858 734	.001 902	.020 692	10.881 197	.091 902	.091 6206
46	52.676 742	574.186 021	.001 742	.018 984	10.900 181	.091 742	.091 4793
47	57.417 649	626.862 762	.001 595	.017 416	10.917 597	.091 595	.091 3505
48	62.585 237	684.280 411	.001 461	.015 978	10.933 575	.091 461	.091 2331
49	68.217 908	746.865 648	.001 339	.014 659	10.948 234	.091 339	.091 1260
50	74.357 520	815.083 556	.001 227	.013 449	10.961 683	.091 227	.091 0284
51	81.049 697	889.441 076	.001 124	.012 338	10.974 021	.091 124	.090 9392
52	88.344 170	970.490 773	.001 030	.011 319	10.985 340	.091 030	.090 8579
53	96.295 145	1058.834 943	.000 944	.010 385	10.995 725	.090 944	.090 7837
54	104.961 708	1155.130 088	.000 866	.009 527	11.005 252	.090 866	.090 7160
55	114.408 262	1260.091 796	.000 794	.008 741	11.013 993	.090 794	.090 6541
56	124.705 005	1374.500 057	.000 728	.008 019	11.022 012	.090 728	.090 5976
57	135.928 456	1499.205 063	.000 667	.007 357	11.029 369	.090 667	.090 5461
58	148.162 017	1635.133 518	.000 612	.006 749	11.036 118	.090 612	.090 4990
59	161.496 598	1783.295 518	.000 561	.006 192	11.042 310	.090 561	.090 4560
60	176.031 292	1944.792 133	.000 514	.005 681	11.047 991	.090 514	.090 4167

$S=1+I$

$S=1+I/12$

9½% RATE I

YEARS	1 AMOUNT OF $1 — The amount to which $1 will grow with compound interest	2 AMOUNT OF $1 PER YEAR — The amount to which $1 per year will grow with compound interest	3 SINKING FUND FACTOR — The amount per year which will grow with compound interest to $1	4 PRESENT WORTH OF $1 — What $1 due in the future is worth today	5 PRESENT WORTH OF $1 PER YEAR — What $1 payable yearly is worth today	6 PARTIAL PAYMENT — The yearly installment to repay $1 with interest	ANNUAL CONSTANT FOR MONTHLY PAYT LOAN — Annual debt service per $1 of loan (Divide by 12 to obtain monthly payment)	YEARS
1	1.095 000	1.000 000	1.000 000	.913 242	.913 242	1.095 000	1.052 2021	1
2	1.199 025	2.095 000	.477 327	.834 011	1.747 253	.572 327	.550 9739	2
3	1.312 932	3.294 025	.303 580	.761 654	2.508 907	.398 580	.384 3954	3
4	1.437 661	4.606 957	.217 063	.695 574	3.204 481	.312 063	.301 4776	4
5	1.574 239	6.044 618	.165 436	.635 228	3.839 709	.260 436	.252 0223	5
6	1.723 791	7.618 857	.131 253	.580 117	4.419 825	.226 253	.219 2963	6
7	1.887 552	9.342 648	.107 036	.529 787	4.949 612	.202 036	.196 1278	7
8	2.066 869	11.230 200	.089 046	.483 824	5.433 436	.184 046	.178 9306	8
9	2.263 222	13.297 069	.075 205	.441 848	5.875 284	.170 205	.165 7123	9
10	2.478 228	15.560 291	.064 266	.403 514	6.278 798	.159 266	.155 2771	10
11	2.713 659	18.038 518	.055 437	.368 506	6.647 304	.150 437	.146 8637	11
12	2.971 457	20.752 188	.048 188	.336 535	6.983 839	.143 188	.139 9648	12
13	3.253 745	23.723 634	.042 152	.307 338	7.291 178	.137 152	.134 2287	13
14	3.562 851	26.977 380	.037 068	.280 674	7.571 852	.132 068	.129 4042	14
15	3.901 322	30.540 231	.032 744	.256 323	7.828 175	.127 744	.125 3070	15
16	4.271 948	34.441 553	.029 035	.234 085	8.062 260	.124 035	.121 7987	16
17	4.677 783	38.713 500	.025 831	.213 777	8.276 037	.120 831	.118 7737	17
18	5.122 172	43.391 283	.023 046	.195 230	8.471 266	.118 046	.116 1494	18
19	5.608 778	48.513 454	.020 613	.178 292	8.649 558	.115 613	.113 8608	19
20	6.141 612	54.122 233	.018 477	.162 824	8.812 382	.113 477	.111 8557	20
21	6.725 065	60.263 845	.016 594	.148 697	8.961 080	.111 594	.110 0921	21
22	7.363 946	66.988 910	.014 928	.135 797	9.096 876	.109 928	.108 5354	22
23	8.063 521	74.352 856	.013 449	.124 015	9.220 892	.108 449	.107 1569	23
24	8.829 556	82.416 378	.012 134	.113 256	9.334 148	.107 134	.105 9330	24
25	9.668 364	91.245 934	.010 959	.103 430	9.437 578	.105 959	.104 8436	25
26	10.586 858	100.914 297	.009 909	.094 457	9.532 034	.104 909	.103 8719	26
27	11.592 610	111.501 156	.008 969	.086 262	9.618 296	.103 969	.103 0034	27
28	12.693 908	123.093 766	.008 124	.078 778	9.697 074	.103 124	.102 2258	28
29	13.899 829	135.787 673	.007 364	.071 943	9.769 018	.102 364	.101 5286	29
30	15.220 313	149.687 502	.006 681	.065 702	9.834 719	.101 681	.100 9025	30

n	$S^n=(1+I)^n$	$S_{\overline{n}}=\dfrac{S^n-1}{I}$	$\dfrac{1}{S_{\overline{n}}}=\dfrac{I}{S^n-1}$	$V^n=\dfrac{1}{S^n}$	$a_{\overline{n}}=\dfrac{1-1/S^n}{I}$	$\dfrac{1}{a_{\overline{n}}}=\dfrac{I}{1-1/S^n}$	$f=\dfrac{I}{1-1/S^{12n}}$
31	16.666 242	164.907 815	.006 064	.060 002	9.894 721	.101 064	.100 3396
32	18.249 535	181.574 057	.005 507	.054 796	9.949 517	.100 507	.099 8330
33	19.983 241	199.023 593	.005 004	.050 042	9.999 559	.100 004	.099 3765
34	21.881 649	219.806 834	.004 549	.045 700	10.045 259	.099 549	.098 9649
35	23.960 406	241.688 483	.004 138	.041 736	10.086 995	.099 138	.098 5934
36	26.236 644	265.648 889	.003 764	.038 115	10.125 109	.098 764	.098 2578
37	28.729 126	291.885 534	.003 426	.034 808	10.159 917	.098 426	.097 9545
38	31.458 393	320.614 659	.003 119	.031 788	10.191 705	.098 119	.097 6803
39	34.446 940	352.073 052	.002 840	.029 030	10.220 735	.097 840	.097 4321
40	37.719 399	386.519 992	.002 587	.026 512	10.247 247	.097 587	.097 2074
41	41.302 742	424.239 391	.002 357	.024 211	10.271 458	.097 357	.097 0039
42	45.226 503	465.542 133	.002 148	.022 111	10.293 569	.097 148	.096 8195
43	49.523 020	510.768 636	.001 958	.020 193	10.313 762	.096 958	.096 6524
44	54.227 707	560.291 656	.001 785	.018 441	10.332 203	.096 785	.096 5008
45	59.379 340	614.519 364	.001 627	.016 841	10.349 043	.096 627	.096 3634
46	65.020 377	673.898 703	.001 484	.015 380	10.364 423	.096 484	.096 2387
47	71.197 313	738.919 080	.001 353	.014 045	10.378 469	.096 353	.096 1255
48	77.961 057	811.116 393	.001 234	.012 827	10.391 296	.096 234	.096 0228
49	85.367 358	888.077 450	.001 126	.011 714	10.403 010	.096 126	.095 9295
50	93.447 257	973.444 808	.001 027	.010 698	10.413 707	.096 027	.095 8449
51	102.357 596	1066.922 065	.000 937	.009 770	10.423 477	.095 937	.095 7680
52	112.081 568	1169.279 661	.000 855	.008 922	10.432 399	.095 855	.095 6981
53	122.729 317	1281.361 229	.000 780	.008 148	10.440 547	.095 780	.095 6347
54	134.388 602	1404.090 545	.000 712	.007 441	10.447 988	.095 712	.095 5770
55	147.155 519	1538.479 147	.000 650	.006 796	10.454 784	.095 650	.095 5246
56	161.135 293	1685.634 666	.000 593	.006 206	10.460 990	.095 593	.095 4770
57	176.443 146	1846.769 959	.000 541	.005 668	10.466 657	.095 541	.095 4338
58	193.205 245	2023.213 106	.000 494	.005 176	10.471 833	.095 494	.095 3944
59	211.559 743	2216.418 351	.000 451	.004 727	10.476 560	.095 451	.095 3587
60	231.657 919	2427.978 094	.000 412	.004 317	10.480 877	.095 412	.095 3262

$$S = 1+I \qquad S = 1 + I/12$$

10% RATE I

YEARS	1 AMOUNT OF $1 — The amount to which $1 will grow with compound interest	2 AMOUNT OF $1 PER YEAR — The amount to which $1 per year will grow with compound interest	3 SINKING FUND FACTOR — The amount per year which will grow with compound interest to $1	4 PRESENT WORTH OF $1 — What $1 due in the future is worth today	5 PRESENT WORTH OF $1 PER YEAR — What $1 payable yearly is worth today	6 PARTIAL PAYMENT — The yearly installment to repay $1 with interest	ANNUAL CONSTANT FOR MONTHLY PAYT LOAN — Annual debt service per $1 of loan (Divide by 12 to obtain monthly payment)
1	1.100 000	1.000 000	1.000 000	.909 091	.909 091	1.100 000	1.054 9906
2	1.210 000	2.100 000	.476 190	.826 446	1.735 537	.576 190	.553 7391
3	1.331 000	3.310 000	.302 115	.751 315	2.486 852	.402 115	.387 2062
4	1.464 100	4.641 000	.215 471	.683 013	3.169 865	.315 471	.304 3510
5	1.610 510	6.105 100	.163 797	.620 921	3.790 787	.263 797	.254 9645
6	1.771 561	7.715 610	.129 607	.564 474	4.355 261	.229 607	.222 3101
7	1.948 717	9.487 171	.105 405	.513 158	4.868 419	.205 405	.199 2142
8	2.143 589	11.435 888	.087 444	.466 507	5.334 926	.187 444	.182 0900
9	2.357 948	13.579 477	.073 641	.424 098	5.759 024	.173 641	.168 9442
10	2.593 742	15.937 425	.062 745	.385 543	6.144 567	.162 745	.158 5809
11	2.853 117	18.531 167	.053 963	.350 494	6.495 061	.153 963	.150 2385
12	3.138 428	21.384 284	.046 763	.318 631	6.813 692	.146 763	.143 4094
13	3.452 271	24.522 712	.040 779	.289 664	7.103 356	.140 779	.137 7418
14	3.797 498	27.974 983	.035 746	.263 331	7.366 687	.135 746	.132 9843
15	4.177 248	31.772 482	.031 474	.239 392	7.606 080	.131 474	.128 9526
16	4.594 973	35.949 730	.027 817	.217 629	7.823 709	.127 817	.125 5082
17	5.054 470	40.544 703	.024 664	.197 845	8.021 553	.124 664	.122 5453
18	5.559 917	45.599 173	.021 930	.179 859	8.201 412	.121 930	.119 9812
19	6.115 909	51.159 090	.019 547	.163 508	8.364 920	.119 547	.117 7511
20	6.727 500	57.274 999	.017 460	.148 644	8.513 564	.117 460	.115 8026
21	7.400 250	64.002 499	.015 624	.135 131	8.648 694	.115 624	.114 0936
22	8.140 275	71.402 749	.014 005	.122 846	8.771 540	.114 005	.112 5895
23	8.954 302	79.543 024	.012 572	.111 678	8.883 218	.112 572	.111 2618
24	9.849 733	88.497 327	.011 300	.101 526	8.984 744	.111 300	.110 0866
25	10.834 706	98.347 059	.010 168	.092 296	9.077 040	.110 168	.109 0441
26	11.918 177	109.181 765	.009 159	.083 905	9.160 945	.109 159	.108 1172
27	13.109 994	121.099 942	.008 258	.076 278	9.237 223	.108 258	.107 2917
28	14.420 994	134.209 936	.007 451	.069 343	9.306 567	.107 451	.106 5552
29	15.863 093	148.630 930	.006 728	.063 039	9.369 606	.106 728	.105 8972
30	17.449 402	164.494 023	.006 079	.057 309	9.426 914	.106 079	.105 3086

n	$f=\dfrac{I}{1-1/S^{12n}}$ $S=1+I/12$	$\dfrac{1}{a_{\overline{n}}}=\dfrac{I}{1-1/S^{n}}$	$a_{\overline{n}}=\dfrac{1-1/S^{n}}{I}$	$V^{n}=\dfrac{1}{S^{n}}$	$\dfrac{1}{S_{\overline{n}}}=\dfrac{I}{S^{n}-1}$	$S_{\overline{n}}=\dfrac{S^{n}-1}{I}$	$S^{n}=(1+I)^{n}$ $S=1+I$	n
31	.104 7813	.105 496	9.479 013	.052 099	.005 496	181.943 425	19.194 342	31
32	.104 3086	.104 972	9.526 376	.047 362	.004 972	201.137 767	21.113 777	32
33	.103 8843	.104 499	9.569 432	.043 057	.004 499	222.251 544	23.225 154	33
34	.103 5033	.104 074	9.608 575	.039 143	.004 074	245.476 699	25.547 670	34
35	.103 1607	.103 690	9.644 159	.035 584	.003 690	271.024 368	28.102 437	35
36	.102 8526	.103 343	9.676 508	.032 349	.003 343	299.126 805	30.912 681	36
37	.102 5752	.103 030	9.705 917	.029 408	.003 030	330.039 486	34.003 949	37
38	.102 3254	.102 747	9.732 651	.026 735	.002 747	364.043 434	37.404 343	38
39	.102 1004	.102 491	9.756 956	.024 304	.002 491	401.447 778	41.144 778	39
40	.101 8975	.102 259	9.779 051	.022 095	.002 259	442.592 556	45.259 256	40
41	.101 7146	.102 050	9.799 137	.020 086	.002 050	487.851 811	49.785 181	41
42	.101 5495	.101 860	9.817 397	.018 260	.001 860	537.636 992	54.763 699	42
43	.101 4006	.101 688	9.833 998	.016 600	.001 688	592.400 692	60.240 069	43
44	.101 2662	.101 532	9.849 089	.015 091	.001 532	652.640 761	66.264 076	44
45	.101 1448	.101 391	9.862 808	.013 719	.001 391	718.904 837	72.890 484	45
46	.101 0351	.101 263	9.875 280	.012 472	.001 263	791.795 321	80.179 532	46
47	.100 9361	.101 147	9.886 618	.011 338	.001 147	871.974 853	88.197 485	47
48	.100 8466	.101 041	9.896 926	.010 307	.001 041	960.172 338	97.017 234	48
49	.100 7658	.100 946	9.906 296	.009 370	.000 946	1057.189 572	106.718 957	49
50	.100 6927	.100 859	9.914 814	.008 519	.000 859	1163.908 529	117.390 853	50
51	.100 6266	.100 780	9.922 559	.007 744	.000 780	1281.299 382	129.129 938	51
52	.100 5669	.100 709	9.929 599	.007 040	.000 709	1410.429 320	142.042 932	52
53	.100 5129	.100 644	9.935 999	.006 400	.000 644	1552.472 252	156.247 225	53
54	.100 4640	.100 585	9.941 817	.005 818	.000 585	1708.719 477	171.871 948	54
55	.100 4199	.100 532	9.947 106	.005 289	.000 532	1880.591 425	189.059 142	55
56	.100 3799	.100 483	9.951 915	.004 809	.000 483	2069.650 567	207.965 057	56
57	.100 3438	.100 439	9.956 286	.004 374	.000 439	2277.615 624	228.761 562	57
58	.100 3111	.100 399	9.960 260	.003 974	.000 399	2506.377 186	251.637 719	58
59	.100 2815	.100 363	9.963 873	.003 613	.000 363	2758.014 905	276.801 490	59
60	.100 2548	.100 330	9.967 157	.003 284	.000 330	3034.816 395	304.481 640	60

10½% RATE I

YEARS	1 AMOUNT OF $1 — The amount to which $1 will grow with compound interest	2 AMOUNT OF $1 PER YEAR — The amount to which $1 per year will grow with compound interest	3 SINKING FUND FACTOR — The amount per year which will grow with compound interest to $1	4 PRESENT WORTH OF $1 — What $1 due in the future is worth today	5 PRESENT WORTH OF $1 PER YEAR — What $1 payable yearly is worth today	6 PARTIAL PAYMENT — The yearly installment to repay $1 with interest	ANNUAL CONSTANT FOR MONTHLY PAYT LOAN — Annual debt service per $1 of loan (Divide by 12 to obtain monthly payment)	YEARS
1	1.105 000	1.000 000	1.000 000	.904 977	.904 977	1.105 000	1.057 7832	1
2	1.221 025	2.105 000	.475 059	.818 984	1.723 961	.580 059	.556 5125	2
3	1.349 233	3.326 025	.300 659	.741 162	2.465 123	.405 659	.390 0293	3
4	1.490 902	4.675 258	.213 892	.670 735	3.135 858	.318 892	.307 2406	4
5	1.647 447	6.166 160	.162 175	.607 000	3.742 858	.267 175	.257 9268	5
6	1.820 429	7.813 606	.127 982	.549 321	4.292 179	.232 982	.225 3476	6
7	2.011 574	9.634 035	.103 799	.497 123	4.789 303	.208 799	.202 3281	7
8	2.222 789	11.645 609	.085 869	.449 885	5.239 188	.190 869	.185 2802	8
9	2.456 182	13.868 398	.072 106	.407 136	5.646 324	.177 106	.172 2103	9
10	2.714 081	16.324 579	.061 257	.368 449	6.014 773	.166 257	.161 9220	10
11	2.999 059	19.038 660	.052 525	.333 438	6.348 211	.157 525	.153 6535	11
12	3.313 961	22.037 720	.045 377	.301 754	6.649 964	.150 377	.146 8969	12
13	3.661 926	25.351 680	.039 445	.273 080	6.923 045	.144 445	.141 3002	13
14	4.046 429	29.013 607	.034 467	.247 132	7.170 176	.139 467	.136 6121	14
15	4.471 304	33.060 035	.030 248	.223 648	7.393 825	.135 248	.132 6479	15
16	4.940 791	37.531 339	.026 644	.202 397	7.596 221	.131 644	.129 2691	16
17	5.459 574	42.472 130	.023 545	.183 164	7.779 386	.128 545	.126 3697	17
18	6.032 829	47.931 703	.020 863	.165 760	7.945 146	.125 863	.123 8673	18
19	6.666 276	53.964 532	.018 531	.150 009	8.095 154	.123 531	.121 6967	19
20	7.366 235	60.630 808	.016 493	.135 755	8.230 909	.121 493	.119 8056	20
21	8.139 690	67.997 043	.014 707	.122 855	8.353 764	.119 707	.118 1518	21
22	8.994 357	76.136 732	.013 134	.111 181	8.464 945	.118 134	.116 7009	22
23	9.938 764	85.131 089	.011 747	.100 616	8.565 561	.116 747	.115 4241	23
24	10.982 335	95.069 854	.010 519	.091 055	8.656 616	.115 519	.114 2977	24
25	12.135 480	106.052 188	.009 429	.082 403	8.739 019	.114 429	.113 3018	25
26	13.409 705	118.187 668	.008 461	.074 573	8.813 592	.113 461	.112 4195	26
27	14.817 724	131.597 373	.007 599	.067 487	8.881 079	.112 599	.111 6365	27
28	16.373 585	146.415 097	.006 830	.061 074	8.942 153	.111 830	.110 9404	28
29	18.092 812	162.788 683	.006 143	.055 271	8.997 423	.111 143	.110 3209	29
30	19.992 557	180.881 494	.005 528	.050 019	9.047 442	.110 528	.109 7687	30

10½% RATE I

n	$f = \dfrac{I}{1-1/S^{12n}}$	$\dfrac{1}{a_{\overline{n}|}} = \dfrac{I}{1-1/S^n}$	$a_{\overline{n}|} = \dfrac{1-1/S^n}{I}$	$V^n = \dfrac{1}{S^n}$	$\dfrac{1}{S_{\overline{n}|}} = \dfrac{I}{S^n-1}$	$S_{\overline{n}|} = \dfrac{S^n-1}{I}$	$S^n = (1+I)^n$	n
31	.109 2761	.109 978	9.092 707	.045 266	.004 978	200.874 051	22.091 775	31
32	.108 8361	.109 485	9.133 672	.040 964	.004 485	222.965 827	24.411 412	32
33	.108 4428	.109 042	9.170 744	.037 072	.004 042	247.377 238	26.974 610	33
34	.108 0910	.108 645	9.204 293	.033 549	.003 645	274.351 848	29.806 944	34
35	.107 7761	.108 288	9.234 654	.030 361	.003 288	304.158 792	32.936 673	35
36	.107 4940	.107 967	9.262 131	.027 476	.002 967	337.095 466	36.395 024	36
37	.107 2411	.107 677	9.286 996	.024 865	.002 677	373.490 489	40.216 501	37
38	.107 0144	.107 417	9.309 499	.022 503	.002 417	413.706 991	44.439 234	38
39	.106 8110	.107 183	9.329 863	.020 364	.002 183	458.146 225	49.105 354	39
40	.106 6284	.106 971	9.348 292	.018 429	.001 971	507.251 579	54.261 416	40
41	.106 4645	.106 781	9.364 970	.016 678	.001 781	561.512 994	59.958 864	41
42	.106 3173	.106 609	9.380 064	.015 093	.001 609	621.471 859	66.254 545	42
43	.106 1851	.106 454	9.393 723	.013 659	.001 454	687.726 404	73.211 272	43
44	.106 0663	.106 314	9.406 084	.012 361	.001 314	760.937 676	80.898 456	44
45	.105 9595	.106 188	9.417 271	.011 187	.001 188	841.836 132	89.392 794	45
46	.105 8634	.106 074	9.427 394	.010 124	.001 074	931.228 926	98.779 037	46
47	.105 7771	.105 971	9.436 556	.009 162	.000 971	1030.007 963	109.150 836	47
48	.105 6994	.105 878	9.444 847	.008 291	.000 878	1139.158 800	120.611 674	48
49	.105 6296	.105 794	9.452 350	.007 503	.000 794	1259.770 473	133.275 900	49
50	.105 5668	.105 718	9.459 140	.006 790	.000 718	1393.046 373	147.269 869	50
51	.105 5102	.105 649	9.465 285	.006 145	.000 649	1540.316 242	162.733 205	51
52	.105 4594	.105 587	9.470 847	.005 561	.000 587	1703.049 448	179.820 192	52
53	.105 4136	.105 531	9.475 879	.005 033	.000 531	1882.869 640	198.701 312	53
54	.105 3724	.105 480	9.480 434	.004 554	.000 480	2081.570 952	219.564 950	54
55	.105 3353	.105 435	9.484 555	.004 122	.000 435	2301.135 902	242.619 270	55
56	.105 3019	.105 393	9.488 285	.003 730	.000 393	2543.755 172	268.094 293	56
57	.105 2719	.105 356	9.491 661	.003 376	.000 356	2811.849 465	296.244 194	57
58	.105 2448	.105 322	9.494 716	.003 055	.000 322	3108.093 659	327.349 834	58
59	.105 2205	.105 291	9.497 480	.002 765	.000 291	3435.443 493	361.721 567	59
60	.105 1985	.105 263	9.499 982	.002 502	.000 263	3797.165 059	399.702 331	60

$S = 1 + I/12$

$S = 1 + I$

11% RATE I

YEARS	1 AMOUNT OF $1 — The amount to which $1 will grow with compound interest	2 AMOUNT OF $1 PER YEAR — The amount to which $1 per year will grow with compound interest	3 SINKING FUND FACTOR — The amount per year which will grow with compound interest to $1	4 PRESENT WORTH OF $1 — What $1 due in the future is worth today	5 PRESENT WORTH OF $1 PER YEAR — What $1 payable yearly is worth today	6 PARTIAL PAYMENT — The yearly installment to repay $1 with interest	ANNUAL CONSTANT FOR MONTHLY PAYT LOAN — Annual debt service per $1 of loan (Divide by 12 to obtain monthly payment)	YEARS
1	1.110 000	1.000 000	1.000 000	.900 901	.900 901	1.110 000	1.060 5799	1
2	1.232 100	2.110 000	.473 934	.811 622	1.712 523	.583 934	.559 2941	2
3	1.367 631	3.342 100	.299 213	.731 731	2.443 715	.409 213	.392 8646	3
4	1.518 070	4.709 731	.212 326	.658 731	3.102 446	.322 326	.310 1463	4
5	1.685 058	6.227 801	.160 570	.593 451	3.695 897	.270 570	.260 9091	5
6	1.870 415	7.912 860	.126 377	.534 641	4.230 538	.236 377	.228 4089	6
7	2.076 160	9.783 274	.102 215	.481 658	4.712 196	.212 215	.205 4692	7
8	2.304 538	11.859 434	.084 321	.433 926	5.146 123	.194 321	.188 5011	8
9	2.558 037	14.163 972	.070 602	.390 925	5.537 048	.180 602	.175 5103	9
10	2.839 421	16.722 009	.059 801	.352 184	5.889 232	.169 801	.165 3000	10
11	3.151 757	19.561 430	.051 121	.317 283	6.206 515	.161 121	.157 1082	11
12	3.498 451	22.713 187	.044 027	.285 841	6.492 356	.154 027	.150 4266	12
13	3.883 280	26.211 638	.038 151	.257 514	6.749 870	.148 151	.144 9033	13
14	4.310 441	30.094 918	.033 228	.231 995	6.981 865	.143 228	.140 2865	14
15	4.784 589	34.405 359	.029 065	.209 004	7.190 870	.139 065	.136 3916	15
16	5.310 894	39.189 948	.025 517	.188 292	7.379 162	.135 517	.133 0800	16
17	5.895 093	44.500 843	.022 471	.169 633	7.548 794	.132 471	.130 2457	17
18	6.543 553	50.395 936	.019 843	.152 822	7.701 617	.129 843	.127 8060	18
19	7.263 344	56.939 488	.017 563	.137 678	7.839 294	.127 563	.125 6957	19
20	8.062 312	64.202 832	.015 576	.124 034	7.963 328	.125 576	.123 8626	20
21	8.949 166	72.265 144	.013 838	.111 742	8.075 070	.123 838	.122 2645	21
22	9.933 574	81.214 309	.012 313	.100 669	8.175 739	.122 313	.120 8668	22
23	11.026 267	91.147 884	.010 971	.090 693	8.266 432	.120 971	.119 6410	23
24	12.239 157	102.174 151	.009 787	.081 705	8.348 137	.119 787	.118 5632	24
25	13.585 464	114.413 307	.008 740	.073 608	8.421 745	.118 740	.117 6136	25
26	15.079 865	127.998 771	.007 813	.066 314	8.488 058	.117 813	.116 7753	26
27	16.738 650	143.078 636	.006 989	.059 742	8.547 800	.116 989	.116 0340	27
28	18.579 901	159.817 286	.006 257	.053 822	8.601 622	.116 257	.115 3776	28
29	20.623 691	178.397 187	.005 605	.048 488	8.650 110	.115 605	.114 7955	29
30	22.892 297	199.020 878	.005 025	.043 683	8.693 793	.115 025	.114 2788	30

11% RATE I

n	$S^n=(1+I)^n$	$s_{\overline{n}|}=\dfrac{S^n-1}{I}$	$\dfrac{1}{s_{\overline{n}|}}=\dfrac{I}{S^n-1}$	$V^n=\dfrac{1}{S^n}$	$a_{\overline{n}|}=\dfrac{1-1/S^n}{I}$	$\dfrac{1}{a_{\overline{n}|}}=\dfrac{I}{1-1/S^n}$	$f=\dfrac{I}{1-1/S^{12n}}$
31	25.410 449	221.913 174	.004 506	.039 354	8.733 146	.114 506	.113 8196
32	28.205 599	247.323 624	.004 043	.035 454	8.768 600	.114 043	.113 4112
33	31.308 214	275.529 222	.003 629	.031 940	8.800 541	.113 629	.113 0476
34	34.752 118	306.837 437	.003 259	.028 775	8.829 316	.113 259	.112 7237
35	38.574 851	341.589 555	.002 927	.025 924	8.855 240	.112 927	.112 4349
36	42.818 085	380.164 406	.002 630	.023 355	8.878 594	.112 630	.112 1774
37	47.528 074	422.982 490	.002 364	.021 040	8.899 635	.112 364	.111 9475
38	52.756 162	470.510 564	.002 125	.018 955	8.918 590	.112 125	.111 7424
39	58.559 340	523.266 726	.001 911	.017 077	8.935 666	.111 911	.111 5591
40	65.000 867	581.826 066	.001 719	.015 384	8.951 051	.111 719	.111 3953
41	72.150 963	646.826 934	.001 546	.013 860	8.964 911	.111 546	.111 2490
42	80.087 569	718.977 896	.001 391	.012 486	8.977 397	.111 391	.111 1181
43	88.897 201	799.065 465	.001 251	.011 249	8.988 646	.111 251	.111 0011
44	98.675 893	887.962 666	.001 126	.010 134	8.998 780	.111 126	.110 8964
45	109.530 242	986.638 559	.001 014	.009 130	9.007 910	.111 014	.110 8028
46	121.578 568	1096.168 801	.000 912	.008 225	9.016 135	.110 912	.110 7190
47	134.952 211	1217.747 369	.000 821	.007 410	9.023 545	.110 821	.110 6440
48	149.796 954	1352.699 580	.000 739	.006 676	9.030 221	.110 739	.110 5768
49	166.274 619	1502.496 533	.000 666	.006 014	9.036 235	.110 666	.110 5167
50	184.564 827	1668.771 152	.000 599	.005 418	9.041 653	.110 599	.110 4629
51	204.866 958	1853.335 979	.000 540	.004 881	9.046 534	.110 540	.110 4147
52	227.402 323	2058.202 937	.000 486	.004 397	9.050 932	.110 486	.110 3715
53	252.416 579	2285.605 260	.000 438	.003 962	9.054 894	.110 438	.110 3329
54	280.182 402	2538.021 838	.000 394	.003 569	9.058 463	.110 394	.110 2983
55	311.002 466	2818.204 240	.000 355	.003 215	9.061 678	.110 355	.110 2673
56	345.212 738	3129.206 707	.000 320	.002 897	9.064 575	.110 320	.110 2395
57	383.186 139	3474.419 445	.000 288	.002 610	9.067 185	.110 288	.110 2146
58	425.336 614	3857.605 583	.000 259	.002 351	9.069 536	.110 259	.110 1923
59	472.123 642	4282.942 198	.000 233	.002 118	9.071 654	.110 233	.110 1723
60	524.057 242	4755.065 839	.000 210	.001 908	9.073 562	.110 210	.110 1544

$S = 1 + I$ $S = 1 + I/12$

11½% RATE I

YEARS	1 AMOUNT OF $1 — The amount to which $1 will grow with compound interest	2 AMOUNT OF $1 PER YEAR — The amount to which $1 per year will grow with compound interest	3 SINKING FUND FACTOR — The amount per year which will grow with compound interest to $1	4 PRESENT WORTH OF $1 — What $1 due in the future is worth today	5 PRESENT WORTH OF $1 PER YEAR — What $1 payable yearly is worth today	6 PARTIAL PAYMENT — The yearly installment to repay $1 with interest	ANNUAL CONSTANT FOR MONTHLY PAYT LOAN — Annual debt service per $1 of loan (Divide by 12 to obtain monthly payment)	YEARS
1	1.115 000	1.000 000	1.000 000	.896 861	.896 861	1.115 000	1.063 3806	1
2	1.243 225	2.115 000	.472 813	.804 360	1.701 221	.587 813	.562 0838	2
3	1.386 196	3.358 225	.297 776	.721 399	2.422 619	.412 776	.395 7121	3
4	1.545 608	4.744 421	.210 774	.646 994	3.069 614	.325 774	.313 0681	4
5	1.723 353	6.290 029	.158 982	.580 264	3.649 878	.273 982	.263 9113	5
6	1.921 539	8.013 383	.124 791	.520 416	4.170 294	.239 791	.231 4939	6
7	2.142 516	9.934 922	.100 655	.466 741	4.637 035	.215 655	.208 6375	7
8	2.388 905	12.077 438	.082 799	.418 602	5.055 637	.197 799	.191 7525	8
9	2.663 629	14.466 343	.069 126	.375 428	5.431 064	.184 126	.178 8439	9
10	2.969 947	17.129 972	.058 377	.336 706	5.767 771	.173 377	.168 7145	10
11	3.311 491	20.099 919	.049 751	.301 979	6.069 750	.164 751	.160 6020	11
12	3.692 312	23.411 410	.042 714	.270 833	6.340 583	.157 714	.153 9980	12
13	4.116 928	27.103 722	.036 895	.242 900	6.583 482	.151 895	.148 5501	13
14	4.590 375	31.220 650	.032 030	.217 847	6.801 329	.147 030	.144 0067	14
15	5.118 268	35.811 025	.027 924	.195 379	6.996 708	.142 924	.140 1828	15
16	5.706 869	40.929 293	.024 432	.175 227	7.171 935	.139 432	.136 9398	16
17	6.363 159	46.636 161	.021 443	.157 155	7.329 090	.136 443	.134 1716	17
18	7.094 922	52.999 320	.018 868	.140 946	7.470 036	.133 868	.131 7954	18
19	7.910 838	60.094 242	.016 641	.126 409	7.596 445	.131 641	.129 7462	19
20	8.820 584	68.005 080	.014 705	.113 371	7.709 816	.129 705	.127 9716	20
21	9.834 951	76.825 664	.013 016	.101 678	7.811 494	.128 016	.126 4293	21
22	10.965 971	86.660 615	.011 539	.091 191	7.902 685	.126 539	.125 0849	22
23	12.227 057	97.626 586	.010 243	.081 786	7.984 471	.125 243	.123 9098	23
24	13.633 169	109.853 643	.009 103	.073 351	8.057 822	.124 103	.122 8802	24
25	15.200 983	123.486 812	.008 098	.065 785	8.123 607	.123 098	.121 9763	25
26	16.949 096	138.687 796	.007 210	.059 000	8.182 607	.122 210	.121 1813	26
27	18.898 243	155.636 892	.006 425	.052 915	8.235 522	.121 425	.120 4809	27
28	21.071 540	174.535 135	.005 730	.047 457	8.282 979	.120 730	.119 8631	28
29	23.494 768	195.606 675	.005 112	.042 563	8.325 542	.120 112	.119 3175	29
30	26.196 666	219.101 443	.004 564	.038 173	8.363 715	.119 564	.118 8350	30

n	$S^n = (1+I)^n$	$S_{\overline{n}|} = \dfrac{S^n-1}{I}$	$\dfrac{1}{S_{\overline{n}|}} = \dfrac{I}{S^n-1}$	$V^n = \dfrac{1}{S^n}$	$a_{\overline{n}|} = \dfrac{1-1/S^n}{I}$	$\dfrac{1}{a_{\overline{n}|}} = \dfrac{I}{1-1/S^n}$	$f = \dfrac{I}{1-1/S^{12n}}$
31	29.209 282	245.298 109	.004 077	.034 236	8.397 951	.119 077	.118 4079
32	32.568 350	274.507 391	.003 643	.030 705	8.428 655	.118 643	.118 0297
33	36.313 710	307.075 741	.003 257	.027 538	8.456 193	.118 257	.117 6944
34	40.489 787	343.389 451	.002 912	.024 698	8.480 891	.117 912	.117 3969
35	45.146 112	383.879 238	.002 605	.022 150	8.503 041	.117 605	.117 1329
36	50.337 915	429.025 351	.002 331	.019 866	8.522 907	.117 331	.116 8984
37	56.126 776	479.363 266	.002 086	.017 817	8.540 723	.117 086	.116 6901
38	62.581 355	535.490 042	.001 867	.015 979	8.556 703	.116 867	.116 5049
39	69.778 211	598.071 396	.001 672	.014 331	8.571 034	.116 672	.116 3403
40	77.802 705	667.849 607	.001 497	.012 853	8.583 887	.116 497	.116 1938
41	86.750 016	745.652 312	.001 341	.011 527	8.595 414	.116 341	.116 0635
42	96.726 268	832.402 327	.001 201	.010 338	8.605 753	.116 201	.115 9476
43	107.849 788	929.128 595	.001 076	.009 272	8.615 025	.116 076	.115 8443
44	120.252 514	1036.978 384	.000 964	.008 316	8.623 341	.115 964	.115 7524
45	134.081 553	1157.230 898	.000 864	.007 458	8.630 799	.115 864	.115 6706
46	149.500 932	1291.312 451	.000 774	.006 689	8.637 488	.115 774	.115 5977
47	166.693 539	1440.813 383	.000 694	.005 999	8.643 487	.115 694	.115 5327
48	185.863 296	1607.506 922	.000 622	.005 380	8.648 867	.115 622	.115 4749
49	207.237 575	1793.370 218	.000 558	.004 825	8.653 692	.115 558	.115 4233
50	231.069 896	2000.607 793	.000 500	.004 328	8.658 020	.115 500	.115 3774
51	257.642 934	2231.677 689	.000 448	.003 881	8.661 901	.115 448	.115 3365
52	287.271 872	2489.320 623	.000 402	.003 481	8.665 382	.115 402	.115 3000
53	320.308 137	2776.592 495	.000 360	.003 122	8.668 504	.115 360	.115 2675
54	357.143 573	3096.900 632	.000 323	.002 800	8.671 304	.115 323	.115 2385
55	398.215 084	3454.044 205	.000 290	.002 511	8.673 816	.115 290	.115 2127
56	444.009 818	3852.259 288	.000 260	.002 252	8.676 068	.115 260	.115 1896
57	495.070 947	4296.269 106	.000 233	.002 020	8.678 088	.115 233	.115 1691
58	552.004 106	4791.340 053	.000 209	.001 812	8.679 899	.115 209	.115 1508
59	615.484 578	5343.344 159	.000 187	.001 625	8.681 524	.115 187	.115 1344
60	686.265 305	5958.828 738	.000 168	.001 457	8.682 981	.115 168	.115 1199

$S = 1+I$

$S = 1+I/12$

12% RATE I

YEARS	1 AMOUNT OF $1 — The amount to which $1 will grow with compound interest	2 AMOUNT OF $1 PER YEAR — The amount to which $1 per year will grow with compound interest	3 SINKING FUND FACTOR — The amount per year which will grow with compound interest to $1	4 PRESENT WORTH OF $1 — What $1 due in the future is worth today	5 PRESENT WORTH OF $1 PER YEAR — What $1 payable yearly is worth today	6 PARTIAL PAYMENT — The yearly installment to repay $1 with interest	ANNUAL CONSTANT FOR MONTHLY PAYT LOAN — Annual debt service per $1 of loan (Divide by 12 to obtain monthly payment)	YEARS
1	1.120 000	1.000 000	1.000 000	.892 857	.892 857	1.120 000	1.066 1855	1
2	1.254 400	2.120 000	.471 698	.797 194	1.690 051	.591 698	.564 8817	2
3	1.404 928	3.374 400	.296 349	.711 780	2.401 831	.416 349	.398 5717	3
4	1.573 519	4.779 328	.209 234	.635 518	3.037 349	.329 234	.316 0060	4
5	1.762 342	6.352 847	.157 410	.567 427	3.604 776	.277 410	.266 9334	5
6	1.973 823	8.115 189	.123 226	.506 631	4.111 407	.243 226	.234 6023	6
7	2.210 681	10.089 012	.099 118	.452 349	4.563 757	.219 118	.211 8328	7
8	2.475 963	12.299 693	.081 303	.403 883	4.967 640	.201 303	.195 0341	8
9	2.773 079	14.775 656	.067 679	.360 610	5.328 250	.187 679	.182 2108	9
10	3.105 848	17.548 735	.056 984	.321 973	5.650 223	.176 984	.172 1651	10
11	3.478 550	20.654 583	.048 415	.287 476	5.937 699	.168 415	.164 1345	11
12	3.895 976	24.133 133	.041 437	.256 675	6.194 374	.161 437	.157 6103	12
13	4.363 493	28.029 109	.035 677	.229 174	6.423 548	.155 677	.152 2399	13
14	4.887 112	32.392 602	.030 871	.204 620	6.628 168	.150 871	.147 7715	14
15	5.473 566	37.279 715	.026 824	.182 696	6.810 864	.146 824	.144 0202	15
16	6.130 394	42.753 280	.023 390	.163 122	6.973 986	.143 390	.140 8470	16
17	6.866 041	48.883 674	.020 457	.145 644	7.119 630	.140 457	.138 1459	17
18	7.689 966	55.749 715	.017 937	.130 040	7.249 670	.137 937	.135 8340	18
19	8.612 762	63.439 681	.015 763	.116 107	7.365 777	.135 763	.133 8463	19
20	9.646 293	72.052 442	.013 879	.103 667	7.469 444	.133 879	.132 1303	20
21	10.803 848	81.698 736	.012 240	.092 560	7.562 003	.132 240	.130 6440	21
22	12.100 310	92.502 584	.010 811	.082 643	7.644 646	.130 811	.129 3526	22
23	13.552 347	104.602 894	.009 560	.073 788	7.718 434	.129 560	.128 2278	23
24	15.178 629	118.155 241	.008 463	.065 882	7.784 316	.128 463	.127 2458	24
25	17.000 064	133.333 870	.007 500	.058 823	7.843 139	.127 500	.126 3869	25
26	19.040 072	150.333 934	.006 652	.052 521	7.895 660	.126 652	.125 6343	26
27	21.324 881	169.374 007	.005 904	.046 894	7.942 554	.125 904	.124 9739	27
28	23.883 866	190.698 887	.005 244	.041 869	7.984 423	.125 244	.124 3936	28
29	26.749 930	214.582 754	.004 660	.037 383	8.021 806	.124 660	.123 8831	29
30	29.959 922	241.332 684	.004 144	.033 378	8.055 184	.124 144	.123 4335	30

12% RATE I

n	$S^n=(1+I)^n$	$S_{\bar{n}|}=\dfrac{S^n-1}{I}$	$\dfrac{1}{S_{\bar{n}|}}=\dfrac{I}{S^n-1}$	$V^n=\dfrac{1}{S^n}$	$a_{\bar{n}|}=\dfrac{1-1/S^n}{I}$	$\dfrac{1}{a_{\bar{n}|}}=\dfrac{I}{1-1/S^n}$	$f=\dfrac{I}{1-1/S^{12n}}$	n
31	33.555 113	271.292 606	.003 686	.029 802	8.084 986	.123 686	.123 0373	31
32	37.581 726	304.847 719	.003 280	.026 609	8.111 594	.123 280	.122 6878	32
33	42.091 533	342.429 446	.002 920	.023 758	8.135 352	.122 920	.122 3793	33
34	47.142 517	384.520 979	.002 601	.021 212	8.156 564	.122 601	.122 1068	34
35	52.799 620	431.663 496	.002 317	.018 940	8.175 564	.122 317	.121 8660	35
36	59.135 574	484.463 116	.002 064	.016 910	8.192 414	.122 064	.121 6531	36
37	66.231 843	543.598 690	.001 840	.015 098	8.207 513	.121 840	.121 4647	37
38	74.179 664	609.830 533	.001 640	.013 481	8.220 993	.121 640	.121 2981	38
39	83.081 224	684.010 197	.001 462	.012 036	8.233 030	.121 462	.121 1506	39
40	93.050 970	767.091 420	.001 304	.010 747	8.243 777	.121 304	.121 0200	40
41	104.217 087	860.142 391	.001 163	.009 595	8.253 372	.121 163	.120 9043	41
42	116.723 137	964.359 478	.001 037	.008 567	8.261 939	.121 037	.120 8019	42
43	130.729 914	1081.082 615	.000 925	.007 649	8.269 589	.120 925	.120 7111	43
44	146.417 503	1211.812 529	.000 825	.006 830	8.276 418	.120 825	.120 6306	44
45	163.987 604	1358.230 032	.000 736	.006 098	8.282 516	.120 736	.120 5593	45
46	183.666 116	1522.217 636	.000 657	.005 445	8.287 961	.120 657	.120 4961	46
47	205.706 050	1705.883 752	.000 586	.004 861	8.292 822	.120 586	.120 4401	47
48	230.390 776	1911.589 803	.000 523	.004 340	8.297 163	.120 523	.120 3904	48
49	258.037 669	2141.980 579	.000 467	.003 875	8.301 038	.120 467	.120 3463	49
50	289.002 190	2400.018 249	.000 417	.003 460	8.304 498	.120 417	.120 3072	50
51	323.682 453	2689.020 438	.000 372	.003 089	8.307 588	.120 372	.120 2726	51
52	362.524 347	3012.702 891	.000 332	.002 758	8.310 346	.120 332	.120 2418	52
53	406.027 269	3375.254 238	.000 296	.002 463	8.312 809	.120 296	.120 2146	53
54	454.750 541	3781.254 506	.000 264	.002 199	8.315 008	.120 264	.120 1904	54
55	509.320 606	4236.005 047	.000 236	.001 963	8.316 972	.120 236	.120 1689	55
56	570.439 078	4745.325 653	.000 211	.001 753	8.318 725	.120 211	.120 1499	56
57	638.891 768	5315.764 731	.000 188	.001 565	8.320 290	.120 188	.120 1330	57
58	715.558 780	5954.656 499	.000 168	.001 398	8.321 687	.120 168	.120 1180	58
59	801.425 833	6670.215 279	.000 150	.001 248	8.322 935	.120 150	.120 1047	59
60	897.596 933	7471.641 112	.000 134	.001 114	8.324 049	.120 134	.120 0929	60

$$S=1+I \qquad S=1+I/12$$

13% RATE I

YEARS	1 AMOUNT OF $1 — The amount to which $1 will grow with compound interest	2 AMOUNT OF $1 PER YEAR — The amount to which $1 per year will grow with compound interest	3 SINKING FUND FACTOR — The amount per year which will grow with compound interest to $1	4 PRESENT WORTH OF $1 — What $1 due in the future is worth today	5 PRESENT WORTH OF $1 PER YEAR — What $1 payable yearly is worth today	6 PARTIAL PAYMENT — The yearly installment to repay $1 with interest	ANNUAL CONSTANT FOR MONTHLY PAYT LOAN — Annual debt service per $1 of loan (Divide by 12 to obtain monthly payment)	YEARS
1	1.130 000	1.000 000	1.000 000	.884 956	.884 956	1.130 000	1.071 8073	1
2	1.276 900	2.130 000	.469 484	.783 147	1.668 102	.599 484	.570 5019	2
3	1.442 897	3.406 900	.293 522	.693 050	2.361 153	.423 522	.404 3274	3
4	1.630 474	4.849 797	.206 194	.613 319	2.974 471	.336 194	.321 9300	4
5	1.842 435	6.480 271	.154 315	.542 760	3.517 231	.284 315	.273 0369	5
6	2.081 952	8.322 706	.120 153	.480 319	3.997 550	.250 153	.240 8893	6
7	2.352 605	10.404 658	.096 111	.425 061	4.422 610	.226 111	.218 3036	7
8	2.658 444	12.757 263	.078 387	.376 160	4.798 770	.208 387	.201 6871	8
9	3.004 042	15.415 707	.064 869	.332 885	5.131 655	.194 869	.189 0431	9
10	3.394 567	18.419 749	.054 290	.294 588	5.426 243	.184 290	.179 1729	10
11	3.835 861	21.814 317	.045 841	.260 698	5.686 941	.175 841	.171 3133	11
12	4.334 523	25.650 178	.038 986	.230 706	5.917 647	.168 986	.164 9550	12
13	4.898 011	29.984 701	.033 350	.204 165	6.121 812	.163 350	.159 7452	13
14	5.534 753	34.882 712	.028 667	.180 677	6.302 488	.158 667	.155 4316	14
15	6.254 270	40.417 464	.024 742	.159 891	6.462 379	.154 742	.151 8291	15
16	7.067 326	46.671 735	.021 426	.141 496	6.603 875	.151 426	.148 7985	16
17	7.986 078	53.739 060	.018 608	.125 218	6.729 093	.148 608	.146 2337	17
18	9.024 268	61.725 138	.016 201	.110 812	6.839 905	.146 201	.144 0519	18
19	10.197 423	70.749 406	.014 134	.098 064	6.937 969	.144 134	.142 1878	19
20	11.523 088	80.946 829	.012 354	.086 782	7.024 752	.142 354	.140 5891	20
21	13.021 089	92.469 917	.010 814	.076 798	7.101 550	.140 814	.139 2137	21
22	14.713 831	105.491 006	.009 479	.067 963	7.169 513	.139 479	.138 0272	22
23	16.626 629	120.204 837	.008 319	.060 144	7.229 658	.138 319	.137 0011	23
24	18.788 091	136.831 465	.007 308	.053 225	7.282 883	.137 308	.136 1120	24
25	21.230 542	155.619 556	.006 426	.047 102	7.329 985	.136 426	.135 3402	25
26	23.990 513	176.850 098	.005 655	.041 683	7.371 668	.135 655	.134 6693	26
27	27.109 279	200.840 611	.004 979	.036 888	7.408 556	.134 979	.134 0851	27
28	30.633 486	227.949 890	.004 387	.032 644	7.441 200	.134 387	.133 5760	28
29	34.615 839	258.583 376	.003 867	.028 889	7.470 088	.133 867	.133 1318	29
30	39.115 898	293.199 215	.003 411	.025 565	7.495 653	.133 411	.132 7439	30

n	$S^n = (1+I)^n$	$S_{\overline{n}|} = \dfrac{S^n-1}{I}$	$\dfrac{1}{S_{\overline{n}|}} = \dfrac{I}{S^n-1}$	$V^n = \dfrac{1}{S^n}$	$a_{\overline{n}|} = \dfrac{1-1/S^n}{I}$	$\dfrac{1}{a_{\overline{n}|}} = \dfrac{I}{1-1/S^n}$	$f = \dfrac{I}{1-1/S^{12n}}$
31	44.200 965	332.315 113	.003 009	.022 624	7.518 277	.133 009	.132 4050
32	49.947 090	376.516 078	.002 656	.020 021	7.538 299	.132 656	.132 1085
33	56.440 212	426.463 168	.002 345	.017 718	7.556 016	.132 345	.131 8492
34	63.777 439	482.903 380	.002 071	.015 680	7.571 696	.132 071	.131 6221
35	72.068 506	546.680 819	.001 829	.013 876	7.585 572	.131 829	.131 4232
36	81.437 412	618.749 325	.001 616	.012 279	7.597 851	.131 616	.131 2489
37	92.024 276	700.186 738	.001 428	.010 867	7.608 718	.131 428	.131 0961
38	103.987 432	792.211 014	.001 262	.009 617	7.618 334	.131 262	.130 9622
39	117.505 798	896.198 445	.001 116	.008 510	7.626 844	.131 116	.130 8447
40	132.781 552	1013.704 243	.000 986	.007 531	7.634 376	.130 986	.130 7417
41	150.043 153	1146.485 795	.000 872	.006 665	7.641 040	.130 872	.130 6513
42	169.548 763	1296.528 948	.000 771	.005 898	7.646 938	.130 771	.130 5719
43	191.590 103	1466.077 712	.000 682	.005 219	7.652 158	.130 682	.130 5023
44	216.496 816	1657.667 814	.000 603	.004 619	7.656 777	.130 603	.130 4412
45	244.641 402	1874.164 630	.000 534	.004 088	7.660 864	.130 534	.130 3875
46	276.444 784	2118.806 032	.000 472	.003 617	7.664 482	.130 472	.130 3404
47	312.382 606	2395.250 816	.000 417	.003 201	7.667 683	.130 417	.130 2990
48	352.992 345	2707.633 422	.000 369	.002 833	7.670 516	.130 369	.130 2627
49	398.881 350	3060.625 767	.000 327	.002 507	7.673 023	.130 327	.130 2307
50	450.735 925	3459.507 117	.000 289	.002 219	7.675 242	.130 289	.130 2027
51	509.331 595	3910.243 042	.000 256	.001 963	7.677 205	.130 256	.130 1781
52	575.544 703	4419.574 637	.000 226	.001 737	7.678 942	.130 226	.130 1565
53	650.365 514	4995.119 340	.000 200	.001 538	7.680 480	.130 200	.130 1375
54	734.913 031	5645.484 854	.000 177	.001 361	7.681 841	.130 177	.130 1208
55	830.451 725	6380.397 885	.000 157	.001 204	7.683 045	.130 157	.130 1061

$S = 1+I$

$S = 1+I/12$

14% RATE I

YEARS	1 AMOUNT OF $1 The amount to which $1 will grow with compound interest	2 AMOUNT OF $1 PER YEAR The amount to which $1 per year will grow with compound interest	3 SINKING FUND FACTOR The amount per year which will grow with compound interest to $1	4 PRESENT WORTH OF $1 What $1 due in the future is worth today	5 PRESENT WORTH OF $1 PER YEAR What $1 payable yearly is worth today	6 PARTIAL PAYMENT The yearly installment to repay $1 with interest	ANNUAL CONSTANT FOR MONTHLY PAYT LOAN Annual debt service per $1 of loan (Divide by 12 to obtain monthly payment)	YEARS
1	1.140 000	1.000 000	1.000 000	.877 193	.877 193	1.140 000	1.077 4454	1
2	1.299 600	2.140 000	.467 290	.769 468	1.646 661	.607 290	.576 1546	2
3	1.481 544	3.439 600	.290 731	.674 972	2.321 632	.430 731	.410 1316	3
4	1.688 960	4.921 144	.203 205	.592 080	2.913 712	.343 205	.327 9177	4
5	1.925 415	6.610 104	.151 284	.519 369	3.433 081	.291 284	.279 2190	5
6	2.194 973	8.535 519	.117 157	.455 587	3.888 668	.257 157	.247 2689	6
7	2.502 269	10.730 491	.093 192	.399 637	4.288 305	.233 192	.224 8801	7
8	2.852 586	13.232 760	.075 570	.350 559	4.638 864	.215 570	.208 4580	8
9	3.251 949	16.085 347	.062 168	.307 508	4.946 372	.202 168	.196 0044	9
10	3.707 221	19.337 295	.051 714	.269 744	5.216 116	.191 714	.186 3197	10
11	4.226 232	23.044 516	.043 394	.236 617	5.452 733	.183 394	.178 6399	11
12	4.817 905	27.270 749	.036 669	.207 559	5.660 292	.176 669	.172 4553	12
13	5.492 411	32.088 654	.031 164	.182 069	5.842 362	.171 164	.167 4124	13
14	6.261 349	37.581 065	.026 609	.159 710	6.002 072	.166 609	.163 2588	14
15	7.137 938	43.842 414	.022 809	.140 096	6.142 168	.162 809	.159 8090	15
16	8.137 249	50.980 352	.019 615	.122 892	6.265 060	.159 615	.156 9239	16
17	9.276 464	59.117 601	.016 915	.107 800	6.372 859	.156 915	.154 4971	17
18	10.575 169	68.394 066	.014 621	.094 561	6.467 420	.154 621	.152 4460	18
19	12.055 693	78.969 235	.012 663	.082 948	6.550 369	.152 663	.150 7051	19
20	13.743 490	91.024 928	.010 986	.072 762	6.623 131	.150 986	.149 2225	20
21	15.667 578	104.768 418	.009 545	.063 826	6.686 957	.149 545	.147 9561	21
22	17.861 039	120.435 996	.008 303	.055 988	6.742 944	.148 303	.146 8715	22
23	20.361 585	138.297 035	.007 231	.049 112	6.792 056	.147 231	.145 9408	23
24	23.212 207	158.658 620	.006 303	.043 081	6.835 137	.146 303	.145 1405	24
25	26.461 916	181.870 827	.005 498	.037 790	6.872 927	.145 498	.144 4513	25
26	30.166 584	208.332 743	.004 800	.033 149	6.906 077	.144 800	.143 8570	26
27	34.389 906	238.499 327	.004 193	.029 078	6.935 155	.144 193	.143 3439	27
28	39.204 493	272.889 233	.003 664	.025 507	6.960 662	.143 664	.142 9004	28
29	44.693 122	312.093 725	.003 204	.022 375	6.983 037	.143 204	.142 5167	29
30	50.950 159	356.786 847	.002 803	.019 627	7.002 664	.142 803	.142 1846	30

14% RATE I

n	$S^n = (1+I)^n$	$S_{\overline{n}} = \dfrac{S^n-1}{I}$	$\dfrac{1}{S_{\overline{n}}} = \dfrac{I}{S^n-1}$	$V^n = \dfrac{1}{S^n}$	$a_{\overline{n}} = \dfrac{1-1/S^n}{I}$	$\dfrac{1}{a_{\overline{n}}} = \dfrac{I}{1-1/S^n}$	$f = \dfrac{I}{1-1/S^{12n}}$	n
31	58.083 181	407.737 006	.002 453	.017 217	7.019 881	.142 453	.141 8969	31
32	66.214 826	465.820 186	.002 147	.015 102	7.034 983	.142 147	.141 6475	32
33	75.484 902	532.035 012	.001 880	.013 248	7.048 231	.141 880	.141 4313	33
34	86.052 788	607.519 914	.001 646	.011 621	7.059 852	.141 646	.141 2436	34
35	98.100 178	693.572 702	.001 442	.010 194	7.070 045	.141 442	.141 0808	35
36	111.834 203	791.672 881	.001 263	.008 942	7.078 987	.141 263	.140 9394	36
37	127.490 992	903.507 084	.001 107	.007 844	7.086 831	.141 107	.140 8166	37
38	145.339 731	1030.998 076	.000 970	.006 880	7.093 711	.140 970	.140 7100	38
39	165.687 293	1176.337 806	.000 850	.006 035	7.099 747	.140 850	.140 6173	39
40	188.883 514	1342.025 099	.000 745	.005 294	7.105 041	.140 745	.140 5368	40
41	215.327 206	1530.908 613	.000 653	.004 644	7.109 685	.140 653	.140 4668	41
42	245.473 015	1746.235 819	.000 573	.004 074	7.113 759	.140 573	.140 4060	42
43	279.839 237	1991.708 833	.000 502	.003 573	7.117 332	.140 502	.140 3531	43
44	319.016 730	2271.548 070	.000 440	.003 135	7.120 467	.140 440	.140 3071	44
45	363.679 072	2590.564 800	.000 386	.002 750	7.123 217	.140 386	.140 2671	45
46	414.594 142	2954.243 872	.000 338	.002 412	7.125 629	.140 338	.140 2324	46
47	472.637 322	3368.838 014	.000 297	.002 116	7.127 744	.140 297	.140 2021	47
48	538.806 547	3841.475 336	.000 260	.001 856	7.129 600	.140 260	.140 1758	48
49	614.239 464	4380.281 883	.000 228	.001 628	7.131 228	.140 228	.140 1530	49
50	700.232 988	4994.521 346	.000 200	.001 428	7.132 656	.140 200	.140 1331	50
51	798.265 607	5694.754 335	.000 176	.001 253	7.133 909	.140 176	.140 1158	51
52	910.022 792	6493.019 941	.000 154	.001 099	7.135 008	.140 154	.140 1007	52
53	1037.425 983	7403.042 733	.000 135	.000 964	7.135 972	.140 135	.140 0876	53
54	1182.665 620	8440.468 716	.000 118	.000 846	7.136 818	.140 118	.140 0762	54
55	1348.238 807	9623.134 336	.000 104	.000 742	7.137 559	.140 104	.140 0663	55

$$S = 1 + I \qquad S = 1 + I/12$$

15% RATE I

YEARS	1 AMOUNT OF $1 — The amount to which $1 will grow with compound interest	2 AMOUNT OF $1 PER YEAR — The amount to which $1 per year will grow with compound interest	3 SINKING FUND FACTOR — The amount per year which will grow with compound interest to $1	4 PRESENT WORTH OF $1 — What $1 due in the future is worth today	5 PRESENT WORTH OF $1 PER YEAR — What $1 payable yearly is worth today	6 PARTIAL PAYMENT — The yearly installment to repay $1 with interest	ANNUAL CONSTANT FOR MONTHLY PAY'T LOAN — Annual debt service per $1 of loan (Divide by 12 to obtain monthly payment)	YEARS
1	1.150 000	1.000 000	1.000 000	.869 565	.869 565	1.150 000	1.083 0997	1
2	1.322 500	2.150 000	.465 116	.756 144	1.625 709	.615 116	.581 8398	2
3	1.520 875	3.472 500	.287 977	.657 516	2.283 225	.437 977	.415 9839	3
4	1.749 006	4.993 375	.200 265	.571 753	2.854 978	.350 265	.333 9690	4
5	2.011 357	6.742 381	.148 316	.497 177	3.352 155	.298 316	.285 4792	5
6	2.313 061	8.753 738	.114 237	.432 328	3.784 483	.264 237	.253 7402	6
7	2.660 020	11.066 799	.090 360	.375 937	4.160 420	.240 360	.231 5611	7
8	3.059 023	13.726 819	.072 850	.326 902	4.487 322	.222 850	.215 3449	8
9	3.517 876	16.785 842	.059 574	.284 262	4.771 584	.209 574	.203 0920	9
10	4.045 558	20.303 718	.049 252	.247 185	5.018 769	.199 252	.193 6019	10
11	4.652 391	24.349 276	.041 069	.214 943	5.233 712	.191 069	.186 1098	11
12	5.350 250	29.001 667	.034 481	.186 907	5.420 619	.184 481	.180 1052	12
13	6.152 788	34.351 917	.029 110	.162 528	5.583 147	.179 110	.175 2345	13
14	7.075 706	40.504 705	.024 688	.141 329	5.724 476	.174 688	.171 2448	14
15	8.137 062	47.580 411	.021 017	.122 894	5.847 370	.171 017	.167 9505	15
16	9.357 621	55.717 472	.017 948	.106 865	5.954 235	.167 948	.165 2124	16
17	10.761 264	65.075 093	.015 367	.092 926	6.047 161	.165 367	.162 9241	17
18	12.375 454	75.836 357	.013 186	.080 805	6.127 966	.163 186	.161 0029	18
19	14.231 772	88.211 811	.011 336	.070 265	6.198 231	.161 336	.159 3838	19
20	16.366 537	102.443 583	.009 761	.061 100	6.259 331	.159 761	.158 0147	20
21	18.821 518	118.810 120	.008 417	.053 131	6.312 462	.158 417	.156 8541	21
22	21.644 746	137.631 638	.007 266	.046 201	6.358 663	.157 266	.155 8677	22
23	24.891 458	159.276 384	.006 278	.040 174	6.398 837	.156 278	.155 0278	23
24	28.625 176	184.167 841	.005 430	.034 934	6.433 771	.155 430	.154 3115	24
25	32.918 953	212.793 017	.004 699	.030 378	6.464 149	.154 699	.153 6997	25
26	37.856 796	245.711 970	.004 070	.026 415	6.490 564	.154 070	.153 1765	26
27	43.535 315	283.568 766	.003 526	.022 970	6.513 534	.153 526	.152 7285	27
28	50.065 612	327.104 080	.003 057	.019 974	6.533 508	.153 057	.152 3448	28
29	57.575 454	377.169 693	.002 651	.017 369	6.550 877	.152 651	.152 0157	29
30	66.211 772	434.745 146	.002 300	.015 103	6.565 980	.152 300	.151 7333	30

15% RATE I

n	$S^n=(1+I)^n$	$S_{\overline{n}|}=\dfrac{S^n-1}{I}$	$\dfrac{1}{S_{\overline{n}|}}=\dfrac{I}{S^n-1}$	$V^n=\dfrac{1}{S^n}$	$a_{\overline{n}|}=\dfrac{1-1/S^n}{I}$	$\dfrac{1}{a_{\overline{n}|}}=\dfrac{I}{1-1/S^n}$	$f=\dfrac{I}{1-1/S^{12n}}$	n
31	76.143 538	500.956 918	.001 996	.013 133	6.579 113	.151 996	.151 4909	31
32	87.565 068	577.100 456	.001 733	.011 420	6.590 533	.151 733	.151 2826	32
33	100.699 829	664.665 524	.001 505	.009 931	6.600 463	.151 505	.151 1037	33
34	115.804 803	765.365 353	.001 307	.008 635	6.609 099	.151 307	.150 9499	34
35	133.175 523	881.170 156	.001 135	.007 509	6.616 607	.151 135	.150 8176	35
36	153.151 852	1014.345 680	.000 986	.006 529	6.623 137	.150 986	.150 7038	36
37	176.124 630	1167.497 532	.000 857	.005 678	6.628 815	.150 857	.150 6060	37
38	202.543 324	1343.622 161	.000 744	.004 937	6.633 752	.150 744	.150 5218	38
39	232.924 823	1546.165 485	.000 647	.004 293	6.638 045	.150 647	.150 4493	39
40	267.863 546	1779.090 308	.000 562	.003 733	6.641 778	.150 562	.150 3869	40
41	308.043 078	2046.953 854	.000 489	.003 246	6.645 025	.150 489	.150 3332	41
42	354.249 540	2355.996 933	.000 425	.002 823	6.647 848	.150 425	.150 2870	42
43	407.386 971	2709.246 473	.000 369	.002 455	6.650 302	.150 369	.150 2472	43
44	468.495 017	3116.633 443	.000 321	.002 134	6.652 437	.150 321	.150 2129	44
45	538.769 269	3585.128 460	.000 279	.001 856	6.654 293	.150 279	.150 1834	45
46	619.584 659	4123.897 729	.000 242	.001 614	6.655 907	.150 242	.150 1579	46
47	712.522 358	4743.482 388	.000 211	.001 403	6.657 310	.150 211	.150 1360	47
48	819.400 712	5455.004 746	.000 183	.001 220	6.658 531	.150 183	.150 1172	48
49	942.310 819	6275.405 458	.000 159	.001 061	6.659 592	.150 159	.150 1009	49
50	1083.657 442	7217.716 277	.000 139	.000 923	6.660 515	.150 139	.150 0870	50

$$S=1+I \qquad S=1+I/12$$

20% RATE I

YEARS	1 AMOUNT OF $1 — The amount to which $1 will grow with compound interest	2 AMOUNT OF $1 PER YEAR — The amount to which $1 per year will grow with compound interest	3 SINKING FUND FACTOR — The amount per year which will grow with compound interest to $1	4 PRESENT WORTH OF $1 — What $1 due in the future is worth today	5 PRESENT WORTH OF $1 PER YEAR — What $1 payable yearly is worth today	6 PARTIAL PAYMENT — The yearly installment to repay $1 with interest	ANNUAL CONSTANT FOR MONTHLY PAYT LOAN — Annual debt service per $1 of loan (Divide by 12 to obtain monthly payment)	YEARS
1	1.200 000	1.000 000	1.000 000	.833 333	.833 333	1.200 000	1.111 6141	1
2	1.440 000	2.200 000	.454 545	.694 444	1.527 778	.654 545	.610 7496	2
3	1.728 000	3.640 000	.274 725	.578 704	2.106 481	.474 725	.445 9630	3
4	2.073 600	5.368 000	.186 289	.482 253	2.588 735	.386 289	.365 1643	4
5	2.488 320	7.441 600	.134 380	.401 878	2.990 612	.334 380	.317 9266	5
6	2.985 984	9.929 920	.100 706	.334 898	3.325 510	.300 706	.287 4339	6
7	3.583 181	12.915 904	.077 424	.279 082	3.604 592	.277 424	.266 4744	7
8	4.299 817	16.499 085	.060 609	.232 568	3.837 160	.260 609	.251 4384	8
9	5.159 780	20.798 902	.048 079	.193 807	4.030 967	.248 079	.240 3180	9
10	6.191 736	25.958 682	.038 523	.161 506	4.192 472	.238 523	.231 9068	10
11	7.430 084	32.150 419	.031 104	.134 588	4.327 060	.231 104	.225 4361	11
12	8.916 100	39.580 502	.025 265	.112 157	4.439 217	.225 265	.220 3930	12
13	10.699 321	48.496 603	.020 620	.093 464	4.532 681	.220 620	.216 4227	13
14	12.839 185	59.195 923	.016 893	.077 887	4.610 567	.216 893	.213 2718	14
15	15.407 022	72.035 108	.013 882	.064 905	4.675 473	.213 882	.210 7556	15
16	18.488 426	87.442 129	.011 436	.054 088	4.729 561	.211 436	.208 7359	16
17	22.186 111	105.930 555	.009 440	.045 073	4.774 634	.209 440	.207 1083	17
18	26.623 333	128.116 666	.007 805	.037 561	4.812 195	.207 805	.205 7924	18
19	31.948 000	154.740 000	.006 462	.031 301	4.843 496	.206 462	.204 7256	19
20	38.337 600	186.688 000	.005 357	.026 084	4.869 580	.205 357	.203 8590	20
21	46.005 120	225.025 600	.004 444	.021 737	4.891 316	.204 444	.203 1537	21
22	55.206 144	271.030 719	.003 690	.018 114	4.909 430	.203 690	.202 5790	22
23	66.247 373	326.236 863	.003 065	.015 095	4.924 525	.203 065	.202 1101	23
24	79.496 847	392.484 236	.002 548	.012 579	4.937 104	.202 548	.201 7272	24
25	95.396 217	471.981 083	.002 119	.010 483	4.947 587	.202 119	.201 4142	25
26	114.475 460	567.377 300	.001 762	.008 735	4.956 323	.201 762	.201 1583	26
27	137.370 552	681.852 760	.001 467	.007 280	4.963 602	.201 467	.200 9489	27
28	164.844 662	819.223 312	.001 221	.006 066	4.969 668	.201 221	.200 7775	28
29	197.813 595	984.067 974	.001 016	.005 055	4.974 724	.201 016	.200 6372	29
30	237.376 314	1181.881 569	.000 846	.004 213	4.978 936	.200 846	.200 5222	30

20% RATE I

n	$S^n=(1+I)^n$	$S_{\overline{n}}=\dfrac{S^n-1}{I}$	$\dfrac{1}{S_{\overline{n}}}=\dfrac{I}{S^n-1}$	$V^n=\dfrac{1}{S^n}$	$a_{\overline{n}}=\dfrac{1-1/S^n}{I}$	$\dfrac{1}{a_{\overline{n}}}=\dfrac{I}{1-1/S^n}$	$f=\dfrac{I}{1-1/S^{12n}}$	n
31	284.851 577	1419.257 883	.000 705	.003 511	4.982 447	.200 705	.200 4281	31
32	341.821 892	1704.109 459	.000 587	.002 926	4.985 372	.200 587	.200 3509	32
33	410.186 270	2045.931 351	.000 489	.002 438	4.987 810	.200 489	.200 2877	33
34	492.223 524	2456.117 621	.000 407	.002 032	4.989 842	.200 407	.200 2359	34
35	590.668 229	2948.341 146	.000 339	.001 693	4.991 535	.200 339	.200 1934	35
36	708.801 875	3539.009 375	.000 283	.001 411	4.992 946	.200 283	.200 1586	36
37	850.562 250	4247.811 250	.000 235	.001 176	4.994 122	.200 235	.200 1300	37
38	1020.674 700	5098.373 500	.000 196	.000 980	4.995 101	.200 196	.200 1066	38
39	1224.809 640	6119.048 200	.000 163	.000 816	4.995 918	.200 163	.200 0874	39
40	1469.771 568	7343.857 840	.000 136	.000 680	4.996 598	.200 136	.200 0717	40

$S=1+I$

$S=1+I/12$

INDEX